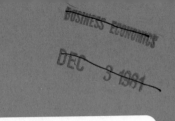

CRUISE MISSILES

RICHARD K. BETTS
Editor

CRUISE MISSILES
Technology, Strategy, Politics

THE BROOKINGS INSTITUTION
Washington, D.C.

Library of Congress Cataloging in Publication data:

Main entry under title:

Cruise missiles.

Includes bibliographical references and
index.

1. Cruise missiles.　2. Atomic warfare.
I. Betts, Richard K., 1947–　.
UG1312.C7C78　　　358'.174　　　81-18149
ISBN 0-8157-0932-3　　　　　　AACR2
ISBN 0-8157-0931-5 (pbk.)

1　2　3　4　5　6　7　8　9

THE BROOKINGS INSTITUTION is an independent organization devoted to nonpartisan research, education, and publication in economics, government, foreign policy, and the social sciences generally. Its principal purposes are to aid in the development of sound public policies and to promote public understanding of issues of national importance.

The Institution was founded on December 8, 1927, to merge the activities of the Institute for Government Research, founded in 1916, the Institute of Economics, founded in 1922, and the Robert Brookings Graduate School of Economics and Government, founded in 1924.

The Board of Trustees is responsible for the general administration of the Institution, while the immediate direction of the policies, program, and staff is vested in the President, assisted by an advisory committee of the officers and staff. The by-laws of the Institution state: "It is the function of the Trustees to make possible the conduct of scientific research, and publication, under the most favorable conditions, and to safeguard the independence of the research staff in the pursuit of their studies and in the publication of the results of such studies. It is not a part of their function to determine, control, or influence the conduct of particular investigations or the conclusions reached."

The President bears final responsibility for the decision to publish a manuscript as a Brookings book. In reaching his judgment on the competence, accuracy, and objectivity of each study, the President is advised by the director of the appropriate research program and weighs the views of a panel of expert outside readers who report to him in confidence on the quality of the work. Publication of a work signifies that it is deemed a competent treatment worthy of public consideration but does not imply endorsement of conclusions or recommendations.

The Institution maintains its position of neutrality on issues of public policy in order to safeguard the intellectual freedom of the staff. Hence interpretations or conclusions in Brookings publications should be understood to be solely those of the authors and should not be attributed to the Institution, to its trustees, officers, or other staff members, or to the organizations that support its research.

Foreword

IN HIS LAST YEAR in office President Carter increased the U.S. defense budget significantly, and President Reagan has further accelerated the buildup of military capabilities. But the Reagan administration has also given priority to domestic economic performance and in September 1981 trimmed its original proposals for defense spending increases. Hence, doubt has been raised about whether the planned military buildup can be sustained. Fiscal constraints on the one hand and concern about the growth in Soviet military power on the other put a premium on analysis adequate to the task of making wise choices about defense expenditures.

The advent of the cruise missile reveals that need in an especially acute form. With recent improvements in guidance and engine technology, cruise missiles have emerged as competitors to ballistic missiles, tactical aircraft, and other weapon systems for a variety of military missions. Depending on the intended purpose, the same missile might be fitted with conventional or nuclear explosives. Strategic and conventional force applications have thereby become closely related. Neglect of cruise missiles by military planners over the past two decades has now given way to measured enthusiasm. Even before their technical development has been completed, cruise missiles have been incorporated in plans for improvements in U.S. and allied strategic forces, as well as several conventional force applications. As a result, the weapon has become enmeshed in European politics and in arms control negotiations with the Soviet Union well before its appearance in any operational form. With these relationships already established, technical opportunity, military purpose, and political context will have to be balanced as plans for using the weapon proceed. Many important decisions are yet to be made, and many implications yet to be discovered.

This book assesses the consequences of cruise missile development in technical, military, and political dimensions. Part 1 describes the special nature, capabilities, background, and costs of cruise missiles compared to other weapons. Part 2 discusses the variety of military missions for which the missile may be suited, the possibilities that other weapons might perform some of those missions more effectively, and various questions about how the cruise missile's strategic and tactical implications might be meshed with arms control. Part 3 outlines the diplomatic and domestic political considerations that have affected the evolution of the cruise missile and plans for its use.

Many people have assisted the development of the analyses in this book. Among those whose criticisms were particularly helpful to the editor are Buddy G. Beck, Robert P. Berman, Bruce Blair, Thomas Blau, Michael Handel, Farooq Hussain, John Kohout, Karl Lautenschlager, Fred McCoy, Clark Murdock, Barry Posen, David Schwartz, Richard Siner, and William D. White. The editor is also grateful to Mary L. Porto for her indirect but invaluable help. A condensed version of Betts's introduction to the volume appeared as an article in *The Washington Quarterly*, vol. 3 (Summer 1980).

John D. Steinbruner, director of the Brookings Foreign Policy Studies program, guided the project from its inception. The manuscript was edited by the Brookings publications staff; its factual content was verified by Clifford A. Wright. Secretarial support was provided by Karin Buchard and Ruth Conrad. The index was prepared by Florence Robinson.

Brookings is grateful to the Ford Foundation for financial support that made this study possible.

The views expressed in this book are those of the authors alone and should not be ascribed to the organizations with which they are affiliated, to the Ford Foundation, or to the trustees, officers, or other staff members of the Brookings Institution.

BRUCE K. MAC LAURY
President

September 1981
Washington, D.C.

Contents

TEXT TABLES

APPENDIX TABLES

TEXT FIGURES

Abbreviations
and Acronyms

ABM	antiballistic missile
ACM	advanced cruise missile
ALCM	air-launched cruise missile
ASALM	advanced strategic air-launched missile
ASAT	antisatellite
ASBM	air-to-surface ballistic missile
ASM	air-to-surface missile
ASW	antisubmarine warfare
AWACS	airborne warning and control system
CEP	circular error probable
CMCA	cruise missile carrier aircraft
DCA	dual-capable aircraft
DSARC	Defense Systems Acquisition Review Council
DSMAC	digital scene matching area correlator
ECM	electronic countermeasures
EOD	externally observable difference
ERW	enhanced radiation warhead ("neutron bomb")
FBS	forward-based systems
FROD	functionally related observable difference
GLCM	ground-launched cruise missile
HLG	High Level Group (NATO)
ICBM	intercontinental ballistic missile
IRBM	intermediate-range ballistic missile
JCMPO	Joint Cruise Missile Project Office

LRTNF	long-range theater nuclear forces
MBFR	mutual and balanced force reductions
MIRV	multiple independently targetable reentry vehicle
MLF	multilateral force
MRASM	medium-range air-to-surface missile
MRBM	medium-range ballistic missile
OSD	Office of the Secretary of Defense
OTH-T	over-the-horizon targeting
PA&E	Office of Program Analysis and Evaluation, Defense Department
RCS	radar cross section
SAC	Strategic Air Command
SALT	strategic arms limitation talks
SAM	surface-to-air missile
SCAD	subsonic cruise armed decoy
SCUD	subsonic cruise unarmed decoy
SIOP	single integrated operations plan
SLBM	submarine-launched ballistic missile
SLCM	sea-launched cruise missile
SNAF	Soviet Naval Air Force
SRAM	short-range attack missile
SSBN	nuclear ballistic missile submarine
SSM	surface-to-surface missile
SSN	nuclear attack submarine
TASM	Tomahawk antiship missile
TEL	transporter-erector-launcher
TERCOM	terrain contour matching
TLAM-C	conventionally armed Tomahawk land-attack missile
TLAM-N	nuclear-armed Tomahawk land-attack missile
TNF	theater nuclear forces
VLS	vertical launching system

Innovation, Assessment, and Decision

RICHARD K. BETTS

TECHNOLOGICAL innovation traditionally plays a crucial role in American defense policy. In its military competition with the Soviet Union after World War II the United States used qualitative advantages in weaponry to compensate for Soviet quantitative advantages in manpower and, more recently, in some elements of nuclear forces. Military, budgetary, diplomatic, and political implications of technological advances, however, are seldom understood and often are not clear until long after new weapons have been deployed.

Ensuring that the full potential of weapon developments is realized and that their inadvertent negative consequences do not outweigh their benefits has become progressively more important. Modern weapon systems are more expensive than their predecessors, so each investment decision has a greater impact on defense capability than in the past. Furthermore, the United States faces an opponent with military power at least equal to its own; and its force posture also affects its relations with its allies. Yet cruise missiles have evolved without a well-defined conception of why they are needed, and without an assessment of their full implications. The programs illustrate how U.S. research and development sometimes operate independent of the policymaking process. Moreover, because there are several variants of the basic weapon, the cruise missile is an issue that cuts across normal jurisdictions in government organization. This makes full strategic assessment extraordinarily difficult.

Richard Betts is a member of the Brookings Foreign Policy Studies program.

Cruise missile technology poses unique challenges for policy planning. First, the missile is extremely versatile, and expectations have expanded about the number of requirements it can fulfill across the nuclear and conventional spectrum of military missions. Second, the technology is maturing at a critical time in East-West relations. Tension has grown between the United States and Soviet Union, anxiety has risen about the military balance, and hopes have receded that negotiated solutions to arms competition will succeed. Third, because of the coincidence of the first two developments, the links between the military and political implications of the technology have become complex—and crucial.

Technological research, development, testing, and evaluation have progressed to the point that critical issues have begun to come into focus. Indeed, important decisions about the deployment of the cruise missile have already been made. Thus the time is particularly ripe for a comprehensive and detailed assessment of the benefits and problems. All of the commitments are not firm. Some are so politically delicate that they may be revised or even reversed. And decisions that are virtually irrevocable will require adjustments in other aspects of force posture and national policy. The technological innovation that provides new options, the strategic conceptualization that provides uses for those options, the political decisionmaking and diplomacy that resolve disputes about strategy, and the interaction among these categories must be evaluated together in order to make sense of the cruise missile's possible promise and disappointments.

Technology: Innovation and Adaptation

The most revolutionary changes in U.S. strategic force posture after those associated with the atomic bomb came in the 1950s and 1960s because of the "confluence of several basic technological advances which came to maturity at more or less the same time—solid-fuel rocket propulsion, high yield-to-weight thermonuclear warheads, inertial guidance, compact solid-state electronics and computers, MIRV and re-entry technology."[1] In the latter part of the century, if exotic developments in directed energy research ever pan out, particle-beam weapons or laser weapons may present even greater changes, possibly shifting the strategic balance in favor of defensive systems. In the immediate future, however,

1. Harvey Brooks, "The Military Innovation System and the Qualitative Arms Race," *Daedalus,* vol. 104 (Summer 1975), p. 78.

the principal weapon innovation is the cruise missile. (Major strategic systems such as the MX and D-5 ballistic missiles will not be available before the late 1980s.) This innovation is peculiar in that it combines new technologies with old, evolutionary rather than revolutionary developments, to yield novel options.

New Wine in Old Bottles

The simple cruise missile (Germany's V-1 buzz bomb) made its debut in World War II.[2] The Allies had experimented with television-steered bombs[3]—forerunners of present-day precision-guided munitions—but matching of such sophisticated guidance developments with cruise missile vehicles was not to occur for decades. Crudely guided cruise missiles were developed and deployed in the 1950s but never appeared reliable or promising enough to compete with emerging ballistic missile systems. The Snark cruise missile, for example, was a fiasco: "The average miss distance was over 1,000 miles. At least one came down in the wrong hemisphere, disappearing somewhere in the interior of Brazil."[4]

What transformed the neglected cruise missile into an important part of U.S. defense programs was uncoordinated, integrative, and synthetic technological innovation, rather than a deliberate effort or an epochal breakthrough.[5] Several developments reaching fruition around 1970, par-

2. The Allied Supreme Commander, Dwight D. Eisenhower, claimed that if the Germans had perfected and used their V weapons half a year earlier the invasion of Europe might not have been possible. *Crusade in Europe* (Doubleday, 1948), p. 260. Defenses against the crude V-1 improved quickly, however, as the Allies used proximity fuses in antiaircraft fire. According to the official history of the wartime Office of Scientific Research and Development, in the last four weeks of V-1 attacks, air defenses knocked down, respectively, 24 percent, 46 percent, 67 percent, and 79 percent of the incoming missiles. "On the last day in which a large quantity of V-1s were launched against British shores, 104 were detected by early warning radar but only four reached London." James Phinney Baxter 3d, *Scientists Against Time* (Little, Brown, 1950), pp. 234–35. The lack of institutional enthusiasm for cruise missiles is reflected in the wisecrack made by an Air Force officer: "Remember, the last side to use buzz bombs lost."
3. Baxter, *Scientists Against Time*, pp. 193–200.
4. Edmund Beard, *Developing the ICBM: A Study in Bureaucratic Politics* (Columbia University Press, 1976), p. 224, n. 15.
5. "The cumulative effect of many small evolutionary improvements in the parameters of component technologies can often be as revolutionary as . . . dramatic basic developments." Harvey Brooks, "The Military Innovation System," p. 78. Technological drift (J. P. Ruina's term), which results in spin-off benefits, "need not result from the decisions of higher authority or the formal R&D machinery at all. It involves minor improvements in systems and components, to cope with minor

ticularly those that substantially improved guidance, made the cruise missile distinctly more attractive than it had been in earlier incarnations: small efficient turbofan engines; microminiaturized electronics; high-energy propellants; small high-yield warheads, both nuclear and conventional; more accurate mapping data; and less radar-reflective airframes. (One primary element—the terrain-contour-matching guidance system—had actually been invented in the late 1950s.)

The newer cruise missile appealed to observers for its apparent wide application. Some of these early expectations were excessive because operational constraints were misunderstood, and some ideas about the ultimate potential for variants of these systems bordered on the euphoric or the fantastic. Two analysts, for example, argued that by reducing the flight range of bombers carrying the missiles, tanker requirements would be reduced (in fact, as long as the missiles are carried on external pylons, greater air drag will *increase* tanker requirements); and looking ahead to an advanced conventional cruise missile, they rhapsodized that "if developed to employ multiple anti-armor warheads, as few as four cruise missiles could search out and destroy up to 200 enemy tanks."[6] Recent testing has led to more modest assumptions about cruise missile virtuosity, at least in the first generation.[7] Technological uncertainties, though, cut in both directions: variation, refinement, and combination of advances may produce remarkably new sorts of weapons.[8]

---

snags which have appeared during development, marketing, deployment, or servicing, but whose cumulative impact can . . . make possible substantial system changes." Harry G. Gelber, "Technical Innovation and Arms Control," *World Politics,* vol. 26 (July 1974), p. 510.

6. Robert L. Pfaltzgraff, Jr., and Jacquelyn K. Davis, *The Cruise Missile: Bargaining Chip or Defense Bargain?* (Cambridge: Institute for Foreign Policy Analysis, 1977), pp. 21, 36. If all the strategic air-launched missiles are carried internally to eliminate the extra drag, the number of deliverable warheads per carrier would be reduced. For another optimistic view of the potential of conventional cruise missiles against mobile targets, see "Cruise Missiles with Laser Radars Studied," *Aviation Week and Space Technology,* December 1, 1980, p. 141.

7. See *Most Critical Testing Still Lies Ahead for Missiles in Theater Nuclear Modernization,* Report to the Congress by the Comptroller General of the United States, MASAD-81-15 (General Accounting Office, 1981), pp. 14–15.

8. A report on the U.S. Air Force study Strategic Missile System (SMS) 2000, which projects *ballistic* missile technology beyond the year 2000, suggests that "a hybrid cruise missile/ballistic system could loiter while operating in the air-breathing mode to assure survivability over protracted periods. Upon receipt of the 'go code,' the weapon transitions to ballistic missile operation to provide for a rapid and reliable penetration capability." Edgar Ulsamer, "In Focus . . ." *Air Force,* February 1981, p. 23.

The cruise missile became appealing despite the greater unit effectiveness of other systems (such as the ballistic missile and tactical aircraft) for two principal reasons: first, during the crucial years of research and development (through the mid-1970s) it was not constrained by SALT agreements; second, and most important, it appeared inexpensive and thus susceptible to deployment in large numbers.[9]

Historically, military establishments usually prefer quantity to quality in weapons—often mistakenly, considering the verdicts of war.[10] After World War II, however, the unmatchable quantity of Soviet conventional forces and the unassailable American superiority in scientific ingenuity encouraged U.S. reliance on technological advantages. The military services became accustomed to the rapid pace of innovation, large research and development bureaucracies burgeoned, and the services became more dependent on science while retaining a mobilization base psychology; planners thus concentrated on maximizing the sophistication of weapon systems—to the point of "gold plating," in the view of critics.[11]

In recent years the pendulum has swung toward concern about quantity. Unit costs of high-performance weapons have climbed geometrically, the technological sensitivity of complex systems has outstripped maintenance capacity (leading to extremely low readiness rates for weapons low in number to begin with, such as state-of-the-art F-14 and F-15 aircraft), and recognition has grown of the advantages the Soviet force posture has derived from sacrificing some elements of quality in the interest of fielding high numbers. Operations research often points to the determinacy of quantity.[12]

9. "Because the weapon was a one-shot deal, expected to perform only once and then for a few hours at most, cheaper materials, lower manufacturing tolerances, and other shortcuts could be made in design and production. The absence of a crew member and associated safety devices, instrumentation and safety factors in engine and airframe further cut weight, complexity, and cost." Kenneth P. Werrell, "The Cruise Missile: Precursors and Problems," *Air University Review*, vol. 32 (January–February 1981), pp. 36–38.

10. See I. B. Holley, Jr., *Ideas and Weapons: Exploitation of the Aerial Weapon by the United States during World War I* (Yale University Press, 1953), pp. 175–76.

11. See Robert J. Art, "Restructuring the Military-Industrial Complex: Arms Control in Institutional Perspective," *Public Policy*, vol. 22 (Fall 1974), pp. 425–28, 431–32.

12. See *Models, Data, and War: A Critique of the Foundation for Defense Analyses*, Report to the Congress by the Comptroller General of the United States, PAD-80-21 (GAO, 1980), pp. 67–70. Calculations such as Lanchester equations rest on engagements between similar weapons (such as tanks versus tanks), which limit their analogy to cruise missiles used against totally different targets.

The appeal of the cruise missile is its potential *combination* of high quality and quantity, with emphasis on the latter. While simpler and further from the cutting edge of scientific advancement than more specialized weapons, the system seems to many observers (mainly civilian strategists) more than adequate for the requirements of its missions. (The limitations of these expectations are explored in part 2.) The simplicity and commonality that make the cruise missile versatile permit economies from very large purchases.[13] Moreover, the cruise missile's adaptability may make it better than other systems for rapid modernization of forces. What is salient, in this view, is not that the cruise missile's technology is efficient, per se, but that the cruise missile will permit faster innovation in "a changing defensive threat environment. A missile design can be modified more quickly than that of a manned aircraft, and performance parameters can be attained which are not economically feasible for manned aircraft."[14] Nevertheless, the military services did not leap to adopt the cruise missile, which raises the difficult issue of the logical relation between technological advance, acquisition policy, and employment doctrine.

Technological Change and Military Doctrine

The quantity-quality trade-off is a useful but oversimplified way of bringing procurement issues into focus. A new weapon cannot be evaluated in isolation because its capability may be unnecessary or redundant. It must be evaluated (a) according to mission requirements and probable combat situations in terms of the three critical ingredients of military efficacy (mobility, striking power, and vulnerability)[15] and (b) relative to the other elements of force posture. Because experience with existing weapons establishes clearer perceptions of their utility, military planners sometimes develop attachments to them that inhibit willingness to expend resources on novel alternatives. In the past, some military innovations have lain dormant for many years before being adopted by defense estab-

13. As time has passed, skepticism has grown about how cheap cruise missiles will really prove to be, compared to alternatives, when costs of the full system (including platforms for delivery) are considered. See Desmond Ball, "The Costs of the Cruise Missile," *Survival,* vol. 20 (November–December 1978), and chapter 4 in this book.

14. John J. Kohout III, "Cruise Missile Carrier or Manned Penetrating Bomber: Must It Be Either Or?" *Air University Review,* forthcoming.

15. See Tom Wintringham, *The Story of Weapons and Tactics: From Troy to Stalingrad* (Houghton Mifflin, 1943), pp. 2–13.

lishments or applied in a meaningful way. Usually this is because authorities do not modify prevailing concepts of strategy or tactics to take account of the new options. "New weapons when not accompanied by correspondingly new adjustments in doctrine are just so many external accretions on the body of an army."[16]

Often it takes the rude and costly awakening of combat to overcome entrenched military interest groups and force the issue. As Rebecca West said, "Before a war military science seems like a real science, but after a war it seems more like astrology."[17] For example, the machine gun was available for over a quarter century before World War I, yet in 1914 each British division had only twenty-four of them! "In view of the scale of expenditures for other types of weapons during this period, it must certainly have been military policy and not limited appropriations which determined the number of machine guns authorized. By the end of 1918 there were over 500 machine guns in each British division."[18] In the nuclear era it is even more vital to anticipate the implications of technology, in order to be able to adapt it quickly to deterrence and to be ready with a doctrine for its utilization if deterrence fails, because the superpowers are unlikely to have the time to make significant adaptations according to experience in war.

New technology, however, does not in itself warrant basic changes in strategic or tactical doctrine.[19] The machine gun experience exemplifies not the stupidity of the British military establishment but the difficulty in making judgments before the test of major war. In 1914 machine guns were heavy and not very reliable. The British had been using them in colonial wars but had found that the rifle in the hands of good marksmen was more effective. In World War I, static trench warfare provided opportunities for enfilading fire, the pressure of total war promoted technological improvements, mass armies with high attrition rates precluded the discipline and marksmanship that had made the infantry rifle a better weapon, and human-wave attacks offered ideal targets for automatic fire. Proper adaptation of the weapon thus depended on both the point it had reached in development and the tactical situation in which it would be employed.

16. Holley, *Ideas and Weapons,* p. 14.
17. Quoted in Frank J. Stech, *Estimates of Peacetime Soviet Naval Intentions: An Assessment of Methods,* N0014-78-C-0727, prepared for the Office of Naval Research (Bethesda, Md.: Mathtech, 1981), p. 1.
18. Holley, *Ideas and Weapons,* p. 16.
19. I am indebted to Michael MccGwire for this and the following paragraph.

The tank may be a clearer example of the considerations that should inform the integration of the cruise missile into doctrine, especially in conventional warfare. The British and French in 1940 failed completely to appreciate the possibilities of armored warfare, while the Germans—who were coming from behind and *had* to develop new concepts—used it to revolutionize their capability. This suggests the U.S. need for innovative use of cruise missiles to counter Soviet superiority in ground forces (and similar to the Russians' use of naval cruise missiles to outflank the West's maritime technological superiority). More precise assessment is critical because, as subsequent chapters show, more sober estimates of the cruise missile's virtuosity lessen the confidence of early enthusiasts for its revolutionary capability, yet the promise of the system is still greater than early skeptics admitted.

As with most new weapons, the cruise missile is being fitted, for the most part, into existing operational concepts. Depending on how overall defense procurement and military commitments develop in the 1980s, this practice may prove to be sensible. But if the missile is to be used effectively for deterrence and defense, it is important to ask whether military doctrine or war plans should be changed. The answer depends in part on whether the missile is an *addition* to nuclear and conventional capabilities or a *replacement* or *substitute* for other systems.

In strategic forces, the air-launched cruise missile (ALCM) has been justified primarily as a support to the role of the bomber by compensating for its declining capacity to penetrate deep into Soviet airspace. (However, if substantial commitments are made to deploy a new penetrating bomber, the question of new uses for the ALCM may become salient.) In theater nuclear forces (TNF) doctrinal adaptation is more challenging, in part because doubts about the coherence of employment doctrine existed long *before* the advent of cruise missiles, and in part because the potential range of the ground-launched cruise missile (GLCM) appears to some (at least to the Russians) to present a significant new dimension of operational capability. Similarly, for NATO war planning the role of cruise missiles with conventional warheads is uncertain because it overlaps the role of tactical aircraft. Finally, use of the sea-launched cruise missile (SLCM) for naval warfare raises doctrinal questions because of the uncertainties about what platforms it should be deployed on and its relation to carrier air power. Chapters 5, 6, and 8, respectively, consider these issues.

There is no automatic relation between technological and doctrinal innovation. In the Soviet Union the Stalin period, for example, was one of stagnation in doctrine but revolutionary change in force structure and planning (acquisition of nuclear weapons, inauguration of missile programs, development of air defenses), while the situation was reversed in the mid-1950s—ferment in doctrine with modest changes in force posture.[20] It is often unclear whether technological push or doctrinal pull dominates. Nor is it evident which tendency *should* dominate. Scientific breakthroughs cannot always be made to order for military planners, and serendipitous discoveries can offer unsought benefits.

The logical relation of strategy to technological change also depends on more general characteristics of national approaches to defense. In one view, the American military establishment usually values flexibility and decentralization and expects great uncertainty on the battlefield; thus the United States "builds weapons to be multipurpose, rather than narrowly specialized, and we expect operations to differ from plans."[21] Emphasis on unit quality and technological substitution for manpower tends to make "technology . . . drive both strategy and doctrine."[22] The Soviet Union views war more as a science, and values centralization, inflexible command, and mass as an offset for uncertainty; "military doctrine is expected to produce weapons requirements to 'pull' technology."[23] (For Americans, both approaches are valid. The former makes sense for the side that feels more at the mercy of uncertainty and expects to be the reactive party in a war, while the latter is more sensible for the side that expects to have the initiative in undertaking combat.)

If the American approach described is valid, the versatility of the cruise missile should make it an unambiguously ideal investment. Other considerations, however, affect procurement. One is opportunity costs. The cruise missile will not be a free good in the U.S. defense budget, piled on top of a force that would be otherwise the same, but may pose trade-offs with alternative weapons. This is the principal reason that the services were not in the vanguard of its proponents: the Air Force did not want to divert commitment from the penetrating bomber and tactical aircraft; the Navy did not want to lose allocations for conventional attack

20. A. W. Marshall, *Problems of Estimating Military Power,* P-3417 (Santa Monica, Calif.: Rand Corp., 1966), p. 18.
21. Richard G. Head, "Technology and the Military Balance," *Foreign Affairs,* vol. 56 (April 1978), p. 547.
22. Ibid., p. 550.
23. Ibid., p. 548.

submarines or other ships. The original impetus for cruise missile development, and the driving force that maintained high priority for the programs, came primarily from the civilian sectors of the Pentagon—research and development offices and secretaries of defense. If buying more cruise missiles requires buying fewer other weapon systems, the United States needs to determine whether its capability as a whole would be better or worse.

Another issue is whether the military utility of a weapon deployment may be neutralized or outweighed by negative political ramifications or by Soviet countering deployments that might otherwise be avoidable. Consider one of the last major departures in the configuration of strategic forces, one that was not even hobbled by service skepticism: multiple independently targetable reentry vehicles (MIRVs). This innovation was not difficult because there was negligible opposition; it appealed to many bureaucratic constituencies, for different reasons.[24] One need not argue that deployment of MIRVs was undesirable, given realistic alternatives, to recognize that ideally (if effective arms limitation had been feasible) confidence in American security might ultimately have been stronger if MIRVs had not been invented. (MIRVs theoretically permit a small number of missiles launched in a first strike to destroy a large number of the enemy's missiles, whereas single-warhead missiles reverse the requirements. Thus, with MIRVs, equivalence in fixed-base ballistic missile launchers favors the side striking first; without MIRVs, the side striking second.)[25] This became clear to some decisionmakers only when the issue was moot—after both the United States and the USSR had tested the system.

Among arms controllers, fears that strategic cruise missiles could have a similar effect have actually ebbed since the early 1970s, but some believe that deployment of the weapons for TNF could eventually boomerang by provoking more threatening Soviet responses. Whether or not this is true (it would not matter if, in the absence of the provocation, the Russians were to allocate that increment of resources to other equally threatening capabilities), and as long as arms limitation agreements re-

24. Ted Greenwood, *Making the MIRV: A Study of Defense Decision Making* (Ballinger for the Program for Science and International Affairs, Harvard University, 1975), pp. 13–50.

25. MIRVs did enhance U.S. second-strike countervalue targeting capabilities, though, by increasing the number of warheads deliverable by SLBMs.

main even remotely possible, it is wise to explore the question thoroughly before all decisions and deployment become irrevocable. Innovation, in short, offers costs as well as benefits. The costs can be neutralized by other complementary and compensating innovations—heavier investment in counter-countermeasures to overcome adversary responses—or effective arms control agreements.

Since the mid-1970s, expectations about the degree to which arms control agreements with Moscow can alleviate Western security problems have declined markedly. The disillusionment is due in part to the deterioration of détente and in part to the belief that the negotiation process cannot cope with the pace of technological innovation. The U.S. cruise missile and the Soviet Backfire bomber, for example, unraveled the 1974 Vladivostok agreement. Continuous qualitative change, even if asymmetrical, may still be stabilizing if it redresses an imbalance or if it contributes more to the innovating side's invulnerability than to the other side's vulnerability. To some observers, cruise missiles are promising because they accomplish both purposes (although there is no evidence that Soviet strategists appreciate prevalent American concepts of the benign characteristics of cruise missiles—that is, their lack of utility for a first strike—that flow from their long flight times). In any case, this sort of stabilization is emergent from competition and not easily compatible with negotiated forms of limitation. Although ALCMs were eventually accommodated within SALT II, that treaty took seven years to negotiate, and then was not ratified. If negotiations are revived, the decision to modernize NATO long-range theater nuclear forces with GLCMs may make a SALT III even more difficult. Thus the challenges of technology are compounded by the complexities and uncertainties of the strategic, diplomatic, and domestic political environments within which policymaking must unfold.

Strategy: Balances and Operations

A mature and realistic national strategy must integrate the imperatives and constraints of three arenas: the military, the international political, and the domestic political. Any formulation that excludes any one of these considerations risks being either irresponsible or infeasible. This section presents the general context within which strategic planning must take place and the broad outline of perhaps the most important of the requirements, the military ones, which decisions on cruise missiles cannot stray far from.

For most of the last thirty-five years the conventional military capabilities of the East for waging a war in Europe have outweighed those of the West (although the size and perceived significance of that advantage has varied over time). This edge is not a predictor of what the situation would be in wartime, because the critical determinant is the behavior of allies. Defections from either coalition—quite likely in any political turmoil severe enough to lead to war—would alter the balance of forces in combat. Without the ability to forecast which alliance would prove less cohesive, however, peacetime indexes of capability are the central military concern.

Three changes in the U.S. strategic position have made the equation change. The first was caused by the Sino-American rapprochement of the early 1970s, which reduced the requirement for U.S. forces to fight a major war in Asia. The tables have turned on the superpowers since the 1950s; it is now Moscow rather than Washington that must worry most about a two-front war. This change, however, did not relieve NATO's requirements, because (a) the Soviet Union built up forces against China without compromising the capabilities of the Warsaw Pact (indeed, after 1968, Soviet formations in Eastern Europe improved); and (b) the reduction of U.S. requirements for contingencies in East Asia was translated more into a reduction of total capabilities than a transfer to reinforce NATO.

The second change is the emergence of parity at best, or Soviet superiority at worst, in strategic nuclear forces. NATO's pretensions that the option for first use of American strategic forces compensates for inadequacy in conventional or theater nuclear defenses are less credible than ever. Whether or not Soviet advantages in a majority of the indexes of nuclear force effectiveness translate into political or military benefits, the consensus in the United States is that the balance should be redressed, especially in capabilities for destroying hard targets.

The third and most recent change is the emergence of a new major front in the Persian Gulf–Indian Ocean area because of Western dependence on Middle Eastern oil, the collapse and alienation of America's proxy (Iran), and the Soviet advance into Afghanistan, which brought their potential for projecting power closer to the Persian Gulf.

The net effect of these changes has been to widen the gap between policy commitments and the military capabilities to back them up. This gap has always existed, although it was narrowest in the 1960s.[26] To estimate how the cruise missiles might contribute to closing the gap, or at least to keeping it from becoming wider, it is necessary to understand how perception of threat has related to the development of both defense programs and concepts of political solutions to military competition, and to appreciate the consequences of uncertainty.

Defense Planning in Flux

American defense strategy has not been clear, consistent, or free of controversy since 1945. Debates about the proper levels and uses of U.S. weapons have often been clouded by disagreements or confusion within the American defense community, and between Washington and allied governments, over concepts of deterrence, assumptions about Soviet aims and capabilities, and the relation between conventional and nuclear forces. These uncertainties have sometimes had beneficial effects, allowing political and diplomatic consensus and thus presenting the West's adversaries with a united front despite underlying dilemmas.

In the past, confusion about the potential of new weapon systems or inconsistencies between declared and actual policies did not lead to disaster because contradictions were not forced into high relief. In the 1950s and early 1960s, when East-West tension was high, U.S. strategists debated the logic of massive nuclear retaliation and the adequacy of conventional forces, but anxieties were often cushioned by a consensus that the United States possessed substantial nuclear superiority over the Soviet Union. There was no consensus on whether such superiority was meaningful, or an adequate offset to perceived conventional inferiority, but it reduced the ranks of those who feared that the West could easily fall prey to Soviet coercion, since those most fearful that deterrence was delicate were the ones who attached the most significance to nuclear superiority. When confidence in nuclear superiority was shaken at the end of the 1950s (the mythical missile gap), the supposed danger was soon neutralized by the Kennedy administration's buildup of nuclear and conven-

26. Robert E. Osgood, *Limited War Revisited* (Westview Press, 1979), pp. 11–14; Samuel P. Huntington, *The Common Defense: Strategic Programs in National Politics* (Columbia University Press, 1961), pp. 7, 22, 35–53.

tional forces; given its expanding economy and relatively modest demands on the federal budget for domestic social expenditures, the United States could devote close to 10 percent of gross national product to defense. In the early 1970s confidence in U.S. military superiority over the USSR ended, but détente and successful SALT negotiations reduced apprehension about the Soviet threat commensurately.

By the end of the 1970s none of those old reasons for a relaxed attitude toward uncertainties in American policy applied any longer. As the 1980s dawned, optimism about negotiated solutions to military competition had largely evaporated. Views of the Soviet threat, in terms of both capabilities and intentions, had become more alarmed than at any time since the Kennedy administration. Even with increases in defense spending and cuts in social programs, the United States will not reacquire a margin of superiority similar to that of the early 1960s: though still large, the gap between U.S. productive potential and that of the Soviet Union has narrowed while domestic demands on U.S. spending have grown dramatically. Moreover, the end of conscription raised the proportion of personnel costs in defense allocations. Meanwhile, Soviet strategic forces grew tremendously without any loss (indeed, with some gain) in Soviet conventional power.

In this situation, with its smaller margin for inefficiency and misdirection, decisions on weapon programs take on heightened significance. The versatility of the cruise missile and the commonality of many of the components of its various types lend it an aura of an easy all-purpose answer for strategic and tactical requirements. However, uncertainties remain. For one, the missiles are still being developed and tested, and whether actual performance matches theoretical performance is still being determined.[27] For another, a gain in overall capability—that is, whether the cruise missile will perform more cost-effectively than alternative weapon systems—is not assured. Finally, American forces have political and image functions as well as operational requirements, and how cruise missiles will fit into these functions is still in doubt.

---

27. Skeptics also point out the difficulties of ensuring reliability in a system dependent on unproved technical refinements (such as interdependent optical and radar-based terrain-following data), the failure rate of early flight tests (eight crashes out of twenty launches for the ALCM), and lack of control over reliability (the unprecedented requirement for storage of sensitive turbofan engines for thirty-month periods without maintenance). See Andrew Cockburn, "The Air-Launched Version of the Cruise Missile: Building on a Foundation of Failure?" *Defense Week,* vol. 1 (June 23, 1980), pp. 1, 9.

Conceptual and Operational Criteria

"How much is enough," in terms of the contributions of the cruise missile to American and NATO defense posture, depends on the conceptual standards for adequacy. These standards must be assessed for several potential arenas of conflict: nuclear war with the USSR, with central strategic systems of intercontinental range; theater nuclear war, at both short and long ranges; conventional war in Europe; war at sea; and conflicts outside the NATO area. In recent years, the principal official guidelines for strategic nuclear forces, in ascending order of the demands they impose on force posture, have been three.

Assured destruction: the capacity to inflict unacceptable damage upon the Soviet Union's economy and population after absorbing a preemptive attack. As a *minimum* requirement, this is the least controversial criterion. Some eminent spokesmen view assured destruction as a *sufficient* standard, though this view has fewer proponents than in the past.[28]

Essential equivalence: "a condition such that any advantages in force characteristics enjoyed by the Soviets are offset by other U.S. advantages. Although we must avoid a resort to one-for-one matching of individual indices of capability, our strategic nuclear posture must not be, and must not seem to be, inferior in performance to the capabilities of the Soviet Union."[29] This is a psychological and political as well as operational criterion and is measured primarily in terms of static indexes.

Countervailing strategy: a range of flexible force employment options. These include the increased capacity to destroy Soviet military forces and command centers, to match a number of conceivable Soviet attack plans, to deny the achievement of any strategic objective such plans might envisage, and to retain substantial forces in reserve. This calls for "calibrating U.S. retaliation to the provocation. . . . No potential enemy should labor under the illusion that he could expect to disable portions of our nuclear forces without in turn losing assets essential to his own military and political security, even if the exchange were to stop short of an all-out destruction of cities and industry."[30] This standard is the most difficult to

28. See McGeorge Bundy, "Maintaining Stable Deterrence," *International Security*, vol. 3 (Winter 1978–79), pp. 6–10, 13.

29. *Department of Defense Annual Report, Fiscal Year 1979*, p. 56; see also *Department of Defense Annual Report, Fiscal Year 1981*, pp. 68–69.

30. *Department of Defense Annual Report, Fiscal Year 1981*, pp. 66–67. Landmarks in the evolution of this emphasis on selective options are: Secretary of Defense Robert S. McNamara's "no cities" counterforce strategy declaration of 1962–

achieve and also the most controversial because of the popular attention focused on it as a result of Presidential Directive 59 in 1980.

The ALCM offers potential—but uncertain—contributions in all three of these areas, probably least significantly for assured destruction. First, given the countervailing strategy, in wartime the assured destruction capability would be held in reserve for an extended period. The aircraft carrying ALCMs are unlikely to survive that long, at least as a coherent force (although some Air Force planners have a more optimistic view of this possibility, whereby ALCMs could be expended early in the war and the carriers could be recycled as regular bombers).[31] Second, if husbanding the capability of assured destruction through a long war is *not* a requirement, other systems—principally submarine-launched ballistic missiles (SLBMs)—are more logical candidates for the largest share of that mission. Since assured destruction mostly involves striking relatively soft area targets, it does not require the accuracy and flexibility of the cruise missile (which supposedly make them useful against hardened point targets). Thus the cruise missile is more capable than necessary for simply inflicting damage on population or economic assets, unless it were

---

64; Secretary of Defense James R. Schlesinger's implementation in 1974 of rapid retargeting capability, principally through the command-data buffer system (National Security Decision Memorandum 242); President Jimmy Carter's Presidential Directive 18 in 1977, resulting from the study of U.S.-Soviet relations and U.S. force posture (Presidential Review Memorandum 10); the targeting review mandated by PD 18, completed in 1978; and the development of plans and systems directed in 1980 to ensure wartime protection of national leadership and survival of telecommunications, reconnaissance, and target acquisition capabilities to support nuclear operations in a long war (Presidential Directives 53, 58, and 59). See also the text of Secretary of Defense Harold Brown's speech at the Naval War College, press release, Office of the Assistant Secretary of Defense for Public Affairs, August 20, 1980, pp. 5–7; Edmund S. Muskie, "U.S. Nuclear Strategy," *Current Policy*, no. 219, Department of State, September 16, 1980; Michael Getler, "Carter Directive Modifies Strategy for a Nuclear War," *Washington Post*, August 6, 1980; Richard Burt, "Better Protection of Leaders in War Ordered by Carter," *New York Times*, August 12, 1980; and Desmond Ball, *Developments in U.S. Strategic Nuclear Policy Under the Carter Administration*, CISA Working Paper 21 (Los Angeles: University of California at Los Angeles, Center for International and Strategic Affairs, 1980).

31. "After an initial SIOP strike mission . . . the missile carrier would return to a surviving base where it could be rearmed with SRAMs and gravity weapons. It would then fly a second mission, this time penetrating the now disarticulated defense environment to accomplish bomb damage assessment and strike surviving targets. . . . Other missile carriers can return . . . and subsequently assume dispersed or airborne alert as a secure reserve." Kohout, "Cruise Missile Carrier or Manned Penetrating Bomber."

more survivable or penetrative than SLBMs, which it is not. To those who still consider assured destruction a criterion for sufficiency, the cruise missile should not appear vital except to the extent that its deployment might save money by forestalling more ambitious modernization programs, such as a new penetrating bomber and heavier and more accurate ballistic missiles.

The most obvious contribution of the cruise missile to U.S. force posture is in essential equivalence. In the 1980s, at least, the USSR will not have cruise missiles comparable to American models. By virtue of their newness, the manner in which they diversify modes of delivery, and their alleged capabilities for destroying hardened military targets (the limits of which are explored in chapter 5), the cruise missile should offset some of the apparent Soviet gains in the strategic balance derived from their massive advantage in ICBM throw weight. At a minimum, the ALCM will mitigate the perception of U.S. strategic inferiority by preserving the role of the bomber leg of the triad.[32] At a maximum, it will encourage the perception of a net increase in capability that will help plug the window of vulnerability before more impressive counterforce capabilities (the MX and D-5 ballistic missiles) become available. (Even if the ALCM is not a satisfactory quick fix it is the *only* fix aside from the Trident I C-4 SLBM currently programmed.) Whether or not such perceptions are warranted, they should be enhanced by the Soviet Union's vigorous complaints about the new threat they feel from the U.S. cruise missile.[33] And if the cruise missile prompts the Soviet Union to invest more heavily in

32. This was the principal consideration that led to earlier favorable assessment of ALCMs. See Alton H. Quanbeck and Archie L. Wood, with the assistance of Louisa Thoron, *Modernizing the Strategic Bomber Force: Why and How* (Brookings Institution, 1976). This study's conclusion that ALCMs could *substitute* for a new penetrating bomber (the B-1) by extending the efficacy of B-52s (or by allowing less capable carrier aircraft to perform similar missions by standing off beyond Soviet air defenses) was controversial. See Francis P. Hoeber, *Slow to Take Offense: Bombers, Cruise Missiles, and Prudent Deterrence* (Washington, D.C.: Georgetown University, Center for Strategic and International Studies, 1977); and Elmo R. Zumwalt, "An Assessment of the Bomber-Cruise Missile Controversy," *International Security,* vol. 2 (Summer 1977), pp. 47–58.

33. In anticipation of the 1979 NATO decision to deploy GLCMs, "a leading West German politician was told by an authoritative Russian that West German acceptance of the new arms would endanger the country's security 'more than Operation Barbarossa did.'" Flora Lewis, "Soviet Warns West on New U.S. Missiles," *New York Times,* November 23, 1979. *Window of vulnerability* refers to the period in the 1980s during which U.S. forces are in their lowest position relative to Soviet forces.

air defenses, it may constrain Soviet allocations to offensive systems, thus enhancing the U.S. position in the more visible elements of the balance.

There is a second dimension of this standard, however, that is more problematic: should theater nuclear forces be equivalent? Chancellor Helmut Schmidt of the Federal Republic of Germany created a stir in 1977 when he argued that parity of U.S. and Soviet central strategic forces required parity at conventional and theater nuclear levels of the military balance.[34] This position contradicted traditional European emphasis on avoiding doubt about U.S. commitment to escalate to the level of intercontinental strikes in the event of war, and Schmidt was subsequently forced to modify his position. The NATO High Level Group resolved that the West need not and perhaps should not *match* all Soviet intermediate-range and medium-range forces, in effect rejecting parity as a standard for long-range theater nuclear forces (LRTNF).[35] As a result, NATO decided to deploy fewer than 600 LRTNF warheads, despite the Soviet potential to deploy about 1,500 by the mid-1980s. Thus essential equivalence could be as divisive a criterion for the role of the GLCM as it is a confidence-building standard for the role of the ALCM.

The contribution of the cruise missile to a countervailing strategy is the most uncertain of all. Its flexibility and accuracy are compatible with such a strategy in principle.[36] But in practice its flexibility depends on bombers being withheld for a substantial time and on mission planning support capabilities remaining intact so they can retarget the ALCMs.

34. "The 1977 Alastair Buchan Memorial Lecture," *Survival,* vol. 20 (January–February 1978), pp. 3–4.

35. John B. Ritch III and Alfred Friendly, Jr., *SALT and the NATO Allies,* Committee Print, A Staff Report to the Subcommittee on European Affairs of the Senate Committee on Foreign Relations, 96 Cong. 1 sess. (Government Printing Office, 1979), pp. 21–22.

36. Accuracy permits use of low-yield warheads, which keep collateral damage down and thus theoretically enhance the capacity to wage nuclear war while holding significant portions of Soviet population and economic assets hostage, thus maintaining deterrence of strikes against U.S. population centers. (The proximity of many Soviet military targets to urban centers, however, would make it extremely difficult to maintain these distinctions.) Flexibility is theoretically enhanced by the capacity to use some ALCMs for defense suppression and, with rotary rack launchers, to select specifically targeted missiles at will, rather than shooting them all at once or in a predetermined sequence. Moreover, storage of ALCMs mounted on pylons allows raising the alert level of bombers much more quickly than if they had to be loaded individually. *Military Posture and H.R. 1872 [H.R. 4040]: Department of Defense Authorization for Appropriations for Fiscal Year 1980,* Hearings before the House Committee on Armed Services, 96 Cong. 1 sess. (GPO, 1979), pt. 3, bk. 1, pp. 646–49.

The GLCM in Europe, which can stay in the field for long periods and will not require elaborate refueling infrastructures or bases to recover in during wartime, could logically be somewhat more applicable for these purposes than the ALCM, although range constraints (which would be aggravated by a retreat of NATO forces on the central front) give the GLCM a smaller potential for target coverage. If ALCMs were used early in the nuclear phase of conflict, saving greater numbers of ballistic missiles for later use, they could more obviously support a long-war strategy. But the demand for weapons capable of great speed in response—principally survivable ICBMs—would probably be highest in that initial phase.[37] Moreover, the counterforce capability supposedly offered by the ALCM is mitigated by its slow flight to target. The Soviet Union would theoretically have ample time to decide to discharge its reserve ICBMs before the ALCMs arrived at the silos. Thus the primary rationales for targeting cruise missiles against ICBMs would be to preclude the reloading of empty Soviet silos for a second salvo and to deny the USSR the option of withholding substantial ensiloed reserves, which in turn would bolster deterrence.

The standards for adequacy for theater nuclear forces have not been articulated as clearly or debated as extensively in public as those for strategic forces based in the continental United States. The consensus that theater nuclear forces contribute to deterrence by supporting the flexible response doctrine (as a bridge between conventional defense and intercontinental nuclear strikes) has been greater than the consensus

---

37. One Navy analyst argues for strategic employment of cruise missiles as superior to ICBMs with MIRVs for the requirements consistent with the countervailing strategy implied by public reports of PD 59: "By selectively retaining spatially separated systems for reserve nuclear forces, the Soviets can widen the required footprint for the average MIRV, leading to a 'virtual attrition' of yield through increased fuel requirements or warhead wastage because of multiple expenditure at isolated targets. The attempt to fire at a nonprogrammed target complex further reduces flexibility for MIRV in that it may preclude optimum warhead-target assignment. The ability to dedicate a single warhead to a single target . . . represents flexibility for the cruise missile." Edward J. Ohlert, "Strategic Deterrence and the Cruise Missile," *Naval War College Review,* vol. 30 (Winter 1978), pp. 27–28. In a long war, however, managing area queues of targets—that is, the gradual collection of targets located so that none of the warheads are wasted (which is more vital when retaliating forces have been degraded by preemption or drawn down by early operations)—is more complex. Either some of the MIRVs must be wasted in order to strike time-sensitive targets, or firing must be postponed until the queue is filled. Ohlert favors sea-launched cruise missiles as an answer to such dilemmas but does not convincingly demonstrate how they would remain sufficiently invulnerable.

about *how* they contribute to deterrence in terms of operational employment plans. Given the reality of mutual superpower deterrence at the strategic level, some American strategists believe tactical nuclear forces offer an *alternative* to strategic forces if the Soviet Army begins to succeed in a conventional invasion. To many European allies, however, the only desirable role for theater nuclear forces if conventional deterrence fails is to serve as a catalyst that ensures that U.S. strategic forces would be drawn into the engagement. Thus policy on TNF has traditionally remained muddled because of the latent contradiction between American and allied interests.

The role of *long-range* TNF beyond the battlefield—including strikes against the western part of the Soviet Union—becomes crucial; this issue involves the GLCMs based in Western Europe, or, if ever deployed, SLCMs earmarked for Supreme Allied Commander, Europe (SACEUR). There are two principal questions in regard to cruise missiles as part of LRTNF in Europe. Do they represent the decoupling alternative that could be in American interest, or the recoupling linkage that is more in European interest? Do they contribute to a separate Eurostrategic balance—a concept extremely controversial in Europe—or are they part of a seamless web of Western escalation potential? (See the discussion in chapter 13.) This ambiguity need not and perhaps should not be resolved, since uncertainty complicates Soviet military planning and buttresses NATO's political solidarity.[38] But the uncertainty is a roadblock to devising either an employment plan or an arms control negotiating position, making the military significance of long-range TNF less separable from the political than any of the other elements of force structure are.

For cruise missiles with conventional armament, the primary conceptual issue is whether or not they will provide new tactical options. The salient question is cost-effectiveness. Do cruise missiles and the platforms required to launch them offer more "bang for the buck" than other systems and platforms (principally land- and sea-based tactical aircraft, aircraft carriers, and surface ships with guns and less expensive missiles)? But more than strategic and theater nuclear forces, whose adequacy is assessed primarily in terms of deterrence theories with large political and psychological components, conventional cruise missile sufficiency depends on operational doctrine (see chapters 6, 7, and 8).

38. Public statements manage to tread carefully around this ambiguity. The *Department of Defense Annual Report, Fiscal Year 1981,* pp. 91–92, notes that LRTNF are designed *both* to operate alone and to prevent any Soviet miscalculation that the USSR could remain a sanctuary during a European war.

Politics: Constraints and Opportunities

Military strategy cannot be devised independent of political considerations. Unilateral initiatives in force posture could guarantee security only in a world where the United States had no need to accommodate sovereign allies, where it could allocate unlimited resources to military power, and where it faced an adversary incapable of countering or neutralizing initiatives with strategic adaptations of its own. None of these conditions exist.[39] Such constraints aside, decisionmakers would still disagree about the proper strategic concepts and procurement choices. Cruise missile programs, more than most other weapon systems, influence politics and are influenced by politics. First, they offer benefits to many constituencies but threaten the preferences of other constituencies. Second, they create an issue at each corner of the U.S.–NATO–Warsaw Pact triangle. And third, they highlight the doctrinal tensions and confusion about the relation between conventional forces, theater nuclear forces, and strategic nuclear forces for deterrence, defense, and negotiation.

If the cruise missile is to be integrated effectively into military policy, therefore, it must pass through three political arenas: (a) U.S. relations with the USSR, including arms control negotiations that could limit either the Soviet threat or Soviet development of options neutralizing U.S. gains from the cruise missile, thus reducing U.S. investment requirements; (b) U.S. relations with NATO allies, whose views and priorities do not always coincide with Washington's; and (c) U.S. decisionmaking on the scale and characteristics of the defense posture as a whole, a maelstrom of competing philosophies, interests, and power bases.

Adversaries and Allies

Hopes that the cooperative elements in the superpower relationship would overtake the competitive ones have declined drastically since the early 1970s. Depending on one's inclinations this can be blamed on a false expectation that the United States could retain its old position in the correlation of forces while building a more stable bilateral relation-

---

39. Some strategic analysts argue that offsetting Soviet improvements pose little threat because the USSR is stretched to its economic limits in military allocations. Even if the Soviet Union has less slack to draw on, however, its political system—more easily than Western legislatures—can squeeze civilian investment and consumption to add to defense investments.

ship; on the relentless buildup of Soviet military power; or on Western
misperception of the actual balance of power and exaggeration of Soviet
assertiveness. In any case, American cruise missile programs have sharply
different significance depending on future relations with Moscow. If there
is no hope of reaching mutually acceptable accommodations on the military balance, a relatively unrestrained U.S. military buildup may appear
the only prudent course. However, even if such a surge is feasible, cruise
missiles may not be as significant a factor as they would be in a more
selective improvement of U.S. forces.[40]

If there is any hope of relieving U.S. defense spending requirements
by inducing Moscow to restrain deployment of threatening capabilities,
two Soviet concerns must be considered (see chapter 11 for an elaboration). The first is whether the cruise missile represents a new or more
intense threat to Soviet targets in a hypothetical American first strike.
Does the ALCM simply *maintain* the efficacy of the declining bomber
force or does it *add* to overall capacity of the triad? And does the cruise
missile increase capability to destroy hard targets and thus put more of
the USSR's retaliatory forces at risk? Many American observers believe
that the ALCM stabilizes mutual deterrence because it is *inherently* a
second-strike weapon. Because it takes hours to reach its target, and
Soviet early warning systems would detect the approach of the carrier
aircraft long in advance of the launch of weapons, Russian leaders would
have ample time to decide to fire their own ICBMs before they came
under attack. No rational attack planner would use such slow weapons
for counterforce preemption, hence Soviet planners should not be concerned that the ALCM is anything but a retaliatory weapon.

Whatever their private assessments of the cruise missile threat, Soviet
leaders give no indication that they view the cruise missile as more benign
than faster weapons; indeed, it is uncertain how far they accept the
prevalent American conceptual distinction between first- and second-
strike weapons. A worst-case planner in Moscow might postulate an
American attack using SLBMs (not highly accurate but fast) and Pershing
IIs (few in number but accurate and even faster) for pin-down strikes to
disrupt the Soviet capability for response; ICBMs and forward-based
aircraft to destroy time-urgent targets; and cruise missiles to finish the job
later on remaining ICBM silos and command posts.

---

40. For a range of options considered by some of the most alarmed critics of
the adequacy of U.S. military posture, see William R. Van Cleave, W. Scott Thompson, and others, *Strategic Options for the Early Eighties: What Can Be Done?* (New
York: National Strategy Information Center, 1979).

The second concern articulated by the Soviet Union is that European-based GLCMs add to the U.S. position in the strategic balance by circumventing the equality in launchers established in the SALT II agreement. This issue resurrects the old dispute between the superpowers about the definition of strategic parity. The Soviet Union prefers to define the relevance of weapons in terms of their ability to reach the opponent's homeland, irrespective of their inherent range. The United States, however, separated from its allies by an ocean, prefers the inherent-range criterion. Otherwise, intermediate-range Soviet weapons (such as the SS-20) could escape constraint and threaten Western Europe, while comparable American weapons would be subject to limitation. To Washington, American forward-based systems counter Soviet theater nuclear forces and are not to be counted with continental-U.S.-based intercontinental ballistic missiles and submarine-launched ballistic missiles against Soviet intercontinental forces. By the Soviet definition, the 464 GLCMs slated for deployment in Western Europe (and which can reach the Russian interior) represent a large addition to U.S. strategic forces. By the Western definition they represent only a modernization response to new Soviet SS-20s and Backfire bombers.

This is the point at which interalliance and intra-alliance politics intersect. The inclusion of the GLCM in the definition of strategic weapons and the exclusion of Soviet medium-range forces would raise the specter of the decoupling of American and Western European security. In the late 1970s, SALT consideration of technological nontransfer and noncircumvention, and the protocol in the SALT II agreement, provoked trepidation in NATO capitals. Assurances from American leaders that the protocol would not be extended and would not inhibit GLCM deployment enraged the USSR. Peculiarly, this quandary leaves the United States at one corner of a triangle in which both its allies and its adversary prefer to regard American theater nuclear forces as strategic—the Russians to limit their vulnerability and maximize their position in the total weapons balance, the Western Europeans to guarantee American commitment to the alliance by guaranteeing the indivisibility of its vulnerability.

The challenge to American leaders in meshing diplomacy and military plans is made more difficult by differences between political and military rationales for long-range TNF and the need to consider a wider range of forces in SALT III discussions. Despite the greater military significance of ballistic missiles, cruise missiles pose the thorniest problem for the mid-1980s because (a) ALCMs will constitute most of the qualitatively new elements in the U.S. strategic force; (b) GLCMs will be greater in number and longer in range than Pershing IIs; and (c) "multi-mission weapons like the cruise missile cannot adequately be counted in an agreement which aims at including all weapons in a specific category because they do not belong to one category alone."[41]

Domestic Interests and Choices

Before the external consequences of cruise missile deployment can be settled, the American government has to decide what priority the weapon should have. Such formulation depends upon the aggregate defense investment, the mix of procurement, and the integration of those choices with arms control schemes.

For those committed to enhancing U.S. capabilities, the cruise missile offers two attractions. First, it can be applied across the spectrum of military engagement: intercontinental strategic, theater nuclear, and conventional. Second, in the 1980s other options at either extreme of the spectrum will be in short supply. New ballistic missiles for strategic forces cannot be deployed in strength before the end of the decade. And without conscription there are special incentives for exploiting improvements in firepower rather than manpower to increase conventional capabilities. These general considerations, however, have not produced unbridled enthusiasm among policy planners (see chapter 12).

Within the military establishment the principal issue is opportunity cost. Throughout the 1970s the Air Force was decidedly unenthusiastic about the ALCM because it appealed to civilian authorities as a substitute for a new penetrating bomber. President Carter rationalized the cancellation of the B-1 in 1977 in large part by the reliance on ALCMs to extend the service life of B-52s for another decade. Since that decision, Air Force planners have accepted ALCMs as a given. They remain somewhat skeptical, however, of more recent suggestions to invest heavily in *conventional* cruise missiles for NATO defense, since such plans might well be implemented at the expense of tactical aircraft.[42]

41. Christoph Bertram, *Arms Control and Technological Change: Elements of a New Approach,* Adelphi Paper 146 (London: International Institute for Strategic Studies, 1978), p. 17.
42. In the mid-1970s some technically oriented analysts believed cruise missiles might completely replace manned fighter-bombers, saving vast sums by eliminating the higher unit cost of aircraft as well as the expensive logistical infrastructure that they require. Kosta Tsipis, "Cruise Missiles," *Scientific American,* February 1977,

Curiously, the arms control community in the mid-1970s joined the Air Force in opposition. The emergence of the cruise missile seemed to threaten SALT—its low cost would make large-scale deployment hard to resist, its range would be hard to verify, and its easier reloadability might make an agreement on limiting numbers of launchers irrelevant.[43] Whereas many Air Force officers were reluctant to believe cost-effectiveness arguments in favor of cruise missiles, many arms control proponents worried that they were *too* cost-effective. They were also reluctant to believe that any alleged stabilization from unilateral deployment of second-strike weapons (even "pure" ones) outweighed the damage to negotiated stabilization (see chapters 9 and 10).

Although SALT II managed to accommodate the ALCM,[44] arms controllers remain concerned about the verification problem posed by conventional cruise missiles as well as nuclear GLCMs and SLCMs. Given the commonality of cruise-missile airframes, it will be extremely difficult to prove to Soviet satisfaction that all cruise missiles should not count as nuclear weapons. Thus, skepticism about cruise missiles persists on opposite grounds—that they are not threatening enough and that they are too threatening. In the eyes of those concerned with improving the U.S.

---

pp. 25–27; Richard L. Garwin, "Effective Military Technology for the 1980s," *International Security,* vol. 1 (Fall 1976), pp. 60–62, 66. These are grandiose views of the military utility of unmanned weapons, which lack the ability to roam the battle area, seek targets of opportunity, or respond to changes in objectives after launch.

43. See, for example, Alexander R. Vershbow, "The Cruise Missile: The End of Arms Control?" *Foreign Affairs,* vol. 55 (October 1976), pp. 136–37, 144. Kosta Tsipis worried that cruise missile development would promote nuclear proliferation and destabilize superpower deterrence by coupling strategic and tactical antisubmarine warfare. "The Long-Range Cruise Missile," *Bulletin of the Atomic Scientists,* vol. 31 (April 1975), pp. 21–25.

44. The SALT II treaty, while placing limits on ALCMs, does not severely constrain U.S. capacity to deploy them. During the term of the treaty the principal constraint on ALCMs is the conversion of B-52s. A new cruise missile carrier will not be available until after the treaty expires. If the Minuteman missile force is really vulnerable to a Soviet first strike, the trade-offs between ballistic missiles and ALCMs posed by MIRV limits are not so disadvantageous. And the protocol disallowing cruise missile deployment in Europe expires before the projected initial operational capability of GLCMs. Some critics assert that the IOC was postponed in order to make the protocol innocuous. This was denied in testimony by Chairman of the Joint Chiefs of Staff David C. Jones. See *Military Implications of the Treaty on the Limitation of Strategic Offensive Arms and Protocol Thereof (SALT II Treaty),* Hearings before the Senate Committee on Armed Services, 96 Cong. 1 sess. (GPO, 1979), pt. 4, p. 1576. The real constraints are the *prospective* pressure from the Soviet Union during SALT III.

position in the military balance, the utility of cruise missiles depends on having them in very large numbers, but successful arms control will inevitably constrain those numbers because until the late 1980s cruise missiles are about all that U.S. negotiators have to bargain with.[45]

As the United States entered the 1980s, resistance to investment in the cruise missile declined. Because of the B-1 cancellation, the distant initial operating capability of the MX, and the perception that SLCMs mounted on surface ships would be more obtainable than comparable levels of striking power from vastly more expensive (and less quickly available) aircraft carrier construction, many elements of the military establishment embraced it as a near-term expedient for reducing the perceived gap between requirements and capabilities. Moreover, the Air Force has less reason to fear the trade-off with manned aircraft since commitment to a penetrating bomber has been renewed, and the consensus has grown that a high-performance plane such as a B-1 derivative (rather than a wide-bodied transport) would be needed as a cruise missile carrier to replace the B-52.[46] If the GLCM permits SACEUR to release dual-capable aircraft for conventional missions at the outset of war rather than hold them back for nuclear missions, Air Force concern about the effect of the cruise missile on the role of tactical air power should be assuaged. Arms control advocates, on the other hand, increasingly focused on staving off

45. The cruise missile was once seen as mainly a bargaining chip to trade away at SALT. See Robert J. Bresler and Robert C. Gray, "The Bargaining Chip and SALT," *Political Science Quarterly,* vol. 92 (Spring 1977), pp. 77–79. The Ford administration subsequently interpreted the 1974 Vladivostok agreement as exempting cruise missiles. One rationale for this course was provided by Colin Gray: "the simplest and most rational American proposal is that cruise missiles of all kinds be excluded from constraint. . . . Range, warhead and (because of the easy-reload potential of cruise-missile launch facilities) even numbers deployed manifestly cannot be verified with any precision. Soviet objections could be met with the following arguments: (1) the treaty would be strictly equitable—should the Soviet Union wish to develop and deploy LRCMs, it would be free to do so; (2) although, for a time, there would be undoubtedly an American advantage in this class of weapons, the United States is not seeking compensation for the vast, and growing, Soviet advantage in ballistic-missile throw-weight, nor for Soviet air defenses and domestic war survival programs." See "Who's Afraid of the Cruise Missile?" *Orbis,* vol. 21 (Fall 1977), p. 529.

46. This argument was based in large part on the slow escape speed of wide-bodied cruise missile carrier aircraft and their greater vulnerability to nuclear effects (from barrages of the aerial sectors through which the carriers would escape) as opposed to a hardened B-1 type carrier. See "Brown Says B-1 'Good Candidate' for Cruise Missile Carrier," *Defense Daily,* August 6, 1980, p. 181. For a contrary view, see Bob Carr, "CMCA: The Confused Missile Carrier Aircraft, Or, How to Pull in Three Directions Simultaneously While Going Nowhere," *Armed Forces Journal International,* February 1980, pp. 68–71.

the MX. Since enhanced U.S. counterforce capability has become politically inevitable, they prefer to have it in slow and more stable cruise missiles than in fast and "destabilizing" ICBMs.

Differences among internal constituencies, however, remain significant for assessing the strategic future of cruise missiles. The heritage of opposition in the Air Force, together with its focusing of innovative energies on manned aircraft, reduces the odds that the service will concentrate on adapting doctrine to make optimal use of cruise missiles. They may become simply accretions, in I. B. Holley's term, or novel concepts for their strategic employment for deterrence and defense may have to come from other groups of planners.[47] Arms control dilemmas also will not go away: the similarity of the missiles' appearance irrespective of the differences in the explosive charges they contain blurs the traditional dichotomies between nuclear and conventional, and strategic and tactical.[48] Something will have to give. If the military utility of the cruise missile is too attractive to compromise, hope for meaningful arms control may not survive, and opponents of arms competition may have to settle for the apparently stabilizing effects of unilateral deployment decisions. On the other hand, if arms-control considerations remain influential, bureaucratic battles may ensue if schemes to permit verification by loading nuclear and conventional versions of the missile with externally observable differences degrade operational efficiency. And if negotiations on theater nuclear forces proceed very far, both military planners and strategists will need to deal with the tension between U.S. war planning and allied views of the proper functions and scale of long-range theater nuclear forces.

Options, Issues, and Decisions

The cruise missile is a reality; it is no longer a potential weapon that can still be shelved. These weapons will have to be integrated into war planning, alliance relationships, and negotiations with the Soviet Union. Many decisions, however, remain to be made (or unmade) if that integration is to be coherent and efficient. Such decisions require a more comprehensive appreciation than has been achieved to date of the links among their technical, strategic, and political implications.

47. Contrary evidence, suggesting innovative approaches to doctrine for cruise missiles within the Air Force, can be seen in Kohout, "Cruise Missile Carrier or Manned Penetrating Bomber?"

48. Richard Burt, "The Cruise Missile and Arms Control," *Survival*, vol. 18 (January–February 1976), pp. 14–15.

The following chapters present detailed discussions of the promise, limitations, and liabilities of cruise missiles. Do they offer a net addition to current military capabilities or simply a replacement for older systems? Will they live up to technical and operational expectations, especially in regard to counterforce capability? Are they more cost-effective than alternative weapons? Should their availability prompt revisions in overall operational doctrines, or is the technological advance they embody modest or familiar enough to simply factor them into traditional employment plans? Are cruise missiles temporary expedients that will be rendered less useful by improvement of Soviet defenses, or will future generations of the missile prove even more capable? Will they buy more in enhanced deterrence and political solidarity of the Atlantic Alliance than they will cost in provocation of Soviet defense planners or aggravation of latent tensions in conceptual solidarity of American and Western European deterrence planners? Because so many types of cruise missiles have been evolving concurrently (with frequent changes of direction), and because they figure in so many arenas of political decision, it is difficult to answer these questions neatly and concisely. Thus some subjects are treated in more than one chapter: chapter 3, for example, gives a chronology of cruise missile programs as background for the detailed discussions that follow on costs and missions (chapters 4 through 8), while chapter 12 analyzes the effect of political and organizational processes on program decisions.

Furthermore, although cruise missile programs have progressed quite far in development, there are still some significant continuing uncertainties in technical data, and estimates of operational capabilities prevent precise answers to any of these questions. For example, sources for chapter 1 attribute much shorter range to the conventional Tomahawk land-attack missile than do sources in chapter 8; and chapters 5 and 6 use different estimates of the number of cruise missiles required to attack airfields successfully. The first example reflects the limitations of an unclassified study, which must rely on publicly available or verbally transmitted data about an evolving technology. The second example reflects the inevitable uncertainty about operational effectiveness of a weapon that has not been fully tested and for which there has been no wartime experience. Rather than obscure the uncertainties, this book lets differing assessments stand. False precision is as bad as inconsistency. Indeed, the aim of this book is to highlight the uncertainties, dilemmas, and contradictions in cruise missile development, to help clarify the choices.

PART ONE

Technology

CHAPTER ONE

Technical Characteristics

JOHN C. TOOMAY

A CRUISE MISSILE is an unmanned, expendable, armed, aerodynamic, air-breathing, autonomous vehicle. Specifying that it is expendable and armed arbitrarily eliminates a number of perfectly rational applications, particularly those of reconnaissance drones, discussion of which would blur the focus of this chapter. Specifying that it is autonomous, that is, that it carries out a programmed mission or guides itself after it is launched, separates it from the family of remotely piloted vehicles and of command-guided vehicles, which are diverse in themselves.

The above definition describes an offensive military weapon for use in furthering U.S. national security objectives. Cruise missiles apparently have qualities which could help attain these objectives, but it is important to understand these qualities. Are they real? Are they technical or political? Are they unique to the cruise missile? Are there weapons that can accomplish the same mission more efficiently? How do costs already sunk in multibillion-dollar weapon systems affect cruise missile uses? What are the future prospects for cruise missiles?

This chapter seeks answers for these questions, by, first, placing modern cruise missiles in historical context; second, explaining the physical principles that differentiate cruise missiles from rocket-powered missiles and the technologies necessary to develop modern cruise missiles; third, describing guidance systems; fourth, speculating on the ideal cruise missiles for certain missions; fifth, describing the cruise missiles being developed; and finally, forecasting the cruise missiles of the future.

John Toomay retired from the U.S. Air Force as a major general and is now a consultant in San Diego.

Past Developments

Although it is almost certain that vehicles meeting the definition of cruise missiles were used in some way as early as World War I, discussions of cruise missiles usually offer the German buzz bomb (V-1) of World War II as the progenitor of the cruise missile.[1] It was certainly the first broad and highly visible (although marginally effective) application, and its design features were precursors to those of modern cruise missiles: jet propulsion (pulse-jet engine),[2] a primitive form of inertial guidance, and relatively slow speed (about 375 miles an hour). But modern cruise missiles fly at altitudes one-tenth those of the V-1, have radar cross sections one hundred times smaller (which reduces detectability), and accuracies two hundred times better.

Technical characteristics of cruise missiles have evolved on a broad front in all the advanced nations, particularly the Soviet Union and the United States, since World War II. (See figure 1-1.) First-generation Soviet cruise missiles have relatively short ranges (due to inefficient engines), large sizes, cumbersome mold lines, and crude guidance, and deployed systems, both air-to-surface and sea-launched, have been continuously upgraded and modified. Recent ones are much more capable, due to supersonic speeds. The Soviet air-to-surface suite goes from the AS-1 through the AS-6, the last being the Backfire bomber antiship missile.[3] The AS-6 is given inertial midcourse guidance and active homing.[4] These air-to-surface missiles have been credited with carrying nuclear weapons since 1961. There is apparently space for a very high-

1. See Ralph Kinney Bennett, "The Missile the Russians Fear Most," *Reader's Digest,* February 1977, pp. 129–32; Juan Cameron, "The Cruise Missile Can Do It All—Almost," *Fortune,* May 8, 1978, pp. 174–84; John Newbauer, "U.S. Cruise Missile Development," *Astronautics and Aeronautics,* September 1979, pp. 24–35. During World War I a 600-pound flying torpedo was built at the Dayton-Wright Airplane Company. See "Cruise Missiles—'Bugs' to Buzz Bombs to B-52 Bomb Bay," Boeing Public Relations Department, Seattle, Washington, December 1980.

2. Pratt and Whitney Aircraft, "The Aircraft Gas Turbine Engine and Its Operation" (Pratt and Whitney Aircraft, East Hartford, Conn., May 1974), p. 34.

3. These and subsequent data on cruise missiles are taken from *Jane's Weapons Systems 1978* (Franklin Watts, 1979), pp. 65, 144, 145, 158.

4. Inertial guidance enables the missile to fly in a manner similar to the automatic pilot of a commercial jet; when the target comes into the coverage of the missile's active system (a radar), the missile homes on the target using the radar returns.

Figure 1-1. *Evolution of the Cruise Missile, United States and Soviet Union, 1951–80*

Soviet Union

Year	Designation	Silhouette	Length in feet
1956	AS-1		27.7
1956	SSC-2b		27.2
1956	SS-N-1		22.5
1959	SS-N-2a		21.5
1960	AS-2		32.9
1961	AS-3		49.1
1962	SS-N-3c		36.5
1962	SSC-1a	Not available	. . .
1965	AS-5		28.2
1965	SS-N-3a		38.5
1967	AS-4		37.1
1967	SS-N-3b		33.5
1967	SSC-1b	Not available	. . .
1968	SS-N-7		23
1970	SS-N-9		29
1970	AS-6	Not available	. . .
1974	SS-N-14	Not available	. . .
1975	SS-N-2c		21.5
1977	SS-N-12		38.5

United States

Year	Designation	Silhouette	Length in feet
1952	Matador		39.7
1956	Regulus I		33
1958	Regulus II		57
1958	Snark		70
1958	Mace		44
1961	Hound Dog		42.5
1970	ALCM/SCAD		14
1970	Harpoon		12.6
1975	Tomahawk		20.5

Source: Based on "U.S. Cruise Missiles," Supplemental Submission by Rear Admiral Walter M. Locke, USN, Director, Joint Cruise Missiles Project, to the House Appropriations Committee, April 30, 1979.

yield weapon, since bomber-type aircraft can carry only one or two of them.

The sea-launched systems are even more numerous. They include the SS-N-1 (no longer at sea), SS-N-2, and SS-N-3 from the 1950s and the SS-N-7, SS-N-9, SS-N-12, and SS-N-19 of more recent vintage. Now in the third generation, such missiles are deployed on a variety of surface and submarine platforms. Nuclear warheads in the kiloton-yield range are assumed. The mission ascribed is always antiship, although theoretically the missiles have some land-attack capability. Analysts on the U.S. side frequently invoke a strategic role for Soviet air-to-surface missiles, particularly those associated with the Backfire bomber, and for sea-launched cruise missiles (whose relative short range is no impediment to attacking U.S. coastal resources).

In the United States there have been two periods of intense activity. The first was immediately following World War II, when some unmanned method for delivering atomic weapons was sorely needed, intercontinental ballistic missiles (ICBMs) having not yet been proven practical. The second began in the 1970s as several advancing technologies gave the cruise missile potentially cost-effective applications, even in the face of continuing progress by the rocket-powered competition.

The intervening period of the late 1950s and all of the 1960s was an era of rocket-powered weaponry, both for intercontinental and short-range use. Cruise missiles were retired in favor of rockets, which were much more reliable and were two to twenty times faster. Consequently, military people with experience in both cruise missiles and rockets were skeptical of the cruise missile advocacy, which began to emerge in the 1970s concurrent with the first strategic arms limitation talks (SALT I).

Physics and Technologies

The fact that cruise missiles are not covered in SALT I motivated their development, but weapon systems do not usually survive on their political expediency alone. The major technical factor which gives the cruise missile an edge over rocket-powered missiles is that, since it breathes air, it does not have to carry an oxidizer and therefore has substantially longer range than a rocket-powered missile of equal weight.

The rocket-powered missile wins on virtually all other counts: it is much faster, it can fly low, it can have lower radar cross section, it can have equivalent accuracy, it is simpler, and it is probably more reliable.[5] But the advantage of the cruise missile is an imposing one. To burn its fuel, a rocket-powered missile must carry oxygen. If it uses a hydrocarbon fuel, the products of combustion are carbon dioxide and water vapor. Thus, the rocket-powered missile must carry enough oxidizer to provide two atoms of oxygen for every atom of carbon and one atom of oxygen for every two atoms of hydrogen. *Fuel for a rocket-powered missile would weigh over three times that needed for a cruise missile to deliver the same energy.*

Current jet fuels yield about 20,000 British thermal units per pound. Pure hydrogen, if it were a practical fuel, provides 50,000 Btus per pound.[6] With both vehicles using hydrogen, the cruise missile would have an even better fuel-to-weight ratio. Since one oxygen atom unites with two hydrogen atoms to form the principal product of combustion (water vapor), the weight advantage of not having to carry along the oxidizer is a factor of eight. This implies that the use of more exotic fuels for cruise missiles may increase their advantage over rocket-powered systems.

The cruise missile has another advantage: for ranges up to several thousand miles the amount of energy needed to push a well-designed cruise missile through the atmosphere is less than the amount required for the rocket-powered missile to reach the same range ballistically.

Technologies that are feasible in themselves cannot always be integrated into an overall system. This is an important point to bear in mind in regard to cruise missile development. Among the technologies scheduled to be used in current cruise missile programs are small efficient jet engines, low RCS (radar cross section), and accurate guidance. Of these, only the small jet engine is peculiar to cruise missiles, but substantial progress has certainly been made in all three areas. The Williams engine used in the family of cruise missiles now in development is a turbofan (more efficient than a turbojet); it weighs about 150 pounds, generates about 600 pounds maximum thrust (about 300 pounds in cruise), and has a specific fuel consumption (SFC) of about one pound of fuel per one

5. The short-range attack missile (SRAM) in its short-range mode flies very low, has extremely low cross section (about an order of magnitude below current cruise missiles), and its solid-state rocket engine is simpler than the small fan-jet of the current cruise missile (flight controls and basic guidance are considered equal in complexity). A rocket-powered vehicle (at velocities below Mach 8, where plasma effects may intervene) can have the same guidance systems as a cruise missile.

6. The National Aeronautics and Space Agency has experimented with hydrogen fuels for aircraft.

pound of thrust per hour. This thrust-to-weight ratio and SFC are not as good as those of bigger engines; nevertheless, they are marked improvements over previous small engines.[7] Such engines are too small to be in demand in the private aviation market.

However, applications of target and reconnaissance drones and development of powered decoys for B-52 bombers kept a small community working during the 1960s. A particular effort in the 1960s by the Defense Advanced Research Projects Agency to achieve manpack jet propulsion also gave impetus to the development.

Guidance and Detectability

Because it flies through air at relatively low velocities, the cruise missile cannot be guided inertially, as the ballistic missile can. The drift of even the best inertial guidance systems (a few tenths of a mile per hour) is too much. The inertial guidance must be aided or updated during the flight by some correcting signal from outside the system. Fortunately, there are available many guidance options which can provide excellent accuracy (several hundred feet) for the delivery of strategic weapons and ample supplementary techniques for providing the pinpoint accuracy (a few tens of feet) required for effective delivery of conventional weapons. In the strategic category—if systems like Loran (long-range navigation system) and the Navstar global-positioning system are discounted because of their potential vulnerabilities to a preemptive attack—there are radar, infrared, and optical mapping schemes.[8] In the tactical category there are all the techniques already used for tactical precision-guided munitions, plus others in development.[9] Only the terrain contour matching (TERCOM) guidance scheme—selected for use in the strategic cruise missiles scheduled for deployment in the U.S. armed forces—and digital scene matching

7. The specific fuel consumption (pounds of fuel per pounds of thrust per hour) of jet engines in commercial airlines is about 0.7. The thrust-to-weight ratio of the General Electric CF-6 engine on the DC-10 (an 8,000-pound engine with 40,000 pounds of thrust) is over five-to-one. Some military jet engines achieve as high as eight-to-one thrust-to-weight ratios (for example, the Pratt and Whitney F-100 engine in the F-15).

8. A radar area correlator has been developed for use on the Pershing II, a theater nuclear ballistic missile.

9. Television, laser, and imaging infrared guidance schemes are best known, but all-weather millimeter-wave and command guidance (Assault Breaker) are receiving emphasis currently. The Navstar global-positioning system is also competitive.

area correlator (DSMAC)—under development for use on a tactical conventional version of the cruise missile—are discussed here.

In its simplest form TERCOM consists of a radar altimeter and a computer. Stored in the computer are digital altitude profiles of parallel strips of terrain from selected locations along the missile's intended flight path. Each set of profiles makes up a terrain contour map. As the missile— steered by a commercial-class inertial navigation system (INS)—reaches the approximate location of a map, the radar altimeter returns generate a real-time altitude profile, which the computer compares with the stored profiles to determine which stored profile the cruise missile just flew across. (Data for both course correction and location with time are needed for the system to fuse its warhead at the right time.) When a correlation is made, the INS is reset and a course correction begins. The missile continues to the next map location, and so on until it reaches the target. Figure 1-2 shows the sequence.

The Defense Department has not released specifics of TERCOM mapping. What follows is derived from estimates of Kosta Tsipis.[10] The ensemble of profiles must be sufficiently large for the missile to intercept the mapped patch, given the drift of the INS; each individual profile must be narrow enough so that the radar altimeter reads the correct altitude even if the missile is not flying down the middle of the strip; and each profile is limited in its length by the drift rate of the INS, since the calculation of more than a few skewed profiles would greatly multiply the processing load.

Since commercial-class INSs have drifts on the order of one mile an hour, and a cruise missile may be launched several hours from landfall from a platform that itself has not received an update for some time, it is clear that the landfall TERCOM map must be twice "several miles" wide (that is, if the missile is flying south, the map must allow several miles to both east and west of the intended point at which the missile intercepts land). Because contour maps are expensive to make, because land gradients are not usually above 10 percent, and because acts of man and nature tend to prevent long-term repeatability of high-resolution measurements, strip widths of a few hundred feet are realistic, allowing strip lengths of many miles. (With INS drift of 100 feet a minute and a velocity of 550 feet a second, the cruise missile would travel over five nautical miles before drifting out of a 200-foot-wide strip.)

10. "Cruise Missiles," *Scientific American,* February 1977, pp. 20–29.

Figure 1-2. *Flight Path of Missile Using Terrain Contour Matching (TERCOM) Guidance*

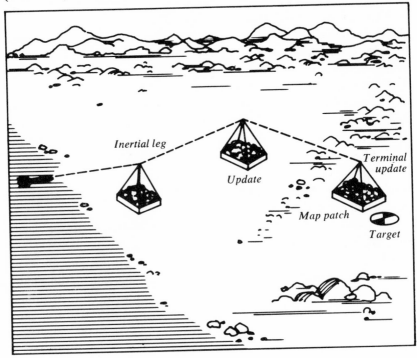

Given a 200-foot-square cell in the altitude profile, a five-mile strip length would give about 150 data points. The correlated profile would then have a "height" of 150 compared to an average "height" of the uncorrelated profiles of about twelve (the square root of 150). Of course ambiguous correlations are possible, but a TERCOM map can be pre-tested for these. If a map yields ambiguities, a new location can be selected.

Because of INS drift, the accuracy delivered by TERCOM deteriorates as the distance from the last fix increases, but at best the accuracy should be on the order of a profile cell size, namely, a circular error probable (CEP) of no less than a few hundred feet.[11]

Contour mapmaking for several thousand cruise missiles is obviously an enormous task: at least a thousand targets, each with several associated TERCOM maps, can be hypothesized. Five thousand five-mile-

11. Ibid., pp. 22, 29.

square maps of 150-by-150 data points would require that over 100 million data points be gathered, evaluated for average radar altimeter characteristics, digitized, and assembled into TERCOM maps.

Maps can be obtained in several ways over friendly territory—by survey teams, by using existing maps, by stereo photography, or by simply flying a radar altimeter over promising terrain. For maps obtained by reconnaissance of denied territory, relative elevation accuracies of perhaps ten feet may be obtained.[12]

Early in the TERCOM development there was much concern about three aspects of mapping. Was there enough terrain in the Soviet Union suitable for making TERCOM maps? Could a proper transform algorithm be developed to make contour data comparable to altimeter returns? If maps could indeed be made, would they be affordable? Answers to these questions seem so far to be favorable.[13] Although most of European Russia is flat, there appears to be adequate variety for good correlations. Extensive flight tests have not only proved that TERCOM works, they have allowed the Defense Mapping Agency—which is responsible for doing all TERCOM maps—to gain experience in generating transform algorithms and in devising ways to generate TERCOM maps more economically. Even so, the cost of TERCOM maps will be around a billion dollars, a substantial portion of the overall program cost.

For tactical conventional applications of cruise missiles, the digital scene matching area correlator supplements TERCOM. The role of TERCOM is to deliver the cruise missile close enough to the target to allow the DSMAC to sense it, perform a correlation, and provide the missile with final guidance instructions. Accuracies equivalent to a few feet are reported.[14]

The early DSMAC system was analog: a stored photographic negative was compared with a photograph taken in flight. The concept was first demonstrated in May 1978 when a Tomahawk cruise missile launched from long range used TERCOM fixes en route. It received its final vernier

---

12. "Elevations are recorded with an accuracy of better than three meters." Ibid., p. 24.

13. "There has never been a false *update* (due to any cause) in the Cruise Missile Program." *Department of Defense Appropriations for 1980,* Hearings before a subcommittee of the House Committee on Appropriations, 96 Cong. 1 sess. (Government Printing Office, 1979), p. 552.

14. Clarence A. Robinson, Jr., "Tomahawk Clears Crucial Test," *Aviation Week and Space Technology,* November 22, 1976. Robinson projects circular error probables of four to ten feet.

guidance instructions from DSMAC and was guided "directly down the middle of the runway under attack."[15]

Analog DSMAC has subsequently been digitized and a competitive-concept validation program is being conducted, using a small piston-engined aircraft. This series of thirty-seven flight tests has been described as going "exceptionally well demonstrating extremely precise updates."[16] Flight tests using DSMAC and Tomahawk missiles were performed in 1979, and a production prototype of DSMAC was demonstrated successfully in the fall of 1980. The technical feasibility of DSMAC is apparently well established, but it has limitations at night and in smoke, dust, and bad weather. The imaging infrared sensor is being investigated as a possibly more cost-effective alternative.

Technology for reducing aircraft and missile RCS, which reduces detectability by enemy air defenses, has been advancing since the 1950s. While much can be done with shaping, ferrites, paints, and other coverings, ferrites are heavy and cumbersome, paints are useful only at relatively high frequencies, and other coverings are delicate and expensive. For *very* low cross-section visibility, dents, joints, and seams are crucial. The stresses of mass production, line maintenance, and years on alert in extreme climates militate against maintaining *very* low RCS. Furthermore, cruise missiles require an engine inlet, which resonates at many frequencies and is difficult to make undetectable.

For effective defense against hard-to-detect cruise missiles, the USSR must develop sophisticated Doppler processing techniques for subclutter visibility. Once these techniques have been acquired further reductions in RCSs will not lead to undetectability. State-of-the-art radars already have prodigious sensitivity, particularly at the relatively short ranges at which cruise missiles would be engaged. The issue is not sensitivity but subclutter visibility and multipath sorting (separating the direct returns from the missile from indirect returns that bounce off the earth at low grazing angles). Subclutter visibility can be made good enough to detect extremely low RCS by improving resolution in angle, range, and Doppler; and multipath can be dealt with in like manner. But in both cases, expensive coherent radars with very sophisticated processing are required. As RCS gets low, designers must worry about other observables such as optical, infrared, and acoustic. Because a cruise missile is small and has a

---

15. *Department of Defense Appropriations for 1980*, Hearings, p. 554.
16. Ibid., p. 555.

small turbofan engine (which has a cool exhaust), its infrared and acoustic observables have low detectability. Clever paints can make it optically insignificant. While rockets have no engine radiation (after boost), their high speeds can cause appreciable radiant skin heating.

The "Ideal" Cruise Missile

The cruise missile defined at the start of this chapter now has a richer set of attributes. With its several-thousand-mile range it can deliver payload more efficiently than a rocket-powered missile, but it must fly slowly (beyond Mach 0.8 its advantage lessens). In navigational accuracy and radar cross section it is competitive. The question now arises, of what utility is such a weapon to our military arsenal? To justify spending the billions of dollars necessary to field new systems we must be able to quantitatively assess their utility. Part 3 of this book examines potential strategies for cruise missile employment. This section highlights the most salient technical attributes that limit or enhance the attractiveness of the cruise missile as opposed to other weapon systems. To put the relative advantage of cruise missiles into perspective, this discussion considers how an ideal version would be designed, irrespective of the actual evolution of U.S. cruise missile programs.

For strategic missions the principal question is how cruise missiles relate to other air-breathing systems, especially the aging B-52 bomber fleet, since there is steadily decreasing confidence in the ability of these aircraft to penetrate Soviet air defenses. While the B-52 can fly low and has long range, it has extremely high RCS and other observables are also high (visual, infrared, and sonic). Although the B-52 has sophisticated electronic and other countermeasures designed to compensate for its high observables, their effectiveness in the face of monotonic Soviet improvements is debatable. The qualities of a properly designed cruise missile are an excellent fit for the perceived deficiencies of the B-52. Where the B-52 might be vulnerable to the Soviet area air defenses because of its high observables and its relatively small numbers (fewer than 350), the cruise missile has low observables and can be deployed in large numbers (more than 3,000 of the strategic version are scheduled to be bought). Furthermore, it can fly lower than the B-52 and has as good or better accuracy.

The penetrating B-52 and the standoff cruise missile are actually complementary, because short-range attack missiles (SRAMs) carried by

B-52s may be needed to penetrate sophisticated terminal defenses. The cruise missile is a hedge against the failure of the B-52 to penetrate *area* air defenses, while the B-52 with SRAMs is a hedge against the failure of the cruise missile to penetrate *terminal* defenses. Unfortunately for the United States, the technology that will allow the Soviet Union to develop look-down, shoot-down interceptors, which will endanger the bomber, is the same technology that will allow terminal defenses to pinpoint cruise missiles in the ground clutter. When the Soviet Union masters that technology, a new era begins.

Given its mission, the principal specifications for the cruise missile can be determined. *Should the cruise missile be the size of a bomber and be launched directly from the United States?* No, because it would not be recallable after being launched on warning, as the manned bomber force is. Furthermore, economies of scale dictate that cruise missiles be taken in a large carrier as close as feasible to the place where they are needed.

What should the cruise missile's range be? It should have sufficiently long range to be able to reach virtually all targets in the Soviet Union after having been launched outside any reasonable Soviet perimeter defense. Reasonable defense perimeters are determined by the effects of the earth's curvature on the detection range of an airborne surveillance radar (at 30,000-foot altitude, the range to the horizon is about 300 miles). The USSR is about 2,000 miles deep from north to south, making about 1,500 miles adequate range for the cruise missile, at least until the Russians develop a more extended defense, which would force carrier aircraft to launch the missiles from a position further back.

How large should the cruise missile be? It should be large enough to deliver a nominal strategic warhead, roughly equivalent to the SRAM, Minuteman III, or Trident, to the specified range. Since the B-52 is an acceptable carrier for the near term, the cruise missile should be designed for carriage on the B-52.

How low should the cruise missile fly? Despite its low RCS, it cannot escape detection by defense radars if it flies high. Low altitude is a powerful aid to penetration since the nap of the earth can reduce the coverage of ground-based radars dramatically. A radar that can detect an aircraft flying at 5,000 feet one hundred miles away will not detect it until it is only twenty miles away if it is flying at 200 feet altitude. Thus a low-flying cruise missile should be able to wend its way around most ground radars without coming into view. Obviously, a cruise missile must fly higher over rough terrain than over smooth. Conveniently for the cruise missile, radar coverage is much poorer over rough terrain. Efforts to make the cruise missile fly low may inordinately increase the probability of a collision with the ground or objects on the ground. For optimum performance, any increase in collisions from flying low should just equal the decrease in attrition from defenses. Since the expectation of attrition is already low at moderately low altitudes (say, a few hundred feet), efforts to go lower, at least in the current environment, seem unwarranted—particularly since design changes in the vehicle's flight control system, engine, wing design, and terrain-following system might be required. Cost or weight increases caused by such changes would have to be evaluated, since they would decrease force size just as much as ground collisions would.

The ideal cruise missile also should be at least as accurate as other strategic weapons. It should fly at its most efficient speed most of the time because speed is far less vital than long range, low flying, and low RCS for penetration. With state-of-the-art engines, fuels, and structures, and the range specified, weight then depends upon the weight of the payload and guidance.

The specifications of the cruise missile actually being procured for the strategic air-launched mission conform fairly closely to these specifications. However, tactical nuclear applications, through cruise missiles deployed with the European theater nuclear forces, raise other questions. Soviet tactical defenses are so competent and so dense that they may exact a greater attrition than the strategic defenses. The cruise missile would certainly do better, however, than the quick-reaction alert aircraft it will replace; and the Pershing II intermediate-range ballistic missile (IRBM) will be a hedge against unexpected effectiveness of the Soviet tactical air defenses.

With the exception that it must be adapted for submarine or surface-ship launch, the cruise missile defined for the strategic air-launched mission is a good fit for the tactical nuclear mission. The cruise missile's range allows it to be launched well offshore and still reach most Warsaw Pact targets outside the Soviet Union. TERCOM guidance is adequate, although modifications to permit ship launch are required. The warhead is also satisfactory, although an option for lesser yields to minimize collateral damage might be appropriate.

The cruise missile best for tactical *conventional* missions is similar to the strategic and tactical nuclear cruise missile, but there are substantive differences. Since TERCOM is useless over water, and since over-the-horizon targeting is a requirement of the antiship mission, other guidance schemes must be found. The antiship cruise missile needs over-the-horizon launch information—which it could obtain from an aircraft, a space satellite, or a submarine—and terminal guidance—which it could obtain with an active radar seeker, as the Harpoon missile does, or with a suite of passive sensors, as precision-guided munitions do. If the range is long or the target is rapidly moving, midcourse updates might also be required; command guidance from an aircraft or satellite communications could be used. Various guidance options are being investigated, with particular attention to the terminal sensors, where passive approaches, including imaging infrared, have advantages.

For other tactical conventional systems (except those for attacking mobile targets) TERCOM guidance can place the missile in the vicinity of the target, but it must be supplemented with terminal guidance. The weight of the conventional warhead—which may be either a single unit or a cluster of submunitions, depending upon the mission—should be one thousand pounds or more. For conventional applications, warhead size must take precedence in the range-payload trade-off. Of course, range requirements are much reduced in tactical conventional applications, and the weight of a tactical warhead plus the weight of a supplementary guidance system just about equal the weight of the fuel which can be off-loaded because of the shorter ranges needed.

Thus the size, weight, and mold lines of the strategic cruise missile require no major changes for tactical conventional roles. (*Strategic* use of conventional cruise missiles against targets in the Soviet Union is a different matter. See chapter 5.) The probable range—about 250 miles—seems sufficient for ground- and air-launched battlefield interdiction. Only the area of coverage of the sea-based land-attack missile will be limited, since launch ships must remain over the horizon and submarines must stay in relatively deep water.

Two technological issues remain. The first is whether the cruise missile is the best carrier for a conventional warhead in these roles. The second is whether the warhead it carries can destroy vital targets. The warhead issue is a thorny one. Fortunately, the cruise missile's success as a warhead carrier is relatively independent of what warhead or submunition is carried. The Defense Department is now addressing the related problems of warhead and submunition technology.[17] As a carrier for explosives,

17. Department of Defense, *Fiscal Year 1981 Department of Defense Program for Research, Development and Acquisition* (Department of Defense, January 1980), pp. I-11, I-12, I-30, I-34, V-14.

the cruise missile has advantages and disadvantages. For long ranges, it has no real competitors. For battlefield close-support and interdiction missions, however, where ranges of a few miles are sufficient and high speed is beneficial (a moving target has no time to move out of danger), the cruise missile has competition from other missiles. As one example, the Assault Breaker program is using the high-speed, rocket-powered, command-guided Patriot missile, the surface-to-air missile of the Army's field air-defense system, to demonstrate a potential solution to the problem of destroying hard, mobile targets.[18]

Current Cruise Missiles

Engineering analysis of mission requirements underlies the weapons acquisition process of the Department of Defense. In 1974 the department began to plan for the development of a family of cruise missiles with common components. In 1977 total responsibility for cruise missile development was placed in a joint cruise missile program office. Now all the cruise missile programs are planned, programmed, and presented to Congress as a coherent whole. At least one cruise missile candidate is in development for each of the potential missions discussed here.

The Harpoon

The United States today has one operational cruise missile, the Navy's Harpoon. The Harpoon is an antiship missile which uses inertial guidance with a radar altimeter in midcourse (for sea skimming) and active radar homing for terminal guidance. It weighs about 1,200 pounds, with a warhead weight of 500 pounds, is powered by a turbojet engine, and has a range of about sixty miles. Harpoon could be sea-, ground-, or air-launched. There is concern that its warhead is too small to be effective against modern warships. There is no nuclear version of the Harpoon.

The ALCM

Of the six cruise missiles in development (see table 1-1), only the air-launched cruise missile is for strategic missions. Boeing Company won the competition for production of this air-launched cruise missile in a fly-

18. Ibid., pp. V-24, V-28.

Table 1-1. U.S. Cruise Missiles under Development

Missile[a]	Mission	Warhead[b]	Launch mode	Carrier	Range (nautical miles)	Guidance[c]
ALCM	Strategic	Nuclear	Air	B-52	1,500	TERCOM
GLCM	Tactical	Nuclear	Ground	Truck	1,300–1,500	TERCOM
TLAM-N	Tactical	Nuclear	Sea	Submarine or surface ship	1,300–1,500	TERCOM
TLAM-C	Tactical	Conventional	Sea	Submarine or surface ship	700	TERCOM plus
TASM	Tactical	Conventional	Sea	Submarine or surface ship	300	INS plus
MRASM	Tactical	Conventional	Air	Tactical fighter	300	INS plus

Source: Rear Admiral Walter M. Locke, Director, Joint Cruise Missiles Project, "Cruise Missiles: A Deterrent with a New Dimension," remarks at the AUVS Symposia, Los Angeles, May 1981.

Note: Acronyms are defined in the glossary.

a. The strategic missile (ALCM) is in production; the tactical nuclear missiles are in the engineering phase; the tactical conventional missiles are in an accelerated engineering phase. All will be capable of subsonic speed. All but the ALCM, which was derived from the earlier SCUD and SCAD, are variants of General Dynamics' Tomahawk.

b. Nuclear warheads weigh a few hundred pounds; conventional warheads weigh about 1,000 pounds.

c. Accuracy of TERCOM is a few hundred feet; accuracy of TERCOM plus and INS plus is a few tens of feet; plus means supplemental precision guidance in the terminal portion of the trajectory.

off with General Dynamics completed in March 1980 after ten flights each. Four of each company's ten flights ended in crashes. Causes of the crashes are correctable and not considered justification for slowing the program. Several more crashes during further testing are attributable to minor engineering difficulties, which affect the system's eventual reliability rather than its inherent viability. As of April 1981, Boeing had completed ten (of nineteen) operational evaluation flight tests, with six successes, including all of the last four flights.

The ALCM is 234 inches long, weighs about 3,000 pounds, and is powered by a 600-pound-thrust turbofan engine. The first squadron of ALCM-equipped B-52s is scheduled to be on alert by December 1982.[19] The missiles will be mounted externally, six on each of two jettisonable wing pylons, while the B-52G will continue to carry SRAMs or gravity bombs in its bomb bay. During this period plans call for the bomber to operate in the shoot-and-penetrate mode—that is, launching its ALCMs first and then proceeding inland to strike targets with its other weapons. By about 1985 the Air Force's 171 B-52Gs (which are getting older as the Soviet air defenses are getting stronger) should be converted to all-standoff systems—fitted for eight additional cruise missiles on a rotary rack inside the bomb bay, giving it a total load of twenty cruise missiles. Both the externally and internally carried ALCMs will be the 234-inch version, the ALCM-B.

Still later, the one-hundred-odd B-52Hs—the most modern of the B-52s and the only ones equipped with fan engines—might be converted to cruise missiles, or a special cruise missile carrier aircraft (CMCA) may be introduced. Previously, it was expected that the CMCA would be derived from a commercial wide-bodied aircraft but a long-range strategic aircraft planned by the Air Force may become a CMCA with such characteristics of the B-1 as nuclear hardness, fast base escape, and long-range flight at low altitudes.

The GLCM

Of the five missiles based on the Navy Tomahawk, the ground-launched cruise missile has received the most attention because of its prominence in alliance politics. Flight testing began in 1980. A production decision is

19. Press release, Office of the Assistant Secretary of Defense (Public Affairs), "Air Force Selects Boeing AGM-86B Launched Cruise Missile," March 25, 1980.

scheduled for 1982 (for a projected 560 missiles, 464 for the NATO nations). Initial operational capability is projected for about late 1983.[20]

Ground-launched cruise missiles are organized in flights of sixteen missiles, four each on four transporter-erector-launchers. The GLCM is about twenty-one feet long (including the 7,000-pound-thrust rocket booster required to accelerate it to flying speed) and has a wingspan of eight and one-half feet.

The TLAM-N

The nuclear version of the Tomahawk land-attack cruise missile was the first of the Tomahawk family in development. It received less emphasis in recent years, but has reportedly been revived by the Reagan administration. The TLAM is almost identical to the GLCM in its specifications. Even the booster required to get the cruise missile up to flight speed is the same, and the launch control systems have a high degree of commonality, including common major hardware components such as the computer, data-storage devices, displays and interface units, as well as the software programs required to operate the system. Its most constraining specification is its twenty-one-inch diameter, required for launch from submarine torpedo tubes, but it can also be launched from surface ships.

The TLAM-C

The conventional Tomahawk land-attack missile is the same as the nuclear TLAM and GLCM in size, shape, weight, launch booster, and launch platforms, but, because of its conventional mission, its warhead is bigger, its range lower, and its guidance is different. The TLAM-C supplements TERCOM with the scene matching area correlator to give the system accuracies on the order of tens of feet. The Navy sees the target of the TLAM-C as enemy airfields, but its role could well be expanded, which would require other submunitions for the warhead and other forms of supplementary guidance. Imaging infrared sensors are already being examined; others, such as millimeter-wave active seekers, might prove extremely valuable. All-weather guidance systems are needed in view of European weather and the smoke and dust of the tactical battlefield.

20. Henry S. Bradsher, "Navy to Proceed on Long-Range Cruise Missiles," *Washington Star,* June 4, 1981.

There are funds in the 1982 budget to continue an operational evaluation of the TLAM-C.[21] The Navy has mentioned an initial operational capability of the submarine-launched version of this system for early 1982.[22]

The TASM

The Tomahawk antiship missile also resembles the nuclear TLAM in outward appearance, weight, launch booster, and launch platforms, but it has even more pronounced differences internally than does the TLAM-C. Its inertial guidance and active and passive seekers allow it to be launched over the horizon in the general direction of a set of targets, to search for targets, to identify friends and turn away from them, and to seek out enemies and attack them with high accuracy. The TASM development program is working to increase the effectiveness of over-the-horizon targeting techniques and to find the best combination of seekers. With twice the warhead weight of the Harpoon and four or five times the range, a quantum improvement in antiship capability is possible. An initial operational capability for the submarine-launched TASM has been scheduled for mid-1982.[23]

The MRASM

The medium-range air-to-surface missile is the latest of the Tomahawk variants. It is to be launched from tactical aircraft against important heavily defended targets, both land and sea. The program is viewed with some urgency by the Defense Department,[24] and a production decision may be made by December 1984. To move the program as fast as practical, the Navy is adapting the Tomahawk air-launched cruise missile, designed for the strategic role, to the MRASM role, using TERCOM and DSMAC

21. Department of Defense, *Fiscal Year 1982 Department of Defense Program for Research, Development and Acquisition* (Department of Defense, January 1981), pp. VII-52–VII-53.

22. Rear Admiral Walter M. Locke, Director, Joint Cruise Missiles Project, "Cruise Missiles: A Deterrent with a New Dimension," remarks at the AUVS Symposia, Los Angeles, May 1981, p. 14.

23. Ibid.

24. Edgar Ulsamer, "A More Liberal, Avant Garde R&D Program," *Air Force*, June 1980. In this article William J. Perry is quoted as saying that the MRASM should "be added to our strike warfare systems as soon as possible" (p. 47).

guidance. The potential effectiveness of other guidance modules, including radar and imaging infrared, is being explored.

The DSMAC is for attacking fixed targets. Whether the MRASM will be able to attack mobile targets depends on the progress of several seeker and command and control technologies. Whether it will be able to stand up to its competitors of somewhat shorter range but very much higher speed (including ramjets and rockets) remains to be seen. Until very recently the Air Force's successes with manned aircraft in four wars tempered its enthusiasm for indirect attack systems such as tactical cruise missiles. But the intensity of Warsaw Pact air defenses, the high cost of modern tactical aircraft, and the extremely high cost of the personnel to operate and support them have gradually led to a reevaluation, particularly for the early part of major engagements.

Future Cruise Missiles

Many weapon systems are effective for as long as twenty years, yet rapid changes in the Soviet threat can require earlier replacement. By the time the ALCM reaches initial operating capability more than ten years will have passed since an organized advocacy for cruise missiles appeared in the Defense Department. Thus the developments for advanced cruise missiles for possible deployment at the end of the 1980s are already under way.

The Defense Advanced Research Projects Agency and the Air Force have active programs to develop the next generation of cruise missiles, which will be designed to maintain penetrativity in the face of improving Soviet air defenses.[25] These area defenses feature Soviet airborne warning and control systems (AWACS) and look-down–shoot-down fighters with advanced missiles equipped with radar seekers, which will be able to reach out long distances from the Soviet borders to attack the cruise missile carriers before the missiles are launched.[26] Soviet terminal defenses feature the new SA-10 missile, a high-performance surface-to-air missile associated with coherent radars having excellent subclutter visibility.

25. Clarence A. Robinson, Jr., "USAF Readies Advanced Cruise Missiles," *Aviation Week and Space Technology,* March 10, 1980, pp. 12–15.
26. Ibid., p. 12.

The ASALM

One potential weapon against the Soviet AWACS is the advanced strategic air-launched missile, an integral rocket ramjet with about Mach 4 high-altitude performance and high-altitude range of several hundred miles (a compromise between the very high speed of the rocket-powered missile and the very long range of the cruise missile). Its terminal guidance system is not yet perfected. Antiradiation homing, alone, is inadequate, because the Soviet AWACS can shut down. On the other hand, an active radar would require rather extensive range and complexity. Several kinds of dual-mode seekers are being examined.

The ASALM is also being considered as a suppressor of airfields and other air-defense targets and as a direct-attack weapon replacing SRAMs.[27] However, to effectively suppress defenses, the ASALM must fly through Soviet high-altitude defenses. Its speed for accomplishing this is marginal and, although it has longer range and much faster terminal velocity than the SRAM, its cross section is higher. Perhaps it will not be competitive with other strategic weapons, and its best application will be tactical. The need is urgent for precision-guided attack weapons for launching from outside the Soviet Union's intense tactical air defenses. The recently instituted MRASM program is a case in point. Although currently based on the Tomahawk, its advanced versions might very well employ ASALM technology.

Advanced ALCMs

To penetrate advanced terminal defenses, strategic cruise missiles may require lower RCSs, higher speeds, greater maneuverability, and penetration aids such as electronic countermeasures, all of which are being studied. The ratio of empty weight to maximum gross weight for the current ALCM-B is about 0.58; well-designed, large aircraft achieve less than 0.5. Its engine has a specific fuel consumption of 1; big fan-jet engines have 0.7. Thus there is much room for improvement in engines, fuels, and structures. Higher-thrust and higher-efficiency engines are being pursued by four Defense Department contractors (Williams, whose F-107 engine is on both ALCM and Tomahawk, General Electric, Teledyne CAE, and Garrett Corporation). Higher molecular-weight fuels, includ-

27. Ulsamer, "A More Liberal, Avant Garde R&D Program," p. 47.

ing boron and carbon slurries, are being explored. Composite structures may hold promise for reducing airframe weight, but since the ALCM-B airframe is only about 20 percent of its maximum gross weight, a substantial reduction would be necessary to have an effect on total weight.

Techniques to lower radar cross section and the detectability of infrared emissions are also receiving attention. Better ways to reduce reflectivity and irradiance of the engine at *all* wavelengths are being vigorously sought. Autonomous sensors for warning and automatic avoidance maneuvers are being investigated, as are electronic countermeasure systems, which may be miniaturized versions of what the bombers now carry.[28] Many of these penetration technologies are extremely expensive and complex, guaranteeing substantial increases in missile unit cost. When it is realized that a fairly simple combination of high speed, low altitude, and low cross section will always penetrate, and that all the efforts to improve the penetrativity of the ALCM are being made because it is inherently slow, there may be some justification for returning to rocket-powered missiles, since their penetration is assured. However, a provision of SALT II counts each rocket-powered missile with a range of over 600 kilometers carried aboard a bomber as a strategic nuclear delivery vehicle. A bomber carrying any number of cruise missiles is counted as a single strategic nuclear vehicle.

Summary

Two technical characteristics of the cruise missile set it apart from its competition: it has long range but slow speed. Its other characteristics— low observables (RCS, infrared, acoustic), low flying, and high accuracy—are shared with its competitors. Its characteristics make cruise missiles ideal for the strategic bomber mission because they can penetrate Soviet defenses after being launched from bombers outside those defenses. Cruise missiles also seem cost-effective as part of a two-pronged theater nuclear force (with the Pershing II).

Other missions visualized for cruise missiles (sea-launched tactical nuclear missiles as well as sea-, land-, and air-launched conventional versions) are not as clearly justified by the technical characteristics. But the uses of cruise missiles depend upon a meld of technical, political, and diplomatic factors. These are examined in detail in the rest of this book.

28. Robinson, "USAF Readies Advanced Cruise Missiles," p. 13.

CHAPTER TWO

Soviet Strategic Air Defense

GORDON MACDONALD, JACK RUINA, *and* MARK BALASCHAK

WITHIN the next few years the United States will start equipping about 150 suitably modified B-52s with twenty cruise missiles each, adding a new dimension to the strategic forces. The air-launched cruise missiles (ALCMs) with long range (thousands of miles) provide the air leg of the strategic triad with about 3,000 independently targetable warheads that place fewer constraints on target choices than an equal number of gravity bombs or short-range missiles. The cruise missile itself is small, is not easily detectable when flying close to the ground, and can carry a nuclear warhead capable of delivering more than one hundred kilotons of explosive power. The cruise missile carrier aircraft, which are large and potentially quite vulnerable, can stand many hundreds of kilometers off the borders of the Soviet Union. However, in the early deployment of the ALCM, some B-52s will be armed with both ALCMs and short-range attack missiles (SRAMs) and are therefore programmed to penetrate Soviet airspace.

The United States abandoned its attempt at a major continental air defense system in the late 1950s when it became apparent that intercontinental ballistic missiles (ICBMs) would be a major component of U.S. and Soviet nuclear forces. It seemed futile to defend against aircraft when there was essentially no defense against missiles. Nuclear-armed ballistic missiles alone could be used to destroy industrial and military targets, and they could also be used to open corridors for bomber aircraft.

In contrast, the Soviet Union, similarly faced with a growing threat

Gordon MacDonald is at the MITRE Corporation. Jack Ruina, professor of electrical engineering, and Mark Balaschak, Ph.D. candidate, are at the Massachusetts Institute of Technology.

from ICBMs, did not stop building up its strategic air defenses. However, until very recently it did not test or deploy strategic defense systems with any substantial capability against low-flying aircraft, even though it was well known that low-altitude penetration was the key tactic planned for U.S. bombers and probably also for British, French, and Chinese bombers.

Because they can remain outside Soviet territory, B-52s carrying cruise missiles are less vulnerable than B-52s carrying short-range missiles or gravity bombs, which must penetrate Soviet territory to deliver their weapons. The small size of the cruise missile and its low-altitude flight profile greatly reduce the probability of detection and tracking by conventional radar although, under specific circumstances, acoustic, infrared, and visual detection and tracking may become feasible at low altitudes. Even though the cruise missile travels at subsonic speeds, its low altitude makes engagement by surface-to-air missiles and by interceptor aircraft difficult. On the other hand, the low altitude makes the cruise missile potentially vulnerable to antiaircraft artillery or to shoulder-held weapons of the Redeye or Stinger heat-seeking type.

The effectiveness of both the present Soviet strategic air defense system and the system with projected modifications is the subject of this analysis, which will focus on the vulnerability of the air-launched version of the cruise missile. NATO, in its program to upgrade its theater nuclear forces, is planning to deploy hundreds of mobile ground-launched cruise missiles (GLCMs) in five European countries, and there has been speculation about the use of sea-launched cruise missiles (SLCMs). In flight the vulnerability of the various cruise missiles is essentially the same, although the basing mode determines their vulnerability before launch. Therefore, Soviet technological developments that may be effective against ALCMs can also be effective against GLCMs and SLCMs. The geographic regions of deployment, however, may have to be somewhat different for ALCM defense than for GLCM defense since the expected cruise missile flight paths would be different.

Although the successful British operations against the German V-1 in World War II might seem relevant to defense against cruise missiles, this is not the case for several reasons. The learning period that was necessary before the defensive measures against the V-1 became effective will not be possible in a nuclear war; the pattern of V-1 attacks remained constant and the V-1 flew at extremely vulnerable altitudes. The current cruise missile is a much more difficult target than the V-1, and defensive technology has improved dramatically, so the V-1 experience is of little use.[1]

The ability of the cruise missile force to cope with Soviet air defenses depends heavily on the role assigned to the missile and on the *operational* capability of the defense system. Here it must be noted that the capability of an air defense system may not be nearly so great as indicated by calculations that assume optimal performance of each technical component. In a system as complex as air defense, the overall performance hinges on how well the many elements of the system, both men and machines, interact, and the system can never be adequately tested. Simulated environments are far different from the real environment of a nuclear war, in which there would be little or no time to adapt systems and people to the nuclear situation. Also, command and control functions can fail even when the individual hardware components of the system are functioning at their best. Consequently, any assessment of the ultimate effectiveness of Soviet defenses against cruise missiles depends as much on U.S. and Soviet doctrine and operational plans (which we cannot evaluate adequately) as on the technical performance of air defense hardware.

Since even a single nuclear weapon can be extremely destructive, there is little question but that the cruise missile force has the capability of destroying about one hundred of the largest Soviet cities containing a total population of about seventy million. Hence concern about the U.S. ability to cope with Soviet urban defenses is minimal. The Soviet air defense would have to be improbably effective to avoid saturation, exhaustion of defensive weapons, and "leakage" of attacking missiles (the fraction that "leaks through" to reach the targets). We see no way that an entire defensive system can be this effective, especially in a nuclear environment. On the other hand, if the cruise missile force must be capable of destroying a large proportion of a much larger number of separate targets, an enhanced Soviet air defense could be very effective.

In planning for cruise missile development and deployment, the United States will have to accept that, whether or not it understands all the purposes of Soviet air defenses or can assess their effectiveness even approximately, these defenses will continue to be massive and constantly upgraded.

1. David L. Briggs, "Some Cruise Missile History: Performance of the Allied Defenses Against the V-1," Lincoln Laboratory, Massachusetts Institute of Technology, December 15, 1977.

Components of an Air Defense System

A modern air defense system consists of a large number of individual components that are integrated by a command, control, and communications system. The technical characteristics of many elements of the Soviet air defense system have been described in the open literature, but there is a paucity of information on Soviet command and control systems. (Details of elements of the Soviet air defense system are given in appendix A.)

Radar

Radar is the primary means of detecting, locating, and tracking enemy targets. Its effectiveness is determined not only by its operating features, but also by such characteristics of the target as size, speed, and altitude.

A conventional pulsed radar determines a target's existence, range, and bearing by measuring the time of transit of a signal sent from a transmitter to the target and back to a receiver. The maximum range at which a target can be detected increases as the antenna area or the transmitter power increases. A radar's ability to detect targets drops rapidly with range because the transmitted radiation must travel two ways (to the target and then back to the receiver) so that the received power varies inversely with the fourth power of range. Therefore, to double the range at which a target of a given size can be detected, the transmitter power must increase by a factor of sixteen. The radar's resolution (ability to separate two closely spaced targets) increases with increasing antenna size and its range with increasing signal band width.

The frequency and therefore the wavelength at which radar operates is a compromise among many factors. Shorter wavelengths (higher frequencies) give better resolution for a fixed antenna size but are harder to generate at high power levels. Short wavelengths (one centimeter or less) are also subject to weather interference, though this interference can be reduced by careful selection of the operating frequencies.

Several factors limit the effectiveness of radar, especially against low-altitude targets. The first is that radar typically cannot see beyond the horizon or over hills and other ground obstructions. Detection ranges, and thus the defenders' reaction time, are shortened for low-altitude targets. For example, a target flying at 500 miles an hour at an altitude of 200 feet directly toward the radar will not be detected until it is fifteen miles away, less than two minutes before it is directly overhead. Elevating the radar antenna on a tower, building, or hill will of course improve its range. Second, reflections from nearby static objects, including the ground itself, may hide targets at the same ranges. This is a particularly limiting problem for tower- or hill-mounted radars and for airborne radars looking down at low-flying targets. Ground-based radars searching for or tracking high-flying, long-range targets have less difficulty handling ground clutter, which in this case is limited to short ranges. Third, signals may follow other paths besides the most direct one from transmitter to target and back to receiver, thereby confusing the radar and associated displays.

The clutter problem can be minimized by taking advantage of the Doppler shift, that is, the shift in the frequency of the reflected signal from a moving target. A Doppler radar filters out reflected signals that show no Doppler shift, so that only moving targets appear on the radar screen, and the radar is said to possess a moving target indicator. Although the principle is old, and its use in radar is about as old as radar itself, the technology for truly effective performance of airborne radar over land against low-flying targets has only recently become available in the United States as a result of major advances in electronic data processing. Doppler techniques are absolutely necessary if an airborne radar is to be effective against low-flying targets. Look-down–shoot-down airborne radars, intended to guide air-to-air missiles, demand full mastery of modern radar transmitter and receiver design and of advanced signal-processing techniques. Use of advanced "chip" technology is particularly important here.

Jamming by the enemy can severely degrade radar performance. Jammers can be designed to overwhelm a target's reflected signal and make a radar screen unreadable, or they can be designed to deceive the radar receiver by creating false targets or by making a real target appear to be where it is not. To be effective, deceptive electronic countermeasures usually depend on a detailed knowledge of the radar to be jammed, so intelligence is an important part of the countermeasures game. Because the jammer power travels only one way, from the jammer transmitter to the radar receiver, the power received at the receiver varies with the inverse square of the distance from the jammer to the receiver. To double the range at which the jammer has a particular effectiveness, jammer power must increase by a factor of four. To restore the status quo, the transmitter power must increase sixteen times. For a given jammer power, there is a certain distance at which the radar can "burn through" the jamming and detect the target. Beyond this range, however, the power situation favors the jammer, because the jammer requires less additional power to increase its jamming effectiveness than the radar does to increase its detection capability.

The effectiveness of jamming can be reduced by careful radar design and also by proper and thorough training of operators. Some modern radar is "frequency agile," that is, it changes the frequency of its transmitted signals at random over a broad range. To be most effective, a jammer must concentrate power at the radar's frequency, so frequency-hopping makes jamming more difficult. Also, radar antennas are highly directional, receiving especially well in a given direction and especially poorly in others. The beams of modern antennas can be adjusted to receive poorly from the direction of the jammer ("null steering"), thereby minimizing the jammer's effectiveness.

A technique that helps when radar is being jammed or when individual radar coverage is limited by low-altitude targets or by small head-on targets is to "net," or provide communication links between nearby radars so they can exchange target data. If one radar receiver has difficulty, data from other receivers may be used. The whole radar network can then perform better than the collection of radars each operating independently. Effective netting requires sophisticated data processing techniques based on solid-state computers.

Radar has special operating problems when there are nuclear explosions nearby even if it remains mechanically undamaged. A nuclear explosion creates an electromagnetic pulse that can damage or destroy the electronic components of radar, and the intense ionization of the air in the area of a nuclear explosion disrupts radar signal propagation to such an extent that radar may be totally blacked out. And products of the explosion such as dust and turbulence lower radar performance. Blackout effects are especially pronounced for low-frequency radars and high-altitude explosions. The details of these effects are not well understood, and so long as the atmospheric test ban treaty remains in effect, they will remain so, making a defender's assessment of the effectiveness of air defense equipment in a nuclear environment uncertain.

Since World War II the performance of radar has greatly improved largely as a result of the development of solid-state electronics. Solid-state devices vastly increase the amount of real-time radar data processing that can be done practicably and also permit realization of large phased-array antennas, which steer the radar beam electronically rather than mechanically.

Radar Cross Section

The radar cross section (RCS) is a measure of how strongly an object reflects electromagnetic waves at any particular frequency. The larger the RCS, the stronger the received signal and the greater the range at which the target can be detected. Received power is proportional to the RCS; if a target's RCS decreases by a factor of ten, the transmitted power (or receiver sensitivity) must increase by a factor of ten for the target to be detectable at the same range. A low radar cross section helps preclude detection.

The radar cross section of an object is determined mostly by size—the larger an object, the larger its RCS—so the first step in reducing the RCS is to keep the object small. The RCS also depends on the angle from which an object is viewed. The RCS of an aircraft is usually smallest when the radar views the aircraft head-on or nearly so; the RCS when viewed from the side is large, and it is still larger when seen from above or below because of the large flat areas presented by the wings and tail. From different aspects, the RCS may vary by a factor of 100. The RCS of an aircraft can also depend on the radar frequency (or wavelength), being particularly high at wavelengths comparable in size to some structural element on the aircraft. Protrusions such as antennas could increase the RCS at high frequencies, and the major structural features of the aircraft increase the RCS at low frequencies.

Apart from limiting size, careful construction is probably the most important step in minimizing an object's RCS. Straight edges, slablike sides, abrupt kinks, and sharply angled joints at places like wing roots should be avoided. By and large this philosophy is consistent with modern aeronautical engineering, except in the design of air intakes. Smoothly rounded blunt intakes are incompatible with many design approaches for sustained transonic and supersonic performance. Engine inlets contribute strongly to an aircraft's RCS. Their elimination (through the use of much heavier non-air-breathing power plants) or their placement above the fuselage helps reduce this contribution, though at a cost in performance. The use of paints, materials, and structures fabricated to minimize reflected electromagnetic energy will lower an aircraft's RCS only for specific frequency bands, but this involves significant weight (and thus performance) penalties and added maintenance problems.

The RCS of the physically small cruise missile is much smaller than that of a conventional bomber, and this is one of the cruise missile's virtues.

The RCS of cruise missiles could be further reduced through the passive measures outlined above and conceivably through active measures in which the cruise missile senses the incoming radiation and sends out signals that mask the reflected signal. The secretary of defense recently reported a "major technological advance of great military significance" in the design of a low-effective-RCS aircraft, Stealth, without giving any details or indicating the costs in performance involved. The practical utility of this recent development in the design of such small aerodynamic vehicles as cruise missiles has not been made public.

Early Warning and Interceptor Control Radar

Radar is used throughout an air defense network. Early warning (EW) radar designed to monitor the routes intruders are likely to use is the front line in such a network. Early warning radars typically have ranges of hundreds of miles (but poor resolution), so that large amounts of space can be surveyed for information about an attacker's numbers, speed, range, altitude, and heading. A fixed radar with a 200-mile range could give from twenty minutes to two hours warning (depending on the location of both the intruder and the unit being warned) of a bomber flying at Mach 0.8 (600 miles an hour) at an altitude of 30,000 feet or more. Because they are currently ground based and widely spaced, EW radars usually have gaps in coverage of low-altitude aircraft.

Soviet deployment of EW radars is typical of their development of air defenses. The Soviet EW radars Tall King, Spoon Rest, and the NYSA-C (see appendix A) were put into the field twenty years ago and are still maintained in large numbers even though U.S. tactical doctrine has evolved to a low-altitude penetration threat. At the same time the Soviet Union has experimented with more advanced systems such as over-the-horizon radars, whose capability against a bomber threat was questionable even in the design phase. Although the Soviet Union has made a large investment in EW radars and continues to upgrade their performance to some extent, the radars seem poorly designed to handle the present U.S. bomber threat, much less a future ALCM attack.

Ground-controlled intercept (GCI) radars have been an important part of air defense since 1940. These radars track both targets and friendly interceptors and provide the latter with guidance information until the target comes within range of the interceptor's own airborne intercept sensors (radar, infrared, or visual). The primary Soviet GCI radars are the

Bar Lock and derivative Big Bar and Big Mesh. These systems have been in use for at least fourteen years and have ranges of about 180 miles for high-flying targets. The GCI radars probably have minimal capability against a low-altitude bomber force and, because of both the low altitude of flight and the low RCS, essentially no capability against the cruise missile.

Airborne Warning and Control System

To upgrade interceptor control and to increase the distance over which the radar can provide early warning, a powerful radar can be mounted on an aircraft flying at an altitude of 30,000 to 35,000 feet. In an effort to better provide control over interceptors during low-altitude operations, the Soviet Union introduced in 1967 the Tu-126 Moss airborne warning and control system (AWACS). There are twelve of these systems in operation. The Tu-126 turboprop airplane carries a radar antenna eleven meters wide, which is used to locate targets and vector interceptors to them. The performance of the radar, named Flat Jack, has been steadily downgraded by observers since the system's deployment. At present it is held to be of limited effectiveness over water and almost totally ineffective over land because of problems of separating returns from the ground from returns from the target.[2] Some modified Moss systems reputedly have limited look-down performance over land.[3] The aircraft is now used primarily in conjunction with long-range interceptors that patrol over the Arctic Ocean in support of naval operations.[4] Most important are reports that a new Soviet AWACS, looking much like the U.S. counterpart, may soon enter service.[5]

The U.S. AWACS, which has been operational since 1977, is installed in a Boeing 707 aircraft with its radar antenna mounted in a thirty-foot "rotodome" on top of the plane. It has an operating frequency of about 3,000 megacycles (ten-centimeter wavelength) and a detection range in

2. J. W. R. Taylor, "Gallery of Soviet Aerospace Weapons," *Air Force,* March 1980, p. 126.

3. *Department of Defense Annual Report, Fiscal Year 1981* (Government Printing Office, 1980), p. 76.

4. David R. Jones, "National Air Defense Force," in David R. Jones, ed., *Soviet Armed Forces Review Annual,* vol. 3 (Gulf Breeze, Fla.: Academic International Press, 1979), p. 32.

5. "New Soviet Air-to-Air Missile," *Flight International,* October 25, 1980, p. 1553.

excess of 200 miles—the distance to the horizon from its operating altitude—and includes design features particularly oriented to handle electronic countermeasures. It has demonstrated its capability to detect and track low-flying aircraft over land.[6] But this capability requires very sophisticated radar transmitter and receiver electronics and advanced data processing equipment. The estimated operational capability of the U.S. AWACS against low-flying cruise missiles is not known but is probably only marginal because of both the low RCS of the cruise missile and the problems of picking the cruise missile out of the ground clutter.

Whereas the Soviet AWACS can in time probably match the U.S. AWACS in some important features, it will probably not operate as effectively over land. The Soviet Union has lagged behind the United States particularly in radar Doppler techniques and in data processing, which is essential to detecting low-RCS objects. It thus appears unlikely that the deployed Soviet radars, including the new AWACS, would be effective in providing early warning or controlling interceptor aircraft in actions against cruise missiles.

The radars described are not the only radars in the Soviet air defense system, only those that are best known. There are 7,000 radars in the Soviet network, with 1,700 more expected by 1989.[7] These numbers, however, may be misleading, since the Soviet Union retains equipment that other countries would retire as obsolescent. In the Soviet Union, these are used as backups to more modern radars, providing overlapping coverage and more diverse frequencies, which make jamming more difficult. The Soviet radar network is currently thought to be improving through the introduction of better data-handling systems and the netting of radars.[8] These improvements will probably not be sufficient to yield significantly better performance against cruise missiles because of the stringent requirements on radar performance and data processing for the detection of low-flying, low-RCS targets.

Interceptor Aircraft

As in other areas of air defense, the Soviet Union has invested heavily in interceptor aircraft. Its strategic air defense force includes about 2,500

---

6. Bonner Day, "AWACS in Operation," *Air Force*, June 1979, pp. 52–56.
7. "Soviets' Nuclear Arsenal Continues to Proliferate," *Aviation Week and Space Technology*, June 16, 1980, p. 69.
8. Ibid., pp. 69–70.

aircraft,[9] about 55 percent of the total tactical inventory. Some of the eight types of aircraft in this force have been operational for two decades (see appendix A). The older aircraft are based in the southern, central, and some in the eastern USSR, where they face technically unsophisticated opponents. Thirty percent of the force is based in the European USSR, with a further 25 percent split between the Moscow and Baku air defense districts—these two areas house important command facilities. The aircraft based in the west are all of the most modern type.[10]

Surface-to-Air Missile Systems

A surface-to-air missile (SAM) system consists of a set of radars to seek out (acquire) and track the target and to track the missile launched by the SAM site, guidance equipment for the missile (which may be on the ground, in the missile, or split between the two), and usually several launchers each with several missiles. There must be communication links from the radars to the launchers. The system's performance is upgraded if there are links to the distant early warning net and to other SAM radars. A description of current Soviet SAM systems is given in appendix A.

The Soviet Union maintains about 12,000 SAMs at over 1,000 sites. Most are deployed around the Soviet border, particularly in the west, and the remainder are used for point defense of cities and military installations.[11] Command centers are defended. As evidenced by the organization of PVO Strany and the large number of SAMs required to defend the missile fields that have 1,500 or so ICBM sites, apparently these are given little emphasis by the air defense system.

A SAM battery's target-acquisition radars are essentially small EW radars, while its fire-control radars, which track both target and missile interceptors, follow a single target constantly with much greater precision and much more agility than that of a typical EW radar. Mechanically scanned radars can be designed to have both surveillance and tracking functions, but this usually means compromises in performance. Modern phased-array radars using solid-state electronics, however, can track one or more targets well while maintaining surveillance over large areas of air space.

9. *Department of Defense Annual Report, Fiscal Year 1981*, p. 77.
10. Robert P. Berman, *Soviet Air Power in Transition* (Brookings Institution, 1978), p. 39.
11. Defense Intelligence Agency, *Handbook on Soviet Armed Forces*, DDB-2680-40-78 (DIA, 1978), p. 11-4.

Organization and Funding

Strategic air defense has a central role in the military forces of the Soviet Union. It is the responsibility of a separate and distinct service branch, the PVO Strany, which is equal in status to the Soviet ground forces, air forces, navy, and strategic rocket forces. It is charged not only with anti-aircraft defense, but also with antimissile and antisatellite defense. Thus the Soviet antiballistic missile system, which is deployed near Moscow (the only Soviet operational ABM system), the ABM research and development program, and the antisatellite (ASAT) forces are under the PVO Strany's command. It is also believed to sponsor research on charged-particle-beam and high-energy laser weapons, suggesting that these weapons may be destined to play a role in air defense.[12]

At present, the PVO Strany consists of between 550,000 and 600,000 men,[13] approximately 16 percent of the active military manpower of the Soviet Union, which makes it the second largest service branch, surpassed only by the ground forces. From 1967 to 1977 the PVO ranked fourth among the service branches in funding allocation with about a 12 percent share of the total military budget.[14]

The PVO is broken down into four operational branches, the Fighter Aviation of National Air Defense (IA-PVO), the Surface-to-Air Missile Troops (ZRV, literally Zenith Rocket Troops), the Radar-Electronics Troop (RTV), which is responsible for operating radars and electronic warfare equipment, and the Anti-Aircraft Artillery Troops (ZA), which existed during and immediately after World War II but whose status is now unclear.

For administrative purposes, the PVO Strany divides the Soviet Union into air defense districts. The Moscow and Baku air districts are those mentioned most often in the Soviet press. Both contain major PVO command posts, though supreme command is normally exercised from Mos-

---

12. David R. Jones, "Air Defense," in David R. Jones, ed., *Soviet Armed Forces Review Annual*, vol. 2 (Academic International Press, 1978), p. 97.

13. International Institute for Strategic Studies, *The Military Balance, 1979–1980* (London: IISS, 1979), p. 9; Central Intelligence Agency, National Foreign Assessment Center, *Estimated Soviet Defense Spending: Trends and Prospects*, SR-78-10121 (CIA, 1978), p. 6.

14. CIA, *Estimated Soviet Defense Spending*, pp. 2–6.

cow.[15] The facilities there, and probably elsewhere, are almost certainly duplicated many times—there are reported to be seventy-five underground command centers within eighty miles of Moscow.[16] It is not known to what extent the boundaries of the air defense districts correspond with the more familiar military districts. Most sources maintain that the country is divided into ten air defense regions, with the Warsaw Pact nations constituting six more, but there is some disagreement about this.[17] However, there is no doubt that the national air defense establishments of the Warsaw Pact countries are part of the PVO Strany network commanded from Moscow.

From what little is publicly known of the PVO Strany and by analogy to other forces, it can be said that control is centralized and that tight communications discipline is maintained. Both measures increase security at the cost of flexibility in what even the Russians maintain will be a fluid battle situation. In part, this may be explained by the limited technical capabilities of Soviet interceptor aircraft. Although centralized command is evident throughout the Soviet military, as Soviet airborne intercept radars increase in range and sophistication (and since a pilot may be able to track his target better than the ground net), the traditionally tight control over Soviet fighter pilots can be loosened; there are already signs of this.[18] As target types multiply, the pilot will be the best judge of how an attack should be pressed. Only time will tell whether this relaxation of the traditional command rigidity is part of a general trend for the whole system.

Not surprisingly, the Soviet air defense network seems primarily occupied with targets from the west and north. As noted earlier, the most modern aircraft are based in the western USSR and constitute roughly 30 percent of the active force; another 25 percent in the Baku and Moscow districts indicate Soviet concern with defending command centers. The Warsaw Pact countries' air defenses add depth to the western bastion. The first EW radars were built overlooking the Baltic and Eastern Europe. Only recently has the Soviet Union begun reshaping its forces to get more complete coverage. As far as is known, there are very light air defenses, or none, associated with the missile fields.

15. DIA, *Handbook on Soviet Armed Forces*, p. 11-3.
16. International Institute for Strategic Studies, *Strategic Survey, 1979* (London: IISS, 1978), p. 13.
17. Jones, "National Air Defense Force," p. 25.
18. *United States Military Posture for FY 81* (GPO, 1980), p. 71.

Assessment of Capability

Any assessment of the effectiveness of an air defense system is necessarily uncertain. Reasonable judgments can be made about the technical capabilities (or at least the maximum capabilities) and design intent of individual components from such simple observables as size, shape of principal features, and in the case of radar, frequency and power. But how well a complex system of components (including many humans in key roles) functions is a different matter. At best, good estimates can be made of the upper bounds of performance based on the assumptions that the components are well integrated, operate reliably, and have no hidden defects and that performance against a large attack can be extrapolated from estimated performance against a single intruder. But optimum performance of any military system is rare, and the more complex a system, the more likely it is to break down. Air defense systems are probably the most complex elements in strategic forces, even more complex than ABMs since humans play so many central roles.

Also, it is extremely difficult to judge the effectiveness of electronic countermeasures such as jammers and electronic counter-countermeasures, when neither has ever encountered the other. The results of a first confrontation of air defense with attacking aircraft have been unpredictable. In the 1973 war in the Middle East it took about seven days of intensive combat before some kind of equilibrium was reached and the attrition rate of attacker against specific air defenses could be estimated with any confidence. But in a nuclear war, there would be no time for equilibrium to be established—the first confrontation is likely to be the last. Estimating performance seems a hopeless task considering that neither the attacking force nor the defending force has experienced a real nuclear environment, nor is there any good way to simulate one for the purpose of training people or testing equipment.

Finally, it should be noted that the nuclear encounter would not involve only aircraft systems and air defenses. Missile-delivered nuclear weapons (submarine-launched ballistic missiles and possibly ICBMs), which would encounter no defense except in the Moscow area as long as the ABM treaty was still in effect, would be very much a part of almost any nuclear war, and they could play a crucial role in defense suppression.

The Current System

The currently deployed Soviet system seems to have been designed only for a high-altitude bomber attack. Early warning radars cover all the important entry areas for bombers from the United States or Western Europe and can detect high-flying aircraft well beyond Soviet borders. Soviet interceptor aircraft and SAM batteries are numerous enough to inflict heavy attrition on any high-altitude attacking force even if the technical performance of the Soviet systems has been overestimated. For a low-altitude (500 to 600 feet) bomber attack the situation is substantially different. Although radar coverage in the northwest sector is dense enough to continue to provide some coverage, large gaps appear where radars are not densely distributed. The capability of Soviet strategic SAMs and current aircraft interceptors would be marginal at best against low-flying bombers.

These judgments are based primarily on geometric considerations (line of sight for radars, interceptor range, and so forth) and what is known of Soviet air defense technology. The U.S. bomber force is heavily equipped with jamming and other countermeasure equipment and relies heavily on short-range attack missiles for nuclear weapon delivery, and this compounds the problem for the defense. Although the operational effectiveness of the U.S. electronic countermeasures is not known, it is obviously expected to be high since a significant amount of the bomber's space and payload are devoted to it. The small, supersonic SRAMs are essentially immune to any current Soviet air defenses. Equipped with SRAMs, a bomber can launch its weapons out of range of any threatening SAM sites; it can in fact use SRAMs to destroy SAM sites in its path, thus clearing the way to the primary target.

The net effect is that a substantial fraction of the weapons carried in a large, well-planned, low-altitude bomber attack against the Soviet Union would probably be delivered to their targets. Highly defended point sites might inflict significant attrition on such an attacking force, but they would be unlikely to survive a heavy attack.

On the other hand, an attack by a small bomber force (of, for instance, British Vulcans), if not assisted with defense suppression from ballistic missiles, might be seriously limited in what it could accomplish. Deep penetration of the Soviet Union through the multiple defense systems would surely be very difficult for a small force (even flying at low altitude), and only a small fraction of the weapons could then be counted on to reach their targets. However, for some military purposes, this might be good enough.

Against air-launched cruise missiles, whether the attack is large or small, the Soviet air defense system now deployed is totally inadequate, and we do not foresee major improvements in Soviet air defense by the time ALCMs become part of the force. With their low altitude, low radar cross section, and long range, only with good luck could any ALCMs be destroyed after launch. The currently deployed Soviet radars do not have the altitude coverage, discrimination against clutter, or range and resolution to provide early warning or track information for interceptors or SAMs. The interceptors do not have a radar and data processing system that can distinguish the cruise missile from ground clutter. The SAMs do not have the ability to attack a low-altitude target, nor can the associated radars pick up low-flying objects. The cruise missile carriers might be better targets for the Soviet air defense system, but the carriers can launch their missiles while well outside the range of Soviet ground-based radars and the quality and numbers of the Soviet Moss, guiding a long-range interceptor such as the Tu-28P, are not adequate to seriously threaten cruise missile carriers arriving from many different directions. It may well be, though, that the Moss, if properly deployed in greater numbers, would be a sufficient threat in certain sectors to require somewhat greater standoff distances for the cruise missile carriers than are now contemplated, thereby eliminating some distant targets from cruise missile coverage.

The Soviet system as a whole has probably not been seen in operation except perhaps in exercises. One exception occurred in 1978, when a South Korean airliner penetrated Soviet airspace in the north. The Soviet claim is that the aircraft flew in Soviet airspace for two hours and failed to respond to numerous signals (the receipt of the signals was not corroborated by passengers or crew). On orders from Moscow, which was convinced that the aircraft was engaged in intelligence collection, it was forced to land.[19] Passengers claim that a single interceptor tailed the airliner for fifteen or twenty minutes before it was forced down.[20] If this is true, the Boeing 707 was over land when it was first intercepted. Such performance against a large, slow aircraft making no attempt to hide and flying at 35,000 feet suggests that the world's largest air defense system may have

19. *Washington Post,* April 26, 1978.
20. *New York Times,* April 26, 1978.

significant operational problems. It has also been reported that early in 1978 a light aircraft managed to land near Leningrad and then escape.[21]

If these two incidents are indicative, the Soviet air defense network seems substantially less capable than the sum of its parts. We can only speculate whether this is due primarily to poorly trained operators, an inadequate command and control structure, unreliable equipment, or some combination of these. Why the Soviet Union has deployed and maintained a vast air defense system with essentially little or no capability against the well-known U.S. bomber threat, low-flying B-52s carrying SRAMs, is puzzling. The system apparently has some capability against a small bomber force, but it has certainly encountered technical difficulties, as demonstrated by the long time required for the development of the SA-10, the first SAM with a design capability against the low-flying B-52 attack. The primary driving force behind the PVO Strany may be the historical concern of the Soviet Union about its airspace. Penetrations by U-2s at the end of the 1950s must have been a deep shock to the Soviet leadership, and undoubtedly one of the PVO Strany's principal missions is to maintain the integrity of the airspace, even though new satellite technologies have long since reduced the need for reconnaissance by air-breathing vehicles. In part, the maintenance of the vast air defense system may be political, assuring the population that the homeland is well defended; elements of the system and exercises are publicized. Also historical is the Soviet emphasis on defense, as well as bureaucratic pressure to maintain a deployed system.

The vast size of Soviet air defense is also puzzling because of the strain the military forces place on a troubled national economy. A diversion of economic support from the PVO Strany to civilian sectors of the economy would almost certainly benefit the nation as a whole, but the power of the Ministry of Defense makes this unlikely. Alternatively, the resources could be used to support the offensive rocket forces or other elements of the military. Such a diversion of resources would certainly be opposed by PVO Strany. Alternative expenditures for defense and damage limitation, such as an increase in civil defense and further dispersion of industry and population, would seem worthwhile, but these measures would require an unusual amount of cooperation and agreement between ministries. We may never know how or why the PVO Strany has won out in the bureaucratic struggles.

21. Jones, "National Air Defense Force," p. 34.

The Next Decade

How might the Soviet air defense system evolve by the next decade, and how might it then be able to cope with a cruise missile attack? Below are listed the important changes in the Soviet system that may be expected.

—Replacement of old interceptor aircraft by additional MiG-23s and MiG-25s and by a new advanced interceptor, to total more than 2,000 modern aircraft—all equipped with look-down–shoot-down radar-missile systems.

—Deployment of up to 100 AWACS aircraft very similar to the AWACS aircraft currently operational in the United States.

—Replacement of old SAM systems (SA-1s and SA-2s) with about 5,000 SA-10 interceptors at 500 sites.

The Soviet air defense system so equipped would present a formidable threat to the current U.S. bomber force (with SRAMs but without ALCMs). Although SRAMs once launched would have little difficulty in penetrating even SA-10 defenses, the bombers would be vulnerable before the SRAMs were launched if the SA-10 should prove to be effective against targets flying below 1,000 feet.

Soviet AWACS aircraft, if they have technical capabilities equal to or greater than those of the 1977 U.S. AWACS and if deployed in sufficient numbers, should be able to readily observe the bomber force, which might then be attacked by long-range interceptors with look-down–shoot-down capability. The Soviet Union would have to develop a new long-range interceptor or the ability to fuel in flight an advanced version of the MiG-25. For most of their missions, attacking bombers would have to penetrate several rings of defense (interceptors and SAMs), each technically capable of shooting them down. Although electronic countermeasures and use of ballistic missiles for defense suppression could certainly thin out the air defenses significantly, the utility of today's U.S. bomber force (without ALCMs) against such an upgraded Soviet air defense system is surely questionable.

The ALCMs are of course intended to maintain the utility of the strategic bomber force for at least another decade. During the initial ALCM deployment, some bombers will be programmed to carry SRAMs and to penetrate the Soviet land mass (though only after the cruise missiles are launched). As Soviet air defenses improved with the measures referred to above, the penetrating bombers would become increasingly vulnerable.

But the future deployments we suggest will take time, since the SA-10, the advanced interceptor, and AWACS are thought to be still under development. Given the history of previous deployments, it should be well into the 1980s before the penetrating bomber is seriously threatened, and by that time many, if not most, of the carriers will be standing off the borders. The most serious penetration problem an ALCM force is expected to face by 1990 is the potential vulnerability of the cruise missile carriers (before missile launch) to an AWACS-controlled, long-range aircraft interceptor attack and the possible vulnerability of cruise missiles to SA-10s while over Soviet territory. Cruise missiles, once launched, are not expected to be seriously threatened by aircraft interceptors or by older Soviet SAMs.

To detect and destroy cruise missile carriers before they launch their missiles would require a large force of AWACS and long-range interceptor aircraft. Fifteen to twenty AWACS aircraft would have to be on station to cover all reasonable approach areas of cruise missile carriers. This would probably require a fleet of eighty to one hundred operational AWACS aircraft assigned to the PVO Strany—an upper limit of the total number expected to be built by 1990. The large numbers are dictated by the times required to get on station and the short duty cycle of several hours a day resulting from the need for maintenance of such complex systems. About 1,000 long-range interceptor aircraft would also be required. There has been some speculation that the Soviet Backfire medium-range bomber with a long-range air-to-air missile might be used in a supplementary role as a long-range interceptor against cruise missile carriers. Although Soviet ships in the North Atlantic and Arctic regions could provide some radar coverage, this would be supplementary coverage only, not complete coverage of feasible approach regions for cruise missile carriers.

Such a forward area defense might be effective in destroying a significant fraction of cruise missile carriers, but if it develops, U.S. countermeasures can surely be expected. By remaining several hundred miles further from Soviet territory, and thereby giving up some targets deep inside the Soviet Union, the carriers could substantially reduce their vulnerability. Cruise missiles could be designed with increased range but at a cost of reduced payload or increased RCS. Also, the Soviet AWACS aircraft, particularly when radiating as they do with high power (therefore particularly detectable at great ranges), are especially vulnerable to attack by long-range interceptor missiles, which might be carried on board the U.S. missile carrier aircraft.

The SA-10 is specifically configured to handle low-altitude aircraft and, at some cost in coverage, might be able to engage and destroy individual U.S. cruise missiles. At this point one can only guess what "leakage" would occur because of SA-10 missile unreliability and problems of clutter rejection, but assigning a 50 percent kill probability to an SA-10 missile launched against a cruise missile within its area of coverage is probably generous to the defense. Protecting a city with SA-10s would require surrounding it with perhaps six to ten SAM sites for each ring of defense. Defending a hundred cities would therefore require several thousand SAM sites, and even then there would be substantial leakage. But it should be noted that ballistic missiles can be used to open corridors for cruise missiles and that any nuclear explosions near defense sites can be expected to degrade their performance seriously.

Recent U.S. government estimates were that a Soviet force of 50 to 100 AWACS aircraft, 500 to 1,000 SA-10 sites with perhaps ten missiles each, and "several thousand" interceptors could destroy half the cruise missile force.[22] These numbers, which probably are not based on detailed analysis, are intended only to approximate the huge investment entailed by a conventional defense against cruise missiles.

In the final analysis the measure of effectiveness of a defense cannot be separated from the strategic doctrine, the goals, and the perspective of both the attacking nation and the defending nation. In the case of a 1990 Soviet defense against a massive cruise missile attack, we can estimate with confidence that if urban-industrial areas are the targets, most major cities would be destroyed by cruise missiles alone. No matter how distributed, a large fraction of soft targets can be destroyed. However, if the attacking force needs to be almost sure (about 80 percent) of destroying a large fraction of a large number of separate targets (say, about 80 percent of 2,000) by cruise missiles alone, then a 1990 Soviet air defense can be effective. Such a defense system could possibly protect some number of hard, valuable sites such as command posts (ballistic missile silos do not at present appear to have extensive air defenses), particularly if the loss of a few was not considered serious.

The strategic air defenses of high-value targets could be augmented by the use of large numbers of tactical SAMs, such as SA-9s with radars or improved versions of the SA-9. An effective hard point defense requires covering all routes to the target as well as having defensive weapons much

22. Press release, Under Secretary of Defense William J. Perry, November 14, 1978.

in excess of the expected attack force to minimize leakage. The large proportion of the present Soviet air defenses devoted to the protection of command centers suggests that an offense-saturating defense may be a Soviet tactic for extremely important hardened military installations.

Potential New Technologies

Technologies currently under development could, in principle, be used to upgrade Soviet air defenses, though they are unlikely to make much contribution before 1990. The number of technologies with possible application to air defense is large, and we consider only the few that might be particularly relevant to defense against an attack force using current or future ALCMs.

Space-Based Radars and Infrared Detection Systems

The Soviet Union has developed space-based radar, presumably to maintain coverage of U.S. naval forces,[23] and might apply such a system to strengthen its air defenses. A space-based radar could provide early warning by maintaining coverage of the carrier aircraft and vector long-range interceptors to the carrier aircraft.

There are fundamental limitations to the utility of space-based radars. The fourth-power dependence of the strength of the returned signal argues for a low-altitude orbit for the satellite, since a satellite, because of its relatively small payload (compared to that of a ground-based installation), has limited power. A system operating in a 200-kilometer orbit would require at least twelve satellites to maintain continuous coverage. The radar would have to have the data processing capability to track a hundred or more carrier aircraft continuously. This is an imposing requirement that may be achievable only through multiplying the number of space-based radars to form a network. As the number of spacecraft increases so does the complexity of the system. The radar must be able to pick the carrier aircraft out of the surface clutter. Since the satellite is looking down, it sees the largest component of the RCS of the carrier, but by 1990 the RCS of the carriers may have been reduced by the use of Stealth technologies that would minimize the effectiveness of space-based

23. "Joint US-Canadian Team Discover Cosmos Debris," *Flight International,* February 4, 1978, p. 278.

radar. Even with current RCS, picking up and tracking a carrier from a space-based radar is a difficult though not an impossible task.

Space-based radars are vulnerable to jamming. In addition to the square law versus the fourth-power law of advantage to the jammer, the ground-based jammer does not have the power limitations of a space-based vehicle. Space-based radars must deal with clutter, and space imposes some limitations on the antenna design. Also, in a low-altitude orbit the satellites are especially vulnerable to destruction by relatively simple anti-satellite systems.

If the use of a space-based radar against carriers is difficult, its use against cruise missiles is truly challenging. The much lower RCS of the cruise missile makes the power and size requirements of the space-based radar well beyond current technology. In the carrier mission, the space-based radar has the advantage of having to pick out the vehicle, for at least a portion of its flight, against an ocean background. This is much easier than detecting a cruise missile in ground clutter. Finally, the data processing requirements for handling 1,000 to 3,000 cruise missiles are far greater than for handling 150 carrier aircraft.

An early warning system might use a space-based infrared detection system. The infrared sensors would pick up the heat generated by the carrier aircraft engines. Such a system, however, has several disadvantages. The data processor must be able to distinguish the heat generated by the aircraft from the heat radiated by the earth or clouds and from sun glints. A high-bypass fan-jet engine can have a cool exhaust, reducing the infrared signal, and heavy cloud cover would effectively hide it from the satellite system. As in the case of radar, the system would have to handle some 150 separate targets simultaneously.

Given its interest in the military uses of space, the Soviet Union may well decide to field a space-based early warning system. Such a system would be complex and vulnerable to a number of countermeasures, including direct attack. In our view, therefore, a 1990 space-based radar or infrared system would provide little, if any, improvement over upgrading present Soviet ground-based early warning systems.

Laser and Particle-Beam Weapons

Numerous reports indicate that there is a major Soviet program to construct lasers or particle-beam weapons.[24] Lasers generate an intense beam

24. "Soviets Build Directed-Energy Weapon," *Aviation Week and Space Technology,* July 28, 1980, p. 47.

of energy at a frequency usually in the infrared part of the spectrum. Lasers can either operate continuously or be pulsed repetitively over a total time of seconds. Particle beams can be generated by equipment similar to that of the accelerators used in experimental high-energy physics. The intriguing advantage of these systems is that the beam propagates at the speed of light so that, once the target is detected, energy can be deposited on it almost instantaneously. In theory, many targets can be handled quickly at a low marginal cost per target.

While superficially attractive, such exotic weapons suffer from severe disadvantages compared with conventional weapons. Laser systems do not perform well in bad weather. Both particle beams and lasers are much more complex than antiaircraft guns or SAMs, and their operation and maintenance would require highly skilled operators. While radiated energy can be transmitted almost instantaneously, destruction of the target requires that it be irradiated for some period of time (depending on the power of the beam). This implies that a specific spot on the target must be tracked during this time and the beam of energy focused on that spot, a task that at the very least requires relatively sophisticated equipment. Finally, the high-energy beam must propagate through an atmosphere that is not homogeneous in its properties, so that maintaining focus is difficult, particularly since the beam deposits energy along its travel path, thereby further degrading its quality and reducing the amount of energy that reaches the target. An additional problem with charged particle beams is that they are deflected by the local magnetic field, which may not be known with precision and which is altered significantly and unpredictably by nearby nuclear explosions.

High-energy weapon systems, using lasers or particle beams, may eventually have a role in space where there is no atmosphere to contend with. However, within the atmosphere, obstacles to such systems are severe. Thus it is highly improbable that these exotic weapons can be used to improve the effectiveness of Soviet air defenses in this century any more than would be possible with traditional technologies.

Alternative Means of Detection and Tracking

Although radar is the generally accepted technology to detect and track air-breathing vehicles, the low RCS of the cruise missile and the possibility that it can be further reduced by the use of Stealth technology may cause the Soviet Union to supplement radar in air defense with infrared and acoustic sensors. Infrared signals are already used in a variety of heat-seeking missiles in both the U.S. and Soviet inventories. Though acoustic detection and tracking of aircraft was first employed in World War I, it has received less attention in recent years because of the effectiveness of radar.

A cruise missile flying at a low altitude will generate an infrared signal both because the engine and the exhaust gases are hot and because the vehicle flying at low altitude generates heat as a result of skin friction with air. A ground-based infrared detector must pick the vehicle out of what is for the most part a cool sky background—an easier task than that of an airborne sensor, which must detect the vehicle against a ground surface that during the day may be warmer than the air. Sensitive infrared detectors are complex systems that usually require the use of liquid nitrogen or helium. The casual reports of U.S. fighter pilots testify to the aggravation and inconvenience caused by cryogenic coolants in tactical situations. A further limitation to the use of infrared is the degraded performance in bad weather.

Infrared detection technology has reached relatively sophisticated levels in various homing devices. With other means available, much less progress has been made in using infrared signatures for tracking. However, the Soviet Union can be expected to continue work on this technology, and at some time in the 1990s it may be sufficiently useful to improve Soviet tracking capabilities. At the same time U.S. countermeasures designed to reduce the infrared signal can be expected, such as cooling the exhaust by increasing the airflow through the engine.

Since the cruise missile flies at low altitudes the acoustical signal it generates could in principle be used for detection, but acoustic tracking systems have several defects. The signal rapidly attenuates as it propagates so that the range over which acoustic detection is possible is limited. The propagation of sound is affected by weather, particularly wind. The temperature structure of the atmosphere may channel the acoustic signal so that it does not reach the detector. The acoustic system must distinguish the cruise missile's signal from other local noises. These limitations make it unlikely that acoustics will significantly improve Soviet air defenses except possibly for early warning.

The Impact of New Technologies on Soviet Air Defense Capability

It appears that the most publicized of possible new technologies, space radars and high-energy weapons, will add little, if anything, in the 1990s to a Soviet air defense against cruise missiles that is expected to consist of more advanced radars, interceptor aircraft, and SAMs. If the United States is successful in reducing the RCS of cruise missiles, the Soviet Union may make a major investment in alternative detection and tracking systems. Such a development is unlikely to be unnoticed by the United States, and appropriate countermeasures to make the ALCM quieter and reduce the infrared signature can be expected.

The size and bureaucratic influence of the PVO Strany may have a significant impact on the course of Soviet technology development. From what we have seen of past Soviet interest in defensive systems, it would not be surprising if developmental work on radiation weapons and space radars for air defense continued long after it was clear that the usefulness of such systems would be marginal.

Analysis of Simplified Defense Deployment

An important feature of the planned U.S. cruise missile force is its size. A possible defense against such a large attacking force is one in which the defense outnumbers the offense, at least around particularly valuable targets. The effectiveness of a defense will depend on the geometry, location of the sites, probability of detection, probability of kill, and so forth. Since all such factors can only be roughly estimated, the general principles of defense can be illustrated by simplified scenarios. If the number of defensive weapons is very large, a system, to be less than prohibitively expensive, must have relatively inexpensive weapons of the SA-7 or SA-9 variety. For the purposes of illustration, we assume a heat-seeking SAM with a range of three kilometers. A longer range missile would not substantially improve the system since the low-altitude flight of the ALCM limits detection range to between ten and twenty kilometers. We thus imagine each site defending a circular territory of about twenty-five square kilometers. We consider two deployments, one defending cities (hundreds of square kilometers) and one defending large areas (a million square kilometers).

City Defense

An illustrative deployment is one in which the defense is intended to protect a hundred cities by defensive rings about each city. The defense must cover all angles of attack because of the maneuverability of the cruise missile and have a sufficient number of sites around each city to provide reasonable protection.

Table 2-1. *Penetration from a Cruise Missile Attack on a Single City*

Number of defensive sites	Kill probability	Penetration rate
200	0.5	0.06
200	0.1	0.66
90	0.5	0.25
90	0.1	0.88
40	0.5	0.50
40	0.1	0.90
20	0.5	0.71
20	0.1	0.95

The following extremely simplified calculations indicate the very large number of weapons required to provide a truly effective defense of cities. The defense is assumed to occupy a region in the shape of an annulus around each city, with the radius of the inner ring of the annulus about thirty kilometers, which keeps engagements away from the target. Table 2-1 illustrates the dependence of the leakage rate (the percentage of cruise missiles that reach the targeted city) on the number of defense sites and on the single-shot kill probability of the defense interceptors.[25] With a kill probability of 0.5 and 200 sites, one out of seventeen missiles aimed at the city will reach it. With only 40 defensive sites and the same kill probability, half the cruise missiles will reach their target. On the assumption that a leakage rate of 0.1 (10 percent of the cruise missiles reach their targets) is acceptable to the defense and that the single-shot kill probability per site is 0.5, the outer ring of the annulus is 48 kilometers and there are 176 sites around each city. A total of 18,000 sites would be required to defend 100 cities. Table 2-2 illustrates the number of missile sites necessary to protect 100 cities from an attack by 1,000 ALCMs (about the number that might survive from a total of 3,400 before a Soviet

25. The defensive sites are in an annulus with inner radius, r, and outer radius r_2. The total number of sites would be $\pi(r_2^2 - r_1^2)/\Delta A$, where ΔA is the area covered by each site. The probability of penetration is $(1 - P_k)^n$, where P_k is the kill probability and n is the number of sites a cruise missile would have to fly over to penetrate the city. An approximation to n is

$$n \approx \frac{r_2 - r_1}{\sqrt{\Delta A}}.$$

With a leakage rate of 0.01, a P_k of 0.5 requires that

$$n \approx \frac{\ln(0.01)}{\ln(0.5)} \approx 7,$$

so that $r_2 \approx 63$ kilometers.

Table 2-2. *Number of Missile Sites Necessary to Protect 100 Cities from an Attack by 1,000 Cruise Missiles*

Kill probability	Surviving cities	Number of defensive missile sites
0.2	80	208,000
0.2	45	135,000
0.2	15	105,000
0.5	85	41,000
0.5	70	37,500
0.5	40	25,000

surprise attack, based on less pessimistic estimates than those in chapter 5), at single-shot kill probabilities of 0.2 and 0.5.

Another problem with such a defensive strategy is its vulnerability to corridor blasting to each city. The corridor blasting (simple saturation of the defense) is assumed to be by cruise missiles, although SRAMs or ballistic missiles might be used for this purpose. If the offense devotes 800 cruise missiles to blasting corridors into 100 cities, 200 cruise missiles remain to attack two targets in each city. This simple offensive tactic renders the ring defense ineffective and illustrates the virtues of a large number of offensive missiles against a limited number of targets.

The situation is very different if the cruise missiles are to attack a large number of targets, each one of which covers a small area and none of which are as individually valuable as the cities. The defense must ensure the survival of a reasonable fraction of the targets. The coverage of the missiles can be made to overlap, increasing the effective kill probability of the system, and in this way decrease the vulnerability of the defense to corridor blasting tactics. With a total inventory of 40,000 missile interceptors, the defense could deploy 40 missiles around each of 1,000 sites. In an attack of 3,000 cruise missiles from a fully generated U.S. strategic force, with 2 cruise missiles to every other site, a kill probability of 0.2 on the part of the defense could reduce the penetration rate to less than 0.01, or 200 targets. The defense could thus protect 800 high-value point targets and exhaust the cruise missile force.

Area Defense

An alternative deployment is one in which the defense sites are uniformly distributed over a large area containing high-value targets such as cities and industrial locations. This deployment reduces vulnerability to corridor blasting, since the route to any target will pass over areas covered by numerous missile sites; a defense in depth reduces the effectiveness of corridor blasting.

We assume the total area covered lies in a circle with a 1,000-kilometer radius, making the defended area a little more than 3 million square kilometers. The attacking force launches 1,000 ALCMs. As above, each interceptor missile is assumed to cover 25 square kilometers. If the kill probability of the individual missile was 0.2, a deployment of 35,000 sites would reduce the leakage to 10 cruise missiles.[26] If the kill probability was 0.1, 40,000 sites would allow 60 missiles to reach their targets. Such a deployment has the disadvantage that all areas outside the area of distributed defense are undefended. The cueing of the operators is much more difficult than in a city defense because of the wide geographic distribution.

Any of the deployments sketched above would require several hundred thousand intelligent and trained personnel. While a "Swiss Army" style of duty, where many of the populace are trained and equipped, might be postulated, such training and maintenance of skills would be a major undertaking. And there is the question of operational effectiveness. While it is easy to set down kill probabilities on paper, it is much more difficult to estimate the joint effectiveness of hundreds of thousands of operators of shoulder-held or similar weapons attempting to detect and lock on low-flying missiles in a nuclear environment. We doubt that any deployment, even of vast numbers, can reduce the vulnerability of cities, and only with great effort can the vulnerability of large numbers of potential targets be reduced.

Conclusions

The Soviet Union has made massive investments in all elements of air defense from early warning radars through SAMs and interceptors. Despite these efforts, the currently deployed system is unlikely to pose a serious threat to the current U.S. bomber force flying low over Soviet terri-

---

26. The sites are assumed to be distributed uniformly over a circle with radius R. The cruise missiles must travel an average distance $R/3$ to reach their targets. If the total number of sites, N, is large enough so that leakage, L, is small, it can be shown that

$$N \approx \frac{3}{2} \pi^{3/2}(- \ln L)R/(P_k\sqrt{\Delta A}).$$

tory, armed with SRAMs, and equipped with electronic countermeasures. In a massive raid most of the B-52s could probably penetrate and reach their targets.

New Soviet air defense systems now being deployed, which are specifically designed to handle low-altitude aircraft, can make the Soviet air defense much more effective against the current U.S. bomber force. But even these systems would be severely limited in handling a large force of low-altitude cruise missiles.

The penetration capability of the cruise missile force results from the large number involved and their low RCS, low altitude of flight, and ability to alter course. The large number makes target handling and data processing difficult for the defense and implies that the attacking force can suffer a high rate of attrition and still deliver many weapons. Since the vehicles are unmanned, constraints imposed by the need to minimize hazard to crews no longer hold. The low RCS of the small cruise missile, which might be made even lower by applying Stealth technology, makes detection and tracking difficult. The low altitude of flight reduces the range at which radar can detect a cruise missile and thus shortens the time during which an engagement can take place. This lessens the effectiveness of SAMs and interceptors. The flexible flight path of the cruise missile means that it can attack a target from any azimuth, which imposes additional geometric requirements on the defense, thereby multiplying the number of SAM sites and radars needed.

An ALCM force appears to be relatively invulnerable to possible Soviet air defenses at least through the middle 1990s if the mission of the force is against a limited number of population centers (a hundred). Corridor-cutting tactics using cruise missiles (or ICBMs, SLBMs, or SRAMs) would be highly effective against city defenses. However, attack on a large number of limited area targets (a thousand) would be more difficult if the Russians concentrated their defenses around these targets and were willing to lose a substantial fraction (more than 30 percent) of the defended sites. An area defense of some million square kilometers is feasible if a leakage rate of 0.01 is acceptable and if some 40,000 simple SAM sites are deployed. But even then, only a fraction of the Soviet Union is defended.

The weakest element of the system is the carrier aircraft. The cruise missile carrier need be no more vulnerable than a penetrating bomber up to the point when the carrier launches its missiles. (The vulnerability of the carrier aircraft before takeoff is not considered here.) After launching its cruise missile, the ALCM carrier can return to its base; it need not carry out the most dangerous phase of the bomber's mission, approaching and penetrating Soviet airspace. The vulnerability of the carrier can be reduced by increasing the range of the cruise missile. The carrier standing a greater distance off the Soviet border increases the volume of airspace that must be defended. Increased range would permit ALCM attacks from a variety of directions, subjecting the air defenses to further stress. For any defined cruise missile force, one can imagine a set of defensive measures that can in theory cope with the threat. However, when comparing the magnitude of the required defense effort to that required to neutralize such an effort (and this is reflected in the relative costs), the offense has an overwhelming advantage in a deterrent role when urban-industrial centers are the targets, but may be severely limited if intended to destroy a large portion of many hardened military sites.

CHAPTER THREE

The History of Modern Cruise Missile Programs

RON HUISKEN

FOR ALL practical purposes, the history of the modern strategic cruise missile began in June 1972 when Secretary of Defense Melvin R. Laird requested $20 million to start developing such a weapon.[1] The request was included in a package of amendments to the 1973 defense budget inspired by the signing of the SALT I agreements.

Laird's request ended a decade of military lack of interest in cruise missiles. During the 1950s the United States had developed a variety of long-range nuclear-armed cruise missiles, including the submarine-launched Regulus I, the ground-launched Matador and Mace tactical systems, the bomber-launched Hound Dog, and the Snark, the only cruise missile of intercontinental range to achieve operational status. In 1957–59, as the United States became increasingly confident of the success of the ballistic missile programs, development work on the cruise missile was sharply cut back, and by 1960–62, with the deployment of the Hound Dog and the Mace B, it essentially stopped. When Secretary Laird proposed the new program, only the Hound Dog was still operational.

The modern strategic cruise missile evolved along two distinct but increasingly interrelated paths. One of these was the submarine-launched (later sea-launched) cruise missile (SLCM) and the other the air-

Ron Huisken wrote this chapter while serving with the Disarmament and Development Committee of the United Nations; he is now with the Australian Department of Defence. The views expressed are his and do not necessarily reflect the policies of either organization.

1. The programs mentioned in this chapter are more comprehensively discussed in Ron Huisken, *The Origin of the Strategic Cruise Missile* (Praeger, 1981).

launched cruise missile (ALCM). The June 1972 proposal concerned the SLCM, but the ALCM has an interesting and relevant history that goes back to 1966–67.

During this period the Air Force conducted a series of bomber-penetration studies from which it was concluded that a replacement for the Quail decoy missile—deployed on B-52s since 1960—would be desirable. A "required operational capability" statement for such a weapon was issued in January 1968, but the Air Force's ambition to develop a pure decoy system was challenged from the outset, notably by Director of Defense Research and Engineering John S. Foster, Jr. The Air Force lost the first round: when the new program got under way in January 1969 it was called the subsonic cruise armed decoy (SCAD). The controversy continued, however, and ultimately resulted in the cancellation of the SCAD program. By early 1971—some eighteen months before the SLCM proposal—tentative consideration was being given to standoff missiles as an alternative to the penetrating strategic bomber. Senator Thomas J. McIntyre, for one, wondered why the B-1 development program could not be stretched by two years to "permit a closer examination of . . . alternatives including . . . a standoff launch capability employing a nuclear armed decoy."[2]

In the meantime, the Navy had begun developing the Harpoon, a short-range antiship cruise missile intended for deployment on surface ships and aircraft. Early in 1971 the Navy added to the development program a third variant, one that would be launched from the torpedo tubes of attack submarines. At the same time, the Navy launched another new program, the advanced cruise missile (ACM). This weapon was also intended for the tactical antishipping role, but its range of about 300 miles was a great improvement over the Harpoon's range of 70 miles. Initially the ACM was conceived as a weapon that would be launched from vertical tubes in a new class of submarines built for the purpose that had twenty tubes per boat. This concept significantly reduced the constraint on size, and the missile was relatively large, about thirty-four inches in diameter.

Sometime during 1971 Foster requested that the Navy examine the possibility of achieving ranges of strategic significance with cruise missiles. The ACM then went through various formulations and emerged as

2. *Fiscal Year 1972 Authorization for Military Procurement, Research and Development, Construction and Real Estate Acquisition for the Safeguard ABM and Reserve Strengths,* Hearings before the Senate Armed Services Committee, 92 Cong. 1 sess. (Government Printing Office, 1971), pt. 1, p. 492.

a weapon twenty-eight inches in diameter, to be fired from horizontal tubes. The 1973 budget contained a modest request for ACM development, but the Navy also attached a $2 million supplement to the 1972 budget specifically for the strategic variant, on the grounds that the concept was sufficiently attractive to be worth pursuing faster than the approval of 1973 funding would allow. Indeed, the strategic cruise missile was already in the big league: in justifying the $2 million supplement a Navy official testified that "the same rationale and sense of urgency that forced us to accelerate [Trident] forces us to proceed as expeditiously as possible with advanced cruise missile development."[3]

In May 1972 the United States and the Soviet Union signed the SALT I agreements, and in response the Defense Department prepared a supplement to the 1973 budget requesting additional funding for strategic programs. One of these requests addressed what was, in effect, an entirely new strategic weapon system—the submarine-launched cruise missile.

Beyond the fact that it would be deployed on submarines, little else about the SLCM had been decided. Four options concerning platforms and mode of launch were under consideration: (1) cruise missiles launched vertically from converted nuclear ballistic missile submarines (SSBNs); (2) cruise missiles launched horizontally from nuclear attack submarines (SSNs); (3) cruise missiles launched horizontally from converted SSBNs; and (4) cruise missiles launched vertically from a new class of SSNs. The candidate missile designs ranged from 21 inches to 32 inches in diameter and from 246 inches to 345 inches in length, with the smaller designs relating to options 2 and 3 and the larger versions to options 1 and 4.[4]

In presenting the SLCM proposal, Secretary Laird expressed a strong preference for option 1, but the chief of naval operations preferred the greater deployment flexibility that would stem from constraining the size of the missile to fit a standard torpedo tube. Accordingly, the Navy pressed for a fifth option: development of a cruise missile with both strategic and tactical applications that would be compatible with all existing potential launch platforms. This option quickly prevailed—the Navy canceled the ACM program in November 1972 in favor of a tactical

3. *Hearings on Military Posture and H.R. 12604,* Hearings before the House Armed Services Committee, 92 Cong. 1 sess. (GPO, 1972), pt. 2, p. 10744.
4. *Fiscal Year 1974 Authorization for Military Procurement, Research and Development, Construction Authorization for the Safeguard ABM, and Active Duty and Selected Reserve Strengths,* Hearings before the Senate Armed Services Committee, 93 Cong. 1 sess. (GPO, 1973), pt. 4, pp. 2635–40.

variant of the SLCM—but it was not until November 1974 that the basic provisions for the new weapon were detailed in an operational requirement document. The document specified a weapon sized to fit torpedo tubes 21 inches in diameter and 246 inches long; capable of both strategic and tactical missions with development priority to be given to the former and, for the tactical version, to surface-ship platforms; and adaptable to launch from land-based platforms.[5] The objectives for range and accuracy, deleted from the published document, were apparently 1,400 nautical miles and a circular error probable (CEP) of 0.1 nautical mile, respectively.[6]

In justifying the SLCM proposal, Secretary Laird leaned heavily on the U.S. experience in negotiating the SALT I accords and their terms, particularly the interim agreement on offensive weapons. Laird believed that the United States had been able to negotiate effectively in SALT I because it had active development or procurement programs in the various areas of weaponry covered by the agreements, namely, antiballistic missiles (ABMs), intercontinental ballistic missiles (ICBMs), and SLBMs. The United States had made an unsuccessful attempt to bring Soviet naval cruise missiles into the SALT I negotiations, and Laird felt that SALT II would produce the same result unless the United States launched a cruise missile program of its own.[7]

John Foster supplemented this theme by pointing out the virtues of a further diversification of the U.S. strategic deterrent and stressing the magnitude of the problem that defense against cruise missiles would pose for the Soviet Union. Foster was so impressed with the potential of cruise missiles that he ranked them ahead of Trident and the B-1 in cost-effectiveness: the SLCM "would add more deterrent per dollar than any other of our schemes."[8]

5. *Fiscal Year 1977 Authorization for Military Procurement, Research and Development, and Active Duty, Selected Reserve and Civilian Personnel Strengths,* Hearings before the Senate Armed Services Committee, 94 Cong. 2 sess. (GPO, 1976), pt. 6, p. 3365.

6. *Fiscal Year 1975 Authorization for Military Procurement, Research and Development, and Active Duty, Selected Reserve and Civilian Personnel Strengths,* Hearings before the Senate Armed Services Committee, 93 Cong. 2 sess. (GPO, 1974), pt. 7, pp. 3652, 3658.

7. *Fiscal Year 1973 Authorization for Military Procurement, Research and Development, Construction Authorization for the Safeguard ABM, and Active Duty and Selected Reserve Strengths,* Hearings before the Senate Armed Services Committee, 92 Cong. 2 sess. (GPO, 1972), *Addendum No. 1,* p. 4244.

8. Ibid., p. 4357.

The Congress did not share this enthusiasm. Several members had long memories and recalled the decisiveness with which the United States had abandoned strategic cruise missiles in the late 1950s on the grounds that they could not compete with ballistic missiles. Another aspect that troubled Congress was that the cruise missiles deployed on Soviet submarines were suddenly depicted as a potential strategic threat, whereas in the preceding ten years (since they were first deployed) the Pentagon had tended to discount their value even in the tactical role. Of similar concern was that a 1,400-nautical-mile cruise missile contradicted the logic behind Trident, a multibillion-dollar program intended primarily to enable strategic submarines to stay farther away from the Soviet Union but still be within range of their targets. Congress was also troubled by the fact that the first agreement to limit strategic arms had spawned a proposal for an entirely new strategic weapon system, and one whose presence or absence could not be determined by existing national technical means of verification. Finally, the Air Force, in attempting to defend its SCAD program, stressed that, in its judgment, a subsonic cruise missile would probably be highly vulnerable to terminal Soviet surface-to-air missile (SAM) defenses. This view contradicted Foster's assessment of the SLCM and added to the already considerable pressure to drop the latter weapon.

The SLCM did survive, of course, but just barely. The original request for $20 million was cut to $6 million, and in the following fiscal year, 1974, only $2.5 million was appropriated. This was accompanied by a directive that the Pentagon thoroughly review the requirement for strategic cruise missiles, particularly the SLCM, before requesting additional funding.[9]

As the above implies, the SLCM was no longer the only strategic cruise missile. In July 1973 the Pentagon canceled the SCAD program and transferred part of its budget allocation to the development of subsystems for cruise missiles. Early in 1974 a program was initiated to develop an air-launched cruise missile for deployment on strategic bombers.

With the complicating factor of a decoy missile removed from the picture, the debate now began to focus more exclusively on whether the ALCM should be viewed as something that would improve the capability of the penetrating bomber, supplement it, or replace it. The debate was further stimulated by the accumulating evidence that the capabilities of cruise missiles would be truly remarkable. When the cruise missile made

9. See A. A. Tinajero, "Cruise Missiles (Subsonic): U.S. Programs," IB 76018 (Congressional Research Service, 1976), p. 19.

its abrupt debut in 1972, there was little firm evidence that really long ranges could be extracted from so small a vehicle or that high accuracies could be achieved at the end of a two- or three-hour journey.

The SCAD program had demonstrated that small turbofan engine technology had made great progress since the early 1960s but that a lot of work remained to be done to optimize these propulsion units for application to cruise missiles. By early 1974 the Navy, at least, was confident that the range objective of 1,400 nautical miles could be achieved even if the SLCM flew the entire distance at low altitude. The second major technological barrier to effective long-range cruise missiles was guidance. TERCOM (terrain contour matching) was selected to supplement inertial guidance.

The TERCOM principle was patented in 1958 and subsequently developed, up to a point, in connection with a weapon known as the SLAM —supersonic low-altitude missile. When this weapon was canceled in 1963, the guidance contractor, E-Systems, kept TERCOM alive with company funds, but no serious prospect for its application in a new weapon emerged until the SLCM was proposed. The first Navy tests began in March 1973, and within a year it became apparent that the accuracy of cruise missiles with TERCOM-aided inertial navigation systems (TAINS) would probably *begin* at the highest accuracies considered feasible with purely inertially guided weapons, that is, at CEPs on the order of 400 feet.

These developments helped to put the SLCM onto a healthier funding track from fiscal 1975 on. In February 1974 the first review of the program by the Defense Systems Acquisition Review Council (DSARC) approved the issue of contracts for the competitive development of prototypes. The Navy selected General Dynamics and LTV and announced that the winner would be selected early in 1976. (The Navy eventually selected the BGM-109 from General Dynamics.)

The rationale for the weapon was still shadowy, however. It was at once an urgent strategic requirement and a "hedge against the development of effective threats to pre-launch survivability of land-based forces, to inflight vulnerability of ballistic missiles and to bomber survivability."[10] Similarly, the idea that the United States was developing a weapon whose advantages included the possibility of covert deployment and the impossibility of distinguishing between the tactical and strategic versions re-

10. *Fiscal Year 1977 Authorization for Military Procurement,* Hearings, p. 3370.

mained a source of discomfort. On the other hand, it was a comparatively inexpensive program—it was, in fact, openly acknowledged that the need for the weapon was not strong enough to justify great expense[11]—and one that could provoke the Soviet Union into a disproportionately costly defense effort. Furthermore, the program was still at an early and flexible stage of development, and probably many people were already considering the SLCM primarily in terms of its spin-off or demonstration effects for bomber-launched cruise missiles. The Navy had been instructed in 1973 to keep in mind as potential launch platforms not only submarines, surface ships, and land vehicles, but also the B-52. And Malcolm Currie, Foster's successor at the Defense Department, viewed cruise missiles in general as a major alternative approach to the penetration of the formidable Soviet air defense system.[12] At DSARC meetings on cruise missiles in December 1974 and March 1975 there was some pressure to cancel the ALCM in favor of an air-launched version of the SLCM.[13] The ALCM survived on both occasions primarily because constraints on size and shape dictated by the respective launch platforms justified separate development, at least through the advanced development phase.

Despite the noticeable drift of interest in the direction of the ALCM, the effort on behalf of the SLCM continued to find a solid rationale for the program. In February 1975 Currie advanced a distinctly new rationale for what was by then being called the sea-launched cruise missile: "A sea-launched cruise missile development provides a desirable augmentation of capability, a unique potential for unambiguous, controlled single-weapon response and an invulnerable reserve force."[14]

The latter element of this rationale flowed easily from the Navy's description of how the SLCM would be employed. By early 1974 the Navy had settled on the SSN as the launch platform for the SLCM and emphasized that SSNs would not, under normal circumstances, be diverted from their primary mission, antisubmarine warfare (ASW). Navy studies indicated that with new-technology ASW torpedoes as many as six of the

11. *Fiscal Year 1975 Authorization for Military Procurement*, Hearings, p. 3639.

12. *Department of Defense Appropriations for 1975*, Hearings before the House Appropriations Committee, 93 Cong. 2 sess. (GPO, 1974), pt. 4, p. 461.

13. *Fiscal Year 1976 and July–September 1976 Transition Period Authorization for Military Procurement, Research and Development, and Active Duty, Selected Reserve, and Civilian Personnel Strengths*, Hearings before the Senate Armed Services Committee, 94 Cong. 1 sess. (GPO, 1975), pt. 4, pp. 2011 ff.

14. *Department of Defense Program of Research, Development, Test and Evaluation, FY 1976* (Defense Department, 1975).

twenty-one or twenty-two torpedo spaces available on an SSN could be allocated to SLCMs without degrading its ASW capability. Since both the submarine-launched version of the Harpoon and the tactical version of the SLCM would be competing for these six spaces, the normal payload of strategic SLCMs should be something less. One official referred to "a couple" of strategic SLCMs per submarine.[15] Currie also pointed out that the developing debate on whether, as a reserve weapon, the SLCM could penetrate Soviet air defenses was largely irrelevant because extensive damage would have already been inflicted by preceding U.S. retaliatory strikes.

The reference to the SLCM's capacity for "unambiguous, controlled single-weapon response" was clearly an attempt to find a slot for the weapon in the so-called Schlesinger doctrine of flexible response and limited strategic options.[16] A clear element of contradiction arises here. Limited options were envisaged as enhancing the deterrent against a full-scale nuclear exchange; in this role a single cruise missile would be pitted against an undamaged and presumably fully alerted Soviet air defense system. In any event, this rationale was not heard of again.

In response to SALT developments and Soviet deployment of the SS-20 intermediate-range ballistic missile (IRBM) the Ford administration's budget for 1978 requested funding to initiate the separate development of a ground-launched cruise missile. The amount requested was a modest $3.9 million, but in amendments to the budget, the new Carter administration boosted this sum to $27.9 million.

An interesting related development was that early in 1976 the SLCM was quietly reclassified as a theater nuclear weapon system, so quietly, in fact, that the House Armed Services Committee was surprised to learn of this development early in the following year.[17] The development program was not affected in any way. It was exactly the same weapon but now cast in the role of an option to preserve the Eurostrategic balance:

The primary need for the land-attack TOMAHAWK is in a theater role where its single warhead, high accuracy capability with resultant low collateral damage, penetrability and survivability make it ideal for use in limited nuclear attacks as a theater weapon. It represents one of the few new systems the U.S.

15. *Fiscal Year 1975 Authorization for Military Procurement,* Hearings, p. 3658.

16. *Department of Defense Program . . . FY 1976,* p. 78.

17. *Hearings on Military Posture and H.R. 5068 [H.R. 5970]: Department of Defense Authorization for Appropriations for Fiscal Year 1978,* Hearings before the House Armed Services Committee, 95 Cong. 1 sess. (GPO, 1977), bk. 2, pt. 3, p. 1099.

could deploy if needed to maintain theater balance in the face of growing Soviet peripheral attack capabilities that include such systems as the BACK-FIRE bomber and the SS-20 mobile ground launched missile.[18]

Whereas the vicissitudes in the SLCM program in 1975–76 were determined largely by external developments, the ALCM was the subject of fierce internal debate. The debate revolved around the relative merits of two studies on how the strategic bomber force should be modernized. In December 1974 the Air Force, in collaboration with the Department of Defense, completed and submitted to Congress the mammoth "Joint Strategic Bomber Study" (JSBS). The second study, prepared by two analysts from the Brookings Institution, appeared about a year later, although Congress had been informed of the preliminary results early in 1975.[19] This mismatch in timing was of little consequence because the production decision on the B-1 had been rescheduled from September 1975 to November 1976.

The two studies arrived at diametrically opposed conclusions. The JSBS demonstrated the cost-effectiveness of the B-1; the Brookings study suggested that the B-1 was unnecessary for the time being and that when a new bomber became necessary it would not have to be as sophisticated as the B-1. A detailed examination of these studies would be out of place here, but it may be worthwhile to identify the specifics and assumptions that in each case were judged to be of central importance to the conclusions reached.

The JSBS, understandably, was ambitious in determining what the strategic bomber force should be able to accomplish; the target base assumed included government controls (national, civil, and political), industrial-economic installations, and military installations. The following is a summary of what was studied and the conclusions reached:

the study methodology subjected each of the equal-cost forces, plus the programmed FY 1980 force, to a survivability and penetrativity analysis. . . . High levels of threat to bomber launch and penetration were postulated and no strategic warning was assumed for U.S. forces in order to present a conservative case for each of the forces. Each of the alternative forces were subjected to the same threat, the same force posturing assumptions, and to a com-

18. *Department of Defense Appropriations for 1978,* Hearings before a subcommittee of the House Appropriations Committee, 95 Cong. 1 sess. (GPO, 1977), pt. 2, p. 235.

19. Department of Defense, Office of Director, Defense Research and Engineering, "Joint Strategic Bomber Study," declassified material, September 1, 1974; and Alton H. Quanbeck and Archie L. Wood, *Modernizing the Strategic Bomber Force: Why and How* (Brookings Institution, 1976).

mon target list. The target value destroyed by each force was the principal measure of merit of the forces. . . .

Force 1. Aircraft programmed to be in the inventory in 1980, including B-52, D, G, H, FB-111A and KC-135 aircraft.

Force 2. The baseline force for costing from which alternative equal cost forces were developed. It consisted of the planned B-1 force programmed to penetrate defenses and attack targets with SRAM [short-range attack missile] and gravity weapons, accompanied by the B-52H fleet employing stand-off cruise missiles [210 B-1s plus 90 B-52Hs].

Force 3. This force was similar to Force 2 in numbers and type of aircraft, but the cruise missiles were replaced by multi-mission missiles capable of air-to-air or air-to-ground attack.

Force 4. A smaller number of B-1s were used in this force, which contained re-engined B-52G/Hs (the B-52I). The entire force was programmed to penetrate postulated air defenses, that is, no standoff cruise missiles were included [180 B-1s plus 255 re-engined B-52s].

Force 5. This force was an all standoff force of a number of wide-bodied jets (similar to the Boeing 747) and the B-52H fleet employing standoff cruise missiles from outside defenses [116 wide-bodied jets plus 90 B-52G/Hs].

Force 6. In this force option, the FB-111G (a "Stretch" FB-111 variant) was substituted for the B-1 in quantities about twice as large as the number of B-1s bought in the baseline case. FB-111Gs penetrated air defenses to attack, while a fleet of B-52Hs launched cruise missiles from outside air defenses.

Force 7. This option contained a smaller number of B-1s (two-thirds of the planned program buy) which penetrated air defenses. A B-52G/H fleet carrying cruise missiles was employed in a standoff role [141 B-1s plus 255 B-52G/Hs].

The results of the study indicated that Forces 2, 3 and 4, containing B-1s in greater numbers, performed substantially better than the other forces. In terms of cost-effectiveness, there was no significant difference between Forces 2, 3, and 4. The study showed that the effectiveness of the B-52I/B-1 combination in Force 4 was close to that of the other forces which contained higher numbers of B-1s. However, the B-52I suffered significant mission degradation from fighters; further, the large force would generate higher O&M [operations and maintenance] costs beyond 1988. Force 5, which consisted only of cruise missiles employed by B-52s and 747-type aircraft, was not as cost-effective as Forces 2, 3 and 4. The "Stretch" FB-111G (Force 6) was clearly non-competitive due to deficiencies in range, payload, and ECM [electronic countermeasures] capability. Force 7, which included a smaller number of B-1s accompanied by large numbers of cruise missiles launched from the standoff B-52G/H fleet, was not as cost-effective as Forces 2, 3 and 4.[20]

20. *Hearings on Military Posture and H.R. 3689 [H.R. 6674]: Department of Defense Authorization for Appropriations for Fiscal Year 1976,* Hearings before the House Armed Services Committee, 94 Cong. 1 sess. (GPO, 1975), pt. 1, pp. 904–05.

The Brookings study essentially went to the other extreme in determining what was required of the strategic bomber force, namely, that this force should be designed and sized to attack fixed industrial and urban targets. To quantify this requirement, the authors resurrected Robert S. McNamara's criterion that the arrival on target of about 400 one-megaton weapons or weapons of equivalent yield (1,200 200-kiloton weapons, for example) would suffice to destroy three-quarters of Soviet industrial capacity and one-third of its population.[21] The study examined the effectiveness of five alternative single-aircraft bomber forces against this criterion: (1) 255 improved B-52s; (2) 200 B-1s; (3) 80 "soft" wide-bodied cruise missile carriers each with fifty ALCMs; (4) 105 hard, fast cruise missile carriers each with thirty-five ALCMs; and (5) 120 high-acceleration cruise missile carriers each with thirty-five ALCMs. On various assumptions regarding alert status, prelaunch survivability, and probability of penetration, it was demonstrated that, based on estimated current threat, all five alternatives could place the requisite 1,200 or so 200-kiloton warheads on target. And finally, the estimated acquisition and operating costs over a ten-year period indicated that option 3 above would be the least costly and option 2 the most costly.[22]

The studies differed on innumerable points of detail but in broad terms there were just two main differences.[23] The first of these concerned the role of strategic bombers and the extent to which bombers could depend on support from the other two legs of the strategic triad in fulfilling their role. The JSBS set a very ambitious objective for the bomber force and assumed that this objective would have to be achieved without assistance. Essentially, the JSBS determined what could be accomplished by a force of 210 B-1s plus the 90 late-model B-52Hs (Force 2) and evaluated other equal-cost alternatives on the basis of their ability to do the same job. The Brookings study, in contrast, asked considerably less of the bomber force and looked for the least-cost way of accomplishing this limited objective. It also assumed that penetration by bombers or bomber-launched weapons would be facilitated by preceding or simultaneous ICBM and SLBM strikes.

The second important difference concerned the relative ability of

21. Quanbeck and Wood, *Modernizing the Strategic Bomber Force,* p. 19.
22. Ibid., pp. 90–92.
23. For a detailed assessment, see Francis P. Hoeber, *Slow to Take Offense: Bombers, Cruise Missiles, and Prudent Deterrence* (Georgetown University, Center for Strategic and International Studies, 1977).

bombers and cruise missiles to survive existing and projected Soviet air defenses. There were really two issues here: the technological capabilities of the U.S. bombers and cruise missiles and Soviet technological capabilities to mount effective defenses against these respective penetrators. The JSBS reflected the Air Force's long-standing judgment that cruise missiles would be highly vulnerable to terminal SAM defenses. Moreover, this study projected major advances in Soviet air defenses with overland airborne warning and control system (AWACS) aircraft, interceptors with look-down–shoot-down capability, and advanced low-altitude SAMs, both fixed and mobile. In such an environment, the survivability of the ALCM was drastically reduced while the B-1 more or less held its own. Significantly, however, the survivability of the B-1 was acknowledged to be extremely sensitive to the effectiveness of its electronic countermeasures. The Brookings study argued that it was unwise to put so much faith in the effectiveness of electronic countermeasures and also postulated future Soviet air defenses against which the ALCM would be less vulnerable.

On balance, proponents of the ALCM—or, more accurately, opponents of the B-1—prevailed. The production decision for the B-1 was deferred once again to permit the incoming Carter administration to review the program. In the 1978 defense budget drawn up by the Ford administration, the rough estimate of the number of ALCMs to be procured had been increased more than threefold. The old figure of 700 missiles was based on the assumption that only B-52s would be armed with ALCMs and that only a small proportion of the B-52 fleet would be suitably modified. The new figure of 2,328 missiles was based on increasing the number of B-52s to be modified and also on the decision to include the B-1 as a launch platform. Before this, the Air Force's position had been that, for the foreseeable future, the B-1 would not require the ALCM.

In January 1977 a pivotal DSARC meeting on cruise missiles took place. Eight years after the SCAD was initiated the Air Force was instructed to give first priority to the development of a full-range airlaunched cruise missile. The objective was to bring the new weapon—the AGM-86B or the ALCM-B—to initial operational capability in December 1980 instead of waiting until July 1981, the target date for the ALCM-A. Even more significant was that the DSARC decided that the ALCM-B would be a stretched or elongated version of the ALCM-A instead of the ALCM-A with an underslung fuel tank. These decisions meant that a new internal rotary launcher would have to be developed;

this, in turn, meant that the air-launched version of the SLCM became a contender for the ALCM role. The decisions also had the effect of pushing the B-1 a little further out into the cold because the aircraft's bomb bays had been designed around the short-range attack missile (SRAM) and could not accommodate the nineteen-and-a-half-foot ALCM-B.

On June 30, 1977, the ax finally fell. President Carter announced that he was canceling the B-1 program in favor of a large force (some 3,400) of long-range ALCMs to be deployed on B-52Gs and possibly, at some future date, on new wide-bodied cruise missile carriers. It was five years, almost to the day, since Melvin Laird had recommended that the United States get back into the long-range strategic cruise missile business. The B-1 decision was followed by a package of amendments to the 1978 budget that included cancellation of the ALCM-A and additional funding for the air-launched version of the SLCM so it would be ready for a competition with the AGM-86B in 1979.

The cancellation of the B-1 was justified primarily by new evidence and judgments in two areas: the relative capabilities of penetrating and standoff bombers to deliver weapons on targets and the size and sophistication of the air defense systems that the Soviet Union would be able to develop and deploy in the future. In the first place, by mid-1977 full-scale models of the cruise missile had had more than a year of testing, and this permitted more confident projections of such characteristics as the weapon's radar cross section and low-altitude capability. Even more important, however, was the reevaluation of the potential threat. Whereas the JSBS had projected defenses that would be highly lethal to cruise missiles, the new judgment was that the defenses the Soviet Union could actually deploy by the time cruise missiles became fully operational (about 1985) would be far less effective.

Jointly these changes had two ramifications. First, cruise missiles deployed on existing platforms (the B-52s) came out as more cost-effective than a force of B-1s when the period of comparison was limited to 1985–90. Second, the reduction in the projected severity of the threat allowed the foreseeable capabilities of second- and third-generation cruise missiles to assume more prominence because time would be available to develop and incorporate such improvements in the missiles as improvements in Soviet defenses dictated. Just as the B-1 had been touted as the bomber weapon system most insensitive to changes in the character of the threat, the new judgment was that "we have come to appreciate that cruise missiles can be improved faster than the Soviets could upgrade their SAM defenses."[24] The secretary of defense encapsulated this last notion as follows: "I have more confidence in our estimates of the effect that the low detectability of the cruise missile will have on Soviet radar than in the effect that the B-1's radar countermeasures would have had."[25]

The reduction in the projected severity of the threat also extended the time period over which suitably modernized B-52s would remain effective as penetrators. Thus while the proposed bomber force would consist predominantly of B-52s carrying long-range cruise missiles, some late-model B-52s and all the FB-111s would remain equipped with SRAM and gravity bombs and would penetrate the Soviet Union.

The long-range strategic cruise missile had clearly come into its own, though deployed on aircraft rather than on submarines as originally envisaged. When Defense Secretary Harold Brown presented his first annual report in February 1978, the ALCM was described as "our highest national priority."[26] The fact that this weapon clearly reflected U.S. technological superiority would help to "improve the world's perceptions of the potency of [U.S.] forces."[27] Furthermore, the size of the contemplated ALCM force and the prospective accuracy of these weapons meant that both static and dynamic indexes of the strategic balance in the 1980s looked much healthier from the U.S. standpoint. In fact, Brown was able to argue that, with the ALCM force factored in, the Soviet Union could not move the balance in its favor by striking first because the U.S. retaliatory counterforce strike would at least restore parity.[28] Projections of the balance made before June 1977, notably those of Paul Nitze, were much more pessimistic.[29]

The cancellation of the B-1 in favor of the B-52/ALCM force meant, of course, that developments in Soviet air defense systems were debated in the context of cruise missile vulnerability. For example, the capability and status of the Soviet SA-10 became a controversial issue immediately

24. *Hearings on H.R. 8390: Supplemental Authorization for Appropriations for Fiscal Year 1978 and Review of the State of U.S. Strategic Forces,* Hearings before the House Armed Services Committee, 95 Cong. 1 sess. (GPO, 1977), p. 89.

25. Ibid., p. 98.

26. *Department of Defense Annual Report, Fiscal Year 1979* (GPO, 1978), p. 119.

27. Ibid., p. 115.

28. Ibid., p. 104.

29. See, for example, Paul H. Nitze, "Deterring Our Deterrent," *Foreign Policy,* no. 25 (Winter 1976–77), pp. 195–210.

after the B-1 decision, as did reports that the Soviet Union had begun to deploy radars mounted on towers several hundred feet high to detect low-flying objects at longer ranges.[30] The Carter administration's commitment to the ALCM was not affected in the least by these challenges. It was readily admitted that the Soviet Union could, in theory, acquire the capability needed to make the first-generation cruise missile seriously vulnerable but such forces would cost $30 billion to $50 billion and take eight to ten years to deploy, ample time for the United States to acquire more ALCMs and saturate even the improved defenses or to develop ALCMs with such features as electronic countermeasures and an automatic reactive maneuvering capability.

The B-1 decision also had important ramifications for U.S. strategy in SALT II. In particular, the range limit for the ALCM of 2,500 kilometers, apparently accepted by the United States in September 1977, seemed too great a concession: potential targets for the ALCM were as far as 2,300 kilometers from the coast. This limitation was slated to go into the protocol of the SALT II treaty, the provisions of which would only be binding for three years, but it was widely felt that it would be politically difficult to break out of this restriction when the protocol expired. U.S. negotiators were therefore obliged to seek at least a higher limit on ALCM range, but, as it happened, the Soviet Union dropped all demands for such a limit in September 1978.

SALT II was signed in Vienna on June 18, 1979. In the treaty, which would expire on December 31, 1985, the main provisions covering cruise missiles were as follows:

1. Any aircraft armed with long-range cruise missiles (defined as a range in excess of 600 kilometers) will count the same as one strategic delivery vehicle armed with MIRVs (multiple independently targetable reentry vehicles).

2. Existing strategic bombers can carry up to twenty cruise missiles each. If a new type of aircraft is deployed with cruise missiles, the average number per aircraft in the whole fleet cannot exceed twenty-eight.

3. Up to 120 aircraft armed with cruise missiles can be deployed without displacing missiles with MIRVs. Deployment in excess of 120 is permitted but only if an equal number of missiles with MIRVs is eliminated.

4. If an aircraft type is deployed as a cruise missile carrier and in other

30. *Aviation Week and Space Technology*, July 18, 1977, p. 7.

roles, the former variant will be given externally observable differences to permit verification.

5. Multiple-warhead cruise missiles are banned.

For the protocol, which would expire on December 31, 1981:

1. Ground- and-sea-launched cruise missiles, if deployed, are limited to a range of 600 kilometers although prototypes can be tested to any range.

One other provision of SALT II is of particular relevance here: the "noncircumvention" clause restricting American allies' access to cruise missile technology. As chapter 13 shows in detail, however, concern about the SS-20 led NATO to decide in December 1979 to deploy 108 Pershing II XRs in West Germany, and 116 flights of ground-launched cruise missiles, each with four missiles, distributed in five countries—the United Kingdom, 40; Italy, 28; West Germany, 24; Belgium, 12; and the Netherlands, 12.

The initial response of the Soviet Union was that the NATO decision to deploy had in principle destroyed the basis for negotiations and not until July 1980 did it soften its position. Initial U.S.-Soviet negotiations on Eurostrategic systems began on October 17; they were short-lived, but the Reagan administration has stated that it intends to start formal negotiations before the end of 1982. Whatever the outcome of these negotiations—and it is difficult to imagine substantial progress until something is done about SALT II—it is clear that a second variant of the long-range cruise missile had found a secure niche in the U.S. military program. The official target for initial operational capability is December 1983 although a six-month slippage in the software program may mean that the first weapons deployed will not have the comprehensive and rapid retargeting capability planned. A total of 572 missiles will be produced through 1988 to support the deployment of 464 weapons.

While the modernization and expansion of NATO's theater nuclear capabilities was being debated, Boeing and General Dynamics were competing for the ALCM contract. The Air Force selected Boeing's AGM-86B in March 1980 to meet the initial requirement for 3,418 missiles. The first squadron of fourteen B-52Gs, each with twelve ALCMs in two clusters of six under each wing, is expected to be operational in December 1982. Subsequently, from October 1985 on, these aircraft will be fitted with a new rotary launcher to carry up to eight more ALCMs internally. Delivery of the last ALCM under the present program is scheduled for

May 1989. Second-generation strategic ALCMs are already under investigation. The development effort will focus on engines and fuels to increase the range to 2,600 nautical miles without increasing the size of the missile. Extensive use will also be made of Stealth technologies to reduce radar cross section and infrared signatures. The development schedule projects test flights in 1983 and a deployment capability in 1986–87.

Meanwhile, the weapon that started the whole business—the SLCM—is on a leisurely development schedule that would permit deployment in 1983. The basic procurement plan was for 135 missiles;[31] some preference is now being shown for vertical launch tubes between the inner and outer hulls of *Los Angeles*-class attack submarines so as to leave the torpedo tubes and internal storage space free for ASW weapons. As has always been the case, however, there are questions about the rationale for the SLCM. At present, there are reports of tentative decisions to produce a significant number, but no official announcement. On the other hand, plans for two variants of the SLCM with conventional warheads are firm. These are now called the TASM (Tomahawk antiship missile) and the TLAM-C (Tomahawk land-attack missile, conventional). The TASM will be carried on *Los Angeles*-class SSNs and *Spruance*-class destroyers. A total of 243 missiles was planned in 1980, but the Reagan administration may increase the number. The TLAM-C, which will have terminal guidance to supplement TERCOM, will be used on submarines and on surface ships. A total of seventy-one of this variant was planned in 1980.[32] Several other variants of the SLCM are under consideration, of which the most imminent is a tactical medium-range air-to-surface missile (MRASM) for joint use by the Navy and the Air Force.[33] This weapon,

31. Before the Reagan administration. *Aviation Week and Space Technology*, November 12, 1979, p. 13; and George C. Wilson, *Washington Post*, August 12, 1980.

32. Information on the TASM and TLAM-C is from *Hearings on Military Posture and H.R. 6495 [H.R. 6474]: Department of Defense Authorization for Appropriations for Fiscal Year 1981*, Hearings before the House Armed Services Committee, 96 Cong. 2 sess. (GPO, 1980), pt. 4, bk. 2, pp. 1496–98, 2310–20. In June 1981 the Reagan administration approved the Navy's plans to deploy the 700-mile TLAM-C on submarines beginning in January 1982. The deployment on surface ships of the 250-mile TASM would follow in mid-1982 and the 1,400-mile TLAM-N in mid-1984.

33. See Jeffrey M. Lenorovitz, "MRASM Development Program Pushed," *Aviation Week and Space Technology*, April 7, 1980, pp. 15–16; and " 'Quick Fixes' Urged to Bolster Defenses," *Aviation Week and Space Technology*, April 21, 1980, p. 153.

plans for which were announced in April 1980, would have a maximum range of about 480 kilometers, and potential launching aircraft include the A-6E, A/L-18, P-3, F-16, and F-111. One consideration driving the range capability is that *any* aircraft carrying a cruise missile with a range in excess of 600 kilometers would become a strategic bomber under the terms of SALT II. The initial version of the MRASM would have TER-COM guidance for attacking fixed targets but a follow-on with an infrared guidance system is contemplated to strike moving targets, particularly ships.

CHAPTER FOUR

Program Costs and Comparisons

JOHN C. BAKER

ATTEMPTS to estimate modern cruise missile costs accurately must recognize that eventual force levels and mission applications are still in flux. This chapter reviews the cost considerations related to specific cruise missile programs; how cruise missiles compare in cost with other systems for performing various military missions; and prospective trends in costs and deployments. (To avoid a distracting clutter of numbers, much of the data behind the analysis has been placed in appendix B.) The discussion provides some tentative conclusions about the cost-effectiveness of cruise missiles, but it does *not* provide a conclusive systems-analysis evaluation. Such a full assessment is precluded not only by uncertainty about force levels and missions, but also by the versatility of cruise missiles, which makes them applicable to missions for which a large number of alternative weapon systems could be used.

An important caveat for the reader to bear in mind is that data on cruise missile program costs are constantly changing and cannot be pinpointed accurately until procurement decisions are final and production gets under way. The figures used in this chapter are the best estimates and extrapolations available at the time of writing; the financial comparisons are therefore heuristic, not definitive. Unless the absolute costs of major program elements change much more radically than others, however, the rough judgments about relative costs should remain reasonably accurate.

John Baker was a research associate in the Brookings Foreign Policy Studies program when he wrote this chapter. He is now at the Pacific-Sierra Research Corporation.

Program Costs

Because cruise missile programs are so diverse and so rapidly evolving, data on program costs are both complex and uncertain. Current figures are likely to change, especially if existing programs are expanded or curtailed by the Reagan administration. In any case, the most relevant measure is the *relative* cost of weapon systems (how expensive cruise missiles are compared to other weapon systems that could perform the same missions), which is examined in the next section of this chapter. This section therefore presents a background discussion of the terms in which estimates should be considered and only a brief summary of the salient elements of recently planned program costs. (For a fuller exposition of data on program components, variations, development, and costs, see appendix B.)

Weapon System Costs

Major weapon system costs accrue over a long time, often decades from initiation to retirement. Expenditures on a weapon system can be broken down into three main types: research and development, production, and annual operating and support costs once deployed. Collectively, these constitute the *life-cycle cost* of a weapon system, the most useful basis for comparing different systems. Annual operating and support expenses (or recurring costs) may eventually total more than the substantial investment costs initially incurred for the research, development, and procurement of the weapon. One problem with cost comparisons is the necessity of factoring out the effects of inflation on program costs. To permit accurate cost comparisons of programs spanning a long period of high inflation, cost figures in this chapter are given in fiscal year 1981 constant dollars whenever possible.

Weapons also can be analyzed in terms of their average unit cost, which is derived by dividing some proportion of the overall program costs by the number of weapons. In the broadest sense, the program's total research, development, and acquisition costs can be prorated to determine the program unit cost. Alternatively, the *average unit flyaway cost* provides the narrowest definition, essentially tabulating the cost of a weapon right off the assembly line. This measure is a useful indicator of how changes in production quantities can affect average unit cost. Both types of measurements are used in this chapter.

Analysis of cruise missile programs involves a few special considerations. A cruise missile is merely the weapon and must depend on a separate launch platform or delivery system. The investment and operating costs of the launch platform must therefore be considered in analyzing the cruise missile's true cost. For some systems, such as the ground-launched cruise missile (GLCM), the cost of the launcher and associated equipment are included in the officially reported costs of the cruise missile program. In others, such as the air-launched cruise missile (ALCM), the platform costs are separately funded. A judgment must be made in such instances about what proportion of the costs of the various functions of the platforms is attributable to the direct support of the cruise missiles.

For this chapter, cruise missile launch platforms will be considered as either "adapted" or "dedicated" delivery systems. The former is one that was deployed primarily for some other military role but has the capability to launch cruise missiles. An example would be the deployment of a few Tomahawk cruise missiles on surface ships whose primary mission continues to be fleet air defense or antisubmarine warfare. In such cases, only the procurement and operating expenses specifically related to the cruise missile are attributed, while the rest of the platform costs are not.

A "dedicated" launch platform is one primarily intended to serve as a cruise missile launcher. If a new delivery system is developed and deployed for this role, all of its investment and operating costs are attributed to the cruise missile. Delivery systems, such as the B-52G bomber, that are converted into cruise missile carriers late in their service lives are considered dedicated only from the time the conversion occurs. Thus the platform's earlier acquisition cost is excluded as a sunk cost, and only the modification costs and operating expenses following its conversion are deemed to be cruise missile related costs.

Finally, confidence in long-term cost projections and complex cost comparisons must be tempered by the recognition that a weapon program can undergo significant changes during its lifetime as a result of unexpected problems of technological complexity, the possibility of changing military requirements, or the influence of institutional and political interests.

Cruise Missile Costs

The U.S. cruise missile program differs from many other weapon programs in its breadth and dynamism. The current effort consists of six specific programs (see appendix B, table B-1), which are interrelated by a common technology. The missiles' military applications have diversified as research and development capitalized on the potential for outgrowths from existing programs. Current cruise missile development began in the 1970s under two separate programs meant to produce three different weapon systems. Today, this has doubled, with four separate programs aimed at deploying six different types of missiles. The basic commonality of components shared by the cruise missiles—airframe, guidance, and propulsion subsystems—also means that changes in the technical characteristics or projected production run of one type of cruise missile can directly affect the unit costs of other variants by altering the economies achievable in purchasing certain subsystems.[1]

Underlying operational concepts and military requirements have been relatively fluid. A good example is the sea-launched cruise missile (SLCM) program that was initiated in 1972 with highest priority on the development of a nuclear-armed land-attack missile. This system is now scheduled to be the *last* of the three SLCMs to become operational. Most of the projected missile purchases and deployment schedules of the cruise missile program are notably different from those outlined even during the past few years.[2] Technical success combined with increasing institutional acceptance of the cruise missile's potential is likely to ensure that currently projected force levels and production rates will also change substantially.

Modern U.S. cruise missile development began in earnest in 1974. Costs were modest through the late 1970s as the ALCM and SLCM programs proceeded through their development phase. Because of their potential for commonality in subsystems and a desire to economize, a Joint

1. For instance, see *Department of Defense Authorization for Appropriations for Fiscal Year 1980*, Hearings before the Senate Armed Services Committee, 96 Cong. 1 sess. (Government Printing Office, 1979), pt. 6, p. 3447.

2. Before the termination of the B-1 bomber, Air Force plans were for production of about 2,300 short- and long-range ALCMs. At one time planned baseline production of the Navy SLCM was about 1,200 missiles split equally between the nuclear Tomahawk land-attack missile (TLAM-N) and the Tomahawk antiship missile (TASM). *Department of Defense Appropriations for 1978*, Hearings before a subcommittee of the House Appropriations Committee, 95 Cong. 1 sess. (GPO, 1977), pt. 2, p. 320. The GLCM program has been reduced from its original objective of 696 missiles to 560. Finally, the deployment dates of all of these missiles have slipped. For example, during 1977 the initial operational capability (IOC) dates for the cruise missiles were listed as June 1981 for the ALCM; June 1980 for the SLCM; and February 1981 for the GLCM. *Supplemental Appropriations for Fiscal Year 1978*, Hearings before subcommittees of the Senate Appropriations Committee, 95 Cong. 1 sess. (GPO, 1977), p. 38.

Cruise Missile Project Office (JCMPO) was established in January 1977 to provide integrated management.[3] It supervised the competition for the ALCM contract and continues to direct the development of the SLCM and GLCM programs and their derivatives. To assure savings, the JCMPO employs competitive contract awards both at the prime contractor level and for the missiles' subsystem components.[4]

To date, a production decision has been made only on the ALCM program (in April 1980); the other programs are scheduled for similar decisions in the next few years.[5] Fiscal year 1981 marked the beginning of a substantial increase in the annual funding levels. Funding can be expected to remain at a level of over $1 billion a year, which should buy about 500 to 700 cruise missiles of various types annually.[6] As planned early in the Reagan administration, the overall U.S. commitment to cruise missiles totals about $11 billion, resulting in the projected procurement of over 4,400 missiles (table 4-1). Excluded from this amount is about $2 billion in the fiscal 1981–85 five-year defense plan for cruise-missile-related costs, covering such items as medium-range air-to-surface missile (MRASM) development, TERCOM (terrain contour matching) mapping costs, B-52G cruise-missile-launcher equipment, and other programs.[7] Also, an additional $1 billion or more can be presumed to be spent by the Department of Energy for development and production of the cruise missiles' nuclear warheads over the same period.

3. "Clements Memo on Cruise Missiles," *Aerospace Daily*, January 24, 1977, pp. 115–16.
4. *Department of Defense Appropriations for 1980*, Hearings before a subcommittee of the House Appropriations Committee, 96 Cong. 1 sess. (GPO, 1979), pt. 3, pp. 504, 517–19.
5. *Hearings on Military Posture and H.R. 6495 [H.R. 6974]: Department of Defense Authorization for Appropriations for Fiscal Year 1981*, Hearings before the House Armed Services Committee, 96 Cong. 2 sess. (GPO, 1980), pt. 4, bk. 2, pp. 1496, 1814.
6. Except where otherwise noted, figures in this chapter are in fiscal 1981 constant dollars.
7. The author's estimates of additional cruise missile costs over the fiscal 1981–85 period include the following major programs and their five-year costs in current dollars: MRASM development and production, $400 million; B-52G bomber conversion to cruise-missile launchers, $400 million; B-52G bomber avionics modernization, $600 million; Defense Mapping Agency expenses for cruise missile guidance map production, $165 million; research and development on an advanced technology cruise missile, $200 million; development and production of the W-80 and W-84 nuclear warheads, $1.3 billion; and development of an over-the-horizon targeting system for sea-launched cruise missiles, $125 million. For sources of program costs, see appendix B.

Table 4-1. *Cruise Missile Unit Costs, Fiscal Year 1981*

Millions of fiscal 1981 dollars

Unit cost measure	Air-launched cruise missile	Sea-launched cruise missile[a]	Ground-launched cruise missile[b]
Flyaway unit cost[c]			
Constant dollars	0.79	1.40	1.92
Current dollars	1.02	1.87	2.67
Program unit cost[d]			
Constant dollars	1.32	4.81	2.80
Current dollars	1.56	5.19	3.79
Addendum Currently projected missile production	3,418	439	560

Sources: Department of Defense, "Selected Acquisition Reports as of September 30, 1980," p. 3; *Hearings on Military Posture and H.R. 6495* [*H.R. 6974*]: *Department of Defense Authorization for Appropriations for Fiscal Year 1981*, Hearings before the House Armed Services Committee, 96 Cong. 2 sess. (GPO, 1980), pt. 4, bk. 2, p. 1498; *Department of Defense Authorization for Appropriations for Fiscal Year 1981*, Hearings before the Senate Armed Services Committee, 96 Cong. 2 sess. (GPO, 1980), pt. 4, pp. 2446–47, 2532–33; and author's conversion of cost figures to fiscal 1981 constant dollars where necessary.

a. To a large degree, the relatively higher unit costs of the SLCM than of the ALCM result from the very small production run assumed for the SLCM. As Tomahawk SLCM production approaches a higher level, such as 1,500 missiles, the average unit flyaway cost should decline to about $1 million in fiscal 1981 constant dollars. See figure 4-1. However, note that data for the SLCM are based on official projections at the start of the Reagan administration; the Defense Department is now reported to be considering a sharp upward revision in SLCM procurement.

b. The unit cost for the GLCM includes the procurement cost of not only the missile but also its associated launch-control center and transporter-erector-launcher. Excluding the latter would probably reduce the GLCM unit cost figures in this table by about 60 percent.

c. Flyaway unit cost is a measure of a system's average procurement cost excluding the procurement cost of support systems and initial spare parts and the "sunk costs" of the weapon's research and development.

d. Program unit cost is a measure of the average cost of a system spread over its "sunk costs" for research and development as well as costs for initial spare parts and military construction.

The ALCM program is more susceptible to economies of scale than the SLCM and GLCM programs, since so many ALCMs (over 3,400) are scheduled to be produced (figure 4-1). The unit flyaway cost for the ALCM, exclusive of warhead, was recently estimated at $800,000 in fiscal 1981 dollars. Since ALCMs are to be deployed initially on "adapted" B-52 platforms, only modification costs are attributable. Delivery system costs are less important than they will be when the time comes for a new, dedicated carrier aircraft.

The SLCMs—both nuclear and conventional—are the most rapidly changing of the three basic cruise missile types. Principally because recent plans were for procuring fewer SLCMs than ALCMs, the average unit flyaway cost of the SLCM is estimated at about $1.4 million. A change in plans toward higher numbers, which is likely, should reduce that estimate. Because of the several variants of missile type and mode of

Figure 4-1. *Average Unit Flyaway Cost of Cruise Missiles in Relation to Number Produced*

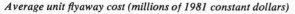

Average unit flyaway cost (millions of 1981 constant dollars)

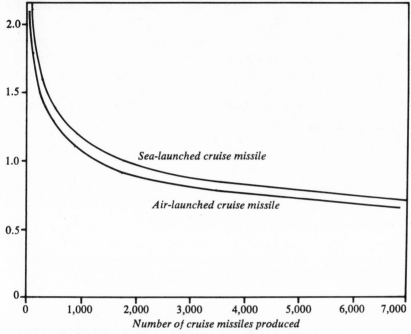

Number of cruise missiles produced

Source: Author's estimates based on Department of Defense projections of the unit costs for air- and sea-launched cruise missiles at the end of 1980, and the assumption of an 85 percent learning curve on increases in production. See appendix B for sources of cruise missile unit costs, and John Rhea, "Tomahawk and ALCM: Cruise Missile Decision Pending," *Sea Power*, December 1976, p. 27.

deployment, the relevant calculations are more complex for the SLCM than for the ALCM and GLCM (see appendix B), and true costs are sensitive not only to the choice of platform, but also to the nature and location of the launcher system.

Costs for the GLCM, much more than those for the ALCM and SLCM, are a function of support equipment, since an entirely new, dedicated launch system (made up of large, multivehicle convoys) must be procured. This has driven the average unit flyaway cost to almost $2 million.

Costs are most critical to conventionally armed cruise missiles because they can inflict much less damage than a nuclear weapon. This makes alternative delivery systems such as manned aircraft, which unlike cruise missiles can be reused numerous times, more clearly competitive. The

MRASM now in development can yield economies by reliance on some components that are cheaper than those for nuclear cruise missiles, but it still seems expensive for conventional missions. Later variants, which might bring the unit cost down $500,000, may be more attractive for large-scale procurement.

Finally, there are several supporting systems that must be considered to appreciate the complete range of costs for cruise missile programs: TERCOM mapping and vertical obstruction data; the computer and communications infrastructures for the theater mission planning system; and over-the-horizon targeting systems for antiship missiles. (See appendix B for more details on these programs and their costs.)

Cost Comparisons

To appreciate how a weapon system's cost affects planning and procurement choices, one must assess the costs in relation to those of other weapon systems capable of performing the same mission. Three general types of weapons can strike targets at long distances: cruise missiles, ballistic missiles, and manned aircraft. In this section cruise missile costs are compared with those of other strategic nuclear forces, theater nuclear and nonnuclear forces, and antiship weapons. The uncertainties in cruise missile programs and the need to take into account a variety of technical and operational considerations (examined elsewhere in this volume) put a genuine cost-effectiveness analysis beyond the scope of this chapter. No attempt has been made to include all possible weapon systems in these comparisons; the cruise missile's versatility and potential applicability for all sorts of missions mean that almost *any* major weapon could be a competitor. The assessment in this section is therefore limited and heuristic rather than definitive.

Before examining the details, it is important to note what these calculations can and cannot reveal. Perhaps most important, by estimating the various systems' life-cycle costs "per weapon," they provide a useful though incomplete basis for identifying potential trade-offs between investments in cruise missiles and other weapons. It is important to remember, however, that these comparisons do not reflect the complex operational environment of combat, which makes mixed forces preferable to the least expensive system. In some instances, it is necessary to go beyond simple cost calculations to make such comparisons valid. In comparing strategic nuclear forces, it is useful to measure the cost of the different weapons against representative target types, since the effectiveness of a particular weapon varies widely depending on what it is targeted against. Unfortunately, reliable public data on relative weapon effectiveness are less available for similar analyses of theater nuclear forces and antiship weapons. Cost comparisons of conventionally armed cruise missiles and tactical aircraft in a sustained nonnuclear conflict, on the other hand, require special assumptions, especially concerning their respective attrition rates, to account for the inherent advantage that a manned aircraft (which can fly multiple missions) might have over a cruise missile (which is a "single-shot" or nonrecoverable weapon).

Although the simple comparisons presented could provide the initial step for such a complete cost-effectiveness analysis, several other variables such as the relative availability, survivability, penetrativity, and reliability of the weapon systems in question must be integrated into the equation more completely than is done in this chapter. Other, less quantifiable considerations are also important, such as the amount of time required to reach the target and the reliability and endurance of command and control systems. Consequently, the basic comparisons in this chapter should help the reader appreciate the implications for strategy and procurement of the operational analyses in part 2 of this book and to arrive at some broader judgments about how cost factors can influence the overall desirability of cruise missiles vis-à-vis other weapon systems.

Strategic Forces

The relative costs of the air-launched cruise missile are included in table 4-2, which shows the major U.S. strategic force systems planned or under consideration for deployment during the 1980s: intercontinental ballistic missiles (ICBMs), SLBMs, and possible new strategic bombers. To facilitate comparisons, the total program life-cycle costs of these weapon systems have been converted into fiscal 1981 constant dollars and prorated on a "per warhead" basis. Two sets of representative targets have been outlined to provide more valid comparisons between the diverse elements of nuclear forces and the roles they are assigned. The first set consists of hypothetical targets at two high levels of hardening against

Table 4-2. Costs of Strategic Nuclear Weapons Required to Destroy Various Types of Targets[a]

Costs in millions of 1981 constant dollars

Target type	ALCM/B-52G cruise missile carrier		ALCM/new cruise missile carrier aircraft[b]		Gravity bomb on B-1 penetrating bomber		Mobile MX ICBM warhead		Trident I SLBM warhead/Trident submarine		Trident I SLBM warhead/Poseidon submarine	
	Number	Cost	Number	Cost	Number	Cost	Number	Cost	Number	Cost	Number	Cost
Hardened[c]												
2,500 psi target	1	8.0	1	6.6–10.4	1.5	22.2	1	20.4	13.5	186.3	13.5	108.0
5,000 psi target	1	8.0	1	6.6–10.4	2.3	34.0	1	20.4	20	276.0	20	160.0
Area[d]												
20 square miles	1.3	10.4	1.3	8.6–13.5	1	14.8	1	20.4	2.1	29.0	2.1	16.8
50 square miles	3.8	30.4	3.8	25.1–39.5	1.3	19.2	2.8	57.1	6.2	85.6	6.2	49.6

Sources: Hard target damage calculations made with General Electric, *Missile Effectiveness Calculator* (Syracuse: GE, Electronic Systems Division, 1965); and area target calculations based on E. Royce Fletcher, *Nuclear Bomb Effects Computer*, prepared for the Energy Research and Development Administration (Albuquerque: Lovelace Biomedical and Environmental Research Institute, 1977). For the assumptions and sources concerning weapon system effectiveness and costs, see appendix B.

a. The following types of weapon systems are assumed: ALCMs carried by a B-52G cruise missile carrier, a 1.1-megaton gravity bomb delivered by a B-1 bomber, MX ICBMs with 335-kiloton warheads deployed in a multiple basing system, and 100-kiloton Trident I SLBM warheads deployed on the existing Poseidon strategic nuclear submarine and the future Trident submarine.

b. The range of cost figures in this column represents the difference between two possible types of dedicated cruise missile carrier aircraft: a fixed-wing variant of the B-1 bomber and one based on a large civilian transport aircraft such as the Boeing 747. The smaller figure relates to the wide-bodied launch platform, and reflects its ability to spread its costs over a larger weapon load of sixty cruise missiles. By comparison, despite the B-1 strategic ALCM launcher's somewhat lower cost per aircraft, its smaller payload of thirty ALCMs results in a higher cost for each weapon it carries. In many cases weapon requirements are expressed in fractional terms, which would not be possible for their actual operational employment. Also, each target is assumed to require at least one complete weapon.

c. Hardened targets include missile silos, command bunkers, and nuclear weapon storage sites. Their physical resistance to a nuclear weapon blast is usually measured in terms of how much pressure per square inch they can withstand. An 85 percent damage requirement was set for the two illustrative targets in this table. Weapon effectiveness against both sets of targets was measured in purely notional terms to highlight the relative effectiveness between the weapons.

d. Area targets include military depots, troop staging areas, airfields, and urban-industrial centers. Attacks on these targets would seek to cover such large areas with sufficient overpressure from the nuclear blast to generally neutralize them. Unless specifically protected, buildings, machinery, and vehicles can be expected to be severely damaged by nuclear blast overpressure levels on the order of 5 to 10 pounds per square inch (psi). The level of 6 psi has been chosen in this table. The figures in the table indicate the exact number of weapons required to achieve at least 6 psi over the entire target area.

nuclear weapon blast effects (2,500 and 5,000 pounds per square inch—psi); these correspond roughly to targets such as Soviet missile silos or command and control bunkers with extremely high blast resistance.[8] Compared to other strategic forces, ALCMs do quite well in terms of the cost and the number of warheads required for destruction. This results from the combination of the ALCM's potentially greater accuracy and significantly lower costs per warhead (see appendix tables B-2 and B-3). Furthermore, the B-52G cruise missile carrier's expenses have been conservatively estimated for this analysis. In addition to expenditures to make the B-52G bomber capable of launching ALCMs, future modification costs associated with the bomber's modernization have been included. Against hardened targets, the ALCM's combination of higher effectiveness and lower cost give it a significant cost advantage over a B-1 using a nuclear gravity bomb.

However, the weapon costs for penetrating bombers can be substantially lower depending on the type developed. The figure in table 4-2 reflects a proposal that the B-1 program be started again, with the goal of deploying a hundred bombers beginning in 1987.[9] If this modest production run was doubled to approximate that envisaged for the earlier B-1 bomber program, cost per warhead might diminish by about 25 percent. Alternatively, at current estimates, procurement of a force of modified FB-111 medium bombers could further reduce costs to about $9 million per warhead.[10] Still, against very hard targets the various ALCM systems retain a simple cost advantage since fewer weapons would have to be placed on the targets.

The value of cost comparisons between bomber-delivered weapons and ballistic missiles is limited by the great disparity in their flight times. For ballistic missiles this is measured in minutes, not hours, as for bombers. In table 4-2 the costs per warhead of the projected mobile MX ICBM are between two and three times that of the various ALCM weapon systems. A significant portion of the mobile MX missile system's cost arises from the multiple basing system planned at the end of the Carter administration. Simply deployed in existing missile silos, the MX ICBM's cost

---

8. See *Department of Defense Authorization for Appropriations for Fiscal Year 1981,* Hearings before the Senate Armed Services Committee, 96 Cong. 2 sess. (GPO, 1980), pt. 2, pp. 547–48.

9. For instance, see *Hearings on Military Posture and H.R. 6495,* pt. 1, pp. 36, 44, 50.

10. Calculations based on ibid., pp. 35, 50.

per warhead could decrease by nearly one-half, although its survivability would be questionable.[11]

The second set shown consists of area targets, which could include military bases or industrial facilities. The figures in the table are based on calculations of the cost and number of warheads required to cover a uniform area with at least six pounds per square inch. The calculations assume the warheads are accurately detonated over their targets and that at least one complete warhead is allocated to each target. Destruction of large, relatively unhardened targets primarily results from the amount of nuclear explosive placed on these targets.[12] Consequently, large-yield weapons, such as the gravitv bombs carried by penetrating bombers, offer the most efficient means of covering area targets. However, depending on the area to be covered, less expensive ALCM and Trident I SLBM warheads also could cover these targets for a comparable total cost because the amount of area destroyed does not increase proportionately with the yield of a nuclear weapon.

The figures in table 4-2 also highlight the salience of platform costs. While all the ALCM carriers are associated with relatively low costs per warhead, underlying distinctions account for the differences. Despite substantial initial investment for developing and producing the ALCM, the cost per warhead of the initial deployment has been fairly modest compared with similar systems (see appendix table B-5). Adapting the ALCM to an existing launch platform, the B-52G, avoids the substantial investment expenditures of a new launch platform. On the other hand, the relatively high operating and support costs of the B-52 raise the overall life-cycle cost per ALCM to about $8 million. The second generation of ALCMs might therefore be carried on new types of aircraft that would require substantial funding for development and production. Missiles on such "dedicated" platforms would be unable to capitalize on the sunk costs of existing delivery systems. The acquisition costs of these platforms seem likely to offset possible savings arising from their lower operating expenses as well as missile-production economies. Depending on the type of new carrier selected, the life-cycle cost per ALCM could therefore be either higher or lower than that of the planned B-52G carrier force. The

11. Without the cost of the multiple basing system, the MX ICBM cost per weapon would decline to about $10 million. Author's estimate based on cost breakdown in *MX Missile Basing Mode*, Hearings before the Senate Appropriations Committee, 96 Cong. 2 sess. (GPO, 1980), pp. 110–11.

12. *Department of Defense Authorization for Appropriations for Fiscal Year 1981*, Hearings, pt. 2, p. 550 note.

higher figure of $10.4 million per warhead against area targets shown in table 4-2 represents an equivalent level of ALCM deployment on a modified version of the B-1 bomber. If deployed instead on large numbers of converted wide-bodied transport aircraft, the cost per warhead would drop significantly since the relatively large number of ALCMs carried by these aircraft would help distribute their costs (see appendix table B-2). Thus simply in cost terms an incentive exists to deploy platforms with greater carrying capacity as a means of offsetting the higher acquisition costs of a dedicated launch platform. But the economy of a wide-bodied ALCM carrier must be weighed against the greater flexibility and survivability that can be offered by the smaller (and more expensive) warfighting aircraft.

Finally, it is worth noting once again that the cost comparisons presented here do not necessarily demonstrate which systems are the most economical or effective for striking strategic targets. That answer depends significantly on operational factors dealt with in more detail in chapter 5, such as force survivability and penetrativity.

Theater Nuclear Forces

Cost considerations were reportedly a factor in the 1979 NATO decision to emphasize GLCMs as the major element of its theater nuclear force modernization plan.[13] The costs of this and some other existing or planned American theater nuclear systems are presented in table 4-3. As in the preceding table, the weapon life-cycle costs have been converted to fiscal 1981 constant dollars and allocated pro rata to a single warhead. But the lack of publicly available information in sufficient detail makes it impossible to measure the cost of these weapons against representative target requirements, as in table 4-2.

On the basis of acquisition costs alone, the two cruise missile systems are the most costly. The conclusion changes dramatically when the long-term operating and support expenses are included; the two cruise missiles then are the *least* expensive on a per warhead basis. Given the high operating and support costs necessary to maintain and operate modern aircraft, the F-111 and F-16 are revealed as the most expensive means of deploying theater nuclear weapons. Broader considerations, such as their military flexibility or political visibility, help explain the U.S. decision to

13. *Department of Defense Authorization for Appropriations for Fiscal Year 1981,* Hearings, pt. 5, pp. 2989, 3018.

Table 4-3. *Cost of Theater Nuclear Weapons*
Costs in millions of 1981 constant dollars

| Weapon system | Average number of weap- ons per launcher | Weapon system costs | | | |
		Acquisition[a] cost per launcher	Annual operating cost per launcher	Life-cycle[b] cost per launcher	Life-cycle[b] cost per war- head or bomb
Sea-launched cruise missile[c]	4	19.7–29.2	0.6–1.0	28.4–44.2	7.1–11.0[d]
Ground-launched cruise missile	4	15.0	1.3	34.5	8.6
Pershing II surface-to-surface missile[e]	2–3	13.4	1.6	37.8	12.6–18.9
F-111 dual-capable aircraft[f]	2	26.2	1.85	54.0	27.0
F-16 dual-capable aircraft[f]	1	10.0	1.0	25.0	25.0

Sources: See the sources listed in appendix B.

a. Includes both the acquisition cost of the launcher and its weapons, although the costs of nuclear warheads and bombs are not available.

b. With the two exceptions noted below, life-cycle costs include both the acquisition cost of the weapons and their launcher, and the operating and support expenses for both over a fifteen-year period. The two columns on life-cycle costs calculate these costs in terms of a single weapon system launcher as well as in terms of a single weapon. The figures in the first life-cycle column include the acquisition cost of a single launcher and its average loading of weapons, in addition to fifteen-year operating and support costs for the launcher and the weapons.

c. The weapon assumed here is the nuclear Tomahawk land-attack missile (TLAM-N). Two launch systems are considered, with the lower cost figure corresponding to torpedo-tube-launched SLCMs carried aboard a nuclear attack submarine. The higher figure represents the procurement and operating costs associated with an armored box launcher on a surface ship.

d. The SLCM program unit cost used in this table is based on the officially projected purchase of 439 SLCMs in the fiscal 1981–85 defense program, although ultimate SLCM production is likely to be much higher. Assuming eventual SLCM production reaches 1,600 missiles, the SLCM's "life-cycle cost per weapon" could decrease to about $5.9 million to $8.4 million instead of the $7.1 million to $11.0 million listed in the table.

e. For this system, a single Pershing II missile and launcher system are assumed, with the addition of one or two reload missiles.

f. The life-cycle costs of the F-111 and the F-16 have been calculated differently from the other systems. Certain sunk costs such as their research and development expenditures and the costs related to the nuclear bombs they would deliver are excluded. The figures used in this table are based on the air-crafts' average unit flyaway costs, which tend to approximate their replacement costs.

retain such aircraft in this role. Not shown in the table is another weapon system capable of theater nuclear strikes—the Trident I SLBM. Its cost per warhead can total $8.0 million if it is deployed on an existing Poseidon submarine (see appendix table B-5).

Although the GLCM actually costs more than Pershing II on a launcher-by-launcher basis, its final cost per warhead is lower partly because its projected support costs are lower. (Since the GLCM has not been deployed before, however, its projected lower operating and support costs may be somewhat optimistic.) Costs per warhead for both missiles would decline if each launcher was deployed with additional reload missiles for refire (as the Pershing I was),[14] although this option is not currently planned. However, for illustrative purposes, Pershing II costs are presented here on the basis of two to three missiles per launcher. In the absence of such deployments, the Pershing II system, at an estimated $37.8 million per warhead and its launcher, would become the most costly U.S. theater nuclear system.

In the narrow context of explicit costs alone, the least expensive system appears to be the TLAM-N sea-launched cruise missile. This advantage, however, is open to question if the probable wartime availability of the TLAM-N is examined. The life-cycle cost advantage of this weapon arises from its ability to capitalize on the sunk costs of existing launch platforms such as the attack submarine (SSN). Yet the costs calculated on this basis assume that these nuclear SLCMs will not serve as on-call theater nuclear strike systems. Such a role would impinge on the launch platform's other mission priorities and require that a larger portion of the launcher's costs be attributed to the TLAM-N, thereby eliminating its apparent cost advantage. In short, significant opportunity costs may offset any apparent advantage enjoyed by the sea-launched cruise missile as a theater nuclear weapon. The same situation exists, however, for *any* multipurpose platform.

Conventionally Armed Cruise Missiles

Nonnuclear cruise missiles are particularly sensitive to variations in cost considerations. It is generally believed that, to be affordable for conventional applications, the unit cost must be significantly reduced. To date, the U.S. effort to develop a nonnuclear version of the cruise missile has focused on the MRASM, although some envision conventional GLCMs (see chapter 6).

Currently, the major system for delivering nonnuclear munitions over long distances is the manned aircraft. Cost comparisons between conventionally armed cruise missiles and aircraft are complicated by several factors—not the least of which is the early state of development of cruise missiles and advanced nonnuclear munitions. Definitive cost comparisons are difficult because the two systems function quite differently. Most

14. Author's estimate derived from Stockholm International Peace Research Institute, *Tactical Nuclear Weapons: European Perspectives* (Crane, Russak, 1978), p. 112.

Table 4-4. Cost of Tactical Aircraft and Nonnuclear Cruise Missiles Required for Attacking Thirty Hypothetical Airfields[a]

Costs in millions of 1981 constant dollars

Weapon system	Number of operational weapons required over 10-day period[b]	Total force life-cycle cost with no attrition	Total force life-cycle cost with 10 percent attrition	Additional force required by 10 percent attrition	Attrition break-even point for cruise missile and tactical aircraft costs[c] (percent)
F-111 fighter-bombers with anti-airfield munitions and average sortie rate of 1.25 a day	48 F-111s	2,725	5,965	60 F-111s	n.a.
Cruise missile systems[d]					
MRASM with F-16 fighter as launcher (3 sorties a day)	1,800 MRASMs/20 F-16 fighters	3,150	3,400	180 MRASMs	2.5
MRASM with F-16 fighter as launcher (2 sorties a day)	1,800 MRASMs/45 F-16 fighters	4,415	4,740	180 MRASMs	5.2
Hypothetical mobile conventionally armed GLCM (lower cost estimate)	1,800 GLCCMs/30 transporter-erector-launchers	4,165	4,500	180 GLCCMs	6.0
Hypothetical mobile conventionally armed GLCM (higher cost estimate)	1,800 GLCCMs/30 transporter-erector-launchers	4,840	5,240	180 GLCCMs	7.5

Sources: Author's estimates based on appendix tables B-4 and B-5.

n.a. Not available.

a. For purposes of analysis, it has been assumed that thirty enemy airfields must be continuously shut down or substantially degraded through the use of antirunway submunitions for a period of ten days. The costs in this table include the acquisition as well as operating and support costs of a force of sufficient numbers to meet this requirement. The antiairfield munitions employed are assumed to be comparable in effectiveness and costs for both tactical aircraft and cruise missiles and are therefore excluded from the cost totals.

b. Does not include new systems required for replacement of original systems lost to enemy air defenses.

c. This is the approximate level of attrition at which the costs of the tactical aircraft force with its replacements equal those of the cruise missile forces. The relative cost advantages of the two forces are graphically illustrated in figure 4-2, below.

d. Medium-range air-to-surface missile (MRASM); and the hypothetical conventionally armed ground-launched cruise missile, referred to here as the GLCCM. The important characteristics and costs of the weapon systems examined in this table are listed in appendix table B-8.

tactical aircraft are not likely to be shot down on their first combat mission; they are expected to return to perform more sorties. In contrast to the reusability of the aircraft, present cruise missiles are considered disposable, destroying themselves in the process of performing their attacks. Static measurements of relative costs on a "per weapon" basis tend to ignore critical aspects of the problem. More accurate cost comparisons must account for this difference and how attrition resulting from enemy defense can affect the relative costs of aircraft and cruise missiles.

For illustrative purposes, table 4-4 postulates a set of common requirements for measuring the costs of aircraft and cruise missiles. The objective of attacking a large number of enemy airfields with munitions intended to degrade or neutralize their operations was chosen as an important mission that both systems could perform.[15] Although based on available information concerning weapon system costs and effectiveness, critical assumptions about various factors were still necessary for purposes of analysis. This constraint and the fact that several important variables such as relative prelaunch survivability are not included make the comparisons in the table limited and heuristic rather than definitive. While the range of alternatives examined could easily be much broader, the analysis deals only with the most likely cases for reasons of clarity and simplicity.

The cost figures in the table assume that two F-111 fighter-bombers must be allocated against each of the thirty hypothetical airfields every twenty-four hours to attack them effectively.[16] Assuming a modest ability to keep these sophisticated aircraft flying (an average rate of 1.25 sorties per day for each aircraft) during wartime results in a requirement for forty-eight operational aircraft (and a few spares). The total life-cycle costs of these aircraft are about $54 million per F-111 (see appendix table B-8), which results in an overall value of nearly $2.7 billion for this force.

Two different types of nonnuclear cruise missiles are compared. One is the planned Air Force MRASM carried by the F-16 fighter. The other is a hypothetical conventionally armed GLCM. As a nonnuclear system

15. *Department of Defense Appropriations for 1981*, Hearings before a subcommittee of the House Appropriations Committee, 96 Cong. 2 sess. (GPO, 1980), pt. 3, p. 1030.

16. Instead of simply calculating the probability of attrition per sortie, the time factor is introduced, because the success of the airfield attack mission is sensitive to the duration as well as the intensity of strikes.

requiring less technical sophistication and support than the nuclear GLCM each missile is assumed to be significantly less expensive. The conventional GLCM is also assumed to rely on a reload capability to substantially reduce the number of transporter-erector-launchers required. To account for uncertainties, two higher cost variants of the MRASM/F-16 system and the conventional GLCM are also presented. The higher cost of the MRASM system arises from a more modest expectation of the F-16's capabilities as a launch platform, and the assumption of 50 percent higher annual operating and support costs per MRASM (see appendix table B-8). Higher operating and support costs also account for the more expensive conventional GLCM.

A total force of 1,800 operational cruise missiles is assumed to be required to match the F-111 force in order to neutralize the thirty hypothetical airfields over a ten-day period. Table 4-4 postulates that three MRASMs with antiairfield munitions would be used to strike enemy airfields every twelve hours, or a total of six each day. For launching the missiles either twenty or forty-five F-16 fighters would be necessary, depending on the assumed launch capacity and sortie rate. Thirty reloadable ground-mobile launchers are assumed in both cases for the conventional GLCM. A small number of spare launchers and missiles were also included. The total life-cycle costs for the four types of forces range from about $3.2 billion to nearly $5 billion in constant dollars, and the overall cost per operational weapon ranges from $1.4 million to $2.2 million.

Of the assumptions underlying the comparisons in the table one of the most important concerns the respective numbers of aircraft and cruise missiles needed to produce equivalent damage against the same target. Six cruise missiles reaching their airfield target are assumed to be as effective as two F-111 fighter-bombers delivering similar munitions. Although this is speculative because of the incomplete state of development of such advanced antiairfield munitions, the estimates in the table are generally consistent with what little information is publicly available.[17] Changes in the relationship would of course significantly alter the cost ratio between the two forces.

A second assumption concerns the relative ability of the two weapon systems to penetrate enemy air defenses. To simplify the analysis, the conservative assumption has been made in table 4-4 that cruise missile

17. Robert D. McKelvey and Edward A. Jordan, "Manned Tactical Aircraft and Conventional Cruise Missile Mission Compatibility and Effectiveness" (San Diego, Calif.: General Dynamics Convair Division, n.d.), pp. 6–7.

Figure 4-2. *Ratio of Tactical Aircraft Costs to Nonnuclear Cruise Missile Costs at Various Attrition Rates*[a]

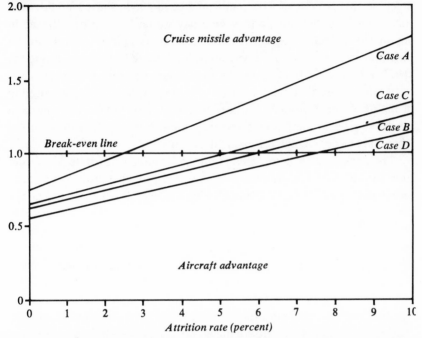

Ratio of aircraft cost to cruise missile cost

a. Case A, lower cost medium-range air-to-surface missile, launched by F-16 fighter; case B, higher cost MRASM, launched by F-16 fighter; case C, lower cost ground-launched conventional cruise missile; case D, higher cost GLCCM.

losses will be equal to those of the F-111 aircraft. Presuming a more favorable rate of penetrativity for the cruise missile than for the tactical aircraft does not substantially change the outcomes shown in the table because large investments are dominant in the costs of each force.

Specifically, what table 4-4 and the related figure 4-2 illustrate is the effect the attrition exacted by enemy air defenses can have on the relative cost relationship of tactical aircraft and cruise missiles. While the higher cost of the aircraft can be spread out over a number of missions, this cost can become unacceptably high as the aircraft's attrition levels begin to increase, thereby expending costly weapon systems for a smaller number of missions. Expressed as a percentage, the attrition rate is a measure of the average number lost in combat over a given number of missions.

Aircraft can suffer attrition through destruction by enemy defenses or simply by suffering damage sufficient to remove them from combat for some period of time. The expense of modern tactical aircraft and the limited numbers available make high attrition rates unacceptable. Even an average attrition rate of 5 percent would be too high, since it would mean that a unit that flew missions twice a day would have to be replaced in about ten days. Consequently, defense planners tend to regard aircraft attrition rates of over 1 or 2 percent as intolerable,[18] although during the 1973 war in the Middle East the high losses of ground-attack aircraft aroused concern that much higher attrition rates might be experienced in a major war in Europe. This does not mean that targets exacting high attrition rates are not considered important, but only that their cost is estimated to be too high for manned aircraft.

The attrition rates considered in this study merely illustrate cost trade-offs between aircraft and cruise missiles, not probable attrition in actual combat. The levels of attrition at which the overall costs of tactical aircraft and cruise missiles become equal is presented in the table and graphically illustrated in figure 4-2 as a ratio of total force costs. Figure 4-2 shows the average attrition rate at which the costs associated with the F-111 fighter-bomber force begin to outweigh those of the various non-nuclear cruise missile forces. However, the attrition break-even line should not necessarily be considered the point at which the use of cruise missiles becomes more desirable. Other factors must also be considered. One is that manned aircraft are much more flexible—they can perform a wider variety of missions than cruise missiles. On the other hand, with high attrition rates, opportunity cost and the loss of highly trained pilots would favor using cruise missiles even if their cost is somewhat greater.

The table and the figure illustrate that, as the attrition rate for tactical aircraft increases, the cost of the aircraft force begins to exceed that of the various cruise missile forces because aircraft replacement costs are far higher. Yet with no attrition, the life-cycle costs of the different cruise missile forces are higher than that of the assumed F-111 fighter-bomber force (table 4-4). For the cheaper versions of the MRASM and the conventional GLCM, the cost advantage shifts in their favor at average attrition rates of about 2.5 and 6.0 percent, respectively. Accordingly, the break-even points come at higher attrition levels for the more costly cruise missile systems. The substantial difference between the lower and higher cost cruise missile systems in table 4-4 illustrates the sensitivity of the

18. Peter Bogart, "The Vulnerability of the Manned Airborne Weapon System," *International Defense Review,* June 1977, pp. 1065–66.

cost ratio to relatively modest changes in assumptions. In particular, because of the large number of cruise missiles, the level of annual operating and support costs per missile can be a significant factor in determining the attractiveness of nonnuclear cruise missile systems vis-à-vis tactical aircraft. Assumptions about the capacity of the F-16 fighter as an MRASM launcher have a similar effect.

Variables not shown in table 4-4 can also be determinants of relative costs. One of the most important is the estimate of the frequency at which the F-111s can mount strikes. If an average sortie rate is increased to 1.5 a day, the break-even attrition point moves somewhat higher,[19] and if the F-111 can average only one mission a day, the cost ratio shifts in favor of the cruise missile forces by increasing the number and cost of the aircraft force. Under the latter condition the lower cost variant of the MRASM system is less expensive than the aircraft force even before attrition occurs. Similarly, the attrition rates at which the other cruise missile forces break even are reduced by as much as one-half.[20]

As noted earlier, another critical factor is the relative effectiveness of the aircraft and the nonnuclear cruise missiles against their targets. In this analysis, their relative effectiveness in attacking airfields is assumed to be 3:1, or three cruise missiles required to do the same task as a single aircraft once they have reached their target. Changes in this ratio dramatically affect their cost relationship. If the ratio is reduced to 2:1 (two rather than three missiles required), the cost advantage shifts substantially toward the cruise missile forces.[21] For the lower cost versions of the cruise missile, the MRASM becomes less expensive than the F-111 force even without attrition, and the conventional GLCM becomes equal in cost at less than 2 percent attrition. Correspondingly, if the ratio shifts the other way (requiring an additional cruise missile), the break-even cost points for the cruise missile force move to even higher (and less probable) average attrition rates. Only the least costly MRASM system would have a break-even point at less than 10 percent attrition for the F-111 alternative. This raises the question of whether bigger cruise mis-

19. The break-even points for the various cruise missile forces would increase as follows: case A, 3 percent; case B, 7.6 percent; case C, 6.8 percent; and case D, 9 percent.
20. The other break-even points would correspondingly diminish to: case B, 3.7 percent; case C, 2.7 percent; and case D, 5.2 percent.
21. Under these assumptions the costs of the lower cost MRASM force (case A) diminish to about $2.5 billion, and the lower cost conventional GLCM system to nearly $3.4 billion.

Table 4-5. *Costs of Long-Range Antiship Weapon Systems*

Costs in millions of 1981 constant dollars

Weapon system	Payload per weapon (pounds)	Average unit flyaway cost (per weapon)	Life-cycle cost[a] (per weapon)	Life-cycle costs of delivering payload			
				1,000-pound payload		4,000-pound payload	
				Number of weapons	Cost[b]	Number of weapons	Cost[b]
Harpoon surface-to-surface missile[e]	500	0.6	2.1–2.8	2	4.2–5.6	8	16.8–22.4
Tomahawk antiship missile[d]	1,000	1.4	3.6–4.0	1	3.6–4.0	4	14.4–20.5
Medium-range air-to-surface missile[e]	650	0.65	1.4–2.2	1.5	2.1–3.3	6.2	8.7–13.6

Sources: See the sources listed in appendix B.

a. These figures include the acquisition costs of the weapon or weapon system (in average unit flyaway costs) as well as their operating and support costs over fifteen years. The range of figures shown for the Harpoon, Tomahawk, and MRASM systems reflects uncertainties about their operating and support costs, in part because of the variety of launch platforms they can use.

b. These two columns measure the relative cost of delivering two levels of payload and provide a rough but useful indicator for comparing the costs of the three weapon systems. The utility of these cost comparisons is somewhat limited because the damage the weapons can inflict depends not only on the size of their payload, but also on other factors, including the material composition of the warhead. As in table 4-2, in some cases the number of weapons required is artificially fractionated to more precisely illustrate the relative costs under consideration (although at least one weapon is allocated per target).

c. It is assumed that this missile is carried on an existing surface ship launcher.

d. The unit flyaway cost of the Tomahawk missile is based on current Department of Defense projections of procuring 439 SLCMs in the 1981–85 defense program. Assuming that production of the missile eventually reaches about 1,500, its average unit flyaway cost should decline to about $1 million per missile, and life-cycle costs should diminish to $2.5 million to $4.8 million for the 1,000-pound payload and to $10 million to $19.2 million for the 4,000-pound payload.

e. This weapon would correspond to the AGM-109I version of the MRASM for attacking naval targets, development of which is only under consideration. Acquisition and operating cost figures are therefore primarily based on the author's own estimates (see appendix B).

siles capable of carrying larger payloads or more effective munitions may be necessary to ensure the cruise missile's effectiveness in the airfield attack mission. Thus despite certain unresolved questions, it appears that based on existing cost projections nonnuclear cruise missiles' utility may vary inversely with the level of attrition suffered by tactical aircraft. In other words, in situations where the attrition of manned aircraft by enemy defenses is high, cruise missiles may offer a relatively less expensive means of attacking certain targets. In the absence of these high attrition rates, tactical aircraft continue to be the least costly means of attack. As the outstanding technical and cost uncertainties discussed in this analysis are reduced, it should be possible to determine more specifically the attrition levels at which the cost advantage shifts between the two types of forces.

Naval Applications

Perhaps the mission most difficult to treat adequately in this chapter is sea control. While at least two new cruise missile variants may have important roles as antiship weapons, several limitations impede comparison based simply on costs. In part this is due to the lack of sufficiently detailed unclassified information outlining the actual effectiveness of these weapons against various targets. Their effectiveness does not necessarily vary with the size of their payloads. Warhead design and material composition are likely to be critical, especially if naval vessels are targets.[22] At sea, the different range capability of the weapons can be a critical factor in determining their value. Target acquisition and the ability to overcome enemy electronic countermeasures are much more important for these weapons than for most land attack systems.

Simple cost comparisons between U.S. antiship weapon systems can nevertheless be revealing. Table 4-5 presents the costs and payload characteristics of the major long-range antiship weapons currently deployed or under development by the United States. Of the three cruise missile systems, only the Harpoon is operational. By assuming two levels of payload requirements, it is possible to gauge more accurately the cost differences between the various weapons. For instance, reaching the specified

22. For instance, because of its special warhead casing, the effectiveness of the 1,000-pound Tomahawk antiship missile is expected to be somewhere between that of current 1,000-pound and 2,000-pound bombs. *Hearings on Military Posture and H.R. 10929: Department of Defense Authorization for Appropriations for Fiscal Year 1979*, Hearings before the House Armed Services Committee, 95 Cong. 2 sess. (GPO, 1978), pt. 3, bk. 2, pp. 1262–63.

levels of payload assumed in the table requires several more Harpoons than other weapons. Missiles with larger payloads such as the Tomahawk SLCM then begin to appear more efficient as the amount of payload required on a target increases. If its lower costs (particularly in estimated support costs) were combined with a modest payload, a MRASM-type weapon would probably be less costly per warhead. While this neglects the possible opportunity costs related to assigning certain carrier-based aircraft to serve as MRASM launchers, there is at present no indication that such undefined costs need be significant.

Finally, a caveat is in order about the level of confidence related to these cost figures. The projected costs in table 4-5 show the MRASM as potentially the least expensive on a per weapon basis. However, it is still only a concept on paper. Whether a MRASM based on current cruise missile systems is ever developed and is capable initially of both antiship and land-attack missions at relatively low cost remains to be seen.[23] By comparison, as the projected purchase of the eventual number of Tomahawk SLCMs grows to more realistic levels, their unit flyaway cost can be expected to decline by as much as 25 percent.

Prospective Trends

The 1980s will witness the assimilation of the cruise missile in its many forms into the American military force structure. The remaining question is merely, to what degree? If only 1980 plans are realized, the United States will procure at least 4,400 air-, ground-, and sea-launched cruise missiles during this decade. Over $11 billion in fiscal 1981 dollars (table 4-6) will be spent directly on these missiles and their launch platforms. But changes in existing plans could double or triple this number over the next decade. Since the ALCM and SLCM programs now provide the necessary technical base, management structure, and production lines, economic barriers to deploying new types of cruise missiles are reduced, and future programs are likely to include the development of new "outgrowth" systems as well as increased production of existing variants. Table 4-6 shows that it would be possible to increase the present commitment to cruise missile acquisition over the next decade to levels about two to four times their present size and cost. Even with only modest extensions of current development and procurement programs, over $22

23. David R. Griffiths, "Proposal Set on Air-to-Surface Missile," *Aviation Week and Space Technology,* December 29, 1980, p. 25.

billion (in 1981 constant dollars) could be budgeted, for a total of nearly 12,000 cruise missiles and their launchers through 1990.[24]

The air-launched cruise missile program is likely to be characterized by both qualitative improvements and quantitative expansion. Acceleration of ALCM deployments provides one means of enhancing U.S. strategic capability in the mid-1980s. The present ALCM production rate could be expanded from about forty to sixty missiles a month without major difficulties.[25] Since the pace of missile production is currently set by the rate of B-52G modifications, accelerated ALCM deployment would necessitate either earlier installation of internal ALCM launchers on the B-52G or the acquisition of an additional cruise missile carrier aircraft. This highlights the issue of whether to deploy a new carrier or simply convert the B-52H bombers into carriers.[26] Although in the past Defense Department officials have favored the former alternative (which would augment the projected force with 1,800 ALCMs), it is possible that a new type of launcher could supplement or supplant the B-52G cruise missile carriers in the 1980s. A deployment date of 1987 for such aircraft was most often noted by the Carter administration.[27] How the Reagan administration will reconcile previous Defense Department plans with its intention to deploy a new penetrating bomber by the mid-1980s is not yet clear.

Defense Department studies have concluded that a new cruise missile carrier with radiation-hardening and fast takeoff is preferable to a converted civilian transport aircraft because of the former's greater survivability.[28] This has led to the proposal that a variant of the canceled B-1 strategic bomber be considered the primary candidate for a new cruise missile carrier if one is required in the 1980s. Capable of mounting thirty ALCMs each, a force of 100 B-1 carriers is estimated to cost about $17 billion in constant 1981 dollars (see appendix table B-5).

24. Author's estimates based on table 4-1. These figures assume the deployment of ALCMs on B-52 bombers, G and H class, the planned GLCM deployment of 560 missiles, about 4,000 MRASMs of various models, and the 1,500 Tomahawk SLCMs (see footnote 7, above).

25. *Department of Defense Authorization for Appropriations for Fiscal Year 1981*, Hearings, pt. 4, pp. 2472–73.

26. Ibid.; and *Department of Defense Appropriations for Fiscal Year 1981*, Hearings before the Senate Appropriations Committee, 96 Cong. 2 sess. (GPO, 1980), pt. 4, p. 910.

27. *Department of Defense Annual Report, Fiscal Year 1981* (GPO, 1980), p. 90.

28. *Department of Defense Authorization for Appropriations for Fiscal Year 1981*, Hearings, pt. 5, pp. 2737, 2969, 3008.

Table 4-6. *Possible Scope and Cost of Cruise Missile Programs through 1990*

Costs in billions of 1981 constant dollars

Program	Type of launcher	Number of launch platforms	Number of missiles	Total acquisition costs[a]
Air-launched cruise missiles				
Currently planned	B-52G bomber	173	3,418	7.7
Probable additions	B-52H bomber	96	2,000	2.7
Possible additions	Strategic ALCM launcher[b]	100–111	3,000–6,650	16.7–21.9
Ground-launched cruise missiles				
Currently planned	Transporter-erector-launcher	Over 116	560	1.7
Probable additions[c]	None	None	None	None
Possible additions[c]	None	None	None	None
Sea-launched cruise missiles				
Recently planned[d]	Attack submarine (torpedo tube)	48	439	2.1
	Surface ship (armored box launcher)			
Probable additions	Attack submarine (torpedo tube)	113	1,070	2.6
	Surface ship (armored box launcher)			
	Surface ship (vertical launching system)			

Possible additions	Attack submarine (hull launchers)[e]	90	500–800	2.8–3.2
	Polaris SSBN conversion[f]	8	570–1,000	2.2
Medium-range air-to-surface missiles[g]				
Probable additions	B-52D bomber and various tactical aircraft	Hundreds	Several thousand	n.a.
Possible additions	Various tactical aircraft	Hundreds	Several thousand	n.a.

Source: Author's estimates based on the sources listed in appendix B.

n.a. Not available.

a. Total acquisition costs include expenses of the acquisition or modification of the launch platform as well as the total investment costs of the relevant cruise missile programs. Operating and support costs for any of these systems are not included. The figures in the table account for not only the operational missiles and their launchers, but also for spare or nonoperating sets.

b. The range of figures depends on whether a B-1 variant (the lower figures) or a version of a wide-bodied transport aircraft (the higher figures) is employed as a new cruise missile carrier aircraft.

c. The particular military and political aspects of the GLCM deployment make it appear unlikely that additional nuclear-armed GLCMs will be deployed. The uncertain eventual deployment in Belgium and the Netherlands may even reduce the planned deployment figure.

d. These numbers reflect the Defense Department's five-year defense plans as submitted in the 1981 budget request. At that time funding was programmed to support the modification of thirty-three SSN-688-class attack submarines to receive Tomahawk SLCMs, and to deploy SLCM armored box launchers on fifteen DD-963-class destroyers. Through congressional action, funding for an additional forty Tomahawk SLCMs was added to the final 1982 budget.

e. This assumes the ninety nuclear attack submarines planned by the U.S. Navy are deployed with hull launchers for cruise missiles or are eventually retrofitted with such a system. A total of eight to twelve hull launchers per submarine is under consideration.

f. Also under consideration at one time was the conversion of the aging Polaris ballistic missile submarines into cruise missile launch platforms with the possibility of carrying about four to seven SLCMs in each of the sixteen launch tubes of the Polaris SSBN.

g. Figures on the eventual size and cost of the MRASM program are not yet publicly available, but it has been unofficially reported that this program could involve several thousands of missiles and cost over $3 billion.

Regardless of which approach is chosen, the missile deployed aboard the cruise missile carrier aircraft by the late 1980s is likely to be an improved version of the present ALCM, the advanced technology cruise missile, which will probably have longer range and reduced detectability. Development of more efficient turbofan engines and higher density fuels are critical to extending the range. Work is also proceeding on advanced guidance and weapon delivery components. Over $500 million in expenditures would be required before the advanced ALCM could become operational in 1986 or 1987.[29] The research and development objectives for the next generation of ALCMs also highlight a basic difference in priorities between the strategic nuclear and the nonnuclear cruise missile programs. Priority in the nuclear-armed ALCM missile program is apparently given to improving effectiveness; nonnuclear cruise missile development focuses on cost reduction. Consequently, future ALCM follow-on systems are likely to exceed the first generation in both technological sophistication and unit costs.

Future trends in the Tomahawk program are more difficult to predict. Uncertainty about projected SLCM deployments is likely to persist until the Navy has a clearer conception of the roles to be accorded to the several Tomahawk variants, and the numbers appropriate to those roles. The SLCMs' prospects seem to turn on whether they are judged a useful—but marginal—means of increasing the wartime flexibility of American fleets, or whether current developments portend more basic alterations to traditional operational concepts and force structure. New outgrowths from the SLCM program could augment planned deployments. One possibility, though not now planned, might be a nuclear-armed version of the Tomahawk antiship missile.[30] The U.S. Navy's interest in such weapons may grow if the number of large Soviet surface ships is increased.

The development of vertical launching systems for surface ships and submarines could enable the United States to deploy a much larger number of SLCMs over the next decade than the 1,700 at present conceivable. Yet perhaps more than for most other types of warfare, naval planning involves difficult trade-offs in the choice of weapon mixes. Recent planning sees the primary missions of the ships and submarines capable of

29. Clarence A. Robinson, Jr., "USAF Readies Advanced Cruise Missiles," *Aviation Week and Space Technology,* March 10, 1980, pp. 12–15.

30. *Department of Defense Appropriations for Fiscal Year 1981,* Hearings, pt. 4, p. 131.

launching SLCMs as fleet air defense or antisubmarine warfare, and their weapon loads should correspond.[31] (The first ships to receive the vertical launching systems are the CG-47 *Ticonderoga*-class cruisers with the advanced Aegis air defense radar system,[32] whose principal mission is defending against antiship missile attacks.) Additional growth in Tomahawk production probably would thus depend either on expanding the fleet beyond the number of ships required for current missions or on accepting new operational concepts or launch platforms. One example of the latter would be the development of a land-based antiship cruise missile system.[33] Deployed along naval choke-points, such a system could help prevent the passage of enemy vessels in wartime. That to date this option has been given little consideration reflects its inconsistency with established institutional preferences for performing such a mission.

For the expansion of SLCM deployments on the existing inventories of Navy ships, mission priorities would have to change. Cruise missiles offer cruisers, destroyers, and attack submarines significantly enhanced capability to inflict damage on enemy land targets. But for nonnuclear conflict, large numbers of SLCMs might be required to achieve the numerous and sustained attacks necessary to neutralize many enemy targets such as air or naval bases. The present air defense and antisubmarine warfare priorities of existing ships and submarines make it unlikely that their weapon loads would be adequate to the task.

There may, however, be other ways to deploy sufficient numbers of SLCMs without degrading the capability of existing forces to perform their missions. One option for additional submarine launchers has been studied. Although this is not very likely, it would be possible to convert eight of the aging Polaris ballistic missile submarines into cruise-missile launch platforms as they are retired from service as strategic ballistic missile submarines in accordance with tacit extension of SALT I limitations.[34] With four to seven SLCMs in each of its sixteen launch tubes, each Polaris submarine would be armed with as many as 64 to 112

31. *Department of Defense Annual Report, Fiscal Year 1981*, pp. 171–76.

32. *Hearings on Military Posture and H.R. 6495*, pt. 4, bk. 2, pp. 1441–43.

33. One of the few official references to this concept appeared in 1977 congressional testimony. *Department of Defense Authorization for Appropriations for Fiscal Year 1978*, Hearings before the Senate Armed Services Committee, 95 Cong. 1 sess. (GPO, 1977), pt. 9, p. 6392. See Michael MccGwire's discussion of the option in chapter 8, below.

34. Ibid., pp. 195–97, 252–53.

Tomahawks.[35] Deployed with either nuclear or nonnuclear cruise missiles, this force would present a significant concentration of naval strike power. But the high cost of this conversion for only a few more years of service life make the prospects for this option seem poor.[36] Perhaps more likely in later years, if the SALT limitations continue in effect, would be conversion of some of the newer Poseidon submarines to cruise missile launchers. If these arms control constraints (which would compel decisions in the late 1980s on the retirement or conversion of these submarines) are abandoned, however, retention as SLBM launchers is far more probable than conversion.

The surface ships with the greatest capacity to carry cruise missiles are also the ones that must perform other critical missions. Thus a more novel concept has been suggested: large numbers of vertical launching system (VLS) modules installed on less expensive transport-type vessels. Such a system would avoid the weapon trade-off problem. Capitalizing on the protection afforded by attachment to a carrier task force, cruise missile transports would supplement the carrier's striking power. Provided with adequate warships as escorts or with shore-based air protection, such platforms also might serve as a lesser substitute in areas where carrier task forces are not available. Any cost estimates for such a hypothetical cruise missile transport are necessarily speculative. However, if such a vessel could carry 500 or so SLCMs, it would cost less per cruise missile loading than most other cruise missile launch platforms (see appendix table B-7) even if the costs of acquiring ships and installing launchers added up to $200 million to $300 million.[37] As with the ALCM carrier, such a notion raises the difficult question of whether military effectiveness is best served by choosing a simple and low-cost (but relatively more vulnerable) launch platform or by relying on a more flexible and survivable (but much more expensive) weapon system.

Perhaps the greatest growth potential of the current cruise missiles is in the recently initiated medium-range air-to-surface missile program.

35. "Submarine Cruise Missile Plan Mulled," *Aviation Week and Space Technology,* June 16, 1980, pp. 119–20.

36. Assuming a service life of thirty years, the Polaris submarines would have an average operating life of six years after their conversion to cruise-missile launch platforms. *Department of Defense Authorization for Appropriations for Fiscal Year 1981,* Hearings, pt. 2, p. 635.

37. If a cruise missile transport's cost and weapon capacity approximated these figures, its cost per weapon loading would be $0.5 million, which is fairly competitive with other launch platforms under consideration.

Unofficial reports place prospective MRASM production at several thousand.[38] Although the MRASM may be the main nonnuclear cruise missile planned for deployment, uncertainties about costs continue to govern the probability of a heavy commitment to nonnuclear cruise missiles. If costs are adequately constrained even as sophistication increases, further nonnuclear variants may be deployed. One is a tactical cruise missile that would attack mobile targets on the battlefield. Under the "Back-Breaker Option-Breaker" program, each missile would be able to destroy several armored vehicles by using a laser guidance system and advanced nonnuclear munitions.[39] Other possible variants for battlefield application could be cruise missiles for reconnaissance or for dispensing chemical weapons.[40]

Unique among current U.S. cruise missile programs is the Air Force's GLCM with its apparent lack of growth potential. One reason is that the present nuclear-armed GLCM is a weapon tied to a very narrow role in one theater. This limitation is compounded by the fact that ultimate GLCM deployment levels in Europe are strongly influenced by political considerations; two potential host countries, Belgium and the Netherlands, have yet to approve deployments on their soil. A negative decision by these countries could further reduce the GLCM program by about 96 missiles and could reopen questions about the feasibility of the whole NATO program of theater force modernization.[41] The GLCM procurement objective was listed in the 1979 budget request as 696 missiles; this was subsequently reduced to the projected purchase of 560.[42]

Conclusions

The massive integration of cruise missiles into the American force structure during the 1980s is in large part due to belief in their relatively low costs. Although this expectation clearly has been exaggerated at times in the past, in general it is probably valid. The central reason for

38. Jeffrey M. Lenorovitz, "MRASM Development Program Pushed," *Aviation Week and Space Technology*, April 7, 1980, p. 16.
39. Philip J. Klass, "Laser Radar Missile Guidance Studied," *Aviation Week and Space Technology*, March 16, 1981, pp. 75–79.
40. Jeffrey M. Lenorovitz, "Other Tomahawk Applications Explored by General Dynamics," *Aviation Week and Space Technology*, March 31, 1980, p. 21.
41. *Baltimore Sun*, June 4, 1980.
42. *Department of Defense Authorization for Appropriations for Fiscal Year 1980*, Hearings, pt. 5, p. 2493.

the affordability of modern cruise missiles in comparison with other weapon systems lies in the missile's inherent technical flexibility, which makes it applicable to a wide range of military roles and capable of deployment on a variety of launch platforms. The commonality of current cruise missile variants reduces program costs in the research and development phase, and the potential exists for significant economies of scale from enlarged production. Savings have also been fostered by competitive procurement practices, which must be continued to avoid unnecessary cost escalation. For the current generation of cruise missiles now nearing deployment, the availability of existing launch platforms made the investment decision much less difficult. Because these missiles can be carried by a wide range of existing delivery systems, the "sunk costs" of which are not attributable to the missiles, the deployment costs of several variants of the cruise missile have been significantly reduced. However, in some cases, savings realized by taking advantage of platform sunk costs may be paid for in less visible costs. Cruise missiles deployed merely as an adjunct on an existing platform can take the space of other weapons or can divert the delivery system from its primary mission.

Future deployments of ALCMs and SLCMs beyond those already planned will probably require dedicated delivery systems, the expense of which would be attributable to the cruise missiles, thereby reducing the cost advantage enjoyed by the current cruise missile programs. Choices of dedicated launch platforms will invariably reflect the tension between military and economic priorities. While the desire to reduce weapon system costs encourages resort to inexpensive cruise missile transporters capable of carrying large numbers of missiles, the desire for military flexibility and combat endurance calls for more expensive war-fighting launch platforms. Unfortunately, public examination of cruise missile costs to date has tended to focus on the weapon's unit cost. In most cases the cruise missile's acquisition cost (excluding the nuclear warhead) accounts for less than 25 percent of the total weapon system cost when prorated per weapon. The costs of launcher acquisition or modification and the life-cycle operating and support costs of the combined system account for the majority of the expense. Because of the large numbers of cruise missiles planned (at least for strategic forces), even relatively small variations in the expected annual operating and support costs will become substantial when multiplied by a ten- to fifteen-year deployment. It is often these expenses that are more difficult to project. Consequently, the question of affordability must be addressed from a broader perspective, such as full system life-cycle costs in comparison with other weapon systems. The limited analyses in this chapter suggest that simply in terms of cost, without factoring in all the operational complexities of actual military planning, cruise missiles compare favorably with other weapons, especially in the case of nuclear systems.

Comparing the costs of nonnuclear cruise missiles with those of other weapon systems is more open to question. Conventional cruise missiles must achieve a high degree of effectiveness by using advanced technologies while simultaneously reducing their acquisition and support costs if they are to be affordable in the quantities necessary for nonnuclear warfare. The margin for error in unit cost increases or less-than-expected capabilities therefore seems much narrower than for nuclear variants. The desirability of nonnuclear cruise missiles in cost terms appears to vary primarily with the attrition suffered in striking heavily defended targets. The cost relationship between cruise missiles and tactical aircraft therefore suggests a natural division of labor based not on the type of target, but on the level of the enemy defensive threat.

Finally, trends indicate that cruise missile deployments and costs may greatly increase over the next decade. Even modest assumptions about the expansion of current programs make it possible to envisage that the costs and numbers of missiles could more than double. Higher levels are likely to require the U.S. military establishment to accept less traditional types of weapon systems and operating concepts to fully exploit the opportunities offered by these new weapons.

PART TWO

Strategy

CHAPTER FIVE

Strategic Retaliation against the Soviet Homeland

BRUCE BENNETT *and* JAMES FOSTER

PUBLIC DEBATE about the merits of the cruise missile as a strategic system has been focused on comparing the system with the alternative of a new manned bomber. The comparisons have emphasized the high cost of a manned bomber, the technologically advanced qualities of the cruise missile, and the relative capabilities of the two systems to penetrate Soviet air defenses. Although it is widely accepted that the cruise missile is more cost-effective, little attention has been given to what it is particularly effective in doing, whether one version is more effective than others, and what the effectiveness trade-offs are compared with other strategic systems. Such assessments are difficult to make since it has never been made clear what purposes cruise missiles are intended to serve in the overall strategic force posture. Comparing the characteristics of the cruise missile and the manned bomber implies only a determination to maintain the "air-breathing" leg of the triad.

The purpose of this chapter is to evaluate the potential utility of cruise missiles in strengthening the capabilities of the strategic force posture to achieve U.S. objectives. This involves identifying the strategic purposes cruise missiles can serve, comparing them with other systems, and evaluating their capabilities in performing the roles for which they are best suited.

Bruce Bennett and James Foster began work on this chapter while on the staff of the Rand Corporation. They are now with the Policy and Management Planning Group.

The Issues

The utility of strategic systems can be assessed in terms of their contribution to three basic dimensions of strategic capabilities. The first involves the particular purposes of maintaining a triad of forces, principally to hedge against failures of some elements of the strategic forces and to improve the survivability of the forces as a whole. The second dimension is achieving force employment objectives—the ability either to successfully attack a set of targets judged to be relevant as a credible deterrent threat or to be successful in conflict if deterrence should fail. The third dimension is how much the system enhances particular force posture characteristics, such as withholdability, endurance, and selectivity in use, which are deemed essential independent of special considerations of target coverage or attack strategy.

These issues also suggest the range of relevant criteria for judging such utility. For example, the utility of a system for maintaining the triad can be assessed by three conditions: high prelaunch survivability and defense penetration in case of a Soviet first strike; the ability to adapt the system to overcome potential Soviet threats against it and to do so at an advantageous cost exchange ratio; and the degree to which a new or improved U.S. system diverts Soviet research, development, and procurement resources that might otherwise be directed against other U.S. systems.

Three components of force employment capabilities help assess the utility of a strategic system. One is the extent to which the system is unique in its ability to attack targets that otherwise could not be struck or that present opportunities for a worthwhile change in attack strategy. A second component is the ability to close gaps in target coverage arising from limitations on the number of weapons likely to survive attack and penetrate defenses or from the need to rely on redundancy in targeting to compensate for uncertain operational capabilities. A third component involves the implications for effectiveness of *how* the system attacks particular sets of targets: the timeliness and size of attack necessary to achieve a successful outcome and the operational uncertainties affecting the readiness, usability, and effectiveness of the system in various situations.

The contributions a strategic system can make to the overall force posture can be assessed on the basis of three attributes that are defined by current strategic doctrinal principles as requirements separate from specific targeting capabilities. These include the capabilities for flexible, controlled, and limited attacks against a wide variety of target types, enduring survival so that a substantial fraction of the forces can be withheld for an indeterminate period of time, and maintaining a strategic reserve force for unforeseen needs and postconflict uses.[1]

The following assessment considers these criteria, with particular emphasis on recently programmed cruise missile forces and current formulations of U.S. strategic policy and requirements, though alternatives will also be considered. Because current programs involve primarily air-launched cruise missile systems, these will receive special attention. Ground-launched and sea-launched cruise missiles—the principal alternatives to air-launched systems—will be assessed to see whether they have the same advantages as, or offset the potential disadvantages of, air-launched systems.

Contributions to the Triad

The decision to procure the cruise missile rather than the B-1 bomber was justified principally on the grounds that it was a more cost-effective way to maintain the air-breathing leg of the triad. This narrow assessment of the trade-offs between the cruise missile and other strategic systems presumes that air-breathing systems perform some unique function. There are, in fact, two potential purposes that these systems can serve for the triad, although the relevance of these purposes depends on the chosen deterrence doctrine, and the ability of cruise missiles to serve them differs for different types of cruise missiles. Nor is it self-evident that a cruise missile force is preferred to a new manned bomber as a means of serving these two purposes.

One aim of current air-breathing systems is to present to an adversary an offensive threat that has vulnerabilities fundamentally different from those of other systems, thereby complicating the adversary's ability to launch an effective surprise attack against U.S. strategic forces. These complications arise because bomber systems pose difficult problems in the timing of attack. A second aim is to exploit the Soviet proclivity to invest heavily in air defenses, which reduces the resources available for

1. *Department of Defense Annual Report, Fiscal Year 1981* (Government Printing Office, 1980).

the development of offensive and defensive systems directed at other elements of the triad.

The timing of attack is difficult because bombers can be launched on warning without a commitment to carry out an attack. This requires the attacker to allow the shortest possible warning time of an attack against bombers and leads in turn to the generally accepted assumption that submarine-launched ballistic missiles (SLBMs), launched from close to U.S. shores, are the most effective means of attacking bomber bases. However, because the flight times of intercontinental ballistic missiles (ICBMs) are much longer than those of close-in SLBMs, the Soviet Union would be faced with the choice between launching its ICBMs first so that they would arrive on target at the same time as the SLBMs and launching both types of missiles simultaneously. In the former case, the bomber (or air-launched cruise missile) would receive a much longer warning time. In the latter case, the probability of receiving unambiguous warning *and* confirmation of a Soviet attack would be increased.

The important point is that the United States would not necessarily have to rely on the uncertain qualities of warning from sensors of a Soviet attack to launch U.S. ICBMs before they could be struck by Soviet missiles. In the most likely case—a simultaneous launch of Soviet ICBMs and SLBMs—the United States would have about half an hour of sensor warning time before an ICBM launch became necessary, and thus would have about fifteen minutes after SLBM detonations on U.S. air bases to launch its ICBM force before the Soviet ICBMs arrived. In this way, the launch-under-attack contingency is quite different from the typical conception of launch on warning with its reliance on uncertain warning information.

Only air-launched cruise missiles (ALCMs) can contribute to this timing-of-attack problem because only they have the attributes of current air-breathing systems. The deployment of sea-launched cruise missiles (SLCMs) would simply increase the number of sea-based systems, which are vulnerable primarily to antisubmarine systems, not strategic offensive systems. The deployment of ground-launched cruise missiles (GLCMs) would pose many of the same problems for a Soviet attack as mobile ICBMs. The advantage of these alternative systems is that they may be more survivable than cruise missiles launched from aircraft—depending on how they are based—especially against a surprise attack (if the GLCMs have been previously dispersed); however, they do not raise timing-of-attack problems. In any case, the value to the United States of making timing of attack difficult for the Soviet Union clearly depends on the desirability of maintaining the risk of, if not official reliance on, launching the ICBM force on warning of a Soviet attack or launching under attack. These options are currently the subject of considerable disagreement, but the vulnerability of the current U.S. ICBM force, which cannot be effectively corrected before the late 1980s at the earliest, means that these options are among the very few open to the United States for most of this decade.

The degree to which timing of attack is difficult for the Soviet Union and the degree to which the air-breathing force can act as a hedge against failures of the other legs of the triad depend on the prelaunch survivability and defense penetration capabilities of the systems involved. The factors determining the prelaunch survivability of weapon-carrying aircraft include (1) the flight time of enemy missiles; (2) the time required for the aircraft to take off and fly beyond lethal nuclear effects; and (3) the time required to obtain and transmit warning information to the force. In evaluating the relative advantages of a cruise missile force versus a new bomber, it should be noted that the characteristics of the U.S. system can only directly affect the second factor, although changes in these characteristics can compel Soviet actions that affect the variables under Soviet control. The Soviet Union can control the attacking missile flight time by launching its missiles closer to U.S. territory or by using depressed trajectory missiles.[2] However, this depends on the launch and flyaway times of U.S. bombers carrying cruise missiles. For example, while a new penetrating bomber like the B-1 has both a faster launch rate and greater resistance to the effects of nuclear weapons, these can be offset, at least in part, by a Soviet submarine force moving closer to the United States. On the other hand, if the Soviet Union should take such actions it would provide clearer strategic warning. Along the same lines, if the Soviet Union were to test its SLBMs in a depressed trajectory mode, this would signal the need to redeploy U.S. forces in a more survivable configuration by moving bases further inland, hardening, and so forth.

2. Many analysts (for example, Alton H. Quanbeck and Archie L. Wood, *Modernizing the Strategic Bomber Force: Why and How* [Brookings Institution, 1976], p. 44) argue that the Soviet Union has never tested a depressed trajectory SLBM and there is no need to worry about such a threat. However, there are various degrees of trajectory depression, some of which certainly should not be difficult for the Soviet Union to use confidently with little or no testing. Lower angles of trajectory depression would certainly require testing and even some changes in software and hardware for the Soviet SLBMs.

On the basis of mid-1970s estimates of the variables affecting aircraft survivability, it was concluded that the B-1's probability of prelaunch survival would be roughly 87 to 95 percent given a nominal 1985 threat, and that the B-52's would be approximately 74 to 90 percent.[3] Several other types of cruise missile carriers have been mentioned, but they are mainly variants on commercial aircraft that would undoubtedly have a still lower prelaunch survival than the B-52.[4] While it is possible that the United States could deploy one of these new carriers or even a more advanced carrier with faster flyaway time and greater hardness, current plans call for the B-52 to be the only ALCM carrier until the late 1980s, and it is unlikely that a new carrier can be developed and deployed before that time in any case. Thus the prelaunch survival probability of the B-52 is the critical consideration. Since studies were made in the mid-1970s, several factors affecting B-52 prelaunch survival have changed. First, it has been discovered that, at least in peacetime, more time may be required to launch the bomber force than was previously expected.[5] Second, the bombers' age makes their performance less reliable. It might not be unusual for only six or seven engines out of eight to start. This could mean aborting aircraft without full power, thereby reducing the size of the force or its overall prelaunch survival since aircraft with less power, and thus less speed, will slow the launching of the rest of the force.[6] Third, the bomber force is now assembled on fewer bases than it was in the mid-1970s, making the bomber takeoff queues longer at the remaining bases. Thus estimates of B-52 prelaunch survivability produced in the mid-1970s cannot be applied to survivability in the 1980s since they tend to overestimate it.

3. Air Force Studies and Analysis, Headquarters USAF, "Assessment of Quanbeck-Wood Report," March 31, 1976, pp. 15–17; Francis P. Hoeber, *Slow to Take Offense: Bombers, Cruise Missiles, and Prudent Deterrence* (Georgetown University, Center for Strategic and International Studies, February 1977), pp. 77–87.

4. Current commercial aircraft are relatively slow to take off and leave a large amount of turbulence behind. By comparison, each B-52 should be able to take off faster, and the delay between consecutive takeoffs should be shorter because of less turbulence.

5. See, for example, the editorial "Two Nuclear Alerts," *Washington Star*, June 11, 1980, which indicates that several false alarms occurred in which alert bombers were not launched even though confirmation that the alarms were false was not received until well after the first bombers should have been in the air.

6. Arthur T. Hadley, "Our Ever-Ready Strategic Forces: Don't Look Closely If You Want to Believe," *Washington Star*, July 1, 1979. Hadley discusses his experience with a B-52 G or H model (a short-range attack missile carrier), at least two of whose engines were very difficult to start, one needing to be started somewhat like "jumping" a dead car battery.

These considerations suggest that there is no clear idea about how large an ALCM force should be to ensure that enough survive a surprise Soviet attack. Several other factors limit the potential size, too. Until the late 1980s part of the B-52 force will continue as penetrating bombers and part will serve as standoff launchers of ALCMs. In the 1990s all B-52s will be cruise missile carriers. In the first phase of ALCM deployment, 151 B-52Gs will carry 12 cruise missiles apiece, giving a force total of about 1,800 missiles. These aircraft would also carry 1,200 to 1,500 bombs and short-range attack missiles (SRAMs), roughly 8 to 10 per bomber. If even half the aircraft were kept on alert (almost twice the current bomber alert level) and the prelaunch survivability was 80 percent, only about 700 ALCMs and 500 to 600 bombs and SRAMs would survive. Of these survivors, perhaps as many as 500 to 600 ALCMs could successfully penetrate Soviet air defenses and detonate on target—a number that does not suggest wide target coverage capabilities. If the force was on generated alert and the prelaunch survival probability did not decline because of longer queues on the runways, as many as 1,400 ALCMs might survive.

In assessing the implications of the growth in the ALCM force in the second phase of deployment, it is important to remember that this growth comes at the cost of a significant reduction in other weapons carried by bombers. While the ALCM force is scheduled to increase by roughly 67 percent (from 12 to 20 per aircraft) in the second phase of deployment, fewer total weapons will be carried by the alert B-52G force since the additional 8 ALCMs per aircraft will replace an average of about 8 to 10 bombs and SRAMS.[7]

In short, the portion of the ALCM force likely to survive a Soviet surprise attack is uncertain but in any case is not large until the second phase of deployment beginning in the late 1980s. Furthermore, given the steadily declining reliability of the B-52 bomber, the prelaunch survivability of an ALCM force deployed on B-52s in the 1990s is subject to serious question. Thus a larger peacetime ALCM force does not necessarily mean a larger surviving force. These problems could, of course, be mitigated by the development of a new ALCM carrier with larger carry-

7. Each current B-52G alert aircraft can carry 4 bombs and 8 SRAMs internally. However, only about 1,500 SRAMs were produced, and some of these have been devoted to the development and operational testing programs. The remainder are spread out over the FB-111 (66 aircraft), B-52H (90 aircraft), and B-52G (150 aircraft) forces. Thus alert forces probably average something less than a full load of SRAMs; we have assumed an average loading of 10 bombs and SRAMs per B-52G or B-52H for this reason.

ing capacity and shorter flyaway times. On the other hand, such a carrier would be expensive, which raises questions about the cost-effectiveness of ALCMs relative to a new manned bomber.

Questions about the relative benefits of ALCMs and a new manned bomber are also raised in considering the second purpose associated with the air-breathing leg of the triad: to stress Soviet air defenses, thereby encouraging the diversion of Soviet resources to improving these defenses. The lower detectability by radar of the cruise missile force and its ability to saturate defenses (in at least some local areas if not nationally) place a heavier burden on Soviet air defenses.

The ALCM/B-52 force as now planned would pose more severe problems for Soviet air defenses than the other cruise missile forces because the B-52 remains a penetrating bomber, and in the first phase of ALCM deployments the potential number of penetrators is substantial. Even if the B-52 were used only as a standoff cruise missile launcher, the B-52/ALCM force would present strong incentives for developing defenses to deal with two types of airborne systems, the carrier and the cruise missile; and an air defense that must deal with different types of airborne systems—especially when one is a significant distance offshore—is considerably more expensive than a defense that can concentrate on one type of system.

These considerations raise some doubts about the argument that a standoff ALCM force is clearly preferable to the development of an effective penetrating bomber force for the period into the 1990s. Reliance on a standoff force would allow the Soviet Union to concentrate its air defense improvements on developing fewer defensive capabilities than would be the case with a mixed force. This is because of the peculiar vulnerabilities and operational constraints of the ALCM system that can be exploited by defensive systems.

First, the ALCM carrier represents an extremely high-value target. Because of ALCM range constraints, the carrier must approach within a few hundred miles of Soviet territory for the missiles to reach deep inland targets. This makes the carrier potentially vulnerable to extended air defense systems guided by an airborne warning and control system (AWACS). This would be an expensive and difficult task for the Soviet Union, but its successful accomplishment could put the ALCM in jeopardy. Second, the cruise missile is likely to be particularly vulnerable to terminal defenses, which may seriously limit its utility in attacking high-value, protected point targets. The lack of electronic countermeasures and other defense avoidance or suppression capabilities could also make the cruise missile more vulnerable to mobile surface-to-air missiles (SAMs). And given the constraints on the range of the cruise missile and on the terrain over which it can navigate effectively, the number of penetration corridors may be limited. These problems would be exacerbated if the cruise missile carrier's prelaunch survivability was low and if concentration of cruise missiles within particular corridors was necessary to saturate air defenses. The Soviet Union could then use SAM barriers along likely corridors of attack and concentrate air defense assets of all kinds in particular areas.

In contrast, the penetrating bomber has range flexibility (within refueling constraints), an ability to exploit electronic countermeasures and other defense avoidance and suppression measures, and rocket-powered missiles, which have greater ability to penetrate terminal defenses. The penetrating bomber is also likely to have greater prelaunch survivability than the current B-52 force and may not represent such a high-value target for enemy defenses before it enters enemy airspace. On the other hand, given the cost differential between bombers and cruise missiles, almost any reasonable defense budget would allow the acquisition of many more cruise missiles than penetrating bombers; defense saturation is in part a function of the total number of penetrators, whether they are bombers or cruise missiles. In fact, any force made up solely of penetrating bombers will almost certainly be too small to saturate Soviet defenses in more than a few local areas. And the bomber has a much larger radar cross section than a cruise missile and should thus be easier to detect.

These arguments suggest that the mixed capability, standoff and penetration, B-52 force planned for the early 1980s is preferable to a primarily standoff force. However, maintaining that mixed capability comes at a cost. The added weight and aerodynamic drag imposed by the externally mounted cruise missiles will place added demands on an already burdened tanker force if the B-52s are to maintain the range necessary to penetrate Soviet airspace, attack a full target set, and then return to a nonhostile location.[8] The B-52s will have to be outfitted with new avionics and penetration-assisting capabilities, and fewer bombers will survive

8. The fuel required by a bomber depends on the mission. Assuming that pilots who have targets in, say, the Moscow area must then have enough fuel to fly out to a friendly airfield makes the fuel requirements quite different from assuming that the plane is ditched as soon as it has covered its targets. Fuel and refueling requirements are thus in part a function of the tactics employed.

strategic attack operations to be reconstituted for subsequent operations. Also, the flexibility of the current bomber force allowing it to be launched on warning of attack and to loiter in anticipation of a recall or attack order may be eroded. Because of the added refueling requirements of the standoff-penetration bomber and the current constraints on tanker capabilities, a mixed force may not have much ability to loiter. This may mean that it must be decided soon after launch whether to recall the force or send it on to attack.

In any case, the mixed standoff-peneration force planned for the first phase of cruise missile deployments will present Soviet air defenses with a greater array of problems than a pure standoff force would. Whether these problems will remain significant in the late 1980s and 1990s depends on whether the B-52H and the FB-111 are retained as penetrating forces, since their ability to penetrate advanced Soviet air defenses is open to question. The development of a new penetrating bomber could affect not only the degree to which Soviet air defenses are stressed but also the degree to which the air-breathing force is able to achieve its target coverage goal.

Force Employment Capabilities

The targeting capabilities of a weapon system derive from four characteristics: the number of systems available, their accuracy, the warhead yield, and the probability that the warheads will hit the targets. These factors determine the kinds and numbers of targets that can be attacked effectively, the confidence that can be placed in the likely effectiveness of the attack, and the collateral effects of using the weapon system against particular targets. The cruise missile is widely considered attractive in all these ways. The planned force of cruise missiles is large, the missile's guidance system gives it high accuracy, which compensates for the low yield of the warhead, and the mix suggests a capability for precise attacks with limited collateral effects.

While these features suggest that cruise missiles could perform a range of important roles, their ultimate utility is their ability to attack classes of targets that represent gaps in the capabilities of other systems or to increase the effectiveness of attacks against targets currently covered by other weapons. The high accuracy of cruise missiles coupled with the limited counterforce capabilities of other strategic weapon systems has led to the suggestion that the cruise missile may be particularly valuable in the counterforce role. More recently, the potential usefulness of cruise missiles was enhanced by the revelation of an official strategic targeting doctrine emphasizing the capability for precise and limited attacks against a range of military, political, and economic targets in a "countervailing strategy." Not only does this strategy substantially increase the potential target list, but it also reveals the weaknesses resulting from the vulnerability of ICBMs and the lack of accuracy and the command and control problems of the SLBM force. However, the cruise missile, too, has limitations that constrain its ability to carry out the missions associated with this new strategy.

The extent of the broader target list was suggested by William Beecher in an article describing the presidential authorization of this strategy. The list included the following Soviet assets:

—700 leadership targets involving underground shelters and therefore, constituting hard targets;

—2,000 strategic force targets including 1,400 ICBM silos plus command-control bunkers, nuclear storage sites, and strategic air and naval facilities most of which are also hard targets;

—3,000 "other" military targets including 500 airfields, military units, supply depots, and key transportation hubs, most of which are soft targets and many of which are large area targets;

—200 to 400 "key factories" which would presumably be war mobilization and production facilities and would be relatively soft area targets.[9]

This list may not include the precise target sets envisioned in the current countervailing strategy, but it does provide a base against which to measure rough requirements for target coverage in this strategy. Because many of the targets on the list are collocated within the lethal radii of at least some nuclear weapons, the number of warheads required to attack them is less than for the total number of targets listed. On the other hand, more than one warhead may be required to destroy some of the targets on the list because of either their hardness against nuclear effects or the size of the target area relative to the yield of the weapons involved. Furthermore, the list does not include the full range of urban-industrial targets normally associated with an ultimate, punitive attack, the capabilities for which are to be held in reserve.

However rough these numbers may be, they do suggest several things about the target coverage potential of the total U.S. strategic force. First, there are some 2,700 hard targets on this list whose exact hardness is

9. *Boston Globe*, July 27, 1980.

unknown and highly variable. Only the Minuteman force and the bombers have any significant hard-target kill capability at present. Because the penetration ability of B-52s is uncertain and there are delays in bomber weapon delivery, the hard-target mission is generally assumed to fall to the ICBM force. However, against very hard targets, only the 300 Minuteman III missiles with the new, high-yield Mk 12A warhead present any significant threat. But even if all 300 were to survive, they would offer only 900 warheads for use against hard targets, and the vulnerability of the force makes relying on it for essential missions questionable.

More than 3,000 soft targets on the list might logically be the objects of SLBM attacks if it were not for two major constraints on using SLBMs this way. First, because of delays in the Trident submarine production program and the possible removal of the Poseidon submarines from the fleet, the number of SLBMs may decline beginning in the late 1980s. The Trident SLBM will have only eight warheads per missile as opposed to the nine-to-ten average of the Poseidons, which will decrease total warheads. This trend will not be reversed until the late 1980s or early 1990s when the Trident II missile is deployed, and only then if twelve to fourteen warheads are placed on each missile. Second, the SLBM force is currently the most survivable strategic force element and is therefore the most logical candidate to be withheld as the ultimate urban-industrial destruction threat and as a reserve force.

The expected decline in SLBM forces in the late 1980s is partially offset by the greater on-station rate of the Trident submarines and the more accurate higher-yield warheads of the Trident SLBMs. The target coverage implications of these changes in the SLBM force are shown in table 5-1. The names in the table refer to the submarine type, while the SLBMs are referred to by their standard model numbers (Poseidon SLBMs as C-3, Trident I SLBMs as C-4, and Trident II SLBMs as D-5). The ability to cover soft point targets is shown by the number of warheads, and the ability to cover moderately hard targets is shown by the kill probability against 100 pounds per square inch (psi) targets and in turn the number of such targets that could be destroyed (assuming that each warhead attacked a separate target).

Several things must be kept in mind in interpreting these numbers. First, they indicate only the number of SLBMs on day-to-day alert; the number of missiles available would increase about 30 percent if the forces were generated. Second, the original creator of the table apparently focused on 100 psi targets to show that the 1992 force, even if it con-

Table 5-1. *Target Coverage Potential of Submarine-Launched Ballistic Missiles*

Year and weapon system	Number of missiles	Percent on station	Warheads on station	Kill probability against moderately hard targets (100 psi)	Targets destroyed
1982					
Poseidon C-3	304	55	1,505	0.6	903
Poseidon C-4	192	55	845	0.71	600
Trident C-4	24	66	127	0.71	90
Total	520	...	2,477	...	1,593
1992					
Trident C-4	288	66	1,521	0.71	1,080
Trident D-5	96	66	887	0.999	886
Total	384	...	2,408	...	1,966

Source: Les Aspin, "Judge Not by Numbers Alone," *Bulletin of Atomic Scientists*, June 1980, p. 32. We have added the column showing the number of warheads to illustrate soft target coverage.

sisted of fewer SLBMs and fewer warheads, could actually destroy more moderately hard targets. In any case, all the numbers in table 5-1 overstate target kill potential because the calculations do not take into account missile reliability or prelaunch survival. Normally, prelaunch survival of the SLBM force is not thought to be a problem; however, if a substantial portion of the SLBMs was withheld, even Soviet antisubmarine capabilities should be able to inflict some attrition on the U.S. nuclear ballistic missile submarines (SSBNs) over the days or weeks that could then be involved. Especially if part of the SLBM force was withheld as an "assured destruction" reserve force, these numbers suggest the limitations of SLBMs in covering even the soft targets in the list noted above.

All this suggests that there will be inadequate coverage of the hard point, soft point, and soft area targets associated with the countervailing strategy. This raises the questions of what targets the cruise missile can be most effective against, and what force size and performance characteristics the cruise missile force must have to be effective against those targets.

A simple means of describing the relative advantages of the various strategic force elements in attacking different target types is to compare the kill probability of different weapon systems against targets of different hardness, taking into account the combined effects of prelaunch survivability, system reliability, defense penetration, and target damage. Table 5-2 summarizes those kill probabilities for a U.S. first strike (in which

Table 5-2. *Kill Probability of U.S. Strategic Weapons in a First Strike against Various Targets*

	Kill probability (percent)				
Weapon system	5 psi target	20 psi target	100 psi target	500 psi target	2,000 psi target
Minuteman II	80	80	80	70	43
Minuteman IIIa	80	80	80	73	48
Titan II	80	80	71	38	17
Poseidon C-3	80	67	30	10	4
Trident C-4	80	77	46	18	7
Gravity bomb	68	68	68	68	64
Cruise missile	68	68	68	67	53
Short-range attack missile	68	68	60	32	14

prelaunch survival is 100 percent), using the yield and circular error probable (CEP) estimates presented in congressional testimony by Paul Nitze.[10] It is also assumed that the probability of the ICBMs and SLBMs arriving on target is 80 percent (arrival probability includes only reliability); for the bombers carrying cruise missiles a combined reliability and probability of penetration of 68 percent is assumed (80 percent reliability and 85 percent penetration probability).

According to the values in table 5-2, all U.S. strategic weapon systems are almost equally effective against Soviet soft targets in a first strike, though the penetration probability of the bomber weapons makes them somewhat less so. Minuteman missiles, gravity bombs, and cruise missiles are relatively effective against targets of 500 psi or more, the Minuteman missiles doing better against the moderately hard targets and the bomber-carried weapons doing better against the very hard targets (2,000 psi). In a U.S. first strike, the cruise missile thus would have a relative advantage against very hard targets, though many other systems are available to compete for this role.

More realistic are the numbers associated with a U.S. second strike against the Soviet Union (table 5-3). The prelaunch survivability of the ICBM is assumed to be 10 percent (consistent with Defense Department estimates for the mid-1980s)[11] and that of the SLBM 95 percent. For the

10. See Paul H. Nitze's statement in *Congressional Record*, daily edition (July 12, 1979), p. S-10078.
11. *Department of Defense Annual Report, Fiscal Year 1981*, p. 6.

Table 5-3. *Kill Probability of U.S. Strategic Weapons in a Second Strike against Various Targets*

Weapon system	Kill probability (percent)				
	5 psi target	20 psi target	100 psi target	500 psi target	2,000 psi target
Minuteman II	8	8	8	7	4
Minuteman IIIa	8	8	8	7	5
Titan II	8	8	7	4	2
Poseidon C-3	76	64	28	10	4
Trident C-4	76	73	44	17	7
Gravity bomb	56	56	56	56	53
Cruise missile	56	56	56	55	43
Short-range attack missile	56	56	49	26	12

bomber–cruise-missile force, a combined probability of survival and penetration of 70 percent is assumed.

Table 5-3 makes it obvious that no element of the ICBM force would be very effective against any type of target after a Soviet first strike, given the low prelaunch survival assumed. The SLBM force is most effective against relatively soft targets of less than 100 psi, as it has an arrival probability much greater than bomber-carried weapons and yet insufficient accuracy to destroy very hard targets. The bomber weapons are best used against hard targets because of their relative accuracy, though SRAMs perform only slightly better than SLBMs. Interestingly, gravity bombs may yet be preferred to cruise missiles in terms of kill probability if they achieve an equivalent probability of arrival (which can be expected with targets that are not terminally defended). This is because their much larger yield can more than offset the accuracy advantage of the cruise missile unless that advantage is large. That is, the CEP of the cruise missile would have to be about 40 percent lower than that of the gravity bomb for the cruise missile to enjoy an advantage. In any case, this simple calculation of the relative targeting advantages of various strategic systems suggests that the cruise missile is more or less equally effective across the range of target types and better than other systems (except gravity bombs) against hard targets.

The most important thing overlooked in this calculation of the preferred targeting emphasis of various strategic systems is that at present far less is known about the performance of the cruise missile than about that of other systems because it is still in development. This, of course, affects judgments about both the preferred targeting orientation and the size of the cruise missile force needed to perform a specific mission. The prelaunch survivability and penetration probability of the cruise missile, its accuracy, and the yield of the warhead can only be estimated.

Uncertainty about yield arises in part from which warhead is chosen. However, whatever the choice, uncertainty will remain, in part, because of the limitations on testing imposed by the various test ban treaties and, in part, because of our limited ability to measure the yield of a warhead accurately. If a new warhead is developed and deployed on part or all of the cruise missile force, the uncertainty will increase because of constraints on testing. It is widely assumed that the cruise missile could use an existing warhead design, specifically a Trident I (100-kiloton) or SRAM (200-kiloton) warhead. A new warhead for the cruise missile is also in design,[12] though its yield will probably be limited to 150 kilotons because larger warheads may not be tested under the currently imposed test ban. Thus a warhead yield of 100 to 200 kilotons is probably the appropriate range to consider.

Uncertainty about the CEP may be difficult to reduce irrespective of testing. Some of this uncertainty is currently due to a new and peculiar kind of guidance system, the performance of which will be better understood with testing, although the testing takes place over well-known and programmed test ranges. Yet the accuracy of a cruise missile, much more than that of a ballistic missile, is sensitive to the flight paths and the location of the target to be attacked. The accuracy of the maps used, the existence of distinctive features of the terrain, and the distance from the target at which the cruise missile can make its last "fix," all critically affect the proximity of the detonation to the target. The cruise missile may be, for example, more accurate in the summer than in the winter, when areas of the Soviet Union may be under heavy snow drifts that change the relative altitude of the terrain features. The accuracy of the cruise missile may also be affected by near-miss SAM attacks that do not destroy the missile but deflect it from its course. The CEP estimates that have been used in the literature vary from as little as 100 feet or less to as high as 600 feet. For analytic purposes it is appropriate to consider at least this wide a range of potential accuracies, though recognizing that the number may be much higher, especially for specific targets.

12. "Nine Nuclear Weapons Devices Scheduled for U.S. Production," *Aviation Week and Space Technology,* June 20, 1977, p. 97.

Figure 5-1. *Cruise Missile Single-Shot Kill Probability in Relation to Point Target Hardness*

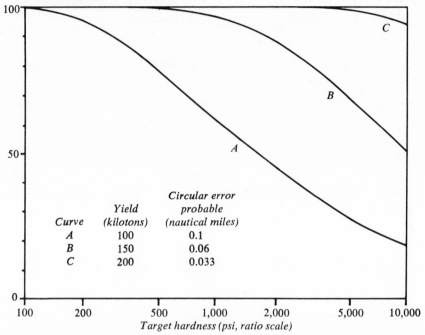

Single-shot kill probability (percent)

Curve	Yield (kilotons)	Circular error probable (nautical miles)
A	100	0.1
B	150	0.06
C	200	0.033

Target hardness (psi, ratio scale)

Based on these estimates of the potential yield and CEP of the cruise missile, we can consider the implications of the uncertainties about its performance characteristics for its ability to attack various target types. Figure 5-1 depicts various mixes of yield and CEP for the single-shot kill probability (SSPK—the kill probability of a warhead that arrives on target and detonates) of the cruise missile against targets of varying hardness. The two outside curves indicate the range of SSPKs associated with the worst and best combinations of yield and CEP. The worst (A, yield 100 kilotons, CEP 0.1 nautical mile) results in a 100 percent SSPK for targets of 100 psi or less, but this falls off rapidly above that hardness and is low for targets whose hardness is in the range associated with Soviet missile silos. At the other extreme (C), a cruise missile with a 200-kiloton yield and a CEP of 0.033 nautical mile (200 feet) will have an SSPK of nearly 100 percent for any conceivable target. In between these extremes (B), a weapon with a 150-kiloton yield and a

Figure 5-2. *Sensitivity of Point Target Single-Shot Kill Probability to Cruise Missile Yield*

Single-shot kill probability (percent)

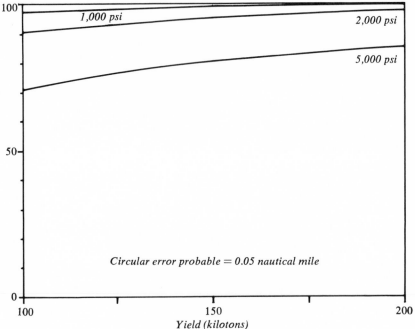

CEP equivalent to 360 feet will have a high SSPK against all targets except those that are superhard.

The message of this figure is that, if the cruise missile can survive and penetrate enemy defenses, it will be able to destroy most point targets even with an unfavorable mix of yield and CEP. However, against hard targets, the effectiveness of the system is sensitive to the ability of the cruise missile to achieve very low CEPs. The relatively greater importance of CEP is illustrated in figures 5-2 and 5-3. For example, for a CEP of 0.05 nautical mile (figure 5-2), variations in the yield of the warhead have little effect on kill probability for targets of 2,000 psi hardness or less and not much more effect for harder targets. Alternatively, for a warhead yield of 150 kilotons (figure 5-3), the CEP of the system is important to its kill probability against targets of more than 500 psi hardness. In any case, the figures indicate that the cruise missile may have to have a CEP of 0.05 to 0.06 nautical mile to effectively threaten Soviet missile

Figure 5-3. *Sensitivity of Point Target Single-Shot Kill Probability to Cruise Missile CEP*

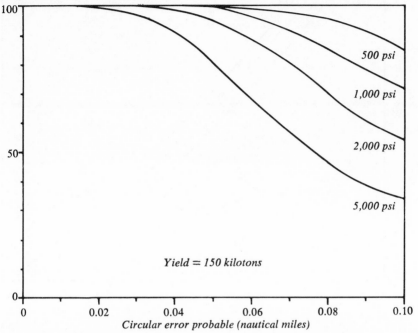

silos. This conclusion is based not only on these calculations but also on previously cited calculations of the size of the cruise missile force potentially capable of surviving a Soviet attack. Likely prelaunch and defense penetration attrition would limit the attacking force to one warhead per missile silo. Thus, unless the single-shot kill probability of arriving warheads is relatively high for the cruise missile against hard targets, planning to launch the weapons against those targets instead of other vital targets may be an inefficient allocation of available weapons.

It is more difficult to assess the kill probability of cruise missiles against urban-industrial assets because such targets tend to be less discrete than point targets, because there is no public target data base, and because the methods for calculating kill probabilities against area targets are less precise. (Destruction of area targets such as urban concentration is, unlike point military targets, a matter of degree.) The lethality of nuclear weapons against soft targets depends primarily on the yield of the weapon

Figure 5-4. *Lethal Area of Cruise Missiles against Soft Targets*

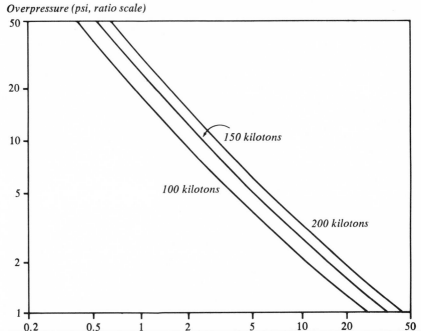

Overpressure (psi, ratio scale)

Lethal area (square nautical miles, ratio scale)

and the overpressure required to destroy urban targets. But claims of the potential effectiveness of Soviet civil defense programs to protect both population and industry have made the overpressure requirement questionable.

Figure 5-4 therefore depicts the lethal area of cruise missiles with yields varying from 100 to 200 kilotons against soft area targets. The figure indicates, for example, that a 200-kiloton warhead would have a lethal area of roughly 6.2 square nautical miles against 5 psi targets, whereas a 100-kiloton warhead would have a lethal area of only 3.9 square nautical miles against the same type of target. A higher yield would provide an equivalent amount of lethal area against harder targets. For example, for a lethal area of 2 square nautical miles, a 200-kiloton weapon would be effective against targets nearly 60 percent harder than targets against which 100-kiloton weapons are effective.

Calculating the potential of a nuclear weapon against area targets is difficult because the lethal area of the weapons does not conform to the size of the target area. This raises the problem of patterning weapons across the target area, an important task if weapons are to be used efficiently.

How much damage can be done to Soviet urban areas with various cruise missile options? Because there is no public urban-industrial target data base for the Soviet Union, two simplifying assumptions are usually made in assessing urban-industrial damage potential. First, the calculations are made easier by assuming that each city represents a single area target.[13] Second, the value of an urban area is assumed to be equal to its population. We use these simplifying assumptions and the data on Soviet population and city size found in Geoffrey Kemp and in *Current Digest of the Soviet Press*.[14]

With population as a surrogate for urban-industrial area targets, figure 5-5 illustrates the number of delivered warheads that would be required to kill various percentages of the Soviet population (in 1970 urban population in the Soviet Union amounted to 48 percent of the total population). The high and low curves show high and low estimates of cruise missile yields paired with the widely accepted highest and lowest estimates of the hardness of urban-industrial targets (10 and 5 psi, respectively). The center curve represents the middle range of a 150-kiloton weapon and target hardness of 7 psi. All cities with a population larger than 10,000 are included in the data set. About 2,400 to 5,400 delivered cruise missiles would be needed to destroy the areas encompassing this population. Alternatively, if only 25 to 33 percent of the population had to be destroyed (consistent with the standard "assured destruction" damage-level assumptions), the required number of warheads detonating on target would vary between 740 and 3,300, with 1,200 a "best estimate" based on the middle-range curve in figure 5-5.

13. If detailed target data were available at a lower level of aggregation, it would clearly be preferable to use them. Since the Soviet Union is a closed society, such information is not readily available.

14. In Geoffrey Kemp, *Nuclear Forces for Medium Powers, Part I: Targets and Weapons Systems*, Adelphi Papers 106 (London: International Institute for Strategic Studies, 1974), the 1970 population is given for all Soviet cities of over 100,000. Kemp also gives the population density for about a dozen cities and suggests that it would be some 9,300 people per square mile for the others. "Preliminary Report on the 1970 Census," *Current Digest of the Soviet Press*, vol. 22 (May 5–July 28, 1970), p. 24, gives the number of cities in each population size range in 1970. From these were taken the number of cities of 10,000 to 100,000, which includes three ranges. These ranges were then divided into two parts each, and an average population calculated for each part. Using the population densities assumed by Kemp, we calculated a land area for all the cities.

Figure 5-5. *Effectiveness of a Cruise Missile Force against Soviet Population*

Percentage of population killed

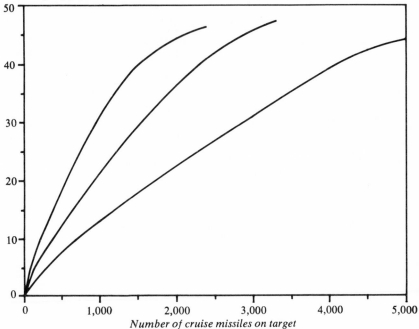

Number of cruise missiles on target

The arrival probability of the cruise missile force is important in planning target coverage. As noted, the prelaunch survivability of the B-52 cruise missile carrier could vary from 74 to 90 percent in the mid-1980s. Similarly, the reliability and penetration probability for the carriers and cruise missiles could each be as high as 90 percent, though they are more likely to fall around 80 percent or even lower.[15] Therefore, the combined arrival probability of a cruise missile could be as high as 80 percent or as low as 50 percent or less. In considering the implications of arrival probability for cruise missile targeting options and force size requirements, we assume the arrival probability to be between 50 and 80 percent.

Most analyses of strategic forces set force requirements for various objectives in terms of delivered warheads, initially assuming a 100 percent probability of arrival (PA). When the arrival probability is less than

15. Alton H. Quanbeck and Barry M. Blechman, *Strategic Forces: Issues for the Mid-Seventies* (Brookings Institution, 1973), p. 73.

100 percent, these analyses then divide the delivered warhead requirement by the arrival probability to determine the actual force size necessary to achieve this objective. This correction factor can be called the coverage multiplier (C); then $C = 1/PA$.

While standard analyses simply multiply C by the delivered weapon requirement to determine the necessary force size, such a procedure ignores the inefficiencies of a less than 100 percent arrival probability. For example, two warheads with an arrival probability of 50 percent are not as effective as one with an arrival probability of 100 percent, since even if they do arrive independently, they will only cover a target with a total 75 percent probability. The difference here must be captured by an inefficiency multiplier, which increases the force requirement enough to offset inefficiency in target coverage.[16] Figure 5-6 shows the potential

16. To extend this example, assume a set of 100 targets. Achieving 75 percent coverage of that target set would take 75 warheads with a 100 percent arrival probability or 200 warheads with a 50 percent arrival probability. While the coverage multiplier would increase the basic requirement of 75 delivered warheads to 150, an inefficiency multiplier of 1.333 would be needed to increase the 150 to the full 200 warheads necessary with a 50 percent delivery probability. If 150 warheads with a 50 percent arrival probability were assigned, 75 would arrive on a target, but only 62.5 targets would receive a warhead—12.5 receiving two warheads, and 50 receiving only one. The assignment of 200 such warheads would mean that 25 targets could be expected to receive two warheads, 50 targets to receive one, and 25 targets none.

Three important points can be derived from the above example. First, inefficiency occurs only when more than one warhead must be assigned to a target in order to achieve a high enough probability of warhead delivery. Thus only if 50 or fewer targets out of the 100 must be covered by weapons with a 50 percent arrival probability need the coverage multiplier be applied. Second, as the coverage requirement increases above the arrival probability and moves toward 100 percent, the inefficiency multiplier increases significantly. Third, the actual effectiveness of an attack that involves an inefficiency multiplier depends in part on the kill probability of the warheads, as some targets will receive more than one warhead, increasing the probability of destroying those targets above the probability with a single warhead as long as the SSPK of each warhead is less than 100 percent.

The latter point suggests that an important difference must be taken into account in calculating the arrival probability against hard point and soft area targets. In the above calculations, it was assumed that a weapon delivered to a soft target would destroy that target as long as it covered the target, and soft area targets were divided into multiple aim points to allow such coverage. Thus for soft targets a second or third warhead delivered would add nothing, being instead an inefficient use of warheads. However, against a hard target, a second warhead normally would increase the kill probability, though by less than it would have increased the kill probability if it had been the first warhead to arrive. For example, if the warhead's SSPK was 80 percent, a second warhead would increase the kill probability against the target to 96 percent, a net increase of 16 percent over the 80 percent damage that it could

Figure 5-6. *Impact of Inefficient Target Coverage on Weapon Requirements*

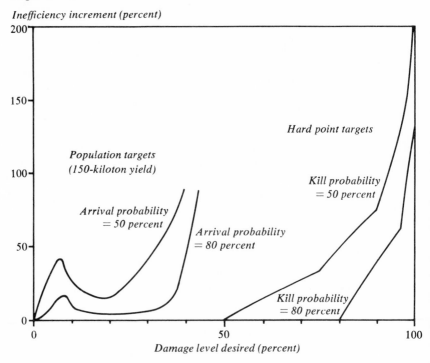

magnitude of the inefficiency multiplier for either hard or soft targets for the two values of arrival probability assumed. For soft area targets, inefficiency begins to creep in even at very low damage percentages because of the differing values of the various target areas, requiring that some be hit by multiple weapons very early. Actually, the values shown for soft area targets are probably too low, since a large part of the data base is assumed to have a uniform population density (requiring uniform weapon allocation rather than multiple targeting of what are really more

---

have done if it had arrived at an undamaged target. The inefficiency in this case is therefore not the loss of the entire SSPK of this warhead, but rather the loss of 64 percent (80 minus 16), or four-fifths, of its potential. Since this loss will vary with the warhead's SSPK, it is better to calculate both the coverage multiplier and the inefficiency multiplier for hard targets on the basis of the warhead's kill probability, which is the product of its SSPK and arrival probability. This procedure is illustrated in the text.

valuable targets).[17] Even with these numbers, though, the magnitude of a potential assured destruction requirement becomes clear: for a warhead arrival probability of 50 percent, the coverage multiplier is 2, and the inefficiency multiplier is about 1.4 (a 40 percent inefficiency increment) at 25 percent fatalities; thus the previously mentioned best estimate of the assured destruction requirement of 1,200 delivered warheads becomes an alert force requirement of about 3,360 warheads (assuming the cruise missile force must perform the assured destruction mission on its own).

The inefficiency multiplier calculations in figure 5-6 for hard point targets is based on the kill probability of the warheads rather than their arrival probability. Since the single-shot kill probability is at most 100 percent, the kill probability of a single warhead can be no larger than the arrival probability, and could be a fair amount less. For example, if the kill probability was 50 percent and the desired damage level against 1,000 uniform hard targets was 80 percent, the coverage multiplier would be 1.6, and the inefficiency multiplier would be about 1.5, which combine to mean that roughly 2,400 warheads must be allocated against the 1,000 targets. Note that because hard targets are assumed to be uniform in value in figure 5-6, there is no inefficiency until the desired damage level is higher than the warhead kill probability, since until that point is reached, there is no reason to allocate more than one warhead per target. However, if some of the hard targets were assigned values higher than the others, inefficiency would begin to become a problem at the point at which multiple warheads were first assigned to the more valuable targets.

The message of the figure is clear. When the arrival probability falls below the rough 80 percent maximum that we assume, force requirements are increased much more quickly than is normally assumed in the strategic literature. That is, not only does the coverage multiplier increase significantly, but the inefficiency multiplier also becomes much larger as the arrival probability decreases. Thus while most of the focus on cruise missiles has been on their accuracy and their relatively high kill probability against even very hard targets, their uncertain arrival probability makes the presumed effectiveness of the force questionable.

In making these calculations we have taken no account of the possible

17. On the other hand, a variation in the density known to the attacker would allow more valuable targets to be struck first, reducing the number of delivered warheads necessary to reach any given damage level. These two effects tend to cancel out, especially if the arrival probability is 50 percent or less.

differences in arrival probability at the various target types. One important reason for these differences is that the Soviet Union is more likely to defend with terminal defenses its more highly valued targets, most of which will be hard point targets. Cruise missiles (and gravity bombs) may be even less effective against Soviet missile silos, leadership bunkers, and other critical targets than the above calculations suggest.[18]

A second important caveat about the effectiveness of any air-breathing force in a hard target kill role has to do with the length of time it takes for such a force to reach distant targets. If the targets were Soviet missiles, the Soviet Union would have considerable time to launch them before cruise missiles or bombers could arrive. On the other hand, it can be argued that the USSR is unlikely to launch its entire missile force. Therefore, even a slow attack by cruise missiles or bombers could destroy withheld missiles and eliminate the ability to reload silos.

By way of summarizing cruise missile requirements for attacking hard targets, we can consider the force size and system effectiveness necessary to attain each of two objectives. One objective would be to achieve a 70 percent damage level against Soviet missile silos (totaling 1,400 targets) either as an acceptable level of second-strike capabilities or as a level that might effectively disrupt whatever force remained if it was not destroyed. The second objective would be to destroy 90 percent of the Soviet silos whether they might contain missiles or not to eliminate the possibility of a Soviet ICBM reserve force. Figure 5-7 illustrates the potential cruise missile force size needed to achieve these alternative objectives at various kill probabilities assumed for a single cruise missile, which take into account the combined effects of prelaunch survivability, system reliability, penetration probability, yield, and CEP.

The range of kill probabilities together with the uncertainty ranges on arrival probability, yield, and CEP defined above can change the force size needed for either of the damage objectives. If, for example, the arrival probability was 80 percent and the single-shot kill probability was 90 percent (a combined kill probability of 72 percent), the lower damage goal would require about 1,350 cruise missiles on alert and the high goal about 2,650. If, however, the arrival probability slipped to 50 percent (a net kill probability of 45 percent), the alert cruise missile force requirement would vary from about 2,850 to 5,450. This means that, with

18. According to chapter 2, there is no evidence of significant air defenses around Soviet ICBM fields. Such defenses could easily be deployed, however, and in any case many hardened command and control centers appear to be defended.

Figure 5-7. *Cruise Missile Requirements for a Countersilo Role*

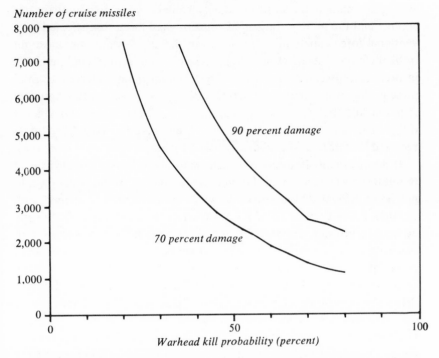

Number of cruise missiles

Warhead kill probability (percent)

the ALCM and even GLCM force sizes nominally considered for the middle to late 1980s, there is considerable doubt about the ability of cruise missiles to carry out effective countersilo attacks even if the time-of-arrival problems are ignored. The ALCM force of somewhat more than 3,000 missiles certainly would not be able to cover a large fraction of the 2,700 hard targets (almost twice as many as the 1,400 silos used in the countersilo calculations above) associated with the countervailing strategy.

Not nearly enough ALCMs can be expected to arrive to cover all of the approximately 3,000 other military targets. How, then, might an allocation of weapons be determined against this target set? One method would be to assign more time-urgent targets in this set to other systems with shorter times of flight. However, many of the remaining targets, such as conventional force assets, are mobile and therefore not readily targetable with cruise missiles. Allocating cruise missiles to fixed military facilities that are not time urgent in general means that the cruise missiles used against other military targets would have limited effect on the course of a strategic campaign. If a strategic attack resulted from an escalating theater conflict and the military targets of concern were those that affected conventional force capabilities, the effects of the attack would be uncertain or likely to have an effect on the conflict only over a protracted period— in both cases because of the inability to target mobile targets. Even if these problems are ignored, 2,600 to 4,800 alert cruise missiles would be required to inflict significant damage on the military targets on this list if their arrival probability was 80 percent, and 5,400 to 10,200 would be required if their arrival probability was only 50 percent.

If the cruise missiles were used against urban-industrial targets instead of military targets, many of the inherent limitations of the system would not be as critical. Urban areas are much more difficult to defend with terminal defenses because of the large areas involved, the ability of the attacker to saturate defenses, and the damage caused if even a few weapons leak through the defenses. On the other hand, if a substantial level of potential damage is thought to be a necessary threat, the cruise missile force size requirement may be relatively large even if the probability of defense penetration is high. We previously calculated the requirement for delivered weapons to destroy 25 to 33 percent of the Soviet population, the level normally associated with an assured destruction attack. Assuming an 80 percent arrival probability for 150-kiloton weapons against a 7 psi hard target area, the alert force requirement is 1,600 to 2,400 cruise missiles. If defenses can drive the arrival probability down to 50 percent, the alert force requirement becomes 3,100 to 5,150 cruise missiles. All of these numbers are higher than planned for day-to-day ALCM alert forces even at the conclusion of phase 2 deployments; thus ALCMs alone would be unable to carry out even an assured destruction attack (though they might come close).

However, the problem with the use of cruise missiles in the urban-industrial attack role is not the potential force size; the damage levels necessary for such a role are always an arguable matter. Rather, the problem is whether the cruise missile can effectively pose the threat of urban-industrial damage required by official U.S. force employment doctrine. Such a threat is supposed to be withholdable and deter Soviet attacks on U.S. cities. But the ALCM force is difficult to withhold without endangering its survivability. Also, assuming that Soviet civil defense activities are well under way or essentially complete by the time attacks start, ALCM attacks on urban-industrial areas may result in lower damage levels (perhaps 10 percent or less in terms of prompt effects) than would otherwise be expected, even if these attacks are much heavier than suggested here. The Soviet leadership would probably be more mobile than the general urban population, making the cruise missiles, with their long flight times, relatively ineffective against leadership-related targets. On the other hand, many of the assets of the urban population and the leadership (housing, records, and other capital assets), as well as industrial facilities, would probably not be as mobile, and fairly high damage levels could be expected against such assets.

In summary, then, a very large cruise missile force would be needed to destroy a large percentage of the Soviet fixed assets associated with any target set. In particular, against the full range of military, political, and urban-industrial targets suggested by a countervailing strategy, the assessments above indicate that it would take between 6,100 and 11,050 alert cruise missiles with an 80 percent arrival probability to cover the entire target base. If the arrival probability was only 50 percent, 12,450 to 23,100 cruise missiles would be needed. Inefficiencies thus mean that more than twice as many cruise missiles would be required to do the job.[19] In any case, the currently planned ALCM purchase can in no way cover all these requirements, nor can it fully meet the requirements for any individual target set.

Contribution to Overall Force Posture

The third dimension by which to assess the utility of cruise missiles concerns the attributes of the overall force posture that are deemed essential and the extent to which the cruise missile contributes to them. As defined by official policy, four attributes are particularly important and provide standards against which to assess the contributions of cruise missiles: (1) the maintenance of overall strategic capabilities that are "essentially equivalent" to those of the Soviet Union; (2) the ability to employ elements of the forces in limited, controlled, and flexible attack operations while presenting incentives for Soviet restraint in response; (3) the ability to withhold a major fraction of the forces as a punitive attack threat without endangering the survivability and effective use of

19. The doubling of required warheads in moving from an 80 to a 50 percent arrival probability is in contrast to a 60 percent increase that would be projected from the coverage multipliers.

the withheld force; and (4) the ability to retain an enduringly survivable reserve force for purposes of managing unpredictable postconflict conditions.

Concern about the strategic balance has come to focus on the mid-1980s "window of vulnerability" suggested by the trend lines of U.S.-Soviet force ratios and on the unilateral Soviet possession of an effective, prompt countersilo capability. Each of these elements is considered important for its potential effects on the perceptions of third parties about the stability of the balance as much as, if not more than, for its implications for the probability of nuclear war.

The planned ALCM deployment will have relatively little effect on the unfavorable trends in force ratios. The large force levels of the United States and the Soviet Union mean that very substantial and unmatched increases by one or the other side would be necessary to affect the trend lines significantly. The deployment of cruise missiles in particular will have less effect than their total number suggests because they will replace weapons already deployed on the B-52 force to a considerable extent.

The cruise missile also offers little relief from the problems posed by a superior Soviet countersilo capability. Even if the cruise missile can effectively threaten hard targets, the uncertain and "slow" counterforce threat posed by cruise missiles cannot offset the qualities of the Soviet first-strike threat. This is true if for no other reason than that the Soviet threat is driving the United States to a very expensive mobile ICBM basing option, and there is no reason to believe that the U.S. cruise missile will have the same effect on the Soviet force posture.

The most important contribution of the cruise missile to the strategic balance may be the effect on perceptions of the balance that derive from the advanced technological qualities of the system. Unless and until the United States deploys the MX missile, the only technologically advanced strategic systems the United States will deploy, unlike the Soviet Union with its plethora of new systems, will be the Trident submarine and missile and the cruise missile. However, because of the attention and publicity that has been given to the cruise missile, much of the advantage to be gained may already have been gained. And if the cruise missile does not live up to its advance billing, the effects may be negative.

In its capabilities for flexible and limited attack, the cruise missile appears to have more disadvantages than advantages. On the surface, its relatively low yield and high accuracy suggest a potential for discriminating and effective limited attacks. However, most important Soviet targets are located well in the interior of the Soviet Union; a cruise missile launched at interior targets will fly over or near many other potential targets and may create confusion about its actual objective. While the damage caused by a cruise missile may be discriminating, it may not be as easy for the Soviet Union to discern the purpose of the attack while it is in progress (and it will be in progress for many hours). This potential problem may be exacerbated because, to ensure defense penetration and target destruction, a large number of cruise missiles may have to be used against specific targets, particularly high-value targets protected by terminal defenses. In turn, these larger numbers would increase the general size of the attack, increase the potential collateral damage, and make it more difficult for the Russians to determine that the attack was indeed intended to be limited.

Retargeting is another dimension important to flexible attack capabilities, because of the difficulty of predicting the contingency and therefore the appropriate targets. A number of technical constraints limit the ability to retarget cruise missiles. Since they depend on terrain maps for their guidance, retargeting would require the availability of these maps for all possible targets, including some that may not have been programmed into massive attack planning. To guarantee accuracy, the maps would have to be detailed enough to give precise terrain fixes fairly close to each potential target. The problem of storing such maps alone would severely limit the capability to retarget an ALCM, especially once its carrier was airborne. Retargeting would also require a wealth of other information, such as defense locations, accessible air corridors, and, for ALCMs, refueling possibilities for the carrier aircraft.

An essential force posture attribute is the ability to withhold a substantial fraction of the forces indefinitely, especially to withhold a credible threat against urban-industrial centers. Two general features of an ALCM make it difficult to withhold without threatening its potential effectiveness. First is, of course, the poor survivability of the ALCM carrier force if left on the ground. On the other hand, it would be extremely difficult to keep this force on airborne alert because of crew fatigue, limits on tanker availability and survivability, and limits on the mechanical endurance of the aircraft. Even if the force was kept on ground alert and was not attacked, crew endurance, maintenance limitations, and logistical requirements would limit overall system endurance, especially if the force was dispersed to increase survivability. Although these limitations are common to any bomber force, the potentially lower prelaunch survival of an ALCM carrier makes them greater for a cruise missile bomber force.

All of these considerations are overwhelmed by the survivability the bomber force gains when launched on warning of attack. Although the cruise missile mounted on the B-52 may decrease the time available for deciding whether to recall the force or to execute the attack because of increased tanker requirements, the fundamental problem in making such a decision is the potentially increased vulnerability of the bomber–cruise-missile force if it is recalled. Considerable time is required to change crews, refuel, and perform maintenance tasks on recalled carriers before they can be launched again. Also, one can only imagine the problems associated with a series of limited attacks, each of which might call for launching the cruise missile force. Again, while these problems are common to any bomber force, the greater support needed by an ALCM force exacerbates them. Although conceivably some bombers could be staged out of reserve airfields, an ALCM force would be likely to quickly lose coherence if forced to adopt such measures.

These weaknesses suggest that the ALCM may not be a good candidate for an enduring reserve role. On the other hand, such a reserve force element could be generated by the recovery and reconstitution of ALCM carriers or aircraft that have aborted their missions. Mobilization of assets is another way to augment the strategic reserve forces by using ALCMs. ALCM carriers that had not been on alert but that had survived enemy attacks could be prepared for use, and in time other aircraft could be modified to carry ALCMs. Of course, a stockpile of cruise missiles would have to be available to arm the force.

If some ALCM carriers are used only in a standoff role, many are likely to survive and may be available for recovery and reconstitution. However, recovery would require, first, the availability of airfields of appropriate dimensions[20] within the range of the aircraft after completion of their missions, and then facilities (tankers and airfields) for staging these aircraft back to bases where they could be reconstituted. Reconstitution would involve supplying the carriers with more ALCMs as well as maintenance, fuel, and other supplies. Furthermore, the effectiveness of

---

20. While B-52s have relatively little trouble finding a runway at which to land, a B-52 loaded with fuel for takeoff requires the use of "landing gear" on each wing, which are separated by about 150 feet. Therefore, a B-52 that is reasonably full of fuel needs a runway at least 150 feet wide for takeoff, and few runways are this wide.

a reconstituted ALCM force would depend on the availability of targeting information and on the ability to establish new ALCM routes (including those occasioned by changes in terrain resulting from nuclear detonations) and program them into the missile guidance systems. Effective reuse of the ALCM carriers thus requires the enduring survival of a wide variety of assets necessary to generate or reconstitute the force and to use it effectively.

While an ALCM force does not appear to have the attributes necessary for withholding, many advocates of cruise missiles argue that SLCMs and GLCMs do have such attributes. However, both of these types of cruise missile would face significant problems as well. With SLCMs, the primary problem is that of command-control. Even for current SLBM forces, receipt of force-execution messages is apparently not very reliable. The SLCM force could be expected to have even more problems; its submarines would have to come closer to Soviet shores to cover comparable targets because of the shorter range of SLCMs than of Poseidon and especially Trident missiles. And the withheld force must be capable of performing a variety of flexible missions against a variety of target types determined during a conflict. Since both execution and targeting information would have to be sent to the SLCM force, messages would have to be considerably more detailed than at present, going beyond the likely capability of the force to receive such messages, especially in a hostile environment. At the same time, the SLCM submarines, which lack reconnaissance, damage assessment, and related capabilities, could not act independently. About the only mission withheld SLCMs could be expected to accomplish would be the destruction of fixed, urban-industrial assets as part of an eventual assured destruction attack, though even then there would be doubt about whether or not the execution message was received (since there would be no reasonable way to send confirmation of its receipt). Beyond these problems, the use of attack submarines as SLCM carriers might divert the submarines from their primary missions for some period of time (unless they were intended to move to their launch points for strategic missions *after* the conventional phase of the war), and the relatively small number of U.S. attack submarines makes this a doubtful strategy. Moreover, moving these submarines in close to the Soviet borders would increase their vulnerability to Soviet antisubmarine warfare; the force could well sustain losses sufficient to prevent its completing all of its missions. Finally, SLCMs would have to be stored in places that would otherwise be used for conventional armaments, and this would reduce the number of engagements a submarine could enter into before being forced to rearm.

The problem associated with withholding GLCMs is one of survivability and security. The GLCMs could not be held at their peacetime bases because there they would be too vulnerable to Soviet attack. They would have to be dispersed at locations well separated from each other and from other potential targets. In these locations, maintaining security for a protracted period of time could be very difficult, as assaults by paramilitary forces or even terrorists would be highly likely. Command and control might also be difficult in such locations; communications could be jammed, and the individual GLCM units would be unable to perform flexible missions independently, as in the case of SLCMs.

Conclusions

Cruise missiles can contribute to the functions of the triad by posing attack complications for the Soviet Union and by giving it an incentive to invest heavily in air defense. The lower prelaunch survivability of the cruise missile force than of a new penetrating bomber would pose lesser first-strike attack problems for the Soviet Union and increase uncertainty about how large a cruise missile force could be expected to survive a Soviet surprise attack. A new, more survivable bomber might also compel actions by the Soviet SLBM force that could, in themselves, provide effective strategic warning—actions that are not as necessary to make the B-52 vulnerable.

Furthermore, the cruise missile force, if it is not complemented by penetrating bombers, does not pose the same number or kind of air defense problems for the Soviet Union. The planned retention of the B-52G as penetrator as well as cruise missile carrier until the late 1980s serves a dual mission purpose but at the cost of further burdening a tanker force of already questionable capability and further limiting the penetration capabilities of the B-52G. The B-52H and the FB-111 may be retained as penetrators through the late 1980s and into the 1990s, but the penetration capabilities of these aging aircraft is questionable. Thus some combination of an ALCM force with a new penetrating bomber would appear to be an optimal choice.

There are potential constraints affecting the use of cruise missiles against virtually all types of targets. To be effective against hard targets, the CEP of the cruise missile must prove to be extremely small, although, since the weapon system is still under development, the reliability of CEP estimates against particular targets is unknown at present. Also, the pre-launch survivability of the force must be very high for there to be enough weapons to cover a significant number of hard targets, and the penetration probability must be very high for the same reason. Even if all of these characteristics are satisfied, the prolonged time of flight of cruise missiles makes their use questionable against hard targets that must be struck quickly. Furthermore, high-value hard targets are more likely to be protected by terminal defenses, which are particularly threatening to cruise missiles. Therefore, cruise missiles probably will not be as effective against hard targets as will some form of ballistic missile.

Use of cruise missiles against other military targets, many of which are soft, is limited by the fact that these targets are mobile, movable, or of value for only a short time. If the purpose of attacking them is to have some near-term effect on the ability of the Soviet Union to carry on a conflict, this limitation may significantly reduce the utility of cruise missiles in this role, for which ballistic missiles (with their shorter time of flight) seem preferable, too.

Cruise missiles may only be effective (as an independent force) against urban-industrial targets, which are generally vulnerable to the missile. Defense saturation makes some "leakage" and resulting damage virtually certain. Whether the planned cruise missile force is sufficiently large to assure the performance of this mission depends on what damage level criteria are established. But there are two caveats. First, the urban-industrial damage threat is supposed to be withholdable for a substantial time, but the cruise missile force cannot be relied on to survive attack and endure for protracted periods and still be ready to act upon orders from the national command authority. The survivability of the force depends on its being used promptly. Second, the submarine-launched ballistic missile is the one most often associated with the withheld threat against urban-industrial targets. If the cruise missiles were used in this role, what would be the purpose of the SLBMs? One alternative might be to use them against other military targets, although accuracy requirements against many of those targets might limit their utility until more accurate Trident missiles, especially the Trident II, entered the force.

In achieving overall strategic balance objectives, the cruise missile would contribute relatively little to offsetting unfavorable trends in the balance or to offsetting the Soviet counterforce advantage. And in its capability for flexible and limited attacks, it has a number of short-comings. In short, the utility of the cruise missile in contributing to the operational purposes of the strategic forces is limited in many respects. It is certainly no cure for current shortcomings in the posture as a whole; rather, solutions to many existing problems have yet to be found. In the meantime, acquisition should proceed in full recognition of the limitations of the system, and the size of the cruise missile force should only match the roles it can realistically perform.

CHAPTER SIX

War in Europe: Nuclear and Conventional Options

ROGER H. PALIN

IN ANY CONFRONTATION in Europe between NATO and the Warsaw Pact, the utility of cruise missiles cannot be assessed from the military standpoint alone, since no weapon system, least of all a nuclear one, can be divorced from the political context. Because cruise missiles have potential application within the full spectrum of NATO military capabilities, they will be subject more than most systems to the many conflicting political considerations that influence NATO strategy.

Long-Range Theater Nuclear Missions

Nowhere is the interaction of political and military factors more complex than in the long-range theater nuclear role. Although NATO declaratory doctrine stresses the capability and resolve to escalate to the ultimate use of strategic central systems if lower options fail, this does not mean that NATO expects to emerge victorious from any nuclear exchange. That a nuclear war cannot be won in the traditional sense has been the consensus view, at least in the West, for a number of years.[1]

Roger H. Palin is a group captain in the Royal Air Force. The views expressed by the author in this chapter are entirely his own and do not necessarily reflect the opinions or policies of any department of the United Kingdom Ministry of Defence. He wrote this chapter as a visiting fellow at the Woodrow Wilson International Center for Scholars in Washington, D.C.
1. See, for example, *U.S. Foreign Policy for the 1970's: A New Strategy for Peace*, A Report to the Congress by Richard Nixon, President of the United States

This is particularly so from a European perspective since the devastation that would result from large-scale nuclear conflict in that densely populated continent would make any victory Pyrrhic. Hence the size and shape of NATO's theater nuclear forces is geared primarily to deterring, not to winning, war.[2] The key question for NATO's planners is how best to deter regional attacks even in cases where no total defense is possible, and, should that deterrence fail, how to safeguard NATO and national interests by discriminating attacks that minimize pressures for further escalation. Although an adequate military capability is necessary for a deterrent posture to be credible, the emphasis is on escalation control: stopping Soviet forces (rather than defeating them decisively) and compelling negotiations on reasonable terms.

Escalation control would obviously prove meaningless in the face of an all-out Soviet nuclear offensive in Europe. However, the modernization of Soviet forces, both conventional and theater nuclear, is expanding the options open to the USSR leadership. To deter such Soviet options, NATO must have the ability to respond both in kind and degree and must also have credible options for the initial and first use of nuclear weapons that fall short of those that would generate an all-out spasm response.[3] Hence there is a need for a range of carefully measured incremental selective employment options short of general nuclear release. Implicit is the

---

(Government Printing Office, 1970), pp. 2–3; and Alain C. Enthoven and K. Wayne Smith, *How Much Is Enough? Shaping the Defense Program, 1961–1969* (Harper and Row, 1971), p. 128. A brief sketch of the evolution of this view can be found in Richard Pipes, "Why the Soviet Union Thinks It Could Fight and Win a Nuclear War," *Commentary,* July 1977, pp. 21–34. See the responses to Pipes's article in *Commentary,* September 1977, pp. 4–26; also Robert L. Arnett, "Soviet Attitudes Towards Nuclear War: Do They Really Think They Can Win?" *Journal of Strategic Studies,* vol. 2 (September 1979), pp. 172–91; and Raymond L. Garthoff, "Mutual Deterrence and Strategic Arms Limitation in Soviet Policy," *International Security,* vol. 3 (Summer 1978), pp. 112–47.

2. The emphasis to be given within NATO's flexible response doctrine to war-winning, war-fighting, and deterrence is a matter of continuous debate among member nations. U.S. analysts tend to stress a war-fighting capability more than their European counterparts. The interpretation of NATO doctrine that follows—written by a European—tends to represent a European viewpoint. However, when measured against the outcome of the NATO deliberations on the modernization of long-range theater nuclear forces, this analysis would appear to represent the prevailing consensus. A useful discussion of divergent views can be found in Stanley Sienkiewicz, "Foreign Policy and Theatre Nuclear Force Planning," *Journal of Strategic Studies,* vol. 2 (May 1979), pp. 17–33.

3. *First use* refers to the first use of nuclear weapons by either side. *Initial use* would be NATO's response to a Soviet first use.

ability to strike targets throughout the Warsaw Pact area, including the western military districts of the Soviet Union, thus denying the Russians the perception of a sanctuary in their homeland during a war in the European theater.[4] Such discriminating strikes attempt to achieve a political and psychological shock effect by attacking key targets with militarily significant results but restricted destruction. The goal is the earliest possible resumption of diplomacy. In this mix of political, military, and psychological factors that impinge on deterrent perceptions, the military impact is not necessarily the prime criterion for deciding appropriate options.

Assessing the military rationale of long-range theater nuclear forces (LRTNF) is further complicated by the bridging function that they serve between nuclear and conventional short-range battlefield weapons and central strategic systems. Battlefield forces derive their deterrent effect by being sufficiently robust to deny an enemy the belief that he can win an easy victory (deterrence by denial), so the military characteristics of these forces are of prime significance. Strategic forces achieve their *ultimate* deterrent effect by threatening an unacceptable level of damage and destruction on an enemy's military, political, and economic base (deterrence by punishment),[5] with emphasis on megatonnage and large numbers of survivable reentry vehicles. LRTNF embody elements of both. They deny an enemy certain military options by attacking key military targets, and they can retaliate in kind at the substrategic level to a limited Soviet nuclear strike. In the former case highly accurate, comparatively low-yield weapons are required, while in the latter different target sets might require larger warhead yields. However, in both roles LRTNF's primary purpose is to contain and slow down the escalation process, and the purely military factors—calculations of damage expectancy, degrees of assurance, and the optimum numbers of weapons to be launched— tend to be dominated by the need to impart the right political signal.

Linking LRTNF to central strategic systems is essential to bolster the credibility of NATO's overall deterrent posture. However, escalation to intercontinental exchange has appeared increasingly implausible ever since the Soviet Union began to achieve a retaliatory capability. The codification of strategic parity between the United States and the Soviet

---

4. *New York Times,* December 13, 1979.
5. Flexible options and enhanced capability to attack hard targets improve the overall credibility of central strategic systems by planning for options short of an all-out retaliatory strike, while retaining assured destruction capability.

Union through the SALT process has reinforced European fears that U.S. central systems may be decoupled from any war within the European theater. Although some U.S. central systems (such as Minuteman III with upgraded guidance and new warheads) might be suitable instruments for a selective response to limited theater strikes, the immediate involvement of such central systems might be too great an escalatory step for the United States to take.

The ability to retaliate with U.S.-owned and -controlled systems from European territory strengthens linkage by making NATO's initial use of nuclear weapons less fearsome for the United States, yet satisfies the Europeans that the United States remains firmly coupled to any nuclear exchange in Europe. Although this U.S. capability to target the Soviet Union from Europe might be considered an attempt to exempt the continental United States from a strategic exchange, paradoxically it serves the opposite purpose because it removes any firebreak between regional and intercontinental war that the Russians might wish to maintain. In Soviet eyes, a U.S. nuclear weapon landing on Soviet territory is strategic irrespective of its launch point, and therefore a response against the continental United States cannot be ruled out.[6]

LRTNF systems also make first use of nuclear weapons more plausible, a threat that is fundamental to NATO's deterrent posture. It is often assumed that NATO's first use would involve battlefield tactical nuclear weapons (TNW) in response to an impending Warsaw Pact success in conventional war. However, NATO could be deterred from the first use of short-range weapons by several factors: the continuous deployment of a considerable Soviet TNW capability, the difficulty of maintaining the safety of friendly troops because of the short ranges and high yields of the majority of NATO's TNW,[7] and the fact that many such weapons

6. For a discussion of Soviet views on the distinction between intercontinental and theater nuclear war and the dilemmas facing the Soviet leadership, see Joseph D. Douglass, Jr., *The Soviet Theater Nuclear Offensive,* Studies in Communist Affairs, vol. 1, prepared for Office of Director of Defense Research Engineering and Defense Nuclear Agency (GPO, 1976). A number of articles in *Pravda* have made Soviet concern clear, stating that NATO's LRTNF modernization would permit the United States to attack Soviet territory without recourse to central strategic systems, while the USSR would lack a similar option.

7. For a comprehensive analysis of NATO's tactical nuclear posture, see Jeffrey Record with the assistance of Thomas I. Anderson, *U.S. Nuclear Weapons in Europe: Issues and Alternatives* (Brookings Institution, 1974); Jeffrey Record, "Theatre Nuclear Weapons: Begging the Soviet Union to Pre-empt," *Survival,* vol. 19 (September–October 1977), pp. 208–11; and Uwe Nerlich, "Theatre Nuclear Forces in Europe: Is NATO Running Out of Options?" *The Washington Quarterly,* vol. 3 (Winter 1980), pp. 100–25.

would undoubtedly land on NATO's own territory. Longer-range nuclear systems with the requisite accuracy and yield would allow NATO more discriminate targeting options beyond the battlefield, thus restoring the credibility of NATO's threat of first use.

There is public misperception that the planned NATO force of ground-launched cruise missiles (GLCMs) and Pershing IIs is a military response to the Soviet SS-20 and Backfire bomber deployments. The layman naturally asks how the Pershing II with its single warhead and range of approximately 1,000 nautical miles[8] equates to the SS-20, each of which has three reentry vehicles and a range on the order of 2,700 nautical miles,[9] and why, if the Backfire bomber is such a threat to Europe, NATO is choosing to move away from theater nuclear aircraft in favor of GLCMs. In reality, the GLCM and Pershing II are not a direct military counter to the SS-20 and Backfire in the sense that they will attack and destroy the Soviet deployments. The asymmetry in effective ranges makes it possible for the Soviet Union to base SS-20s outside the range of GLCMs and still be able to cover targets throughout Western Europe. Even if the bases were in range, SS-20s are road-mobile and could be deployed away from their bases, making it difficult for NATO to find and target them. Similarly, although GLCMs have sufficient range to attack some Backfire airfields, their long flight time would allow the Soviet bombers to launch unscathed should the raid be detected.

Rather, LRTNF modernization, in the form of the GLCM and Pershing II, is essential to maintain overall balance in the face of the rapid, sustained modernization of all aspects of Soviet armed forces. The qualitative improvements to Soviet LRTNF, which go beyond the systems that have been threatening NATO for many years, afford the Warsaw Pact an extended range of military options that outmatches NATO's and thus undermines the credibility of NATO's chain of escalatory responses. Strategic equivalence at the intercontinental level, coupled to a considerable numerical imbalance at the conventional level, serves to emphasize this gap. Furthermore, the SS-20 and Backfire and other Soviet theater nuclear systems have been exempt from arms limitation negotiations while some NATO theater systems have been included, thus reinforcing Euro-

8. This range is quoted in a *New York Times* article cited in Clarence Robinson, Jr., "Pershing 2, Tomahawk Split Congress," *Aviation Week and Space Technology,* May 15, 1978, pp. 18–20.

9. International Institute for Strategic Studies, *The Military Balance, 1980–1981* (London: IISS, 1980), p. 89. An SS-20 armed with fewer than three reentry vehicles would have an increased range.

pean fears about a growing theater imbalance.[10] NATO therefore requires weapon systems that offer options similar to those the SS-20 and Backfire afford the Soviet Union, not only to overcome the military limitations of NATO's current LRTNF assets but to reforge the deterrent chain and to create a stronger position for future arms limitation negotiations. Unless NATO deploys some comparable systems, there is no incentive for the Soviet Union to agree to arms control limitations on its theater nuclear systems. The Backfire and SS-20 have thus become linked in public with the LRTNF modernization decision, but they are not the sole military rationale for the choice of GLCMs and Pershing IIs.

Combining Political and Military Requirements

Besides the need for an expanded range of options in response to SS-20 and Backfire deployments, a further major political requirement was to bolster NATO alliance cohesion, particularly after the damage done by the neutron bomb debate. The key to the choice of the GLCM lies in Article 5 of the North Atlantic Treaty, which states that an attack on one nation shall be considered an attack on all, thus implying a unity of NATO territory. Hence it is logical to select a weapon system that can be accommodated by as many European NATO nations as possible, involving maximum participation, political visibility, and sharing of risk. The Pershing II could not meet these criteria because it would be short of range unless based in West Germany, and a longer range medium-range ballistic missile (MRBM) would not have been available until the mid- to late 1980s. Very few nations would be able to participate in deploying the sea-launched cruise missile (SLCM) unless a dedicated NATO naval

10. The U.S. Poseidon warheads available to NATO were included in the strategic totals agreed to in SALT II; the protocol limited GLCMs to 600 kilometers; the Pershing I, 1,000 nuclear warheads, and some dual-capable F-4s were included in option 3, which was tabled by NATO at the mutual and balanced force reduction talks in Vienna. (This option was subsumed by NATO's decision to withdraw 1,000 warheads, announced in December 1979 at the time of the LRTNF modernization decision.) By contrast, Soviet theater-oriented medium-range and submarine-launched ballistic missiles have been excluded from negotiations in either forum, and the Backfire bomber is subject to relatively minor limits on its radius of action, although these constraints were not included in SALT II. See Roger P. Labrie, ed., *SALT Hand Book: Key Documents and Issues, 1972–1979* (Washington, D.C.: American Enterprise Institute for Public Policy Research, 1979). A discussion of the theater nuclear balance can be found in IISS, *The Military Balance, 1980–1981,* pp. 116–19.

force were created. A submarine-based force would not be identifiably different from U.S. and U.K. strategic forces, and sea-based systems do not attract the same political visibility as land-based systems. An air-launched cruise missile (ALCM) force would require a dedicated force of carrier aircraft, and basing on the European continent would leave them vulnerable to tactical air attack. Selecting airfields solely in the United Kingdom, where that threat is reduced, would obviate multinational participation.

By contrast, deploying GLCM flights within the territory of five European NATO nations might strengthen alliance cohesion and reduce the Soviet Union's options for selective retribution in both peace and war. Furthermore, the number of deployed GLCM flights means that in order to stage a preemptive strike intended to take out all GLCMs within the European theater, the Soviet Union would have to attack on such a scale as to invite almost guaranteed retaliation from the United Kingdom's strategic submarine-launched ballistic missile (SLBM) forces, perhaps France's *force de frappe,* and quite probably a proportion of the U.S. central systems.

Two considerations with more political value than military utility are the desire to limit collateral damage and the need to ensure high prelaunch survivability—although the latter is vital for military reasons also. In recent years NATO apparently has paid increasing attention to the restriction of collateral damage from theater nuclear strikes.[11] The Soviet reaction might be more rational if NATO's strikes did not inflict widespread damage on the civilian population. In addition to serving humanitarian concerns, discriminate targeting sends a less ambiguous political signal, and restricting the size and yield of theater strikes is a clearer demonstration of restraint, yet both these actions retain the threat of escalation. Unfortunately, NATO's current long-range theater nuclear systems do not combine the required accuracy and low yield for extremely discriminating attacks.

Good prelaunch survivability for weapons and their associated command, control, and communications enhances the credibility of NATO's overall deterrent posture. Excessive vulnerability in any one link of the deterrent chain undermines confidence in the strength of the whole. LRTNF are particularly important in this regard since they may need to survive protracted periods of hostilities at lower levels of conflict against

11. This was perhaps most noticeable in public reports of the neutron bomb debate.

a wide variety of threats. Soviet literature stresses an enemy's theater nuclear forces as a primary target to be sought out and destroyed with the utmost speed. Certainly LRTNF should not be seen as vulnerable to a preemptive attack, particularly by conventional forces.[12]

The ultimate logic of the argument might lead to a sea-based, subsurface force where survivability is currently almost assured. However, selective nuclear release options would leave submarines that fire only a partial missile load highly vulnerable. The small number of airfields on which a theater nuclear force of ALCMs might be based would be well known and could be targeted selectively. Thus ALCMs are more vulnerable than NATO's conventional air forces, which are more dispersed, and the Warsaw Pact would have to launch much stronger attacks to neutralize them. Mobile GLCMs, on the other hand, are deployable to any number of unpresurveyed operational sites during a period of tension, and if given adequate protection against attacks by saboteurs would not suffer these limitations, assuming survivable command, control, and communications.

Thus it is clear that determination of the size and composition of NATO's LRTNF has to balance occasionally conflicting requirements. The force must be large enough to afford NATO a number of selective options, each so structured as to impart the required political signal without ambiguity. The force should also be dispersed widely for survival. Yet it should not be large enough to persuade either the Russians or the Europeans to believe that a nuclear war might be limited to Europe, thus leading to the apparent decoupling of U.S. strategic systems. The composition of the force, particularly MRBMs based on West German soil,

---

12. For example: "The primary objectives of armed combat in the theaters will be the nuclear weapons of the enemy. Without eliminating or neutralizing these nuclear weapons it is impossible to count on successful conduct of any military operations, offensive or defensive, in the theaters." V. D. Sokolovskiy, *Soviet Military Strategy,* 3d ed., Harriet Fast Scott, ed. and trans. (Crane, Russak, 1975), p. 291. The emphasis on anticipation, surprise, and decisive action that permeates Soviet military literature indicates that should hostilities appear imminent, the Warsaw Pact would seek to preempt NATO's theater nuclear weapons, either by conventional or nuclear means. This should not be confused with a "bolt-out-of-the-blue" attack occurring without any previous political or military warning. The two scenarios generate different requirements for prelaunch survivability. The former assumes some indicators allowing timely dispersal decisions to be taken; to safeguard against the latter requires a proportion of strategic systems (such as SLBMs) to be at constant readiness. This distinction is well made in *The Future United Kingdom Strategic Nuclear Deterrent Force,* Defence Open Government Document 80/23 (London: Ministry of Defence, 1980). See also Nerlich, "Theatre Nuclear Forces in Europe."

should not appear to the Soviet Union to pose a disarming first-strike capability, and yet the force should have sufficient size and strength to encourage the Soviet Union to be genuinely interested in arms limitation.

In speculating on the target sets that might be included in the LRTNF selective employment options one must bear in mind the political goal: to achieve resumption of diplomatic activity. This requires creating a psychological climate in which the Russians' instinct to retaliate is tempered by the knowledge that the damage of the initial strikes, though significant, is limited, and that an excessive response would inevitably be met by escalation, if necessary to the use of intercontinental systems. Targets must be of sufficient significance to have an immediate impact on Soviet thinking without being so critical as to provoke a spasm response. Hence suitable target sets might consist of military installations removed from dense civilian areas, for example, isolated naval bases and airfields (particularly those associated with theater nuclear strike operations), reinforcements, logistic supply depots, tactical command, control, and communications centers, railway marshaling yards, nuclear storage sites, lines of communication choke-points such as key railway bridges, fixed air defense sites, army and divisional headquarters, and combined-arms army rear assembly areas.

Targets deliberately excluded in the interests of escalation control would presumably include command and intelligence centers concerned with the highest levels of Warsaw Pact leadership and vital elements of strategic capability such as intercontinental ballistic missile silos. Key nodes in industrial plant and critical components of the oil distribution or electricity supply networks could well be included in follow-on options should initial strikes fail to achieve their purpose. Destruction of such targets would not have an immediate effect on the battlefield situation, although the loss of such targets would seriously hinder the Soviet Union's ability to sustain war in Europe for a lengthy period. Finally, GLCMs will retain a countervalue threat, complementary to the U.K., U.S., and French nuclear ballistic missile submarine forces, which the USSR cannot ignore.

A Solution to Current Inadequacies?

Current theater assets are inadequate to meet all the preceding criteria. Since the withdrawal of Mace, Jupiter, and Thor in the 1960s, NATO has relied primarily on in-place aircraft and SLBMs. Airfields, however, are increasingly vulnerable to expanding Soviet interdiction capabilities, and while this might be overcome in part by airborne alert, the reliance on air-to-air refueling would add yet another vulnerable link to the deterrent chain. Aircraft are also subject to weather constraints, and their ability to penetrate deep into the Soviet Union is becoming suspect in the face of the increasingly sophisticated Soviet air defenses. As a supplement, 400 Poseidon warheads are available to the Supreme Allied Commander, Europe (SACEUR), as is the U.K. Polaris fleet.[13] These, however, have neither the flexibility nor responsiveness required, due to command, control, and communications limitations inherent in subsurface operations, and have lower accuracy than surface-launched missiles. Moreover, use of submarine-launched ballistic missiles would blur the distinction between theater and strategic use, which could defeat the political purpose of sending unambiguous substrategic signals.[14] Of equal importance is the dichotomy between nuclear and conventional requirements caused by relying on long-range dual-capable aircraft (DCA); at the very time maximum conventional air effort is needed in support of land and air battle, DCA must be held back for possible nuclear operations. In a vicious circle, this makes holding the war at the conventional level more difficult, thus accelerating the likelihood of nuclear war, which in turn requires increasing numbers of shorter-range DCA to be withheld.

How then would GLCMs improve the situation, and what are their limitations in the LRTNF role? GLCMs are considerably more accurate than existing nuclear missile systems; their variable yield allows them to be precisely matched to targets, thus limiting collateral damage; and their single warhead allows less wastage than might occur with SLBMs armed with multiple independently targetable reentry vehicles (MIRVs). Unlike Pershing IIs, GLCMs have the range to cover vast tracts of Soviet territory as far east as Moscow. Their proposed mobility, ability to operate from dispersed unpresurveyed sites, and quick activation enhance pre-launch survivability. Because of their slow flight time, they cannot reasonably be perceived by the USSR as a first-strike force. They will be able to operate at all hours and in all weather conditions. By substituting GLCMs and Pershing IIs for some older tactical nuclear weapons, NATO would achieve a more balanced force with an increased number of options at

13. Details on NATO theater nuclear forces are to be found in IISS, *The Military Balance, 1980–1981.*

14. A further problem associated with Poseidon SLBMs, each of which carry eight to ten warheads, is the need to avoid wasting reentry vehicles. This requires sufficient appropriate targets simultaneously available within the footprint of the missile. For a useful discussion of the problem of nuclear target queuing, see Lt. Cdr. Edward J. Ohlert, USN, "Strategic Deterrence and the Cruise Missile," *Naval War College Review,* vol. 30 (Winter 1978), pp. 21–32.

medium and long ranges. The planned 108 Pershing IIs and 464 GLCMs could permit a large number of DCA to be released from quick-reaction-alert status. The synergistic effect of this would be considerable. It would give NATO increased long-range nuclear options and a significant boost in conventional tactical air capability, and at the same time retain flexibility for using DCA in nuclear operations against mobile targets.

GLCMs, however, are not without limitations. Their slow flight time makes them unsuitable for time-sensitive targets and for targets at extreme ranges. This could allow the Soviet Union to react before NATO weapons arrived, particularly if the Russians did not play according to the rules of NATO's game theory. Nor can GLCMs be targeted reliably against Warsaw Pact forces that are on the move, which would limit usefulness against targets such as reinforcement armies. The ability to retarget GLCMs effectively will depend on the availability of a comprehensive matrix of terrain contour matching (TERCOM) maps, on which the missile depends for accurate navigation, and on current, detailed knowledge of all ground obstacles in all likely areas of operations. The terrain must be suitable and unique to each flight profile, and maps must steer flight paths away from likely areas of defense concentration. New routes can be prepared quickly to take into account intelligence on the latest deployment of mobile defense systems, but how to transmit the new data tapes to the dispersed launcher sites in secure, survivable, and timely form remains unresolved.

It is not known whether the terrain and weather conditions in which cruise missiles have been tested in the United States realistically represent those in Eastern Europe and the Soviet Union, nor how nuclear conditions might affect the reliability of TERCOM as a means of guidance. There will also be increasing doubts over time about the continued reliability and serviceability of missiles deployed as complete systems from the manufacturer and subject to minimum testing in the field. Ground sabotage could be a serious threat once the missiles leave the relative physical security of their base areas, and logistic resupply might also be vulnerable. Off-base deployment training in peacetime might have to be limited to avoid offering a focal point for public antinuclear opposition, and similar considerations could impede timely decisions to deploy the missiles to their dispersed sites in times of rising tension.[15]

15. Choosing a ground-launched system to attract maximum political visibility thus presents a paradox: that very visibility could work against NATO's interests and is one reason why some have argued for sea-based missiles.

Perhaps the major limitation of GLCMs in the LRTNF role is the potential ambiguity of the political signal intended by their use. Because their long-term ability to penetrate the evolving and expanding Soviet air defenses is uncertain, it is difficult to judge how many missiles to launch to achieve the desired effect. If defense suppression weapons were planned in coordination with cruise missile strikes to aid penetration, analysis of Soviet perceptions and reactions would be further complicated, because the Russians would be less certain the strike was limited. The cruise missile's ability to change course and to strike targets throughout the Warsaw Pact area as far east as Moscow also could make it more difficult for the Russians to predict the intended target. If the number of cruise missiles launched is reduced to lessen the ambiguity of the signal, the uncertainty of how many will arrive on target makes damage expectancy and consequent Soviet reactions difficult to assess. By contrast, the ballistic flight profile of the Pershing II can be predicted soon after launch, and its speed of flight and current near certainty of arriving on target eases the calculation of damage and reactions.

The ambiguity inherent in GLCMs, unlike the Pershing II, argues that they are not the optimum weapon for widespread use in NATO's initial long-range employment options, but rather are more suited to follow-on options when raid sizes are likely to be larger, more targets are likely to be attacked, and the distinction between theater and strategic use of cruise missiles becomes blurred. The choice of GLCMs for the LRTNF modernization program is a good example of how purely military factors —flexibility, ability to penetrate, damage expectancy, and speed of response and execution—are dominated by other considerations. A new extended-range mobile MRBM would arguably have been a preferred solution. However, the GLCMs' limitations as a politico-military instrument of escalation control are outweighed by their earlier availability, the difficulties they pose for optimization of the Soviet air defenses, their lower cost and manpower requirements, their political visibility, and their effect on NATO cohesion.

Conventional Applications

NATO requires a robust conventional capability for many reasons: to defend vital NATO territory; to deter the Warsaw Pact from assuming successful operations in Europe could be limited to conventional weapons; and to raise NATO's nuclear threshold. Other reasons include uncertainty about Soviet reactions to a NATO first use of nuclear weapons; the devastation that would occur in Western Europe in even a limited nuclear exchange; a growing popular aversion in many European nations to all things nuclear; and the lack of credibility to both sides of a deterrent posture based on an instant nuclear response to even limited aggression. The potential accuracy of cruise missiles when equipped with terminal guidance and modern conventional warheads, allied to their autonomy, extended range, and endurance, could contribute significantly to NATO's conventional capabilities in areas where NATO now depends on nuclear weapons or the effectiveness of current conventional systems is increasingly suspect.

However, realization of this potential will depend on the successful development of appropriate conventional warheads—earth-penetrating, runway-cratering, and hardened construction munitions—and of the guidance and target-seeking technology to give the required accuracy. Sufficient resolution will be required to recognize the assigned target without being vulnerable to adverse weather effects or enemy jamming. While development of the guidance systems using imaging infrared, millimetric radar, and laser apparently progresses well, there is considerably more doubt about the development of the warheads.

All this must be done at a cost that is more affordable than that of suitable alternative weapon systems. Clearly the use of a cruise missile to deliver 1,000 pounds of conventional high explosive on a one-way mission at a unit price of $1 million would not be cost-effective for many targets. Research is therefore concentrating on the development of submunitions and unitary warheads embodying highly specialized weapons technology matched to specific target categories. Besides the various fusing problems that must be resolved, the crucial question is whether small submunitions packing the right punch can be developed so that large numbers can be carried in each cruise missile, reducing the number of missiles required. Whether such submunitions can be developed is still uncertain, and therefore comparisons of cruise missiles' relative cost-effectiveness with other delivery systems can only be tentative.

There is similar uncertainty about other suggested uses of cruise missiles. Some analysts have suggested that cruise missiles could revolutionize future warfare by taking control of many phases of the battle—airspace surveillance, target detection, classification and designation, and even command and control of attack cruise missiles.[16] However, successful development of the requisite technology and its embodiment in cruise missiles is by no means certain and is sure to be complex, lengthy, and costly. Furthermore, the dependence of such a complex system on a comprehensive communications network, vulnerable to jamming, deception, and physical destruction, throws serious doubt on the practicability of such ideas.[17] Nonetheless the military potential of conventionally armed cruise missiles should not be ignored. There are some practical applications of developments that show promise of being available in the mid- to late 1980s.

The Forward Edge of the Battle Area

The political constraints governing the structure and employment of LRTNF should not apply in the same degree to a force of conventionally armed cruise missiles. Once political authority to cross the inner German border were given, conventional weapons would probably be used against a wide range of military targets in non-Soviet Warsaw Pact territory whose destruction or disruption would have a direct effect on the land-air battle.

Offensive operations on the modern battlefield will almost certainly be highly maneuverable and dynamic because of the ever-present threat of nuclear weapons and the high degree of mechanization of both sides' ground forces. Enemy attacks are likely to take place along a wide front and in great depth, utilizing surprise and mobility to the maximum. Soviet motorized rifle and tank divisions of combined-arms armies are trained to move from widely dispersed assembly areas, reach their line of attack simultaneously with other forces, deploy into combat formation, and initiate the assault, all without stopping. The primary goal of leading echelons would be to probe for weaknesses in NATO's defensive line, seeking to punch through the covering forces and to penetrate quickly and in depth before there is time to reconstitute a viable defense. NATO

16. For representative samples, see Richard L. Garwin, "Effective Military Technology in the 1980s," *International Security,* vol. 1 (Fall 1976), pp. 50–77; "Missiles, Missiles, and Missiles," *Business Week,* August 11, 1980, pp. 76–81; and Ohlert, "Strategic Deterrence and the Cruise Missile," p. 29. The conclusion of some of these theorists is that there will be no need to develop the next generation of tactical fighter aircraft.

17. The possible effects of an electromagnetic pulse generated by an exoatmospheric nuclear burst could also be significant.

defensive strong points would be bypassed to sustain the advance for later encirclement operations. Dispersed battle formation would be used before contact with NATO forces to reduce the unit's vulnerability to nuclear, artillery, or air attack, and motorized rifle troops would remain mounted in their armored fighting vehicles for as long as practicable. Equally maneuverable reserves and second-echelon units of the leading formations would follow shortly behind the first echelon to exploit successful breakthroughs, deflect counterattacks, liquidate forces remaining in the enemy's most forward defensive positions, or replace first-echelon units that have lost their fighting capacity. Airborne assault troops and large numbers of helicopter gunships are likely to be used extensively.[18]

In the highly fluid circumstances around the forward edge of the battle area (FEBA), cruise missiles would seem to have little use, except perhaps in defense suppression and reconnaissance. The speed and variable direction of advance are always likely to outpace the ability of cruise missiles to counterattack, due to the time needed for mission planning and their comparatively slow flight. One potential application consists of cruise missile canisters, launched from aircraft out of range of the Soviet leading air defense elements, which would dispense submunitions in the general area of the FEBA to detect and attack individual tanks.[19]

This development is intended to overcome some of the limitations that bedevil tactical aircraft's current contribution to the immediate battlefield through close air support. The basic problem for close air support remains how to concentrate sufficient and timely firepower anywhere along the FEBA to counter any number of critical enemy thrusts, when the choice of axes and timing lies with the enemy. Tanks and artillery are never likely to be available to NATO in sufficient numbers, mobility, or range to cover all possible points of penetration.[20] For this, use of the air is essential. However, aircraft are particularly vulnerable if they employ dive tactics against ground targets. Moreover, in this role, which requires coordination with the fire and movement of friendly troops, they depend

18. The Soviet concept of operations for war in Europe is well set out in the series "Soviet Military Thought," translated and published under the auspices of the United States Air Force, in particular, A. A. Sidorenko, *The Offensive: A Soviet View* (GPO, 1973); N. A. Lomov, ed., *Scientific-Technical Progress and the Revolution in Military Affairs: A Soviet View* (GPO, 1975); and V. Ye. Savkin, *The Basic Principles of Operational Art and Tactics: A Soviet View* (GPO, 1974).

19. "Missiles, Missiles, and Missiles," pp. 78–79.

20. Details of current developments in field artillery can be found in Patrick F. Rogers, "The New Artillery," *Army*, July 1980, pp. 27–33.

on an intermediary forward air controller, who is himself vulnerable to enemy fire and who must rely on communication links with the aircraft, which can be jammed.[21] Autonomous cruise missile operations would dispense with the need for forward air controllers, but, as already stated, are likely to be too slow to keep pace with events. If air patrol were used to speed response times, an intermediary link would be required, as for aircraft, to allocate targets. Cruise missiles are too slow, cannot yet differentiate enemy from friendly tanks, and are not flexible enough to attack targets of opportunity, an essential requirement in a fast-moving battle situation. Therefore they could contribute little to this crucial mission.[22]

Defense Suppression and Reconnaissance

In a defense suppression (DS) role, however, cruise missiles or drones could play an extremely useful role over the forward battle area and deeper into enemy territory, where Warsaw Pact armies possess a comprehensive array of air defense weapons, many of which (such as the SA4, 6, and 8) rely on search and acquisition and/or tracking radars. DS drones could employ reactive electronic countermeasures (ECM) covering a wide band of frequencies, or they could be programmed to detect and attack radars emitting on specific frequencies. For use over the battlefield, relatively inexpensive drones could be constructed with small piston engines, unsophisticated detection equipment, and small light high explosive warheads. Longer-range DS cruise missiles, launched in coordinated raids with manned aircraft carrying large weapon loads, would help to offset a serious shortfall in NATO's current ECM capabilities and would also help to relieve the need for attack aircraft to carry self-screening ECM pods at the expense of their maximum ordnance load.

21. A full debate on the problems associated with using tactical aircraft in the close air support role is outside the scope of this chapter. For a full discussion, see Group Capt. Ian Madelin, RAF, "The Emperor's Close Air Support," *Air University Review,* vol. 31 (November–December 1979), pp. 82–86; Wing Cdr. Jeremy G. Saye, RAF, "Close Air Support in Modern Warfare," *Air University Review,* vol. 31 (January–February 1980), pp. 2–21; and the extensive correspondence in *Air University Review,* vol. 31 (May–June 1980), pp. 94–105.

22. A more promising line of development, dispensing with the cruise missile's attributes of autonomous flight and long range, would be to marry cruise missiles' autonomous terminal guidance to rocket-propelled missiles to be launched from aircraft outside the range of Warsaw Pact air defenses. The intelligence of the human operator would be retained, aircraft survivability enhanced, and accurate hitting power increased.

Reconnaissance cruise missiles employing electro-optical or forward-looking infrared detection systems with secure data link transmission to the intelligence center could also play a useful role over wide areas of enemy territory. Over the immediate area of the battlefield, reconnaissance cruise missiles would need to be able to transmit their information directly and securely to commanders in the field so that timely defensive counteractions could be taken. This would require a large network of receiver systems for optimum interpretation and exploitation, and might not be cost-effective compared to other ground-based line-of-sight systems. Remotely piloted recoverable drones (not strictly cruise missiles) might be more practical. It might also be possible to include target-designating laser systems in such drones to guide cannon-launched munitions.

Reconnaissance cruise missiles for use deeper into enemy territory would be a useful supplement to NATO's manned reconnaissance aircraft, which are few in number, limited in range, affected by weather, and constrained by time-consuming pilot debriefing, interpretation, and dissemination procedures. Although cruise missiles flying on preprogrammed profiles at heights that allow an effective search would be vulnerable to air defenses, they would be no more so than manned aircraft, and would be considerably cheaper and free from weather constraints. Moreover, the cruise missile's endurance would afford extended time on patrol, although secure near real-time transmission of intelligence would be essential. On the other hand, cruise missiles are unlikely to be able to reconnoiter other than preplanned target areas and therefore would be less flexible than manned aircraft for gathering intelligence on targets of opportunity and slower to respond to requests for immediate reconnaissance sorties. Moreover, sophisticated reconnaissance equipment is hardly expendable, which would argue for a recoverable missile. In principle, however, cruise missiles offer a complementary potential for acquiring detailed intelligence within and beyond the range of airborne systems that employ broad area coverage from behind the FEBA, and ground-based systems mainly concerned with operations in the battlefield area.

Targets behind the First Echelon

Operations beyond the immediate area of the battlefield would still be mobile, although possibly not as fast and fluid as on the battlefield itself, while the threat of nuclear weapons would dictate dispersal of forces.

Since a war of attrition is generally agreed not to be in the West's interests, NATO must concentrate on attacking the forces and target sets that present immediate danger. While halting the Warsaw Pact first echelon will naturally be the overriding priority, NATO will also need to prevent the rapid deployment forward of enemy operational reserves geared to exploit areas in the NATO defensive chain seriously weakened or broken by first-echelon assaults. NATO must block the movement of the enemy's second echelon and thus disrupt the coordination of the offensive. Attacks on the divisional elements that Warsaw Pact tanks need (artillery, engineering, infantry, and immediate logistic support such as petroleum, oil, lubricants, and ammunition), units that employ softer-skinned vehicles and present more vulnerable targets, would seriously degrade the operational effectiveness of their forces. A concerted attack on the command and control organization, particularly divisional and army headquarters, could upset the timing of the combined-arms offensive and force delegation of responsibility for initiative onto ever-lower command levels.[23] Other important target categories include theater nuclear forces, reinforcement armies, and airfields. Nuclear surface-to-surface missiles (SSMs) and airfields supporting theater nuclear operations must be attacked quickly, as well as forward airfields supporting helicopter gunship operations, tactical air command posts, early warning and ground control units, and surface-to-air missile (SAM) sites and their associated radars. It will be equally important to block the forward deployment of reinforcements from Poland and the western military districts of the Soviet Union.

What can conventionally armed cruise missiles contribute to these operations beyond the battlefield? The dispersal and concealment of most ground force targets in this area, their rapid movement when deploying from assembly areas, and the unpredictable timing and axes of the enemy's tactical movements would seem to limit the potential utility of cruise missiles and would point to the use of manned tactical aircraft because of their speed of response, ability to attack multiple and moving targets, larger payload that can include more than one type of weapon, and ability to cover wide areas quickly in an ever-changing battle situation. Moreover, the ability of aircrews to react to the unforeseen, adapt

23. The potential weakness in the combined-arms approach has been well analyzed in John Erickson, "Soviet Combined-Arms: Theory and Practice," University of Edinburgh, Defence Studies, September 1979; and Douglass, *Soviet Theater Nuclear Offensive*, pp. 69–97.

tactics to the prevailing situation, and update tactical intelligence through visual sightings is vital.

One possible use for cruise missiles beyond the battlefield, currently being studied, is to search likely areas for tank concentrations and to launch submunitions designed to attack individual tanks automatically.[24] However, the cruise missiles' dependence in this role on fixed and easily identifiable approach paths such as roads would make them vulnerable to air defense units deployed in advance of the reinforcement columns. Also, tanks so far removed from the battlefield should be able to employ relatively simple countermeasures—thermal blankets, infrared decoys, or steel nets. On the other hand, cruise missiles could play a useful role if they were programmed to report the relevant coordinates of any cluster of tanks detected and act as target designators or scatter mines in front of the columns. Manned aircraft could then be scrambled, armed with area weapons to attack the softer-skinned elements of the combined-arms divisions.

However, more promising targets for conventional cruise missile attack are heavily defended high-value fixed installations, against which attacks by manned aircraft are likely to become increasingly difficult and expensive. The increased vulnerability of manned aircraft to the growth in Soviet air defenses, particularly around important targets, and NATO's limited aircrew and aircraft resources emphasize the need to develop less wasteful means of attacking such targets. Furthermore, for some targets such as airfields, current aircraft payload and weapons characteristics require very large numbers of sorties, which can be by no means assured, to disrupt Warsaw Pact air operations. Runways and essential support infrastructure are vulnerable to interdiction, bad weather might impede effective air operations, and air commanders may be forced to allocate all available aircraft to more pressing tasks. This latter consideration is particularly true in the initial stages of hostilities, when many aircraft capable of more than one role (such as the F-16) would probably be required to support air defense or battlefield operations.

Much of the cruise missile's potential comparative advantage over manned aircraft will depend on the frequency spectrum chosen for the terminal guidance and on the successful development of the next generation of warheads and submunitions. In principle, however, appropriate

24. "Missiles, Missiles, and Missiles."

targets for the next generation of conventional cruise missiles might include the following: airfields; selected command and control centers, including air defense zonal and district command posts; frontal aviation and tactical command posts and relatively static headquarters; forward nuclear storage sites and hardened SSM sites; and fixed air defense sites, including SAM, early warning radars, and ground control intercept sites. In addition, because of their low specific fuel consumption and enhanced range, cruise missiles could attack targets that lie outside the range of most current and planned NATO manned aircraft and are now primarily targeted with nuclear weapons. Examples are the railway bridges over the Oder-Neisse, Vistula, and Bug rivers, the destruction of which could cause considerable delay to the forward deployment of reinforcing armies, and possibly the rail transfer areas inside the Polish-Soviet borders where the railway gauges change and reinforcement forces must transfer from one rail system to another.

The substitution of cruise missiles for manned aircraft in certain roles is an emotional subject for professional air force planners, which cannot be resolved definitively at this stage in cruise missile developments. Nor can analyses of relative cost-effectiveness between different weapon systems ever be entirely satisfactory because of the number of variables involved that require subjective judgment. However, in principle the relative merits of the two systems can be assessed against certain important parameters—for example, accuracy, survivability, life-cycle costs, and infrastructure support—to demonstrate what advances conventionally armed cruise missiles could bring to offensive air operations. Of the targets enumerated above, airfield attack will serve as an appropriate example.

Airfield Attack

In principle, a cruise missile should be more survivable in flight than an aircraft because its radar cross section and infrared, noise, and visual signatures are less observable. As Warsaw Pact air defenses develop, cruise missiles should lend themselves to the simpler and cheaper incorporation of appropriate countermeasures. Furthermore, cruise missiles should be able to carry out attacks at night and in all weather conditions without radiating actively, thus enhancing survivability in the face of terminal defenses. Similarly, cruise missiles, not being dependent on runways, should be able to launch more successfully during hostilities.

Cruise missiles have two advantages in accuracy. Those that are not shot down will not be put off their aim by terminal defenses—a possibly significant factor that affects manned aircraft—and cruise missiles will have less trouble dispensing submunitions at correct intervals for efficient cutting of the runway and taxiway since no allowance needs to be made for aircraft safety or variable flight attitudes. This also facilitates attacking key points on an airfield, such as the petroleum, oil, and lubricants storage tanks, operations bunkers, or engineering support centers, that are likely to be camouflaged against the human eye. For a given criterion of damage, higher accuracy reduces the over-target submunition requirements, which, combined with greater survivability, significantly reduces the number of missiles needed.

A further important consideration is that cruise missiles are expendable, while aircraft and their crews are not. This makes the normally inverse relationship between attrition rates and sortie generation a moot problem. Furthermore, missiles needed to saturate defenses would be instantly available (provided stocks were sufficient), whereas if aircraft are to realize their potential for more than one sortie, they must survive the return flight to their bases, where they will require time for servicing, rearming, and possibly repair.

The advantages of aircraft, besides those already enumerated, lie in the flexibility afforded by having a human operator: the ability to change tactics, react to threats en route, reattack a target or attack secondary targets, and carry out postattack reconnaissance. Also, aircraft weapon loads are larger, possibly three or four times the individual load of a cruise missile. On the other hand, some tactical concepts require attack aircraft to be supplemented by a number of supporting aircraft—fighter escort, defense suppression, air-to-air refueling, and possibly an airborne command post. By contrast, the cruise missile's autonomy and stealth dispense with the requirement for these supporting systems.

Besides these operational arguments, cruise missiles should show an overall cost saving. Comparisons of unit price serve little purpose at this stage, since claims that conventionally armed cruise missiles can be produced for $1 million to $2 million could well be premature, and aircraft attrition figures, a key factor in any relative cost equation, cannot be known before actual conflict. However, a cruise missile force with capability approximately equivalent to a squadron of aircraft should have considerably lower life-cycle costs. There would be savings in manpower, aircrew training, engineering and servicing schedules, and space, fuel, and infrastructure support for peacetime training. Against this should be offset cruise missiles' requirement for far more detailed mapping data and planning, with an associated need for computers and highly qualified manpower.

Such then is the balance of advantages offered by cruise missiles in the airfield attack role. However, there are several significant aspects of tactical air operations in which cruise missiles cannot substitute for manned aircraft. The formidable variety and number of targets that cruise missiles cannot engage includes leading-echelon armies in the event of a breakthrough, forward and rear assembly areas and columns deploying from them, divisional and regimental headquarters, operational reserves, mobile nuclear forces, the logistic train supporting helicopter gunship operations, and second-echelon forces on the move forward. Other important tasks that require manned aircraft include engaging enemy airborne assault and interdiction aircraft in the air, providing fighter escort, countering amphibious operations on the flanks, supporting NATO counterattacks, and, most important, providing immediate air support in situations requiring the timely arrival of concentrated fire support. Thus cruise missiles essentially complement manned aircraft by taking on fixed targets against which the cost-effectiveness of aircraft may be declining, while releasing aircraft to attack mobile and dispersed targets more suited to their unique characteristics.

Offensive Counter Air and Interdiction

The target categories that might be appropriate for cruise missiles fall generically under the NATO definitions of offensive counter air and interdiction, two roles whose value is increasingly questioned. Critics portray an offensive counter air campaign as a war for its own sake and argue that a war for air superiority has little relevance to the ground battle. They also argue that interdiction that denies resupply to enemy forces at the front until they collapse is no longer relevant in Europe due to the diversity of the transport net, the forward stocking of essential logistic supplies that allows combined-arms armies to operate autonomously for considerable periods, and the time lag before such interdiction affects the situation on the battlefield.

Should such charges have substance, the rationale for developing tactical cruise missiles would be undermined. However, without a NATO offensive counter air campaign, Warsaw Pact frontal aviation forces, supplemented by long-range aviation and Soviet naval air forces, potentially could gain total air superiority over NATO territory and thus prevent NATO's effective forward defense. Moreover, NATO's capability to conduct an offensive air campaign forces the Warsaw Pact to devote considerable resources to air defense that might otherwise be allocated to offense. NATO's counter air campaign is not therefore designed to achieve total air superiority, but to reduce the sortie generation potential of Warsaw Pact offensive air forces.

The growth in Warsaw Pact frontal aviation forces and their introduction of third-generation aircraft with greatly increased payloads and the range to attack targets throughout the depth of NATO territory offer the Warsaw Pact interdiction options that NATO cannot afford to ignore. Attacks on Warsaw Pact airfields at the outset of hostilities, besides bottling up aircraft on the ground, would force the diversion of aircraft already airborne to other bases, which would become overcrowded and even more lucrative targets, or to highway strips where continuous operations are more difficult to maintain. Currently NATO must allocate large numbers of tactical air sorties to airfield attack, and this can be done only at the expense of other equally high-priority missions. Conventionally armed cruise missiles, by attacking airfields, command posts, and ground control intercept sites, could usefully disrupt frontal aviation operations, reduce their sortie rates, and free DCA to destroy aircraft in the air.

An interdiction campaign deep into enemy territory is needed because the advent of current generations of precision-guided conventional weapons increases the importance of reserve and reinforcement forces. The Warsaw Pact forces' shorter land lines of communication, compared to NATO's longer sea and air lines of communication, gives them a decided advantage.[25] The shorter the warning time, the more vital it becomes for NATO to be able to interdict Warsaw Pact reinforcement forces early in any hostilities. The multiplicity of roads in the western parts of East Germany and the Pact forces' proven capability for river crossing makes interdiction of their lines of communication close to the battlefield

25. Consider: "Thus, high tempos of attack may lead to a disruption of the mobilization deployment of the enemy army, of the massing of forces necessary for a successful defense and of the approach of reserves from other continents." Savkin, *Basic Principles of Operational Art and Tactics*, p. 173. Also, "The significance of these reserves under the conditions of modern war grows decisively." Lomov, *Scientific-Technical Progress and the Revolution in Military Affairs*, p. 138.

almost impossible, short of the use of nuclear weapons.[26] Farther east, however, their rapid forward deployment depends on relatively few railway lines, all of which must cross major rivers. Destruction of these railway bridges early in the war would delay the advance of reinforcement forces considerably and leave those forces vulnerable to follow-on air attacks. (However, current-generation cruise missile accuracies are probably insufficient to put a bridge out of action for a worthwhile time unless massive numbers are launched against each bridge.)[27] In sum, the value of interdiction lies in attacking communication choke-points, rather than the classic interdiction of supplies practiced in previous wars, and early interdiction in the east is likely to be more beneficial than later interdiction farther west. Cruise missiles could help NATO to pursue that option below the nuclear threshold.

Targets in the Soviet Union

One possible use of conventionally armed cruise missiles would be to attack a range of military targets in the Soviet Union that currently can be attacked only with nuclear weapons. However, considerations of military effectiveness, cost, and possible counterproductive impact on Soviet perceptions might outweigh the potential gain of this step. It is interesting to speculate on this possibility, however, since it raises the specter of strategic conventional warfare, about which there has been little debate since the advent of nuclear weapons.[28]

There are strong arguments in favor of such a capability. It would increase NATO's range of options, and could raise the nuclear threshold by delaying the use of LRTNF. By holding high-value targets in the Soviet Union hostage to conventional weapons, NATO would deny the Russians sanctuary for waging a conventional war in the European theater. Attacking appropriate air defense sites would leave the Soviet Union

26. Soviet tactics for crossing water obstacles are well described in Sidorenko, *The Offensive*, pp. 177–99.

27. Dropping a bridge span is the normally accepted criterion of damage; to achieve this the aim point selected is normally a bridge pier, one of the abutments, or a span itself. In all cases extreme accuracy is required: about three meters for an abutment or probably one meter for a bridge pier, depending on the type of bridge construction. The charge weight of explosive required is also large; for example, a gap of at least thirty-five meters must be blown in a bridge span because of the capabilities of Soviet bridge-laying equipment.

28. Many of the early writers on cruise missiles foresaw this potential, but there has been no detailed analysis.

more vulnerable to subsequent conventional operations by long-range aircraft such as the F-111. Furthermore, military targets close to civilian areas might be attacked in the early stages of hostilities without the excessive collateral damage that accompanies nuclear attacks. Because the Russians would be uncertain whether a NATO raid detected crossing the European-Soviet Union border was nuclear or conventionally armed, their contingency planning would be complicated, they would be less sure about their response, and there might be further time for political negotiation.

Deeper examination of this use of cruise missiles reveals a number of contrary considerations, however. One difficult problem is the range-payload trade-off. If the missile is to travel more than several hundred kilometers, the size of the warhead would have to be reduced to accommodate more fuel, thus reducing the probability of kill against the target. Beyond such tactical considerations are political restrictions. Attacks across the Soviet Union border are presently considered a different level of conflict, so the employment of conventionally armed cruise missiles for such attacks could be subject to political control as stringent as that governing nuclear forces. Such control could detract from the military utility of these forces by constraining the military commander's choice of targets and reducing the number of weapons launched below that required to achieve the requisite level of damage. As a means of escalation control, however, conventional weapons would be insignificant compared to nuclear weapons, whose effect in maintaining and restoring deterrence would be of a different order of magnitude.

If military commanders were to be allowed relatively free rein in target selection once border-crossing authority had been granted, the value of such a force would have to be justified by its contribution to direct defense. To cover adequately the number of suitable targets in the Soviet Union, the force would have to number thousands of missiles, which would be very expensive and would affect the procurement of other high-priority equipment. Airfields and air defense sites would have to be attacked repeatedly. Radar antennae, for example, can be replaced relatively quickly if spares are prestocked. The range of the Backfire bomber and Soviet transport aircraft would allow operations to be conducted throughout the European theater from any number of bases deep in the Soviet Union. The destruction of command, control, and communications bunkers in the Soviet Union might have a serious effect on the battlefield due to the Soviet leadership's tight centralized control, but they are likely to be buried deep and hardened beyond the effective capabilities of conventionally armed cruise missiles. For longer-term effects, many logistic supply and supporting systems would have to be attacked. Such a strategic conventional capability would also imply a shift in policy toward a war of attrition, which European nations in particular would be unwilling to adopt. Therefore, it would be important for such a capability to have an immediate effect on the battlefield situation. It may be postulated that selective use of nuclear weapons would not be authorized until shortly before NATO armies were threatened with defeat, or NATO was about to lose its nuclear counterstrike capability or vital territory. If so, then a key question is whether a long-range conventional cruise missile force attacking targets in the Soviet Union would be able to delay those moments significantly.

An assessment of Soviet perceptions is equally important. The manifest capability to threaten targets in the Soviet Union with conventional weapons would arguably enhance conventional deterrence. However, deterrence might fail. Since it would require considerable political resolve for the Russians to initiate hostilities within Europe, it is difficult to see how the disruption of some military targets in the Soviet Union could dent their determination to pursue their chosen path. Once such hostilities had begun, the use of conventional rather than nuclear weapons to attack targets in the Soviet Union would hardly enhance deterrence and, particularly if launched in less than optimum numbers, might be interpreted by the Soviet Union as a lack of resolve to escalate. Chemical warheads might have greater deterrent value, but NATO undoubtedly would not authorize first use of chemical weapons and the necessarily retaliatory nature of such weapon-warhead combinations could obviate their use when most needed.[29]

A more plausible option would be to target key installations in the military complexes closer to NATO territory that are likely to play an important part in Warsaw Pact operations from the outset of hostilities:

29. The use of chemical weapons is explicitly prohibited by the Protocol on the Use in War of Asphyxiating, Poisonous, and other Gases and on Bacteriological Methods of Warfare, signed in Geneva on June 17, 1925. However, owing to reservations by signatories, the protocol in effect prohibits only first use of chemical weapons. See S. J. Lundin, "Confidence-building Measures and a Chemical Weapons Convention," in Stockholm International Peace Research Institute, *Chemical Weapons: Destruction and Conversion* (London: Taylor and Francis; New York: Crane, Russak, 1980), p. 141.

for example, the Kola Peninsula, the Baltic and Black Sea fleet ports, and supporting airfields. Conventional cruise missiles could be deployed in Norway and Denmark to get around Nordic refusal to station foreign forces or nuclear weapons on their soil and to strengthen the deterrent effect of NATO's forces in the northern region, which is particularly vulnerable to surprise land and amphibious attack.[30] This could also help NATO to act in the important Norwegian and Baltic seas and demonstrate at the outset that war could not be restricted to NATO and non-Soviet Warsaw Pact territory. Similarly, targets in the Black Sea fleet ports and key targets in the Kiev and Odessa military districts could be covered by long-range cruise missiles based in NATO's southern region. While border-crossing authority would still be involved, such a force of cruise missiles would be clearly limited in numbers and intended purpose. Besides being more affordable for NATO, this step could be rationalized politically as an evolutionary development of current conventional capabilities rather than a revolutionary doctrine of strategic conventional warfare.

Launch Modes for Conventional Cruise Missiles

One of the military attractions of cruise missiles is that they can be launched from a variety of platforms, thus enhancing operational flexibility while complicating an enemy's offensive and defensive task. Considerations for basing conventional cruise missiles are substantially different from those for LRTNF. Requirements for control and security, as well as prelaunch survivability, are not so stringent, and the total number of missiles involved is much greater. A mixed force taking advantage of all possible launch modes would have considerable appeal, but proliferation on such a wide scale would hardly be justifiable for the limited role previously discussed for cruise missiles in Europe. Furthermore, certain basing options that might be attractive to the United States in the exercise of its global responsibilities have less merit when considered from the standpoint of a war in Europe, where cruise missile operations can for the

30. For an analysis of the vulnerabilities of NATO's northern flank, see Jacquelyn K. Davis and Robert L. Pfaltzgraff, Jr., *Soviet Theater Strategy: Implications for NATO*, United States Strategic Institute Report 78-1 (Washington, D.C.: USSI, 1978).

most part be preplanned. Each basing mode has certain military advantages and disadvantages, as well as a number of nonmilitary considerations—arms control, political, single-service preferences, and, in some options, legal.

Sea-Launched Cruise Missiles

Although it should be possible to install cruise missiles on a variety of surface or subsurface vessels, for a number of reasons sea-launched cruise missiles are not a good choice for land-attack missions in Europe. Deployment of these weapons on U.S. general purpose naval forces is not practical because they are unlikely to be in the right place when required. The variety of maritime tasks that European navies would have to undertake in the buildup to and during hostilities would occupy to capacity the number of ships planned to be available to NATO. Adding cruise missiles to surface ships for land-attack missions would constrain their operational flexibility by requiring them to operate within range of the intended targets or requiring long sea passages, possibly through contested waters, in order to reach their designated launch positions, which would also be within range of Soviet land-based air power. Submarines would be less vulnerable, and the ability to attack key maritime installations with conventional submarine-launched cruise missiles would dispense with the need to sail large carrier groups in the north Norwegian Sea waters. However, cruise missiles might be installed primarily at the expense of the torpedo inventory, which would detract from their primary antisubmarine warfare role.

An alternative would be to arm coastal shipping with cruise missiles. Although the use of commercial ships is unlikely due to contractual and legal difficulties, it might be possible to convert such shipping for manning by regular naval personnel and thus be able to operate merged with all other shipping in the area. However, a coaster armed with two or three hundred cruise missiles would be a lucrative target, counteracting to some degree the advantages of anonymity. Smaller craft, such as Hovercraft, patrol boats, or barges, would provide less attractive targets and would be difficult to detect and attack if operated in both coastal and inland waterways, such as the lakes, canals, and rivers of western Germany. The relatively restricted nature of inland waterways would facilitate ground sabotage, however, and major rivers and lakes might be encircled by the enemy. The most promising sea-launched option would appear to be patrol boats operating in friendly coastal waters. However, considerable investment in new hulls and extra manpower would be required, making the sea-launched option more expensive than either the air- or ground-launched option.[31] Since either of the latter could adequately cover the relevant target sets, the extra cost of investing in SLCMs would probably not be justified.

Air-Launched Cruise Missiles

Air-launched cruise missiles would have a number of advantages. The increased number of potential launch points would complicate the task of Soviet air defense planners, and the cruise missiles could be deployed quickly from one theater to another. The cruise missile's range would allow its parent aircraft to fly shorter distances and thus act as a force multiplier by facilitating more sorties. It would also extend the effective range of aircraft whose radius of action is limited when carrying a full weapon load. Similarly, the effective range of the cruise missile would be increased by that of the aircraft, reaching targets deeper in the Soviet Union. This would be of particular significance if a SALT III agreement were to apply range limitations to ground- or sea-launched missiles similar to those negotiated in the protocol to SALT II. The costs of modifying tactical aircraft to carry and fire cruise missiles might be less than those for the special launcher units and booster motors required for GLCMs and SLCMs, and utilizing the aircraft's advantages (range, high-speed dash, agility, ECM) might dispense with the need to design such features into the next generation of cruise missiles, thus reducing unit costs. Well-established command and control facilities already exist at military air bases, and since security regulations applying to conventional warheads are less stringent than for nuclear weapons, conventional missiles could be prestocked at military and possibly civil air bases, enhancing survivability and interoperability between NATO's various air forces.

On the other hand, arming tactical aircraft with cruise missiles would confront air commanders with the crucial dilemma of what percentage of scarce air assets to allocate to different roles. Carriage on aircraft would also vitiate the cruise missile's inherent autonomy by subjecting it to the aircraft's limitations of weather, vulnerability, and runway requirements.

31. It is also relevant that U.S. naval manpower has already been stretched too thin in recent years to make such options very practical.

The prelaunch survivability of the missile would be only as high as the survivability of its parent aircraft. The development of a dedicated carrier aircraft designed to operate outside the range of Soviet air defenses would overcome some of these limitations, but, as with dedicated sea platforms, would be costly in money and manpower.[32] Alternatively, it might be possible to modify large military aircraft—such as transports, tankers, or early warning or maritime patrol planes—to carry ALCMs as a secondary role. But cost and the need for a lengthy modification program for aircraft already scarce in number and fully committed to their primary role would appear to rule this out.

Ground-Launched Cruise Missiles

Ground-launched cruise missiles would free both ships and aircraft to carry out their primary roles, and by using mobile operations, they could be more survivable than ALCMs on fixed bases. GLCMs could be held at a high state of readiness for lengthy periods, armed with warheads matched to their preplanned targets, and available for immediate use in all weather conditions. This would free air commanders to allocate manned tactical aircraft to immediate support of land armies while simultaneously using cruise missiles for essential offensive air and interdiction tasks. Deployed GLCMs would, however, be more vulnerable to sabotage than if based on protected airfields. The need for a booster motor, transporter-erector-launcher, and launch control center raises the overall cost, and as dedicated systems they would require extra manpower, particularly if the mobile concept were adopted. Average support costs per missile fired could be reduced, however, if provisions were made to reload transporter-erector-launchers with extra rounds. Moreover, as separate systems, no lengthy modification program affecting operational availability would be required. Significantly, this form of deployment would mean that no European NATO nation could argue that it did not have suitable launching platforms.

Much of the extra cost associated with the GLCM derives from the concept of mobile operations, which requires large convoys of vehicles, including launch control centers and transporter-erector-launchers, and

---

32. An interesting possibility would be the modification of USAF B-52Ds, rather than developing cruise missile carriers based on civilian transport aircraft. See chapter 7.

extra security personnel. While this is essential for the nuclear GLCM force, the prelaunch survivability criteria for conventionally armed GLCMs would not be so stringent, particularly since many of them would be launched in the early stages of any conflict. Operating from fixed sites would reduce costs considerably. A less sophisticated launcher with a rapid reload capability could be developed. If it were deployed on airfields, existing command and control facilities, logistic supply networks, ground security personnel, and protection against air attack could be utilized. Because it would not need runways, the force could in theory continue operations even when the airfield was under conventional attack.

Conceptually it is difficult to argue against ground basing as the preferred option, provided no excessive cost is incurred. However, some important considerations could combine to weigh against this option. First is the problem of differentiating conventionally armed missiles from those armed with nuclear warheads for the purpose of arms control verification. Because current conventional cruise missile design, based on the Tomahawk, allows a direct trade-off between warhead size and fuel load, differentiation is impossible within current national technical means of verification. Even if the follow-on generation of cruise missiles is observably different, verification difficulties would still arise if they were designed to fire from launchers similar in outline to those for nuclear missiles. Since the West does not have under development or test a GLCM that is observably different from the nuclear Tomahawk, restrictions on conventionally armed GLCMs could well be established largely by default in the next round of arms limitation talks. A continuation of the current definition of a cruise missile to include both nuclear and conventional armament, in conjunction with the numerical limits that may be placed on nuclear GLCMs, would effectively rule out the deployment of conventionally armed GLCMs.

A further barrier to the deployment of a conventionally armed GLCM force lies in the 600-kilometer range limitation in the protocol to SALT II. Although the protocol range provisions are unlikely to be carried forward in toto into any SALT III agreement because of the importance of the NATO LRTNF modernization program, it is conceivable that a 600-kilometer range limit on observably different conventional GLCMs could be included in order to establish some differentiation between nuclear and conventional categories. However, such a limitation would seriously degrade the utility of these missiles due to the definitions of a cruise missile's range in SALT II and the missile's guidance, which requires a zigzag course to enhance in-flight survivability.[33] When a further allowance is made for deployment well behind the FEBA to ensure prelaunch survivability, the effective range of the missiles is reduced to about 300–400 kilometers, rather than 600. Thus, to avoid a negative arms control impact on any future deployment of conventionally armed long-range GLCMs, the West would have to renegotiate the 600-kilometer range limitation (or range definition) and develop a missile observably different from the nuclear GLCM.

A second obstacle to the choice of conventional GLCMs is the skepticism among air forces. Because they are aware of the problems associated with long-range counter air and interdiction operations, they question the ability of weapons as small as cruise missiles to carry out effectively tasks that manned aircraft, with their larger payload, find difficult. There is also an understandable reluctance to add to tightly constrained budgets provisions for a weapon system with unproved effectiveness and uncertain total costs, especially if existing weapon programs— especially aircraft—have to be excised or pared. But if objections about effectiveness and costs are met, and some aircraft program has to be pared to accommodate a cruise missile program, an ALCM force has certain advantages. Not only are ALCMs likely to be cheaper, but their force-multiplier effect on sortie generation capability and the lower aircraft attrition that could be assumed would partially make up for the aircraft that had been replaced.

A further hurdle to the GLCM lies in the fact that NATO forces are based on the size and shape of national forces. Most nations wish to retain full flexibility within their own forces to cover as many roles as national budgets will allow, despite the assignment of the major proportion of those forces to NATO and the resultant potential division of labor among nations. Hence individual countries may well be wary of committing large

33. Second agreed statement to paragraph 8 of Article 2 of the treaty: "The range of which a cruise missile is capable is the maximum distance which can be covered by the missile in its standard design mode flying until fuel exhaustion, determined by projecting its flight path onto the earth's sphere from the point of launch to the point of impact." Reproduced in Labrie, *SALT Hand Book*, pp. 621–50. See testimony of Harold Brown and David C. Jones in *Military Implications of the Treaty on the Limitation of Strategic Offensive Arms and Protocol Thereto (SALT II Treaty)*, Hearings before the Senate Committee on Armed Services, 96 Cong. 1 sess. (GPO, 1979), pt. 4, pp. 1557–59.

sums of money to forces with only one application, not only because of the opportunity costs of capabilities forgone, but also for fear that in the planned lifetime of the equipment changes in Soviet tactics might make that single-role system obsolete. They might prefer to invest in the air-launched variety because the aircraft's versatility would be preserved for other tasks if the cruise missile became obsolete.

Although these pressures will conspire to create support for the air-launched option, I believe that the imperative remains to deploy a force of conventionally armed GLCMs that can be used at the very outset of hostilities in all weather conditions. Should other considerations of arms control, national force structure, and budgets drive the main thrust of cruise missile development toward the air-launched variety, then a mixed force should be established with a large enough ground element to operate while the demands on tactical aircraft are most intense. Once the initial surge demands on tactical aircraft have been met and the coordination of Warsaw Pact air defenses has been dislocated, air commanders might then be in a position to allocate a proportion of available aircraft to offensive counter air and interdiction tasks. Arming these aircraft with ALCMs would reap the force-multiplier advantages already described.

It is difficult to quantify precisely the numbers of cruise missiles required, since probabilities concerning prelaunch survivability, ability to penetrate Warsaw Pact defenses, and eventual damage effects are extremely complex. Moreover, no one can predict the course or duration of the conventional stage of any conflict, and assessments of attrition to enemy and friendly forces, an important criterion in such calculations, are largely subjective. However, from 800 to 1,000 GLCMs, targeted against Warsaw Pact main operating bases, key railway bridges, headquarters, and fixed air defense sites, might suffice for the first two days of hostilities.[34] This would free manned tactical aircraft to attack mobile and dispersed targets on and behind the battlefield. Perhaps 300 to 350 ALCMs for each subsequent day of conventional hostilities would suffice.

---

34. Author's estimate, based on an arbitrary selection of airfields and bridges derived from ordnance survey maps and assumptions on numbers of headquarters and air defense sites that might be appropriate for cruise missile attack. These rough calculations assume an average of five to eight missiles are used against each airfield (depending upon the type of aircraft operating from the field) and two to three against each bridge, air defense site, or headquarters. If less conservative estimates about the number needed to close an airfield were used, requirements would be lower.

Benefits of a Conventional Cruise Missile Force

A small force of long-range conventionally armed ground-launched cruise missiles for preplanned attacks against the high-value military assets discussed could contribute significantly to NATO's capabilities at the outset of any war in Europe. The size of the force could be limited to that required to attack fixed targets for a certain time, after which further coverage of those targets might be assigned to aircraft with other conventional ordnance, or to nuclear weapons if the Warsaw Pact chose to continue hostilities. The synergistic effect would be considerable. Even if the backup force of ALCMs were not deployed, the 800–1,000 GLCMs would release aircraft for battle support and air defense that are currently earmarked for offensive counter air and long-range interdiction roles. Because targets allocated to the former roles are closer to the FEBA and would result in less attrition than against heavily defended point targets, perhaps 2,000–3,000 additional aircraft sorties could be made in the opening days of a war. At the same time, GLCM attacks could disrupt the coordination of the Warsaw Pact's offensive and degrade its potential for mounting perhaps twice that number of offensive sorties per day.[35] This would reverse the present asymmetry in available air power and have a significant effect on the land battle.

Further advantages would accrue from such a force. The ability to attack essential interdiction and offensive counter air targets at the outset of hostilities would be of particular significance if NATO had a short warning time. All available tactical air resources would necessarily be allocated to defensive counter air and close air support to prevent an immediate enemy breakthrough, allowing Warsaw Pact reinforcements to deploy forward with impunity unless NATO were to use nuclear weapons. If the Pact deployed reinforcements earlier so as to overcome the threat posed by a cruise missile force, NATO's warning time would be increased, which would facilitate timely mobilization decisions. The fact that NATO could attack with conventional cruise missiles targets that can currently

35. Author's estimate, based on IISS, *The Military Balance, 1980–1981*, table 5, p. 113, assuming 50 percent of available NATO fighter ground-attack aircraft are allocated to offensive counter air and interdiction tasks, and aircraft fly two or three sorties per twenty-four hours. Soviet offensive air sortie potential is even more difficult to assess since the number of dual-role interceptor fighters allocated to offensive missions and the numbers of armed helicopter sorties available cannot be predicted with any certainty.

be targeted only with nuclear weapons might also force the Warsaw Pact to continue investing resources in air defense that might otherwise be devoted to developing offensive weapons. Allocating long-range counter air and interdiction targets to cruise missiles would also dispense with the need to develop the follow-on generation of aircraft dedicated to these roles and allow tactical aircraft development efforts to focus on the relatively narrower, though still demanding, operational requirements of battlefield support.

If NATO were to adopt this concept and seek to persuade nations to establish a cruise missile force for deployment throughout the European NATO countries, a common fund could be established that might safeguard the force from the vicissitudes of national budgetary planning (although the experience with the NATO E-3A aircraft provides a somewhat unhappy precedent). Collaborative production between Europe and the United States could be encouraged, taking advantage of previous U.S. research and development, saving European costs, and giving a much-needed boost to allied cooperation in the field of weapons acquisition. A conventionally armed and limited-range force would evoke none of the domestic political antipathies associated with nuclear weapons. Such a force would enhance integration of NATO defense posture, making it more than just an accumulation of national technologies and armaments, and would demonstrate a level of standardization in equipment and tactical operations beyond anything so far accomplished. Besides its contribution to NATO's direct defense, it would thus be a visible demonstration of alliance cohesion and resolve.

Implications for Future Cruise Missiles

There are a number of important factors to consider in defining the broad parameters for the design of the next generation of cruise missiles. The size and shape of the Tomahawk, which forms the basis of current conventional developments in the United States, prevents a large enough conventional warhead from being carried to the required ranges when flying at low level.[36] It is also not yet clear whether sufficiently small sub-

36. Details on the air-launched conventionally armed cruise missile based on the Tomahawk currently under development can be found in Mark Hewish, "Tactical Missile Survey, Part I: Ground Targets," *International Defense Review*, vol. 13, no. 6 (1980), p. 861.

munitions packing the right punch can be developed so that enough munitions can be carried in a Tomahawk missile to achieve the required damage. Moreover, the Tomahawk's lack of agility, due to its tubular shape, small wings, low power-weight ratio, and guidance system, limits its ability to follow terrain and use evasive routing in more than rolling terrain without flying so high that it would be vulnerable to enemy defenses. The proposed terminal guidance for the conventionally armed land-attack Tomahawk is scene matching, which could be degraded by weather conditions. Night operations will require artificial illumination, which would also increase its vulnerability.[37] Although seeking to make use of existing Tomahawk production facilities makes economic sense, a unit price of approximately $1 million a missile (although this might be reduced significantly if large numbers were ordered) would be unlikely to attract many buyers.

Requirements for the next-generation cruise missile could include a range of 1,000 nautical miles, greater agility to allow for a smaller radius of turn and more effective terrain following, and the potential to carry integral ECM to aid penetration. The weight of warhead required might vary between 1,500 and 2,000 pounds, depending on the target and appropriate type of munition. Certainly the large number of submunitions to be carried dictates a larger volumetric capacity.[38] Such specifications would lead to a larger missile (perhaps 30 percent larger), which would require a more powerful engine. Terminal guidance must meet the conflicting demands of fine resolution for target discrimination and invulnerability to enemy jamming and adverse weather effects; millimetric radar and long-wave infrared show promise. Alternatively, a forward-looking laser system could be used for target detection and homing (thus increasing accuracies to the order of one meter), which could also update the inertial navigation, thus dispensing with the need for TERCOM. It would also allow closer terrain following and thus increase survivability. To keep ahead of evolving Warsaw Pact air defenses, the missile would need radar-absorbing materials to attenuate electromagnetic waves. Configuration shaping to reduce the radar cross section would significantly decrease the probability of being detected and engaged.

37. General Dynamics, "A New Dimension in Conventional Air Power: MRASM: Medium-Range Air-to-Surface Missile," document 06080571-58, p. 20.

38. The tubular shape of the Tomahawk makes carriage of large numbers of submunitions difficult. Thus the next generation of missiles should not necessarily be tubular.

These development requirements would increase costs, but costs can be reduced by using cheaper materials (such as aluminum), turbojet rather than turbofan engines (provided the missile retains sufficient range), and simpler navigation systems (the current guidance system accounts for up to one-third of current unit costs). Production orders in the thousands would also bring economies of scale. If such missiles could be produced at the unit price of $1 million (and development efforts are geared to reducing this substantially), their greater individual punch and range would reduce the number required and could make them relatively cost-effective.

Considerations of cost, range, and vulnerability are likely to rule out giving land-attack cruise missiles a supersonic capability. At high levels, where a supersonic cruise missile might have sufficient range, detection by radar or space-based infrared sensor is relatively assured, and such missiles are vulnerable to hypersonic surface-to-air missiles. At low altitudes, even a large cruise missile would have limited range flying at supersonic speeds. Furthermore, agility is less at higher speeds and full advantage cannot be taken of terrain masking. The combination of higher flight profile and increased infrared and noise emission would mean a higher probability of detection. By contrast, subsonic low-altitude cruise missiles take advantage of many of the sensor limitations that degrade radar performance—terrain masking, horizon limits, and background clutter—and enhance their survivability.

An alternative would be to convert surplus aircraft such as F-100s, F-105s, F-104s, or F-4s to remote control for a one-way mission in much the same way that they are currently converted for use as target drones. Modification would be limited to the installation and integration of the necessary guidance systems with the aircraft controls, data bank, and terminal guidance. This would allow large payloads to be carried, with scope for integral ECM, on highly agile platforms. Weapons currently under development for manned aircraft, which might be too large for cruise missiles, could be carried, thus saving parallel development work. Such large aircraft would be much more detectable by Soviet radars, although their enhanced agility might more than offset this. On the other hand, the timely availability of large numbers of surplus aircraft could depend on the compliance of a variety of nations, and this option is unlikely to appeal to industry since the scope for advancing technological developments is less than with cruise missiles.

Because each cruise missile can be used only once, one major concern is their relative cost-effectiveness. Recoverable missiles have been proposed, on the assumption that the increased cost of development would be more than offset by the greater overall military effectiveness of each missile. This assumption has not been verified with a full cost-benefit analysis, but at first sight there are a number of uncertainties. The extra cost of developing the recovery system could be considerable. Although recovery systems are used for test missiles, there is no certainty that such systems would be suitable in combat conditions. Besides the recovery units, a large infrastructure would be required. Extra computer capacity and increased flight-planning time would also be required. Missiles would remain vulnerable to interception on their return flight, and airspace coordination for the control of returning friendly aircraft, already a major problem, would be exacerbated. While recovering reconnaissance and ECM defense suppression missiles has obvious merit, a recoverable system for attack cruise missiles would be hard to justify.

Conclusion

It is still too early in the development of cruise missiles for more than tentative conclusions to be drawn. However, it is apparent that cruise missiles could contribute significantly both to deterring confrontation between the Warsaw Pact and NATO and, in the event of war, to direct defense. Nuclear GLCMs promise to help restore the integrity of NATO's deterrent posture. While they might not be the ideal weapon system to meet the particular needs of NATO's sophisticated theater nuclear doctrine, they make an excellent choice when other important considerations of time, cost, alliance cohesion, and response to SS-20 and Backfire deployments are taken into account. Should a longer-range MRBM become available in the long term to replace them, nuclear GLCMs will have played an essential interim role.

Major questions surround the future of conventionally armed cruise missiles for conflict in Europe. Although an analysis of Warsaw Pact target sets, viewed against current NATO limitations, can show in conceptual terms the potentially significant boost conventional cruise missiles could bring to NATO capabilities, it is by no means certain that such missiles can be developed effectively at affordable cost. Until specialized submunitions are tested satisfactorily and mated with a sufficiently accurate terminal guidance system, cruise missiles will suffer in cost-effectiveness comparisons with manned aircraft. Even if these requirements are met, it is still unlikely that sufficient intelligence can be built into a cruise missile to cope with the fast-moving, unpredictable pattern that is likely to characterize a future conflict in Europe. Cruise missiles are therefore likely to be most usefully employed against static installations of high military value, freeing tactical aircraft for battlefield support. The importance to NATO of an offensive counter air and interdiction capability, however, argues strongly that development of conventionally armed cruise missiles should be among the highest of NATO's priorities.

CHAPTER SEVEN

Local Conflicts
in the Third World

RICHARD BURT

As THE 1980s get under way, it is becoming clear that the potential for military conflict is growing in nearly every region of the world. Contrary to analyses popular in the United States only a few years ago, the usefulness of force in international politics seems to be on the rise, particularly in the regions of the nonaligned, or the third world.

Several factors have heightened the probability of violence in these countries. The Soviet Union's capacity to use its power in the third world has grown, as demonstrated in Angola in 1975, Ethiopia in 1978, and Afghanistan in 1979. The fading of pax Americana has confronted former U.S. clients with new security concerns and has fed the regional ambitions of other local powers. Economic, social—and in some areas religious— pressures are feeding centrifugal tendencies, undermining postcolonial political arrangements and widening and intensifying disputes, which can be further fueled by external intervention. To complete this gloomy picture, third world countries are acquiring military equipment at an unprecedented rate; transfers of advanced technology, such as high-performance combat planes and precision-guided munitions, to less developed nations are now almost commonplace.

The modern, long-range cruise missile (like most advanced American weapon systems developed since World War II) was not developed for

Richard Burt is director of politico-military affairs in the Department of State. He wrote this chapter while serving as a reporter for the *New York Times,* before entering the government. The views expressed are strictly his own and do not necessarily reflect the position of any agency of the U.S. government.

use in local wars. Both the Boeing air-launched cruise missile (ALCM) and the General Dynamics Tomahawk cruise missile are designed primarily as nuclear delivery vehicles for strategic roles against targets in the Soviet Union or as theater weapons in a high-intensity conflict between the Atlantic Alliance and the Warsaw Pact in Central Europe. But the flexibility of cruise missiles—like that of the aircraft they could replace—suggests that they might possess military utility beyond their contribution to Soviet-American strategic deterrence or the maintenance of stability in Europe. When the B-52 bomber rolled off the production line in 1955, few observers foresaw that it would be used to deliver conventional munitions in Vietnam some fifteen years later. A decade ago, moreover, very few analysts recognized the B-52's current utility in maritime missions, including mine-laying. It is not surprising, then, that the potential relevance of new cruise missile technology for local conflicts in the third world has received only scant attention.

In analyses of the impact of new cruise missiles, writers either have focused on the Soviet-American nuclear dimension or, in describing possible deployment in other contexts, have made extravagant claims. It has been suggested in some naval circles, for example, that if the United States deployed thousands of cruise missiles on surface ships, submarines, and forward-deployed aircraft around the world, the Navy's carrier fleet would become obsolete. (Indeed, noting the Soviet Navy's widespread deployment of cruise missiles in the early 1960s, some analysts have asserted that Moscow, early on, decided that it did not have to match the United States in carrier power, a point that obviously needs to be reconsidered in the light of Moscow's more recent deployment of carriers.) In a similar vein, it has been argued in arms-control circles that the spread of cruise missiles to third world countries would be sure to raise the risks of nuclear proliferation.

The purpose of this chapter is to explore what effect cruise missiles are likely to have on military environments in the third world and, in particular, what role they are likely to play in future local conflicts. To explore this problem, four clusters of questions are addressed:

1. Are existing cruise missile designs relevant to local conflict conditions? What design changes are necessary (and feasible) to give cruise missiles more utility in conventional roles in local conflicts?

2. In what circumstances might local powers desire cruise missiles? How serious a threat is the possible proliferation of cruise missiles in the third world?

3. How might the United States use cruise missiles in a conflict with a local power? What are the broad implications for U.S. force structure of using cruise missiles in local conflicts?

4. How might the United States use cruise missiles in a local conflict involving Soviet forces? In particular, how might they be exploited in a conflict with the Soviet Union in the Persian Gulf area?

Before these questions are analyzed, some definitions are necessary. *Local conflict* is a vague term. For purposes here, it refers to nonnuclear combat outside Central Europe. Local conflicts in the third world can be small-scale civil wars in which external forces are invited in by one or another party, as was the case in Angola in 1975. But they can also be full-scale wars between local powers, for example, the 1973 war in the Middle East; a conflict in which one of the superpowers is directly involved, for example, the war in Vietnam or the Soviet invasion of Afghanistan; or a limited conflict involving both superpowers, like a Soviet invasion of Iran that triggers a local American response. In a case in which both superpowers are engaged in combat, a local conflict could obviously become the opening phase of a global war.

It is also necessary to define cruise missile. Since the 1950s both the United States and the Soviet Union have deployed cruise missiles, ranging from the U.S. intercontinental missile, Snark, to the Soviet short-range antiship missile, Styx. Both systems are unmanned and armed and use air-breathing propulsion. What is clearly different about the new Boeing and General Dynamics designs are their relatively small size, low radar reflectivity, long range, high accuracy, and possible low cost. Cruise missiles used in local conflicts may exploit all of these characteristics or only some of them, but the quality of modern cruise missiles that sets them apart from earlier systems is their high accuracy at relatively long ranges.

Cruise Missile Design

Superficially, the attributes of Boeing's ALCM and General Dynamics' Tomahawk that make them so versatile and effective (see chapter 1) seem well suited to long-range strike missions, particularly in the less demanding air-defense environments of the third world. This said, it is important to recognize the drawbacks of cruise missiles in nonnuclear roles. One of the most important is their limited payload, measured in weight and space. At a range of more than 500 miles, a Tomahawk is unable to deliver a warhead exceeding 1,000 pounds or a munitions package exceeding about seven cubic feet. Against all but the most heavily defended, high-value targets, this is clearly not a cost-effective means of delivering ordnance. (Ground-attack aircraft, such as the A-7 and the F-4, are capable of delivering three or four times the payload of a cruise missile at these ranges and, of course, they can be reused.) At more than $1 million per copy, cruise missiles in nonnuclear conflicts would be too costly to use against most targets and for saturation attacks against well-defended, high-value targets.

Thus, a critical question—to which there is no clear answer as yet—is whether existing cruise missile designs should be used for conventional missions or whether a new generation, optimized for that role, should be acquired. The Navy is now examining the possible deployment of a land-attack version of the Tomahawk SLCM (sea-launched cruise missile), the TLAM-C (Tomahawk land-attack missile–conventional), which would be armed with a single, 1,000-pound, high-explosive warhead. The TLAM-C could be deployed aboard existing attack submarines and new surface combatants fitted with vertical launch tubes. The Air Force has tested an airfield-attack version of the Tomahawk, whose fragmentation munitions crater runways and render them temporarily inoperable. But it is apparently not clear whether the Tomahawk, even at ranges of 500 miles or less, could carry the payload to be competitive with aircraft in attacking high-value, fixed targets, such as airfields, petroleum oil-lubricant (POL) facilities, radars, and command bunkers.[1]

To be most effective, cruise missiles will have to be tailored to the new generation of munitions now under development in the United States and Western Europe, which includes small air-delivered mines, cluster bomb units, and terminally guided submunitions. Dispensers for most of these munitions require either a few thousand pounds of payload or twenty or so cubic feet, requiring a larger airframe than the Tomahawk and the ALCM but using many of the same components. Consequently, there is some support within the aerospace industry for rapidly developing a larger version of one of these missiles. The Air Force and the Navy, meanwhile,

1. The first test of a cruise missile in a conventional land-attack role was conducted in May 1978. A Tomahawk flew 400 miles and attacked an airfield with submunitions, relying on terrain contour matching (TERCOM) navigation. After dropping eleven bomblets on a runway, it flew back over the target area, simulating a damage-assessment photo run. Further tests are now in progress, but a definitive assessment of the missile's utility in the airfield-attack role has not been made. See John Newbauer, "U.S. Cruise Missile Development," *Astronautics and Aeronautics,* September 1979, p. 29.

have asked military contractors to prepare initial designs based on the Tomahawk for a medium-range air-to-surface missile (MRASM), which could deliver heavier conventional payloads. However, the MRASM would have only about thirteen cubic feet of usable payload space.

Another important technical issue, which also has a bearing on cost, is accuracy. American long-range cruise missiles are being equipped with enormously sophisticated guidance systems (terrain contour matching, or TERCOM, and digital scene matching area correlator, or DSMAC), which may achieve accuracies on the order of ten to twenty meters.[2] For TERCOM to work properly, however, highly detailed maps of the missile's desired course must be prepared and stored in its computer. Maps of potential target areas in the Soviet Union and Eastern Europe are now being prepared for use with the B-52 ALCM and the NATO GLCM (ground-launched cruise missile), but using cruise missiles in conflicts elsewhere would essentially require mapping the world, which would be incredibly costly.

For contingencies in the third world, then, it might be preferable to rely for guidance on precision-positioning technology. Delivery vehicles, whether missiles or aircraft, would receive signals from radio beacons, which would enable the on-board guidance equipment to establish the position of the vehicle in relation to the target so that course corrections could be made. By the mid-1980s, the United States is scheduled to have deployed the global-positioning system, an arrangement in which Navstar satellites in high orbits will enable ships, aircraft, and ground forces to determine their location within ten meters. The global positioning system will be vulnerable, in theory, to antisatellite attacks and thus not ideal for strategic or theater nuclear roles. But Soviet use of antisatellite systems in local conflicts is unlikely, so global-positioning technology might provide a more efficient and less costly alternative to TERCOM guidance for the use of cruise missiles outside Europe or the Soviet Union.

Third World Powers

Over the last decade, precision-guided, antiship missiles have proliferated in the navies of the West, the Warsaw Pact, and the third world. Possessing over-the-horizon ranges of fifty kilometers or more, these missiles augment the coastal defenses of small states significantly while

2. Imaging infrared sensors, which will allow the missiles to verify targets, are under development. The system would match sensory information of the target area with stored information to make last-minute course changes. Ibid., p. 30.

making larger navies more vulnerable. Deployed on land or on fast patrol boats, missiles like the French Exocet (which has been purchased by more than ten nations) and the Israeli Gabriel give small states an unparalleled capability to reduce naval access by larger powers. The spread of anti-ship missiles to small powers and the Soviet fleet poses particular problems for the U.S. Navy's prime power-projection instrument, the attack carrier. Indeed, the vulnerability of major surface combatants to antishipping missiles has become one of the Navy's primary rationales for deploying land-attack cruise missiles on surface ships and submarines.

But third world deployment of antishipping missiles should not be seen as a prelude to their acquisition of long-range naval attack systems, such as the Tomahawk SLCM. Targeting a naval vessel thirty kilometers away is far easier than engaging a target hundreds of kilometers away. Acquiring a moving target at great distance at sea and then engaging it is probably beyond the means of third world navies during the coming decade. In the foreseeable future, then, coastal third world states will be able to do little more than keep outsiders from coming close to their shores.

Most third world nations would face even more daunting problems in using long-range cruise missiles for land attack. The basic problem would be developing a system roughly comparable to the ALCM or the Tomahawk. Although indigenous defense industries in the third world have grown steadily over the last decade, no state (with the possible exception of Israel) is likely to master the microelectronics and computers for the guidance systems, let alone the metallurgical and precision machining of the missile's small turbofan engine. And even in the unlikely event that a state secured a Tomahawk-like system from the United States or another supplier, it would face another difficulty—generating the mapping information necessary for using TERCOM or gaining access to a precision-positioning guidance system.

The central reason that few third world nations will be interested in acquiring long-range cruise missiles is that they already possess the means of carrying out ground-attack missions. More than thirty nonaligned countries in the third world have advanced aircraft capable of delivering payloads of 1,000 pounds or more over ranges exceeding 500 miles. For many of these states these capabilities are not only sufficient for tactical strikes on or near the battlefield, but in most cases allow them to target the cities and industries of regional adversaries. Although the air defenses of some countries in the third world are likely to improve over the coming decade, aircraft will continue to serve as reliable penetrators.

Despite this, two arguments are made for the likely proliferation of long-range cruise missiles in the third world. First, states bent on becoming nuclear powers might perceive cruise missiles as potential delivery systems for nuclear weapons. There are several problems with this argument. For one, given the relatively small payload of modern cruise missiles, aircraft in a relatively benign air-defense environment would appear as cost-effective in the nuclear role as in the conventional. In the rare case where aircraft penetration seems doubtful, a would-be nuclear power is much more likely to turn to ballistic technology, as India has done, rather than to cruise missiles. Also, new nuclear powers would find it difficult to produce not only the components of the cruise missile itself but the small and relatively lightweight warheads it requires. Finally, although the ballistic missile is less accurate than a precision-guided cruise missile, its technology is more accessible—and accuracy, after all, would not be the predominant concern, since such states would probably allocate nuclear warheads to countervalue targets.

The second argument is that some third world powers might be interested in obtaining a strategic conventional capability with cruise missiles —the capacity to destroy high-value political and economic targets at long distances with a minimum of collateral damage. Israel, for example, with its asymmetries in population and geography vis-à-vis its Arab adversaries, would not want a Middle East war to escalate to the point of exchanging blows—nuclear or conventional—against population centers. At the same time, the capacity to undertake discrete and painful attacks against such Arab targets as oil fields and pumping centers might provide Israel with bargaining leverage before or after a conflict got under way. Long-range cruise missiles, particularly in the lethal air-defense environment of the Middle East, might then appear the most suitable system. Israel, with its well-developed technological base and its formal and informal ties to the American research and development establishment, is also one of the few nations in the third world capable of mastering cruise missile technology.

In the Far East, Taiwan and South Korea might have the incentives and skills to investigate cruise missiles for the long-range strike role. Taiwan, confronting the People's Republic of China across the strait and gradually losing its access to American arms (especially strike aircraft), might view cruise missiles as providing a surgical attack capability, which could keep Beijing from launching an invasion. South Korea, facing an invasion from the north, might view cruise missiles as the best option for attacking heavily defended air bases and logistics sites across the border. For all three of these third world nations, large numbers of conventional cruise missiles would be necessary and would impose a heavy and perhaps unacceptable financial burden.

The United States

The potential use of cruise missiles by the United States offers more intriguing possibilities. Without certain access to land bases around the world and with American power-projection capabilities centered in only thirteen aircraft carriers, the United States could put Tomahawk land-attack cruise missiles (TLAMs) on a variety of naval vessels. In situations where the United States lacked carriers, TLAMs, the Navy contends, would provide an offensive capability where none existed. The Navy maintains that TLAMs, in tandem with carriers, would enhance the capability of carrier aircraft in local conflicts. The deployment of ALCMs on long-range aircraft, such as the B-52 or the P-3, for use in remote third world conflicts is also receiving attention.

Apportioning carrier air power among potential theaters is indeed one of the most difficult problems the Navy faces in the coming decade. Following the Iranian revolution and the Soviet invasion of Afghanistan, the United States, in a rare instance since World War II, was forced to withdraw a carrier from the waters off Northeast Asia and another from the Mediterranean in order to have two carrier battle groups in the Indian Ocean. Similar situations are likely to arise in the 1980s in the Middle East, Southeast Asia, the Korean peninsula, and the Caribbean.

But the crucial question for the United States is what widespread deployment of TLAMs or ALCMs would add to U.S. military capabilities in dealing with conflicts in the third world. To answer this question, it is important to distinguish the scale of the conflict. The first, or "lesser," category might include small inaccessible conflicts, such as the 1975 Angolan civil war, in which small increments of military force could prove decisive and the American objective might be merely to prevent outside intervention. A second category would include large intense conflicts, say, in the Middle East or the Persian Gulf, where intense fighting took place and American interests were tied clearly to the outcome.

In an Angolan-style contingency, the capacity to undertake a limited number of strikes against fixed military targets ashore would be of uncertain value. A surface combatant or submarine armed with cruise missiles would not affect the course of a confused and quickly shifting guerrilla campaign in which only ground forces would make a difference. In some conflicts it could have symbolic force. A vessel standing off from a regional conflict would cast the sort of "shadow" an aircraft carrier casts, affecting the risk calculus of local actors and, more important, the intervention of outside powers. In addition, conventionally armed cruise missiles could strike the ports and air bases these outside powers would use to introduce troops and military equipment, thus sending a spectacular political message to both local actors and outside powers. (B-52s equipped with conventional ALCMs appear best suited for such missions because of their relatively short transit times. But even aircraft could not respond immediately unless reconnaissance was available to provide targeting information.) However, the United States would still have to decide how far it was willing to escalate its involvement if the demonstration of resolve failed to deter the Soviet Union from intervening directly with Cuban proxies. In the final analysis, the presence or even the use of cruise missiles in conflicts like that in Angola or the 1979 South Yemeni incursion into the Yemen Arab Republic would only buy the United States time. After damaging some fixed targets, U.S. air or naval forces would affect the course of the conflict very little; ground forces and sustained air operations would be required if this became the objective. Cruise-missile-equipped aircraft or vessels on the scene might provide the "breathing space" for American forces while amphibious, airborne, or carrier air units moved to the scene.

The role of cruise missiles, particularly TLAMs, in larger conflicts with local powers must be seen in a different light. What is envisioned here is not a civil war or a regional conflict involving small numbers of poorly equipped regular troops or guerrillas, but an intense war between well-equipped forces that affected central American interests, such as those in the Persian Gulf. In this contingency, Washington would not be as worried about becoming embroiled in "another Vietnam." The goal would be to terminate the conflict in a way favorable to American interests, and the United States would probably be ready to bring a full panoply of force to bear. Cruise missiles would have to compete with other systems, primarily air power. Tactical aircraft possess important advantages over TLAMs. In an Iraqi attack on Saudi Arabia, for example, the targets would be armored and infantry forces moving across the Saudi border. Aircraft equipped with precision-guided munitions and area weapons would be indispensable for finding armored columns and interdicting them. Even against lightly defended fixed targets, such as air bases and command posts, aircraft would offer advantages over cruise missiles because of their superior payload and reusability.

This said, there would be some specialized missions in which land-attack cruise missiles could complement the role of aircraft. For sustained antiarmor air operations against Iraqi forces moving into Saudi Arabia, American aircraft operating from carriers in the Arabian Sea or from Saudi bases would need a capacity to knock out Iraqi air power quickly and effectively. Strikes against Iraqi air bases, which are well defended by Soviet surface-to-air missiles, could tie up large numbers of American aircraft, and counterair operations could exact an unacceptably high attrition, but cruise missiles targeted on SAM sites around air bases and other heavily defended targets could lower the number of follow-up sorties required. In this way, cruise missiles would provide the conventional-warfare equivalent of corridor cutting in strategic nuclear warfare. A few hundred TLAMs and ALCMs on a few platforms—B-52s, surface ships, or attack submarines—would fill the requirement.

The Superpowers

Although the United States and the Soviet Union have yet to fight a limited war in the third world, this contingency cannot be counted out in the coming decade. In the 1973 war in the Middle East, the Soviet Union is reported to have made preparations for intervening with ground forces, a step that could have triggered a corresponding American response (and indeed, it did provoke the U.S. worldwide alert). And in early 1978 the Carter administration considered deploying a carrier task force in the Red Sea to threaten the Soviet air- and sealift to Ethiopia in its conflict with Somalia.

In the wake of the Soviet invasion of Afghanistan, the possibility of a Russian thrust against Iran and other oil-producing states in the Persian Gulf has emerged as a central concern. Recognizing the political and logistical constraints on deploying a large American force in the area, most analysts conclude that the way to counter Soviet intervention in the Gulf is to disrupt military operations until American and allied airlift and sealift can tip the local force balance. Since no large U.S. land-based combat force would be present in the region as a Soviet attack got under way, the United States would have to depend on aircraft for the following missions:

—intercept Soviet transport aircraft as they moved troops and equipment into the area;

—disrupt the landing of Soviet transport aircraft;

—interdict Soviet personnel, equipment, and supplies being moved into the region along land routes;

—insert troops to seize and defend critical points like air bases, ports, oil-production complexes, and lines of communication;

—conduct surveillance;

—control sea lines of communication while denying them to the enemy;

—create a logistical network capable of supporting sustained operations.

Navy F-14s and Air Force F-15s, equipped with air-to-air missiles, would intercept Soviet troop transports flying into the region. Ground-attack aircraft, A-10s and A-7s, along with B-52s from Diego Garcia and perhaps Egypt, Israel, and Somalia, could interdict land forces at key choke-points and strike airheads in Iran or further south. Aircraft armed with a new generation of conventional munitions, including long-range air-to-air weapons, cluster-bomb dispensers, air-delivered mines, and terminally guided submunitions, might execute a containment and disruption strategy in the Gulf.

Land-attack cruise missiles could perform important though limited roles in such a strategy. In the opening phase of a large-scale Soviet assault, the U.S. Navy would probably be reluctant to move carrier battle groups close to the fighting for fear of being attacked by cruise missiles aboard Soviet vessels or by Backfire bombers and other long-range Soviet aircraft based in the north. (Also, the Gulf's narrow width and erratic winds cause operating problems for carriers.) In this situation, cruise missiles aboard U.S. aircraft or submarines in the Gulf could attack Soviet airheads. Once the air and naval environment had stabilized and carrier forces could operate within range of the conflict, aircraft could take over this role. However, cruise missiles could continue to be used to attack heavily defended air bases, staging areas, and choke-points, which would exact high attrition were aircraft used. As in the Iraqi contingency described above, small numbers of cruise missiles used to damage Soviet SAM sites and to crater Soviet-controlled runways could reduce the number of sorties needed for follow-up attacks, thus freeing aircraft for interdiction missions against land forces.

Cruise missiles could also be used in more decisive (and more risky) attacks on air bases, staging areas, and command posts on Soviet soil, which would clearly be better protected against air attack than the more temporary facilities to the south. Of course, attacking targets on Soviet soil with even conventionally armed cruise missiles would constitute a major escalatory step, but the military payoffs would be high: if specialized submunitions became available, they could render Backfire bomber bases inoperative (at least temporarily), and seriously hamper air transport operations. Even if the constraints on actually implementing this option in the event of a Soviet attack were high, the capability to exercise this option might have some deterrent effect in Soviet deliberations over whether to initiate large-scale attack.

Attacking targets on enemy home territory would be far less constrained if that enemy was other than the Soviet Union. Should North Korea attack South Korea, for example, ground-launched cruise missiles assigned to American forces could perform deep penetration missions into North Korea, freeing tactical aircraft for use close to the battle area. In Southeast Asia cruise missiles could be used to conduct deep-strike missions against air bases, command posts, and other critical targets in Vietnam, freeing sea-based air power to interdict a Vietnamese invasion of Thailand.

Nuclear Missions

While it is useful for analytical purposes to distinguish local conflicts involving one or both of the superpowers from direct encounters between the superpowers, it is dangerous otherwise, even for defense-planning purposes, to make this distinction. In reality even the smallest local conflict contains the risk of escalation. Third world guerrilla conflicts may tempt Soviet or American involvement, but it is hard to see these situations escalating beyond the nuclear threshold. But at the other end of the local conflict spectrum, a Soviet invasion of Iran would open up the possibility. Indeed, in discussing the Carter doctrine for defending Western interests in the Persian Gulf, senior officials have been careful not to rule out the possibility of a nuclear response in the event of Soviet aggression.

The use of nuclear threats in local conflicts has important implications for cruise missiles. Perhaps overdesigned for most conventional roles, the new generation of cruise missiles is particularly well suited to theater warfare and to nuclear and chemical weapons delivery, as their small size and launch weight offer mobility and their high accuracy makes possible limitation of collateral damage.

In an era of nuclear parity (or even what Senator Sam Nunn has described as "clinging parity"), it is not clear how far beyond Europe Washington should want its "extended" nuclear deterrent to reach. As Soviet nuclear capabilities grow and the conventional forces of third world powers expand, American nuclear threats will be less credible and more risky, although it would probably be a mistake to completely denuclearize American power-projection forces in the third world. Maintaining nuclear-capable aircraft and cruise missiles will not reduce requirements for effective conventional forces, but the options of nuclear and chemical responses might be a deterrent to escalation.

There are also operational and economic arguments for blending nuclear and conventional (as well as chemical) capabilities into the same systems. In the 1950s and 1960s budgetary largesse and technological imperatives generated specialized weapon systems for specific military roles: intercontinental ballistic missiles (ICBMs) were deployed for strategic nuclear missions, while aircraft were classified as either strategic or tactical, depending on their range and payload. But spending constraints now and in the future make such specialization difficult to justify, while technology is creating opportunities for much greater flexibility. The Tomahawk cruise missile might be capable of missions ranging from destroying a Soviet intercontinental ballistic missile silo with a nuclear warhead to cratering a runway in Angola with conventional ordnance. (Flexibility is not limited to cruise missiles; a new strategic bomber is likely to be designed with a variety of conventional roles in mind.)

The actual flexibility of cruise missiles will depend on how they are deployed and the associated equipment developed for their use. In a conventional role they will require advanced munition-and-guidance packages compatible with many different environments. Development of a new generation of binary chemical agents and insertable nuclear components may allow missiles earmarked for conventional missions to be used for nuclear and chemical roles. Thus a cruise missile force deployed for local conflicts would be relevant in the event of escalation; with alteration in their configuration and role, these systems could take on new assignments in an expanded, high-intensity conflict.

Arms Control

Contrary to some arguments, the widespread deployment of cruise missiles by the United States or other industrial powers is unlikely to lead to their proliferation in the third world. For economic, technological, and operational reasons, few third world countries are likely to view cruise missiles as offering important advantages over existing means of delivering conventional munitions, even if they seem obtainable at reasonable cost.

Rather than conventional and nuclear proliferation, the most important arms control issue is how American exploitation of cruise missiles is likely to affect the strategic arms limitation process. The SALT II treaty and the associated protocol (now discarded by the Reagan administration) restricted the deployment of cruise missiles, including their use in theater warfare. If, as critics of the protocol argued, this provision had been extended pending a new agreement or incorporated into a new treaty, NATO's program for deploying 464 ground-launched cruise missiles by the mid-1980s would have had to be scrapped.

For American options in local conflicts in other parts of the world, however, the proposed restrictions on ALCMs and SLCMs were the most troubling. The protocol banned deployment of long-range SLCMs until after 1981, which would have effectively ruled out deployment of nuclear and conventional TLAMs aboard surface ships and submarines if the protocol provisions had been extended. Even without the protocol, however, the treaty would have constrained deployment of ALCMs for local contingencies through 1985 by limiting their deployment to heavy bombers and by treating nuclear-armed and conventional ALCMs alike for verification purposes. The United States would have been able to deploy conventionally armed ALCMs on B-52s and other aircraft, but only within the SALT ALCM ceiling. Under these circumstances, it was unlikely that the conventional role for ALCMs would have been exploited.

The potential SALT constraints on the deployment of nuclear and conventional cruise missiles is important for local contingencies. Moscow will surely seek constraints on cruise missiles like those in the 1979 treaty and protocol, since the strategic cruise missile along with the Trident submarine-launched ballistic missile constitute the main component of the American program for strategic modernization in the early 1980s. These limits could impinge on the use of cruise missiles in third world conflicts.

The same is true of any American-Soviet agreement covering long-range theater nuclear systems in and around Europe. An accord that accommodated NATO's plans for stationing GLCMs in Western Europe might be used by Moscow to ban their deployment elsewhere.

In the long term, cruise missiles may have a major influence on arms control. They have already raised havoc with efforts to identify them as a strategic weapon. Deployment of hundreds and perhaps thousands of conventional or dual-capable cruise missiles for theater contingencies would exacerbate this problem. Their use in all global contingencies would compound the problem even more. Although from an American perspective these systems would only have a tenuous relationship with the central strategic balance, in Soviet eyes they would surely be viewed as a new and threatening class of forward-based systems—and with some justification. Deployment of ALCMs and TLAMs capable of delivering nuclear, chemical, and new classes of conventional munitions would pose impossible verification problems.

For arms limitation negotiations to survive, the United States may have to forgo opportunities for deploying a new generation of multirole aircraft and ballistic and cruise missiles. The security advantages of keeping SALT alive should be balanced against the benefits derived from exploiting American technological advantages. If a decision is made to forgo some cruise missile applications to obtain a new SALT agreement, it should exact substantial Soviet concessions.

In the short term, the collision of SALT and new military technologies like the cruise missile will confront American decisionmakers with some difficult choices. In the long run, however, existing arms control enterprises should be examined to determine whether they are becoming obsolete and whether new negotiating enterprises, capable of accommodating flexible weapons, are needed.

Conclusions

Not surprisingly, cruise missiles are not a panacea for American problems in handling local conflicts in the third world. In small, remote conflicts, cruise missiles aboard attack submarines, surface ships, and long-range aircraft would provide the United States with a quick-reaction land-strike capability it might otherwise lack. How useful such a capability would be is open to question. A small cruise missile strike would demonstrate American resolve, but in some regions it could also set off an escalatory process that the Soviet Union or a local power, instead of the United States, could dominate. In any event, cruise missiles will be able to serve at best as complements to, not as surrogates for, ground forces and strike aircraft in brushfire wars, where the ability to detect, track, and engage small mobile targets is essential. The same is true for larger-scale conflicts. In intense local wars, only aircraft could generate the heavy and continuous firepower necessary to blunt advancing ground forces. But cruise missiles used for specialized missions could enhance the effectiveness of strike aircraft while reducing the vulnerability of launch platforms, particularly carriers.

The question then, is not how far cruise missiles can be exploited to replace aircraft, but whether an effective combined-arms doctrine can be elaborated. In third world conflicts, as in Central Europe, that doctrine should emphasize the use of small numbers of cruise missiles against important, well-defended targets in the interior, while larger numbers of aircraft are assigned counterair and ground-attack missions on or near the battlefield. Working out a doctrinal division of labor between cruise missiles and strike aircraft will be difficult because the Air Force and the Navy have long emphasized deep-penetration roles in designing aircraft and structuring forces. But a cruise missile employment concept that emphasized their utility as a supplement to instead of a competitor with aircraft could ease bureaucratic resistance to their introduction.

The flexibility of cruise missiles offers both opportunities and risks in local conflicts. While carrier-based aircraft have long been nuclear-capable, they are not as competent for strategic nuclear missions as cruise missiles. The deployment of cruise missiles in local conflicts is thus likely to be viewed as more provocative than the use of aircraft, despite the latter's greater lethality in most conventional roles. In conflicts adjacent or close to Soviet territory, cruise missile employment will raise escalatory possibilities that could lead Moscow to exercise restraint. By the same token, the presence of U.S. cruise missiles in a local crisis involving the superpowers could lead to Soviet preemptive attacks on American forces, widening the scope of the conflict and forcing Washington to either reciprocate or back down.

But if cruise missiles are to be used for local conflicts, a decision will have to be made soon whether to rely on the current Tomahawk and the ALCM or to create a new generation of missiles better adapted to conventional munitions delivery. There are good arguments for both, and until some technical questions are answered, a firm answer will not be possible. For example, it is not clear whether existing cruise missiles possess sufficient size and payload to carry out effective conventional strikes against targets such as air bases. It is also unclear what types of munitions (cluster bomblets, minelets, new point and area munitions) would be most efficient in different missions; are minelets a more effective way to disrupt air-base operations than cratering a runway? Guidance technology is also uncertain. Should map-matching systems be relied on in every region, or are there less costly but equally effective alternatives, such as precision-positioning using Navstar satellites or command aircraft? Another uncertainty is how quickly and at what cost a new class of larger, but possibly more austere, cruise missiles for conventional applications could be developed and deployed.

Testing and evaluating Tomahawk and ALCM systems in conventional (and chemical) roles should be given a high priority, and initial steps should be taken to deploy them aboard platforms that could accommodate cruise missiles quickly and cheaply: B-52s, DD-963 carrier escorts, and attack submarines.[3] However, far-reaching proposals, such as constructing cruise missile launch tubes in the hulls of new attack submarines or outfitting new surface ships with vertical launchers, should be deferred until a decision is made about whether the existing generation or a new generation of missiles will be relied on in local conflicts. At the same time, conventional applications will depend heavily on the progress in developing new area and point munitions. The United States lags behind some smaller states, such as West Germany, in testing and deploying new munitions.

Maximum commonality for nuclear and conventionally armed cruise missiles for theater and strategic roles would hold down costs and should not be prematurely abandoned for fear of burdening arms control. Even if the decision is not to fully exploit the flexibility of cruise missiles, the technology represents one of the few bargaining chips the United States will possess in the near future in talks with the Soviet Union.

3. A force for contingencies outside Europe might consist of 1,140 cruise missiles: 600 ALCMs (fitted externally on seventy-five B-52Ds) and 540 TLAMs (240 on thirty DD-963s and 300 on ten nuclear-powered attack submarines).

CHAPTER EIGHT

The Tomahawk and General Purpose Naval Forces

MICHAEL MCCGWIRE

IF FLEXIBILITY and versatility are the ideal qualities of a general purpose weapon system, the Tomahawk cruise missile might seem the answer to an admiral's prayer. It has a long reach and a large payload, it can be nuclear or conventionally armed, it can be used against ships at sea and targets on land, it can be fitted aboard surface ships and submarines, and it can be emplaced ashore or carried by aircraft. On first impression it appears to be a universal weapon, and it has even been suggested that it will revolutionize naval warfare.

First impressions are sometimes misleading. Certainly, the Tomahawk will be a welcome addition to the fleet, but close inspection belies many of the claims made on its behalf. Some of its limitations stem from its antecedents. Its design was optimized to deliver a nuclear warhead at very long range and constrained by the requirement that it fit a submarine's torpedo tubes. Since its primary application will be in the antiship and conventional land-attack roles, the importance of the latter has waned considerably. But other limitations apply to cruise missiles in general and are inherent in maritime warfare.

The Tomahawk's immediate effect will be to improve the U.S. Navy's antisurface capability at a time when the Soviet Navy is building up its surface forces, and this is reason enough for the prudent introduction of the system throughout the fleet. It will also improve the U.S. capability

Michael MccGwire is a senior fellow in the Brookings Foreign Policy Studies program. Robert P. Berman provided important assistance at the initial stages of this analysis.

231

for military intervention in distant sea areas, for which there appears to be a growing political demand. But the Tomahawk's most important effect will be to focus the U.S. Navy's attention on the cruise missile as a generic weapon system. This will encourage the scale of investment in research and development needed to explore and exploit its full potential technological capability and operational application.

Because the Tomahawk is suboptimal, it is important not to constrain the characteristics of future systems by designing important elements of current new construction around the present missile; this applies particularly to its storage and launch facilities. Also, planners must be sensitive to the new opportunities in ship design and force structure that these future systems will allow. It is in this area that the Tomahawk is likely to be revolutionary.

This chapter has two objectives. One is to explore the Tomahawk's potential and limitations to illuminate the immediate decisions that have to be made about the procurement and deployment of these missiles. The other is to clarify the issues as an aid to estimating future requirements. The underlying analysis is unavoidably complex. The Tomahawk has to be seen as at least three separate systems, whose potential differs according to launch platform and whose usefulness is tied to circumstances. This requires reviewing most types of naval operation and the various ways in which navies can be used worldwide in war and in peace. A three-stage approach has been adopted: a summary of how Tomahawks could be used; an assessment of the usefulness of these roles and the costs involved; and a discussion of how Tomahawks should be deployed, what the analysis suggests about the system's limitations, and what this implies for future requirements.

For twenty-five years after World War II the U.S. Navy largely disregarded the potential of the surface-to-surface cruise missile (SSM) as an antiship weapon. This policy was reversed in the early 1970s, and in the three and a half years ending in December 1980, 100 surface ships, 29 submarines, and 7 squadrons of aircraft were equipped to launch the sixty-nautical-mile Harpoon antiship missile.[1] Meanwhile the Tomahawk missile had been developed, and in 1981 operational test and evaluation began of the conventionally armed Tomahawk land-attack missile (TLAM-C) and the Tomahawk antiship missile (TASM).[2] Plans

1. Conversation with officials in the U.S. Department of the Navy.
2. On the basis of two recent reports, the TLAM-C is assumed to have a range of 600 nautical miles. The *Virginian Norfolk Pilot* of June 7, 1981, quoted "600

call for the submarine-launched versions of these missiles to start entering service in 1982, and the surface-launched versions in 1983.[3] Although the nuclear-armed land-attack variant (TLAM-N) dropped from public discussion during 1980, development funding continued and deployment by mid-1984 is now planned.[4]

The Navy is planning to retrofit the Tomahawk to *Spruance*-class (DD 963) destroyers, nuclear-powered cruisers, and most submarines, as well as to any battleships that are withdrawn from reserve. The missile will also be carried by the new Aegis-equipped *Ticonderoga*-class (CG 47) cruisers and by the *Adams*-class replacement (DDGX). By the mid-1980s, the U.S. Navy could have a family of four SSM systems at sea, which could be launched from surface ship or submarine (see table 8-1).

There could also be air-launched variants of the missiles, the Tomahawk version being known as the MRASM (medium-range air-to-surface missile).[5] These are not, however, discussed in this chapter since they represent the extension of an existing capability rather than a new one. For the same reason, no consideration is given to the Tomahawk as a means of delivering antisubmarine weapons.

The submarine-launched Harpoon and Tomahawk are both designed to use existing torpedo stowage racks and launching tubes,[6] but there is talk of modifying the 688-class attack submarines (SSNs) to carry eight

---

miles" after interviewing two U.S. admirals, while the *Baltimore Sun* of June 5, 1981, quoted "700 miles" after a briefing by Department of Defense officials; the 100-mile discrepancy can be explained by the different sources, 600 nautical miles being equal to 691 land (statute) miles. On the basis of discussions with officials in the Department of Defense, this analysis assumes that the 600 nautical miles refers to target rather than flight range. It should be noted, however, that in recent tests the Tomahawk flew 500 terrain-matching miles to strike a target 300 miles from the launching submarine; *New York Times,* July 13, 1981.

The TASM's target range is given as 250 nautical miles ("Tomahawk Ready for the Warpath in the '80s," *Surface Warfare,* vol. 5 [March 1980], p. 15), but it has the same engine, airframe, and warhead as the TLAM-C. It can therefore be assumed to have a comparable flight range, which is taken to be 500 nautical miles.

3. *Department of Defense Appropriations for Fiscal Year 1981,* Hearings before the Senate Appropriations Committee, 96 Cong. 2 sess. (Government Printing Office, 1980), pt. 4, p. 129.

4. A Defense Department spokesman, as reported in the *Baltimore Sun,* June 5, 1981. He said that it is hoped that by 1985 600 TLAM-Ns will be deployed at sea.

5. The MRASM is primarily a land-attack missile, but an antiship variant is under development by the Navy.

6. A nuclear attack submarine might be expected to carry twenty to twenty-five torpedoes.

Table 8-1. *U.S. Surface-to-Surface Missile Systems*

		Warhead		
Role	Type	Conventional (*pounds*)	Nuclear (*kilotons*)	Range[a] (*nautical miles*)
Antiship	Harpoon	500	. . .	60–100
	TASM	1,000	200	250
Land-attack	TLAM-C	1,000	. . .	600
	TLAM-N	. . .	200	1,500

a. The TASM's target range of 250 nautical miles has been applied to both the conventional and nuclear variants despite the latter's potentially greater flight range, since it is assumed that over-the-horizon targeting will be the limiting factor. There has been no mention of a nuclear TASM, but the capability is inherent in the system.

to twelve vertical missile tubes externally.[7] The surface-launched Harpoon is designed to use the magazines and launchers of existing antisubmarine and surface-to-air missiles, or to be fired from lightweight canister-launchers specially fitted in other ships. The surface-launched Tomahawk initially will be carried in elevating armored box launchers fitted to the upper deck. However, a modular vertical launching system is being developed that can store and fire all these different missiles, providing increased magazine capacity and a new degree of flexibility in the choice of the initial missile load.[8]

The Antiship Missile

The TASM offers the U.S. Navy a new means of disabling surface ships at long range. Its value against third world navies is limited because of the environment in which it would have to operate and the characteristics of local forces. The discussion therefore focuses on the weapon's potential against Soviet surface forces.

7. This would be done by incorporating the tubes into the existing forward main ballast tank area without lengthening the submarine or imposing operational constraints. *Hearings on Military Posture and H.R. 6495 [H.R. 6974]: Department of Defense Authorization for Appropriations for Fiscal Year 1981,* Hearings before the House Armed Services Committee, 96 Cong. 2 sess. (GPO, 1980), pt. 3, p. 222.

8. For details of this launch system, see Lt. Cmdr. Rodney P. Rempt, "Vertical Missile Launchers: Part I," *United States Naval Institute Proceedings,* vol. 103 (October 1977), pp. 86–89, and (December 1977), pp. 105–07; and Capt. John W. Kinnier, "Vertical Launch: Up and At 'Em," *Surface Warfare,* vol. 5 (March 1980), pp. 16–19.

Capabilities and Constraints

It is hard to be precise about how many 1,000-pound warheads would have to strike a warship to achieve a "mission-kill" (preventing the ship from carrying out its intended mission)[9] since it depends on the target's type and size, where the missile hits, the level of damage control, and the amount of fuel remaining in the missile, which compounds the effect of the high explosive. There is, however, a general relationship with the ship's length, and as a very crude measure for Soviet ships one might allow one warhead for the first 300 feet of length, plus an additional warhead for each additional 100 feet. These figures are on the generous side, and it may of course be possible to take out a critical system such as the main search radar with special weapons. The Soviet Union, however, is well aware of this weakness, and besides the emphasis on redundancy, its weapon systems are designed to fail by stages.

To achieve a misson-kill these warheads would first have to penetrate the enemy's defenses, and because missiles can be shot down, deceived, or confused, successful penetration depends on overburdening the defense's target-handling capability. The latter is related to the speed of the incoming missile (which dictates the available reaction time), the number of fire-control channels (which determines the number of targets that can be handled simultaneously), and the rapidity with which missiles can be detected and designated and weapon systems retargeted. Again, it is impossible to be precise about the number of missiles required to achieve saturation, as it will differ between ship classes and fleet formations, but some indication of this "price of admission" can be inferred from the types of antiair weapons and the number of separate fire-control systems a ship carries.[10]

9. For example, mission-kill for a carrier might result from damage to the flight deck or the disabling of the command, control, and communications links with its aircraft; for an Aegis-equipped ship (or a Soviet *Kynda*-class ship), the loss of its radars; for all ships, the loss of maneuverability.

10. Most classes of Soviet warships entering service since 1970 have been fitted with two medium-range and two to four short-range gun systems, and most of the larger types also carry two medium-range and two short-range surface-to-air missile (SAM) systems; note that the terms *medium* and *short* imply ranges for guns very different from what they imply for missiles. Both kinds of short-range systems are seen as being primarily antimissile, but the SA-N-3 medium-range SAM is unlikely to have much capability against low-flying SSMs; however, a new type of medium-range SAM is carried by the new *Sovremenny*-class ships, and this may have an antimissile capability. The Soviet Navy still lacks a primary radar comparable to Aegis, but it would be prudent to assume that each of the SA-N-6 fire-control radars on *Kirov*-class ships can handle more than one target at a time.

Crude calculations along these lines are set out in table 8-2, which illustrates the scale of requirements, although it makes no specific allowance for the success of enemy deception measures, for U.S. electronic countermeasures, or for TASM system failure. The table highlights the sharp rise in the number of TASMs needed to saturate the defenses of the more modern ship, a trend that will continue as new Soviet classes enter service and existing ones are back-fitted with antimissile defense systems.[11]

The TASM can be seen as an alternative to the submarine torpedo, though the latter is somewhat cheaper.[12] The TASM has a much longer reach than the torpedo, which allows the submarine, in most cases, to launch the missile from beyond the range of enemy countermeasures. However, assuming that the submarine can get within range to fire its torpedoes, the chances that a missile or a torpedo will obtain a hit against older classes of warship are roughly comparable, a judgment based on balancing such characteristics as terminal-homing capability, speed differential, and the weapons' vulnerability to detection and countermeasures. Against a more modern ship, the hit probability tilts in favor of the torpedo because the greatly improved antimissile defenses raise the "price of admission" for the missile. This, of course, has to be balanced against the greater difficulty of getting within torpedo firing range. However, if a hit can be achieved, the torpedo is much more likely than the missile to disable the target. Although both warheads are comparable in size, the torpedo's explosion is tamped (and hence focused) by the sea and takes place in the vicinity of the propellers or under the ship's keel. Even if the explosion does not break the ship's back or open the hull to the sea, shock damage will affect plant, machinery, and systems through-

11. Although not directly analogous, an illustration of this trend is provided by the use of the Styx SSM (Soviet SS-N-2) in the third world. In 1967 two Egyptian missiles sank an Israeli destroyer (taken by surprise), and in 1971 nine Indian missiles sank one Pakistani destroyer and disabled another. However, the Israelis assimilated the lesson of 1967, and in the 1973 Arab-Israeli war, when missile boats were pitted against each other, the Israelis sank ten Arab units and, although their Gabriel missiles had half the range of the Styx, sustained no losses themselves. This invulnerability was secured mainly by high-speed maneuver combined with electronic countermeasures (including chaff), and relatively few missiles had to be destroyed by close-in ship defenses. See Capt. William J. Ruhe, "Cruise Missile: The Ship Killer," *United States Naval Institute Proceedings,* vol. 102 (June 1976), p. 46; and B. Telem, "Israel's Guided Missile Fast Attack Craft in Yom Kippur War," *Naval Forces,* no. 2 (1980), pp. 24–32.

12. U.S. Navy sources give $845,000 as the 1980 contract price for one Mk 48 torpedo; the TASM costs about $1 million. *Hearings on Military Posture and H.R. 6495,* p. 306.

out the ship. Also, a single submarine carries enough torpedoes to disable the largest surface ship and the rate of fire is not critical. But it may not be able to carry enough missiles to do so and the rate of fire is critical. If the submarine can use only its torpedo tubes for missile launch, it is limited to firing four at one time, which leaves nothing to spare over the price of admission for destroyer-sized units delivered in the 1970s, and it would have little chance of penetrating the defenses of larger or more modern units.

The TASM also provides a partial alternative to the carrier strike aircraft. Its low flight profile and its small size and radar cross section, combined with the absence of pilot reaction to enemy fire, give it an advantage over the aircraft against heavily defended targets such as ships and naval formations. The aircraft has the advantage in reach, payload, and target location and identification, as well as increased flexibility in the target area. However, if the TASM was provided with midcourse guidance (and there are no technical reasons for not doing so), its reach would be comparable to the unrefueled aircraft, and they could be used together.

Target location is a major problem for the TASM, since the enemy target must first be found and identified, and then allowance made for its movement during the missile's time of flight. With the 60- to 100-nautical-mile Harpoon, this is manageable. A majority of surface ships now carry radar-fitted helicopters, and submarines should be able to locate the enemy by using on-board sensors, except in narrow, congested waters;[13] target movement during the seven-minute maximum time of flight is not significant.[14] Providing over-the-horizon targeting out to the full range of the 250-nautical-mile TASM is more difficult. Operating in company with carriers, surface ships would have no problems, but submarines usually work independently and their on-board sensors can only reach out to about 50 nautical miles. For surface ships, shipboard helicopters could provide an independent (though intermittent) all-round capability out to about 150 nautical miles, with a single direction capability of perhaps 175 to 200 nautical miles.[15] It takes the missile half an hour to fly 250

13. The submarine would rely primarily on its passive acoustic sensors, which would not be effective in shallow or congested waters.

14. Maximum displacement from the missile's flight path would be three to four miles, which can be covered by the homing system's angle of look.

15. The maximum ceiling for contemporary helicopters is about 20,000 feet, which gives a radar horizon of about 160 nautical miles. The helicopter's endurance (about two and a half hours) and cruising speed (about 140 knots) do not allow it to maintain station far from its parent ship.

Table 8-2. *Estimated Antiship Missile Requirements*

Class of ship	Delivery begun[a] (1)	Length (feet) (2)	Warheads necessary to disable[b] (3)	Medium-range SAMs (4)	Short-range SAMs (5)	Medium-range guns (6)	Short-range guns (7)	Top Sail radar (8)	Missiles necessary to saturate (9)	Mission requirement (10)
						Price of admission[c]				
Riga	1952	300	1	...	...	...	...	...	0	1
Petya	1962	265	1	...	...	1 76x4	...	...	0.33	2
Skory	1950	395	2	...	...	...	1 45x4	...	0	2
Kotlin	1955	420	2	...	...	...	2 45x4	...	0	2
Kildin	(1975)	415	2	...	...	2 76x2	2 57x8	...	0.66	3
SAM Kotlin	1966	420	2	1 N1	...	...	2 30x4	...	0.66	3
Kanin	(1969)	455	2–3	1 N1	...	...	1 57x8; 2 30x4	...	0.66	3
Kynda	1962	465	2–3	1 N1	...	2 76x2	...	...	0.66	3
Kashin	1962	470	2–3	2 N1	...	2 76x2	...	...	0.66	3
Kashin	(1975)	480	3	2 N1	...	2 76x2	2 30Gx2	...	2.66	6
Kresta I	1966	510	3	2 N1	...	2 57x2	...	...	0.66	4
Moskva	1967	625	4	2 N3	...	2 57x2	...	Yes	1.33	6

									Missiles^c	
Kresta II	1969	520	3	2 N3	...	2 57x2	2 30Gx2	Yes	3.33	7
Krivak	1970	410	2	...	2 N4	1 76x4	...	...	2.33	5
Sverdlov CC	(1972)	690	5	...	1 N4	...	4 30x4	...	2.33	8
Kara	1972	570	4	2 N3	2 N4	2 76x2	2 30Gx2	Yes	5.33	10
Kiev	1975	900	7	2 N3	2 N4	2 76x2	4 30Gx2	Yes	7.33	15
Kirov	1980	755	5–6	2 N6	2 N4	1 100x2	4 30Gx2	Yes	12	18

Source: Author's estimates.

a. When a class has undergone a conversion or a major modification, the date is given in parentheses and indicates the delivery of the modified version.

b. The number of warheads that must strike home to achieve a mission-kill is calculated on the basis of: the ship's length in feet minus 200, divided by 100.

c. The "price of admission" is the number of missiles necessary to saturate a ship's defenses. It is assumed that during a concentrated attack lasting three minutes, the weapon systems listed below could each shoot down the number of missiles shown; other systems are assumed to have no capability against low-flying missiles. The first figure in columns 4–7 shows the number of separate fire-control systems; it is followed by the type of weapon; for guns (columns 6 and 7), the figures denote the bore in millimeters and the number of barrels controlled by each system. The numbers of missiles credited to each system are added (this is not a probability analysis) and arbitrarily multiplied by 0.66 to produce the number necessary for saturation. It is stressed that the following are assumptions:

Designator	System	Number of missiles
N4	SA-N-4 twin launcher, Mach 2, range 9 kilometers, height down to 10 meters	1.5
N6	SA-N-6 vertical launcher, Mach 6, range 30 kilometers, height down to 10 meters	3.0
30	30-millimeter twin automatic, Drum Tilt fire control, 240 rpm, range 3 kilometers	0.5
30G	30-millimeter Gatling automatic, Bass Tilt fire control, 3,000 rpm, range 3 kilometers	1.5
57 76 100	Medium-range 57-millimeter twin, 120 rpm; 76-millimeter twin, 60 rpm; 100-millimeter single. Ranges 12 to 15 kilometers. The 76-millimeter's greater capacity for proximity fusing is assumed to balance out the 57-millimeter's higher rate of fire and more flexible fire-control system	0.5
Yes	The presence of Top Sail radar is assumed to indicate an improved target-handling system	1.0
...	The target-handling capability of the Kirov-class ships is assumed to be a further improvement	1.0

nautical miles; by this time the target could be 17 miles away from its initial position.

The problem of target movement during the TASM's time of flight has been met by giving the missile a search capability.[16] It has not yet been possible to provide TASM-armed units with an organic over-the-horizon targeting capability. Instead, a system, under development for some time, uses a mix of existing area-search sensors and surveillance systems, which are linked through a data processing and display system code named "Outlaw Shark"; this system will pass target data to TASM-armed ships. The whole system is expected to be fully operational by the time the TASM enters service in 1982–83.[17] The major problem is to correlate, fuse, and relay enemy and other surface information fast enough to provide near real-time (without delays in processing) target data. At present, this is being tackled by upgrading the capabilities of existing sensors and by improving data processing and distribution procedures, but later, additional sensors and surveillance satellites will be available.

Launching modes affect the TASM's potential, and each of these is discussed separately. No consideration is given to the use of nuclear warheads, but if they were available it would considerably reduce the number of missiles required to achieve a mission-kill.

The Submarine-Launched TASM

The TASM offers the submarine a qualitatively new antisurface weapon whose standoff capability makes it unnecessary to negotiate perimeter defenses. To ensure a mission-kill against most of the modern classes of surface ships, five or more missiles have to be launched so as to arrive on target nearly simultaneously. Against the largest units, the requirement rises to fifteen to eighteen missiles, which is more than a single submarine is likely to carry, let alone launch at one time. However, against soft-

16. Based on the initial target location data, the TASM's inertial guidance system is programmed to close the target's initial position and then fly a standard search pattern covering future target movement, using active radar. The missile is programmed to home on specific types of targets and to disregard all others.

17. *Department of Defense Appropriations for Fiscal Year 1981,* Hearings before a subcommittee of the Senate Appropriations Committee, 96 Cong. 2 sess. (GPO, 1980), pt. 4, pp. 125–28. The Outlaw Shark system is part of an ocean surveillance and information system and involves computer-to-computer links providing naval units with all-source ocean surveillance data.

skinned amphibious forces, the exchange rate could be closer to one ship per missile.

Where TASMs can be stored in externally fitted launch tubes, this new capability could be added to existing ones. Where TASMs have to share torpedo storage and launching facilities, this may be at the expense of the antisubmarine weapons.

There are five main ways in which this new capability could be used. The first is the traditional mission of attrition against enemy surface forces and supplies, which is greatly facilitated by the combination of submerged concealment, nuclear mobility, and a standoff, terminally guided weapon.

Second, there is a new possibility for area interdiction. A TASM-armed unit can threaten the use of almost 200,000 square miles of sea, or passage through waters less than 500 nautical miles wide, and the submarine platform allows this capability to be deployed in areas where U.S. surface ships could operate only in force, if at all. In the Norwegian Sea, for example, forward-deployed submarines could attack warships seeking to extend the Soviet maritime defense perimeter or interdict the passage of amphibious assault forces whose mission was to seize important islands and stretches of coast.

The third way is the escort role with the submarine acting as an antisurface picket, deployed away from the main surface force in the direction of the threat from missile-armed surface units.

The fourth is the submarine's involvement in a general fleet engagement, which is covered in the later discussion of surface-ship TASMs.

Fifth, there is the mission of attacking Soviet ballistic missile submarines (SSBNs) in their defended bastions in the northwest Pacific and the Greenland and Barents seas. TASMs could be used to attack the surface element of the antisubmarine area-defense system that protects these bastions. However, the antisubmarine warfare (ASW) ship will be only one of a diversity of Soviet sensors deployed in depth, and a variety of weapon-delivery systems will be available on call. Many submariners believe that in such circumstances concealment is still the submarine's strongest suit and that the dangers of betraying its presence far outweigh the possible advantages. But in the years ahead the defenses may become so dense that it becomes necessary to physically disrupt them, in which case a submarine-launched standoff weapon such as the cruise missile is clearly preferable to a relatively close-range system like the torpedo. However, the TASM's full range seems excessive for this task.

The Shore-Based TASM

Surprisingly, there has been little consideration of shore-based TASMs, yet they could provide additional offensive power at no cost to existing maritime capabilities. They would introduce a completely new factor to Soviet threat assessments and complicate the Soviet Navy's problem in critical sea areas.

The Western allies occupy all or part of the coastline of the Norwegian Sea, the Mediterranean, and the Sea of Japan. The missile's reach of 250 nautical miles means that land-based TASMs could directly threaten surface operations in what the Soviet Union considers key strategic areas. TASMs could make the Aegean Sea, an area the Soviet Union considers an outer defense zone, untenable by surface ships in war, and should persuade the Soviet Navy to relocate its peacetime anchorages to less threatened (and less well-placed) waters. A 250-nautical-mile TASM based on Italian, Greek, or Turkish territory could cover about two-thirds of the eastern Mediterranean, leaving only the Gulf of Sidra (Libya) and the southeasternmost segment uncovered. A 500-natutical-mile TASM could cover the whole Mediterranean from friendly shores.

TASMs emplaced on Norwegian, Danish, and Icelandic territory could cover the Norwegian Sea up to 72° N, except for a narrow strip down the center, north of the Arctic Circle. Stretch the TASM's operational range to 300 nautical miles, and coverage would be complete. This would not require emplacement on politically sensitive Bear Island but would use Jan Mayen Island and the coast of Greenland.

Domestic sensitivity to such deployments in the Norwegian Sea area might have to be overcome, but this is likely to diminish as the Soviet surface buildup becomes increasingly obtrusive. Nor is it essential that land-based TASMs be pre-positioned. For example, missiles could be flown into Iceland during a crisis buildup, joined with simple trailer-launchers stockpiled at Keflavik air base, and deployed by road to pre-surveyed coastal sites.

The Surface-Ship TASM

The TASM's potential aboard surface ships is more complex than might be expected and is discussed in the context of three types of situation: confronting enemy missile units, peacetime escalation, and the general fleet engagement.

CONFRONTING SOVIET MISSILE UNITS. Until recently, the long-range missiles carried by Soviet surface ships represented a relatively minor and outmoded fraction of the overall threat and the least dangerous of the three launching modes, both in numbers (less than 15 percent of the total)[18] and method of employment. In the Norwegian Sea, for example, behavior during exercises has suggested that they would be held back as a final line of defense or until the carrier had been partially disabled by submarine attack. However, the relative significance of this element of the threat is likely to increase in the years ahead,[19] and in the event of general war and the loss of Soviet shore-based air facilities, these missile-armed surface units will assume a new importance.

A TASM-armed surface ship could be in a position to directly counter the threat from an enemy missile unit if three conditions could be fulfilled: the TASMs had a sufficient advantage in range to strike home before the enemy unit could launch its missiles at the designated target; the opposing forces were initially outside missile range of one another (a "meeting engagement"); and the TASMs could penetrate the enemy's defenses either by subtlety or by saturation.

TASMs can be expected to maintain their advantage over the short- and medium-range (60 to 100 nautical miles) Soviet SSMs now being fitted in various distant-water surface units. But it is hard to ensure an inherent range advantage over long-range systems (250 to 350 nautical miles) like the SS-N-12 and SS-N-19, since reach can be increased by relatively simple improvements in fuel, airframe, and miniaturization, as well as by trading speed for range.

To protect the main force from such long-range systems, TASM-armed surface ships could be used as antimissile pickets, but they would be ex-

18. Apart from the newly delivered *Kirov*-class battle cruiser, the only surface ships now carrying long-range SSMs are the two *Kiev*-class, four *Kresta I*-class, and four *Kynda*-class ships.

19. In the 1960s, 56 submarines carrying 368 long-range launchers and 8 surface ships carrying 48 launchers were delivered. In the 1980s the annual delivery of submarine launchers is unlikely to be more than two or three times the number of surface launchers. Meanwhile, the current delivery rate of Backfires to the Soviet Naval Air Force (15 a year) suggests that the number of strike aircraft armed with air-to-surface missiles is likely to drop.

posed and vulnerable to attacks from all sources. Unlike the radar pickets in the Pacific in World War II, which fulfilled their function by providing early warning of air attack even if they were sunk in the process, the anti-missile picket will have failed in its purpose if it does not disable the enemy missile platform or cause it to expend its missiles.

The foregoing adds up to saying that only in a limited range of circumstances will surface-ship TASMs be able to disable an enemy missile unit before it launches its weapons, and the more usual situation will involve an exchange of missile fire. In some cases, where the enemy unit carried reloads or held back part of the initial loading, such an exchange could forestall the launch of these remaining missiles, although the TASM's thirty- to fifty-minute time of flight makes this a sanguine prediction. In other cases, where the SSM was not the predominant component of the enemy's capability, a successful missile exchange could degrade the enemy force's antiair or antisubmarine capability.

PEACETIME ESCALATION. There is an increasing possibility that, through the pressure of events rather than a desire to initiate a conflict, a competitive show of naval force in the third world will escalate to an exchange of fire and perhaps lead to a limited engagement between Soviet and U.S. naval units. In such circumstances the presence of TASMs aboard U.S. surface ships would be important for its impact on Soviet perceptions and for the options it gave the U.S. force commander. The presence of Soviet surface missile units would provide a matching capability, but even if the direct threat came from Soviet SSM-armed submarines, the overall U.S. posture would be improved by the ability to attack the accompanying Soviet surface ships, even though they offered no direct threat. If it did come to an exchange of fire, the TASM offers a means of symmetrical and graduated response, whether carriers are present or not. It is less overwhelming than an air strike, and the weight of an initial missile attack can be calibrated to show resolve without swamping the Soviet defenses. It is a less blunt weapon than the submarine torpedo, which is liable to sink (rather than just damage) its target, and the submarine may itself become a casualty as it closes to within torpedo firing range.

The most likely scenarios involve the interposition of naval forces by one side to deter maritime access by the other, such access being required for trade, logistic support, or perhaps direct military intervention. The practical value of the TASM will depend on whether U.S. forces are seeking access themselves or trying to prevent Soviet forces from gaining access. In the latter case, the TASM, with its long reach and large pay-load, can provide a useful means of forceful dissuasion, and from a start with a single missile, the number of rounds per salvo can be increased as necessary. However, when U.S. ships are faced by a Soviet interposition force, the primary requirement is to secure U.S. use of the sea, and this places first priority on antimissile defenses. Only the interposer will be in a position to exploit a relative advantage in missile range, since it is the interposer that establishes the intrusion perimeter, while the intervener will be holding its fire, hoping to call the interposer's bluff.

THE GENERAL FLEET ENGAGEMENT. A general engagement between the concentrated forces of the opposing navies could arise in two kinds of situation. One would take place at the onset of war between forces maintaining "continuous company," as they have done for some years in the Mediterranean and, more recently, in the Indian Ocean. The other would be a "meeting engagement" after the outbreak of war, probably brought about by a U.S. attempt to push back the Soviet maritime defense perimeter in the Norwegian Sea and in the northwest Pacific.

Surface-ship TASMs offer an efficacious way of dealing with the Soviet ships (combatants and support units) that are within missile range of the main force at the onset of hostilities. It would not be sensible to use TASM-armed surface ships to hunt down Soviet units that were outside missile range, principally because many of the latter would have a speed advantage. Such ships are best dealt with by other means such as carrier and shore-based aircraft and by shore-based TASMs when they are available, as they could be in the Mediterranean. One can envisage a continuously updated master strike plan that allocates Soviet surface targets to different weapon platforms and systems. The aim would be to dispose of them all as soon after the start of war as possible.

Operations designed to secure U.S. command of an area such as the Norwegian Sea must include the process of pushing back the Soviet defense perimeter—a meeting engagement. Soviet area defenses are echeloned in depth, with submarines as the primary element, followed closely by aircraft but with surface ships becoming an increasingly important component of the antisubmarine and antisurface teams, both in their own right and as a means of providing the submarine with "combat stability."[20]

20. This term, *boevaya ustoichevost'*, is taken to mean the provision of a favorable operating environment, including keeping enemy antisubmarine warfare forces away from the submarines. The role of surface ships in providing submarines with combat stability and the Soviet Navy's need for more surface ships were major ele-

In such circumstances, the disabling of Soviet surface ships would destroy the synergism of the all-arms approach and make Soviet submarines more vulnerable to Western antisubmarine forces.

One can thus visualize operations where TASM-armed submarines move into the contested area well ahead of the battle group in order to attack Soviet antisubmarine surface ships, after which U.S. antisubmarine forces would be able to dispose of Soviet antisubmarine and cruise missile submarines more easily. In these circumstances TASM-armed surface ships would complement the aircraft carrier, helping to dispose of enemy surface units that come (or remain) within 250 nautical miles of the advancing force.

A more novel concept would be to exploit the TASM's potential range of 600 nautical miles or more to reach deep into the Soviet defense zone and disable Soviet surface forces before U.S. submarines tried to penetrate Soviet antisubmarine defenses and before U.S. battle groups came within range of Soviet surface-ship missiles. Besides incapacitating the surface component of the defense team, the TASM onslaught would deprive the Soviet Union of its command and control facilities afloat and deny its submarines the combat stability it values so highly. However, carrying out such a concept would require a very large number of missiles, perhaps some 225 today, rising to more than 600 by the end of the decade.[21] To use sea-based platforms for this attack would only make sense if the United States had lost control of the land adjoining the Norwegian Sea and could not make use of TASMs emplaced ashore. This implies that the United States would be operating in an extremely hostile environment and would need large numbers of air-defense and antisubmarine missiles with a correspondingly large number of launchers to ensure the survival of the force.

---

ments in Admiral Gorshkov's argument challenging the allocation of resources in the ninth Five-Year Plan; this is contained in his series of eleven articles in *Morskoj sbornik* (Naval Review) between February 1972 and February 1973. See my "Naval Power and Soviet Oceans Policy," in *Soviet Oceans Development,* Committee Print, prepared for the Senate Committee on Commerce and National Ocean Policy Study, 94 Cong. 2 sess. (GPO, 1976), pp. 116–20. For specific reference to this requirement, see S. G. Gorshkov, "Voenno-morskie Floty v Voynax i Mirnoe Vremya" (Navies in War and Peace), *Morskoj sbornik,* February 1973, p. 21.

21. These crude estimates are arrived at by applying the figures in table 8-2 to two-thirds of the combined strength of the Northern and Baltic fleets and allowing 50 percent for system failure. The 1990 figures are an extrapolation using current building rates and proportional interfleet distribution. They are intended to illustrate the scale of the problem and are not assumed to be accurate.

Target Location and Command and Control

In some of these scenarios existing resources, using available procedures, can provide over-the-horizon targeting and command and control. For example, the current means of area surveillance can provide shore-based TASMs with target data, and the availability of carrier-based reconnaissance is implicit in the antisurface picket role and for units involved in a general fleet engagement. In other cases, the launch platform can rely on its own sensors, as when, for example, the submarine operates independently in its traditional role of attrition warfare or the surface ship uses its helicopter when faced with medium-range enemy missiles. But several scenarios would require special arrangements. These include submarines carrying out area interdiction in hostile waters, submarines penetrating Soviet antisubmarine warfare defenses (if they wish to engage beyond the range of their own sensors), and surface ships operating independently against long-range enemy missiles.

The difficulties of providing over-the-horizon targeting in the latter cases are obviously considerable, particularly if the United States cannot rely on the continuing availability of land- and space-based systems after the onset of war. But the existing availability of over-the-horizon targeting and command, control, and communications resources in the other scenarios should not mean ignoring the considerable problems involved in engaging an enemy at these ranges. They are complex enough for a single platform using its own sensors, but as the United States moves to integrate data from a variety of sources and to coordinate the fire from different platforms to ensure the simultaneous arrival of sufficient missiles on target for defense saturation, new problems abound. These questions have barely been addressed, let alone resolved, and the concept of a force commander orchestrating a fleet engagement with an enemy some 500 miles away is far from reality.

The Land-Attack Missile

The Tomahawk offers the U.S. Navy a new means of projecting force ashore that could be carried by all submarines and by surface ships of frigate size and larger. Consideration is limited here to the role of the TLAM carried by general purpose naval forces. The reach and destructive capacity of the nuclear and conventional versions are so different that the 1,500-nautical-mile TLAM-N and the 600-nautical-mile TLAM-C must be viewed as completely different weapon systems.

Capabilities and Constraints

The TLAM is most directly comparable to the carrier strike aircraft, and the missile's low flight profile and small radar cross section give it a major advantage against well-developed air defenses, such as those of the Soviet Union. The aircraft, however, has an important advantage in its targeting flexibility, since the TLAM is limited to attacking previously surveyed fixed targets. Even then, providing TLAM ships with up-to-date terrain contour matching (TERCOM) data is a demanding requirement. It should be less difficult for the TLAM-N since there are a finite number of targets for which a nuclear weapon is suitable, but the number of potential targets for the TLAM-C's 1,000-pound conventional warhead is almost limitless, and the weapon also needs digital scene matching area correlator (DSMAC) data to obtain the necessary accuracy. Meanwhile, there is the more general problem of linking shipboard TLAMs with the main TERCOM network. Particularly if launched against targets in Eastern Europe or western Russia, TLAMs will fly substantial distances over friendly territory, requiring the provision of TERCOM data not needed by ground-launched and air-launched cruise missiles. If timeliness is a requirement, TERCOM "stepping stone" maps will have to cover a wide range of possibilities, since there is no way to know where general purpose naval units will be at the onset of war. As a further complication, it is unlikely that the landfall stepping stone will lie on a direct path joining the ship and its target, and this may require a significant track diversion, limiting the missile's reach and delaying the time on target.

The TLAM-N has a greater reach than the carrier strike aircraft and provides a cost-effective alternative for delivering nuclear weapons. The aircraft can compensate for the range advantage by in-flight refueling, but it cannot offset the missile's capability for submerged launch, which allows a single submarine to pose a scale of threat that on the surface would require a carrier battle group. Even then, missile-armed aircraft of the Soviet Naval Air Force (SNAF) would have a range advantage of 200 nautical miles over TLAM-Ns deployed with the main surface force.

The TLAM-C's range is roughly similar to that of the carrier aircraft, but its reach is little more than one-third that of SNAF strike aircraft. It is, however, comparable to that of the Flogger D (MiG-27), which is the most likely "worst-case" threat from third world countries. The TLAM-C's potential against third world states is very different from its potential against the Soviet Union, because the nature of the targets and the type of opposition are so dissimilar. Third world defenses are much less extensive, dense, diverse, and sophisticated, and they cannot reach far out to sea. More important, in the third world the number of critical military targets and the availability of alternative facilities will be limited, relatively few will be effectively hardened, and the capacity to repair extensive damage will be restricted. This means that the target set is vulnerable to 1,000-pound warheads and can often be covered by a manageable number of missiles.

The opposite tends to be the case in the Soviet Union. For example, to keep the runways of a SNAF base out of action could require an impact rate of three missiles during each twelve-hour period. If these numbers were doubled to allow for system failure and defense attrition, the requirement would be twelve missiles per airfield every twenty-four hours. This means that to neutralize for five days the SNAF bases that can fly strikes against U.S. forces in the Norwegian Sea would take about a thousand missiles.[22]

Realistic estimates of the TLAM-C's comparative cost-effectiveness are hard to arrive at, and figure 4-2 in the chapter by John Baker gives some indication of how sensitive aircraft costs are to attrition rates. There are also the matter of how one defines "effectiveness" and the central importance of timeliness. While it may be notionally cheaper to deliver a certain weight of munitions or strike a given number of targets with "reusable" aircraft, the numbers of carrier strike aircraft and of their sortie rates are strictly limited. In war, time is of the essence and concentration of force a primary principle. A simultaneous attack on a large number of targets would create far greater disruption and be far more cost-effective than if spread out over a period of time. The longer it takes to carry out a strike plan, the more slowly the enemy will be weakened, the longer U.S. ships will have to loiter in danger, and the more likely counterattacks are to be successful.

22. This assumes one base per SNAF regiment in the Northern and Baltic fleets. The existence of 16 regiments of 10 medium bombers is deduced from the total of 210 SNAF strike and fighter-bomber aircraft; *Department of Defense Annual Report, Fiscal Year 1980* (GPO, 1979), p. 93. Of these, about 45 are Su-17 Fitter Cs or Ds; International Institute for Strategic Studies, *The Military Balance, 1980–1981* (London: IISS, 1980).

Nuclear Land Attack

Proposals for the use of the TLAM-N fall into three main categories: strategic deterrence and war-fighting; the land battle; and the naval battle. In all cases, the central question is not whether general purpose forces *could* be used in these ways, but whether they *should* be, given the operational costs involved, their relative effectiveness in these roles, and the availability of alternative weapon platforms.

STRATEGIC DETERRENCE AND WAR-FIGHTING. The TLAM-N's 1,500-mile range, subtended from waters where U.S. naval forces operate regularly, covers important parts of the Soviet Union. TLAM-Ns aboard general purpose units could therefore add to the overall deterrent posture of the United States. However, the value of such weapons for war-fighting and as a means of assuring "escalation dominance" is questionable. The most obvious problem is that general purpose units, if being used as such, are unlikely to be in the right place at the right time. There is the difficulty of ensuring the availability of the relevant TERCOM data. Controlling the use of strategic weapons becomes more difficult as the weapons are deployed to lower echelons. These TLAM-Ns therefore could not be included in the single integrated operational plan (SIOP), nor could they be counted on for follow-up strikes, because of uncertain availability, command, control, and communications limitations, and restricted flexibility in targeting.

Casting general purpose units in this role would adversely affect the flexibility with which they could be used. Normal peacetime control procedures would be tightened. The operational freedom of attack submarines would be constrained by the need to remain in continuous communication. Inevitably, TLAM-Ns aboard surface ships and submarines would become part of the rhetoric of domestic reassurance, and these units would become less general purpose and more part of the U.S. deterrence posture. U.S. attitudes toward the political symbolism of such units would change, reducing the willingness to risk them. Soviet evaluations would also change, perhaps increasing the pressure to escalate and use nuclear weapons at sea.

THE LAND BATTLE. Because of their uncertain availability, naval TLAM-Ns cannot be counted on to support the land battle on the main fronts, where timing will be crucial; and in a fast-moving engagement, the argument that they would "come in handy" is irrelevant for a weapon that is only useful against fixed targets. The missile's potential is somewhat greater on the flanks, where TLAM-armed general purpose forces could be assigned specifically to support the land battle. But if a firm requirement for such support exists, there are more cost-effective ways of meeting it than by tying down valuable naval platforms. For example, northern Norway could be covered by ground-launched cruise missiles (GLCMs) emplaced in Scotland and the routes south to the Persian Gulf could be covered from Turkey.

THE NAVAL BATTLE. TLAM-Ns can hamper the Soviet Union's use of the sea by attacking its naval bases and support facilities and can contribute to securing U.S. use of the sea by striking SNAF airfields. A nuclear warhead would disable an air base for a significant period; even with system failure and defense attrition, about thirty-two missiles deployed on about four platforms should be sufficient to cover the main SNAF bases serving the Northern and Baltic Fleet areas. To blunt the initial Soviet attacks, TLAM-Ns would have to be deployed several hundred miles ahead of the force being protected, which would mean using submarines as launch platforms. All this is practicable, but begs the question of why special arrangements are needed to strike SNAF bases when they are already covered by the SIOP. It is of course conceivable that by the time U.S. carrier battle groups were ready the damage from such a strike could have been repaired, but if this is a serious possibility, there are other ways of coordinating the timing of strategic or theater nuclear strikes to meet the requirement to strike SNAF bases.

The TLAM-C and the Soviet Union

Targets within the Soviet Union are relatively inaccessible to the 600-nautical-mile TLAM-C; besides being well hardened and defended, their overall vulnerability is reduced by the Soviet emphasis on redundancy and restorability. The value of TLAM-Cs will therefore depend on the ability to identify vital links in the various Soviet operational systems that are vulnerable to precisely delivered payloads (tailored, if necessary, to the specific target), are relatively few in number, and cannot easily be replaced or repaired.

The TLAM-C aboard general purpose forces could not be counted on to make a contribution in the main central and southern European theaters. It might, however, provide northern Norway with support in the absence of aircraft or of GLCMs emplaced further south. It could also be used to interdict a Soviet thrust through northwest Iran, although to get within missile range of the northern passes would require forces in the Persian Gulf. In the Far East, it could be used to disrupt the reinforcement of the Kuril Islands by attacking Soviet embarkation ports.

The TLAM-C would not be very effective against hardened naval base facilities, which are difficult to disable with high explosives,[23] and support facilities afloat would be widely dispersed and not amenable to TERCOM targeting. There might, however, be certain key links in the shore elements of the fleet command, control, communications, and intelligence system that would be vulnerable to such attacks.

Of more immediate operational importance is the SNAF missile strike capability. It is generally accepted that countering this threat by attacking the airfield with TLAM-Cs is not practical because of the large number of missiles required to keep runways out of action and the delayed impact of attacks on maintenance and logistic facilities. There are two other approaches. One is to use TLAM-Cs to suppress air defenses, which would allow fully effective carrier air strikes against SNAF bases. In such circumstances, TLAM-C strikes could be launched by ships of the main force since aircraft and missile ranges would be comparable, but these strikes would have no effect on the initial Soviet attacks because of the Soviet range advantage.

The other approach, which would have some hope of at least blunting the initial attacks, is to identify and attack vulnerable links in the SNAF concept of operations, using forward-deployed launch platforms. A fruitful field for such targets may be the system for providing command, control, and intelligence, which has to fuse reconnaissance data from a variety of sensors (including satellites), provide navigational support, and combine and direct the various forces committed to a coordinated attack. Another vulnerable link may be the ground control elements that direct the fighters escorting the strike aircraft.

---

23. The assumption that bases are hardened rests in part on Soviet practice in other fields and in part on the practice of countries such as Britain, which put many support facilities below ground in Malta and Gibraltar, and Sweden, which tunneled into the sides of fjords to provide docks, workshops, and stores. The difficulties of attacking such facilities is illustrated by Allied air attacks on the German ports in the Bay of Biscay in World War II. For instance, the German submarine pens in Brest received nine direct hits with 12,000-pound bombs (compare the Tomahawk's 1,000-pound warhead), but no serious damage was done. S. W. Roskill, *The War at Sea, 1939–1945*, vol. 3: *The Offensive, Part II, 1st June 1944–14th August 1945* (London: Her Majesty's Stationery Office, 1961), p. 133.

The TLAM-C in the Third World

The TLAM-C's reach is more than adequate for most third world scenarios, and its capability for punitive strikes is obvious. More interesting is its potential to disrupt a state's defenses sufficiently to allow U.S. forces to achieve a lodgment ashore without benefit of carrier air support. The missiles could ensure the passage of seaborne intervention forces with preemptive strikes against the coastal state's maritime defense systems. Timing would be all-important, and one can envisage a series of attacks, the first of which might take place several days before the main task force came within striking range from the shore, using submarine-launched TLAM-Cs against naval facilities in the expectation of catching defending warships in port. If, however, the naval threat was relatively slight, it might be better to preserve surprise and save the initial attack for use against airfields. This would be timed to arrive on target shortly before U.S. forces came within range of a shore-based air strike, in an attempt to catch aircraft on the ground while limiting the time available to repair base facilities. Submarine-launched TLAMs would ensure surprise, but surface-launched missiles could also be used, since TLAM-Cs would have a range advantage over most third world strike aircraft.[24] The next round of attacks would be directed at offshore surveillance radars and coastal defense systems, each strike being delayed as long as possible to limit the opportunities for repair or replacement. During the landing phase and once troops were established ashore, TLAM-Cs could be used to interdict the movement of reinforcements to the battle zone by attacking vital links in the lines of supply such as bridges, tunnels, and fuel depots, or to make problems for the enemy by striking at instruments of governmental control such as central broadcasting facilities.

Against limited opposition, this type of intervention could be successful, because the circumstances provide for premeditated attacks timed to catch the opponent at a disadvantage. By degrading the enemy's capability for air attacks on U.S. naval and ground forces so that they could be handled by air-defense weapons at the force and unit level, TLAM-Cs could substitute for both the fighter supremacy and the strike functions of the carrier. And close air support of the land battle could be provided by

24. The United States could not, however, assume surprise since the Soviet Union would be in a position to pass satellite surveillance data to countries that were potential targets.

helicopter gunships and Harrier V/STOL (vertical or short takeoff and landing) aircraft operating from *Tarawa-* or *Iwo Jima*-class amphibious assault ships.

The availability of a carrier to support the intervention would allow a division of labor between aircraft and missile, each doing what it does best. The combination would be most fruitful against strong forces ashore that could pose a serious air or maritime threat to the intervention. In such circumstances, TLAMs could be given full responsibility for dealing with fixed ground targets, reducing the requirement for aircraft in the land-attack role and allowing more to be deployed to air superiority and maritime warfare tasks.

Evaluation

The discussion so far has focused on how Tomahawk missiles carried by general purpose units *could* be used, but two types of questions need to be addressed before conclusions can be drawn about how they *should* be used and hence about deployment policy. One concerns the relative value of the different roles discussed above—an assessment that must take into account the other ways of performing them. The other concerns the opportunity costs involved. There are the financial costs, of course, but in discussing the Tomahawk's potential value at this stage, operational costs are probably more important. Tomahawks will be competing with other systems for finite on-board resources and, except where it can use unexploited facilities such as deck space and top weight in certain surface ships or ballast space and buoyancy in certain submarines, it will be fitted at the expense of other weapon systems. For example, in surface ships with a vertical launching system Tomahawks will be competing for launcher tubes with antiair and antisubmarine missiles, and this raises the question of whether the end result will be an overall increase in capability.

Securing and Preventing the Use of the Sea

Maritime warfare is about the use of the sea: using it for one's own purposes and preventing its use to one's disadvantage. Naval forces can secure the use of the sea against attempts at obstruction and prevent the use of the sea by others. Naval forces are also employed to project force ashore, exploiting the access provided by the sea. These are the three basic naval missions.

It used to be true that if, by battle or blockade, a nation could prevent enemy warships from using the sea, ipso facto its use was secured for that nation's own purposes, and these two different missions were generally treated as one. In fact, neutralizing the enemy's fleet was viewed as the primary naval mission. It was akin to drawing one's opponent's trumps at bridge, and ensured that he would never be able to upset one's plans by contriving a local superiority of naval force.

This apparent harmony between missions was first undermined by the submarine, and as the scope of maritime warfare has widened to include a growing array of land- and space-based systems, it has become increasingly important, when analyzing operational requirements, to distinguish between the final objectives of securing and preventing the use of the sea. There are two reasons for this. First, the primary naval mission is *not* to prevent the enemy from using the sea, but rather to secure one's own use. Second, there are many circumstances where the use of the sea by enemy warships is not greatly to a nation's disadvantage, and it would be a misapplication of resources to try to prevent it.

If a naval unit or force cannot secure its own use of the sea, it cannot secure the use of the sea for others, nor is it in a position to project force ashore or to prevent the enemy from using the sea. It is in this sense that securing the use of the sea is the primary mission. Sometimes it is an end in itself, as in securing the passage of seaborne supplies or of an amphibious assault force. Sometimes it is a means to an end, as in striking targets ashore or disrupting the enemy's coastal supply lines. But in all cases it is a necessary condition.

This has implications for ship and force design, a process that involves a balancing of mission priorities and a trade-off between capabilities. On land, this is exemplified by the offsetting of firepower, mobility, and protection so as to produce the optimal mix for a given set of circumstances. The comparable trio at sea could be taken as "to float, to move, to fight," except for the crucial distinction that the ordering of these factors is fixed, each being a necessary condition to its successor. The distinction reflects the fundamental difference between the two combat environments: land warfare is over territory and naval warfare is over use. It is necessary to survive long enough (to float, to move) to be in a position to achieve (to fight for) the objective. This does not mean that survivability has absolute priority in ship design, any more than protection overrides all other factors in tank design. But there is a critical difference between the military significance of a ship and that of a tank, stemming as much from the total numbers available as from the differences in size and complexity of individual units. Major surface combatants are simply not expendable in the way tanks are, the loss of a frigate or destroyer being akin to the loss of a whole battalion or more. A carrier task group is comparable to a division, and a multicarrier task force to an army. These are significant military assets, and survivability in the form of a self-defense capability is a primary requirement.

This military significance, combined with the political symbolism of naval units, means that in a peacetime confrontation at sea the requirement changes from survivability to invulnerability. The intensity of the missile threat in limited confrontations is likely to be relatively low, but the importance of being able to protect against such a threat with certainty is very high. A missile exploding inboard in peacetime represents a defeat, no matter how much damage is wrought on the enemy. To be politically imposing in crisis circumstances, major naval assets must be able to protect themselves against significant symbolic damage.

Invulnerability at the lower levels of threat also reduces the danger of escalation. It maximizes U.S. flexibility and, by raising the costs of success, inhibits the Soviet Union from initiating hostilities.

Now that securing one's own use of the sea has been established as a necessary condition, a distinction must be drawn between this and securing such use as a final objective, since the latter is one of the three basic naval missions and their relative priority is not fixed. At the national level this will be consistent, being determined by a country's geostrategic situation and the nature of its maritime interests; for the United States, the mission of securing use has overall priority. But at the operational level, the relative priority of the three missions will change according to circumstances, and in the meantime the other two missions can also be means to an end. Preventing an enemy from using the sea may be a way of securing one's own use—for instance, by disabling forces that are seeking to prevent it. Similarly, projecting force ashore may contribute to securing use —for instance, by striking air bases and diminishing the weight of enemy attack—or contribute to preventing the enemy's use—for instance, by striking at enemy naval bases. This reinforces the need to distinguish between means and ends and identify final objectives and is particularly important when evaluating a new weapon like the Tomahawk in relation to alternative systems.

The Structure of Force Defense

There are different ways of securing the use of the sea; the submarine, for example, relies mainly on concealment and evasion. This is more difficult for surface ships to achieve, and they have to be able to counter enemy attempts at obstruction actively. One way is to prevent the opposing forces (enemy weapon platforms) from using the sea or air. Another way is to prevent enemy weapons from striking home. In practice, a mix of both is used. To reduce the final weight of attack to manageable proportions, the defense of surface forces in high-threat areas has to be layered and reach out as far as possible. It starts with the attempt to disable or distract the enemy's weapon platforms before they reach their launch position and, through various intervening stages, ends with terminal defenses that seek to destroy or divert any surviving missiles or torpedoes. The actual structure of force defense reflects judgments about the relative utility of countering the projectile itself (for example, the missile or the torpedo), disposing of the launch platform, or attacking the platform's home base. One type of competition for finite shipboard resources is between the different weapon systems used in these different elements of the defense.

The emphasis placed on countering the different links in the chain of threat is properly determined by calculations of the comparative advantages of competing systems at each level. It should not be assumed that the further one can reach toward the ultimate source of attack, the better, but neither can the possibility of disposing of a significant part of the threat at one time, by striking directly at the source, be ignored. Success, however, may require that the enemy be caught in place, as the Egyptian air force was in 1967 (but not the American carriers in 1941), and in such cases the possibility represents a tactical opportunity and not the basis for force planning. But where the projectile cannot be countered, as with the artillery shell, attacking the source may be the only means of defense. In any case, the allocation of resources to the different links in the threat chain should assume an alerted enemy whose defenses get more effective the closer one gets to the source of attack. The factors of time and space are also relevant. There is no point in investing heavily in the means of attacking opponents' bases if they have no need to use the naval bases for the duration of an engagement or if they have an advantage in aircraft range that allows them to mount their main strikes while their air bases are beyond the reach of U.S. forces.

Comparative advantage is the dominant consideration when structuring force defense. But where both sides are evenly matched, the advantage will lie with the one who fights closest to "home," a dictum that is even more relevant if the geostrategic circumstances favor the enemy. This means that, in theory at least, priority in force defense should be given to building outward from the center, adding extra layers only as necessary for the terminal defenses to be able to handle the expected weight of attack. Not only is this theoretically the most cost-effective way of securing the use of the sea, but it allows the greatest flexibility in how one chooses to use it. In practice, other considerations intervene, but it is important to be clear about the advantages of being able to counter the projectile itself. First, the engagement takes place at the peak of one's power gradient, which observes the principle "concentration of force." Second, no effort is wasted on projectiles that are not destined to reach the target area because of system failures of various kinds, which observes the principle "economy of effort." And third, the defense has available a range of evasion, deception, and confusion techniques, which are not applicable to other links in the threat chain. The further one reaches toward the source of attack, the more one is limited to "destruction" as the only effective countermeasure and the greater the scale of destruction required to achieve useful results.

The structure of force defense must also take account of the time horizon. In certain circumstances it may be theoretically more effective, in the long term, to strike at the source of threat rather than concentrate defense around the force. But where the Soviet Union is concerned, it is the short term that is important, because the Soviet concept of operations involves concentrating the maximum weight of attack in the initial stages of a general engagement. If the United States is unable to secure its use of the sea in the short term, there will be no long term.

Securing the Use of the Sea

By disabling Soviet surface ASW forces, TASMs can contribute to U.S. submarines' use of the sea in certain circumstances, primarily those of penetrating area defenses. But the primary U.S. concern is the Soviet threat to U.S. surface forces, posed mainly by the submarine torpedo and by cruise missiles launched from aircraft, surface ships, and submarines. Since the Tomahawk has no capability against the submarine, the discussion focuses on its potential as a counter to air- and surface-launched missiles. These can be destroyed or diverted by terminal defenses, and the question to be addressed when calculating antimissile defense requirements for the force is the extent to which Tomahawks can be counted on to dilute the threat. They have the capability to strike at missile-armed surface ships and at the systems that support missile-armed aircraft.

THE THREAT FROM SOVIET NAVAL STRIKE AIRCRAFT. Although the TLAM-N could be used to disable SNAF airfields once nuclear weapons were released, there is no good reason to tie down submarines in this role when it can be performed by the dedicated forces allocated to the SIOP and the theater nuclear strike plan. There appears to be no strong argument for treating SNAF airfields differently from other such targets.

If a limited number of critical links in the SNAF's operational structure, which are vulnerable to conventional attack and are hard to replace or restore, can be identified, the TLAM-C could be an effective means of degrading the SNAF's strike capability. What is known of Soviet concepts of operation suggests that such links must exist. Besides such precision strikes, the TLAM-C could be used to make limited sporadic attacks on the air bases themselves in order to disrupt preferred procedures and introduce uncertainty and complications into Soviet plans.

Using the TLAM-C to suppress air defenses in support of carrier strikes on SNAF bases is not a good idea, because the value of such strikes is dubious and there are more effective ways that carrier aircraft can contribute to securing the use of the sea in such circumstances. The tendency is to assume that, since each base supports ten aircraft, there should be a ten-to-one advantage in attacking at the source. But even in theory this would only apply if Soviet aircraft could be caught on the ground or were unable to redeploy between bases. None of these conditions is likely to obtain in a conventional conflict. The practical question is whether a given number of carrier aircraft over a given period of time can put more Soviet strike aircraft out of action by attacking their bases or by attacking the aircraft before they launch their missiles in the vicinity of the force being defended. A broader question is what mix of carrier aircraft contributes most to securing the use of the sea in the face of an intense air, submarine, and surface threat.

The aircraft mix in a standard carrier air wing is usually made up of thirty-four attack, twenty-four fighter, twenty antisubmarine, and about fifteen special-purpose aircraft. For most of thirty hours, as the carrier steams to get close enough to launch its strike, the attack aircraft stand idle, defense against SNAF strikes being the responsibility of the twenty-four fighters.[25] Assuming that the carrier manages to survive until within launch range, perhaps half the fighters will then have to accompany the attack aircraft, denuding the carrier force when it is closest to the enemy. The Soviet range advantage will also allow the launching of an attack on the carrier force from other bases to coincide with the return of the strike aircraft, when the battle group will be at its most vulnerable.

The concept of striking SNAF bases with carrier aircraft thus flouts the principle "security of the rear" in order to attack heavily defended and thoroughly hardened air bases at a maximum distance from "home." The alternative concept of attacking enemy aircraft in the vicinity of the carrier observes the principles "concentration of force" and "economy of effort" and reaps the advantage of fighting close to home. It applies the lesson that had to be relearned in both world wars of the advantages that accrue from concentrating the defense around the convoy and forcing the enemy to come to you and fight on your own ground.

Dropping the requirement to attack SNAF bases with carrier aircraft has other attractions. It allows the question of the optimal aircraft mix in the air wing to be addressed from first principles, taking full account of the Tomahawk's strike capability. For example, the number of fighters now carried could be doubled, or perhaps the reallocation should be broader and involve proportional increases in fighter, ASW, airborne early warning, and electronic warfare aircraft.

THE THREAT FROM MISSILE-ARMED SURFACE SHIPS. The TASM's major contribution to securing U.S. use of the sea will be the indirect one of complicating Soviet calculations and inducing a caution that would otherwise be absent.

To diminish the weight of a missile attack by enemy surface units, the TASM would have to strike home before the missile unit launched its initial salvo, or at least before it had time to reload. These conditions could be met by the submarine picket and by surface ships in a meeting engagement where the TASM had the greater reach. But they could not be met in other circumstances, notably "continuous company." Hence TASMs carried by surface ships of the main force cannot be counted on as threat dilutant when assessing requirements for antimissile defense.

---

25. These figures indicate the proportions of different types aboard a carrier battle group, not the total numbers that would be available for a particular operation. On the one hand there will be a minimum of two, and possibly four, carriers in company. On the other hand there will actually be fewer fighter aircraft per air wing because of unserviceability and operational attrition.

Even in cases where TASMs could strike home in time, there is the separate question of relative cost-effectiveness. The attraction of attacking the launch platform lies in the potential exchange rate, which was very favorable against the earliest classes of Soviet missile units since they were relatively poorly defended and carried large missile loads. But the high price of admission for more modern Soviet warships has brought the rate down to 1:1 or worse, and this must be compared with the exchange rate of U.S. antimissile defense missiles against incoming SSMs. Furthermore, the antimissile defense missile can handle missiles from *all* sources, which provides maximum flexibility, whereas the TASM's potential is limited to countering those carried by surface ships.

The mistaken impression that the TASM offers a general counter to the missile-armed surface ship stems in part from the tendency to view the cruise missile as a technological extension of the long-range gun. This is misleading. Understanding the missile's potential contribution to both securing and preventing the use of the sea will be furthered by clarifying the distinction between a naval artillery duel and a missile exchange. With both the gun and the missile, the warship designer–force planner must achieve the appropriate balance between offensive and defensive capabilities (which are better termed the capacity for penetration and protection), but the factors involved are different. With the gun, armor plating provided the only means of protection against the incoming shell, armor could only be carried by larger ships, and it could still be circumvented by innovative shell design. In such circumstances, offense was the *only* effective means of defense, and the emphasis in naval design shifted almost wholly to penetration. With the missile, only in a limited range of circumstances will the ability to penetrate serve as an indirect means of protection. On the other hand, the ability to shoot down or deceive the incoming projectile means that direct protection has been restored as a viable option. Furthermore, the capacity for self-protection is not restricted to larger ships (as was the case with armor) but extends to smaller units, in the form either of point-defense weapons or of area-defense systems protecting the whole force.

There are other distinctions. With the gun, because there was no effective protection against the shell, not only was it necessary to disable the enemy as a means of diverting its aim or stemming its fire, but it was essential to do so before the enemy disabled you. This placed a premium on large broadsides and high rates of fire, not because these were necessary to penetrate the enemy's defense (that requirement determined the caliber of gun and design of shell), but because the circular error probable (CEP) of ballistic rounds was large and (other things being equal) the chance of scoring a damaging blow was directly related to the number of shells fired at the target.

For the cruise missile, terminal accuracy is not a problem but penetration is. One element of that problem is the need to outwit the defense's attempts to deceive and deflect the incoming missile, and success largely depends on the sophistication of the terminal guidance system. The other and less tractable element of the problem is the need to overwhelm the defense's attempts to physically destroy the incoming missile, and success depends on exceeding the enemy's target-handling capability, the latter being a function of numbers and time.

The same factors that put a premium on high rates of fire also put a premium on the gun's reach, since a range advantage meant that you remained invulnerable while the enemy was denied its only means of protection. With missiles, a range advantage likewise offers invulnerability to the other ship's projectiles, but it does *not* deny the enemy the means of protection against your missiles. The 1973 Israeli experience demonstrated that, as long as the side with the shorter reach can protect itself against the incoming missiles, it can still go on and win.[26] The ability to penetrate therefore remains critical.

As a final point it should be remembered that the tactical realities of naval warfare involve more than matters of comparative reach and the balance between penetration and protection. Target location and identification are vulnerable to deception and decoy, while the effectiveness of attack and defense is influenced by skill in maneuver.

Preventing the Use of the Sea

In the short term, the importance of preventing the Soviet Union from using the sea depends on the extent to which such use is to U.S. disadvantage; hence there can be no automatic presumptions about the value of this mission. In some cases Soviet use of the sea may even work to U.S.

26. The Egyptian Styx missiles had a much longer reach than the Israeli Gabriels and were launched from outside the latter's range. No hits were scored, and the Israeli's speed advantage allowed them to overhaul the Egyptian *Osa*-class ships and sink most of them. Telem, "Israel's Guided Missile Fast Attack Craft." The relevance of this experience lies not in the *way* in which the Israelis went on to win, which would not apply to U.S.-Soviet engagements, but in the fulfillment of the *prior* requirement of ability to counter the enemy's missiles.

advantage if it ties down forces that might otherwise obstruct U.S. use. In the long term, however, the attrition of enemy forces becomes an objective in its own right.

Attacks on Soviet naval bases could hamper Soviet use of the sea and if the United States can impair Soviet submarine support facilities, this will contribute in the long term to securing U.S. use of the sea. It is not clear, however, that this is an appropriate role for either variant of the TLAM. The arguments advanced for leaving SNAF bases to the SIOP and the theater nuclear strike plan apply still more forcibly to naval bases, since there is no requirement for operational coordination. So, too, does the general line of argument against using TLAM-Cs and conventional carrier air strikes against main base structures and support facilities. It is hard to close ports and bases with high explosive, but it is relatively easy to do so with mines. There may, however, be a role for the TLAM-C against links in the command, control, and communications structure if these can be identified.

The TASM can contribute to preventing the USSR's use of the sea by disabling Soviet surface ships, a task that has received relatively low priority within the U.S. Navy until recently. The importance of the mission as an end in itself varies widely with circumstances, although the long-term objective of enemy attrition ensures for the antisurface role a significant minimum value. The basic mission assumes its greatest importance in circumstances of peacetime confrontation and, at the other end of the scale, in the broken-back phase of a nuclear war, when the mobile firepower of surface ships would take on a new significance. In many other situations, the longer term objective of enemy attrition would provide the primary justification, as, for example, when the opposing forces were in continuous company. While the dominant requirement would be to emerge from the battle unscathed (secure U.S. use of the sea), long-term advantages would accrue from disabling as many Soviet surface ships as possible.

When there was no immediate advantage to be gained from preventing Soviet use of the sea and long-term attrition became the primary objective, cost-benefit considerations (financial and operational) would come into play. For example, while it would be sensible to use shipboard TASMs to disable Soviet surface units at the onset of war in the Mediterranean, this does not mean that a special operation, with enemy attrition as the objective, could be justified in the Norwegian Sea. It could, however, be justified as preventing Soviet use of the area, although shore-based TASMs offer a better alternative. The latter could prevent use by posing a standing threat, which would need to be implemented only a few times, whereas a special operation would involve a fleet engagement, with all that implies in missile expenditure and ship casualties.

This brings out the point that the TASM's most important attribute will be to *inhibit* Soviet surface operations. Its effectiveness as a means of actually preventing them is much less certain because of the high price of admission demanded of Tomahawks and the difficulty of ensuring a sufficient concentration of missiles in the target area. An exception to this lukewarm assessment is the use of TASMs against soft-skinned amphibious forces.

Strategic Nuclear Missions

There is no strong argument in favor of general purpose naval units' contribution to the overall U.S. nuclear deterrence posture, but there are several against. They could not be relied on as strategic or theater nuclear forces, and the *practical* value of a nuclear reserve dispersed throughout the fleet is very questionable. If there are actually fewer nuclear weapons than required to assure general deterrence and escalation dominance, this would be best remedied by dedicated systems using the optimal basing mode, which may or may not be seagoing.

The concept of using the TLAM-N as a means of focused or proportional deterrence is flawed.[27] In peacetime such a declaratory policy could encourage the action the United States is trying to deter. In wartime it is hard to substantiate how the process could possibly work.

There are three kinds of objection to giving general purpose naval forces a long-range nuclear strike capability. One is the effect it would have on the flexibility of employment of U.S. ships and submarines, in-

---

27. It is argued, for example, that Soviet air strikes against U.S. carriers operating in the Indian Ocean can be deterred by the threat of TLAM-N attacks on the relevant air bases. Apart from the physical problems of penetrating alerted defenses focused on a known sector of attack, there are the perceptual ones of whether the Soviet Union would share the U.S. view of proportionality and distinction between "central" and "tactical" systems, and therefore refrain from escalation, and why the United States in turn would not be deterred by the threat of a "proportional" Soviet escalation. The more serious objection is that such a declaratory policy could make U.S. carriers *more* liable to attack by assuring the Soviet Union that the U.S. response would be not only limited but also one that could be contained if the Soviet Union made the necessary defense preparations.

cluding the willingness to risk them in peacetime operations. Another involves the implications for arms control, which are not invalidated by the problem of verification. And the third is the effect on Soviet naval requirements. If past performance is any guide, the dispersion of a strategic nuclear strike capability throughout the U.S. Navy would evoke a vigorous Soviet response. It would create a new impetus to achieving a worldwide general purpose naval capability that is not inherent in the current Soviet concept of operations or in the present structure of Soviet wartime naval requirements.[28]

These particular objections do not, however, apply to the carrier. It already suffers from the disadvantages of high target value and political symbolism; it already carries nuclear weapons that could be used against the Soviet Union; and it already has the command, control, and communications facilities and procedures for directing nuclear strikes. Placing TLAM-Ns aboard the carrier[29] would not incur new political costs or impose new operational constraints. This is not to cast the carrier as a contributor to strategic deterrence and war-fighting, because the problem of being in the right place at the right time and the TERCOM-related difficulties still apply. But TLAM-Ns would provide the carrier with an additional capability that could be used, for example, against SNAF airfields.

28. It is widely accepted that the Soviet Navy's shift to forward deployment in the mid-1960s was prompted by the sharp increase in the Polaris program authorized by President Kennedy on taking office. This, combined with the continuing strike carrier building program, resulted in a marked rise in the sea-based proportion of U.S. strategic delivery systems. Unquestionably, the Soviet move forward in strategic defense has undermined the U.S. Navy's worldwide predominance. While the exact nature of the Soviet response to a proliferation of TLAM-Ns cannot be predicted, it is relevant that, as a by-product of the debate in the early 1970s over the adequacy of the resources being allocated to naval construction, the concept of sea power entered the mainstream of Soviet analysis, and there was also a notable increase in the Navy's political clout. For the time being, Soviet naval procurement continues to be determined by wartime requirements, particularly the need to secure command of the outer defense zones as a means of protecting the SSBN bastions, which are located close to home. However, proponents exist for still larger naval forces and an increased naval role in the pursuit of overseas objectives in peacetime. A requirement to counter TLAM-Ns would provide these advocates with powerful new arguments for additional resources and for developing a naval policy where peacetime employment became a major factor in determining overall requirements.

29. Horizontal launchers could be fitted at the forward end of the carrier below the flight deck, at no cost to the number of aircraft carried, but at the sacrifice of some accommodation and storage space.

Projecting Force Ashore

Naval support for the land battle with the Soviet Union could be provided by TLAMs, but this falls mainly into the category of convenience
rather than necessity. The problems of providing the necessary TERCOM
and DSMAC data are significant, and in most cases alternate means are
available to provide the same support. It is on the maritime flanks that
the access provided by naval units may offer a comparative advantage in
the provision of conventional support: northern Norway, the Kuril chain,
and the routes south to the Persian Gulf. Except perhaps in the Persian
Gulf, the arguments for TLAM-Cs in this role are not strong.

The TLAM-C could, however, play an important role against third
world countries. It can be used in combination with carrier operations,
either increasing the effectiveness of manned aircraft or allowing a reallocation of aircraft to maritime warfare roles, and it can be used on its own.
For several years there has been talk of surface forces armed with land-
attack missiles compensating for the shortage of carriers.[30] However, the
primary role of such ships would be to launch punitive strikes, which in
most cases can be carried out more effectively by land-based bombers,
assuming that such attacks are considered to have real political utility.

A more interesting possibility is the use of TLAM-Cs to disrupt the
target state's defenses sufficiently to allow appropriately equipped U.S.
forces to achieve a lodgment ashore and then to interdict the reinforcement of the battle area. This would not be possible in the immediate

30. The short-lived concept of the nuclear-powered strike cruiser (CSGN)
which was first reported publicly in November 1974 (Clarence A. Robinson, "Mis-
sile-Equipped Strike Cruiser Studied," *Aviation Week and Space Technology*, November 18, 1974, pp. 14–15) and formally canceled by the incoming secretary of
defense in February 1977. The 17,000-ton CSGN was to carry the Aegis antiair system, eight Tomahawks, and sixteen Harpoons, plus the proposed new lightweight
8-inch gun. The CSGN was intended to operate either as part of an all-nuclear carrier
task force or as an independent means of projecting force ashore should a carrier
not be available. The battleship concept involves the four *Iowa*-class now in reserve
and the most ambitious proposal requires the removal of the after turret and some
of the after superstructure, and constructing a two-runway, V-shaped, V/STOL ski-
jump flight deck on the after part of the ship with the arms of the V running forward
and outward on either side of the after superstructure. A 320-missile vertical launching battery would be set in between the arms of the V. For a photograph of a model
of this conversion and further references to this brainchild of Capt. Charles Myers,
USN (rtd.), see *United States Naval Institute Proceedings*, vol. 106 (November
1980), p. 131.

future, since U.S. forces are so geared to working with fixed-wing air support as to be at a loss without it, but the capability could undoubtedly be developed.

Conclusions

The conclusions fall into three parts: the Tomahawk's potential value and its deployment; the system's limitations and the implications for future requirements; and a final summing up.

Deployment

Any attempt to draw conclusions about the Tomahawk's potential value to the Navy must start with the caveat that it is an immensely complex subject in which the issues are not clear-cut and an exception can be found to most assertions. Before considering TASMs and TLAMs separately, three general points can be made.

Except in a limited range of circumstances, the Tomahawk cannot contribute to countering immediate threats to the survival of U.S. naval forces. As these threats continue to increase throughout the world, so does the requirement for self-protection. For political reasons, U.S. surface ships should have a self-defense capability that is completely reliable in low-intensity encounters and effective in high-intensity situations within the context of force defense. This requirement should take priority in the allocation of resources and in the design of ships and force structures. The fitting of Tomahawks to surface ships must not be at the expense of the ships' ability to defend themselves.

The second point is that the Tomahawk's strike capability allows a reconsideration of the apportionment of roles in the carrier air wing. The importance of the carrier aircraft's contribution to the nonstrike aspects of maritime warfare has been steadily increasing, but at present over one-third of the air wing is configured for the strike role. If Tomahawks could take over at least part of that responsibility, the overall capability of the carrier battle group would be significantly increased.

The third point is that the Tomahawk's value in most scenarios, particularly those involving the Soviet Union, depends on the availability of large numbers of missiles, and these will have to be provided without impairing force survivability.

ANTISHIP MISSILES. Two problems are central to the use of TASMs. One is the provision of over-the-horizon targeting data and meeting the requirements for command integration and command, control, communications, and intelligence. The other is the need to provide for a missile salvo large enough to saturate the target's defenses, if necessary by coordinating the fire of several platforms.

Where space and top weight allow, the deployment of TASMs aboard all surface ships can be justified on the grounds that this will be advantageous in peacetime confrontation with Soviet naval forces and, in more general terms, will complicate Soviet threat assessments and induce added caution.

Given the availability of the torpedo and the Harpoon, the deployment of TASMs aboard submarines can only be justified on a selective basis for tasks that require their long reach. One such task is area interdiction in waters where there is a high air threat. A more doubtful candidate is the task of antisurface picket, since there are probably more cost-effective ways of covering that threat. In both cases the submarine would have to be fitted with external launch tubes to provide the necessary size of salvo. TASMs might also be deployed aboard a limited number of attack submarines for use when penetrating area antisubmarine defenses, but only if they were significantly more cost-effective than Harpoons in this role.

The operational arguments in favor of emplacing TASMs in coastal sites covering strategic waters are clear. The missile's reach undercuts the advantage of a mobile platform, and with no space and weight constraints there need be no difficulty in providing the necessary size of salvo. Such land-based emplacements would also bring psychological benefits. The missiles would be a positive demonstration of the geographic advantage of the West and an assertion of the primacy of its interests in these strategic areas.

LAND-ATTACK MISSILES. The central problem for the TLAM is the timely provision of the launch platform with TERCOM and DSMAC data, and difficulties with this limit the flexibility of the system's employment.

The TLAM-C can help meet two important naval requirements: diminishing the air threat to U.S. naval forces by attacking links in the SNAF's operational structure, and improving U.S. capability to intervene in the third world.

It is impossible to estimate the number of TLAM-Cs needed to disrupt SNAF operations, since the target set is not known. The missile would have to be deployed aboard submarines, and since there is no requirement for concentrated fire, missiles could be launched from torpedo tubes. Submarines would also have to be used if tactical surprise was necessary when intervening in the third world. The most important conclusion to be drawn is that if the submarine force is to discharge its existing tasks as well as these new ones, more submarines will be needed.

The deployment of TLAM-Cs aboard all surface ships operating with carriers would augment the force's intervention capability. If Soviet interposition seemed likely, the requirements for the TLAM-C would have to be balanced against those for the TASM in terms of launcher availability.

The overall intervention capability of the United States could be extended by using surface groups armed with TLAM-Cs independently of carriers. The formation of such groups around a strike cruiser or missile-armed battleship could not be justified if their purpose was just to carry out punitive attacks (there are other ways of doing this), but it could be if it made an amphibious assault without carrier support possible. It is sometimes claimed that if a carrier was not available, the amphibious assault group would not be either, but it is not hard to visualize a situation where all the carriers were tied down in situations that did not require the landing of men. Carrying out landings without conventional air cover against limited opposition would have implications for antiaircraft weapons at the force and unit levels, and these need to be addressed.

There seems to be no urgent requirement to deploy TLAM-Ns aboard general purpose forces. The arguments in favor range from "come in handy" to "nice to have," rather than "necessary," but the penalties for such deployment outweigh the possible advantages. This is not to deny the convenience of having TLAM-Ns aboard submarines deployed to disrupt SNAF operations with TLAM-Cs—if the war became nuclear they could immediately strike at the air bases themselves. But since this nuclear requirement is already covered by dedicated forces, it is a matter of operational convenience rather than necessity. The exception is the carrier, which would incur no new operational or political penalties by carrying TLAM-Ns. There is deep prejudice against placing extraneous weapons aboard these ships, but TLAM-Ns could be a cost-free addition and would improve the carrier's capability significantly.

Limitations and Possibilities

The trade-off between reach, penetration, and kill is central to missile design, and the appropriate balance will differ between roles. One of the

Tomahawk's deficiencies is that the same engine-airframe unit is being used for three very different missions.

For the antiship missile, penetration is much more important than reach. Defense against enemy missiles does not depend on having longer reach, which yields tactical advantage in only a few situations, and then only if penetration can be ensured. Poor penetration raises the price of admission to levels where it becomes hard to assemble a large enough salvo and magazine capacity becomes a significant factor in the simplest engagement. Problems of over-the-horizon targeting and coordinating time on target are magnified by the combination of long range and the many missiles necessary to achieve penetration.

Penetration depends on the enemy's target-handling capacity, which is a function of time and numbers; the shorter the time available to react, the fewer the missiles needed to saturate the defenses. This reaction time depends on missile speed and detectability, with speed being more important at sea. For shipboard radars, the horizon imposes an absolute detection limit on missiles flying low over the sea, and once past a relatively small cross section, an increase in missile size will not lead to significantly earlier detection. Missile speed is therefore the primary aid to penetration, and it is relevant that among the deficiencies of Western SSM systems the Soviet Union specifies the missile's subsonic speed.[31] As an indication of their probable ability to counter such missiles, it is relevant that each generation of Soviet SSMs and ASMs has seen a significant increase in speed, which now stands at Mach 2.5 as against the Tomahawk's 0.9.

Speed and range are inversely related and both are conditioned by missile size. If radar cross section is not critical to detectability, one constraint on size falls away, but that of magazine capacity remains. However, if greater speed leads to improved penetration and a drop in the price of admission, the pressure on magazine space will be reduced, allowing more flexibility in the choice of missile size.

There is a strong argument in favor of antiship missiles' having very high speed when within range of terminal defenses. The advantages of

---

31. A Strokin, "Protivokorabel'nye rakety: dostoinstva i nedostatki" (Antiship Missiles: Capabilities and Limitations), *Morskoj sbornik*, November 1980, p. 86. The other deficiencies noted by the author were: vulnerability to ship's fire; inadequate target discrimination; and inadequate defense against enemy electronic countermeasures. This article appeared in the section "Foreign Fleets" and is reputedly based on material published in the foreign press, but it reads like a Soviet evaluation.

long range, with all the attendant problems of targeting and command and control, are much harder to identify. Ideally, the missile's propulsion system would combine a reasonably fast transit speed over a long range with a high-speed dash capability in the terminal area. If that is not possible, speed is more important than range.

For TLAM-Cs, speed is less important as an aid to penetration than detectability is, since the defenses it has to negotiate are not limited to the terminal area, nor are they concentrated there as they are at sea. The TLAM-C's small radar cross section was determined in part by the necessity to penetrate the sophisticated defenses of the Soviet national air defense system, as was the expensive emphasis on minimizing reflectivity. The penalty is in payload, and it is the unfavorable ratio between payload and missile cost that would restrict the value of this missile against the third world. The air defenses of third world states are quite different from those of the Soviet Union, and if the most likely application of the conventional land-attack missile is in such areas, it would be sensible to exploit the advantages of a less hostile environment in order to use a bigger missile with a larger payload.

The very different balances between the reach, penetration, and destruction capabilities required for different missions means that using a common engine and airframe, as the Tomahawk does, incurs heavy penalties. This commonality has certain advantages in cost and production, military supply ashore, and stowage and launching at sea. But these are not sufficient to outweigh the operational drawbacks. The TASM's poor penetrativity can only be compensated for by using twice as many missiles as would otherwise be required, with all that implies for procurement costs and missile stowage and launch requirements.

Looking to the future, one can see the need for systems tailored more closely to specific roles, with perhaps a basic division between weapon delivery (strike) and surveillance-search (think) vehicles, and further divisions within the strike category. If this should be the case, it must be determined whether the design of different missiles or remote piloted vehicles should be constrained by the requirement that they fit a common launcher. Specifying that the Tomahawk should fit a torpedo tube was an economical way of meeting the original requirement to launch a limited number of strategic nuclear missiles, but as the program was extended to include the TASM and TLAM-C variants it entered a vicious circle. The limited speed and payload necessitate the fitting of external tubes to submarines so that they can carry or launch sufficient missiles to accomplish their missions, and the result is the worst of both worlds. At the same time surface ships have been fitted with specially designed armored box launchers that could have been any size.

Constraining missile design is not the only issue concerning common launchers. The analysis has highlighted the competition for space and weight between the Tomahawk and the antiair and antisubmarine systems aboard surface ships, and it is not clear that having the different missiles share the same vertical launching system launcher-stowage battery makes the best use of these scarce resources. The argument about flexibility is less persuasive because in many circumstances the maximum number of *all* types of missiles available will be needed, and the physical requirements for launching quick-reaction antiair and antisubmarine weapons are different from those for long-range SSMs. Has enough imagination gone into devising different ways of launching SSMs and different ways of using the ship's structure for stowage? For example, a floating vertical launching system was developed by the U.S. Navy in the 1960s, and this would allow the SSM to be stowed horizontally (like torpedoes) right aft, and "laid" from the stern of the ship while under way.[32] And the very simplicity of the Harpoon launcher suggests other opportunities for stowage and launch aboard ship, quite separate from the complex vertical launching system.[33] The answers are by no means clear, but these are fundamental considerations that have major implications for future ship design and force structure.

To Sum Up

The Tomahawk offers some interesting new capabilities but is handicapped by its genesis and the inevitable design constraints. These inadequacies must not be perpetuated by basing future ship design on this suboptimal system. Its most important long-term contribution will be to force the U.S. Navy to focus its attention on the cruise missile as a versa-

32. A floating launch method code named "Project Hydra" was developed in the early 1960s. It successfully launched a range of different missiles, but the program was canceled in 1965 as no longer needed. See John E. Draim, "Move MX Missiles Out to Sea," *National Review,* December 12, 1980, pp. 1500–01, 1526–27. Captain Draim, USN (rtd.), was the program manager of Project Hydra.

33. For example, it has been suggested that missiles could be mounted vertically on the outside of deckhouses and the main superstructure, or in the case of carriers, on the underside of the angled deck sponsons. Some armoring would be necessary.

tile weapon system and to explore its full potential and that of other unmanned systems, including tactical ballistic missiles. By reducing the Navy's dependence on the fixed-wing aircraft, these systems could make significant changes in fleet structure possible.

By taking over part of the strike role, the Tomahawk may allow a re-allocation of carrier aircraft between tasks, enhancing the force's ability to secure the use of the sea, and it offers new opportunities for preventing Soviet use of the sea, particularly if friendly coasts bordering strategic sea areas are exploited. Its most important short-term effect will be to improve the U.S. Navy's antisurface capability at a time when the Soviet Navy is building up its surface force in numbers and effectiveness. It will improve the U.S. capacity for military intervention in the third world, for which there appears to be a growing political demand. But it should not be seen as a means of bringing yet more nuclear weapons to bear on the Soviet Union for deterrent or war-fighting purposes. If there is a genuine deficiency in this respect, it can only be met by dedicated systems and not by general purpose naval forces.

CHAPTER NINE

Arms Control: Toward Informal Solutions

GEORGE H. QUESTER

ARMS CONTROL advocates often cite cruise missiles as a cause for concern. The intention of this chapter is to subject such concern to some critical scrutiny.[1] Why are cruise missiles considered to be a problem? Perhaps the problem lies in a misstatement of the ultimate rationale for arms control.

Arms control is a phrase used differently by different observers. Some apply the term only to formal negotiations for the limitation or reduction of weaponry. Some would procedurally broaden the concept to include any tacit bargaining backed by verification by national means, that is, by technological or other monitoring processes giving each side some assurance about what the other is deploying in weapons.

Finally, some would treat either negotiations or verification as simply inputs to arms control, not necessarily having merit in their own right (any more than straightforward disarmament has merit in its own right), but to be judged instead by how they affect certain very important outputs. These crucial arms control outputs would be to diminish the likelihood of war, reduce the destructiveness of war (if it were nonetheless to occur), or reduce in peacetime the political, social, and economic costs

George Quester is professor of government and director of the Program on Peace Studies at Cornell University.
1. Good general discussions of the arms control implications of cruise missiles are to be found in Richard Burt, "The Cruise Missile and Arms Control," *Survival*, vol. 18 (January–February 1976), pp. 10–17; and Alexander R. Vershbow, "The Cruise Missile: The End of Arms Control?" *Foreign Affairs*, vol. 55 (October 1976), pp. 133–46.

of military preparedness. This chapter will touch on each of these interpretations of arms control while leaning toward an interpretation that stresses outputs, rather than formal negotiations or reliable monitoring. What effects have cruise missiles had on the negotiation of arms limitations? Do they interfere with monitoring and thus disturb arms race stability and drive up the total numbers of weapons procured? Do they facilitate preemptive counterforce attacks against the other side's strategic forces, thereby upsetting crisis stability and making some forms of general war more likely? Do they upset deterrence stability, or instead contribute to it, thus discouraging any deliberate aggression by the Warsaw Pact forces against America's NATO allies?

Past SALT Negotiations

The history of strategic arms negotiations contains past sensitivities about territories and basing modes that make it difficult for the United States and the Soviet Union to develop agreements about cruise missiles.[2] The fundamental characteristic of what have variously been referred to as gray area weapons, long-range theater nuclear forces (LRTNF), or forward-based systems (FBS) is asymmetry. NATO forces have based nuclear weapons in Western Europe that could be delivered by missile or aircraft to attack targets within the USSR. The Soviet Union has no corresponding nuclear warheads aimed at the United States except those based within the USSR itself or on board submarines of the Soviet Navy. (It was the Soviet effort to deploy some of these nuclear forces forward to Cuba, in what might have seemed analogous to Western deployments to West Germany, Italy, Greece, or Turkey, that produced the missile crisis of 1962. The American success in that crisis hence was crucial to making the FBS question what it is today.)

Making the picture somewhat less asymmetrical, the USSR has long possessed nuclear weapons aimed at targets in Western Europe, including the launching bases for the Western nuclear forces. (The United States could of course easily direct a nuclear attack at Cuba, Grenada, Vietnam, or any other satellite of the Soviet Union, in many cases using delivery systems not included in the limitations negotiated in SALT I or SALT II.) Soviet negotiators have thus many times argued that forward-based

2. For a comprehensive account, see Thomas W. Wolfe, *The SALT Experience* (Ballinger, 1979).

systems should be counted as part of any reckoning of equality of strategic forces for the two sides, since a missile's origin would make little difference to a Soviet or American city in World War III. (If missiles based on submarines cruising in the Atlantic are to be counted, why should not missiles on the continent of Europe?) However, the complications and disadvantages of accepting such a claim would be very great for the United States. Some of the relevant forces (those of Britain and France) are not under American control. Even if those that are under American control could under some special circumstances reach targets in the western Soviet Union, they are more normally described as playing a tactical role. They are intended to reach military facilities in Eastern Europe that would support a war being fought on that continent.

Western Europe is not only special as a base from which missiles and bombers can be launched. It is also a densely populated and enormously valuable piece of land, unfortunately very open to direct armored attack by forces of the Soviet Union. Negotiated arms control would have been easier with regard to cruise missiles (and for SALT I and SALT II) if Europe had been situated elsewhere, so that neither side might ever have felt a need to deploy any of its tactical or strategic nuclear weapons there.

Americans who think the details of SALT I or SALT II show Russian toughness and cleverness at negotiation can cite a number of counts to support their argument. In SALT I, there was the decision to freeze the missile totals simply as they were in 1972, which gave the USSR more total ballistic missile launchers than the United States (2,350, compared to 1,700). The Jackson amendment then signaled a clear congressional desire for more explicit parity in the future, but in the proposals for SALT II (where manned bombers were included in the totals of parity), there were no restrictions on the Backfire bomber and a certain number of heavy missiles were allowed on the Soviet side for which the United States had no equivalent. However, an appraisal of Soviet negotiating prowess would have to be balanced by the American success at keeping forward-based systems entirely out of SALT I and also keeping most forms of such European-based systems (including ground- and sea-launched cruise missiles after 1981) unlimited by SALT II.

The United States quite steadfastly and successfully rebuffed all Soviet efforts to get European-based nuclear forces included in the text at SALT I. Cruise missiles were not much involved in this; their technology seemed at a low point at the beginning of the 1970s, because earlier systems such as Snark, Matador, and Mace had been found lacking when compared with ballistic missiles or manned bombers. (It should be noted, however, that early Mace cruise missiles with a range of 1,500 miles were deployed in concrete bunkers in Germany until 1969.)

When the 1974 Vladivostok summit meeting between Leonid I. Brezhnev and President Gerald R. Ford signaled the outlines of a possible SALT II agreement, the cruise missile option began to look more interesting again to U.S. Navy and Air Force planners and to Secretary of State Henry Kissinger, who apparently wished to develop it as a bargaining chip in case the Russians became too obstinate in their negotiating posture.[3] Nonetheless, at Vladivostok the only possibility of an explicit reference to such systems was in the proposal for a limit of 600 kilometers on airplane-launched missiles. Kissinger afterward stated that this applied only to air-launched *ballistic* missiles, but the Russians insisted it applied to air-launched cruise missiles (ALCMs) as well.

The Soviet Union can hardly have been said to have given up the FBS issue without something in return, of course: their concession at Vladivostok was explicitly tied to the United States' dropping its demands that the Russians' SALT I advantage in heavy missiles be terminated. Soviet acquiescence also required an agreement to very high totals for both sides, which led many arms control commentators to criticize the Vladivostok accord for being meaningless as an arms restraint.

The cruise missile played a more prominent role in the deterioration of Soviet-American relations that set in after Vladivostok. American intelligence estimates had concluded that the Russians' Backfire bomber could reach the United States from bases in the Soviet Union, so pressure mounted to include it in the total of Soviet forces to be constrained by treaty limits. The Soviet response was to insist again that more extensive limits be applied in turn to the totals of American cruise missiles: those carried on board aircraft were to be counted against American treaty totals and those based on land or sea were to be substantially limited in range. Since a restriction on sea-based cruise missiles, or in particular on land-based cruise missiles, would intrude substantially into the domain of European-based theater nuclear forces, a fair amount of concern emerged in NATO capitals about the military and political impact of what might eventually be negotiated at SALT by the United States and the USSR.

3. For details, see Strobe Talbott, *Endgame: The Inside Story of SALT II* (Harper and Row, 1979), and also see Robert Emmet Moffit, "The Cruise Missile and SALT II," *International Security Review*, vol. 4 (Fall 1979), pp. 271–93.

After the initial Soviet rejection of the Carter SALT initiatives in 1977, the cruise missile issue seemingly became more important for a time to all concerned. Soviet proposals increasingly called for bans not only on the deployment of longer-range cruise missiles, but also on any sharing of this technology with allies. Such a ban on sharing could again be viewed in various ways. If one regarded Germany, France, or any other European NATO state as a staunch and loyal ally of the United States, the ban on sharing technology would simply protect the Russians against a disguised American acquisition of hundreds of additional missiles. If they were handed over to a NATO ally as a conventional weapon system, there might be little to stop the United States from accepting them back sometime later as a gift to expand its strategic nuclear arsenal. From the Western European view, however, such a ban on transferring weapons or technology might instead imply that the United States shared a Soviet distrust of European nuclear proliferation, or—assuming that there might be important uses for such cruise missiles with conventional warheads—that the United States was ready to sacrifice its allies' military options in this conventional category merely to reassure the USSR on the strategic nuclear side in order to seal the deal on SALT II.

It is still debated whether the final SALT II package, as signed in June 1979 (but then withdrawn from consideration for Senate ratification in January 1980), was more a concession by one side or the other. Aircraft with cruise missiles mounted on them were to be counted against the total of multiple-warhead-equipped launch vehicles, dampening any Western inclination toward extensive investment in air-launched cruise missiles with conventional warheads. This restriction also cast doubt on whether enough such nuclear-armed ALCMs could be procured to renew the bomber leg of the triad convincingly in the face of imminent vulnerability of the land-based missile leg.

Cruise missiles based on submarines or on land, while not counted in the totals of strategic forces, were to be limited in range to 600 kilometers, but by a protocol to the SALT treaty that was to remain in effect only until December 1981. Those seeing this as a concession to Moscow argue that Soviet negotiators were sure to demand an extension of this protocol, so it would set a precedent that would hurt the United States and its allies in the end. Carter administration spokesmen were inclined to brush off this protocol provision as a piece of meaningless window dressing to satisfy the Russians, since no American-made land-based or sea-based cruise missiles were slated for deployment before 1982 in any event.

Moreover, the formal NATO decision of December 1979 to deploy ground-launched cruise missiles (GLCMs) of a range of 2,500 kilometers could be viewed as locking the United States into a commitment stronger than the counterpressures in the implicit precedent of the SALT protocol.

Past Theater Negotiations

Until the mid-1970s, the United States had been determined for years to keep the subject of theater nuclear forces (TNF) such as cruise missiles out of SALT and arms limitation negotiations in general. Since that time, however, two kinds of changes have occurred in this attitude.

One is a proposal that was made during the negotiations on mutual and balanced force reductions (MBFR), which have been under way since 1973 in Vienna, involving representatives of European states in both NATO and the Warsaw Pact and the United States and the Soviet Union. These negotiations, working up from the other end of the weapons spectrum compared to SALT, have been mainly concerned with totals of troops, tanks, and tactical aircraft and thus have only occasionally considered theater nuclear forces. However, in December 1975 the discussants were asked to consider NATO's "option III" proposal: a reduction of 1,000 U.S. nuclear warheads, 54 nuclear-capable F-4 quick-reaction-alert aircraft, 36 Pershing I ballistic missiles, and 29,000 American troops in exchange for a reduction of 68,000 Soviet troops and 1,700 Soviet tanks.

The second change is more recent: the Russians have begun deploying a new multiple-warhead intermediate-range missile, the SS-20, in place of earlier single-warhead medium-range missiles—the SS-4 and SS-5—deployed early in the 1960s. This development has captured a fair amount of Western attention and led to proposals that such deployments be halted in exchange for restraints on Western TNF.

A major argument of this chapter will be that the pairing of Western nuclear warheads with Soviet tanks, as suggested in the 1975 MBFR proposal, is more real and significant than pairing with systems such as the SS-20, which is a more political proposal and a distraction. In the MBFR negotiations, as was the case at SALT, the specific delivery system of cruise missiles did not seem to be a real option in its earliest presentation. However, as the cruise missile began to look more promising militarily after 1975 and was pulled into SALT, so it will also be pulled into future regional arms control negotiations.

The Impact of the SS-20

The Russians' SS-20 is the most prominent in an array of modern theater nuclear weapons systems. It can be viewed as threatening to the European NATO states in several ways, although the real nature of these threats is open to some debate.[4] First, the SS-20 can strike at European cities, which strategically amounts to no real change from what was already available to the Russians in their array of missiles and aircraft. However, their investment in a newer and more modern version of such intra-European overkill could be a politically disturbing move in a period generally supposed to be characterized by détente and arms control.

In fact, the SS-20 may simply be the second and third stage of the failed SS-16 intercontinental missile, and the Russians may be aiming it at Europe for lack of anything else to do with these components. Even if there were thus no new hostile intent toward Europe, for the Russians to keep on putting such missiles into place—at a rate of one new launcher a week in 1980—must nonetheless be seen as provocative. Since the SS-20 has multiple warheads, the effective total of Soviet nuclear destructive power aimed at Western Europe is clearly on the rise, a fact that Soviet statements about the arms situation in Europe often tend to gloss over.

A second consideration is that the mobile SS-20 will be less vulnerable to counterforce strikes by the forces of the United States and its NATO allies. Militarily this can be seen as a setback for the West, in terms of who would "win" any future war fought between NATO and the Warsaw Pact. From the point of view of arms control, however, it might be considered desirable in that it would reduce temptations and Soviet fears of preemptive attack.

A third threat is that the SS-20 will have much more accurate warheads, posing a greater threat of counterforce attack at the existing tactical nuclear forces of NATO or conventional forces, even though its own vulnerability to counterforce assault will be reduced. Such accuracy might allow the preemptive destruction of all the existing NATO nuclear armed missile forces and all the air bases from which NATO-manned aircraft could deliver such weapons. Particularly important, some observers fear that the SS-20 might now be so accurate as to allow a surgical preemptive counterforce strike without extensive collateral damage to the surrounding population and landscape of West Germany and Western Europe.

4. For a very balanced German assessment of the extent of European military concerns, see Karl Kaiser, "Security: A European Perspective," *Trialogue,* no. 21 (Fall 1979), pp. 16–20.

The last point is very debatable, just as it is very important. If the collateral damage in a Soviet preemptive first strike with theater nuclear weapons could not be contained, then either the damage to West German real estate would be likely to lead to an all-out American retaliation amounting to general war, or it would do so much to destroy the prize of Western Europe that the Russians would be robbed of any prospective fruits of aggression. In either case, the weapons involved would make little political difference.

Anyone confronting the European balance of forces must take seriously the strictly military problems, and likely outcomes, of wars that could arise under a wide variety of circumstances. Deliberate Soviet aggression is only one of the possibilities. Wars that began as a result of some kind of accident or a local crisis entirely out of Moscow and Washington's control could still provoke the use of such modern weapons as the SS-20 and GLCMs. Yet much of the decisionmaking about theater nuclear weapons and cruise missiles will depend more on the political shadow of military possibilities than on the military possibilities themselves. Thus, it has always been most important to NATO that no one on either side conclude that aggression is an easy option for Moscow, for this would produce a "Finlandization." If a reflective analysis of the SS-20 shows that it does not pave the way for any easy Soviet moves westward, then much of its threat to the West will evaporate.

The real impact of the SS-20 is thus not fully settled. There is more concern about the political than the military impact, but the deployment of this new missile (along with the Backfire bomber and several other advanced Soviet tactical aircraft also capable of delivering nuclear warheads) now unquestionably figures in consideration of the cruise missile by the United States and its allies. The terms of the trade in which NATO has been seeking to use any of its European-based nuclear weapons as the bargaining chip has thus shifted, now involving Soviet nuclear forces as well as conventional ones.

Negotiation Offers and Responses

The NATO Council decision on December 12, 1979, completed a carefully assembled and orchestrated package of deployment moves and arms reduction negotiation offers. The council proposed to deploy 464 nuclear-armed cruise missiles and 108 nuclear-armed advanced Pershing II theater ballistic missiles. Having rescinded the earlier option III proposal, NATO also unilaterally reduced by 1,000 the total of nuclear warheads deployed in Europe and offered to negotiate a limitation of such Western cruise missile deployments with the USSR in exchange for a reduction of the Soviet deployment of the SS-20.[5]

The Soviet posture on this in late 1979, before the December 12 meeting, was to warn menacingly against any deployment of such advanced TNF, to offer a ground force reduction and negotiations on possible restraints in its TNF if a ban on cruise missiles could be accepted, and to announce a unilateral withdrawal of up to 20,000 Soviet troops from East Germany. Then, after the NATO decision of December 1979, the Russians petulantly announced for a time that further negotiations along these lines would be impossible if the NATO deployments were implemented.[6]

The allied decision to ignore Soviet demands before the December meeting was interpreted in some quarters as a hard-line rejection of negotiations, and the Soviet vehemence after that decision as the same. The ensuing Soviet invasion of Afghanistan and President Jimmy Carter's withdrawal of the SALT II treaty from the Senate then put the seal on what appeared for the time being to be a low point in negotiated arms restraints.

Hopes were resuscitated when contacts aimed at TNF negotiations began in the fall of 1980. NATO indecision on going ahead with a cruise missile deployment, evidenced by the Netherlands and Belgium at the December 1979 meeting and underscored by worried speculation on the possibility of West German delay, might have been viewed by some as encouraging continued negotiations. However, it would have been seen with alarm by others—most significantly, in the United States—who fear a "self-Finlandization." What these people object to is that the Russians would be allowed to keep the SS-20s they already have, while the West would prematurely give up the TNF improvements that might seem the natural counterweight to the SS-20 and the Backfire, thus surrendering the chip without getting any bargaining leverage out of it.

Prospects for agreement are constrained, even if the West bargains resolutely, by some asymmetries in the hardware at issue. The United

5. For details, see Mark Brent and William H. Kincade, "NATO Decides: New Arms and Arms Control in Europe," *Arms Control Today*, vol. 10 (February 1980), pp. 1–2, 6–10.

6. For relevant portions of the key Soviet statement, see excerpts from President Brezhnev's speech of October 6, 1979, in *Survival*, vol. 22 (January–February 1980), pp. 28–30.

States seems to be well ahead of the Soviet Union in the development of cruise missiles, simply because the crucial technological inputs are precision and miniaturization. The proposed NATO response to the Soviet Backfire (a manned aircraft) and the SS-20 (a ballistic missile) thus came in the form of an advanced ballistic missile (the Pershing II, which because of its speed to target can raise new arms control problems of its own) and the cruise missile.[7]

Most significant, however, is the basic disagreement between the United States and USSR over whether Western LRTNF should be distinguished from Soviet theater systems because they can strike Russian territory. This asymmetry is of course not new, having been in effect in some form ever since the first of what the Russians call FBS were deployed to Western Europe. It stems from long-standing U.S. commitments to the defense of the European NATO states to the extent of possible escalation to nuclear warfare. It in the end derives from the most basic asymmetry of all: that Western Europe is still in danger of invasion by forces that can easily be brought in by railroad from the Soviet Union. No piece of Communist-governed territory faces the same threat of invasion by forces of the West.

Arms Race Stability: The Monitoring Problem

Even if each of the two superpowers could be very certain of how many cruise missiles the other possessed, in light of the above, they might encounter difficulty in negotiating "fair" quotas for any treaty. However, the arms control impact of any extensive procurement and deployment of cruise missiles has even broader pessimistic implications.[8] Even if the two sides could agree on some kind of fair ratio of force strengths, the technology of the cruise missile raises problems of monitoring and verification. Capable of being fired from many different kinds of launchers, such missiles lack the anchor that previously had allowed each side to monitor the number of its adversary's ballistic missiles—the visibility of the silos or submarines specially fitted to fire ballistic missiles.

7. Christopher Paine, "Pershing II: The Army's Strategic Weapon," *Bulletin of the Atomic Scientists,* October 1980, pp. 25–31, presents a very skeptical view of the logic of the Pershing II deployment.
   8. A pessimistic forecast of the impact of cruise missile development on the SALT process can be found in Lawrence Weiler, "Strategic Cruise Missiles and the Future of SALT," *Arms Control Today,* vol. 5 (October 1975), pp. 1–4.

The attainment of a monitoring capability in the 1960s is sometimes viewed as the single greatest asset of arms control. The technological achievement of satellite reconnaissance, and the political understanding by which the two superpowers tolerated and dignified such reconnaissance, may have allowed procurements of intercontinental ballistic missiles (ICBMs) to remain lower than they would have been otherwise. Whenever a critic of the process states that arms control logic has merely dignified and codified the arms race that would have occurred otherwise, he is omitting this very important influence. Other things being equal, to know how many weapons an adversary holds, regardless of political hostilities, is likely to reduce the amount of weaponry one feels a need to obtain.

A strong emphasis on monitoring among arms controllers is also a response to decades of American rejection of Soviet disarmament proposals that omitted international inspection or verification. The U.S. government year after year had to remind the neutral gallery that the USSR was not as inherently open as the United States, so that some form of verification would be needed if the Russians were not to get away with enormous cheating. Arms controllers since the 1960s have shown agreement with this broad American position, in part because it was correct and sensible and in part because they wanted to differentiate themselves from naive believers in unilateral disarmament. In view of this background, it is ironic that American arms controllers should indict the cruise missile mainly for its verification difficulty. And it is a switch in roles for Defense Department defenders of the cruise missile to brush off such problems, for in most earlier rounds of arms negotiations, they have been the most vigilant proponents of assured verification.

An interesting example of how earlier postures present problems in future negotiations is that of "counting rules," a SALT I breakthrough that induced the Russians to concede that all of a particular class of ballistic missiles would have to be charged against the limit of those allowed with multiple independently targetable reentry vehicles (MIRVs), once *any* of that class had been test-fired in that mode. Since there would be no other means to reassure the other side that a particular missile lacked MIRVs, except a lack of test-firings, this could be a perfectly reasonable rule. However, this rule then gave the Russians a strong card to play in SALT II, allowing them to demand similar counting rules for cruise missiles, such as counting all GLCMs, including those conventionally armed, as if they were nuclear. The relatively greater openness of the West might have provided the Russians with other means of confirming whether a cruise missile was conventionally armed or limited in range, but the United States has now been put into the position of fighting off the logic of this counting rule.

Short-Term versus Long-Term Gains

Any American assessment of the monitoring issue on the cruise missile is complicated by certain considerations. The United States begins with a clear lead in cruise missile technology, while the USSR still has an inherent and ongoing advantage in its ability as a closed society to evade effective verification. For the short run, the difficulties in verifying the number, range, or payload of a cruise missile might thus entirely fall on the Soviet side. For the longer term, assuming that the Russians and their allies will finally master the technology needed to design smaller cruise missiles, such verification might instead become a burden for the West. Critics of the cruise missile have argued that the United States must thus contemplate the possibility that the Russians will also eventually have such missiles. As other chapters note, there are important strategic arguments why the cruise missile may not become the Soviet chosen instrument, but a failure to think through the long-run implications of short-run negotiating victories or deployment moves would still surely seem ill advised. As a parallel example of a short-term gain that might be neutralized when the Russians acquire a matching ability in the long term, the scheme for multiple-aim-point basing for the MX missile would severely test the ability to verify Soviet force totals once they were to move to a similar "shell game," raising fears that there could be many more than one missile in place for each group of twenty-three silos. Another example (this time somewhat less cheering to the arms controllers) could emerge in the satellite reconnaissance systems cited above, which have allowed short-run moderation in the arms race by reliably monitoring the construction of missile silos, but only at the longer-term price of giving each side precise knowledge of the locations of such silos. This knowledge unfortunately matches up with the enhanced accuracy of ICBMs armed with MIRVs to generate preemptive instability. It would of course be a mistake to assume that this fallacy of the last move always produces bad results. If American submarine-based missiles were to be followed inexorably by Soviet submarine-based missiles, it would be in a procession that arms controllers generally welcomed. How would they rate such a procession of American, and then Soviet, cruise missiles?

Arms controllers looking ahead even in the 1960s could have predicted (and did so) that a move to MIRVs, by one side or by both, would be destabilizing because it would increase the attractiveness of striking first in any situation of uncertainty or crisis. However, at the point when the United States has large (possibly unverifiable) totals of cruise missiles, and then the USSR has them as well, will this be as clear a loss in crisis stability? Or, on the other hand, could it amount to an enhancement of crisis stability, that is, a decreased likelihood of the war nobody wanted? It might be good to entertain a little skepticism about whether difficulties in monitoring the cruise missile would really be such a direct problem.[9] It would be unfair to blame the coming loss of verifiability entirely on the cruise missile, for the general trend in strategic weapons has been, as noted, in the same direction.

The Search for New Means of Monitoring

It would seem that the capabilities of satellite reconnaissance that have provided arms race stability by monitoring now threaten something even more precious—crisis stability. Submarine-based missiles continue to escape this tough choice, because the adversary's reconnaissance satellites can surely tell whether the West is launching an additional missile-firing submarine without being able to spot the submarine when deployed. It is difficult, however, to imagine any mode of land-basing for strategic delivery vehicles, cruise or ballistic, that can offer the same combination of assurances. Thus it would surely be wise to expend some creative genius in making monitoring and verifying possible again for the next generation of weapons systems. Much of the rationale for the complicated "racetrack" system for the basing of the MX intercontinental missile stemmed from the hope that the United States could thus achieve the crisis stability im-

---

9. Would an unverified arms race become as open-ended in extent, infinite in its drain on the participants' economic resources, and sure to cause war as has been predicted? This view is of course too pessimistic. The U-2 and the reconnaissance satellites that followed may well have allowed American presidents from Dwight D. Eisenhower through Jimmy Carter to spend less than they would have otherwise spent, but the savings were finite. Even today some parts of the arms buildup are unverified; each side simply levels off under this handicap at a somewhat higher and more precautionary level of military preparedness.

pact of multiple aim points without also upsetting arms race stability, that is, without leaving the Russians genuinely in the dark about the total number of U.S. missiles.

Some similar creativity is being applied in search of ways to monitor differences between conventional and nuclear-armed cruise missiles or between shorter- and longer-range cruise missiles so that the Russians will not be in a genuine state of uncertainty about the size of the U.S. strategic force. Such functionally related observable differences (FRODs) would indeed reduce some of the tensions discussed here. However, the pessimistic assumptions of arms controllers may still be realistic: the margin of confidence in the monitoring of weapons totals, both for ballistic and cruise missiles, may be less in the 1980s. An important part of my argument is that this possibility can not per se veto a decision to deploy cruise missiles, for it does not per se dictate that such a deployment will upset the sum of the ultimate purposes of arms control. Moreover, arms control is not the *only* consideration in any case.

The Impact on Crisis Stability

Cruise missiles could deliver a conventional warhead with accuracy to a Polish railway junction, but missiles of a very similar design could also deliver a nuclear warhead with accuracy to a Russian missile silo.[10] Would the addition of cruise missiles, whose number, range, and nature of warheads could be monitored, thus pose a destabilizing threat to the assured second-strike forces of the USSR and increase the risk of mutually unwanted escalation once a war had broken out? If the new generation of cruise missiles can reinforce NATO defenses (and thus contribute to deterrence stability), could it also be accused of upsetting crisis stability by possibly stampeding the Russians into earlier launches of their strategic ballistic missiles?

The reality of this particular concern is in some doubt. It is commonly noted that the slowness of the cruise missile's flight to target makes it a poor first-strike weapon. If detected by early-warning radar, it gives Moscow hours rather than minutes in which to launch Soviet ICBMs. The

---

10. For a good overview of the more general spread of new technological possibilities in weaponry, see Richard Burt, *New Weapons Technologies: Debate and Directions*, Adelphi Paper 126 (London: International Institute for Strategic Studies, 1976); and Paul F. Walker, "New Weapons and the Changing Nature of Warfare," *Arms Control Today*, vol. 9 (April 1979), pp. 1, 5–6.

cruise missile might be devastatingly accurate, but it simply would take too long to get there. Compared to medium-range ballistic missiles such as the Pershing II and to the most accurate of U.S. ICBMs such as the MX, the cruise missile might thus be credited with an arms control advantage precisely because of its slowness. This is only a partial reassurance, however, for it simply amounts to pushing the Russians into a very slow and deliberate launch-on-warning policy. This is not at all the same as the fondest dream of some advocates of mutual assured destruction and strategic stability: that both sides feel so unthreatened by counterforce attacks that they can deliberate days or weeks before launching retaliatory strikes.

However, at least such cruise missiles would not be crossing over the USSR on their way to their tactical limited war targets in Poland or East Germany, so the Russians could wait to see that their silos were not being attacked. If the approach path did not reassure the Russians against an attack at the strategic counterforce level, perhaps the smaller numbers fired might do so, or the timing might suffice, since the Western cruise missiles would dive into their Eastern European targets hours before they could have hit the Soviet silos. Cruise missiles thus cannot be totally dismissed as a threat to crisis stability merely because they are slow to target. If a launch-on-warning policy is not attractive, then there are objections to any system that attaches much significance to warning. Yet the tensions imposed on the USSR by such systems are surely less than might be imposed by the MX or Pershing II.

There was a time when it was considered important to assure American ability to retaliate on second strike against Soviet value targets, but also to let the USSR have an assured second-strike capability against American targets: this basically was a logic of being content with mutual assured destruction. The mood of American strategic thinking is now considerably changed in light of Soviet force buildups and their continued doctrinal attachments to concepts of war-fighting and victory.[11] Americans welcoming the additional options offered by the accuracies of the MX or cruise missiles do not endorse the idea of counterforce preemptive strikes against Soviet missile silos, for they acknowledge that this might create a greater likelihood of all-out war. But they advocate taking some

11. A good overview of the issues here can be found in Desmond Ball, *Developments in U.S. Strategic Nuclear Policy Under the Carter Administration*, ACIS Working Paper 21 (Los Angeles: Center for International and Strategic Affairs, University of California, 1980).

risk by instilling possibilities of Soviet nervousness, on the theory that the West needs a large array of targeting options to deter the Russians and in particular to avoid accepting political intimidation in the face of Soviet strategic pronouncements and force buildups. Such options might include industrial targets, military bases, command posts, or shelters for the Communist elite. I should stipulate, however, that I still approve of assuring the Soviet Union against countersilo strikes. The price paid (in loss of crisis stability) for these additional targeting options could be too high, especially given the accuracy and speed of the MX ballistic missile.

The more important point here, however, is that an American acquisition of cruise missiles might not be so objectionable even by this more demanding mutual assured destruction arms control standard. Indeed, the cruise missile, when fitted with longer-range and nuclear warheads, also contributes tremendously to crisis stability, since it renews the bomber leg of the American strategic retaliatory triad and offers many other basing modes for retaliation against the USSR. Thus the prospect of American Minuteman vulnerability should become less bothersome. Many of the platforms for launching strategic cruise missiles can be made mobile enough to complicate Soviet targeting. If the cruise missile were not likely to be so very accurate, it might be unambiguously rated as stabilizing because it would maintain the assured destruction potential of the United States.

Deterrence by Denial: Conventional Options

Arms control should not be shaped into a doctrinaire or mindless opposition to every kind of weapon. For example, the cruise missile can impose enormous problems of negotiation, definition, and monitoring, but it is also rich enough in options to offer some solutions to some problems. A very complicated net assessment will be required.[12] A good illustration of the way in which cruise missiles could positively affect the military balance is their use with *conventional* warheads or with limited ranges, so that Eastern Europe—but not the Soviet Union itself—could be attacked. If the accuracy of such cruise missiles were as good as anticipated, this might provide a substantial conventional augmentation of NATO defenses in a manner not nearly so likely to escalate into an all-out thermonuclear exchange (see chapter 6).

12. An elaborate statement of some possibilities here can be found in Colin S. Gray, "Who's Afraid of the Cruise Missile?" *Orbis*, vol. 21 (Fall 1977), pp. 517–31.

Given the likely increase in cost of cruise missiles and the likely deployment of defensive weapons against them, it might strike some analysts as wildly unrealistic that they should be squandered in the delivery of conventional warheads.[13] Discussions of war scenarios of the European theater frequently refer to the fact that published Soviet military doctrine assumes that nuclear weapons might be used from the very outset of such combat. However, one might consider the use of B-52s in the Vietnam War. Who would have predicted in 1961 that this splendid vehicle for delivering the H-bomb to the Soviet Union over a range of 10,000 miles would be consigned instead to delivering "iron bombs" of TNT over the short range from Thailand to Vietnam? Such a utilization of the B-52 made sense as part of an effort to avoid escalation to more general war and as part of an unsuccessful effort to cripple the Communist advances in the south by attacking the logistical lines from the north that supported them. Like the B-52, the cruise missile may be used at shorter range and with conventional warheads. (Indeed, conventional cruise missile programs are now the most dynamic of those in development.) Also like the B-52 and most other aircraft, however, the cruise missile will not permit any assurance that such weapons could be used *only* in these modes. Any cruise missile can be stretched in range by readjusting the balance of warhead weight and fuel weight (as well as by adding some auxiliary fuel tanks). One way to reduce warhead weight, of course, is to go to nuclear warheads.

Arms controllers would thus worry about what could confirm the inclination to limited use and assure the other side of a less escalatory targeting approach. The reassurance is not impossible to find. Each side in any limited war must rely not just on predetermined limits of its adversary's weapons and military capacity, but also somewhat on the adversary's good sense. Limited war does not entail being disarmed so much as refraining from the use of the various weapons available. Such mutual recognition of the opponent's good sense is of course reinforced by what Thomas Schelling identified as the core of tacit communication, the ongoing day-by-day pattern of restraint that implicitly signals an intention to continue restraint.[14] If the first cruise missiles fired in a European war were to aim at railway bridges in Poland and land with conventional

---

13. For a skeptical analysis of the "cheapness" of cruise missiles, see Desmond Ball, "The Costs of the Cruise Missile," *Survival*, vol. 20 (November–December 1978), pp. 242–47.

14. Thomas C. Schelling, *The Strategy of Conflict* (Harvard University Press, 1960).

rather than nuclear detonations, the Soviet leadership would be getting a signal that the West had for the moment chosen to try to keep the war nonnuclear. (This of course assumes that the Soviet attackers also would have elected not to use nuclear weapons, which would similarly be a signal to the West.) The pattern of where the cruise missiles landed would similarly be a signal of what the geographical limits to the exchange were slated to be.

In summary, it is entirely possible that preoccupation with the SALT process has led to an exaggeration of the significance of monitoring and prior limitation of military arsenals, as compared with the possibilities of mutual restraint in the use of such arsenals. Cruise missiles may hurt the former, but they may lend themselves to the latter.

Deterrence by Punishment: Nuclear Proliferation?

The arms controllers' concern about cruise missiles is that any shorter-range conventional missiles might be turned into longer-range nuclear missiles, but normally this concern has not led to a fear that the United States would be equipped with a menacing first-strike counterforce capability. The fear has instead been expressed that cruise missiles will increase the temptations toward nuclear proliferation. The Russians' opposition to the deployment of such weapons has focused particularly on GLCMs, which they have sometimes claimed, in a rare display of humor, stood for "German-launched cruise missiles." The allies of the United States, for reasons noted above, might have a very serious claim to such weapons. If a very accurate conventional cruise missile could hit key targets to frustrate a Soviet tank advance, who could be against letting the Germans or French or South Koreans (or Communist Chinese) have access to it sooner or later?

The problem is similar to the proliferation question posed by the spread of nuclear power reactors around the world. What is useful for peaceful nuclear purposes can also be used to make nuclear warheads; what is useful for delivering conventional warheads to target can also be used to deliver nuclear warheads. The United States finds it easier to withhold sensitive peaceful nuclear power facilities where the economies of scale are great, for then it is plausible that an entire portion of the nuclear fuel cycle (uranium enrichment, for example) should remain in American hands. The need to question the motives or reliability of foreign governments is avoided. When the economies of scale are not so strong, however, it becomes much more difficult to hold back what is so sensitively dual purpose.

Similarly, when B-52s were used for tactical purposes in Vietnam, this did not produce a chorus of requests for such weapons from the NATO states, South Korea, Australia, or Thailand. Because the economies of scale in managing a weapon system like the B-52 are enormous, however, the United States could have diverted any such request by noting that the entire array of these bombers could be managed much more effectively if kept within the U.S. Air Force. Cruise missiles, by contrast, will probably not be governed by such economies of scale and may lend themselves to efficient deployment and operation by separate national forces.

One way to avert concern about nuclear proliferation would be to limit the Western investment to sea-based cruise missiles, deployed in waters off Western Europe and dedicated to the tactical purpose of NATO, like the currently dedicated U.S. Navy Poseidon submarines. There should be less concern about the development of a "German-launched cruise missile" when the vehicle is not physically deployed in close proximity to non-American forces.[15]

Submarine-based cruise missiles would be just as invulnerable to Soviet attack as the Poseidon, and would permit absolute maintenance of American control, thus lessening concern about nuclear proliferation. Yet this possibly would mean that they are also as unsatisfactory as the Poseidon for the calming of European apprehension about U.S. support and Soviet intentions in Europe. The claim has been made that the Poseidon submarines are "not visible enough." Submarine-based forces could surely be made visible by commissioning the production of documentary films for European television that would show the crews at their controls and test-firings of ballistic and cruise missiles from below the surface. Periodic port calls of such submarines could also be arranged to remind everyone that a number of such vessels were in the vicinity.

This approach still might not assuage the European planners' concern, however. At the heart of their complaint about the Poseidon submarines'

15. This point leads to the final rub on the arms control and strategic impact of deploying cruise missiles. Ground-launched cruise missiles pose the greater threat of a tendency toward nuclear proliferation. Yet, as part of maintaining the peace in Europe, the United States has all along probably (without ever fully admitting it) wanted and welcomed *some* of this tendency toward proliferation in this area, at least by the British and French.

visibility is that the missiles have not been deployed into a position that by itself would increase the likelihood of their use. Since the 1950s, Europeans have seen American tactical nuclear weapons deployed so that Soviet forces would in effect have to trip over them in the process of a forward move into West Germany and Western Europe. This presence of American tactical nuclear weapons in the combat zone (along with the existence of the British and French nuclear weapons forces) might make it impossible for an American president to limit nuclear escalation to European territory. Soviet planners simply cannot be as sure of a U.S. president's command and control over nuclear weapons use when the weapons are land-based in the path of a Soviet tank advance, instead of sea-based in the waters off Europe. In short, modern strategy may imply that the most important characteristic of some weapons may not be what targets they could hit, but where they are based.

Cruise missiles could thus contribute to preventing a Soviet conquest of Western Europe in two drastically different ways. First, if effective, they might allow the crippling of the Soviet military potential in a very clean and nonescalatory way by delivering nonnuclear warheads with great accuracy to military targets upon which the Soviet ground advance depended. The second way is enormously different, based on almost opposite premises about the likelihood of escalation. The presence of cruise missiles with *nuclear* warheads in the NATO area would reinforce Soviet expectations that any war would be messy and likely to escalate, that Western Europe and much of Eastern Europe as well would be severely damaged in the process of any struggle, and that the ensuing escalatory process might well lead to all-out war. This would be classic deterrence by punishment rather than deterrence by denial.

Future Theater Negotiations

Taking all considerations into account (rather than adopting a partial definition of arms control that focuses only on formal negotiations or verifiability of totals), one might reasonably conclude that the cruise missile is not a disaster and might even be more of a solution than a problem. If the primary goal is to deter war in the first place, as well as reduce the costs of war and peacetime preparedness, the cruise missile in some of its possible deployments may contribute to the end goals of arms control.

Yet one must ask whether negotiated agreements might not offer better possibilities than a simple advance with deployments in the absence of negotiations and agreements.[16] Such agreements, if properly formulated, might deliver a still greater contribution to the goals just noted. The NATO decision in December 1979 to deploy GLCMs in Europe also proposed negotiations between the United States and the Soviet Union for limitations on both sides' theater nuclear weapons.

Negotiations about theater nuclear systems such as cruise missiles could be envisaged in at least four forms. The first would be to handle the entire issue within a revived SALT process. This could be done by treating such vehicles as strategic in potential and recognizing that the primary Western capability in this area will remain American for the short run— but perhaps not in the longer run, if France or other U.S. allies develop their own cruise missile technology. Participation in these negotiations would remain limited to the United States and Soviet Union. (This in effect is the negotiating approach endorsed at the December 1979 NATO Council meeting.) The negotiators might have to include in the American quota of theater forces those of American allies such as Britain and France. Such a formula would address Soviet arguments about functional parity and noncircumvention while allowing Paris and London to feel relatively independent. However, it might meet resistance in the U.S. Congress even if the administration in power accepted it.

Second, one could alternatively pull cruise missiles (especially since their warheads can be conventional as well as nuclear) into the MBFR negotiations, which heretofore have been mainly devoted to discussions of conventional arms. An obvious criticism of this option is that it would tend to make an already complicated MBFR much more complicated. The MBFR discussions have not progressed to a point that would allow a breakthrough on theater nuclear weapons, but instead have been bogged down in complicated arguments about asymmetries at the conventional level. However, I would argue that the ultimate source of the arms control problem here is at the conventional weapons level, and thus MBFR might be the *logically* appropriate place to do the negotiating. To reduce tank totals might be the best first step toward reducing theater nuclear weapons totals, or even avoiding a heavy investment in conventionally armed cruise missiles.[17]

16. See Coit Dennis Blacker and Farooq Hussain, "European Theater Nuclear Forces," *Bulletin of the Atomic Scientists,* October 1980, pp. 32–37, for a valuable overview of the arms control issues in the TNF deployment.

17. A very imaginative set of possibilities for stabilizing the European confrontation can be found in J. I. Coffey, *New Approaches to Arms Reduction in Europe,* Adelphi Paper 105 (London: IISS, 1974).

Third, a new forum could be created specifically to discuss nuclear weapons based in Europe or aimed at Europe (sometimes suggested as TALT—"Theater Arms Limitation Talks"),[18] with participation by all the interested parties in Europe, yet perhaps not quite as many as the participants in MBFR. Because the British and French would be agreeing to negotiate the future of their own independent strategic forces, which are hardly redundant in capability, there is a distinct possibility that both Paris and London would elect not to take part.[19] This is the format that the Russians seemed to be leaning toward recently, perhaps on the assumption that Western disarray would give them some negotiating advantages missing at SALT, and might have been suggested in the Schmidt-Brezhnev meeting in July 1980. It might even be more desirable for the ultimate interests of the West.

A fourth approach would simply let the issues be sorted out by a kind of tacit bargaining and informal exchange of unilateral moves, in the hope that no great misunderstandings are imposed thereby. This would avoid the intensive litigation and finger-pointing that are typically a part of formal negotiations on gray area systems. As those concerned with arms control continue to focus on formal negotiations, it is important to discuss the possible advantages of a more informal, tacit approach. Unilateral moves may reduce the kind of constituent attention that generates agonies about parity or nourishes the use of bargaining chips. The East-West dialogue has been committed to formal negotiations for more than a decade now, but one should not forget that a less formal and explicit exchange can continue while attention is directed to proposals for formal negotiations. Ironically, such a less formal exchange may be under way even as this is being written.

Unilateral Moves

History will surely not mark 1979 and 1980 as halcyon years for arms control. Yet it is interesting to note that during that time two matching unilateral disarmament moves were undertaken, somewhat in accord with the earlier Western proposals advanced in the Vienna negotiations, despite the justified sense of a breakdown of negotiations and an end to

18. See Robert Metzger and Paul Doty, "Arms Control Enters the Gray Area," *International Security,* vol. 3 (Winter 1978–79), pp. 17–52.

19. For an informed British assessment of new weapons delivery options, see Ian Smart, "British Foreign Policy to 1985: Beyond Polaris," *International Affairs,* vol. 53 (October 1977), pp. 557–71.

détente at SALT and elsewhere. The NATO delegations offered their option III MBFR proposal in 1975. As the negotiations dragged on, this proposal to reduce NATO theater nuclear weapons strength, paired with reductions in Soviet conventional ground forces, was offered again in several versions, all explicit statements of the coupling of Soviet threat and NATO response. When Brezhnev tried to head off the NATO Council endorsements of cruise missiles with his announcement in October 1979 of a unilateral withdrawal of 1,000 tanks and 20,000 men, this was in some ways a de facto acceptance of a scaled-down version of the NATO MBFR proposal. When NATO went ahead in December 1979 with its plans to upgrade theater nuclear forces, including the deployment of cruise missiles, the Soviet uproar about that decision somewhat masked two facts: the Soviet troop withdrawal had not been officially rescinded,[20] and the NATO move had included a net reduction of 1,000 NATO nuclear warheads.

What Is the Real Threat?

Any decision on the appropriate format for negotiations should largely be determined by the strategic problem to which the weapons in question are directed. For example, which threat are cruise missiles (and other NATO theater nuclear weapons) really meant to address? Is the problem really embodied in the Soviet TNF or in the latent superiority of Soviet tank and ground forces?[21] Is the problem the kind that can ever be discussed frankly and directly in NATO position statements? Is the problem as much political as military?

It surely would be a strategic mistake to define numerical parity in TNF systems as the Western goal for negotiated arms restraints on the European front. If the Russians possessed no TNF at all, but fielded their current array of tank forces, NATO would still want some TNF, for all the reasons noted so often in the past twenty-five years. Conversely, what if the Russians had no such potent offensive ground forces, but were

20. If a substantial reduction in Soviet ground force strength were to be achieved (it would have to go considerably further than Brezhnev's recent offers), this would remove much of the *strategic* need for ground-launched cruise missiles and for other new missiles assigned the theater nuclear role. It would also eliminate much of the argument for extensive development of conventionally armed cruise missiles.

21. An earlier perspective on the continuing problems here can be found in Wolfgang Heisenberg, *The Alliance and Europe: Part I: Crisis Stability in Europe and Theatre Nuclear Weapons,* Adelphi Paper 96 (London: IISS, 1973).

equipped with their current array of SS-20s? There might then be little or no strategic need for NATO to have any TNF of its own. It is the Soviet threat of seizing Western Europe, rather than the threat of destroying it with nuclear warheads, that is the core of the problem. Soviet SS-20s can destroy targets in Ireland, just as Soviet missiles can destroy targets in Australia, but since occupation of such areas is not plausible, there is no need for a responsive locally based nuclear force. Most discussions of the TNF problem, including Chancellor Helmut Schmidt's 1977 speech at the International Institute for Strategic Studies (IISS) in London,[22] can thus be accused of exaggerating the interlock between Soviet and NATO nuclear forces.

The worst Western fear about strategic balance can hardly be that the Soviet theater nuclear weapons are militarily superior to NATO's.[23] Rather, it is the possibility that Soviet forces might be able to conquer Europe *without* escalating to the use of nuclear weapons (and that the USSR would be so strong at the strategic level that it could deter the United States from escalating). Unless one assumes (against the great bulk of the evidence) that the USSR could use its theater nuclear systems such as the SS-20 and Backfire and still obtain an undamaged prize, there is little rational motive for Soviet nuclear aggression against Europe.[24]

A Position for the West

The Western arms control negotiating stance should follow the logic outlined above. The United States and its NATO allies should generally avoid getting pulled into a comparison of totals of LRTNF systems with a view to some kind of parity. Even the December 1979 NATO decision, so much denounced by the Russians, does not envisage numbers of GLCMs and other Western theater weapons matching the total number of SS-20 warheads. Rather the negotiating formulas offered by the West should address *ratios of reductions* on the two sides, starting from the status quo at any particular moment. For the sake of political appear-

22. Helmut Schmidt, "The 1977 Alastair Buchan Memorial Lecture," *Survival,* vol. 20 (January–February 1978), pp. 3–5.

23. A detailed compilation of the direct confrontation of NATO and Warsaw Pact theater nuclear forces, together with a discussion of arms control possibilities, can be found in Metzger and Doty, "Arms Control Enters the Gray Area."

24. See Herbert F. York, "The Nuclear 'Balance of Terror' in Europe," *Bulletin of the Atomic Scientists,* May 1976, pp. 8–16; and Frank Barnaby, "War-fighting Weapons for Europe," *Bulletin of the Atomic Scientists,* March 1980, pp. 8–10.

ances, the West could offer to reduce cruise missile totals in exchange for reductions of SS-20 totals or even for a withdrawal of SS-20s to positions out of firing range of Western Europe.[25]

But more important would be a set of parallel offers of Western forbearance on theater cruise missile deployments in exchange for reductions in Soviet tank totals, since the tanks are more important than the Soviet TNF. This should quietly be made clear to the Soviet Union, and could also be made clear in the structuring of the negotiating formulas. The Russians would have to give up a great fraction of their theater nuclear potential before NATO could afford to give up most of its own TNF capability. A major reduction in Soviet ground force strength would also allow a major reduction in Western theater nuclear potential. The Western proposals, by discussing ratios of reduction rather than agreed-upon totals at which to begin and end, would avoid the stigmas of supposed inequalities. Such ratios of reduction would reflect the importance of what Western Europe has feared most all along, rather than what is only symbolic and political. The negotiations of SALT III on theater nuclear weapons should thus resemble more the style of SALT I and less that of SALT II, since the Jackson amendment made it imperative that the two sides end at numerically identical totals of launchers.

The second important step for Western arms control negotiating strategy is to move where possible away from the SALT framework, which implicitly reinforces the Soviet claim that theater nuclear weapons are to be thought of mainly as forward-based elements of the total of strategic forces. The West might have been better off if it had tried to steer the "Eurostrategic" discussion of theater nuclear forces and European-based cruise missiles into the MBFR format instead of SALT. Although something may have been lost in the greater complexity of negotiations involving so many powers, the central message would have been what the West has known all along: its European theater nuclear forces are linked directly to the menace of Soviet ground attack more than to any balance of Soviet versus American central strategic forces.

25. It was a mistake for the West to make so much of an issue of the SS-20, just as it may have been a mistake earlier to forgo the possibilities of a mutual ban on the testing of multiple warheads for intercontinental missiles. It was similarly a mistake for the Russians to deploy the SS-20 if they were serious about détente and arms control, just as it was a mistake—vis-à-vis SALT—to deploy such an array of new intercontinental weapons. For a somewhat parallel view on the West's position, see Klaas G. de Vries, "Responding to the SS-20: An Alternative Approach," *Survival*, vol. 21 (November–December 1979), pp. 251–55.

For a variety of reasons, Western European expressions of concern about the SS-20 and other Soviet theater systems aimed at Europe have led to requests to include such weapons in a potential SALT III round of Soviet-American negotiations. Rather than commit itself to this blending of strategic and Eurostrategic issues, it might have been much more to the West's advantage to leave the two areas decoupled, with limitations addressed to the strategic balance and weapons based in Europe left undiscussed. With Western European complaints about SALT II ironically reinforcing Soviet demands that European-based forces be counted in SALT, it is perhaps too late to get back to this format. Yet, as much as possible, this is still how the United States should strive to frame the terms of discussion.

Functionally related observable differences might help here, if it became clear that the Soviet Union could distinguish between theater and central nuclear forces or between nuclear and conventional cruise missiles. Any accomplishments in FRODs should therefore be utilized to ward off the applications of counting rules against NATO and the United States, avoiding the inclusion of theater-based cruise missiles in negotiations that do not address Soviet tank totals. Even if such FRODs do not materialize so clearly, however, the general thrust of Western negotiating strategy should be to press the Russians to acknowledge the difference in functions of the different kinds of Western cruise missile deployments, which Moscow still has many means of verifying.

Where FRODs genuinely allow conventionally armed cruise missiles to be distinguished from nuclear or shorter-range from longer-range, the West must demand that the differences be accepted by the USSR. Where such differences are less clear, the West may have to give the Russians the same counting rule concession as that extracted in the past, but then must demand large totals of nuclear-capable (and presumably nuclear-armed) cruise missiles until the Soviet Union makes reductions in conventional force strength. Cruise missiles will remain necessary either way as long as the Soviet potential for a tank attack on Western Europe remains so extensive and seemingly unchecked.

Future SALT Negotiations

The problem is somewhat different with regard to strategic cruise missiles, however, for the ultimate goal in deployments of (and negotiations about) such vehicles would be to keep all such strategic weapons from ever being employed. The nuclear weapons deployed by NATO are intended primarily to deter the use of Soviet conventional weapons. The nuclear weapons assigned to the U.S. Strategic Air Command are intended primarily to keep Soviet strategic nuclear weapons from being used.

At the level of strategic nuclear forces, there might have been far less need to preserve the strength of the bomber force by equipping B-52s with standoff cruise missiles had it not been for the enhanced threat to U.S. land-based missile forces posed by the accurate warheads equipped with MIRVs and mounted on the Soviet SS-18 and SS-19 ICBMs. Students of American strategic policy might disagree as to why this Soviet ability to attack Minuteman silos is so disturbing but agree that it is the source of American irritation. Believers in a mutual assured destruction posture would worry simply that the residual of retaliatory capability left in penetrating bombers or submarines might not suffice. Analysts who question the adequacy of relying simply on countervalue retaliatory capabilities would rather point to escalation scenarios and crisis situations in which the United States would be handicapped if it did not have a similar capability for precision attacks against Soviet missile silos.

The MX ballistic missile offers a parallel to the cruise missile as a part of the response to Soviet missile accuracies. Some Americans welcome the MX mainly because it might be deployable in modes that escape the accuracy of Soviet ICBMs; others would welcome it just as much because it offers hard-target-kill capabilities comparable to those of the Soviet strategic forces. Some American analysts similarly welcome air-launched strategic cruise missiles because their basing modes might escape the threat of Soviet preemptive attack, while others appreciate more the additional targeting options they offer against the USSR. The MX and the cruise missile are quite similar in terms of the issues of monitoring and verifiability discussed earlier. It is not easy to see how Minuteman vulnerability can be redressed without some recourse to the kind of deployment that upsets the most demanding standards of verification by national means.

Any mobile basing of land-based ballistic missiles generally threatens to seek survivability at the price of compromising monitoring capability, just as a shift to long-range nuclear-warhead cruise missiles tends to do. The option of shifting all land-based missiles to submarines is costly and worrisome for other reasons, such as the possibility of breakthrough in antisubmarine warfare. An earlier ban on the testing and deployment of

MIRVs would have allowed the superpowers to retain the verification inherent in silo-based ballistic missiles without threatening the survivability of such systems, but the MIRV systems of both the United States and the Soviet Union have now been tested enough to erode any arms control reassurance in that respect.

Even if an imminent Soviet option of destroying one leg of the U.S. strategic triad were not strategically meaningful, Americans and Europeans would worry that American presidents would be intimidated in future crises by the mere chance that the Russians would use their ICBMs this way, especially if the United States had no reciprocal option for disarming the Soviet land-based missile force. As either an accessory to or a substitute for the B-1 bomber, long-range cruise missiles can thus do a great deal to reduce American anxiety about a Soviet first strike at the Minuteman silos (if one has a more optimistic assessment of ALCMs' counterforce capabilities than that presented in chapter 5).

Two Contingencies

The uncertain future of SALT II poses two separate contingencies for the MX and cruise missile. Would multiple-aim-point basing of the MX serve to ensure the survivability of U.S. land-based missiles if SALT II is ratified, and if its constraints on Soviet warhead fractionation are extended in a follow-on agreement? Possibly yes. Would it do so if SALT II instead becomes null and void, and the Russians deploy much larger totals of heavy missiles with more fractionated payloads? Very possibly not. On the other hand, would the deployment of ALCMs ensure the retaliatory capabilities of U.S. central strategic forces within the limits of a duly ratified and mutually binding SALT II? Since B-52s equipped with cruise missiles would have to count against the total of U.S. missile launchers equipped with MIRVs, some calculations would suggest that this option would make no great contribution. Perhaps the largest contribution would be simply to vary the avenues of retaliatory attack that Moscow would have to prepare for.

But what if SALT II is not ratified and binding, as currently appears almost certain? With the totals of ALCMs, conventional or nuclear, no longer limited by treaty, the potential of such an American force could indeed serve as a convincing supplement to or replacement for the more vulnerable land-based missile force (at least compared to what the situation would be without any modernization of the bomber force). The chances of winning U.S. Senate ratification of the SALT II agreements were uncertain even before the Afghanistan invasion and the election of Ronald Reagan. Barring a dramatic resuscitation and expansion of the SALT process, a reliance on ALCMs as an important part of the American strategic deterrent may be inevitable.[26]

Critics of the past handling of the SALT process can of course indict the U.S. interest in ALCMs and cruise missiles in general as being a major cause of SALT II's imperiled status. By this view, the U.S. desire for short-run superiority led to an unnecessary contentiousness about the Soviet Backfire bomber, thus delaying the SALT process so much that the trivial issue of a few thousand Russian troops in Cuba could derail the agreement. The essential goal of arms limitation may all along have been to assure both sides that they cannot benefit from a first strike; this clearly has become more difficult with the enhanced accuracy of ICBMs. It might therefore have been preferable to design an MX that was only mobile, and therefore ensuring American force invulnerability, but was not so accurate, and therefore not so threatening to Soviet forces. As noted, it might have been desirable to avoid the perfection of ICBM accuracy and multiple warheads in the first place. This is not the place to go extensively into these issues, except to note that the way they evolved makes it less likely that any negotiated arms limitation can now allow the United States to dispense with cruise missiles.

The political form of the negotiation issue is often stated as a demand that the Russians be limited to numerical parity by any one of a large number of yardsticks. The more important strategic form of the issue, however, may be to ensure crisis stability: neither side could attempt or fear a first strike in a political crisis. One of the difficulties of any negotiations on arms control, as opposed to a simple set of unilateral moves on each side, is that the political sensitivity and importance of numerical parity may be elevated at the expense of the more important strategic question of stability.

Translating this into more specific proposals for a negotiated arms control posture, one approach would be to show a willingness to trade off the solution to the problem against the cause of the problem. Cruise missiles could be given up in exchange for a substantial reduction in the number of Soviet heavy missiles, the ICBMs that when armed with

26. For a series of imaginative suggestions on reviving SALT, and also for making progress in negotiations on theater nuclear forces, see Alton Frye, "How to Fix SALT," *Foreign Policy*, no. 39 (Summer 1980), pp. 58–73.

MIRVs threaten the survivability of American land-based missiles. As the Soviet threat to American land-based missile forces was eased, it would then become less necessary for the United States to undertake compensating measures to ensure its force survivability or to try to match Soviet capabilities by adding to American hard-target capabilities. This might be easier if SALT II were to be ratified by both sides, but it would be appropriate policy in any event. Yet what if the Russians show themselves unwilling to give up their heavy missiles armed with MIRVs, as is not unlikely with or without SALT II? Would this be a disaster and setback for arms control or more a setback in the progress of formal negotiation?

Cruise Missiles for Stability

Cruise missiles could still be a net plus, in the end, because they would reensure stability. If they could not be counted to Soviet satisfaction, this would be a loss, but not a total one. As the monitoring and verification capabilities of the 1960s and 1970s are eroded by the inherent characteristics of cruise missiles, the lid on the arms race would be lifted, but it would not be totally off. The United States might have to be assumed by the USSR and others to have acquired more deliverable warheads than before, but obviously not infinitely more. Policing the totals of the U.S. strategic arsenal and the dividing line with its theater forces would be difficult for any foreign power, but not hopelessly so, because the United States and its allies continue to constitute an unusually open society. Where FRODs did not solve the problem, the *New York Times* and *Aviation Week and Space Technology* would make the differences "observable."

If the ideal basing mode for all theater and tactical cruise missiles were to be on the ground or at sea, there might be a more reliable means for distinguishing between these forces and central strategic forces. This is not a likely possibility, however; the first theater nuclear forces assigned to Europe will be GLCMs, but it is possible that these will be supplemented over time by theater ALCMs. The most promising form of conventionally armed cruise missiles for NATO defense is also likely to be an ALCM. If the logic of the counting rule is not outweighed by the development of reliable FRODs, something more political and less technological may have to fill in the difference. If FRODs could be developed that clearly distinguish between the strategic forces of the United States (to be traded off only for reductions in Soviet heavy missiles) and theater forces (to be traded off only for reductions in Soviet ground forces), they should be refined and adopted in American development and deployment policies. If no such clear distinctions can be found, the U.S. SALT III negotiation posture should still implicitly assume that Moscow has ways of knowing which systems are assigned to strategic roles and which are more tied to the European theater. The Soviet Union was induced to accept such distinctions in SALT I and to some extent in SALT II, so the West should quietly press them to accept these distinctions again.

This is not quite the same as suggesting that the United States should "stonewall" all the USSR's demands that counting rules and noncircumvention clauses be applied to the total of U.S. strategic forces. Some kinds of cruise missiles may always have to be charged against a SALT total, if only because Moscow has demanded this so much and because the United States and its allies have chosen to move down this road. Rather, it is most important to measure the reality of Soviet apprehension about verification and not do much more than is required in response. FRODs, or simple common sense, must keep the logic of the Russian demands from pulling even the most tactical and theater-specific applications of cruise missile technology into the SALT totals.

Defending Europe is a different problem from deterring a Soviet first strike against the United States. At the strategic level, it has been in the American and Western European interest to get the two problems somewhat intertwined. At the negotiating level, the interest perhaps should have been to keep them separate.

Lessons for the Arms Control Policy Process

There are many lessons to be extracted from the handling of cruise missiles and other theater nuclear weapons to date, some of them perhaps relevant to avoiding undesired outcomes in the future. Formal disarmament negotiations may solve some problems more effectively than does the procurement of new weapons, but there are also ways in which such negotiations have created problems. Formal negotiations may make governments excessively litigious, thus hurting both sides, or excessively clear in their logic, perhaps hurting themselves most. The mere knowledge that a formal contract is in the offing makes each side reluctant to abandon any weapons that are becoming obsolete (since they might be traded for something as bargaining chips) and more contentious about any adjustments in posture introduced on the other side. If there had not been negotiations under way in SALT and MBFR, would the West have been so upset about the SS-20 or the Russians about the GLCM?

The current U.S. cruise missile program grew in part as a bargaining chip, when Secretary of State Henry Kissinger and civilian leaders in the Pentagon urged the military services to go ahead with it even when they were not yet enthusiastic about its technological prospects. Then when some elements of the defense community became enthusiastic in later years, the chip could no longer easily be bargained away.[27] And, as noted, the process of introducing some necessary tidiness to SALT also irritated Western Europeans and perhaps made them request weapons options that otherwise could have been dispensed with.

In the history of Soviet-American negotiations on arms control there have been times when clarity of logic was on the Western side and others when clarity contributed to strengthening the Soviet position. The case of TNF (or FBS) may be one favoring the Russians. Formal negotiations in general tend to produce greater clarity as well as greater litigiousness. Yet the logical tidiness of formal SALT negotiations when addressed to theater nuclear weapons options has led to a weakening of the Western position. Western European expressions of anxiety about the provisions of SALT II have paradoxically come closer to giving the Russians what they long have been demanding, the inclusion of FBS in SALT. Perhaps the Russians deployed the SS-20 deliberately to serve as a prod to achieve this, or perhaps the effect was inadvertent. In either case, it has cast just enough political shadow over Europe to induce anxious public statements that in the end may lead to Soviet-American negotiations specifically addressed to restricting the replacement for the unrestricted F-4.

A less formal style of arms negotiation not only might have led to lower degrees of weapons procurement on each side (and thus fewer bargaining chips), but also might have left the Western position stronger. The recommendation is thus that the West should edge back to the fuzziness whereby gray area systems were left gray, rather than being defined as black or white. There is nothing inherently unacceptable about this for

---

27. For an early skeptical view of whether cruise missiles could be anything more than a bargaining chip, see Center for Defense Information, "The Cruise Missile: A Weapon in Search of a Mission," *The Defense Monitor*, vol. 5 (September 1976), pp. 1–8.

the USSR. There is no reason why some of these issues cannot be left gray—more informally negotiated—for another decade or two.

To the extent that the issues of cruise missiles and theater nuclear forces in general are political rather than strategic, much of the problem obviously derives from the perceived indecisiveness of the Carter administration on many issues, most explicitly the neutron bomb.[28] Yet some similar start-stop indecisiveness has appeared on the European side as well: Chancellor Schmidt's commitment to TNF modernization has not been as clear or consistent as some might have hoped. Assaying West German preferences on such issues has been just about as difficult as determining American preferences. All the NATO partners will always agree on the bottom line, however: Soviet conventional invasions of Western Europe should be prevented at the same time that the initiation of an all-out thermonuclear war is avoided. But the questions of how to achieve this, what weapons to deploy, where they are to be deployed, what negotiating postures to take, and what negotiating forum to prefer will always be much harder to sort out.

28. Students of the longer-term issues of Western European defense may feel a sense of déjà vu, on both the issues of military strategy and the political treatment of such issues. The deployment of tactical nuclear weapons in the first Eisenhower administration produced some of the same East-West tensions and intra-NATO debates. Similar confusions showed up in the later discussions about deploying first-generation Jupiter and Thor missiles to Western Europe in response to an imminent Soviet missile-gap advantage after Sputnik. Uwe Nerlich, "Theater Nuclear Forces in Europe: Is NATO Running Out of Options?" *Washington Quarterly*, vol. 3 (Winter 1980), pp. 100–25, presents a very useful (albeit more pessimistic) overview of the historical development of the NATO nuclear issue.

CHAPTER TEN

Arms Control: Negotiated Solutions

WILLIAM H. KINCADE

DESPITE what some observers view as marginal military justifications and ill-defined operational requirements for them, modern cruise missiles represent a technology that is likely to be increasingly exploited throughout the remainder of this decade. As other contributions to this volume have made clear, whatever cruise missiles' specific merits in comparison with competitive systems, they have proved convenient answers to a number of politico-military questions. Senior decisionmakers in the U.S. government have consistently seen them as relatively reliable, low-cost solutions to the vexing condition of superpower strategic parity. They have pushed cruise missiles when fine-grained operational analysis and service preferences appeared to stand in their way, because cruise missiles promise to expand U.S. deliverable warheads at the fastest rate and least cost—an appealing combination for cost-conscious defense secretaries, budget directors, and presidents. The armed services, at times reluctantly, have sought to make a virtue of this situation by finding for cruise missiles tactical or conventional applications that filled their non-strategic needs.

Though speculation about costs suggests that cruise missiles may not

William Kincade is executive director of the Arms Control Association. He acknowledges the generous assistance of Alton Frye, Raymond L. Garthoff, and Herbert Scoville, Jr., while absolving them of responsibility for the flaws that remain despite their aid.

be as cheap as once thought, they still offer, in contrast to alternatives, considerable potential for cost savings, if the advantages of component commonality, mission flexibility, long production runs, and sunk research and development (R&D) investment are maximized. The imperative for senior decisionmakers, then, is to assure such cost benefits by directing the services to exploit cruise missile technology to the hilt. If the stimulus given to modern cruise missile development by former defense secretaries Melvin R. Laird and Harold Brown is any indication, the interest in promoting the cruise missile will remain more or less constant at high levels of government, whichever party controls the White House. Like multiple independently targetable reentry vehicles (MIRVs), to which the cruise missile is often compared in arms control analysis, cruise missiles represent a seemingly inexpensive, quick technological fix in a period of steeply rising procurement costs.

Yet, judging from the cruise missile experience of the last decade and to a lesser extent from the MIRV case, the exploitation of the cruise missile's potential will proceed in a context of ill-defined operational concepts, objectives, and missions. The diversity of the roles and limitations of cruise missiles suggested elsewhere in this collection testifies to this. Cruise missiles, moreover, will enter service at a time when there is little consensus among specialists on nuclear weapons employment and procurement policies or objectives (despite the Carter administration's updating of targeting policy in Presidential Directive 59), when the trend toward counterforce capability is creating new perceptions of instability or vulnerability, when the standard of adequate surveillance has been raised, and when virtually any technically conceivable scenario is often regarded as plausible. All of these factors affect decisions on cruise missiles, though hardly in a felicitous way.

Any effort to negotiate limits on cruise missiles will suffer seriously, perhaps fatally, from this combination of high-echelon political interest and continuing uncertainty and disagreement about specific cruise missile functions. In the absence of an agreed conception of the particular contribution of the cruise missile to Western security, the United States will be ill positioned to obtain internal agreement on acceptable limits, much less agreement with its allies. Moreover, if avoiding expenditures is one of the strongest attractions of negotiated security agreements for American presidents and defense secretaries, then the potentially low costs of the cruise missile will remove an important element of the arms control imperative.

Why Limit Cruise Missiles?

But why, we must ask, should the United States want to limit its exploitation of a technology that promises both a significant near- or medium-term technological advantage over the USSR and a relatively low price tag? Traditionally, one of the U.S. goals for arms control has been stability, an elusive notion with multiple connotations that has never seemed especially persuasive in its more abstruse forms to Soviet specialists and is increasingly disputed in the West.[1] At the most general level, the idea of an equilibrium between the two superpowers—the scorpions in a bottle—appears quite attractive. The application of this idea to specific weapons or force configurations is, however, highly problematic. The fact that no consensus exists in the West on how to detect, define, measure, or influence military stability is reflected in quite contradictory assessments of the impact that cruise missiles would have on stability.[2]

1. For the differences and similarities in Soviet and American conceptions of the nuclear stalemate, see Raymond L. Garthoff, "Mutual Deterrence and Strategic Arms Limitation in Soviet Policy," *International Security,* vol. 3 (Summer 1978), pp. 113–47; and Fritz Ermarth, "Contrasts in American and Soviet Strategic Thought," *International Security,* vol. 3 (Fall 1978), pp. 138–55, especially pp. 145–46. For a critique of various American conceptions of stability, see Colin S. Gray, "Strategic Stability Reconsidered," *Daedalus,* vol. 109 (Fall 1980), pp. 135–54.

It should not be inferred from the discussion of the concept of stability that there is *no* agreement on it between Americans and Russians. The ability of the United States and the USSR to come as far as they have along the path of negotiated limits surely rests on the mutual appreciation of national decisionmakers in Moscow and Washington that, in general, an equilibrium of forces is safer than endlessly jockeying for an advantageous but often ephemeral position, and that some force structures are, in the abstract, more provocative in a crisis than others. Beyond this important but rudimentary agreement, there has been relatively little accord on what constitutes an equilibrium, how to achieve it, or which weapons are most provocative and which least.

As is illustrated by the disagreement among Westerners or Americans about a stable balance of forces and stabilizing or destabilizing weapons, answers to these more fine-grained questions are heavily determined by perspective and must ultimately be worked out (if only synthetically) at the bargaining table. This is especially so, since, as George Quester points out, some forms of stability conflict with others. What needs to be avoided, then, is the canonizing of stability as some sort of absolute, the academic elaboration of the ideal beyond what is politically or militarily useful, and the search for precision in an area where only first-order approximation is possible.

2. Compare, for example, George Quester's assessment in this volume (chap. 9) and that of Alexander R. Vershbow, "The Cruise Missile: The End of Arms Control," *Foreign Affairs,* vol. 55 (October 1976), pp. 133–46.

Secondary justifications for the limitation of cruise missiles would include, with varying degrees of cogency, avoidance of the following:

1. Soviet countermoves that could complicate the U.S. and NATO defense problem and increase the Western defense burden;

2. A degradation of military surveillance capacity likely to result from wholesale deployment of ambiguous and readily concealed weapon systems;

3. The deepening of fissures within and between NATO governments, especially between the United States and Western Europe;

4. The domestic dissent likely to result in time from an aggravated nuclear competition, sharply rising defense budgets, or an expanding U.S. share of NATO defense costs;

5. A more defensive U.S. posture regarding international arms limitation commitments (such as the Nuclear Nonproliferation Treaty, the pledge to conclude a chemical warfare agreement, and the comprehensive nuclear test ban initiative).

If cruise missiles are viewed not in isolation but as the first wave of generations of flexible, concealable, and unclassifiable weapons, then the first and second items above assume even greater significance. Both bear directly on the nature of the strategic environment the United States will have to face in the next ten to twenty years.

Cruise Missiles in Context

The superpowers now face a strategic environment that is changing in an evolutionary but nevertheless radical fashion, primarily because of the miniaturization and microminiaturization of weapon components or subsystems and the related increasing capacity to proliferate weapons, either conventional or nuclear, of very high reliability, accuracy, and destructive force. Reliable, long-range, and accurate mobile missiles, advanced cruise missiles of several types, encapsulated missiles, antisatellite weapons, as well as hybrids such as rocket-ramjet missiles, are only the most prominent strategic systems that could emerge in the next five to ten years, as indicated in the list of U.S. R&D initiatives below.[3]

3. *Fiscal Year 1982 Arms Control Impact Statements,* Statements Submitted to the Congress by the President Pursuant to Section 36 of the Arms Control and Disarmament Act, Joint Committee Print, House Committee on Foreign Affairs and Senate Committee on Foreign Relations, 97 Cong. 1 sess. (Government Printing Office, 1981).

Nuclear weapons
B-83 gravity bomb
W78 missile warhead
WXX missile warhead (MX)
Trident II missile warhead

Ballistic missiles
Missile experimental (MX)
Trident II submarine missile
Pershing II missile
Medium-range ballistic missile (MRBM-X)

Cruise missiles
Air-launched cruise missile
Ground-launched cruise missile
Land-attack, sea-launched cruise missile
Advanced air-launched strategic cruise missile

Delivery vehicles
Cruise missile carrier
Penetrating bomber (Stealth)
New missile submarine, SSBN-X

Ballistic missile defense
Low-altitude defense (LoAd) (inner space)
Homing overlay experiment (outer space)
Nonnuclear kill

Space defense
Antisatellite systems (ASATs)
Satellite survivability systems

Directed energy (beam) weapons
High energy laser program
Charged particle beams

Command and control, communications and intelligence,
  warning and assessment
Ballistic missile early warning system (BMEWS) upgrade
Integrated operational nuclear detonation reporting system
  (IONDS)
Gryphon, Tacamo, and extremely low frequency (ELF) naval
  strategic command, control, and communications intelligence
  (C^3I) systems

Pave Paws submarine-launched ballistic missile (SLBM) radar
warning system

Continental United States over-the-horizon (CONUS OTH-B)
radar warning system

Worldwide military command and control system (WWMCCS)
upgrade

Associated with these new weapons are broad advances in command and
control facilities—the central nervous system of modern warfare—that
will substantially improve weapon performance but also expand the
range of crucial and vulnerable targets, and possess their own limitations
in terms of high production and maintenance costs, combat reliability,
and personnel training.

Also under development are improved warheads, maneuvering reentry vehicles, a new penetrating bomber, a new medium-range ballistic
missile, and advanced antiballistic missile (ABM) defenses. On the
farther horizon are a supersonic cruise missile, remotely piloted vehicles,
the "rail" gun (a type of ballistic ordnance that overcomes many of the
limitations of conventional artillery and is thought to have significant
antiarmor and antisatellite potential), and various types of beam weapons, which, if they overcome engineering obstacles, are likely to augment,
not supplant, projectile weapons.[4]

While the United States now appears to have the lead in several of
these new technologies, it is only in the area of modern cruise missiles
that the Soviet Union has, as yet, shown little interest. The nature of
technological competition in the past, shown in table 10-1, however, does
not inspire great confidence that the American technological advantage
will prove very durable or meaningful. While table 10-1 does not illustrate the generally higher performance and reliability of American systems, it remains unclear whether the higher performance distinction
makes much of a difference in actual combat. To some degree, qualitative advantages can be overcome by substituting quantity. In addition,
the less sophisticated Soviet systems may prove more serviceable in battle
than their comparatively more complex and delicate American counterparts.

4. A longer analysis of new technologies and their possible impact appears in
William H. Kincade, "Over the Technological Horizon," *Daedalus,* vol. 110 (Winter
1981), pp. 105–27.

Table 10-1. *Superpower Competition in Offensive Nuclear Weapons,
1945–80*

Innovation	U.S.	USSR[a]
Fission explosion (atomic bomb)	1945	1949
Intercontinental bomber	1948	1955
Fusion explosion (hydrogen bomb)	1952	1953
Deliverable hydrogen (thermonuclear) weapon	1954	1955
Nuclear-powered submarine	1954	1958
Operational short-range cruise missile (sea- and ground-launched)	1955	1958
Operational intercontinental cruise missile	1958	Not to date
Test of intercontinental ballistic missile (ICBM)	1958	1957
Operational ICBM	1960	1959
Operational submarine-launched ballistic missile (SLBM)	1960	1957[b]
Solid propellant ICBM	1962	1968
Test of multiple reentry vehicle (MRV)	1962	1968
Test of multiple independently targetable reentry vehicle (MIRV)	1968	1973
ICBMs with MIRVs operational	1970	1975
Test of modern, long-range cruise missiles	1976	1979
Operational ICBM with high accuracy	1980	1980

Source: Data compiled by the author.
a. Some dates are approximate.
b. These early Soviet SLBMs, like the Soviet ICBMs, were far inferior in operational characteristics, including reliability, to American counterparts and were fitted awkwardly in the hulls of existing conventionally powered submarines. Their existence was enough, however, to fuel fears of a missile gap, especially in an environment marked by primitive surveillance capability. As coming generations of weapons elude surveillance techniques in being or in prospect, the reoccurrence of intelligence gaps of this type becomes a greater possibility.

Impact on the Strategic Environment

The advent of a significant number of these new technologies will give an unprecedented flexibility to strategic and theater nuclear warfare. The comparative order that has been imposed on the strategic environment by the inherent limitations of current weapons is likely to be erased, as will be many of the distinctions that have been the basis of Western nuclear strategy. The concepts of firebreaks, escalation control, and limited nuclear options, for example, all depend on distinctions between tactical, theater, and strategic systems or between conventional and nuclear explosives, which will gradually be undercut by emerging technologies, cruise missiles in particular.

Escalation control, to take one instance, requires the Soviet perception that the United States is withholding weapons capable of greater violence but is prepared to use them if the USSR does not confine its own operations to the lower levels of violence. Hence, the control of escalation from the use of battlefield nuclear weapons to the use of theater nuclear weapons—if it can be achieved at all—could be further complicated by the introduction of more weapons, nominally classified as strategic, theater, or battlefield, yet each capable of and known to be assigned to missions under each contingency.

Developing a new doctrine consistent with both American and NATO interests could prove more arduous than it was to gain acceptance for the present amorphous one, given the polarization within the U.S. strategic community, the discernible differences between Americans and Western Europeans on East-West relations, and the greater attention now being paid to these matters by elite groups on both sides of the Atlantic.

Scenarios formerly considered implausible or marginal are likely to acquire more widespread credence. The fear of a Soviet submarine missile attack on U.S. Strategic Air Command (SAC) bases and coastal areas, with warning times under ten minutes—long thought to be prevented by the difficulties of firing a ballistic missile in a depressed or high-energy trajectory—will become a more significant possibility if the USSR eventually replaces its aging antiship cruise missiles with modern variants. With the emergence of ballistic missiles of constrained or unconstrained mobility—perhaps encapsulated like the land-mobile MX—and cruise missiles of longer range, the problem of strategic break-out will assume greater plausibility.

Though U.S. cruise missiles have until now been constrained in range by the necessity of fitting them to existing B-52 rotary launchers or submarine torpedo tubes, Soviet designers need not observe these limitations when they come to designing their own versions. Though there are few signs of Soviet interest in modern cruise missiles, as Raymond Garthoff points out in chapter 11, it would be imprudent to predicate the future of American security on the hope that the USSR will somehow elect to deny itself this promising new technology. The 1979 Soviet test of an ambiguous long-range, air-breathing aerodynamic vehicle from an aircraft (which circumstantial evidence strongly suggests was a Backfire bomber) may presage not only an interest in developing modern cruise missiles but also the difficulty of bringing such weapons under adequate surveillance.

The Soviet Union not only has experience with its own earlier-generation cruise missiles and the example of American improvements, it will have a powerful prestige incentive to develop cruise missiles, if they become the dominant new technology of the 1980s. Given the political mileage the Russians have sought from achieving parity in modern ballistic missiles, there is little warrant for believing that they will unilaterally forgo a technology that will increasingly be perceived as a new wave in nuclear warfare.

Should the Soviet Union make a significant commitment to cruise missiles, especially for use beyond theater operations, the virtues that make them attractive to American planners will quickly become less so. Their mission flexibility, interchangeability, and adaptability; ease of concealment and production; and capacity for speedy reloading could seriously complicate surveillance for military intelligence purposes. The limitations of older technology that made it possible to estimate adversary orders of battle with reasonable confidence will be missing. Intelligence analysts will have to make generous allowances on the high side, counting ships, submarines, and aircraft capable of carrying modern cruise missiles as strategic or theater nuclear forces rather than tactical weapons. Improved intelligence collection and evaluation, which have made a neglected contribution to American force planning and security, will suffer. As a consequence, the quality of decisionmaking also is likely to suffer in an environment of heightened threat perception and greater information uncertainty. American self-confidence and feelings of relative safety may decline still further.

If for military or other considerations the USSR does decide to omit modern cruise missiles from its arsenal or to produce them in only limited numbers, it will doubtless act in other areas both to combat U.S. cruise missiles and to allay any suspicion that the Soviet Union is somehow falling behind the United States again. The products of such actions cannot be predicted precisely—they may include fitting the Backfire with land-attack rockets (or, indeed, cruise missiles) to make it a true strategic threat or investing in intercontinental ballistic missiles (ICBMs) of unconstrained mobility—but it is hard to imagine that the response will be benign in terms of Western security interests, even if the West sports a wide array of cruise missiles.

Implicit in the view of many who argue for greatly expanded U.S. deployment of nuclear weapons of all types—strategic, theater, or tactical; offensive or defensive—is the notion that this would aid the creation of an equilibrium of forces, no matter what countermoves the Soviet Union makes in response. The underlying premise of this stability through saturation or planned proliferation approach seems to be that only when one side exhausts every deployment opportunity can it feel comfortable that it has covered all risks and attained a full-scope deterrent.

Something like this view is also implied in the arguments that the United States should set in motion a massive strategic rearmament that would eventually force a chastened Soviet Union to bargain away its assets in return for relief or would permit the United States to substantially outgun the USSR if the Russians fail to be intimidated. Setting aside the very real question of whether the Russians could be intimidated by this behavior, the maximum deterrent approach entails costs, risks (especially in terms of accidents), and a loss of controllability and calculability that Americans and their leaders have historically rejected. Such an approach would certainly prejudice stability in the near and medium term, if not ultimately.

Implications for Defense Planning and Arms Limitation

What these reflections suggest is, first, that an edge in a new technology, even a substantial one, does not necessarily translate to a gain in security and may even produce a net loss, and, second, that the chief purpose of arms limitation negotiations in the 1980s will be to retain or restore order in the strategic environment. This order has hitherto been taken for granted because it arose from the nature of strategic, theater, and tactical nuclear weapons and improved intelligence more than from conscious management. Without such strategic orderliness or predictability, the tasks of strategic planners will be almost infinitely complex due to the proliferation of conceivable strategic and theater threats. Budget planners will be similarly taxed as they find a wider and deeper range of contingencies that must be met.

The widely recognized need to improve and augment Western conventional forces across the board will run head-on into expanding requirements for strategic forces to meet this richer array of potential threats, a prospect that is already quickening the interest of some senior U.S. military officers in strategic arms limitation. Meanwhile, the Western Europeans, whose desire to avoid heightened East-West tensions is already pronounced, may find it increasingly expedient to consider different relationships with Moscow rather than bear the political and economic burdens of an aggravated nuclear rivalry.

Heretofore, cruise missiles have been viewed more or less in isolation as answers to specific and immediate political and military requirements. Too little attention has been paid to the longer-range and interactive effects of their deployment in the context of the political, strategic, and intelligence environments. Only toward October 1980, when East-West talks on theater nuclear forces (TNF) were first under way, did the Carter administration begin to grapple in earnest with the complex surveillance and verification problems of theater cruise missiles. This delay contrasted with the attention to verification well before and throughout SALT; it was prompted by the bureaucratic separation of the SALT and TNF teams, ad hoc decisionmaking, and the lack of a comprehensive view of the role of cruise missiles in Western security.[5]

When modern cruise missiles are seen, not as a unique advantage for specific missions, but as the first and perhaps most important of a series of technological innovations that will dominate the strategic and theater nuclear environment of the 1980s, the value of negotiated, reciprocal restraint becomes more evident. Too single-minded and narrow a focus on the technical virtuosity of cruise missiles obscures this important reality. While there has been some confusion on this score in attempts to deal with strategic air-launched cruise missiles (ALCMs) in SALT, the problem is most magnified where theater applications of cruise missiles are concerned. This chapter emphasizes the long-range theater nuclear forces (LRTNF) dimension of cruise missile arms control.

Preliminary Steps

The impending reduction of predictability and calculability in the strategic and theater environments—coupled with the high opportunity costs and direct costs of an unrestrained rivalry in emerging nuclear weapons technologies—may provide sufficient incentive to sustain the talks on LRTNF. If so, the course of such discussions will be extremely arduous, probably more so than the SALT negotiations of the last decade.[6] It may be useful to reflect on some of the lessons of those negotiations; whatever ingenuity negotiators may display at the bargaining

5. See Philip A. Odeen's analysis of security policy integration and coordination in the Carter administration in "Organizing for National Security," *International Security,* vol. 5 (Summer 1980), pp. 111–29.

6. It is assumed for the purpose of this discussion that the superpowers will continue to observe the major provisions of the SALT II regime or replace it with something substantially similar.

table, the results could be nullified if the broader political errors of the SALT process are not avoided. American and Soviet negotiators bear multiple burdens in this connection, since the good faith of the parties, the astuteness of the diplomats, and the quality of the agreements must be made manifest to both Western European and North American publics.

While it is imperative to begin a negotiation with a clear notion of desirable outcomes and a set of sensible proposals to put on the table, concern for these matters should not preclude attention to equally fundamental preliminaries: a lingua franca for discussions, a common currency of exchange, and agreement (tacit or explicit) on permissible measures for monitoring compliance. Much of the SALT process was devoted to these basics. Yet neither attentive nor mass publics were forewarned of the need for and difficulties of establishing these prerequisites between two antagonistic and suspicious powers whose strategic forces appear superficially similar but in actuality are quite disparate. In the end, the agreements, while substantial in terms of the obstacles they overcame (including some self-imposed hurdles such as the 1977 comprehensive proposals), were so much less than anticipated or advertised that critics on both the left and right could term them inadequate and the center could not be mobilized on their behalf. The early promises of new departures and better, faster results typically associated with incoming American administrations only fosters these unrealizable expectations.

Therefore, it should be made clear to officials and publics that the first order of business in any LRTNF talks will be agreement on the framework, what the discussions cover and do not cover, how included systems are to be categorized and counted, and how (to the extent it can be foreseen) any limits on these weapons are to be monitored. In addition, as far as possible, it will be useful to lay out in general terms the anticipated sequence of negotiations, assuming that it will be even more necessary in LRTNF than in SALT discussions to approach complex issues piecemeal.

No ironclad program for negotiation can or should be expected. Yet agreement on general terms of reference will have the benefits of allowing trade-offs between phases of the talks, of establishing a loose schedule for negotiators and their principals, and of informing Western publics that negotiated security agreements, like any other important diplomatic endeavor, represent a painstaking, time-consuming process of sorting out and matching separate and tangled interests. If these matters can be settled more or less satisfactorily—and it will be no easy task—then the actual discussions of limits and constraints will be facilitated. And securing the necessary public acceptance of the process will also prove easier.

TNF Negotiating Format

The suspension of SALT II and the advent of a new U.S. administration have raised the question of whether nuclear arms limitation, if it is to be resumed, should follow established lines or adopt new ones. The issue is especially pertinent to any negotiations on cruise missiles, since SALT II left many issues related to these weapons to future talks.

Certainly, political advantages would accrue to the Reagan administration if it could demonstrate that its approach to SALT II was fundamentally, not cosmetically, different. In principle, the range of options runs from beginning afresh by scrapping the offensive weapons limitation process as it has evolved (and perhaps the ABM treaty, as well), to making minor changes in and ratifying SALT II while developing positions for a renewed round of TNF talks or SALT III negotiations.

The first approach permits both sides to begin discussions with a clean balance sheet; however, new approaches will doubtless take time, and old concerns will not go away just because the negotiating table has been cleared off. The less radical approach trails clouds of both political glory and infamy, depending on the observer's perspective on different negotiations.

By now, the Reagan administration should have discovered that its ability to innovate in strategic arms limitation is constrained by factors relating to technology, economics, the defense industrial base, other defense budget imperatives, and the continuity of Soviet strategic concerns. This suggests some sort of intermediate approach that combines the clear benefits of SALT II with what flexibility the new administration does have.

Since the protocol to SALT II—which in the main addressed future negotiations on TNF issues such as cruise missiles—was set to expire at the end of 1981, one avenue might be to negotiate an interim executive agreement in lieu of the protocol. This interim agreement, which would not require ratification, would address the ground rules for negotiation, not their substance. First, it would recognize that the current protocol has been, practically speaking, overtaken by events. Second, it would stipulate that both parties would observe the remaining provisions of the SALT II treaty (minus the protocol) pending the negotiation of SALT III, thereby removing to some degree the uncertainty and opportunity for misunderstandings that arise from the ambiguous status of the treaty. Third, it would lay down in broad terms the objectives, classes of weapons, and negotiation phases for SALT III (that is, the ground rules for TNF discussions). And, fourth, it would stipulate that SALT II would be resubmitted for ratification when SALT III negotiations successfully reached some preestablished stage, perhaps the conclusion of the first package of trade-offs. This approach would probably require some change in the termination date for SALT II, now set in 1985.

The political benefits to the Reagan administration of this approach would be great. It would preserve the benefits of SALT II while tying its final acceptance to progress in SALT III, where attention would quickly focus. It would, at the same time, yoke the Soviet interest in SALT II to its interest in TNF limits, thereby providing a double incentive to serious negotiation. It would mute the differences between the United States and its Western European allies over the combined SALT-TNF issue. It would raise Ronald Reagan's stock with the American public—a historical inevitability with progress in nuclear arms control—without requiring the immediate resubmission of SALT II to the Senate. It would permit the Defense Department to concentrate on more pressing manpower and conventional forces issues. And it would preempt critics of Reagan's strategic policy, who, ironically, are well positioned to make as much trouble if Reagan disdains progress in strategic arms limitation as Reagan and others made for President Jimmy Carter because of his apparent preoccupation with this issue.

Cruise Missile Negotiations: Problems

The LRTNF talks involve asymmetries and other problems already encountered in SALT but affecting theater nuclear forces to a far greater degree. First, there is the difficulty of distinguishing adequately between strategic, theater, and tactical weapons or between long-, intermediate-, medium-, and short-range systems. Related to this is the fact that many weapons are capable of carrying conventional or nuclear ordnance (dual-capable) and of performing several types of missions (multiple-mission), earning them the sobriquet of "gray area system."[7] In part, the superpowers in SALT were able to temporarily finesse their disagreements on these distinctions by putting off the discussion of disputed weapons to later talks. The time for those later talks has now arrived.

7. For a summary of these weapons, see Robert Metzger and Paul Doty, "Arms Control Enters the Gray Area," *International Security*, vol. 3 (Winter 1978–79), pp. 17–52.

Counting weapons may create difficulties, anomalies, and distortions in terms of assessing force postures or concluding negotiated security agreements, but weapons are, realistically, the only currency of exchange. Some agreed means must thus be found of defining, classifying, counting, and trading off among weapons despite the fact that on each side there are often unlike systems serving unlike, multiple objectives. Whether the current division between long-range and other theater nuclear forces will prove durable may well depend on the superpowers' willingness to postpone discussion of disputed systems or to initiate simultaneous discussions on the two types of TNF.

The characteristics of theater nuclear weapons also make them more difficult to fit into neat orders of battle and precise verification schemes. This is now more true of dual-capable, multiple-mission aircraft but will also pertain to cruise missiles when they are deployed. By comparison, intercontinental-range bombers, stationary ballistic missile launchers, and ballistic-missile-launching submarines proved relatively easy to detect, assess, and count with available surveillance systems—one of the major factors that made the SALT process possible.

Though innovation in surveillance technology proceeds, it will not be of a character that will permit easy distinctions as to type of warhead (conventional or nuclear), maximum range, or probable target. Because of their mobility, concealability, and lack of visible revealing characteristics, aircraft and missiles of intermediate range or below will be difficult to locate and evaluate. The capacity to extend the range of aircraft and to fit nuclear as well as conventional weapons on ships, submarines, and aircraft further complicates surveillance and verification, especially the very high standard set for verification in the SALT II debate.

In addition to these problems, and the larger disparities in superpower interests, LRTNF talks face three related asymmetries or incommensurabilities:

1. Although the 464 ground-launched cruise missiles (GLCMs) and 108 extended-range Pershing II ballistic missiles the United States plans to deploy in NATO countries in the 1980s are politically responsive to the ongoing deployment of Soviet mobile ballistic missiles (SS-20s) and medium-range bombers (Backfires), they are not directly responsive militarily in the sense that they serve identical missions and can be traded one against the other.

2. As just suggested, the upgrading of U.S. theater nuclear forces is prospective, while the Soviet improvement of analogous forces has been

in progress for several years, creating a temporal disparity sure to bedevil negotiations.

3. There are several military-geographic asymmetries, the most prominent of which is the fact that the Western GLCMs and Pershing IIs threaten Soviet territory, at least the most populous and industrialized portions, while the SS-20 and the Backfire do not threaten U.S. territory or do so only marginally.

Other, more arguable (but certain to be argued) asymmetries include the facts that the Soviet Union can redeploy SS-20s and Backfires from the east to augment its European-oriented forces, and that the United States withdrew earlier-generation cruise missiles (the Mace and Matador) from Europe over a decade ago, while the Soviet Union is only now withdrawing earlier-generation ballistic missiles (the SS-4 and SS-5). Finally, there has been the previously mentioned disparity of interest *within* the U.S. government, with the armed forces generally preferring more tactical applications and senior officials favoring the strategic and theater nuclear versions.

Practically speaking, the precise solutions to these problems of incommensurability would have to be worked out through the ingenuity of the bargaining table, which in SALT II proved quite considerable, and through internal coordination. Some notion of the form these solutions might take can be gained, however, by asking what it would take to conclude a successful negotiation on LRTNF, including cruise missiles.

Strategic Air-Launched Cruise Missiles

First, a successful LRTNF negotiation would require some fundamental U.S. decisions on what, in the array of cruise missile options now available, is most important to preserve and what is more dispensable. For the time being at least, it seems fair to assume that the long-range air-launched cruise missile designed for use on standoff strategic bombers is here to stay. Also for the time being, it seems premature to address the supersonic, developmental, advanced strategic air-launched missile equipped with a rocket-ramjet engine, though doubtless the Soviet Union will be thinking about it in the course of negotiations at the strategic or theater level.

The ALCM precedent in SALT II has several important implications for any future cruise missile negotiations. The ingeniousness of the counting rule that likens ALCM-carrying aircraft and ICBMs armed with

MIRVs lies in the fact that it imposes an equal subceiling on and therefore requires trade-offs between two different weapons that each superpower respectively wishes to deploy in significant numbers. Thus, it yokes together the dynamism in the two countries' respective strategic programs, permitting flexibility to each while establishing a limit on both.

If the United States were to maximize its ALCM force under this rule, it would have to do so at the expense of increasing its ICBMs armed with MIRVs and a likely maximization of similarly mounted Soviet ICBMs. Conversely, Soviet fulfillment of its ICBM MIRV potential would be at the future expense of deploying a significant ALCM force and full exploitation of the U.S. ALCM option. This exemplifies the essential logic of the SALT process.

If the present administration were to avoid strategic arms limitation altogether or design a new agreement that omitted such a felicitous feature, it is hard to imagine that it could somehow unilaterally achieve a better outcome for the United States. Indeed, were the SALT II treaty in effect, one method of capping the Soviet potential for adding more reentry vehicles to each of its land-based missiles (fractionation, currently viewed as the greatest Soviet strategic threat) would be to propose an additional protocol to the agreement tying the average number of ALCMs permitted each U.S. aircraft to the number of MIRVs on Soviet ICBMs. Thus, if the Russians further limited their MIRVs on land-based missiles, they could count on additional limitations on the U.S. ALCM force.

While some may argue that there is an inequity in matching limits on a presumptive first-strike weapon (ICBMs armed with MIRVs) with limits on a presumptive second-strike weapon (ALCM aircraft), it is probably more theoretical than real. First, under the proposed regime, the United States would retain the option of substituting its ICBMs armed with MIRVs for ALCM carriers if it so desired. Second, in the event of protracted nuclear warfare, the value of a recoverable force of ALCM aircraft would in principle increase more than the value of the Russians' reloadable silos, because the latter are stationary and perhaps more vulnerable targets. Third, current agreements must look to future technology; as a new ALCM carrier and new varieties of long-range ALCMs (especially supersonic or rocket-ramjet cruise missiles) are developed, the classification of ALCMs as second-strike weapons will become progressively less meaningful.

The sacrifice of some U.S. ALCMs now that the United States has a lead in this technology may be offensive to the primitive appetite for technological and numerical superiority, but it seems a wise trade-off, considering that skillful use of the ALCM-MIRV leverage can be used to constrain both Soviet fractionation and eventual Soviet deployment of present-generation or advanced ALCMs. To put the issue another way, in the absence of SALT II or something like it, the United States faces the prospect that over the next decade the Soviet Union will maximize its fractionation potential *and* produce its own standoff ALCM carrier. To repeat the immutable logic of arms control: save for an uncharacteristic change in Soviet determination, no correlation of strategic forces occurring as a natural product of unrestricted competition can plausibly be imagined that will be better than the one arrived at by mutual agreement. None of the critics of SALT II have satisfactorily explained how, in its absence, the balance of forces would tip in favor of the United States, given the proven ability and determination of the USSR not to be outclassed in this area of national power.

Without such a subceiling linking these two systems, then, one is hard pressed to conceive a sensible way in which the Reagan administration can restrict Soviet fractionation while, in Defense Secretary Caspar W. Weinberger's words, it is "rearming America." Proposals that the United States insist on the right to deploy heavy missiles, reopen its Minuteman ICBM production line, or find a rapid way of deploying the MX are all likely to speed, not limit, Soviet fractionation and deployment of additional ICBM launchers. If the United States is seriously concerned about preventing implementation of the Soviet fractionation program and ICBM throw weight, it will have to offer a serious bargain, rather than an inducement to Soviet acceleration. The ALCM trade-off recommends itself not only because of its evident negotiability but also because it involves a system crudely parallel to Soviet fractionation in that it rapidly multiplies nuclear weapons yet can be readily throttled back.

The SALT II ALCM-MIRV counting rule may also provide an attractive precedent for TNF negotiations. Linking dissimilar systems for which each of the negotiating parties has a different preference and a healthy fear of the other's preference tends to harness competitive drives to work for restraint rather than open-ended rivalry. It makes clear that both parties face the prisoner's dilemma of game theory. A system wherein the likely effect of each unilateral move to maximize individual advantage can be more straightforwardly seen in the context of the adversary's countermoves makes the internal logic of the strategic competition more visible.

In designing TNF bargaining packages, therefore, consideration should be given to such pairings, rather than to equal ceilings on similar systems in which the parties have dissimilar interests or capabilities. Whether U.S. cruise missile limits can be yoked to the Warsaw Pact tank limits, as George Quester suggests in chapter 9, remains doubtful, primarily because it would be difficult to sell this arrangement to Western publics. Yet the basic logic is sound: what one party wants most for itself must be tied to what it fears most in the other's arsenal.

The packages of limits suggested further on in this essay, though they group more or less similar systems together, might be arrived at indirectly in TNF negotiations by linking dissimilar weapons. Limits on Soviet SS-20 deployment, for example, might be tied to limits on Western deployment of forward-based, nuclear-capable, theater-range aircraft, rather than to GLCMs or the Pershing II. The demands on ingenuity in designing and negotiating such provisions will be substantial, but, as with the SALT II feature that links ALCM aircraft with ICBMs armed with MIRVs, so too would be the rewards of success.

Ground-Launched Cruise Missiles

It seems likely that there is little enthusiasm among the military for the ground-launched cruise missile and that the interest of senior Western decisionmakers in the GLCM is prompted primarily by political considerations. Therefore, it would appear possible to gain agreement within the U.S. government and the NATO alliance to limit GLCMs to the lowest level consistent with Soviet concessions on the SS-20 and Backfire— the forces that initially gave rise to NATO's politico-military concerns. Although it is GLCMs that would be more or less formally on the LRTNF agenda, it seems unlikely that any Soviet negotiator averse to wintering in Siberia would accept as anything more than a temporary settlement a proposal that constrains GLCMs but leaves the West free to deploy instead unlimited sea- or air-launched cruise missiles of a type or range different from the ALCM. These other missiles must also be addressed, directly or indirectly.

Other Cruise Missiles

The harder nuts to crack are the hybrid cruise missiles: the Tomahawk land-attack missiles, both nuclear and conventional (TLAM-N and

TLAM-C), the Tomahawk antiship missile (TASM), and the medium-range air-to-surface missile (MRASM). From the standpoint of LRTNF talks and nuclear arms reduction in general, there would be little objection to the tactical, conventionally armed variants if they were not generally so difficult to distinguish from longer-range, nuclear versions (with which they are presumptively interchangeable), thus causing so many problems for test-phase surveillance, heretofore a primary method of nuclear arms limitations verification. (One answer, though not necessarily a very palatable one, might be to follow the de facto SALT II precedent for ALCMs and count all cruise missiles, or those above 600 kilometers in range, as nuclear tipped, while using a size formula to make range distinctions. This might force the Russians to replace their antiship cruise missiles with modern models more like U.S. versions.)

In principle, however, it should be possible to integrate functional differences in the design of these missiles or their launch platforms—analogous to those provided for standard bombers and ALCM carriers in SALT II—that would facilitate their identification as different from long-range nuclear missiles, when combined with other aids to verification. Nevertheless, such design tasks are not easy ones, especially in connection with submarines, and time has already been lost by the failure of the Carter administration to give prompt attention to these problems. Moreover, the heightened climate of suspicion that exists between the superpowers could provoke mutual concern that the United States and the USSR (if it turns to modern cruise missiles) are clandestinely developing or producing nuclear versions of such missiles *without* observable and distinguishing design features. To reduce such concern, any approach to verification and distinction problems that relies on design features will have to be buttressed by other limitations and aids to surveillance.

If satisfactory design features can be developed for discriminating between cruise missiles with tactical ranges and conventional warheads and those with longer ranges and nuclear explosives—such as dimensional limits that preclude fuel loads for long ranges—the remaining U.S. problem is to determine the value of the long-range nuclear cruise missile (TLAM-N). There seems to be some doubt as to the utility of this variant, particularly on submarines, where it would compromise either strategic or antisubmarine warfare missions. Doubts of another kind may also arise as to the wisdom of making surface vessels strategic launch platforms by equipping them to fire the TLAM-N. Any ship so equipped becomes a strategic target, and any port where the ship calls may share the same fate. The Russians are already thought to have assigned ICBMs to important

U.S. Navy targets (ballistic missile submarines and attack aircraft carriers). Soviet naval defenses, including the naval aviation version of the Backfire, might make the deployment of standoff surface cruise missile platforms a poor use of available U.S. combat hulls. Other roles hypothesized for the TLAM-N, chiefly shore bombardment against the Soviet Union or lesser powers, simply do not seem sufficient to justify its deployment; better weapons are available that do not compromise the ability of submarines or surface vessels to perform other more likely missions.

If these doubts prevail, the value of the TLAM-N might best be established by what the Soviet Union would be willing to concede for an outright ban on such weapons, including the obsolete but always modernizable Soviet naval cruise missiles (at least those of ranges with theater or strategic implications). Since the simplest Soviet option for expanding strategic capability, and one of greatest concern to the West, is ballistic missile warhead fractionation, the quid pro quo for such a ban might be MIRV limits on LRTNF or lower MIRV limits on ICBMs. Alternatively, restrictions on intermediate-range ballistic missiles, ICBM mobility, or deployment areas could be demanded.

Verification Problems

Successful LRTNF negotiations would also require negotiated aids to verification that go well beyond those just addressed. Though both sides face real difficulties in terms of the comparatively greater mobility and concealability of emerging theater systems, the difficulty of verification is greater for the USSR because it is the United States that is proposing to deploy first a family of especially ambiguous systems, the modern cruise missiles. Over the long term, however, it is likely to be in the American interest to nail down cruise missile verification problems.

Military surveillance or verification is always aided, first, by a ban on flight testing and, if that is unachievable, as it is now, by a ban on deployment. Low deployment numbers, geographical restrictions, launch platform restrictions, prior announcements of modifications or redeployments, exchanges of data, and agreements on production rates are all aids to verification for which there is a precedent. All will probably have to be brought into service in overlapping combinations to undergird effective LRTNF agreements on cruise missiles, given the limitations of satellite and other unobtrusive surveillance techniques.

Except for the GLCM, which could be loaded on a more austere platform than currently planned, the systems of greatest immediate interest in LRTNF talks—SS-20, Backfire, and Pershing II—do not pose insuperable verification problems. Yet it seems unlikely that either side will want to tie itself to limitations on these weapons without associated verifiable limits on other weapons (particularly other aircraft and ships equipped with missiles). The particular combination of acceptable verification measures needed to support an LRTNF limitation regime would be even more intricate than required for SALT, and such measures are difficult to specify in advance. Nevertheless, a viable verification package does not seem impossible conceptually, so long as it is designed before deployment of the more ambiguous type of cruise missiles. Verification measures might combine range limits in the form of size restrictions, limits on deployment areas and the rate and amount of permissible redeployment, and functionally related or externally observable differences, as well as counting rules that assume the "worst case."

If an overall United States-NATO position on cruise missiles and a package of plausible verification measures can be arranged in a timely way, the most problematic remaining hurdle is the development of a framework within which the asymmetrical features of the current East-West force postures can be made sufficiently equivalent to permit trade-offs. Establishing such a framework is difficult enough in regard to the weapons of major interest, but becomes even more taxing when establishing some metric of equality among these systems because it would throw into sharper relief the disparities in other theater nuclear forces.

However, the purpose of arms control is not to create neatly symmetrical balances along static indicators of military strength. This is a perversion of the objective, which is first, to reduce the dangers of a nuclear war when it is unwanted by both sides, and second, toward that goal and the reduction of the overall military burden, to bring greater predictability to the nuclear environment. In addition, both sides lived with a number of asymmetries in the European theater before the final phases of SALT II and the development of Backfires, GLCMs, SS-20s, and extended-range Pershings. Finally, the asymmetries in force levels in Europe could become even greater without arms control than with it.

Framework for Agreement

The ultimate key to a framework for negotiation is, as always, creating a match between the greatest fears of the antagonists. The West's greatest fear is of the increased threat to centralized NATO nuclear weapons storage areas and operating bases—as well as of the loss of escalation control or dominance—thought to be caused by extensive Soviet deployment of the mobile multiple-warhead SS-20. Whether the concept of escalation control ever had much operational value, it has become largely an artifact of the political and strategic imagination, owing to the blurring of distinctions along an escalatory scale the Russians may never have accepted anyway. Undoubtedly, the storage and operating bases are becoming more vulnerable, as are all nuclear warfare support facilities, under the pressure of greater missile accuracies. But this condition can best be alleviated by warhead stockpile redundancy and dispersal and by arms control, not by countering with more U.S. or NATO launchers, which, if Presidential Directive 59 is any guide, will pose a similar threat to counterpart Soviet facilities.

The greatest Soviet apprehension stems from the improved ability of NATO's GLCMs and Pershing IIs to strike key military targets in the most consequential western districts of the USSR and especially the decreased warning time (time-to-target) of the Pershing IIs. The Russians also fear a putative unilateral advantage that these factors confer on the United States when parity has been negotiated at the strategic level. The West has given little more credence to this concern than the Russians have given to NATO fears of the SS-20 deployment, claiming that the numbers of NATO systems do not constitute a first-strike threat. To the reasonably detached observer, there is a quality of youthful unrealism in the positions of both antagonists.

Assuming these concerns are not disingenuous, however, and that the expressed interest in negotiating limits is sincere, the achievement of an LRTNF accord will hinge on finding a level of SS-20s and Backfires and of GLCMs and new Pershings that each side can tolerate in combination with other restrictions, even though strictly speaking these weapons are incommensurate. Only bargaining can determine such levels. In other words, the proper balance of such forces in Europe is largely a political issue, for it is only in the political realm that the apparent military asymmetries can be adjusted, if at all.

Achieving such a solution, however, will soon become impossible if the Soviet Union does not curb its controversial SS-20 deployment rate before negotiations proceed. Though it may be true that the West lost negotiating opportunities earlier and that Soviet restraint would be hard to justify in terms of their military objectives, the political reality now is that no meaningful negotiations are possible if the SS-20 is deployed at a rapid rate.[8] The appearance that the Soviet Union is seeking a one-sided advantage by simultaneously building new weapons, condemning prospective NATO deployments, and calling for talks cannot be ignored by any Western government if it wishes to remain in office. What is needed to achieve fruitful LRTNF discussions is a politically and militarily relevant signal of earnestness. Troop reductions or simple removal of older missiles will not provide that signal.

From this analysis emerges a tentative outline for a theoretical agreement that might guide the development of Western negotiating positions:

1. Preliminary agreement on a moratorium or substantial slowdown of SS-20 missile deployment.

2. A combined deployment ceiling for launchers of SS-20s, SS-4s, SS-5s, or equivalent missiles (including future GLCMs) capable of striking Western Europe and a separate combined ceiling for launchers of GLCMs and Pershings (old and new), probably but not necessarily equal to the Soviet missile ceiling. The United States would agree to a ceiling as low as possible consistent with Soviet willingness to curtail SS-20 deployments and to dismantle SS-4s and SS-5s and would also agree not to maintain GLCMs and new Pershings in the United States above numbers required for training (assuming that SS-20 redeployment from the Far East could be adequately constrained by provisions noted in point 8 below).

3. Fractionation or MIRV limits on all theater missiles deployed in Europe by either side.

4. A ceiling on Backfires based within range of Western Europe and on equivalent NATO bombers (such as the F-111 and Vulcan) based within range of western Russia and the Warsaw Pact countries, with a separate ceiling or subceiling on naval aviation bombers based within range of targets in Western and Eastern Europe, classified by bomb load and range.

5. A ban on the TLAM-N and current or future Soviet naval cruise missiles capable of carrying out equivalent missions.

6. A ban on air-launched nuclear cruise missiles of greater than 600-kilometer range other than the strategic ALCM as provided for in SALT II.

7. Freedom to deploy other types of cruise missiles not provided for in an LRTNF or SALT agreement.

8. See Raymond L. Garthoff, "Brezhnev's Opening: The TNF Tangle," *Foreign Policy,* no. 41 (Winter 1980–81), pp. 82–94.

8. A package of verification aids, including: (a) exchanging data on numbers and types of LRTNF covered by the accord and establishment of an agreed data base; (b) establishing primary European operating bases of LRTNF; (c) setting numerical limits on the number of LRTNF weapons that can be deployed in the European theater in a given period; (d) requiring prior announcement of redeployments of weapons covered by an agreement; (e) providing externally observable or functionally related observable differences on all cruise missiles permitted by this and other agreements; and (f) identifying production facilities and rates for systems covered by the agreement.

9. Agreement on additional systems to be negotiated in future TNF discussions and to undertake negotiations by a date certain, with the proviso that failure to meet this deadline or agree to its extension will nullify the provisions of this agreement.

While such a general formulation leaves many specific military questions and matters of negotiability unaddressed, it appears to provide for the stated long-term political and security concerns of NATO and the Soviet Union while recognizing that there is an important difference between military and security interests. Its success depends on the Soviet Union's seeing that its long-term security interest lies in treating LRTNF in their European context and regulating deployment of new systems numerically and geographically to avoid Western proliferation of nuclear theater and strategic cruise missiles. It depends, as well, on the United States' and its NATO allies' seeing that their long-term interest lies in using their technological virtuosity as a lever, rather than a counterpoise, to assure limitation and regulation of the robust Soviet military production base in both current and future offensive nuclear weapons.

Implications for the Future

While many of the difficulties associated with LRTNF negotiations lie in the task of sorting out forces that have evolved in response to differently perceived military and security imperatives and opportunities, the problem of the cruise missile in particular reflects a larger difficulty that may occur with greater frequency in the near future. This is the problem of negotiating calculability in strategic and theater nuclear environments when the pace of innovation varies between adversaries. SALT, in its earlier phases, benefited from the roughly parallel development of the major categories of delivery vehicles, particularly in the late 1950s and

1960s, and even more from the fact that when talks opened the two parties were able to foresee a condition of numerical and qualitative parity in offensive and defensive systems.

If arms limitation is to make a significant contribution to American security, those hoping to further it cannot merely wait, perhaps in vain, for similar propitious circumstances to evolve naturally. Instead, they must seek to manage innovation so as to avoid new threats to the United States and its allies. This means, in part, avoiding or minimizing the temporal gaps and problems of incommensurability so well reflected by attempts to balance existing Russian SS-20s and Backfires against prospective NATO GLCMs and Pershing IIs.

From the point of view of security, economy, and military intelligence or verification, the most effective form of arms control is preclusion: banning weapons or limiting them to very low levels before they are deployed. This is also the best means of preventing incongruous packages of negotiating items such as in the LRTNF talks, where it is difficult to find the common framework for trade-offs that underpins the ABM treaty of 1972 or, to a lesser degree, SALT II.

In some measure, the superpowers have already been backing into the device of preclusive arms limitation. The little-regarded Antarctic, seabed, and outer space treaties and the environmental modification convention[9] are preclusive in their thrust, though with potentially significant loopholes. And the ABM treaty, the SALT II provisions covering ALCMs and fixed ballistic missiles on the beds of internal waters, and the anti-satellite weapons talks all sought to deal with weapons before, or in the initial stages of, deployment; they were much facilitated by this approach.

If the superpowers are able to sustain the process of joint management of the technological competition, the self-conscious adoption of this approach will be necessary to regulate the many disparities that afflict the LRTNF talks. Limitations of R&D programs are not required; indeed, a vigorous R&D program is essential to enduring arms limitation, since it provides a major inducement to compliance by ensuring against the violation or abrogation of agreements. What is needed, however, is a

9. The Antarctic Treaty, 12 U.S.T. 794, 402 U.N.T.S. 71; Treaty on the Prohibition of the Emplacement of Nuclear Weapons and Other Weapons of Mass Destruction on the Seabed and the Ocean Floor and in the Subsoil Thereof, 23 U.S.T. 701; the Treaty on Principles Governing the Activities of States in the Exploration and Use of Outer Space, including the Moon and Other Celestial Bodies, 18 U.S.T. 2410, 610 U.N.T.S. 205; and the Convention on the Prohibition of Military or Any Other Hostile Uses of Environmental Modification Techniques, TIAS 9614.

mechanism for mutual technological foresight, for exploring negotiating possibilities, and for negotiation agenda-setting.

A possible basis for such an effort is the Standing Consultative Commission (established by the ABM treaty) or some subunit thereof. The purpose of such a unit would be to test the willingness of either superpower to undertake talks on emerging technologies, to define the most appropriate framework for grouping or addressing such innovations, and to establish the most useful sequences for talks. Arrangements for such an initiative could be integrated in an LRTNF agreement or pursued in tandem. Given current levels of scientific and technical intelligence, there is no reason why such a forum would reveal military secrets. Its function would be merely to explore at a conceptual level the desirability and feasibility of talks on undeployed types of military technology such as precision-guided and maneuvering reentry vehicles or directed energy weapons. Each side could table subjects for discussion and could draw appropriate conclusions for its own R&D efforts from the other's willingness or unwillingness to take up the offer. Even if such a mechanism produced few or no agreements, discussions could have a confidence-building effect (as compared to the present approach of speculation, hypothesis, and second-guessing) and help inform costly investment decisions at the prototype or production stage.

Though in part discredited as an image of the strategic competition in the period before parity, the action-reaction dynamic is likely to be more apt as a description of this rivalry in the period ahead, as each side struggles to gain marginal leads over its adversary and to offset the foe's apparent gains in other areas.[10] The MX as a response to Soviet heavy missiles and the GLCM–Pershing II combination as a response to the SS-20 and Backfire are cases in point; Soviet replies to these Western reactions remain unclear but will doubtless be forthcoming.

In an era of technological dynamism and accelerating costs for incremental gains in strategic capability—a capability that may not enhance security but only increase risks—the need to explore creative methods of managing the competition will become even more pressing. The case of the cruise missile in particular and the LRTNF talks in general bear out the contention that security negotiations must be as innovative as military technology.

10. For an effort to debunk this model, see Albert Wohlstetter, "Is There a Strategic Arms Race?" *Foreign Policy,* no. 15 (Summer 1974), pp. 3–20; and "Rivals But No Race," *Foreign Policy,* no. 16 (Fall 1974), pp. 48–81.

PART THREE

Politics

CHAPTER ELEVEN

Soviet Perspectives

RAYMOND L. GARTHOFF

THIS CHAPTER presents a discussion of Soviet interest and achievements in cruise missiles, some possible Soviet reactions to U.S. development and deployment of various kinds of cruise missiles (countering by defenses, by emulation, or by other means), and other ways in which these missiles may affect Soviet perceptions and actions, both political and military, including Soviet views on the impact of modern cruise missile technology on prospects for arms control.

Soviet Interest in Cruise Missiles, the 1940s through the 1970s

Following World War II, Soviet military development efforts included research and experimentation with a wide range of new potential weapons, including cruise missiles (largely based on the German V-1). During the late 1940s and 1950s, greater attention was given to ballistic rockets than to cruise missiles, a priority that probably reflected the long-standing Russian tradition favoring artillery.[1] Thus the United States—in line with its tradition of reliance on air power—tested and deployed theater land-attack weapons such as the Air Force's Matador and Mace medium- and intermediate-range cruise missiles, the Navy's Regulus I and II submarine- (and potentially surface ship-) based cruise missile launchers, and even

Raymond Garthoff, formerly a member of the U.S. SALT delegation and U.S. Ambassador to Bulgaria, is a senior fellow in the Brookings Foreign Policy Studies program.

1. For a review of contemporary Soviet views on early missile systems, see Raymond L. Garthoff, *Soviet Strategy in the Nuclear Age* (Praeger, 1958), pp. 221–37.

the intercontinental strategic Snark. During this time the Soviet Union concentrated on a series of ballistic missile successors to the V-2, which led to its priority in testing and deploying medium-range ballistic missiles (MRBMs) and in testing intermediate-range (IRBMs) and intercontinental ballistic missiles (ICBMs) in the late 1950s.

Cruise missiles were not, however, neglected. In particular, although the United States continued to stress naval carrier-based aircraft, the Soviet Union—lacking experience with aircraft carriers—developed and deployed in the 1960s a series of submarine- and surface ship-based cruise missiles to provide tactical offensive and defensive fleet support. Similarly, for tactical naval and ground force support, the Soviet Union developed airborne cruise missiles.

By the 1970s the USSR had in operation several hundred seaborne launchers for cruise missiles, and several hundred naval and tactical air-to-surface cruise missiles, with operational ranges up to a few hundred miles. The Soviet Union also adapted naval surface-to-surface cruise missiles for land-based coastal defense, and for some years deployed with army field forces tactical ground-launched cruise missiles (GLCMs) adapted from a naval missile. Although some research and testing had been conducted, the Soviet Union did not develop or deploy strategic or long-range land-based or aircraft-borne cruise missiles.

The United States, by contrast, had by 1970 deactivated all its land- and sea-based tactical and strategic cruise missile launchers and retained only an obsolescing cruise missile (Hound Dog) for launching from strategic bomber aircraft.[2]

The year 1970 offers an unusual opportunity to gauge Soviet (and U.S.) interest in cruise missiles, inasmuch as it was marked by bilateral U.S.-Soviet strategic arms control negotiations to limit current and future "strategic" weaponry.[3] As indicated above, neither country had strategic

2. Earlier U.S. deployment of sea-launched cruise missiles (SLCMs) and intercontinental cruise missiles (ICCMs) had not been extensive (ten Regulus SLCM launchers on five submarines and thirty Snark ICCM launchers), but over 200 Matador and later Mace medium- and intermediate-range ground-launched cruise missile launchers had been deployed in both Europe and the Far East in the 1960s.

3. For comprehensive accounts of the SALT I negotiations, see John Newhouse, *Cold Dawn: The Story of SALT* (Holt, Rinehart and Winston, 1973); Gerard C. Smith, *Doubletalk: The Story of SALT I* (Doubleday, 1980); and Raymond L. Garthoff, "SALT I: An Evaluation," *World Politics*, vol. 31 (October 1978), pp. 1–25. The author has also drawn on his own participation as a member of the U.S. SALT I delegation.

cruise missiles in its arsenal at that time, except the missiles on bomber aircraft that were considered part of the respective strategic bomber weapon systems. Moreover, there were no GLCMs (except for some Soviet coastal defense units). Cruise missiles on Soviet surface ships were designed to serve purely a tactical antiship role. The only existing system that required consideration was the Soviet sea-launched cruise missile (SLCM) force carried on submarines. The United States decided that even though the Soviet submarine-borne SLCMs, totaling at that time about 350 launchers, were intended for an antiship role, they nonetheless had a *capability* for attack against strategic targets on land if appropriately deployed and thus should preferably be limited.

The first U.S. SALT proposals in April 1970 therefore included provisions to limit all but short-range submarine-borne SLCMs to "an agreed number" (which was not specified; the United States had in mind the existing Soviet level of 350, or less), to ban any GLCMs of medium (1,000 kilometers) or greater range, and to prohibit any additional MRBMs or IRBMs. Air-launched cruise missiles (ALCMs), as bomber armament, were not mentioned. (Heavy bombers, but not medium bombers, were to be limited as part of an aggregate of strategic offensive delivery systems.)

The Soviet Union, not surprisingly, argued vigorously against limitation of its SLCMs on the grounds that they were tactical antiship weapons, not strategic weapons. (At the same time, the Soviet Union argued that U.S. carrier-based nuclear delivery aircraft had a strategic capability and should be limited, while the United States disagreed.) The USSR also favored counting strategic air-launched ballistic and cruise missiles as individual strategic weapons rather than counting only the bomber that carried them. GLCMs were not in contention and were scarcely discussed.

In August 1970 the United States introduced a revised comprehensive proposal providing no limitations on cruise missiles except for a ban on intercontinental cruise missiles (ICCMs). SLCMs and GLCMs with shorter than intercontinental range, as well as ALCMs, were to be completely unconstrained. Before the attempt to negotiate a comprehensive strategic offensive and defensive arms limitation was set aside nine months later, agreement had virtually been reached on this putative disposition of the question of cruise missiles in SALT. The Soviet Union agreed to a ban on intercontinental cruise missiles (while observing that there were no longer any deployed and that such a system was obsolete), and accepted with satisfaction the absence of limits on its SLCMs. The

Soviet Union did not even raise the question of limiting GLCMs with shorter than intercontinental range. ALCMs per se also were not discussed, and the question of bomber weapons remained only a potential issue (although one that became important in SALT II after 1974). This early consensus on cruise missiles fell by the wayside, however, when efforts to reach a comprehensive SALT agreement on strategic offensive and defensive arms were abandoned in May 1971.

Positive Soviet interest in cruise missile systems through 1971, as reflected both in Soviet weapon development and deployment programs and in the SALT exchanges concerning possible constraints on such programs, was thus confined to tactical air- and sea-launched systems. Any Soviet concern about future U.S. strategic cruise missile systems was sufficiently muted so that the Soviet Union did not seek limitations. Clearly, the Soviet military and political leaders did not foresee an imminent revolution in cruise missile technology.

At present the Soviet Union has a number of relatively primitive air- and sea-launched cruise missile systems; it has no long-range or strategic cruise missile systems that are operational or, so far as is publicly known, under development. By 1980 the Soviet Navy had about 45 nuclear-powered and 23 diesel-powered submarines carrying a total of about 450 cruise missiles with operational ranges up to about 600 kilometers. A giant new Soviet submarine (Oscar class) armed with antiship cruise missiles was launched in 1980. Several hundred Naval Aviation and Long-Range Aviation bombers are equipped to launch air-to-surface cruise missiles, also with operational ranges up to about 600 kilometers, and are principally used for naval missions.

Soviet Views on U.S. Cruise Missile Programs

As a result of the renaissance in cruise missilery during the 1970s, the Soviet Union has had to weigh the opportunities and risks of the advent of this new technology. Its response to date has been based on the belief that the potential disadvantages of cruise missiles far outweigh possible advantages, without prejudice to future development and procurement decisions that the USSR would make if the technology was not limited by agreement. The Soviet attitude is influenced by the fact that the United States has taken the lead in developing these weapons. Soviet leaders today would not agree to the permissive nonlimitations in SALT that they were prepared to accept a decade ago; they have mounted vigorous efforts through persuasion, pressure, and negotiation aimed at curbing American and NATO pursuit of modern cruise missile systems.

Soviet concerns about the new cruise missile potential are political, military, and economic—in many respects, a mix of all three. Underlying the Soviet response is a rising Soviet political and military concern since the late 1970s that the United States is seeking to reacquire strategic superiority. Although cruise missiles are not seen as the principal or driving element, they are viewed in the context of a broad U.S. arms buildup including MX, Trident I and II submarine-launched ballistic missiles (SLBMs), the Minuteman III Mark 12A warhead, ALCMs, and the NATO long-range theater nuclear forces (LRTNF) with GLCM and MRBM (Pershing II) components. In particular, the LRTNF are perceived as an intended circumvention of the SALT II equal limits on intercontinental forces capable of striking the territories of the United States and the Soviet Union. GLCMs are believed to present specific problems, but they are also viewed as part of a broad design to seek global U.S.-NATO military superiority over the USSR-Warsaw Pact.[4] The pursuit of new cruise missile programs is also considered by many military and political commentators in the Soviet Union to prejudice SALT and

4. See V. K. Sobakin, *Resheniya NATO i sudby voyennoi razryadki v Evrope* (The NATO Decisions and the Fate of Détente in Europe) (Moscow: Znanie, 1980), pp. 42–64 (hereafter cited as *Resheniya*); Lt. Gen. N. Petrov, "A Hopeless Course—The US and NATO Attempts to Upset the Military Balance," *Pravda,* June 16, 1980; N. Yur'ev, "For Europe—A Stable Peace, Security and Cooperation," *Mirovaya ekonomika i mezhdunarodnyye otnosheniya* (World Economics and International Relations), no. 4 (April 1980), pp. 45 and 54–55 (hereafter *MEIMO*); [Lt. Col.] L. Nechayuk, "The Pentagon Eurostrategic Creations," *International Affairs,* no. 4 (Moscow: April 1980), pp. 125–26; Eng. Col. N. Grishin, "Cruise Missiles: The NATO Variant," *Krasnaya zvezda* (Red Star), June 18, 1980; and Vyacheslav Boikov, "Cruise Missiles and Futile Hopes," *New Times,* no. 6 (February 1980), pp. 12–13. For a recent discussion that specifically focuses on GLCMs, see [Lt. Gen. retd.] M. A. Mil'shtein, "Some Characteristics of Contemporary U.S. Military Doctrine," *SShA* (U.S.A.), no. 5 (May 1980), pp. 11 and 17–18. Literally dozens of articles in military and political journals in the latter half of 1979 and in 1980 stressed this perceived U.S. aim of superiority in discussions of NATO's LRTNF decision in December 1979 with respect to both GLCMs and Pershing II MRBMs. The same contention of a general pursuit of superiority with specific reference to ALCMs is made in Eng. Col. V. Kirsanov, "Air-Based Cruise Missiles," *Zarubezhnoye voyennoye obozreniye* (Foreign Military Review), no. 10 (October 1979), pp. 47–52 (hereafter *ZVO*).

détente, and indeed to reflect a conscious desire by certain influential Western circles to torpedo détente in general and SALT in particular.[5] The LRTNF deployments, specifically including deployment of GLCMs, are said to threaten to upset an existing balance of theater nuclear forces in Europe between NATO and the Warsaw Pact.[6] Moreover, the strategic significance of NATO's planned LRTNF deployments have a broader strategic impact as seen from Moscow; such forces are interpreted there not only as an augmentation of NATO theater forces with new weaponry, but also as a new military threat to the Soviet Union itself (especially in conjunction with other U.S. programs for weapons with high counter-force capabilities) that would adversely affect the global U.S.-USSR strategic balance.[7]

Soviet commentaries ascribe to the United States a motive of seeking to negotiate from a position of strength by acquiring cruise missiles and other new weapon programs as "trump cards" or bargaining chips, then using that position to obtain Soviet concessions.[8] Many accounts impute

5. For example, see "Cruise Missile Program Dangerous to Peace," *Radio Moscow,* Domestic Service, May 3, 1980, in Foreign Broadcast Information Service, *Daily Report: Soviet Union,* May 5, 1980, pp. A7–A8 (hereafter FBIS); V. Shein, "Behind the Facade of 'Modernization,'" *SShA,* no. 3 (March 1980), p. 14; O. Bykov, "The Main Problem of All Humanity," *MEIMO,* no. 3 (March 1980), p. 15; Col. M. Ponomarev, "The Militarist Course of NATO," *Krasnaya zvezda,* December 16, 1979; Y. Gudkov, "Pulling the Wool Over Our Eyes," *New Times,* no. 52 (December 1979), p. 9; Eng. Lt. Col. L. Nechayuk, "The Pentagon Steps Up the Arms Race: Missile Fever," *Krasnaya zvezda,* May 26, 1977; Nechayuk, "Aims Pursued by the Pentagon," *Krasnaya zvezda,* May 5, 1976; Col. M. Ponomarev and V. Berezin, "The Pentagon's Missile Programs," *Krasnaya zvezda,* February 20, 1977; V. Vinogradov and V. Berezin, "The Pentagon's Dangerous Actions," *Krasnaya zvezda,* April 4, 1976; Eng. Col. (Res.) S. Pavlov, "The Pentagon's Strategic 'Trump Card,'" *Krasnaya zvezda,* April 21, 1977; and "Staking on Strategic Cruise [Missiles]," *Aviatsiya i kosmonavtika* (Aviation and Cosmonauts), no. 10 (October 1977), p. 46.

6. Petrov, "A Hopeless Course"; Mil'shtein, "Some Characteristics of Contemporary U.S. Military Doctrine," p. 11; Bykov, "The Main Problem of All Humanity," p. 15; Nechayuk, "The Pentagon Eurostrategic Creations," pp. 125–26; Yur'ev, "For Europe—A Stable Peace, Security and Cooperation," p. 45; Ponomarev, "The Militarist Course of NATO"; and Ponomarev and Berezin, "The Pentagon's Missile Programs." Again, as mentioned in note 4, there are dozens of other articles attributing this same purpose to NATO's LRTNF decision in general; the articles cited here make particular reference to GLCMs or cruise missiles in general.

7. See Raymond L. Garthoff, "Brezhnev's Opening: The TNF Tangle," *Foreign Policy,* no. 41 (Winter 1980–81), pp. 82–94.

8. Boikov, "Cruise Missiles and Futile Hopes," p. 13; [Col.] Lev Semeiko, "Does NATO Need the 'Euromissiles'?" *New Times,* no. 44 (October 1979), p. 5; Y. Gudkov, "Continent of Peace or Nuclear Launching Pad?" *New Times,* no. 45 (Novem-

even more ominous U.S. designs for the use of superiority, and the LRTNF deployment is believed to increase the risks of war.[9] For example, the GLCM is said to have a high potential for surprise because of its mobility, difficulty of its detection, and its accuracy and to represent a first-strike weapon (although this argument is made more frequently concerning the Pershing II).[10] Owing to its high accuracy, the GLCM is said to have a counterforce capability against such targets as ICBM silos.[11] Indeed, one account explicitly attributes higher expectations of kill probability to cruise missiles than to Polaris and Minuteman ballistic missiles.[12] The most authoritative statement was made by First Deputy Minister of Defense and Chief of the General Staff Marshal Nikolai V. Ogarkov, who declared in a speech in 1980 to a Soviet military audience that the NATO plan for LRTNF missile deployment "not only would disrupt the approximate balance of medium-range nuclear systems that has been created in Europe, but would also lead to a sharp qualitative change in the political-military situation, since it would create the threat of a surprise suppression of the launches of our strategic nuclear forces."[13]

The qualities of GLCMs have been summed up in *Red Star* as follows: "the great destructive power of their nuclear charges . . . difficulties of detection in flight . . . ease of camouflaging, owing to the small size of the missiles and their launchers, concealing them from existing means of technical detection . . . their number and basing locations are extremely difficult to verify, and that facilitates their employment for a surprise attack."[14] Some Soviet accounts do note U.S. views that some characteristics of cruise missiles, in particular long flight time to target, may make them better suited for follow-through attacks than for a first strike.[15]

---

ber 1979), p. 18; and I. Chistyakov, "U.S. Cruise Missiles," *Voyenno-istoricheskii zhurnal* (The Military Historical Journal), no. 3 (March 1979), p. 75.

9. For example, see Shein, "Behind the Facade of 'Modernization,' " p. 13.

10. Maj. Gen. V. Larionov, "Grave Heritage: The Outgoing U.S. Administration's Military Policy," *Krasnaya zvezda,* January 4, 1981; Boikov, "Cruise Missiles and Futile Hopes," and Ponomarev, "The Militarist Course of NATO." See also Theo Sommer, an interview citing G. Arbatov, *Die Zeit,* April 4, 1980.

11. See Kirsanov, "Air-Based Cruise Missiles," p. 50.

12. Chistyakov, "U.S. Cruise Missiles," p. 78.

13. Marshal Nikolai V. Ogarkov, "In the Interests of Combat Readiness," speech to a meeting of leading command and political personnel of the Soviet Army and Navy on June 3, 1980, *Kommunist vooruzhennykh sil* (Communist of the Armed Forces), no. 14 (July 1980), p. 26.

14. Ponomarev, "The Militarist Course of NATO."

15. Kirsanov, "Air-Based Cruise Missiles," p. 51.

Cruise missiles would, however, increase uncertainties in Soviet assessment of the size and objective of a nuclear attack from Western Europe. Some accounts ascribe synergistic effects to GLCMs and Pershing II MRBMs, with their differing capabilities combined (in ways not defined) to enhance overall effectiveness.[16]

Because published Soviet commentary has been keyed so closely to Western developments, particularly to NATO's decision on LRTNF, it does not provide a balanced consideration of such factors as the doctrinal implications of distinctions between, say, the relative preemptive or first-strike capabilities of cruise missiles as compared with ballistic missiles. The distinction is evident to some extent in the particular stress on the first-strike potential and short warning times of medium-range ballistic missiles such as the Pershing II; first-strike capability is also attributed to the GLCM because of the difficulty in detection both before and after launch and its expected high accuracy.

Soviet comments on the challenge of modern cruise missiles to air defenses suggest concern about the new demands such missiles will place on defense systems.[17] The most confident statements are public pronouncements made by senior commanders of the Air Defense Forces (PVO), whose responsibility it is to provide air defense, and in most cases, these remarks seem to be addressed to ALCMs.[18] Other Soviet commentators are more cautious, implying a lack of faith in the country's air defense system. One military writer, for example, in an article dealing with recent developments in ALCM, short-range attack missile, and advanced strategic air-launched missile technology concludes that "they are all designed to break through strong air defense systems and strike them from various distances. . . . It is difficult to say at the moment to what extent the hopes of the foreign military specialists are justified, how suc-

16. Col. Yu. Chaplygin, "Behind the Facade of 'Modernization,'" *Pravda,* January 4, 1980; and Nechayuk, "The Pentagon Eurostrategic Creations," p. 126.

17. Nechayuk, "The Pentagon Steps Up Arms Race"; Kirsanov, "Air-Based Cruise Missiles," p. 50; and Chistyakov, "U.S. Cruise Missiles," pp. 77–78.

18. For example, see Col. Gen. Ye. Yurasov, "Responsible for the Sky of the Motherland," *Izvestiya,* April 13, 1980; Col. Gen. of Aviation I. Podgorny, "Sentries of the Sky," *Trud,* April 8, 1979; Marshal of the Air Force A. Koldunov, "Defenders of the Skies of the Motherland," *Zarya vostoka* (Dawn of the East) (Tbilisi: April 9, 1978); Lt. Gen. Artillery Yu. Kulikov, "Reliable Shield of the Motherland," *Sovetskaya Belorossiya* (Soviet Belorussia) (Minsk: April 9, 1978); and Col. Gen. V. Sozinov, "Always in Combat Readiness," *Sovetskaya Rossiya* (Soviet Russia), April 10, 1977.

cessful development and testing will be and what final results will be achieved."[19] Many Soviet observers have noted the expected high penetration capabilities and high accuracy of cruise missiles.[20] Articles in various military journals have also acknowledged the missile's small radar profile,[21] its ability to maneuver evasively and to fly below radar scanning levels,[22] and the low infrared emissions of its propulsion system[23]—all factors that seriously complicate detection and interdiction by defenses.

When considering possible war scenarios, Soviet military writers do not limit consideration of GLCMs to their role in the initial phase of a war. Soviet views on the probably extended nature even of a general war lend weight to considerations of extended survivability and reconstitution of various nuclear strike forces, and land- (and sea-) based cruise missile systems may be seen as important in this context.

Soviet literature stresses that GLCMs would circumvent and evade SALT ceilings on intercontinental forces targeted on the United States and the Soviet Union.[24] Indeed, one reason for the U.S. revival of cruise missiles since 1972 is said to be the SALT I Interim Agreement in that year, which limited ICBMs and SLBMs but not GLCMs or SLCMs. As

19. Maj. Gen. Artillery V. Zhuravlev, "Air-to-Ground Missiles," *Krasnaya zvezda,* September 30, 1975. See also Col. Gen. A. Sozinov, "Sentries of the Sky," *Sovetskaya Rossiya,* April 8, 1979.

20. Grishin, "Cruise Missiles"; Nechayuk, "The Pentagon Eurostrategic Creations," p. 126; Kirsanov, "Air-Based Cruise Missiles," p. 50; Capt. 1st Rank V. Konstantinov, "U.S. Cruise Missiles," *ZVO,* no. 3 (March 1978), pp. 10–11; Eng. Major Ye. Klimovich, "Cruise Missiles," *Voyennyi vestnik* (Military Herald), no. 3 (March 1978), pp. 121–22; and Chistyakov, "U.S. Cruise Missiles," pp. 77–78.

21. Nechayuk, "The Pentagon Steps Up the Arms Race"; Konstantinov, "U.S. Cruise Missiles," p. 15.

22. Eng. Col. V. Konstantinov and Eng. Sr. Lt. A. Bokov, "Cruise-Missile-Terrain-Matching Guidance Systems," *ZVO,* no. 4 (April 1980), pp. 52–56; Col. I. Mikhailov and Capt. 2d Rank K. Kostin, "U.S. Ground-Based Cruise Missiles," *ZVO,* no. 7 (July 1980), pp. 43–45; Kirsanov, "Air-Based Cruise Missiles," p. 51; Konstantinov, "U.S. Cruise Missiles," p. 15; Nechayuk, "The Pentagon Eurostrategic Creations," p. 125; Boikov, "Cruise Missiles and Futile Hopes," p. 12; and an illustration borrowed from the Italian journal *Il Giorno,* in *New Times,* no. 45 (November 1979), p. 19.

23. Konstantinov, "U.S. Cruise Missiles," pp. 10 and 15.

24. Boikov, "Cruise Missiles and Futile Hopes," p. 12; Yur'ev, "For Europe—A Stable Peace, Security and Cooperation," p. 55; Chistyakov, "U.S. Cruise Missiles," p. 75; Eng. Col. A. Latukhin, "The Truth about the Eurostrategic Weapons," *Voyenniye znaniya* (Military Knowledge), no. 2 (February 1980), p. 31; Pavlov, "The Pentagon's Strategic 'Trump Card' "; and see Eng. Capt. 1st Rank (Res.) N. Shaskol'sky, "One More Guided Missile," *Krasnaya zvezda,* September 10, 1975.

one Soviet observer put it: "The Pentagon saw in this a loophole for circumventing SALT-1 and gaining unilateral advantages."[25] This argument is made a fortiori in connection with the 1979 NATO decision to develop and to deploy GLCMs, following by only six months the signature of the SALT II treaty and protocol.[26] In addition, there are Soviet suspicions of Western coercion by a threat ultimately to deploy an unlimited number of U.S. cruise missiles (GLCMs) in Europe.[27]

In a series of discussions in Moscow in the fall of 1980, the author noted the stress placed by Soviet interlocutors on the broad impact that cruise missile technology could have in stimulating military competition and complicating arms control. One retired senior officer, after criticizing the destabilizing effect of the first-strike capability of the Pershing II, stated that he was even more concerned about the overall effects of unleashing GLCM and SLCM cruise missile technology—by both the United States and the Soviet Union and eventually by other countries also.

SLCMs received relatively early attention in Soviet commentary because of their prominence as the first modern cruise missile program proposed and funded by the United States beginning in 1972. The reasons attributed to the United States for interest in cruise missiles, despite their lower speed, range, payload, and "theoretical interceptability" in comparison with ballistic missiles are lower cost, great flexibility of deployment of launchers given their small size (on strategic or tactical aircraft, surface ships, submarines, and mobile land launchers), the absence of need for costly special carriers such as nuclear powered submarines for SLBMs, and their unprecedented accuracy. Also, despite subsonic speed, such missiles are regarded as difficult to intercept because of low radar cross section and low-altitude flight profile. In addition to all these advantages, the deployments would evade the limits on strategic weapons established in the SALT II treaty.[28]

Soviet attention was directed toward ALCMs in the mid-1970s and

25. Boikov, "Cruise Missiles and Futile Hopes," p. 12; and see Pavlov, "The Pentagon's Strategic 'Trump Card.' "

26. Aleksandr Bovin, *Radio Moscow*, Domestic Service, October 16, 1979, in FBIS, *Daily Report: Soviet Union*, October 17, 1979, p. AA-2; and Valentin Falin, TV Studio Nine, *Radio Moscow*, October 13, 1979.

27. Sobakin, *Resheniya*, p. 58; and see [Col.] L. Semeiko, "Washington's 'Eurostrategic' Gamble," *Novoye vremya* (*New Times*), no. 27 (July 1980), pp. 8–9.

28. Alexei G. Arbatov, *Bezopasnost' v yadernyi vek i politika Vashingtona* (Security in the Nuclear Age and the Policy of Washington) (Moscow: Politizdat, 1980), pp. 167–70.

GLCMs in the late 1970s as they became part of more active programs. From 1975 to 1978 Soviet emphasis was placed on ALCMs, paralleling the emphasis in the SALT II negotiations on that system.[29] GLCMs were given greatest prominence by 1979 and 1980, as NATO approached and then arrived at a decision to deploy these weapons as part of the alliance's LRTNF.

From the Vladivostok agreement of 1974 until 1979, strategic cruise missiles (eventually defined for SALT purposes as missiles with ranges greater than 600 kilometers) were a subject of great controversy in the SALT II negotiations. The Soviet Union pressed from 1974 until 1978 to count each ALCM missile as one unit under the overall ceiling on numbers of strategic launch vehicles. Eventually the USSR agreed to include ALCM-carrying heavy bombers as single launcher units, and the United States agreed to include ALCM carriers in a subceiling category with ballistic missiles having multiple independently targetable reentry vehicles (MIRVs).

Although the Soviet Union long pressed for a complete ban on long-range GLCMs and SLCMs, the United States was prepared to accept only a ban on deploying such weapons, or on testing them with multiple warheads, for a limited time period to the end of 1981 (a limitation included not in the body of the 1979 treaty but in a protocol with that limited duration). The Soviet Union made clear its intention to seek additional limitations in future negotiations, which it expected would occur during the protocol period, but conceded much of its leverage by accepting a longer-term SALT II treaty (effective, if it had been ratified, until the end of 1985). Continuing Soviet interest virtually ensures that any future SALT or LRTNF negotiations will include consideration of long-range cruise missiles.

Soviet military concern about the advent of modern high-performance long-range cruise missiles thus stems from the belief that global and European theater nuclear balances will be upset by the addition of these new systems to the Western arsenal unless there are new countervailing Soviet military programs. In the Soviet view, deterrence is based on war-fighting capability, and the established mutual deterrence will be weakened if cruise missiles (and other new weapon systems) disturb the military balance. Thus strategic, as well as tactical, considerations underlie the Soviet

29. For a review of the history of the ALCM issue in the SALT II negotiations, see Strobe Talbott, *Endgame: The Inside Story of SALT II* (Harper and Row, 1979), pp. 103–07, 125–31, 181–89, 210–12, 224–25, 231–34, and 271.

military and political reactions to cruise missilery. The GLCM in particular (and, should it be developed and deployed, also a theater-range SLCM) threatens to disturb the existing balance of LRTNF—which, from the Soviet standpoint, includes U.S. fighter bombers in Europe and other forward-based means of delivering nuclear weapons. Moreover, as noted above, to the extent that such weapons are perceived to have a first-strike capability against strategic targets in the USSR, they affect the intercontinental strategic balance as well as the theater balance. Hence the Soviet Union is better able to accept the ALCM as one more intercontinental weapon system weighed in the intercontinental balance and limited in SALT; the GLCM and, putatively, the SLCM are not accepted as strategic weapons in the West and are not taken into account in SALT. To Western rejoinders that the Backfire and the SS-20 affect the theater balance, the Soviet Union argues that they represent merely modernization of existing systems.[30] (The Soviet Union does not regard as a serious argument that the Backfire affects the intercontinental balance; nor does it deploy, train, or target the Backfire for such missions.) The GLCM would, in fact, constitute a new U.S. land-based capability threatening targets in the Soviet Union for the first time since the Thor and Jupiter IRBMs and Mace cruise missiles were withdrawn in the 1960s.

In addition to these political and military issues, and stemming from some of them, are Soviet concerns about additional economic outlays. Soviet commentaries point out that the development and deployment of the cruise missile, especially the GLCM, means adding a completely new type of weapon, and not merely modernization.[31] While this is held to be pernicious, it is said—sometimes with explicit comparison to MIRVs— that this escalation in the arms competition will not yield any advantage to the security of the deploying country because it will be matched in some (unspecified) way.[32] The cruise missile thus promises to add to the costs and risks of a continuing upward spiral of arms competition without gaining anything for anyone.

How the Soviet Union will respond is problematic. Although, as noted above, certain military leaders have publicly expressed confidence in their

30. See Garthoff, "Brezhnev's Opening."

31. "Review," Tass International Service, *Radio Moscow,* January 10, 1980; Nechayuk, "The Pentagon Eurostrategic Creations," p. 125; Ponomarev and Berezin, "The Pentagon's Missile Programs"; Yur'ev, "For Europe—A Stable Peace, Security and Cooperation," p. 55; and Sobakin, *Resheniya,* pp. 43–45.

32. Boikov, "Cruise Missiles and Futile Hopes," p. 12; and Grishin, "Cruise Missiles."

ability to defend against at least the ALCM threat, those leaders are undoubtedly more concerned privately and more conservative in their internal presentations of requirements for new and additional air defenses. Requirements could include new radars, new types of surface-to-air missiles, and more discriminating look-down–shoot-down radar capability for jet interceptors. This effort might, incidentally, lead to increased Soviet tactical antiballistic missile (ABM) capability—a possibly important consideration that has not been given attention.

The challenge of long-range cruise missiles to the air defenses of the Soviet Union—GLCMs, SLCMs, and ALCMs—must be considered in the light of the strong, not to say inordinate, historical Soviet emphasis on defense of the homeland. Air defense has consistently been given high priority since the 1930s, and especially since World War II. Following the SALT I treaty and subsequent protocol, with provisions banning a nationwide ABM defense and permitting only a single deployment of 100 ABM launchers, the United States accelerated its reduction of air defenses of North America, but the Soviet Union has continued to maintain and improve its defenses. To be sure, Soviet military planners see other potential air threats, for example, from China and Western Europe. But the imperative to build defenses persists and will undoubtedly influence Soviet leaders to authorize new defenses against cruise missile threats, even though this compounds pressures on the economy.

The total additional outlay for future Soviet defense needs is difficult to project; Western estimates for the costs of upgrading Soviet strategic defenses to counter the cruise missile challenge have ranged from $10 billion to $50 billion.[33] The economic burden of such new defenses is no doubt one source of the unhappiness of the Soviet political and military leaders over the advent of this new offensive technology, for which they probably see little need and in which the United States moreover currently holds a considerable advantage. At the least, upgrading means a substantial and unwanted increase, or reallocation, of Soviet defense expenditures.

In addition to increased outlays for defenses to counter hostile cruise missile systems, the Soviet Union would seek to offset U.S. deployments (especially the NATO deployments of GLCMs) by increasing its offensive forces. One possible response, although not necessarily the most likely, would be to develop and deploy Soviet cruise missiles (the pros-

33. See Robert Emmet Moffit, "The Cruise Missile and SALT II," *International Security Review*, vol. 4 (Fall 1979), p. 277.

pects for which are discussed below). It should be stressed that the precise Soviet response (or, more likely, responses) may vary depending not only on the perceived military threats presented by ALCMs, GLCMs, and conventional and nuclear SLCMs, but also on the political-military context. In response to the NATO GLCM deployment, the Soviet Union may wish to deploy a new demonstrative matching offensive system. In the case of ALCMs, the response may be concentrated on devising appropriate air defenses. The Soviet Navy, on the other hand, may be designed and deployed not only to counter antiship cruise missiles, but also to counter potential land-attack SLCMs. Thus the advent of land-attack SLCMs might affect future Soviet fleet deployment patterns and, indeed, the composition of the Navy. In tactical terms, GLCMs (and SLCMs) may prompt increased attention to target acquisition and enhancement of preemptive capabilities. The Soviet Union seeks, even if countermeasures are not fully effective, to deny a "free ride" to any potential attack system or attacker.

Thus both in military and political terms, apart from possible attractions of new cruise missile technology to meet perceived Soviet military requirements, the advent of modern Western cruise missiles is virtually certain to elicit a wide range of Soviet military responses.

Soviet Views on Cruise Missiles and Arms Control

Apart from political and military and related economic responses to U.S. cruise missile programs, Soviet commentators also have expressed concern about the negative impact of cruise missile technology on future prospects for arms control. This concern is not limited to Soviet positions in strategic arms control negotiations (and related political maneuvering) aimed at inhibiting or limiting U.S. deployment of cruise missiles. For such bargaining, the USSR would have to relinquish comparable opportunities, and given the disparity in interest and achievement in cruise missiles, might also have to make concessions on other matters. The Soviet Union has clearly indicated its readiness at least to accept reciprocal limitations in order to head off some American programs. These Soviet apprehensions about the impact on future arms limitation and other arms control interests warrant further attention.

The Soviet Union argues that, above all, cruise missile systems will present insurmountable difficulties for verification—in the words of one leading Soviet analyst, difficulties so severe that they "would hinder or even preclude arms limitations."[34] This objection is particularly addressed to GLCMs and SLCMs[35] because they are small, mobile, and easily camouflaged,[36] and also because "it is impossible to distinguish strategic cruise missiles from tactical ones by their external features."[37]

One can speculate on the extent to which the Soviet leaders are disturbed about possible obstacles to future arms limitations posed by cruise missiles and the extent to which they see this as an argument that would appeal to Western audiences who might oppose such programs for that reason. Given, however, the strong Soviet interest in limiting U.S. SLCM and GLCM deployments, and in particular the expressed interest in LRTNF arms limitation negotiations, it is quite probable that at least some Soviet officials are indeed troubled about the prospect that U.S. cruise missile development and deployment will prejudice possible future negotiated limitations. This point was included in Secretary General Leonid Brezhnev's authoritative report to the Twenty-sixth Congress of the Communist Party of the Soviet Union in 1981, when he noted that "rapid and profound changes are occurring in the development of military technology. Qualitatively new types of weapons, primarily weapons of mass destruction, are being developed—types of weapons that can make control over them and therefore also their agreed limitation extremely difficult if not impossible." In the same speech, Brezhnev proposed a moratorium on deployment in Europe of medium-range weapon systems, specifically including "ground-based strategic cruise missiles."[38]

Proliferation of cruise missile technology to other countries is another important source of Soviet uneasiness. Although undoubtedly the Soviet Union would have liked to preclude possible U.S. transfer of cruise missile technology to its allies in the SALT agreement, that was not acceptable to the United States. The Soviet Union remains concerned about such transfer, even if only for delivery of conventional weapons. Soviet

34. Georgy A. Arbatov, "US Foreign Policy on the Threshold of the Eighties," *SShA*, no. 4 (April 1980), p. 50; see also Arbatov, *Radio Moscow*, May 2, 1980, in FBIS, *Daily Report: Soviet Union*, May 5, 1980, pp. A1–A2; and Sobakin, *Resheniya*, p. 44.

35. See Boikov, "Cruise Missiles and Futile Hopes," p. 13; Nechayuk, "The Pentagon Steps Up the Arms Race"; and Shaskol'sky, "One More Guided Missile."

36. Boikov, "Cruise Missiles and Futile Hopes."

37. Nechayuk, "The Pentagon Steps Up the Arms Race."

38. L. I. Brezhnev, "Report of the C.P.S.U. Central Committee to the XXVI Congress of the C.P.S.U. and the Immediate Tasks of the Party in the Fields of Domestic and Foreign Policy," *Pravda*, February 24, 1981.

leaders also believe that other states will be tempted to develop cruise missile technology, compounding Soviet defense requirements.[39]

Another specific concern expressed is the heightened risk of accidental outbreak of war. One Soviet commentator noted that the false November 6, 1979, North American Air Defense (NORAD) alert warning of a Soviet missile attack on the United States was triggered by an error in programming the wrong computer with a simulation tape for training—an error that was discovered and corrected only after six minutes. But, in the Soviet view, Eurostrategic missiles, including land-based cruise missiles, "do not afford that opportunity" because they can reach targets in a matter of minutes.[40] This argument is evidently more applicable to the Pershing II MRBM with its flight time of only about five minutes to Soviet territory; the Soviet Union has stressed that fact, but as noted above, the argument has also been extended to GLCMs inasmuch as they may escape timely detection.

Potential Future Soviet Interest in Cruise Missiles

At present, the Soviet Union would prefer to reach an arms limitation agreement with the United States to ban long-range GLCMs and SLCMs, as would temporarily have been done until the end of 1981 under the protocol to the 1979 SALT II treaty, and to limit ALCMs, as would have been done by that treaty if it had been ratified. Regardless of the fate of the SALT II treaty and protocol, the Soviet Union at this point would probably be prepared in any negotiation to give up prospects for these weapons if the United States would also agree to do so. In view of the fact that the United States is proceeding with a substantial ALCM program and has forged a NATO decision to proceed in the mid-1980s with deployment of intermediate-range GLCMs, the Soviet leaders must recognize that the chances for agreement on a ban on GLCMs are slim indeed, and on ALCMs virtually nil. There is not much more prospect for banning SLCMs given the momentum of such programs and the current hiatus and future uncertainty with respect to strategic arms limitation negotia-

39. Vinogradov and Berezin, "The Pentagon's Dangerous Actions"; and "The Task of Limiting Strategic Arms: Prospects and Problems," *Pravda*, February 11, 1978.
40. Boikov, "Cruise Missiles and Futile Hopes," p. 13.

tions. The numbers of launchers for such weapons might be limited by a negotiated agreement if adequate verification could be provided.

No evidence exists, at least on public record, to indicate active Soviet development of strategic long-range ALCMs, SLCMs, or GLCMs based on technology comparable to that being developed by the United States. The Soviet Union has continued to develop improved short- to medium-range air-launched and sea-launched cruise missiles based on traditional technology. Soviet military leaders are actively following U.S. development of advanced cruise missile weapons, if only to be abreast of their capabilities and to design countermeasures. They may also be, or become, interested in acquiring such systems.

ALCMs

A truly strategic standoff ALCM would have been less likely to be developed by the Soviet Union if the SALT II treaty had been ratified. Under the 1979 treaty, the United States and the USSR would have been allowed, under a 1,320 subceiling, any combination of strategic missiles equipped with MIRVs—ICBMs, SLBMs, and air-to-surface ballistic missiles (ASBMs)—and heavy bombers equipped with ALCMs with a range greater than 600 kilometers. Because there would have been a further subceiling of 1,200 for MIRV-equipped ICBMs, SLBMs, and ASBMs, in effect there would have been a "free ride" for 120 ALCM-carrying heavy bombers (although in place of 120 other strategic launchers). Additional ALCM-carrying heavy bombers beyond 120 could have been deployed but only in substitution for MIRV-equipped ICBMs, SLBMs, or ASBMs. ALCMs were also limited to no more than 20 on each existing type of bomber, and in the future if new carriers were introduced to an overall average of 28 per carrier. There were no maximum-range restrictions; all ALCMs with ranges over 600 kilometers would have been included, as would any bomber carrying such ALCMs. Testing or deployment of ALCMs equipped with MIRVs also would have been banned.

The low density of air defenses of the continental United States might reduce the perceived need for ALCMs. On the other hand, ALCMs could extend the combat radius of the heavy bomber fleet. ALCMs might extend significantly the strategic potential of Backfire (Tu-22M) medium bombers. (This could not have been done under the SALT II treaty, which would have banned ALCMs with ranges above 600 kilometers from all except heavy bombers, without further reducing existing forces, because testing and equipping the Backfire with such ALCMs would have converted it to a recognized heavy bomber type and brought Backfire under the overall ceiling.) Without the constraints of the SALT II treaty, however, the Soviet Union might expand its Backfire fleet and equip some Backfires, Bears, and follow-on heavy bombers with ALCMs.

SLCMs

The Soviet Union, with a long and active history of cruise missile deployment on submarines and surface ships, is continuing to improve tactical antiship systems of various ranges. It is possible that the USSR will develop an interest and a capability in strategic land-attack SLCMs. It would probably be misleading, however, to assume that because there are many Soviet surface and subsurface naval platforms and tubes they would necessarily be converted to a land-attack role. The Soviet Union has extensive antiship torpedo and cruise missile launchers because of perceived requirements. Moreover, as the U.S. Navy expands (and if it develops an additional SLCM strategic role) the Soviet Union is likely to see its antiship requirements rise rather than fall. In short, strategic SLCMs will have to compete with other naval weapon systems rather than simply inherit their assets.

One possible outcome of any emerging Soviet naval interest in land-attack SLCMs might be authorization for such a system to be used against port and naval base targets. This would be focused on a long-standing naval target requirement, which might be conceded without a bureaucratic struggle as extensive as a strategic SLCM concept could prompt, although this, too, could engender opposition from the Naval Aviation and the ballistic missile-launching submarine components now probably sharing in this mission.

Notwithstanding the caveats discussed above, a Soviet strategic land-attack SLCM could significantly enhance Soviet capabilities and might be developed and deployed. Such a system would be able to take advantage of the geographical asymmetries of the two countries, and even a modest medium- or intermediate-range SLCM force could threaten a wide range of military and other targets in the United States. It would add a new dimension to the attack threat against the continental United States, even though a redundant one. It could also augment SLBMs in hedging against the growing U.S. counterforce threat to the fixed land-based Soviet ICBM force.

GLCMs

The failure of previous Soviet land-based cruise missile systems to compete successfully with ballistic missiles in the 1950s and 1960s may not augur well for the future prospects of GLCMs. To be sure, substantial differences in cost and effectiveness could bring a different outcome. Another serious competitor will be the Frontal Aviation (the tactical air arm), which has been substantially upgrading its conventional and nuclear attack capabilities, and probably also the Long-Range Aviation (the strategic air force), most of which comprises medium bombers assigned to conventional and nuclear strike missions in a given theater.

The deployment of large numbers of nuclear-armed GLCMs in NATO in the 1980s, as currently planned, will not only stimulate the USSR's review of its plans and posture to assure no degradation in capability in the European theater, but will also raise the question of demonstrative counterdeployments. This is especially the case given the Soviet view that the Western move is intended to upset an existing parity and balance. Whether these countermeasures will include Soviet GLCMs is, however, uncertain—the Soviet decision is not known to the United States, and in all probability the decision has not yet been made in Moscow.

Despite the above considerations, unless GLCM deployment is curbed by negotiated arms control, it is highly likely that the Soviet Union will eventually deploy large numbers of GLCMs in Europe, the Far East, and southern USSR.

Concluding Observations

The U.S. approach to the new cruise missile technology, as is discussed elsewhere in this book, has been affected by the political-military strategic context and by domestic U.S. and allied institutional and political considerations. The evolving strategic relationship between the United States and the Soviet Union has in recent years been characterized by an unprecedented emergence of overall strategic parity and also by an unprecedented role for arms control. Arms control in the 1980s may, however, be of less concern than it was in the 1970s, and in any event the attention that has been given to arms control implications of cruise missile technology has been directed more to possible limitations on current systems than to future developments. Also, the significance for the Soviet Union of the theater nuclear situation in Europe and of the implications of the cruise missile technology for that situation has not been given sufficient attention in the West. The United States and NATO have seized upon this available technology to help redress a perceived Western shortcoming in the theater nuclear balance. In dealing with this current political-military problem, the impact on Soviet programs or on arms control prospects has been given less attention.

The Soviet perspective on advanced cruise missile technology is still in a formative stage. The Soviet Union has reacted to a situation in which the United States has a clear lead in development and deployment plans and decisions, and this has reinforced Soviet preferences for restraint and negotiated arms control. But as U.S. deployment proceeds, and as opportunities for arms control diminish, Soviet preferences will shift toward acquisition of advanced cruise missiles and their adaptation to Soviet military requirements (as well as engendering other Soviet countering or offsetting military and diplomatic measures). The concern that the Soviet Union has about some features of the new technology (such as counterforce applications, increased defensive outlays, and potential spread to other countries) will be accommodated, and the Soviet Union will seek ways to capitalize on the new technology to serve its needs and interests.

The attraction of cruise missile technology, especially GLCMs and SLCMs, which is based in part on apparent lower cost and early availability for new high-performance weaponry, may be leading to decisions in the early 1980s that the West will regret by the end of the decade. Eventual Soviet deployments of GLCMs, possibly on a massive scale, would more than wipe out any gains of early NATO deployment. Similarly, long-range land-attack SLCMs could add new perceived threats to Europe, North America, and in the third world, far outweighing the value of the addition of this weaponry to Western arsenals. Perhaps there is no alternative. But this is far from clear, given the current Soviet interest in arms control of this technology. It would be most unfortunate if the West, by assuming that no constraints were possible, became responsible for that very outcome.

CHAPTER TWELVE

The Domestic Politics of Cruise Missile Development, 1970–1980

ROBERT J. ART *and* STEPHEN E. OCKENDEN

FOR THE LAST ten years, cruise missiles have played a bewildering variety of roles in the United States. To the arms control community, they have come to represent the most recent example of the inexorable technological imperative that drives the arms race. To the proponents of greater military spending, who fear that the United States is becoming second best, they have epitomized the American technological edge that barely

Robert Art is dean of the Graduate School of Arts and Sciences, Brandeis University. Stephen Ockenden, whose work on this chapter was done at the University of Minnesota, is now legislative assistant to Senator David F. Durenberger, who does not necessarily share the views expressed in this chapter.

The authors are indebted to Michael MccGwire, Glenn Snyder, and Kenneth Waltz for their perceptive comments on an earlier draft of this article. The bulk of the material in this chapter is based on two hundred interviews with government officials who have been directly involved with one or more aspects of the cruise missile. Stephen Ockenden conducted one hundred of these interviews in 1977 and 1978, concentrating primarily on the Air Force and the Navy. Robert Art conducted one hundred in 1980, concentrating primarily on SALT, NATO, and the ground-launched cruise missile. Nevertheless, the chapter is truly a collaborative effort. Most of the material, especially the political nuances, cannot be found in the written public record; therefore intensive interviewing (with confidentiality guaranteed) was necessary to reconstruct and analyze what had happened. Because participants differ in their perceptions, the authors stipulated that all information received from their interviews be confirmed by at least two persons, each in a different bureau or office, before considering the information reliable. They have also tried to reconfirm interview data with citations from the public record when possible.

enables compensation for the Soviet Union's quantitative superiority. To the military services, they have been unwanted competitors in the perennial Pentagonal fights for scarce funds. To the technology community, they have been another gadget with which to demonstrate its engineering wizardry. And to those heavily involved in the hautes politiques of American foreign policy, they have been alternately a bargaining chip, an unwanted complication, and a godsend for tough political problems.

Cruise missiles have played these many roles in the varied arenas of American politics because they appear to be relatively cheap, promise great performance, and, most important, are adaptable to a broad range of military uses. Perhaps unique among the major weapon systems developed by the United States since World War II, cruise missiles have been an important factor in a large number of political arenas. Table 12-1 shows the six types of cruise missiles that were under development from 1970 through 1980 and the six political arenas in which each version figured. The variety of arenas and multiple versions of the missile in each one make a complicated story. Although it is the political intricacies— and the conclusions drawn from an analysis of them—with which we are concerned, this chapter will focus initially on the three modes of launch —air, land, and sea.

The following four propositions summarize the politics of cruise missile development in the United States from 1970 through 1980:

1. Without exception, the military services did not want cruise missiles if they threatened their respective dominant missions or ate into their scarce funds, both of which were in general the case. The long-range air-launched cruise missile (ALCM) was rammed down the throat of the Air Force. The Army refused to accept development responsibility for the ground-launched cruise missile (GLCM). The Air Force consequently got stuck with it and viewed it as a "national mission"—one it performed for the country, but that had little value for its own missions. The Navy—specifically, the carrier admirals—did not want the Tomahawk antiship missile (TASM) because it represented a clear and present danger to the mission of the carrier-based aircraft.

2. The cruise missile would not have proceeded as fast and as far, if indeed at all, had it not been for the intervention and support of high-level political figures in the Pentagon, the White House, and even the U.S. Department of State. For individuals operating at this level in the American government, the driving factors were negotiations with the Soviet Union on SALT I and II, the concern expressed by NATO's

Table 12-1. *Cruise Missile Types and Political Arenas*

Political arenas	ALCM[a] (A and B) (Air Force)	GLCM[b] (Air Force)	TASM[c] (Navy)	TLAM-N[d] (SLCM) (Navy)	TLAM-C[e] (Navy)
SALT II politics	×	×	...	×	...
NATO politics	...	×	...	×	...
Office of the Secretary of Defense versus service politics	×	×	...	×	...
Intraservice politics	×	...	×	×	...
Executive-congressional politics	×	...	...	×	×
Intraexecutive politics	×	×	...	×	×

a. Short-range air-launched cruise missile (ALCM-A); long-range air-launched cruise missile (ALCM-B).
b. Ground-launched cruise missile.
c. Tomahawk antiship missile.
d. Tomahawk land-attack missile, nuclear armed (TLAM-N); sea-launched cruise missile (SLCM).
e. Tomahawk land-attack cruise missile, conventionally armed.

European members about the reliability of America's foreign policy and the credibility of the U.S. nuclear umbrella over them in the era of strategic parity between the superpowers, and White House anticipation of adverse congressional action on SALT II if this new technology were not developed to its fullest.

3. Technological innovation therefore did not create an irresistible force. It may be, as Samuel P. Huntington once said, "what is technically possible tends to become politically necessary."[1] Technological innovation, however, only creates the necessary, not the sufficient, condition. At every crucial stage in the development of each type of cruise missile, high-level political intervention was necessary either to start it or to sustain it. As a consequence of this dichotomy between service resistance and high-level political pressure, the American government during the SALT II negotiations from roughly 1973 until 1977 was bargaining hard for systems that the services did not want.

4. Finally, Congress was the arena in which intraservice and Office of the Secretary of Defense (OSD)–service disputes were resolved on the surface, but it is by no means clear that members of Congress always

1. Samuel P. Huntington, "Arms Races: Prerequisites and Results," in Carl J. Friedrich and Seymour E. Harris, eds., *Public Policy: A Yearbook of the Graduate School of Public Administration, Harvard University* (Cambridge, Mass.: Graduate School of Public Administration, 1958), p. 71.

knew what was going on in the Pentagon or that Congress prevailed. The role of Congress in the politics of cruise missile development during the 1970s remains the most difficult about which to generalize. Congress intervened at three crucial points during this decade and played the role of ally, lobbyist, judge, and gadfly, but an overall assessment of congressional influence in this case remains elusive. The decade of the 1970s was supposedly the era of congressional activism in defense matters, based on a quality and depth of staff that Congress theretofore had not possessed. That decade has been heralded as the decade of micromanagement, an intimate and continuous congressional involvement in the details of Pentagon policy. Congressional actions on the cruise missile during this period by no means fully support this view. Congress was heavily involved in the details of cruise missile development, but such involvement did not radically affect, deflect, or alter the course of the cruise missile. The more traditional view of Congress is the most sensible here: Congress exerted influence less by mastery of detail than by executive anticipation of likely congressional reactions to its proposed actions. And what the executive spent the most time anticipating were the general political contours on Capitol Hill.

The Air Force and the Air-Launched Cruise Missile

Since its inception, the United States Air Force has identified itself intimately with the manned strategic bombardment mission. It is this mission that provided the rationale for the separation of the Air Corps from the Army, that sustained Air Force identity and budgetary levels throughout much of the post–World War II era, that has driven the Air Force to press periodically for the modernization of the manned strategic bomber, and that was threatened by the long-range air-launched cruise missile in the early 1970s. In order to understand why the ALCM came about, the manner in which the Air Force reacted to it, and how the matter was finally resolved, it is first necessary to begin with the Air Force's plans in the 1960s to replace its aging B-52 fleet.

The Penetrating Bomber and the Air Force in the 1960s

Manned strategic bombers can attack the enemy either by penetrating hostile airspace and flying directly to their targets, or by standing off at great distances and releasing weapons that fly to the targets. The penetration mode provides flexibility because each bomber can fly alternate routes, conduct postattack reconnaissance, and recommit its weapons load as necessary. The price of flexibility comes quite high because penetrating bombers are expensive to build and operate. Their susceptibility to detection and destruction imposes stringent and hence costly requirements on designers. Although range and defensive armament requirements are less stringent for the standoff mode, such bombers sacrifice flexibility, and their net weapons yield is diminished because a large portion of each weapon's weight is dedicated to the propulsion and guidance systems.[2] Air Force doctrine has consistently favored the penetrating bomber, preferring the advantages of flexibility. Moreover, for many years the guidance and propulsion problems of long-range standoff weapons were considered too complex for solution. Consequently, since 1945 the Air Force has devoted a great deal of effort to improving the penetration capability of the manned bomber.[3]

Events of the 1960s began to conspire against this traditional preference. Hoping to replace the B-52, the Air Force devoted its research efforts in the late 1950s to a follow-on aircraft that could fly higher and faster than any previous bomber. The result was the B-70, a bomber that could fly in excess of Mach 3 and at an altitude of 70,000 feet. In 1960, however, just as the Air Force was ready to commit funds to full-scale production of the B-70, the Russians dramatically demonstrated that the basic concept of the high penetrating bomber was obsolete. By shooting down the high-flying U-2 piloted by Francis Gary Powers, they showed that the B-70 too would be vulnerable to air defenses and thereby forced the Air Force to rethink its commitment to the penetrating bomber.[4]

2. On the merits of the standoff and penetrating missions, see G. K. Burke, "A Case for the Manned Penetrating Bomber," *Air University Review*, vol. 28 (July–August 1977), pp. 15–26; and the testimony in *Department of Defense Appropriations for 1973*, Hearings before a subcommittee of the House Committee on Appropriations, 92 Cong. 2 sess. (Government Printing Office, 1972), pt. 4, pp. 317–19.

3. Neil R. Falk, "The Manned Bomber: Its Evolution and Future Use in the United States Strategic Offensive Force Concept" (Air Command and Staff College, Air University, Maxwell Air Force Base, Alabama, May 1971); Michael Brown, "Patterns of Organizational Decision-Making: Cases in the Development of the U.S. Strategic Bomber," paper delivered at the 20th Annual Conference of the International Studies Association, Toronto, Ontario, March 1979; and Air Force Manual 1-1, *United States Air Force Basic Doctrine* (August 14, 1964).

4. Alain C. Enthoven and K. Wayne Smith, *How Much Is Enough? Shaping the Defense Program, 1961–1969* (Harper and Row, 1971), pp. 243–51; Robert E. Hunter, "The Politics of U.S. Defense 1963: Manned Bombers versus Missiles," in Morton H. Halperin and Arnold Kanter, eds., *Readings in American Foreign Policy* (Little, Brown, 1973), pp. 191–202; and Brown, "Patterns of Organizational Decision-Making."

The Air Force responded to the U-2 incident in two ways: it began to develop a series of short-term modifications to the existing B-52 fleet, and it instituted a long-term study designed to produce a more effective manned penetrator. Most of the effort initially went into refurbishing the B-52 for low-altitude penetration by modifying the avionics and wings and by adding two types of defensive weapons—an air-to-surface missile (Hound Dog) and a decoy missile (Quail).[5] Although both missiles were developed before the U-2 incident and hence were not optimized for low-level penetration, they added significantly to the life of the B-52. With a range of 600 miles, the Hound Dog gave the B-52 an ability to suppress enemy defenses; with a range of 250 miles, the Quail drew some defenses away from the mother aircraft. Each missile extended the range at which the bomber's weapons could be released and, moreover, augmented the low-level penetration capability of the B-52. Neither, however, yielded a long-range standoff capability: only two Hound Dogs were carried aboard a B-52, and the ranges of both missiles were too short to reach most targets within the Soviet Union from beyond its borders. Thus, although the Air Force modified the B-52 for low-level flight, the service remained committed to the penetration mode.[6]

While work progressed on a short-term response to the U-2 incident, the Air Force began a series of conceptual studies for another manned bomber. After several years, the Air Force recommitted itself to the penetrating bomber in the guise of the advanced manned strategic aircraft (AMSA). It was this action that subsequently shaped how the Air Force viewed the cruise missile. The AMSA was to be a modern, small, versatile, supersonic bomber optimized for low-level dash, but flexible enough to fly at high altitudes. Early criteria established that the AMSA would have twice the range and five times the payload of the FB-111 and more than twice the speed of the B-52. The AMSA was to outperform any previous bomber and was to have the costly, if not potentially contradictory, characteristics of short takeoff, high speed, and a low-level terminal

5. On early studies and programs designed to refurbish the B-52 for low-level penetration, see John F. McCarthy, Jr., "The Case for the B-1 Bomber," *International Security,* vol. 1 (Fall 1976), pp. 78–97; and "Controversy Over the B-1 Bomber Program," *Congressional Digest,* vol. 55 (December 1976), p. 294.

6. Characteristics of the Quail and Hound Dog can be found in Roger E. Linnee, "SRAM and SCAD—New 'Tough' for an Old 'Buff' " (Air University, May 1973); "Quail Need Studied in Light of SRAM," *Aviation Week and Space Technology,* May 10, 1976, p. 129; and "SCAD Subsystems Awards Planned by Summer," *Aviation Week and Space Technology,* February 21, 1972, p. 87.

dash.[7] As early as 1968, therefore, systems analysts within the Department of Defense began to express concern over the costs of the AMSA. Nonetheless, the Air Force obtained approval for the award of a development contract to Rockwell Aviation in June 1970, and the AMSA was renamed the B-1.[8]

The B-1 and the Subsonic Cruise Armed Decoy

Even with formal approval, the Air Force could not deploy the B-1 for several years. In the interim the B-52 had to be maintained and modernized by upgrading its defensive weaponry; the Hound Dog and Quail had been designed in the 1950s. Modernization, however, entailed two key constraints. First, the follow-on defensive weaponry to be put on the B-52 also had to be compatible with the B-1. Second, such weaponry could not challenge the penetration mission. For the B-1, in short, the new defensive weaponry would be a predictable technological advance, not a radical reorientation in concept, to facilitate, not obviate, the role of the strategic penetrator.

For the Hound Dog, innovation proceeded quickly and with little difficulty, largely due to the political skill of the development team. Not without reason, the Hound Dog's replacement was named the short-range attack missile (SRAM), a small supersonic weapon designed to be carried within the bomber's weapons bay. These characteristics sacrificed range (30 to 100 miles for the SRAM, compared with 600 for the Hound Dog) for a substantial gain in high-speed performance and in the bomber's weapons load. This trade-off was by no means irrational (it clearly resulted in a superior offensive capability), but it was also not coincidental.[9] The SRAM was designed specifically as a defense suppression weapon to assist bombers in the penetration mission. Its short range would have

7. "New AF Strategic Bomber Under Study by McNamara," *Air Force Times*, November 23, 1966, p. 11; and Francis P. Hoeber, *Slow to Take Offense: Bombers, Cruise Missiles and Prudent Deterrence* (Washington, D.C.: Center for Strategic and International Studies, Georgetown University, 1977), especially p. 4.

8. Walter Andrews, " 'Split-Decision' Paper on New AMSA Bomber Now Before Secretary Nitze for Approval," *Armed Forces Journal International*, November 23, 1968, p. 5; Charles W. Rogers, "The National Security Decision Process: A B-1 Case Study" (Air University, April 1978).

9. Details on the SRAM can be found in Linnee, "SRAM and SCAD"; Edgar E. Ulsamer, "New Dimension in Nuclear Deterrence," *Air Force and Space Digest*, December 1969, pp. 65–72; and Edgar E. Ulsamer, "SRAM: The Last Word in Defense Suppression," *Air Force and Space Digest*, February 1972, pp. 28–34.

made it useful for little else. The SRAM project team was careful to moderate any claims and to downplay any characteristics that might threaten existing Air Force doctrine. As one of the team noted:

The trick in any innovation is to balance the demands of the innovators with the political reality. We always took care to list modifications as "refurbishments" rather than as "upgrades." We kept everything as incremental as possible. It's a lot less threatening that way.[10]

Due both to the technological superiority of the SRAM over the Hound Dog and to the political skill of the SRAM design team, the new weapon won ready acceptance within the Air Force and entered full production in 1972. By contrast, from the outset the project to replace the Quail decoy became mired in controversy, which shaped the Air Force attitude toward long-range cruise missiles throughout the 1970s. The Quail replacement became wrapped up in intraservice and Defense Department politics that struck at the heart of the rationale for the penetrating bomber.

The controversy began with the fact that the Quail was not an optimal decoy for a low-level penetrating bomber. Having been designed in the 1950s, when penetrating bombers flew at high altitudes, the Quail could be a decoy for a bomber only in high-altitude flight and therefore could be used for only a portion of the B-52's flight profile. Because of its size, moreover, the Quail could be carried only in limited numbers aboard each aircraft. By the mid-1960s, the Air Force clearly recognized that it needed an advanced decoy to augment the low-level penetrating bomber of the future.[11] As a result, the Air Force, the Strategic Air Command (SAC), and corollary agencies within the Department of Defense undertook a series of studies between 1967 and 1969 to establish the criteria for a decoy that would be capable of operating in the projected environment of Russian defenses. Of the many criteria arrived at, one was critical: the new decoy had to be compatible with the rotary launching rack developed for the SRAM. Bomber operations, it was concluded, would best be served if the new decoy, like the SRAM, were carried within the weapons

10. Interview, August 9, 1977. Also *Department of Defense Appropriations for 1971,* Hearings before a subcommittee of the House Committee on Appropriations, 91 Cong. 2 sess. (GPO, 1970), pt. 1, pp. 599–604. Confirming evidence was also obtained in interview, July 12, 1977.

11. James R. Bridges, "An Analysis of USAF Training and Training Equipment Policies for SRAM and SCAD" (Air University, May 1974); James H. Haessler, "Advanced Decoy Missiles for Bomber Penetration" (Air University, May 1972); Linnee, "SRAM and SCAD"; and Edgar E. Ulsamer, "SCAD—Electronic Stand-In for the B-52," *Air Force,* November 1972, pp. 43–47.

bay of a penetrating bomber and were made interchangeable with the bomber's armaments. It was this interchangeability criterion that created the controversy over the new decoy and later over the long-range cruise missile.[12]

Requiring that the new decoy fit the SRAM launcher imposed severe constraints on its size, volume, and weight, and hence on its range. Yet it was clear that the decoy had to travel much farther than the SRAM: a decoy limited to a one-hundred-mile range would provide only a few minutes' protection against Russian defenses. Therefore, Colonel Archie L. Wood, a member of the study group formed to examine decoys in 1967, proposed that the decoy be propelled by one of the small turbofan engines then under development by Williams Research Corporation and by other contractors. If it lived up to its promise, this engine would give a range of at least 500 miles. Concurrently, however, a private research organization suggested adding a nuclear warhead to the decoy in order to ensure that the Russians would be forced to expend resources on destroying those missiles even if they were recognized by radar as decoys.[13]

To senior Air Force officers, of course, a decoy with a long range and armed with a nuclear warhead sounded very much like a standoff weapon. Moreover, there were serious questions about the technological feasibility of propelling and guiding a cruise missile over such long distances. Then skeptics of the penetrating bomber within the Department of Defense Office of Program Analysis and Evaluation (PA&E) quickly seized upon Wood's concepts as an alternative to the costly B-1. In short, the decoy quickly became transformed from a straightforward augmentation of the B-52's penetration capability into a potential competitor to the penetrating mission itself and hence to the B-1 aircraft.[14]

The Air Force responded by monitoring and managing the program's development as closely as possible in order to ensure that the decoy did not become a full-fledged standoff weapon. The Air Force Systems Command took the unprecedented step of acting as subsystems integrator, a role normally reserved for the prime contractor. It placed the decoy project within the Systems Program Office designated for Reconnaissance, Strike and Electronic Warfare. Such close monitoring ensured that

12. Interviews, July 28, 1977; August 4, 1977. Also Ulsamer, "SCAD—Electronic Stand-In for the B-52," p. 47.
13. Interviews, July 28, 1977; August 4, 1977. Also Ulsamer, "SCAD—Electronic Stand-In for the B-52," pp. 44–47.
14. Interviews, July 12, 1977; July 13, 1977; July 28, 1977; and August 4, 1977.

the decoy—now named the subsonic cruise armed decoy, or SCAD—would remain an augmentation of, rather than a replacement for, the penetrating bomber.[15] The missile that ultimately emerged from this process was a scant 168 inches long and 21 inches in diameter. With a nuclear warhead, it would have a range of roughly 1,000 miles.[16]

Within this context the SCAD entered its final and fatal controversy. In June 1972, Secretary of Defense Melvin R. Laird asked for and received supplemental appropriations to begin work on weapons that would provide assurances against any failure in the newly signed SALT I treaty. Among such programs was a vaguely defined strategic cruise missile for the Navy. Laird had first heard of cruise missile technology while serving on the House Appropriations Committee. His enthusiasm was fed both by Navy aides and by analysts in PA&E. He also felt that the Air Force was resisting the concept in order to protect the B-1. Laird therefore hoped that high-level OSD support for a new Navy cruise missile program would force the Air Force to develop its own long-range cruise missile.[17]

For the moment, his hopes came to naught. Throughout 1972 and 1973, the debate grew more intense between those who wished to see the new Air Force decoys unarmed (subsonic cruise unarmed decoy—SCUD) and those who wished to see them armed (SCAD). At issue, of course, was the role of the penetrating bomber. A decoy with a 1,000-mile range and a nuclear warhead could grow into a standoff weapon. The advocates of such a development were explicit in their quest for a standoff replacement for the B-1. The issue, therefore, had fully crystallized. Both sides in the SCAD-SCUD debate wanted to force a resolution. Thus, on April 13, 1973, at a meeting of the Defense Systems Acquisition Review Council (DSARC), analysts from PA&E confronted analysts from the Air Force and urged that the decoys either be fully armed or canceled outright; PA&E saw unarmed decoys as a waste of money. Ironically, rather than

15. On the role of the development office, see Michael L. Yaffee, "USAF Unit Seeks Integrator Role," *Aviation Week and Space Technology,* May 10, 1971, pp. 14–15; "ASD to Keep Major SCAD Responsibility," *Aviation Week and Space Technology,* June 26, 1972, pp. 139–40; and Ulsamer, "SCAD—Electronic Stand-In for the B-52," pp. 44–47.

16. "B-52 Ideas Sought," *Air Force Times,* March 8, 1972, p. 18; "New SCAD Contracts Awarded by USAF," *Aviation Week and Space Technology,* July 17, 1972, p. 15; and *Fiscal Year 1973 Authorization for Military Procurement, Research and Development, Construction Authorization for the Safeguard ABM, and Active Duty and Selected Reserve Strengths,* Hearings before the Senate Committee on Armed Services, 92 Cong. 2 sess. (GPO, 1972), pt. 4, pp. 2363–77.

17. Interviews, July 13, 1977; July 28, 1977; August 16, 1977; August 22, 1977. Also *Fiscal Year 1973 Authorization,* Addendum No. 1.

trying to control the SCAD program any longer, the Air Force proposed that because the costs of the decoy had grown so prohibitive, it should be canceled and, even more, that the missile was no longer needed by the B-1. The result was foreordained: on July 6, 1973, Deputy Secretary of Defense William Clements notified Congress that the SCAD would be terminated.[18]

The B-1 and the ALCM-A

If the Air Force had, for the moment, killed a standoff missile, it had by no means generated public enthusiasm for the B-1. The bomber was running into an increasingly heavy opposition that was less concerned with doctrinal subtleties than with the B-1's ever-growing costs and decreasing performance. Over several years the B-1 had fallen behind schedule, below requirements, and over its original cost ceilings. Moreover, at the specific urging of Secretary Laird, Congress in late 1973 directed the Air Force, first, to coordinate its cruise missile research programs left over from the SCAD project with those of the Navy and, second, to investigate a standoff application for such missiles.[19] The cost

18. Limited information on the SCAD-SCUD question can be found in *Fiscal Year 1974 Authorization for Military Procurement, Research and Development, Construction Authorization for the Safeguard ABM, and Active Duty and Selected Reserve Strengths,* Hearings before the Senate Committee on Armed Services, 93 Cong. 1 sess. (GPO, 1973), pt. 2, pp. 1026, 1171–72; *Department of Defense Appropriations for 1974,* Hearings before a subcommittee of the House Committee on Appropriations, 93 Cong. 1 sess. (GPO, 1973), pt. 7, p. 488; "Armed Decoy Project Scrubbed," *Air Force Times,* July 25, 1973, p. 34; and "DOD Halts SCAD Development as Costs Rise, Need Is Debated," *Aviation Week and Space Technology,* July 16, 1973, p. 22. Further information about DSARC was derived from two separate interviews on July 13, 1977; interview, July 28, 1977; and interview, August 16, 1977. See also Henry D. Levine, "Some Things to All Men: The Politics of Cruise Missile Development," *Public Policy,* vol. 25 (Winter 1977), pp. 117–68.

19. On B-1 performance gaps, see Dana Adams Schmidt, "Air Force Cuts B-1 Bomber Plan to Save Money, Speed Work," *New York Times,* February 12, 1971; "Controversy Over the B-1 Bomber Program," pp. 297–305; "Air Force Stretches B-1 Program, Ups Cost by $80 Million," *Aerospace Daily,* July 13, 1973, pp. 65–66; J. Phillip Geddes, "Rockwell International's B-1 at a Critical Point," *Interavia,* February 1975, pp. 132–38. On congressional action, see "Air Force, Navy to Develop Cruise Missile," *Aviation Week and Space Technology,* August 20, 1973, p. 24; A. A. Tinajero, "Cruise Missiles (Subsonic): U.S. Programs," Library of Congress Issue Brief 76018 (Congressional Research Service, 1978), p. 2; Fiscal Year 1974 Defense Authorizations Conference Report, October 16, 1973, and Fiscal Year 1974 Defense Appropriations Conference Report, October 13, 1973, especially pp. 32–36. Confirming and additional information came from interviews, July 8, 1977, and August 11, 1977.

to the Air Force of these two actions was clear: it had begun to lose control over the development of bomber-launched weapons. The culmination of this trend came in a directive from Deputy Secretary of Defense Clements to the Air Force on December 19, 1973, that required it to begin the development of a formal ALCM program using SCAD propulsion technology and the terrain-contour-matching navigation under exploration by the Navy.[20]

What had largely been implicit in the SCAD-SCUD debate was thus now explicit. The Air Force was being challenged to defend its B-1 bomber against a shift in doctrine. Opponents of the B-1 could now focus their efforts on the standoff solution to bomber modernization rather than merely express their concern over cost and performance figures. The Air Force's answer to the challenge, however, was ingeniously simple: they brought the SCAD back to life.[21] The weapon the Air Force offered as an ALCM was structurally identical to the SCAD, which it had earlier claimed would be insufficient for a standoff missile because of its small size and its design as a decoy. There was no search for a new design to meet the congressional and Defense Department directives because the ALCM-SCAD hybrid had the advantage of limited range. Within the Air Force, high-level opposition was directed, not at cruise missiles per se, but rather at *long-range* cruise missiles that could threaten the development of a penetrating bomber. Use of the SCAD airframe for a cruise missile thus served both to answer demands from outside actors and to keep the B-1 alive in the face of mounting opposition.

Ironically, however, it was Air Force efforts to save the B-1 that ultimately contributed to its demise. In an attempt to put the challenge of the ALCM to rest once and for all, the Air Force, at OSD direction, initiated a comprehensive study of bomber alternatives in August 1973. For the ensuing sixteen months, the Air Force, in conjunction with representatives from the OSD and the Joint Chiefs of Staff, worked on the widely heralded Joint Strategic Bomber Study (JSBS). The study looked at seven possible mixes of existing and potential aircraft, each armed with a varying number of gravity bombs, SRAMs, and ALCMs. Not surpris-

20. *Fiscal Year 1975 Authorization for Military Procurement, Research and Development, and Active Duty, Selected Reserve and Civilian Personnel Strengths,* Hearings before the Senate Committee on Armed Services, 93 Cong. 2 sess. (GPO, 1974), pt. 7, pp. 3704, 3718, 3629.

21. "SCAD Replacement Pact Near," *Aviation Week and Space Technology,* August 5, 1974, p. 19; and Clarence A. Robinson, Jr., "Cruise Missile Guidance Bids Near," *Aviation Week and Space Technology,* January 21, 1974, pp. 18–19.

ingly, the study concluded that the best possible force consisted of penetrating B-1 bombers rather than a force of standoff cruise missile carriers.[22]

The critical assumption of the JSBS was that the United States would spend a sum of money equal to that dedicated for B-1 construction. In other words, the study concluded that once cost was fixed at that level, a B-1 fleet put twice as many warheads on target as the next best fleet of bombers. This assumption necessarily gave the expensive B-1 bomber an advantage in marginal rates of return because the study failed to address the question of how many warheads on target should be factored into the computer model. In addition, the study made a number of questionable assumptions about American-Russian offensive-defensive interchanges and remained unduly optimistic in its assessment of American defensive electronic warfare capabilities. The results of the JSBS were so controversial that what the Air Force had hoped would be the definitive case in favor of the B-1 instead quickly became a rallying point for its opponents. Gleeful critics in Congress found it difficult to refrain from referring to the study as the "Joint Strategic B.S."[23]

In the meantime, the Navy's cruise missile program began to show great promise. Because the Navy did not constrain its missile to the dimensions of the SRAM launcher, it had greater range and could be a clear alternative to the Air Force cruise missile for the air-launched mission. As a result, the DSARC in late 1974 ordered that the Air Force ALCM project be phased back and closely coordinated with the Navy project.[24]

22. U.S. Department of Defense, Office of Director, Defense Research and Engineering, "Joint Strategic Bomber Study," declassified material, September 1, 1974. Also *Department of Defense Appropriations for Fiscal Year 1976*, Hearings before the Senate Committee on Appropriations, 94 Cong. 1 sess. (GPO, 1975), pt. 4, pp. 444–45; McCarthy, "The Case for the B-1 Bomber"; and Archie L. Wood, "Modernizing the Strategic Bomber Force Without Really Trying: A Case Against the B-1," *International Security*, vol. 1 (Fall 1976), pp. 98–116.

23. Interviews, July 28, 1977; August 11, 1977; June 19, 1980; and June 20, 1980. Also see Clarence A. Robinson, Jr., "USAF Manned Bomber Need Challenged," *Aviation Week and Space Technology*, March 24, 1975, pp. 18–19.

24. Clarence A. Robinson, Jr., "Navy to Act on Cruise Missiles," *Aviation Week and Space Technology*, August 13, 1973, pp. 12–14; J. Phillip Geddes, "The Air-Launched Cruise Missile," *Interavia*, June 1976, pp. 580–83; "DDR&E Said to Favor AF ALCM Cancellation; Switch to Navy SLCM Version," *Aerospace Daily*, October 29, 1974, p. 306; "Key Decisions on Cruise Missiles Near," *Aviation Week and Space Technology*, November 15, 1976, pp. 24–25; and "AF, Navy Officials Agree on Tomahawk Cruise Missile Advantages," *Aerospace Daily*, November 22, 1976, p. 108.

Thus the Air Force was steadily losing control over the ALCM program. It was caught in an impossible bind. If the Air Force did nothing to improve the range of its own missile, Defense Department officials could always turn to the Navy. If instead the Air Force began to increase the range of its ALCM, it would shoot itself in the foot. Either way, the B-1 would be undercut.

Although the B-1 was subject to cost overruns and performance failures, it was a superlative aircraft. The real question was whether it was sensible to purchase 244 of these planes at $80 million to $100 million apiece when equally effective alternatives might be available for substantially less money.[25] Matters came to a head in mid-1976 when Congress adopted a measure designed to appease both critics and supporters. After several attempts to kill the B-1 outright, House and Senate conferees directed that procurement funds for the first eight B-1s be allocated at the rate of only $87 million per month through January 31, 1977. Although this would not terminate expenditures on the troubled program, it would ensure that the next administration would have the chance to evaluate the aircraft before buying it in bulk.[26]

In the interim, the Air Force tried to solve the challenge of a long-range Navy cruise missile by extending the range of its own missile, but not to the point that the rationale for the B-1 would be threatened. At a meeting of the DSARC on January 9, 1977, however, shortly before the Carter administration assumed office, the OSD directed the Air Force to develop an extended-range ALCM by stretching the fuselage of its prototype missile and to give the extended-range missile (ALCM-B) priority over the shorter-range ALCM-A. Finally, the OSD ordered that the Air Force project merge with the Navy cruise missile program in a Joint Cruise Missile Project Office, but with the Navy in control. The

25. On cost overruns and technical characteristics of the B-1, see "Controversy Over the B-1 Bomber Program"; John L. McLucas, "The Case for a Modern Strategic Bomber," *AEI Defense Review*, vol. 2 (1981), pp. 13–24; "USAF Cuts B-1 Maximum Speed," *Aviation Week and Space Technology*, June 16, 1975, p. 18; *Fiscal Year 1978 Authorization for Military Procurement, Research and Development, and Active Duty, Selected Reserve and Civilian Personnel Strengths*, Hearings before the Senate Committee on Armed Services, 95 Cong. 1 sess. (GPO, 1977), pt. 1, p. 578; and Nicholas Wade, "Battle of the B-1 Bomber: How a Coalition Beat High Odds to Bring Down Costly Plane," *Washington Post*, July 31, 1977.

26. See Katherine Johnsen, "Conferees Compromise on B-1 Funding," *Aviation Week and Space Technology*, September 6, 1976, p. 41.

Air Force had thus been ordered to build a true standoff missile, with Navy supervision to ensure compliance.[27]

The stretched fuselage of the ALCM-B made the missile incompatible with the doctrine of penetration because it extended the ALCM's range to 1,300 miles or more. It also made the missile incompatible with the design of the B-1 because the aircraft had been built with three separate weapons bays, each just large enough to carry a SRAM launcher. The extension of the ALCM's length by five feet meant that it could no longer be carried internally. External mounting on wing pylons, however, would give the B-1 a substantially larger radar cross section, cut its speed and range, and thereby make it unsuitable for low-level penetration. With the B-1, therefore, the Air Force faced two choices: either not carry the ALCM-B at all or undermine the principal design features of the aircraft.[28] Consequently, in order to save the B-1, the Air Force fell back on the B-52, the plane it had hoped to retire from service, proposing a mixed force of penetrating B-1s armed with SRAMs and ALCM-As and stand-off B-52s armed with the long-range ALCM-B. The mixed force would mean a smaller purchase of B-1s than the 244 originally envisioned, but it would still keep the penetrating mission alive under the rationale of diversifying the bomber force.[29] By early 1977, therefore, the stage was set for the final confrontation.

Bomber Politics and the ALCM-B

Immediately upon assuming office, President Jimmy Carter reduced the planned 1977 purchase of B-1s from eight to five and ordered Secretary of Defense Harold Brown to undertake still another analysis of the

27. Deputy Secretary of Defense William Clements, Memorandum, January 14, 1977; "Services to Merge Cruise Missile Efforts," *Aviation Week and Space Technology,* April 4, 1977, p. 16; and "Cruise Missile Order," *Aviation Week and Space Technology,* January 24, 1977, p. 17.

28. Cecil Brownlow, "Quantity Cruise Missile Production Set," *Aviation Week and Space Technology,* February 21, 1977, p. 20; "Boeing USAF Missile Effort Set; $6.7 Million Obligated," *Aviation Week and Space Technology,* March 14, 1977, p. 23; and "USAF Pushes Long-Range Cruise Missile Version," *Aviation Week and Space Technology,* April 18, 1977, pp. 19–20.

29. *Department of Defense Appropriations for 1978,* Hearings before a subcommittee of the House Committee on Appropriations, 95 Cong. 1 sess. (GPO, 1977), pt. 2, pp. 315–19; *Fiscal Year 1978 Authorization,* Hearings, pt. 9, pp. 6104–05.

B-1 in order to investigate other alternatives to the bomber modernization question. In turn, Secretary Brown directed his assistant secretary for program, analysis, and evaluation, E. C. Aldridge, to chair the Modernization of the Strategic Bomber Force Study, with inputs from the Air Force, the Joint Chiefs of Staff, the Office of International Security Affairs, and the Office of Defense Research and Engineering. The study was transmitted to Brown on May 11, 1977.

Brown asked the group to focus on two critical factors. First, he wanted a reassessment of the intelligence estimates about Russian air defenses and therefore directed that the analysis examine the likelihood that the Russians might soon deploy look-down–shoot-down radars capable of countering low-flying penetrating bombers. Second, he asked the group to determine whether the low radar cross section of the cruise missile would be an effective counter to such defenses. The study then analyzed two main alternative approaches to modernizing the bomber force: B-52s armed with cruise missiles and deferral of B-1 production, or B-52s with cruise missiles and continuance of B-1 production. This made it possible to analyze three types of forces: a pure penetrating bomber force, a pure cruise missile force, and a mixed force of penetrators and standoff bombers armed with cruise missiles.

In his memorandum transmitting the study to Secretary Brown, Aldridge stressed the overall conclusion of the group's efforts: "cost-effectiveness analysis does not provide a clear choice among the three types of forces; therefore, factors other than cost-effectiveness must be relied upon to make the decision." Three additional conclusions were offered: (1) for the next ten years, penetrating bombers were likely to be able to penetrate Russian air defenses; (2) for this period, the B-1 and the B-52Gs and Hs would be equally cost-effective as penetrators, but after that, the B-52 would be closed out by improvements in the Soviet Union's air defenses, but the B-1 would not; and (3) "a mixed force hedges against defense improvements that could be uniquely effective against either penetrating bombers or cruise missiles."

The difficulty in reaching a firm recommendation on which of the three options to take stemmed from the inability to determine how much Russian air defenses would improve after the ten-year period that the group took as its focal point, which carried the analysis through 1990. The study did conclude that the B-1 would be able to penetrate Russian air defenses longer than the B-52, but ultimately that it too would no longer be effective. It could not, however, say with certainty how much longer and therefore could not specify the time when the B-1 would be closed out. Thus, although the study could not choose one option as clearly superior, it did recommend continued production of the B-1 at a reduced rate to preserve the mixed bomber force as the best hedge against the uncertainties about Russian defenses. On the basis of this analysis Secretary Brown recommended to the president that he continue production of the B-1, but not at the rate requested by the Air Force.[30]

Brown's recommendation was reviewed during May and June at the White House by staff from the National Security Council and the Office of Management and Budget. Three factors clearly affected the general perspective with which the staff viewed the entire issue.[31] First, of course, was President Carter's stated opposition to the B-1 during his campaign. Any analytical case for continued production of the plane would have to be compelling if the president were to reverse himself on what had become the political symbol of his attitude toward defense spending. Second was the relation between what would be decided on the B-1 and the ALCM on the one hand and the SALT II treaty negotiations with the Soviet Union on the other. After the Russians' summary rejection of the March comprehensive proposal, the United States had proposed to the Soviet Union in late April a "three-tier" approach in which ALCMs with a maximum range of 2,500 kilometers would be permitted. It would be unfair to conclude that the administration was preserving the long-range ALCM option because it had already decided to cancel the B-1. But it would not be unfair to conclude that the administration was trying to preserve this option should it decide to cancel the B-1 penetrator and opt for the standoff force of B-52s armed with long-range cruise missiles. Third,

30. Information on the 1977 studies was derived from interviews, August 1, 1977; August 3, 1977; August 8, 1977; July 19, 1980; July 21, 1980; and July 23, 1980. These interviews supplemented and clarified the severely sanitized version of the April 29, 1977, *Modernization of the Strategic Bomber Force* obtained by the American Foundation of Scientists through the Freedom of Information Act and made available to the authors. Also Harold Brown, "The B-1 Cruise Missile Decision," *Commanders Digest*, September 15, 1977; press conference by Harold Brown, July 1, 1977; *Hearings on H.R. 8390: Supplemental Authorization for Appropriations for Fiscal Year 1978 and Review of the State of U.S. Strategic Forces; also Reprogramming Action Nos. FY 78-2 P/A, FY 78-3 P/A, and 78-4 P/A*, Hearings before the House Committee on Armed Services, 95 Cong. 1 sess. (GPO, 1977); and *Department of Defense Appropriations for 1979*, Hearings, pt. 1, p. 373.

31. This account of White House decisionmaking on the B-1 is based on interviews held on June 19 and July 21, 1980. For the relation between SALT II negotiations at the time and the B-1/ALCM decision, see Strobe Talbott, *Endgame: The Inside Story of SALT II* (Harper and Row, 1979), pp. 83–106.

and directly related to the second, were concerns over the political and strategic implications of the increasing vulnerability of the Minutemen. Key White House officials were unanimous that the United States could not put all its eggs into one strategic basket, the sea-based deterrent force. No decision had yet been made on the MX program. Carter's closest advisers wanted to make certain that, whatever the president decided about the B-1, the bomber leg of the triad would be kept effective. If the B-1 were to be canceled, therefore, a major program to keep the air-breathing component of the strategic forces viable was essential. The political ramifications, both at home and abroad, of failure to modernize both the bomber and the land-based force would be unacceptable. Thus, the first factor inclined Carter toward cancellation of the B-1. The second enabled him to do so without undue SALT II complications with the Soviet Union. And the third mandated that he had better have a defensible "big-league" program to preserve the bomber force if he did.

Carter's advisers presented the president with four options: (1) the Air Force case, argued eloquently by Chief of Staff General David C. Jones, for a force of 244 B-1 bombers at a cost of at least $30 billion; (2) the standoff or pure cruise missile force, with cancellation of the B-1 and any other plans to build a penetrating bomber, with the B-52s serving as the platforms for long-range ALCMs in the near term, and with an undefined follow-on platform when the B-52s wore out; (3) the arms control option of doing nothing for the bomber force, which meant canceling the B-1, living with aging B-52s, and ultimately accepting a two-legged triad; and (4) the curtailed B-1 force, which entailed a slowing of the development of the B-1, a careful look at its costs and capability, an imposing of less stringent requirements on it for penetration, speed, and range, and a production purchase of seventy to seventy-five.

On substantive grounds, none of the president's advisers recommended the first option. Each was highly skeptical of the Air Force's cost estimates and did not trust its assurances about the long-term ability of the B-1 to penetrate the likely improvements in Russian air defenses. Although the B-1 had a lower radar cross section than the B-52, nevertheless it was still large enough that it would have to rely on electronic countermeasures (ECM) that threw out a great deal of electromagnetic energy. The fear was that in time the Russians would improve their high-speed computer ability enough to be able to triangulate the electromagnetic energy generated by the B-1's ECM and thereby pinpoint its location. Secretary Brown was asked point-blank by the president "whether ECM will cut the mustard over the next twenty to thirty years." Brown could not guarantee that it would. White House analysis, in short, had reconfirmed the conclusion of the OSD's modernization study: the technical case for the B-1 was marginal. Jones, speaking for the Air Force, said nothing to alter that view. He knew that the Air Force case had two large soft spots—underestimation of costs and overestimation of penetration capability. He therefore chose not "to get into an analytic tennis match" with Brown, but rather to stress the perceptual dimension—that the United States had to be number one militarily in the world, that it could and therefore should build the world's best bomber, that it had already started to modernize the sea-based deterrent and was thinking about how to do so for the land-based force, and that now was the time to begin modernization of the bomber force. But the analytical and technical case against full-scale production of the B-1 was too strong, and the president could, with good conscience, reject it. As one adviser close to this decision stated: "I'm sure the president remembered his campaign promise, but the technical case against the Air Force proposal was compelling."

The third option was the preferred choice of those who were concerned about the arms control implications of cruise missiles. But because of concern about the increasing vulnerability of the Minuteman force and because the administration was not yet in a position to make a decision about the proposed MX (technical experts had just told the generals that the covered-trench deployment for the MX was highly vulnerable to attack), that option was summarily rejected by Carter and his advisers. At home and abroad, the political costs of allowing the strategic deterrent to become two-legged, or to appear to be slowly going entirely to sea, were intolerable.

The decision, therefore, came down to a choice between the second and fourth options. Brown, Zbigniew Brzezinski, and ultimately Bert Lance privately and strongly urged Carter to select the fourth option. Political and substantive factors lay behind their recommendation. Politically, some sort of B-1 program would strengthen the president's hand in selling a SALT II accord to the hard-liners in Congress, keep up the pressure on the Russians to negotiate, and lessen the pressure from the Air Force for the MX. (The B-1, moreover, was more clearly suited for retaliation, while the MX had first-strike overtones.) Substantively, reservations about how well a long-range cruise missile would perform, when one had not yet been dropped out of a B-52 and when the guidance problems were still formidable, made total reliance on an unproved weapon look too risky. A curtailed production of the B-1, moreover, would preserve the option of a mixed force that still remained the best hedge against future uncertainties. A more modest B-1 than that proposed by the Air Force, produced at a more modest rate, would enable the president to give the Air Force a new bomber, but also to say that he had kept his campaign promise because he had changed the program with respect to both cost and capability. Carter's advisers had fashioned the fourth option in order to give the president the ability to have his political cake and eat it too.

The president, however, had built up too strong a political investment in opposing production of the B-1 and perhaps also an ingrained dislike of it. He was impressed with the promised performance of the long-range ALCM. And perversely enough, as one participant put it: "The existence of the B-1 made the cruise missile option feasible." If the promise of the long-range ALCM were not fulfilled, the administration could resurrect the B-1. Thus, on June 30, the president canceled production of the B-1 and ordered development of the long-range ALCM to be accelerated. But concomitantly the B-1 was to be kept in development and flying, avionics were to be put in and tested, and the progress of the program was to be monitored closely. Whether politics per se decided the fate of the B-1 remains unclear. What is clear is that the case between the long-range ALCM and the B-1 was so close that politics *could* have decided it.

Once the final decision was made, development of the ALCM-B proceeded apace. The Air Force had no choice but to proceed with the only remaining development project that could keep the bomber viable. Ironically, the Air Force itself eventually cooled on the B-1, though not on a penetrating bomber. A reevaluation of bomber needs by the OSD in 1978 once again raised the choices among a pure force of penetrators, a pure force of standoff bombers, and a mixed force. Although the Air Force continued to believe in the merits of the penetrating bomber and the B-1 program had been kept alive as a technology base, Air Force officials had begun to switch their preferences to a high-altitude penetrator for the 1990s. Indeed, 1980 saw the unusual situation of such congressional critics of the B-1 as Senators John C. Culver and George S. McGovern demanding the development of a new manned penetrator based on the B-1 airframe. Some in the Air Force preferred to develop an interim penetrator based on the FB-111 for use in the 1980s. These differing viewpoints reflected either ignorance or knowledge of the Stealth technology program, which was designed to reduce the radar detectability of penetrating aircraft. By late 1980, the United States had committed itself to a standoff cruise missile bomber, but was once again exploring a penetrating bomber because of the belief that a mixed force was the best hedge against Russian air defense improvements.[32]

In retrospect, the ALCM-B was so long delayed because of the threat it presented to the Air Force's preferred mission of penetrating strategic bombardment. Indeed, so highly did the Air Force value its doctrine and new penetrator that it took the combined efforts of many in Congress, the Department of Defense, and the White House to force adoption of a long-range standoff cruise missile. The ALCM-B might have been built with far less difficulty and delay had its original proponents recognized and adapted to the dominant thinking within the Air Force. But these proponents had conspicuously forced crucial trade-offs into the open and in the process had deliberately challenged the central doctrine of the Air Force. Such zealotry delayed rather than promoted the service's acceptance of the inevitable. This story contrasts significantly with the behavior of the Navy cruise missile innovators.

The Navy and the Sea-Launched Cruise Missile

While the Air Force has a relatively tight hierarchical structure, the Navy has long been more decentralized and organized around three autonomous factions or "unions"—the surface fleet, the carrier fleet, and the underwater fleet. This decentralized structure shaped much of the politics of cruise missile development within the Navy because it gave cruise missile proponents there more freedom to maneuver than their Air Force counterparts had.

For most of the post–World War II era, admirals with an aviation background have dominated the Navy. Because aircraft carriers had proved their worth in World War II, the Navy subsequently organized itself around carrier attack groups, with the main function of the surface fleet being the support of the aviation arm. The bulk of the forward striking power of the Navy was concentrated in aircraft, and consequently the lion's portion of the Navy's budget was consumed by the carrier fleet. The

32. The 1978 Office of the Secretary of Defense bomber study was discussed in an interview, July 23, 1980. Information about the new bomber debate and the Stealth technology issue can be found in the *Congressional Record,* daily edition (July 1, 1980), pp. S9097–9104; "Pressure for New Bomber Rises in Congress," *Aviation Week and Space Technology,* February 11, 1980, pp. 12–14; "Congress and the Manned Penetrating Bomber Debate," *The Backgrounder,* no. 125 (Washington, D.C.: The Heritage Foundation, August 12, 1980); and "*Journal* Testimony on Stealth Leaks Before the House Armed Services Investigating Subcommittee," *Armed Forces Journal International,* October 1980, pp. 11–18.

Russian Navy, by contrast, was unable to match the American Navy in aircraft carriers. Instead, Soviet naval planners opted for relatively primitive and inexpensive surface-to-surface missiles as the principal means by which to exert long-range striking power. Even small patrol craft, when armed with long-range antiship missiles, could pose a significant threat to enemy fleets, a fact quickly recognized by Soviet naval officers who were forced to counter the American naval threat with limited resources. The surface-to-surface missile fulfilled the role for the Soviet Navy that the kamikaze had fulfilled for the Japanese: inexpensive air-breathing surface-to-surface weapons were designed to shatter a vastly superior enemy.[33]

For much of the postwar era, the American Navy tended to downplay the threat posed by Soviet antiship missiles because the aviators claimed that their aircraft could destroy Russian missile platforms before the missiles could be launched, or, failing that, could shoot down incoming missiles with such weapons as the F-14/Phoenix system and its predecessors. Dominant doctrine held that U.S. surface vessels did not need long-range surface-to-surface capabilities of their own. At stake was both a roles-and-missions assignment and a claim to a substantial portion of the Navy's budget. So long as the aviation arm continued to dominate the Navy, the chances of adopting a long-range surface-to-surface missile (SSM) remained slim.[34]

The Missile Challenge to the Surface Fleet in the 1960s

By the early 1960s, however, the continued emphasis on carrier forces provoked increasing dissatisfaction within the surface fleet. Several officers began to argue that the Russian antiship missile had to be taken

33. On the Navy's structure and factions, see Elmo R. Zumwalt, Jr., *On Watch: A Memoir* (Quadrangle, 1976). On postwar Soviet naval doctrine and force structure, see Norman Polmar, *Soviet Naval Power: Challenge for the 1970s* (New York: National Strategy Information Center, 1972); and Christoph Bertram, ed., *Power at Sea: I: The New Environment,* Adelphi Paper 122 (London: International Institute for Strategic Studies, 1976). Also "Navy Facing Anti-Ship Missile Challenge," *Aviation Week and Space Technology,* February 21, 1972, pp. 60–66; George Rogers, "Anti-Ship Warfare," *International Defense Review,* vol. 11 (1978), pp. 347–50; and William J. Ruhe, "Cruise Missile: The Ship Killer," *United States Naval Institute Proceedings,* vol. 102 (June 1976), pp. 45–52.

34. Interview, August 24–25, 1977. Also Robert D. Colvin, "Aftermath of the *Eilat,*" *United States Naval Institute Proceedings,* vol. 95 (October 1969), pp. 60–67; and Zumwalt, *On Watch,* p. 81. Further confirmation was obtained in interviews, July 12, 1977; August 9, 1977; and May 6, 1978.

seriously. Others argued that the surface Navy had for too long been subordinated to carriers. Dissent became vocal, and any incidents that dramatized the vulnerability of the surface fleet were likely to serve as rallying points to challenge the dominant doctrine.[35]

The Cuban missile crisis provided the first rallying point. During the course of preparing contingency plans for a possible invasion of Cuba, the Navy had to confront the fact that small *Komar-* and *Osa*-class patrol boats, armed only with Styx missiles, could hide out in the lengthy Cuban shoreline and threaten devastation of an invasion fleet. The Navy was forced to acknowledge the capabilities of antiship cruise missiles. This crisis spawned a series of study projects designed to augment terminal defenses against incoming missiles and to upgrade the air-to-surface capabilities of the aviation arm.[36] The most significant development was the agreement by Secretary of the Navy Paul H. Nitze to undertake a major research program on surface-to-surface missiles. The formal idea behind this initiative had originated with Captain Worth Bagley, then an assistant to Nitze, and Captain Elmo R. Zumwalt, Jr., then director of the Navy's Division of Systems Analysis. Nitze agreed in principle to the Bagley-Zumwalt proposal in 1966, which laid the groundwork for the Navy's eventual adoption of the sea-launched cruise missile (SLCM).[37]

A second major rallying point occurred on October 22, 1967. On this date, the Israeli destroyer *Eilat,* while patrolling off Port Said, was sunk in a matter of minutes by four Styx missiles launched from an Egyptian *Komar*-class patrol boat riding at anchor behind the Port Said breakwater. Here was dramatic evidence of the value of the Russian investment in surface-to-surface missiles.[38] Because the sinking of the *Eilat* was so shocking, it prompted immediate research by the Navy. Efforts focused both on short-term upgrading of the terminal defense capability of Navy vessels to shoot down incoming missiles and on longer-term efforts to procure an improved air-to-surface missile to attack enemy missile platforms.

35. See Levine, "Some Things to All Men," pp. 145 and 151. Also see Zumwalt, *On Watch,* p. 81.

36. Interview, August 24–25, 1977. Also see Michael L. Yaffee, "Navy Condor Ready for Pilot Production," *Aviation Week and Space Technology,* July 30, 1973, pp. 44–46.

37. Interviews, July 14, 1977, and August 1, 1977. Also Zumwalt, *On Watch,* p. 81.

38. On the *Eilat* incident, see Colvin, "Aftermath of the *Eilat*"; Brooke Nihart, "Harpoon: Navy's Answer to Soviet Missile Boats," *Armed Forces Journal International,* November 16, 1970, pp. 22–23; and "Navy Facing Anti-Ship Missile Challenge," pp. 60–66.

Admiral Thomas H. Moorer, the chief of naval operations (CNO), had long been concerned that Russian missile ships threatened the fleet; but he was convinced that the best response was a superior air-to-surface missile, not a new extended-range surface-to-surface missile for the surface fleet. Since 1966 he had therefore sponsored several study programs and had drafted a standing operational requirement (O.R.) for a new air-to-surface missile.

The surface sailors wanted an extended-range SSM as quickly as possible. They had Nitze's 1966 agreement for support, but they recognized that in the immediate future the chances of developing an SSM were not good. Admiral Moorer had chosen to respond to the *Eilat* incident by enhancing the capabilities of the carrier fleet, not those of the surface fleet. The 1966 Nitze directive, moreover, was not specific. It would take time to translate this document into a full-fledged program. Therefore, if the surface fleet were to press hard at the outset for its own SSM program, it would certainly face a funding conflict and probably provoke a more serious and debilitating roles-and-missions dispute with the aviators.[39]

The advocates of a new SSM quickly perceived that the best strategy was to "satisfice," not maximize—to adapt an air-to-surface missile to SSM applications rather than press for a completely new weapon. This would both minimize conflict and create the opening wedge for a genuine surface-to-surface missile. Consequently, the decision was made to treat Nitze's directive as an addendum to the standing operational requirement for a new air-to-surface missile, which was then revised in 1967 to include both a surface- and an air-launch capability. The surface sailors had gotten their foot in the door. But the aviators had extracted a significant concession, for as Admiral Zumwalt recalls:

> The most significant string attached to this order was the verbal message relayed to me through the aide system that the missile was to have a range of no more than fifty miles if it was to be acceptable to the CNO. Evidently, the aviators' union was still nervous about its prerogatives.[40]

The range limitation constrained the surface fleet more than the aviators. An air-launched missile could be carried to the general vicinity of its target and released from a distance of fifty miles without unduly en-

39. On Moorer's views, see Nihart, "Harpoon." Further information about the internal political situation within the Navy was obtained from interviews, July 14, 1977; August 22, 1977; August 23, 1977; August 24–25, 1977; and May 6, 1978.

40. Zumwalt, *On Watch*, p. 81. Also R. Meller, "The Harpoon Missile System," *International Defense Review*, vol. 8 (February 1975), pp. 61–66; and Nihart, "Harpoon."

dangering the aviator. The aviators had little reason to press for a longer missile range and indeed every incentive to press for a shorter range. They were justifiably skeptical about releasing missiles from over-the-horizon distances because the guidance problems at such distances were still unsolved. Only the surface fleet wanted the longer ranges, the only means by which the surface fleet on its own could fire at Soviet missile ships before they fired their missiles at American ships. Yet so long as the aviators were developing the new tactical missile, a dramatic increase in range was not likely to come about.

It therefore became clear to the surface fleet proponents that their only hope lay in ensuring that the new air-to-surface missile would have as much growth potential as possible; thus it was crucial to make certain that the new missile was fitted with an air-breathing, not a rocket, engine. (A rocket engine was constrained in range because of the weight added by the need to carry its own oxidizers.) Yet the quest for an air-breathing engine had to be conducted in such a way as to avoid alarming the aviators. This, in turn, required a tacit alliance with the aviators against the ordnance division of the Naval Material Command. As one participant made clear:

We recognized that if we were going to get cruise missiles, we would have to maximize the chance that there would be an air-launched cruise missile. The fundamental obstacle would be the carrier Navy. The major bureaucratic challenge would therefore be tasking the O.R.

If the O.R. were sent to NAVORD [Naval Ordnance Systems Command], it would have failed because of carrier opposition and because NAVORD couldn't do anything right anyway. If it were sent out as an advanced weapon, it would go to R&D, where it would have languished forever. So it was drafted as an O.R. to the advanced group of Air-05 [the Material Acquisition Division of the Air Systems Command].[41]

This manipulation set in train the program that ultimately produced the Harpoon cruise missile. The Naval Air Systems Command (NAVAIR) took the lead in exploring design concepts for the new air-to-surface missile ordered by Admiral Moorer, accepting the proviso that the new missile would also be capable of surface launching. By 1971, competitive airframe contracts had been awarded to two companies; by 1974, a development contract had been awarded for an air-breathing turbojet engine. Thus by the early 1970s the surface fleet proponents of an extended-range ship-to-ship missile had allied themselves with the aviators to push

---

41. The quotation is from interview, August 24–25, 1977. Further confirmation came from interviews, August 22, 1977; August 23, 1977; and May 6, 1978.

for a new air-to-surface missile. While the Harpoon missile was not a true extended-range SSM, it represented a victory for the surface fleet dissidents, but what they ultimately sought was the longer-range Tomahawk, not the Harpoon.

Intraservice Politics and the Tomahawk Missile

After assuming the duties of chief of naval operations, Elmo Zumwalt tried to interest the service in a submarine-launched antiship cruise missile. At nearly the same time, Melvin Laird wanted to develop a strategic cruise missile for insurance if the SALT I treaty failed. It was the confluence of these two stimuli that produced the program for the Tomahawk missile—one that did not readily fulfill the expectations of either Zumwalt or Laird, but aptly fulfilled the needs of the surface fleet.

Shortly after becoming CNO, Zumwalt appointed Admiral Robert Kaufman to chair an ad hoc panel on a submarine-launched antisurface ship interim missile. The Kaufman panel's charge was to investigate both a new antiship missile and for later development a new submarine to carry it. The panel was formed in September 1970 and ordered to report by November.[42] The Kaufman panel wanted to propose cost-effective alternatives for an attack submarine that would succeed the recently completed SSN-668 class. But in order to accommodate both antisubmarine torpedoes and antiship missiles, the panel deemed it necessary to increase the hull size of the new submarine. Moreover, because the antisubmarine mission was valued most, the submarine commander would have to keep his torpedo tubes fully loaded with antisubmarine weapons at all times. This, in turn, pushed the Kaufman panel to recommend that the new antiship cruise missile be launched from vertical tubes. This would have the added advantage of extending the range of the missile because vertical tubes could be made larger in diameter than torpedo tubes, thereby allowing a larger missile engine. In its final report the Kaufman panel called for a new tactical antiship missile that would be launched from a new submarine, called the submarine tactical antiship weapons system (STAWS).[43]

42. *Naval Nuclear Propulsion Program—1971*, Hearing before the Joint Committee on Atomic Energy, 92 Cong. 1 sess. (GPO, 1971), p. 18. See also Levine, "Some Things to All Men," pp. 127–28.

43. Some details on the Kaufman panel and the STAWS proposal can be found in Levine, "Some Things to All Men," pp. 128, 147–50; and in *Fiscal Year 1975 Authorization*, Hearings, pt. 7, pp. 3660–61. Further details were provided by interviews, August 15, 1977; August 29, 1977; and September 2, 1977.

After the panel returned its recommendations, the Naval Air Systems Command, then overseeing development of the Harpoon, was asked to investigate the design of the proposed tactical antiship missile. In April 1971, a NAVAIR study group returned a report recommending that the new missile take one of three general configurations: an encapsulated Harpoon for vertical launch; a follow-on to the Harpoon with twice the payload and a range of 120–140 miles; or a strategic land-attack cruise missile with a 1,600-mile range. The submariners were not interested in the last proposal. They were well satisfied with the Polaris and Poseidon missiles, and moreover they were skeptical that any air-breathing missile could obtain the ranges mentioned by NAVAIR. Nonetheless, the NAVAIR studies convinced Admiral Zumwalt that a long-range cruise missile could be built with relatively little difficulty. He therefore ordered studies to be conducted on developing an advanced cruise missile (ACM).[44]

At this point, Admiral Hyman G. Rickover, the "father of the nuclear Navy," entered the picture. He had begun development of a new 60,000-horsepower reactor in 1968 and wanted to mate this engine with the STAWS proposal. He had become convinced, moreover, that the Navy needed to enhance cruise missile capability. He began to lobby within the Navy and before several congressional committees for a fully dedicated cruise missile submarine based on his reactor, the STAWS design concept, and the advanced cruise missile proposals coming out of NAVAIR. Rickover thus sought to redefine the STAWS from an inexpensive attack submarine into a dedicated or single-purpose expensive submarine, and, in doing so, to sell his newest reactor to the Navy.[45] Rickover's interest served to sustain the advanced cruise missile project in the face of possible opposition because the divergence in design between the advanced cruise missile and the ongoing Harpoon program had led to a decision to

44. On the NAVAIR studies, see *Department of Defense Appropriations for Fiscal Year 1973*, Hearings before the Senate Committee on Appropriations, 92 Cong. 2 sess. (GPO, 1972), pt. 3, pp. 1445–47; and *Fiscal Year 1973 Authorization*, Hearings, pt. 4, pp. 2446–48. For a description of one of the design concepts proposed, see "Navy Explores New Cruise Missile," *Aviation Week and Space Technology*, September 13, 1971, p. 23. Further information was derived from interviews, August 22, 1977; August 23, 1977; and August 24–25, 1977.

45. See Rickover's testimony in *Department of Defense Appropriations for 1972*, Hearings before a subcommittee of the House Committee on Appropriations, 92 Cong. 1 sess. (GPO, 1971), pt. 8, pp. 19–23; *Department of Defense Appropriations for 1973*, Hearings before a subcommittee of the House Committee on Appropriations, 92 Cong. 2 sess. (GPO, 1972), pt. 9, pp. 42–45; and *Naval Nuclear Propulsion Program*, Hearing, pp. 13–19, 52–61, 219–21.

create another entirely separate advanced cruise missile project office. This was set up under Captain Walter M. Locke, the guidance project officer in the old Harpoon office, and placed administratively under NAVAIR. The Naval Ordnance Systems Command (NAVORD), however, wanted to obtain control of the ACM program under the rationale that it was the appropriate parent organization for developing surface-to-surface missiles. This argument was sound in terms of the formal organization charts, but weak in terms of practical bureaucratic politics, for NAVORD faced two determined opponents in Admirals Zumwalt and Rickover.

Zumwalt insisted on developing a cruise missile for use aboard surface vessels. He recognized that, because of the power within the Navy of the carrier admirals, his best chance lay in letting the innovators in NAVAIR develop a missile such as the Harpoon, which could later be adapted to other applications. Rickover believed that NAVAIR was more imaginative and efficient than NAVORD. The result of this high-level sponsorship and interest was that the ACM program office remained under NAVAIR, where work proceeded rapidly.[46] Although Rickover's sponsorship served to keep the ACM project alive, ironically it proved the kiss of death for the STAWS program. STAWS had grown under Rickover's prompting into an expensive proposal that contradicted Zumwalt's commitment to purchasing a larger number of less costly ships, not fewer more costly ones. The STAWS program was quietly dropped in 1972.[47]

Although the original impetus had disappeared with the STAWS concept, the research on cruise missiles was pushed forward at Zumwalt's personal insistence. At this point, Secretary of Defense Melvin Laird sought from Congress an authorization for a vaguely defined strategic cruise missile (SCM) for possible use aboard those Polaris submarines retired from the fleet under the terms of SALT I. The ACM office had itself explored a strategic variant of cruise missiles. Because the two programs—the ACM and the SCM—shared a common technological orientation, it made great sense to consolidate them into one program. Politics, however, was of even greater importance than shared technology. Zumwalt and the advocates of a long-range antiship missile knew they

---

46. The story of the separation of the ACM from the Harpoon office and of NAVORD's attempts to gain control was obtained in interviews, August 19, 1977; August 23, 1977; August 24–25, 1977; August 29, 1977; and May 6, 1978.

47. *Fiscal Year 1974 Authorization,* Hearings, pt. 4, p. 2676, and *Fiscal Year 1975 Authorization,* Hearings, pt. 7, pp. 3660–61.

could better protect their program politically if they consolidated it with Laird's missile. On its own the tactical antiship variant of the ACM faced an uncertain future. Although as yet it was only an internal study concept, its critics within the Navy were powerful and numerous. The strategic cruise missile, however, was directly sponsored by the secretary of defense, even though Laird was as much interested in inducing the Air Force to explore ALCM technology as he was in finding a good use for retired Polaris submarines.

Therefore, if the ACM could be integrally linked to Laird's missile and treated simply as a technological derivative rather than a wholly separate program, its future would be better assured. It was thus only sensible to arrange a marriage of convenience.[48] And in the process Zumwalt had created a tacit alliance with Laird. Combined with Zumwalt's manipulation, Laird's intervention thus set the Navy on a nearly irreversible course. By November 6, 1972—the date of the consolidation order—the surface fleet proponents of a new surface-to-surface missile had effectively won their battle, even if they did not realize it at the time. There were many bureaucratic obstacles and technological uncertainties still to overcome, but the consolidation tied a weak proposal to a strong one and vastly increased the likelihood that the Navy would produce a long-range surface-launched antiship missile.

Ironically, it was the strategic variant that proved the most troublesome aspect of the entire project. Although Congress fully endorsed the antiship missile, the justification for the strategic variant appeared unclear, and the weapon came under severe criticism. Defense Department officials had been initially interested in the SCM-ACM project in order to keep up research on turbofan propulsion after the demise of the SCAD project, but this rationale disappeared with the revival of the ALCM-A project. Thus, the technological justification for the strategic missile that the Defense Department could present to Congress was quite tenuous, and the strategic rationale appeared weak. Congressional critics feared that a nuclear-armed cruise missile aboard attack submarines would jeopardize the antisubmarine warfare mission and add nothing to the sea-

48. The phrase *marriage of convenience* comes from Levine, "Some Things to All Men," p. 154. For more on the strategic cruise missile program, see Nihart, "Harpoon"; Thomas J. Canfield and Raymond A. Kellett, Jr., "Cruise Missile: An Examination of Development Decisions and Management" (thesis, Naval Post-Graduate School, 1978), particularly p. 42; and *Fiscal Year 1974 Authorization,* Hearings, pt. 4, pp. 2636, 2672. Also see *Fiscal Year 1973 Authorization,* Addendum No. 1, pp. 4244, 4340–41.

based strategic deterrent. The 2,000-mile range of the missile would require the submarine that carried it to operate closer to Russia's shore-lines than the Poseidon-armed strategic ballistic missile submarines in order to hit the same targets. Yet the Navy had sought for years to extend, not decrease, the range of its strategic missiles in order to increase the operating ocean space of its strategic submarines and reduce their vul-nerability to detection. Moreover, if the attack submarine was to be used in the strategic deterrent mode, then it would become a platform dedi-cated to retaliating against Russian cities, not to killing enemy subma-rines. It was no surprise, therefore, that in July 1973 Congress froze fund-ing for the strategic SLCM; and the Senate later eliminated the entire project. House and Senate conferees agreed in late 1973 to restore fund-ing for the strategic program, but only with the proviso that the Navy de-velop a clear rationale for it and simultaneously explore tactical antiship cruise missiles.[49]

The fuzziness in the Navy's official mission for the SLCM, however, was not mindless. What was strategic nonsense to Congress made effec-tive politics within the Navy. The conceptual flexibility of the Navy cruise missile program offered innovators the means to overcome significant obstacles within the Navy in their quest for a long-range surface-to-surface missile. It offered Defense Department officials an opportunity to spur Air Force work on the ALCM. It did not unduly raise the hackles of the carrier lobby because of its very fuzziness. It later permitted the Navy to compete for the ALCM mission, made a ground-launched ver-sion readily available, and resulted in an antiship missile. Had not such flexibility existed from the outset, the technologists might well have pre-maturely closed their designs; and the opponents of a surface-to-surface missile might very well have killed it. So long as the strategic cruise mis-sile, however vaguely defined, was perceived as the lead program within the Navy, the tactical antiship version could be treated as a fortuitous spin-off. Although the Navy drafted a requirement for a tactical version of the cruise missile in November 1974, it distinctly paced this program behind the one for the strategic cruise missile. Before late 1974, there-fore, the Navy repeatedly emphasized that it had no requirement for a tactical antiship missile. After late 1974, when it had developed such a

---

49. Robinson, "Navy to Act on Cruise Missiles"; "Air Force, Navy to Develop Cruise Missile"; and the report of the Appropriations conference committee for Fis-cal Year 1974, House Report 93-588 (December 20, 1973), pp. 32–36.

requirement, the Navy repeatedly stressed that it was merely investigating an inexpensive derivative of the strategic program initiated by Secretary Laird.[50]

Such moderation in pursuit of an antiship missile extended to the design features of the SLCM as well. Until late 1976, development plans called for mounting a Harpoon turbojet engine rather than the more capable turbofan engine on the antiship version of the cruise missile. As later testimony was to indicate, the turbofan engine was the superior choice for an antiship missile. By adhering to the turbojet engine during the early stages of development, however, the proponents of the antiship missile minimized the visibility of their program and hence their challenge to the carrier fleet.[51]

Finally, the carrier fleet was not the only source of potential opposition to an antiship missile. The missile was also downplayed before Congress, where the early stages of development posed two problems. First, although Congress itself had urged in 1973 that a tactical antiship missile be built, the costs of such a program alone would have been prohibitively high. But if the missile was treated as merely one of a generic set of missiles, including the strategic version, development costs could be amortized over several programs and thereby kept low. Second, it was crucial to make the SLCM and the shorter-range Harpoon look as dissimilar as possible. If Congress had felt so inclined, it could have canceled the Harpoon, which had suffered cost overruns, in favor of the more capable SLCM. But this would deny the Navy a surface-to-surface missile capability in the near term and also threaten to open fully the roles-and-missions dispute between the carrier and surface fleets. Proponents of the antiship version of the SLCM could always downplay their ultimate goal of obtaining a truly long-range antiship missile out of the SLCM program by pointing to the fact that they had the Harpoon. If the Harpoon was

50. See the testimony in *Fiscal Year 1975 Authorization,* Hearings, p. 4245, and *Fiscal Year 1975 Authorization,* Hearings, pt. 7, pp. 3666–67. See also chap. 3 in this book.

51. See the testimony in *Fiscal Year 1975 Authorization,* Hearings, pt. 7, pp. 3634, 3636, and especially 3684–85. Compare to the testimony in *Hearings on Military Posture and H.R. 5068 [H.R. 5970]: Department of Defense Authorization for Appropriations for Fiscal Year 1978,* Hearings before the House Committee on Armed Services, 95 Cong. 1 sess. (GPO, 1977), bk. 2, pt. 3, p. 1105; and also Michael L. Yaffee, "Cruise Missile Engine Design Pushed," *Aviation Week and Space Technology,* July 7, 1975, pp. 41–43.

killed, they would be forced into the open. Thus, from both a cost and a bureaucratic perspective, it was better to downplay the antiship missile and press for the strategic missile. As one observer noted:

> It's not unfair to say that at first the strategic missile was forced down the Navy's throat. It had to be pushed, but you can say that it provided the impetus for Tomahawk. It got us the bucks. We couldn't have carried the tactical SLCM on our own.[52]

The Strategic SLCM in Search of a Mission

For a variety of reasons, therefore, the Navy chose to emphasize the ill-defined strategic cruise missile rather than any specific derivatives. The missile played a role within the Navy, not as Melvin Laird had intended, but rather as the vehicle by which intraservice disputes could be deferred until the antiship missile became a fait accompli. So as not to raise the hackles of the carrier admirals, the surface fleet made the submariners the spear carriers in this campaign. They were forced to go before Congress each year to defend a program for themselves that they did not want. Aside from their skepticism about the promised performance of the SLCM, the submariners were downright hostile to the operational implications of a strategic SLCM for their boats. The principal rationale offered for the weapon was that it would provide a strategic nuclear reserve aboard attack submarines for use in controlled responses in limited nuclear wars or in a third strike. The submariners also found themselves citing such dubious merits as the weapon's leverage in arms control negotiations.[53]

52. The quotation is from interview, August 23, 1977. Further evidence came from interview, August 24–25, 1977. Also see the testimony in *Hearings on Military Posture and H.R. 11500* [*H.R. 12438*]: *Department of Defense Authorization for Appropriations for Fiscal Year 1977*, Hearings before the House Committee on Armed Services, 94 Cong. 2 sess. (GPO, 1976), pt. 1, p. 840; *Hearings on Military Posture and H.R. 5068*, Hearings, pt. 2, p. 347; *Department of Defense Appropriations for Fiscal Year 1978*, Hearings before the Senate Committee on Appropriations, 95 Cong. 1 sess. (GPO, 1977), pt. 4, p. 547; and *Fiscal Year 1976 and July–September 1976 Transition Period Authorization for Military Procurement, Research and Development, and Active Duty, Selected Reserve, and Civilian Personnel Strengths*, Hearings before the Senate Armed Services Committee, 94 Cong. 1 sess. (GPO, 1975), pt. 10, p. 5171.

53. *Fiscal Year 1975 Authorization*, Hearings, pt. 7, pp. 3620, 3628, 3686–87; *Fiscal Year 1976 and July–September Transition Period Authorization*, Hearings, pt. 10, pp. 5130–31; and *Hearings on Military Posture and H.R. 11500*, Hearings, pt. 1, p. 188.

To have built a submarine-launched strategic nuclear missile could have meant forcing attack submarines to offload valuable antisubmarine weapons in order to prepare for a mission that had little, if any, justification. To fire the SLCM at a target deep in the Soviet Union, moreover, would entail moving the attack submarines in toward enemy coastlines, thereby increasing the risk of detection. The firing of a SLCM would generate bubbles and acoustic signals that could reveal the submarine's location. In addition, because guidance alignment required at least twenty minutes after the missile was loaded into a torpedo tube, a submarine could fire only infrequent salvos while assuming high risks of detection. Finally, if the strategic SLCMs were to be integrated into the single integrated operational plan, attack submarines, like strategic ones, would be forced to keep in more frequent contact with SAC headquarters, thereby risking detection and sacrificing considerable operational flexibility.[54] Simply put, submarines could not be simultaneously attack and strategic.

Members of Congress were quick to notice such difficulties, but curiously enough there was little risk to the Navy that the SLCM program would be canceled, precisely because it was flexible and vague enough to gain wide support. It could serve as a technology program for advocates of increased research and development in Congress or the Defense Department. It could serve as a SALT bargaining chip for persons concerned with American-Russian arms control talks. It could serve as another addition to the strategic nuclear forces for those who were pressing for nuclear superiority. It could serve as the baseline technology for those who wished to see modernization of NATO's long-range theater nuclear forces. And it could serve as a prod to the Air Force for those who wished to accelerate the ALCM. The Navy's strategic cruise missile was a weapon system for all seasons precisely because it had no clearly defined mission. Few people in the Navy, particularly among the submarine forces, ever wanted the strategic SLCM. But few in the Navy were motivated strongly enough to work for its cancellation, and many outside the Navy, especially in the OSD, pushed strongly for it.[55]

54. J. Phillip Geddes, "The Sea-Launched Cruise Missile," *Interavia,* March 1976, pp. 260–64; Alexander R. Vershbow, "The Cruise Missile: The End of Arms Control?" *Foreign Affairs,* vol. 55 (October 1976), pp. 133–46; and *Fiscal Year 1975 Authorization,* Hearings, pt. 7, p. 3657. Further information was obtained in interviews, July 27, 1977; August 1, 1977; August 15, 1977; July 23, 1980; July 25, 1980; July 29, 1980; and July 30, 1980.

55. Interviews, July 7, 1977; July 8, 1977; July 21, 1977; and August 15, 1977.

By 1976, however, after the tactical antiship missile had gained considerable momentum, the environment was safe enough for the proponents of the antiship missile to come out in the open. Thus, in a highly significant shift in testimony, Admiral James L. Holloway III, the CNO, repeatedly argued in 1976 that the Navy had to pursue a tactical missile, even if the strategic variant were banned by Congress or by arms control negotiations.[56] This testimony opened the door for a major realignment in the Navy's cruise missile programs. The conference committee of the Armed Services Committees steered money toward the tactical SLCM and provided funds for a turbofan rather than a turbojet engine, thereby considerably extending the range of the antiship missile. Simultaneously, of course, the Navy moved quietly to drop the turbojet engine from its tactical variant. Thereafter, in response to congressional criticism about the utility of a strategic cruise missile, the Navy changed its tack. It gave the program a new name—the Tomahawk—and presented two variants —a conventionally armed Tomahawk antiship missile (TASM) and a nuclear-armed land-attack missile (TLAM). The latter was indistinguishable in design and capability from the earlier strategic cruise missile that had drawn such congressional criticism, but in order to preserve the variant, the Navy changed its mission. Rather than being targeted only against strategic targets within Russia, the TLAM would be a worldwide theater nuclear weapon. Later on, the Navy, under pressure from Secretary of Defense Brown, further refined the TLAM into the TLAM-N (the nuclear variant) and the TLAM-C (the conventional variant).[57]

In short, the decisions taken in 1976 formalized a chain of actions and decisions that had been carefully orchestrated over the preceding three years in the quest for a new extended-range antiship missile. Full recognition was given to the TASM by the Department of Defense in January 1977, at the DSARC stage II meeting, when Deputy Secretary Clements ordered the development of the TASM, the GLCM, and the ALCM, and a slowdown on the TLAM. Although Secretary of Defense Brown subsequently slowed the development of the antiship missile pending progress in over-the-horizon target-acquisition technology, the fundamental point

56. *Department of Defense Appropriations for Fiscal Year 1977*, Hearings before the Senate Committee on Appropriations, 94 Cong. 2 sess. (GPO, 1976), pt. 1, pp. 665–66; and *Department of Defense Appropriations for 1977*, Hearings before a subcommittee of the House Committee on Appropriations, 94 Cong. 2 sess. (GPO, 1976), pt. 2, pp. 130–32.

57. *Conference Report*, H. Rept. 1305, 94 Cong. 2 sess. (GPO, 1976); and *Hearings on Military Posture and H.R. 5068*, Hearings, bk. 2, pt. 3, pp. 1099, 1105.

remained unchanged. The surface fleet dissidents had won a major victory by 1976 and had successfully challenged the carrier admirals, the dominant group within the Navy.

Ironically, since 1976 the successor to the strategic cruise missile has remained a weapon largely in search of a mission. The TLAM has been viewed as a possible weapon for use in non-NATO theater nuclear contingencies (the worldwide mission), as a possible candidate for nuclear warfare at sea in defense of the fleet (the global sea control mission), and, to this day, as a strategic reserve. In order to develop the TLAM without signaling to NATO that the United States might develop the capability to put NATO's long-range theater nuclear forces (LRTNF) out to sea,[58] the Department of Defense, under the specific urgings of Congress, has promoted the TLAM-C, which was to serve as the airframe technology base for the TLAM during the sensitive negotiations over NATO's LRTNF modernization. The TLAM-C is now offered as a candidate for precision attacks against high-value shoreline targets, a mission equally dubious in view of the extraordinarily high costs of each missile. Although both versions of the TLAM remain vaguely defined and subject to continuing controversy, the Navy and the Congress have fully accepted the TASM. In short, the case of the Navy sea-launched cruise missile demonstrates that skill at bureaucratic politics can often overcome immense obstacles to weapons innovation.

Salt II and NATO's Theater Nuclear Forces

Until 1977, the Air Force and the Navy were resistant, if not hostile, to the development of long-range air- and sea-launched cruise missiles. The former threatened the mission of the penetrating bomber; the latter, the missions of both fleet aircraft and attack submarines. And yet, at the same time, because of the dynamics of SALT II negotiations, it was the long-range versions that most interested the Defense Department, the White House, and the State Department. By late 1976, the same pattern of developments began to happen to the ground-launched version. The White House, the OSD, and ultimately the State Department began to worry about both the Europeans' reactions to SALT II and their increasing concerns about the emerging imbalance in theater nuclear forces.

58. This point will be fully explained in the last section of this chapter.

Especially the latter factor pushed high-level civilians toward development of the ground-launched cruise missile, a system that neither the Army nor the Air Force wanted. In order to understand the dichotomy between service attitudes toward these three systems on the one hand and those of civilians at the pinnacles of executive power on the other, it is necessary to look at the SALT II negotiations and their effects on the NATO alliance.

Cruise Missiles in SALT II Politics

From 1973, when negotiations on a SALT II accord began in earnest, until June 1979, when the Treaty on the Limitation of Strategic Offensive Arms was signed between the United States and the Soviet Union, the cruise missile figured centrally in the packages put together by the executive and offered to the Russians. Initially, the ALCM was the most prominent, but by 1976 the SLCM and GLCM had developed equal visibility. All three versions played roles: first, as bargaining chips by which to wrest concessions from the Russians; second, as political lubricants with which to gain the acceptance by Congress and the NATO allies of a SALT II accord; and, third, as significant military options to be protected in their own right because of their presumed enhancement of America's strategic retaliatory forces.

Over this seven-year period, the executive branch developed a seemingly endless number of SALT II packages to offer the Soviet Union. Many never saw the light of day. Three proposals, however, stand out because they were presented formally to the Russians, they affected Russian attitudes toward subsequent American proposals, and they highlight the larger political considerations that motivated high-level civilians and shaped their attitudes toward cruise missiles. The first is Henry Kissinger's offer of January 1976 and subsequent offers to count American bombers armed with cruise missiles as part of the 1,320 launchers mounted with multiple independently targetable reentry vehicles (MIRVs) permitted each party by the 1974 Vladivostok accord in exchange for constraints on the Russians' Backfire bomber. The second is the Carter administration's March 1977 comprehensive proposal, in which all cruise missiles were to be limited in range to 2,500 kilometers in exchange for deep cuts in both sides' overall strategic launchers and in Russia's heavy missiles. Third is the three-tier proposal made in April 1977 by the United States, in which ALCMs were limited in range to

2,500 kilometers, and SLCMs and GLCMs to 600 kilometers if they were deployed during a three-year period.[59]

In seeking to produce a SALT II accord, Gerald Ford and Henry Kissinger confronted three central problems: first, how to produce an agreement that would satisfy the equal overall aggregates proviso attached by the Senate to the SALT I treaty; second, what to do with the newly emerging cruise missile technology that had not been covered by SALT I, was being pushed by the Pentagon, and was increasingly worrying the Russians; and third, how to treat the Backfire bomber that appeared to some as an intermediate-range plane not capable of hitting the United States, to others as capable of being upgraded to reach the United States, and to the Russians as a system that should not be counted in the SALT II aggregates because it fell into the same category as America's theater nuclear forward-based systems (FBS) deployed in Europe. The Russians were particularly vehement about the Backfire issue, since in SALT I they had agreed to exclude FBS even though those systems could target the western military districts of the Soviet Union. The Backfire, they maintained, could not target the continental United States. The Americans were now asking them to count in the overall aggregates weapons that could not hit the United States while simultaneously insisting that weapons that could hit Russia should not be counted. It was the asymmetry in the American position that piqued the Russians.

The questions of overall aggregates, Backfires, and cruise missiles came to a head at Vladivostok in 1974. Kissinger's attitude toward the cruise missile remains unclear. Some say he viewed it only as a chip to be bargained away, but because of Pentagon resistance and Russian interest it instead became a chip that refused to go away. Others maintain that he never intended to trade away the cruise missile, particularly the ALCM, but only to use it to extract concessions from the Soviet Union because he accepted the then prevailing view that it would assist in preserving a mixed force of penetrators and standoff bombers.[60] The Russians, however, wanted to ban all cruise missiles with ranges over 600 kilometers, whether they were ground-, sea-, or air-launched. The United

59. This account of SALT II draws from Talbott, *Endgame,* especially chaps. 2–7, but differs in some key respects on the American negotiating position on cruise missiles before 1977.

60. Talbott, *Endgame,* pp. 31–37; Thomas W. Wolfe, *The SALT Experience* (Ballinger, 1979), pp. 171–78; and interviews held on June 26, June 27, and July 30, 1980. Our interviews incline us to believe that Kissinger held to the second view.

States countered (orally, according to some at Vladivostok, but certainly immediately afterward in an exchange of letters) that the air-launched ban applied only to ballistic, not cruise, missiles. To sweeten the pot, Kissinger agreed to count heavy bombers in the overall ceiling of 2,400 strategic launchers. The Soviet Union agreed to exclude FBS from the overall aggregates in return for the United States' dropping its insistence on a cut in Russia's heavy intercontinental ballistic missiles.

From January through September 1976, the Ford administration made three proposals to the Soviet Union in order to reach an accord on these two issues.[61] In January 1976 Kissinger flew to Moscow and proposed to limit the Russians to a total of 250 Backfires for five years, in return for which the United States would agree to count heavy bombers armed with cruise missiles in the subceiling agreed to at Vladivostok. ALCMs with ranges over 2,500 kilometers and SLCMs and GLCMs with ranges over 2,000 kilometers would not be deployed. The Russians countered with a 600-kilometer limit for the SLCM and GLCM and apparently did not oppose the 2,500-kilometer range limit for the ALCM. Based on an initiative by the director of the Arms Control and Disarmament Agency, Fred C. Iklé, and Secretary of Defense Donald H. Rumsfeld, the United States offered another proposal in February to break the January deadlock on the cruise missile issue. ALCMs would be treated as in the January offer. In a separate protocol, tied to an agreement about the Backfire, was the offer to limit *deployed* SLCMs and GLCMs to 600 kilometers, but to permit flight testing on both up to ranges of 2,500 kilometers. That offer was repeated again in September. The Ford administration, in short, had "invented" the protocol that was to figure so prominently in the Carter administration's April 1977 three-tier approach, which in turn ultimately became the basis of the 1979 SALT II executive agreement. The NATO allies were informed about the January proposal, but were not aware of the details of the February and September initiatives.

Thus through 1976 the U.S. government was clearly protecting the standoff bomber option and preserving its flexibility on SLCMs and GLCMs. It had developed a consensus on the military value of the long-range ALCM, at least among high-level civilians, but had given little thought to the military utility of the sea and ground versions.

The September 1976 proposal was the last made by the outgoing Ford administration. From a variety of motives, newly elected President

---

61. Information on these three proposals comes from two interviews on June 25 and 27, 1980. Talbott, *Endgame,* has recorded part of the January proposal, but makes little mention of the February and none of the September initiatives.

Jimmy Carter decided at the outset not to take the Vladivostok agreement with the September additions as the basis for resuming negotiations with the Soviet Union. Instead, he put forth what came to be called the comprehensive proposal. It called for deep cuts in the overall strategic launchers permitted both sides (from 2,400 to somewhere between 1,800 and 2,000); a reduction in launchers mounted with MIRVs (from 1,320 to somewhere between 1,100 and 1,200); an entirely new subceiling on ICBM launchers equipped with MIRVs (550); a reduction in Russia's heavy missiles (from 300 to 150); exclusion of Backfire from the overall strategic launcher ceiling as long as Russia adhered to restrictions on its range; and a 2,500-kilometer range limit on all types of cruise missiles deployed during the time the treaty would be in force.[62]

Carter's motives in offering such a radical proposal were complex. In his election campaign he had called for reductions in the superpowers' nuclear arsenals and had attacked the style and substance of Kissinger's diplomacy. He had, moreover, to deal with the relentless buildup in Russia's heavy missiles that many thought posed a threat to America's Minuteman force, a problem that neither the SALT I treaty nor the Vladivostok agreement with the September additions had solved. He had, finally, to respond to the pressures from Senate hard-liners, led by Henry M. Jackson, to obtain an agreement that was more beneficial to the United States than either SALT I or Vladivostok. Secretary of Defense Brown took the lead in pushing for an approach that would meet these goals through deep cuts. Brown's proposal gave Carter what he needed: an approach that had his own political stamp on it, not Kissinger's, and that responded to both his own arms control instincts and his political needs of the moment. The proposal also gave Brown what he wanted: a reduction in the vulnerability of Minutemen that would be achieved by deep cuts in Russia's heavy missiles and limits on testing rather than by increases in U.S. forces. Strategic logic nicely dovetailed with political needs. It was a beautifully crafted compromise.

The only problem, of course, was that the Russians summarily rejected it, not even bothering to offer any counterproposals. They insisted on returning to Vladivostok as the basis for negotiations. Because the Carter

---

62. The terms of the comprehensive proposal and why it was proposed come from Talbott, *Endgame*, chap. 3. The Joint Chiefs of Staff (JCS) were asking for only a 1,500-kilometer limit on the ALCM in order to protect the B-1. Talbott (p. 61) quotes a JCS officer thus: "We figured that a 1,500-kilometer limit on ALCMs was sure-fire insurance that we would get the B-1, because without the B-1 the limit made no sense."

administration thought it had no choice, it returned to matters as they had been left by Ford and Kissinger. It offered a "new" proposal in April 1977 that combined a three-tier approach: a treaty, a protocol, and a statement of common understandings. ALCMs would appear in the treaty, limited in range to 2,500 kilometers. SLCMs and GLCMs would appear in the protocol, limited in range to 600 kilometers if they were deployed, but to be tested at ranges up to 2,500 kilometers. The treaty would last through 1985; the protocol through the end of 1981. Any reductions on overall strategic launchers would be modest.

The similarity between Carter's April proposal and Ford's September offer is not accidental: having failed in its radical approach, Carter simply resurrected the final Ford package. This account makes clear what many have claimed: the Carter administration might very well have reached early agreement with the Soviet Union (although not with the U.S. Senate) on a SALT II accord had it accepted the Vladivostok agreement with the September additions as the starting point for negotiations. Carter was initially pushed by political needs and strategic concerns not to do so. He picked up the pieces by taking his predecessor's approach when forced to do so. The final SALT II accord of June 1979 largely resembled the April proposal, except that the ALCM range limits were dropped. More than most have realized, the final accord reflected the handiwork of Henry Kissinger.

European Concerns about America's Nuclear Umbrella

In its early negotiations with the Soviet Union, the Carter administration had preserved the 2,500-kilometer limit for the ALCM because it did not know what it would decide about the B-1. Once the administration decided to cancel production, the long-range ALCM became essential for the preservation of an effective strategic bomber force in the 1980s. The case for the SLCM and GLCM was more complex because it involved political considerations vis-à-vis not only the Russians but also the Europeans.[63]

63. The account that follows of NATO's long-range theater nuclear force (LRTNF) modernization is based on fifty-seven interviews held from June through October 1980. The material is drawn from a larger work in progress by Robert Art and Simon Lunn, *NATO in the Age of Strategic Parity*, which attempts to trace and analyze the LRTNF decision of 1979 in its broadest aspects as it was made in eight NATO countries. For a good overview of the broad outlines of the decision, see Fred Kaplan, "Warring Over New Missiles for NATO," *New York Times Magazine,*

The Russians appeared to fear the SLCM and GLCM even more than the ALCM and took a much tougher negotiating posture on them. In the case of the ALCM, the Soviet Union could at least detect standoff bombers through its reconnaissance satellites and surmise that cruise missiles had been fired from them, even if it could not track the missiles once they were launched. Cruise missiles fired from mobile ground launchers or submerged submarines, however, would be practically impossible to see, even with the most sophisticated satellite and other capabilities. The eventuality that hundreds, if not thousands, of SLCMs and GLCMs could be fired at long ranges from either Western Europe or at sea against the Soviet Union appeared to offer the Americans the chance to upset the strategic nuclear balance in a dramatic fashion. The Soviet Union therefore insisted that both the SLCM and GLCM, if they were deployed before 1982, be limited to a range that would reduce, if not eliminate, their strategic threat to Russia. In order to reach an agreement with the Soviet Union on an overall SALT II treaty, the United States conceded on deployment ranges, but preserved its right to flight test SLCMs and GLCMs at much longer ranges.

In agreeing to the 600-kilometer deployment limit and preserving the 2,500-kilometer testing limit, the Carter administration felt that it had pulled off a great negotiating coup.[64] In the middle of 1977, SLCMs and GLCMs had not even completed development. They would not be ready to deploy until 1982 at the earliest, about the time when the protocol provisions limiting their deployment ranges would self-destruct. In fact, the protocol had been carefully designed to end precisely when the administration thought the GLCM and SLCM would be ready for full-scale production and deployment. The United States, therefore, had not given anything away to the Russians. Not only had it preserved a military option for the future, but it also had retained its ability to develop that option fully during a period of supposed restraint.

What seemed a great negotiating coup to the Americans, however, appeared to the Europeans to be a great potential giveaway. They worried

December 19, 1979. Also see David N. Schwartz, "U.S. Policy and NATO's Strategic Dilemma" (Ph.D. dissertation, Massachusetts Institute of Technology, 1980), chap. 8; and chap. 13 in this volume. For an official rationale on why GLCMs and Pershing IIs were to be deployed in Europe, see Office of the Secretary of Defense, "Modernization and Arms Control for Long-Range Theater Nuclear Forces," U.S. Rationale Paper, October 16, 1979.

64. Two interviews, June 25 and July 22, 1980.

that the United States had set a dangerous precedent: they feared that upon expiration of the protocol the United States would cave into Russian pressure and extend it. To the Europeans, matters were made worse by the other provisions and lapses of the April three-tier proposal. The United States had preserved the long-range ALCM option for its central strategic systems. It had done nothing to constrain Russia's deployment of two weapons—the SS-20 and the Backfire—that most threatened Western Europe. Although the issue of the Backfire was not yet settled, the Europeans knew that the United States was working quite hard to ensure that its range would not be intercontinental. Hence, the United States appeared to be magnifying the long-range theater nuclear force threat to the Europeans in order to reduce the long-range strategic threat to its own territory.[65] The fact that the Europeans had not been consulted about the protocol before it was presented to the Russians only made them more suspicious.

Throughout the spring, summer, and fall of 1977, the Carter administration went to great lengths to deal with these suspicions by sending to Europe a series of joint State-Defense Department briefing teams. The problem with these trips, however, was that the United States was too honest in its views about the sea and ground versions of the cruise missile. Under the lead of the State Department, the Carter administration was trying to educate the Europeans about the cruise missile, to explain the state of American thinking about the GLCM and SLCM (which was not very advanced at the time), and to show that the cruise missile was not the answer to all of NATO's problems. The attempt to be honest, however, only made the problem worse. The Europeans, particularly the Germans, thought that the Americans were trying to talk them out of cruise missiles for NATO, not educate them about their merits and demerits. The problem in part was that the Europeans had become accustomed to the United States taking the lead in nuclear matters. They were not used to "participatory consultation" at the formative stages of an administration's thinking. But because the administration had not informed the Europeans about the protocol before presenting it to the Russians, it had no choice but to engage in some type of consultation to repair the political damage that had been done. The difficulty was that the administration did not yet know what it wanted to do with cruise missiles, and it knew that the Europeans did not know what they wanted to do with them.

65. Two interviews, June 24, July 21, and July 24, 1980.

The Europeans only knew that they did not want to be forced to do *without* them before they had a chance to look closely at them.[66]

The differences in views on these matters were rooted in the difference in national perspectives and military circumstances that have characterized the NATO alliance since its inception. The Europeans' military dependence on the United States has always made them acutely sensitive to the slightest shifts in America's military policy. At the outset, President Carter set a tone in military matters that did little to assuage this sensitivity. First, in his campaign and after, he expressed a desire to banish nuclear weapons from the face of the earth. Second, three months into office, he offered a SALT II package to the Russians that seemed designed to provoke their rejection. Third, from the beginning, he put heavy pressure on the British, the French, and especially the Germans to restrict their sales of nuclear power-generating equipment so as to minimize the likelihood that nuclear weapons could be made from it. The first unsettled the Europeans because their security rested centrally on nuclear deterrence. The second threatened the viability of a détente in which they had a great economic stake. And the third appeared to be a not so subtle attempt by the United States to prevent the Europeans from commercially exploiting a technology in which they were developing an edge over the Americans.

Finally, American-European and especially American-German relations were strained to the hilt by Carter's handling of the enhanced radiation weapon, or what became known as the neutron bomb, in mid-1977.[67] The sensitivities of European governments to their publics' growing unhappiness with all things nuclear required crafting an elaborate scenario for NATO acceptance of the neutron bomb. By changing his mind at the last minute, President Carter undercut Chancellor Helmut Schmidt, who had worked hard and spent much political capital with his fellow European Social Democrats to line them up behind deployment of these weapons. Carter also undercut his own State Department, which had worked for months to devise an acceptable means for the European governments to accept these weapons.[68] Carter's reversal reinforced the Europeans' perception of him as vacillating and his government as uncoordinated and, worse, called into great doubt the ability of the United States to lead

66. Four interviews, June 24, June 27, July 21, and July 22, 1980.
67. Four interviews, June 25, June 27, July 21, and July 22, 1980. See chap. 13 of this book for a fuller account.
68. Two interviews, July 22 and July 24, 1980.

NATO. The neutron bomb fiasco largely determined both the resolve and manner with which the Carter administration approached the LRTNF case, making clear three important requirements: first, to be absolutely clear about what the Europeans really wanted; second, to regain American leadership within NATO; and, third, to prove that NATO could collectively make clear-cut decisions.

These events may have enhanced Europe's unease about the reliability of the United States, but the unease was there to begin with. A deeper concern was at work—the credibility of the American nuclear umbrella—for which the cruise missile had become the tangible political symbol. Would the United States risk New York for Hamburg now that the two superpowers had reached strategic parity? This was the underlying issue that Carter's actions during his first fourteen months had further aggravated. But strategic parity was enshrined in the SALT I treaty of 1972 and thus predated Carter. By 1975 the Europeans had begun seriously to ponder the strategic consequences for them of superpower parity. The substance of the 1977 protocol and the manner in which it had been revealed crystallized these fears. Just as the SS-20 had come to symbolize the growing Russian threat to Western Europe that America's central strategic systems were not counteracting, so did American actions on the GLCM and SLCM come to symbolize America's unwillingness to counter that threat *within* Europe. Carter had made a difficult problem worse, but he had not created it.

After Schmidt made a speech before the International Institute for Strategic Studies in London in October 1977 proclaiming the SS-20 to be a great threat to Western Europe, the Carter administration knew that it had to take Europe's concerns about the SS-20, the Backfire, and the protocol's limitations on the GLCM and SLCM seriously. Taken together, these symbolized to the Europeans the disadvantageous position in which they would find themselves if a SALT II accord were concluded along the April three-tier approach. Strategic parity would be enshrined, but nothing would be done to redress a perceived imbalance in the LRTNF balance in Europe that threatened to open up a "gap in the spectrum of deterrence" in favor of the Soviet Union.[69] If deterrence rested upon the ability to match the enemy's moves with similar ones at every step of the escalation ladder, then NATO would shortly be missing a rung. Even though the Carter administration assured the Europeans that a response

69. Office of the Secretary of Defense, "Modernization and Arms Control for Long-Range Theater Nuclear Forces."

by the Soviet Union with its LRTNF could and would be met with an American strategic counterresponse, the Europeans were not assured.

The Carter administration found itself in a bind. It could not push cruise missiles on the Europeans because, by doing so, it would be admitting that America's strategic systems were not sufficient to protect them. Besides, the administration was not certain whether the Europeans really wanted cruise missiles. State Department officials in particular were wary of repeating the multilateral nuclear force (MLF) debacle of the early 1960s. After the neutron bomb fiasco, the MLF precedent heightened this sense of caution throughout the American government. The administration did not want to force on the Europeans nuclear forces that they initially appeared to want but ultimately might reject. At the same time, however, the United States could not tell the Europeans that they could not have cruise missiles because that would further inflame their fears about a superpower condominium at their expense. The logic of the situation dictated that the administration could neither force upon, nor deny to, the Europeans the cruise missiles constrained in the protocol.[70]

Parallel to this bind on cruise missiles was the ambiguity over the coupling-decoupling argument. Strategically, one could argue that an American deployment of new LRTNF would fill in the gap in the deterrent spectrum because at every step in the deterrent or escalation ladder every Soviet action could be met in kind. Strategically, however, one could also argue that the deployment of long-range systems in Europe would decouple events on the European battlefield from America's nuclear umbrella. Such systems would enable the United States to hit Russia from Europe, thereby avoiding use of its strategic forces and allowing the United States to wage a nuclear war with Russia but confining the devastation to Europe and Russia. By deployment of LRTNF in Europe, the United States could conduct a limited nuclear war confined to the central front.[71] On military grounds, both arguments made sense. But because the issue at heart was a political one, it was political attitudes that determined which view would prevail. And, as one participant in this decision remarked, because of the central role in the alliance played by the Germans, "coupling was whatever the Germans said it was."[72]

Given the political difficulties associated with taking one line or the other, the administration invented the High Level Group (HLG) to

70. Four interviews, June 24, July 21, July 22, and July 28, 1980.
71. Two interviews, July 23 and July 28, 1980.
72. Interview, July 24, 1980.

plumb the depth of European concern about decoupling and interest in cruise missiles.[73] It met from December 1977 through March 1979 and was chaired by Assistant Secretary of Defense for International Security Affairs David E. McGiffert, who initially maintained American neutrality on the cruise missile. However, at the second meeting of the HLG in February 1978 at Los Alamos, a consensus developed among the middle-level politico-military representatives that some type of hardware response to the SS-20 and the Backfire was necessary.[74] Once this consensus had emerged, the United States took the lead in the staff work necessary to determine the available options. In the Pentagon, PA&E conducted a cost-effectiveness study on the alternatives of deploying GLCMs, SLCMs, and ALCMs on tactical aircraft, a new medium-range ballistic missile, and an extended-range follow-on to the Army's Pershing I, the Pershing II.

The study did not conclude that any one option was clearly superior on both cost and military grounds. The ultimate decision to deploy both GLCMs and the Pershing II came as a consequence of considering both military and political factors. On military grounds, it was decided that a mix of both ballistic and cruise missiles was advantageous because of the hedge against improvements in Soviet air defenses that such a mixed force would provide. The Pershing II was preferred because its cost estimates looked more reliable than those for the MRBM and it had an earlier initial operational capability. The ALCM on tactical aircraft suffered from all the vulnerability problems that tactical aircraft stationed in Europe had. The GLCM was not cheaper than the SLCM if dedicated platforms were not built for the latter, but the GLCM had the political advantage of being highly visible when deployed on land. SLCMs looked to the Europeans much as did the Polaris submarines that had been assigned since the early 1970s to the supreme allied commander of NATO's forces: they were available, but they were invisible. Military factors called for a mixed force; political factors called for a visible and early-deployed land-based force.[75]

True to form, once the decision had been made to deploy the GLCM, the secretary of defense had trouble finding a service to give it to.[76] The Army had earlier rejected interest in taking on development of the

---

73. Four interviews, July 21, July 25, and July 28, 1980.
74. Three interviews, July 25, July 28, and October 22, 1980.
75. Four interviews, June 24, July 23, and July 25, 1980.
76. Five interviews, June 18, June 26, July 25, and July 28, 1980.

GLCM. It feared a roles-and-missions fight with the Air Force over whether the GLCM was akin to an artillery shell for interdiction, in which case it fell into the Army's province, or whether it was akin to a strategic projectile (the Air Force's province). The Army in the mid-1970s was also more concerned with building up its conventional capability in Europe. The opportunity costs of having to pay for another system dedicated solely to the nuclear mission (besides the Pershing II) were too great. Finally, the Army feared that it might be put in the position of developing a system that would never be deployed: along with the decision to deploy LRTNF was a decision to pursue arms control negotiations with the Soviet Union in order to limit both sides' deployment of these forces. In the late 1970s, it was not completely clear whether GLCMs were a chip to be bargained away or a system to be deployed.

For its part, the Air Force wanted nothing to do with the GLCM. It, too, was worried about paying for the costs of developing what might turn out to be a bargaining chip. It wanted to continue with the modernization of its tactical fighter forces, to which it had committed a large fraction of its budget in the 1970s. It had no taste for a mission that involved pushing around in the mud a cumbersome weapon that moreover required no pilot to fly it. Largely because the Army already had the Pershing II and because the GLCM could not be given to the Navy, the Air Force got stuck with it. Air Force enthusiasm for the GLCM has been reflected in the spending priority attached to it: the Air Force has consistently put the GLCM near the bottom of its budget priorities, only to have PA&E allocate more dollars to it. Just like the ALCM and the SLCM, the GLCM was a weapon that none of the services wanted. It was pushed upon the Air Force because of the larger political decisions taken by the Carter administration.

Conclusions

The overriding conclusion from the above analysis is inescapable: not one of the present versions of the cruise missile was readily embraced by any service. The Air Force accepted the long-range ALCM only because the president ordered it to do so. It reluctantly accepted the GLCM, but viewed it as a national, not an Air Force, mission and consistently gave it low priority during the annual budget negotiations with the secretary of defense. The Army successfully fought having to accept the GLCM, not only because it already had the Pershing II, but also because Secretary of Defense Brown and his predecessors agreed with Army leaders, especially Chief of Staff Creighton Abrams, that the highest priority had to be put on rebuilding the Army after Vietnam and on refurbishing America's ground forces in Europe. The Navy fought the SLCM if dedicated platforms were required to carry it and, if not, had to grasp for rationales to justify its existence. The TLAM-C came into being only because Secretary Brown unilaterally put money into the Navy's budget to develop it. The TASM was the only version that one powerful subgroup within any of the services enthusiastically desired, but the Navy surface fleet had to proceed cautiously and indirectly to get it. Thus, all of the present five versions of the cruise missile owe their existence largely to the political incentives—born of SALT II politics, NATO alliance considerations, and the political needs of presidents—that caused high-level political appointees within the executive branch to push for their development. It was these factors that converted the technologically possible into the politically necessary.

In terms of *intraservice* politics it is clear why no service readily embraced cruise missiles. The dominant group within each service—the strategic bombers in the Air Force, the carrier admirals in the Navy, and the NATO–conventional arms lobby in the Army—opposed any cruise missile variant that threatened what it conceived to be the service's central mission. Within the arena of intraservice politics, the dominant group must always negotiate the allocation of resources with the other subgroups and parcel out a reasonable amount to them. The dominant group, however, will firmly resist those innovations that threaten its claim over the bulk of service resources, question the relevance of its wisdom and experience, and, ultimately, menace it with obsolescence. In this respect, military organizations differ little from other bureaucracies. They are highly resistant to radical change. And, for that reason, political intervention from the outside is necessary if radical change is to occur. This overall conclusion, central though it is, does not exhaust the lessons to be derived from a decade of development of the cruise missile. There are three more.

First, intraservice politics does not take place in a void. Changes in both the external balance of military forces and the perceived nature of the military threat vitally affect the political balance among the service subgroups contending for their share of resources. Clearly, the military climate of the seventies differed from that of the fifties and sixties. Nuclear weapons were where the money was in the fifties, and each service and all its major subgroups got into the nuclear business. With the flexible response doctrine of the sixties, the services obtained more nuclear weapons and large increases in their conventional forces. In the early sixties, both interservice and intraservice competition was dampened by real budget increases that made the nuclear and conventional buildup simultaneously possible. In the late sixties, the Vietnam War created a consensus for the allocation of resources to the conventional effort.

For the services in the seventies, the overriding factors were the tremendous growth in Russia's strategic nuclear forces and buildup in conventional forces, the depletion of America's conventional capability (especially in Europe) due to Vietnam, the failure to invest in the modernization of conventional forces, and, finally, a severe budgetary stringency exacerbated by high and continuous inflation. For a time, the political elite was able to enforce restraint in the amount of resources allocated to the strategic nuclear forces and thereby emphasize their modernization rather than expansion. But because Russia's vastly expanded strategic forces gave it a security shield behind which it could exert conventional forces on a global scale, the United States began to pay greater attention to the effects of strategic equivalence on the conventional balance. As had been the case in the early sixties, concern was expressed that greater stability at the strategic level (a low probability of general nuclear war between the superpowers) increased the likelihood of tactical instability (conventional wars on the peripheries).[77] Particularly in the Air Force and the Navy, this development enhanced the political position of those who argued for an improved conventional war-fighting capability.

However, there were concerns about nuclear forces as well. The SALT II accord of 1972 was not universally accepted as desirable; nor was there agreement that strategic nuclear parity obtained, in good part because no political consensus existed on what was meant by parity. Furthermore, concern about the size and continuing modernization of Russia's strategic nuclear forces spawned changes in beliefs about the uses and levels of the U.S. strategic forces. It also produced much analysis on what the change in the strategic nuclear balance meant for the theater nuclear force balance. These concerns about nuclear forces did not diminish the po-

---

77. In a report to Congress on how it saw the changed environment, the Army put it succinctly: "In the spectrum of warfare, nuclear war is the least likely occurrence. The importance of conventional forces has moved to the front." *New York Times,* February 23, 1981.

sition of those who argued for more attention to conventional forces. However, the severe budgetary stringency that prevailed in the seventies intensified interservice competition for the defense pie and intraservice competition over the nuclear versus the conventional missions. The latter was especially the case within the Air Force and the Navy.

In this complex military environment, the balance of political forces within each service began to shift. The balance shifted least within the Army largely because of widespread acceptance within it of the primacy of the conventional mission. GLCMs devoted to a long-range theater nuclear mission ranked low in Army needs. A significant segment even wanted to give up the Pershing I and certainly not develop the Pershing II, because such labor-intensive systems would magnify the Army's manpower problems. The Navy began to shift its emphasis away from nuclear power projection against the Soviet homeland to protection of the surface fleet and control of the seas. As a consequence, the surface and submarine fleets gained political power at the expense of the carrier admirals. The Air Force witnessed the political coming of age of the Tactical Air Command, which assumed a position of near equality with the Strategic Air Command. Tactical interdiction and air superiority have always been valued in the Air Force, but they took a prominence in peacetime (compared to the strategic bombing mission) not previously characteristic of the Air Force. The changes in the political balance of forces within each service should not be overstated, but neither should they be underestimated.

These changes in the military environment and in the politics of intraservice competition unambiguously favored only one version of the cruise missile: the TASM. A conventional weapon dedicated to the protection of the surface fleet, it was in tune with the greater emphasis placed on control of the seas. The ultimate fate of the TLAM-C is not clear. Although it is conventionally armed, its high unit cost makes its military worth still debatable. The ALCM-B was so much caught up in the vortex of SALT II and presidential-congressional bomber politics in the seventies that it was lifted out of the arena of intraservice politics. The TLAM-N and the GLCM are single-purpose, theater-based, nuclear systems. In general, but especially in periods of fiscal stringency, the services have consistently preferred to deploy dual-purpose systems capable of both a nuclear and a conventional mission. With the greater concern for the conventional balance in the seventies, the services considered theater-based nuclear systems as a necessary evil. Theater nuclear weapons must be bought in order to be able to fight what the services see as the most likely war—a conventional one. Theater nuclear systems must be deployed for deterrent, not for war-fighting purposes.

Because of the crosscurrents in the military environment of the seventies, the only easily discernible trend within all of the services is a greater emphasis on conventional war-fighting capabilities. It is precisely this trend that largely explains Army resistance to the GLCM and lack of enthusiasm for the Pershing II, Navy ambivalence about the TLAM-N and significant support for the TASM, Air Force unhappiness with the GLCM, and, presumably in the eighties, Tactical Air Command ecstasy over a conventionally armed medium-range air-to-surface missile. The dynamics of intraservice politics explains the central conclusion of this chapter, that civilian intervention was required for development of the cruise missile.

A second conclusion concerns the relevance of bureaucratic politics. As commonly understood, this phenomenon refers to the pulling, hauling, and tugging that goes on in the executive branch over a given issue, with the resultant policy often one that none of the participants initially or even eventually desired. The outcomes of cruise missile development in the seventies, however, occurred in spite of, not because of, bureaucratic politics. Within the services there was a great deal of bureaucratic politicking, most of it ultimately to little avail. The Air Force did not want the ALCM-B. It was forced to take it. The Air Force did not want the GLCM. It was forced to take it. The Navy had little enthusiasm for the TLAM. It was forced to take it. Only in the case of the TASM does bureaucratic politics explain a great deal about the final outcome. Even here, as in the other cases, outside political intervention was necessary to produce the outcome that the politicians wanted.

In terms of the scope of bureaucratic politics within the executive branch, the GLCM case is the most interesting because it fully involved all the main national security participants: the Defense Department, the State Department, the Arms Control and Disarmament Agency, and the White House. Yet all the major participants, with the possible exception of the Joint Chiefs of Staff and NATO's supreme allied command, were initially dubious about the need for more nuclear weapons in Europe. The State Department and the Arms Control Agency may have been more skeptical than their counterparts in the Pentagon—PA&E and

International Security Affairs—but only in degree. All came to support the deployment of more theater nuclear weapons in Europe largely because the Germans pushed hard for them. Faced with pressure from without, the United States government acted more like a unitary actor on this issue than a house divided. The divisions that did occur revolved more around the issues of how many weapons to deploy and under what rationale than on the decision of whether to deploy them. As with most pivotal issues in American foreign policy since 1945, there was more unity at the top than commonly thought.

Finally, the third conclusion to be drawn from this case concerns its implications for the congressional role in weapon systems decisions. Formally, the power of the purse has always given Congress the authority and the capability to play major roles in American foreign and defense policy. Yet in the past Congress has not always availed itself of this opportunity. In recent years, it has become a virtual cliché to assert that Congress has assumed a prominent, if not dominant, role in national security policy. To support this view, analysts have typically pointed to such events as the 1969 antiballistic missile debate, the Cooper-Church amendment limiting American involvement in Indochina, the passage of the War Powers Resolution of 1973, the refusal to provide promised assistance to the government of South Vietnam, and the Turkish arms embargo. Coupled with the growth of micromanagement in defense programs, these events are taken as signs of a new activism in Congress.

It is clear that in the 1970s Congress significantly expanded its oversight ability in defense matters. Hearings before the Armed Services Committees were carried on by numerous subcommittees, each of which had authority over defense programs in a specific area. Such subcommittee specialization not only yielded extensive and intensive information, but also constrained the ability of the Department of Defense to reprogram money from function to function because each subcommittee authorized programs and established budgetary ceilings in a highly detailed fashion. In the past decade, moreover, there was a major growth in the quantity and quality of professional staff. Over 18,000 staffers, many with advanced professional training and considerable executive experience, were employed in the standing committees, the offices of individual legislators, and such investigative arms as the Congressional Research Service, the Office of Technology Assessment, the Congressional Budget Office, and the General Accounting Office. Finally, passage of the Congressional Budget and Impoundment Control Act of 1974 gave Congress a significant institutional advantage.[78] It was now possible for Congress as a whole to set budgetary priorities in advance of appropriations rather than build budgets from the bottom up in disaggregated committee fashion. In short, Congress in the seventies acquired the capability to constrain, manage, or even initiate highly detailed programs and policies.

Because the cruise missile program began in the late 1960s and early 1970s, when congressional activism in defense first came to the fore and congressional analytical capability was beginning to expand, it is useful to use this case in order to draw tentative conclusions about the effectiveness of congressional micromanagement in defense matters. Our analysis casts doubt on the view that Congress's influence, if not its role, somehow changed radically in the seventies. An assessment of three specific congressional interventions in the cruise missile program illustrates the point.

First, in 1972 and 1973, Congress acted as an ally of the secretary of defense by authorizing research on long-range cruise missiles. The program was pushed by Secretary of Defense Laird for reasons related to SALT II. It was necessarily vaguely defined, given Laird's ulterior motives. Latitude for congressional micromanagement was extremely limited because the program was in early development. The connections between the SCAD, SCM, and ACM programs were ill defined. In this instance, congressional funding was vital to the success of the cruise missile program. The congressional role, however, was one of a supporter, not a meddlesome backseat driver. The second significant intervention occurred in 1976 when Congress ordered the Pentagon to accelerate the tactical antiship missile and demanded that it clarify the rationale for the land-attack version. In this instance, the congressional actors thought they had acted as a judge of the worth of several programs. As our analysis made clear, however, the Navy had little interest in a land-attack program that had served largely to camouflage the activities of the surface fleet. Few Navy officials were disheartened by Congress's displeasure over the land-attack version. Although Congress had made it harder for those high-level Defense Department officials who wanted to build the land-attack missile, this action did not kill that version. Unknowingly, it had acted as an ally of the surface fleet proponents of the antiship missile and, therefore, had done little to alter the preferences of the Navy activists.

The third intervention occurred in 1979 when Congress forced the Pentagon to initiate development of the TLAM-C program. In this in-

78. P.L. 93–344.

stance, Congress acted as a successful lobbyist because it started a program that very few in the OSD or the Navy wanted. The background for this action began in earlier years. In 1976, as in 1972, the Senate Armed Services Subcommittee on Research and Development had taken the lead in criticizing the TLAM-N and reducing its funding. In 1976, as in 1972, the House Armed Services Committee, always more enthusiastic about new technologies than its Senate counterpart, had restored some funding for it. The program had limped along in the Pentagon, however, because no one quite knew what to do with it.

Some incentives were present, however, to keep it going. Until mid-1976, the Navy surface fleet used the TLAM-N to protect the TASM. After these proponents no longer needed it to protect the TASM, the OSD kept it alive because by then America's NATO allies were expressing interest in SLCMs and GLCMs. The OSD kept the TLAM-N going during 1977 and 1978, but had lost enthusiasm by 1979 once it knew the NATO High Level Group had chosen the GLCM over the SLCM. In anticipation of the December 1979 NATO ministerial meeting, where NATO was formally to approve the GLCM's deployment, the OSD downplayed the SLCM and accelerated the GLCM. During the summer and fall of 1979, the Carter administration was highly sensitive to any actions that might threaten an affirmative decision in December. Specifically, the administration worried about what was called the "SLCM escape-hatch scenario"—the fear that, because deployment of land-based cruise missiles was proving to be politically difficult within Europe, the governments there might seize upon any pretext to back away from the consensus they had reached within the HLG on the GLCM. The administration thought that if it funded the TLAM-N, then its NATO allies might use this to "go to sea" with the cruise missile in order to defuse the political opposition that was building on the GLCM. The House Armed Services Committee, however, wanted the TLAM-N built. The compromise reached between Secretary Brown and the committee was to accelerate development of the TLAM but in the conventional version.[79] Once again, it was high-level politics—this time a mixture of congressional-executive and American-European politics—not service interest, that forced development of a cruise missile.

The meaning of these three specific congressional interventions is difficult to assess. In its first intervention, Congress clearly allied with the

79. Three interviews, on July 25, July 29, and July 30, 1980.

executive to fund a program even though one of its houses was highly skeptical of its stated mission. In its second intervention, Congress slowed development of a program that most in the Pentagon were happy to see slowed. Only in its third intervention did Congress force the hand of a reluctant Pentagon. Clearly Congress was attuned to both technological details and the fine points of larger military purposes. Congress also gave the administration what it wanted more often than not. Only once was micromanagement employed, in the sense of intervening to run a program in a fashion the executive opposed. The three key congressional programmatic interventions on the cruise missile during the 1970s do not impressively support the conclusion that Congress has become the defense micromanager. But that does not mean that Congress had little influence. It affected the program in its specifics more through support of than opposition to executive preferences. Continuity with the past thus appears stronger than a sharp break with it. Congress functioned more in the traditional roles of lobbyist, gadfly, supporter, and arbitrator than as detailed manager of ongoing programs.

Why, then, did the United States develop cruise missiles when none of the services wanted them? The answer, quite simply, is that the politicians did, and their preferences prevailed. The final word on the broad politics of cruise missile development in the seventies is this: had it not been for politics, the cruise missile in all its present versions might never have existed.

CHAPTER THIRTEEN

NATO Alliance Politics

GREGORY F. TREVERTON

MUCH of what passes for European concern in transatlantic relations is in fact a reflection of U.S. anxieties or uncertainties. Given the degree of European dependence on the United States, that is inevitable and hardly surprising. Cruise missiles have been and are likely to continue to be such a concern. Because the United States found it difficult to decide whether cruise missiles could improve its defenses and why, Europeans had still more difficulty sorting out their interests. The difficulty extended to nuclear cruise missiles; in the future it will bear most heavily on conventional options.

Transatlantic deliberations over cruise missiles took place under the pressure of the SALT II negotiations. Indeed, the discussions might not have taken place at all if SALT had not occurred. The Europeans were in the position of entreating the United States to protect European interests in cruise missiles without knowing what those interests were or how important they might be. Their primary concern was not what cruise missiles might do to their enemies but what their American friends might do to them.

One set of cruise missile issues appears to be settled among the allies, in principle if not in practice. With NATO's December 1979 decision to deploy 464 continental-range cruise missiles in Western Europe, the NATO allies have committed themselves—and the United States in particular—to that nuclear mission. Such a role will thus have to be preserved in any arms control discussions. In particular, even if SALT II

Gregory Treverton, currently assistant director of the International Institute for Strategic Studies, London, is joining the faculty of the John F. Kennedy School of Government at Harvard University.

comes into effect in a form like that agreed upon in June 1979, the protocol provisions on cruise missiles—a range limit of 600 kilometers on ground- and sea-launched cruise missiles (GLCMs and SLCMs, respectively)—will have to expire before the new GLCMs begin to be deployed in Europe in 1983. The allies will debate whether they should be prepared to scale down their planned deployment in response to measures of Soviet restraint on the SS-20 or other continental nuclear systems, and they may agree in a SALT III or other arms control negotiations to limits on the numbers of continental-range cruise missiles. Opposition in Western Europe to the stationing of the cruise missiles may even mean that the December 1979 decision is never implemented. But the principle of U.S. continental-range cruise missiles armed with nuclear weapons, ground-based in Europe, is likely to stand.

A number of other arms control issues remain, however, which will require future decisions about the missions of cruise missiles in European defense. The central question is the role of conventional cruise missiles. The SALT II protocol pertained to both nuclear and conventional cruise missiles; similarly, the SALT II treaty defined *any* airplane carrying *any* cruise missile with a range of more than 600 kilometers as a multiple-warhead launcher to be counted under the appropriate subceiling.[1] The United States clearly could not help its allies perform the military tasks that it had committed itself not to do. Hence bilateral U.S.-Soviet provisions for cruise missiles will affect not only U.S. deployments but will also bear on independent decisions by European countries to the extent that they depend on some transfer of U.S. cruise missile technology.

Simply stated, decisions by the allies about cruise missile provisions in arms control should be governed by determinations of military utility, not the reverse. However, recent history is not comforting on that score. Cruise missiles were welcomed by Henry Kissinger in 1972 explicitly as an arms control bargaining tool. Since then their fashionability in NATO defense establishments has waxed and waned in a way that hardly corresponds neatly to military analysis.

This chapter reviews the recent history of cruise missiles in the context of the NATO alliance, with a focus on two related episodes. The first is discussions among the allies on cruise missiles during SALT II. In the process of deciding about cruise missile missions the United States sought both to share those assessments with Europeans and to reassure its allies

1. The SALT treaty is reproduced in *Survival,* vol. 21 (September–October 1979), pp. 217–30.

that their interest in cruise missiles would be taken into account. For much of SALT II it succeeded in doing neither, though the eventual outcome was acceptable. The second episode overlaps the first. It is the deliberations that led to NATO decisions—regarding both force deployments and arms control—on theater nuclear forces (TNF) in December 1979. In both cases I examine how well the United States and its allies did at planning forces and handling arms control implications. I then turn to assessments of those processes, with a discussion of other instances, in particular the multilateral force (MLF) of the early 1960s and the neutron warhead dispute of 1977–78. Finally, I speculate about what recent events suggest for the handling of the alliance cruise missile issues that lie ahead.

The Ambiguity of the Technology

The flexibility, and hence ambiguity, of cruise missile technology makes difficulties between the United States and its European allies inevitable in discussing related issues. Cruise missiles blur the neat categories into which weapons have been sorted, and this is to a large extent but not exclusively due to arms control.[2] Cruise missiles can be either nuclear or conventional, tactical or strategic. There is often no external way to know which choice to make: much depends on how much fuel the missile carries and thus on how range is traded for warhead payload.

The ambiguity is not without precedent. Many of the short-range missile and artillery systems and aircraft of both NATO and the Warsaw Pact have had dual capabilities from the beginning. Systems labeled strategic are variable in range; the Soviet SS-11 is an obvious case. But such examples did not blur categories to the same extent as cruise missiles did. For many weapons it was possible to be certain, from satellite photography and other observations, of either the range or the type of warhead, though perhaps not both. Or, as in the case of intercontinental ballistic missiles (ICBMs), systems could be used for purposes other than their intended missions but at such waste that any concern was hypothetical.

Cruise missiles, however, were both inherently ambiguous and inexpensive, at least in early estimates, suggesting a major exception to existing

2. See, for example, Richard Burt's early discussion, "The Cruise Missile and Arms Control," *Survival*, vol. 18 (January–February 1976), pp. 10–17.

categories. That posed a problem in principle for the arms controllers, even as military planners remained uncertain about the purposes that cruise missiles might serve.

The early alliance history of cruise missiles contains one intriguing footnote, suggesting that the technology was much less prominent then. In the late 1950s when NATO decided to deploy U.S. medium-range ballistic missiles (MRBMs) in Western Europe (and eventually deployed a total of 105 Thors and Jupiters in Britain, Italy, and Turkey), the Federal Republic of Germany refused to accept Jupiters on its soil. As chapter 15 makes clear, the reasons were strikingly reminiscent of the German TNF debate of the late 1970s: West Germany was the primary location of most short-range TNF already and did not want to be further singled out. Moreover, the Federal Republic of Germany wanted NATO to pursue opportunities to negotiate with the Soviet Union.[3] In the early 1960s Helmut Schmidt, then a young member of parliament, opposed accepting the Jupiters, primarily on technical grounds that were similar to those in the 1970s: Thors and Jupiters would be vulnerable, and it was better to rely on U.S. submarine missiles or silo-based Minutemen.[4]

In the 1970s debate the assertion was frequently made that to deploy continental-range TNF on West German soil was unprecedented, and thus deployment would constitute a new situation. Yet between 1962 and 1969 there were in fact as many as ninety-six Mace B cruise missiles deployed in hardened and dispersed sites in the Federal Republic of Germany.[5] These missiles had a range of 1,500 miles and a warhead with a force of more than one megaton; they were intended for NATO defenses against attacks by Eastern Europe and for the U.S. Strategic Air Command against the Soviet Union. Despite its range, the Mace was referred to as tactical. The German debate of 1957–58 was sweeping and addressed the entire German role in the alliance; the Mace and its predecessor, the Matador, entered in the debate, especially in the 1958 Bundestag session, but they did not occupy a prominent position as did the Thor and

3. The nuclear debate in Germany during this period is well described in Catherine McArdle Kelleher, *Germany and the Politics of Nuclear Weapons* (Columbia University Press, 1975), pp. 60–121.

4. See Helmut Schmidt, *Defense or Retaliation: A German View* (Praeger, 1962), pp. 27–43. However, Schmidt soon regretted the decision not to accept Jupiters, arguing that even "soft" missiles would have been better than none and would have served as a spur to do better in a second generation of systems.

5. See Uwe Nerlich, "Theatre Nuclear Forces in Europe: Is NATO Running Out of Options?" *Washington Quarterly,* vol. 3 (Winter 1980), p. 121.

Jupiter. Chronology may have been much of the reason: the Matador had been in Europe since 1954 and did not have sufficient range to reach Moscow, while the Mace was not scheduled to arrive until 1962, after the nuclear debate had subsided. Still, the Mace was deployed, and the Jupiter was not. Ballistic missiles clearly were the preferred technology.

Cruise Missiles, SALT II, and Europe

Cruise missiles were included only marginally in the futile attempt of the Carter administration in April 1977 to reshape the SALT dialogue. Moscow did express interest in an overall ceiling of 2,200 launchers, provided that cruise missiles were included and Backfires excluded, but the U.S. fallback position precluded this condition. For its part, the Soviet Union was uninterested in simply deferring cruise missiles to SALT III.

In the effort to pick up the pieces after the April disaster, the United States returned to an earlier position of a three-part formula for SALT II—a treaty, a protocol of limited duration, and a statement of principles for SALT III. Cruise missiles were relegated to the protocol, with other issues that were too important to defer yet too difficult to solve definitively in the treaty. As initially conceived, the protocol was to ban deployment of ground- or sea-launched cruise missiles with ranges of more than 600 kilometers, with air-launched cruise missiles (ALCMs) limited to 2,500 kilometers, the range limit suggested for all cruise missiles in the comprehensive April proposal. These range limits bore only indirect relation to military analysis. Six hundred kilometers was established in response to the Soviet insistence, already expressed, that SALT should not permit GLCMs within range of the Russian homeland, but 2,500 kilometers for ALCMs was a longer range than even the Pentagon requested; 1,500 would have sufficed with the B-1 bomber as the carrier, and the B-1 was still under consideration in April.

During 1977 European uneasiness with the provisions of SALT II, especially the protocol, increased. It became clear that the protocol would ban GLCM and SLCM deployment for a period, although such weapons could not be deployed before the end of the protocol. It was also clear that the Soviet Union was asking for a nontransfer provision much like that contained in the antiballistic missile (ABM) treaty, a detailed listing of the technology that the United States was precluded from transferring to its allies.

Throughout 1977 and 1978 the United States frequently repeated the same reassurances. GLCMs and SLCMs could not be deployed during the period of the protocol in any case, and so the ban on deployment had no effect. Testing of those systems would be permitted, however. The United States would not consider the provisions of the protocol a precedent for future negotiations, and the Senate would not permit the protocol to be automatically extended. Washington insisted that it would not accept a nontransfer provision; it did agree to a general noncircumvention clause, but only to close the negotiations. Well in advance, the United States showed its allies the version that was eventually agreed upon. It argued that the language only made explicit what was implicit in any treaty—that the parties agree not to evade its terms by helping other countries do what they themselves had agreed not to do in the treaty.

None of these efforts was entirely successful. Europeans turned American arguments around. If the protocol was so inconsequential, why bother with it? And why had the Soviet Union seemed to cooperate? If Europeans, West Germans in particular, sometimes sounded overly legalistic by insisting that the protocol would constitute a precedent even if it expired, they were correct that it would not only put cruise missiles on the agenda for future SALTs but would also suggest one possible way to treat them. That concern could not be made to disappear until NATO had committed itself to some notion of how it might employ cruise missiles.

One U.S. effort in particular illustrated the difficulty of reassuring Europeans on arms control while the planning for cruise missile missions still lacked concreteness. In the summer and early fall of 1977 the United States prepared a paper on cruise missiles to circulate among the allies in NATO. It grew out of the concerns of the allies in SALT II, but was framed by the United States as a discussion of possible uses for cruise missiles. It outlined the arguments against as well as in favor of cruise missiles. It was thus in part an attempt to dampen enthusiasm about cruise missiles without distorting the potential of the system.

However, Europeans were skeptical of the paper and regarded it as an effort to promote SALT II. To them the paper's cautionary arguments about cruise missiles were a reflection not of realistic military assessments but of a conscious U.S. decision to deemphasize the significance of possible cruise missile options. After all, the United States in June 1977 had just made the decision to add ALCMs to the bomber component of its strategic triad. Now it seemed to be saying that cruise missiles were good for the United States but not for Europe. These concerns were expressed at a special meeting of the NATO Nuclear Planning Group (NPG) in October 1977 and again at the NATO winter meetings of foreign and defense ministers in December 1977.

West German Chancellor Helmut Schmidt's celebrated speech to the International Institute for Strategic Studies in London in October 1977 is a bench mark exemplifying European concern.[6] His call for parity at other levels of armament, because SALT had codified parity in strategic nuclear weapons, probably is a reflection of his concern about the course of SALT II. Europeans like Schmidt had more qualms about the political symbolism of the emerging SALT II treaty than about specific provisions. Measures that were agreed upon before or during the SALT "breakthroughs" in September 1977—when it was decided that the United States would include cruise missiles in SALT while excluding the Soviet SS-20, would treat air-launched cruise missiles differently from those that might be based in Europe, or would include provisions for the Backfire that would ensure its use exclusively against Europe—all seemed to suggest to the Soviet Union that the security of the United States and that of Europe could be treated separately.

These concerns were at the heart of NATO's nuclear dilemma. With the withdrawal of the Thor and Jupiter from Europe in 1964 and the demise of the MLF in 1965, NATO decided, more or less consciously, to locate most of its strategic nuclear deterrent—its weapons capable of striking the Soviet homeland—not in Europe but rather "offshore," that is, in U.S. bombers, submarines, and land-based missiles. Shorter-range nuclear systems in Europe were to serve as adjuncts to conventional defense and, more important, as a critical middle rung on the escalation ladder, "coupling" the U.S. strategic deterrent with the defense of Europe.[7]

Yet the dilemma was inescapable because most of NATO's strategic nuclear weapons were located an ocean away from the likely point of Soviet attack in Western Europe. Europeans could not be sure that an American president would put U.S. cities at risk to defend Europe. Those

---

6. Schmidt's speech is reprinted in *Survival,* vol. 20 (January–February 1978), pp. 2–10.

7. This background is discussed further in Gregory F. Treverton, "Nuclear Weapons and the 'Gray Area,' " *Foreign Affairs,* vol. 57 (Summer 1979), pp. 1075–89.

doubts intensified as the Soviet Union began to equal the United States in nuclear strength and continued to deploy a wide range of new weapons for use against Western Europe.

SALT also played a role in increasing European doubts, since the negotiations also underscored what was being left out—in particular Soviet continental-range systems, like the SS-20, often labeled Eurostrategic weapons. It was tempting, for Europeans especially, to argue that there should be a rough balance in such systems; that temptation was visible between the lines of Schmidt's speech. Yet talk of Eurostrategic weapons and balances carried dangers for NATO, apparent in the TNF discussions and in debates even today. NATO needed weapons to make credible its doctrine of flexible response rather than to match or counter particular Soviet weapons on a one-to-one basis. Moreover, the focus on a Eurostrategic balance ultimately suggested that Western Europe could be separated from the central U.S. strategic deterrent, just the result Europeans sought to avoid.

The United States continued its efforts to reassure Europeans through 1978. After the Soviet Union achieved its major cruise missile aim in September 1977—the inclusion of ALCMs under the multiple independently targetable reentry vehicle (MIRV) ceiling—a year later, in September 1978, it fell back a step on cruise missiles. It agreed to unlimited ALCM range in return for a strict limit of 600 kilometers on GLCMs and SLCMs. The United States argued previously that the range limits should be "operational"—that is, the straight-line distance between the missile launching sites and the intended targets, not necessarily the distance missiles would actually fly on a given mission—and take into account evasive measures. Characteristically, the Europeans were more interested in the principle of how cruise missiles would be treated than in the technical details; thus the Soviet concession on ALCM range was not particularly encouraging but neither was the strict limitation on GLCMs and SLCMs especially damaging.

There remained only one cruise missile issue to be tied up in SALT II. That was the question of conventional cruise missiles, which was directly related to the desire to protect options for use in Europe. In 1977 the U.S. SALT working group developed the idea of a statement, to be agreed upon by both the United States and the Soviet Union, that at the end of the protocol either country could deploy conventional cruise missiles on airplanes other than so-called heavy bombers, without those cruise missiles being counted in the MIRV limit of 1,320. Obviously such a provision was unverifiable and, furthermore, it was bound to be attacked by the Soviet Union as seeking unilateral advantage.

As time went on and the suggested U.S. provision delayed the negotiations, those who had supported it in the Pentagon and the White House began to have second thoughts. Because it was clearly unverifiable it was conceivable that, for instance, the Soviet Union could add alleged conventional cruise missiles on Backfire bombers at the end of the protocol. It was not clear that it was in the U.S. interest to create such a possibility.

It soon became apparent that the issue would be important to Europeans only if the United States made it so. Again, the United States was projecting its own concerns on its European allies and doing so when conventional cruise missile missions were not yet defined. The U.S. Joint Chiefs of Staff were not attached to the particular form of statement regarding cruise missiles at the end of the protocol period, only to their desire that the period not be automatically extended when it expired and to the principle that SALT did not include conventional weapons. When President Carter gave those assurances, the United States changed its position slightly and treated conventional and nuclear cruise missiles alike in both the SALT treaty and protocol.

Cruise Missiles and Continental TNF

The second of the two important episodes in the history of cruise missiles is the deliberations that led to NATO decisions on TNF.[8] Consideration of longer-range TNF, and the role of cruise missiles therein, began during discussions of SALT II. Indeed, it is fair to say that SALT II was important in setting the TNF discussions in motion, particularly in guiding them. Concern about the incoherence in NATO's TNF posture had existed since the deployment of the weapons, and there had been increasing criticism of the preponderance of vulnerable, short-range systems.[9] But SALT focused the discussion on the continental-range spectrum— weapons capable of reaching Western Europe from the Soviet Union, and vice versa.

8. The primary source for this account is newspaper articles on the NATO deliberations, supplemented by background interviews with officials who took part. I also draw upon my own memory of events while I was a National Security Council official in 1977–78.

9. See, for example, Jeffrey Record, "Theatre Nuclear Weapons: Begging the Soviet Union to Pre-empt," *Survival,* vol. 19 (September–October 1977), pp. 208–11.

In May 1977 the heads of government in NATO agreed to a major program of defense improvements, the Long-Term Defense Program (LTDP). One task force of the LTDP was to deal with theater nuclear forces. The alliance's nuclear body, the Nuclear Planning Group (NPG), took charge of the TNF exercise and, at a meeting in October 1977, created the so-called High Level Group (HLG) of defense ministry officials to undertake a comprehensive review. TNF had been under study in the alliance in one form or another for most of the previous decade, and U.S. Secretaries of Defense James R. Schlesinger and Donald H. Rumsfeld had pressed concern about TNF modernization before the Carter administration began.[10]

After 1977 the focus on the continental range of the TNF spectrum emerged. The United States apparently initiated an exchange with its allies during the summer on the issue of whether existing sea-based systems, in particular U.S. Poseidon-carrying submarines assigned to NATO, provided adequate links between Europe and the U.S. central strategic deterrent. In August, British Secretary of State for Defence Fred Mulley wrote to his U.S. counterpart, Harold Brown, arguing that the answer was no. Mulley's letter made the two arguments that ran through subsequent NATO deliberations: that NATO's existing continental capability was based on aging, land-based aircraft in need of modernization and that some increase in continental forces was called for to provide an additional rung in the escalation ladder. The thinking in Bonn was similar; the West Germans emphasized the psychological threat posed by the SS-20 and the adverse implications for Europe of SALT II as it was then taking shape. Besides directing attention to continental-range TNF, SALT again contributed to European concern that the United States and the Soviet Union would reach agreement by trading systems of special interest to Europeans—cruise missiles—for American needs in central strategic systems.

At this point the United States was somewhat ambivalent. In December 1977 Secretary of Defense Harold Brown assured European NATO members that although he did not know how cruise missiles might fit in NATO defense, no options would be given up in SALT II. In the winter and spring of 1978, the Department of Defense was prepared to embrace the HLG consensus in favor of increasing the number of continental-

---

10. See, for example, Lothar Ruehl, "The 'Grey Area' Problem," in Christoph Bertram, ed., *The Future of Arms Control: Part I: Beyond SALT II,* Adelphi Paper 141 (London: International Institute for Strategic Studies, 1978), pp. 25–34.

range systems based in Europe, a proposal first expressed at a meeting in Los Alamos, New Mexico, in February 1978 as "evolutionary upward adjustment."[11] However, the U.S. government was wary; its initial reaction was dominated by two concerns: that the continental-range issue should not further complicate SALT II, and that the alliance was not ready to reach decisions on issues that touch basic NATO nuclear doctrine and practice.

By 1979 the official U.S. view had shifted toward accepting the NATO consensus of the previous spring, a sign of the seriousness of the United States in addressing allied concerns as much as an indication of clear U.S. preference. In the spring of 1979 the HLG reached agreement on a total force size of 200 to 600 warheads. The total size of a new force was bound to be quite arbitrary in any case. The simple obsolescence of existing systems, like Britain's Vulcan bombers, indicated one need. By their nature and by the logic of their deployment, the new missiles were intended for selective employment, not as part of a general NATO nuclear strike. Still, the basic question was how many targets in Eastern Europe and the Soviet Union would be allocated to new systems instead of—or in addition to—existing weapon systems, especially the NATO-assigned Poseidons or other central U.S. systems. The ultimate decision was bound to be political: too many new warheads would suggest the capability to fight a nuclear war limited to Europe, while too few would not be credible or worth the political trouble of deploying.

In summer 1979 the United States suggested a total force of 572 warheads, at the high end of the HLG 200–600 range, apparently expecting that NATO discussions might reduce that figure and that subsequent arms control negotiations might further pare it. Once a particular number that had been kept secret became known, however, it was difficult to change. The precise number was a marginal factor in the European debate about the new weapons, but it might have been slightly easier for the Dutch and others to defend the NATO outcome if it had come closer to the middle of the HLG range, which by then was public knowledge, or if the range itself initially had been broader.

The predominance of cruise missiles in the NATO decision—464 of 572 warheads—appears to have resulted from reasonable, straightforward calculations. Cruise missile technology had matured, was moving

11. Stephen R. Hanmer, Jr., "NATO's Long Range Theatre Nuclear Forces: Modernization in Parallel with Arms Control," *NATO Review*, vol. 28 (February 1980), pp. 1–6.

to deployment in the air-launched mode, and could be easily and fairly cheaply adapted to other basing modes. The Pershing II ballistic missile, an improved Pershing with extended range, was already under development. Moreover, since the new Pershing could be used on the existing transporter-erector-launcher, its cost was competitive. But with a range of 1,000 miles it was a candidate for deployment only in the Federal Republic of Germany. By contrast, the first generation of an entirely new medium-range ballistic missile was not as attractive. It would have cost more than the cruise missile, and there was skepticism about whether it could have been ready for deployment by 1984. Certainly a missile with terminal guidance and thus extremely high accuracy could not be ready until 1987.[12]

From a military perspective, some mix of systems was useful as a hedge against advances in Soviet defenses. What is not entirely clear is why other types of cruise missiles, in particular SLCMs, fell by the wayside. Cost and survivability may have been determining factors. Cruise missiles on surface ships were of dubious survivability, were expensive if new fast boats had to be built for them, or both. Moreover, the approach was too similar to that of the MLF, hence smacked of political gimmickry. Submarine-launched missiles would be survivable but expensive, either directly if new submarines were built or indirectly if current attack submarines were converted to the cruise missile role.

The argument for the visibility of land-based systems played an important role, especially early in the HLG discussions. How could Europeans have greater confidence in SLCMs under the sea than in Poseidons similarly located? Yet there are hints that Americans and Europeans were caught in a game of mirrors: West Germany felt that the United States preferred ground basing, while the United States argued that only ground-basing would be tangible enough to reassure West Germany.

Certainly modernization that included some continental-range cruise missiles gave proof that the United States would not extend the SALT II protocol's limits on cruise missiles. At that point the SALT and TNF stories converge. Surely that consideration played a part in ensuring that cruise missiles would be included, but it was not dominant, at least not on the basis of the testimony of officials involved. By the latter stages of the HLG discussions, moreover, efforts by the U.S. administration to reassure Senate hawks about SALT II further removed some of the European con-

12. Ibid. See also Communiqué, Special Meeting of Foreign and Defence Ministers, NATO, Brussels, Belgium, December 12, 1979.

cern about the protocol. Processes in the NATO alliance provided for a thorough review of options and rationales. The HLG, for instance, looked at a variety of systems and basing modes, and its two years of deliberations meant there was time for a political consensus to form on the emerging technical choices. Its key participants were defense officials from the NATO capitals. Chaired by the Pentagon, the HLG operated on the basis of U.S. leadership, rather than on the NATO principle of consensus, so the European allies had no formal veto in the process. In practice, however, the distinction was slight. There was broad agreement on the need for action, and the long process of analysis provided the chance to iron out most differences. However, the majority of the staff work was done by the United States; Britain occasionally submitted a paper, the Federal Republic of Germany seldom did, and the other countries did not participate at all. The neutron warhead dispute of 1977–78 was much on the minds of those engaged in TNF discussions, those in Washington in particular. The United States left little doubt, at least from the beginning of 1979 onward, of the direction it wanted NATO to take, but did so without bullying the Europeans.

Much of the last year of HLG discussions was devoted to basing, both mode and location. Because GLCMs had a relatively long range and were to be deployed in peacetime on NATO air bases, most European NATO countries were potential locations. Norway and Denmark were ruled out by their long-standing policies against basing NATO nuclear weapons in peacetime, and in 1977–79 Greece was not yet a participant in the NATO military command. Turkey had been a host to NATO MRBMs in the 1950s and 1960s, but this time it was in the midst of domestic turmoil and was still somewhat estranged from NATO and the United States because of the lingering aftermath of its Cyprus invasion in 1974 and the U.S. arms embargo. Turkey was thus an interested bystander but stated that while short-range TNF made sense for its defense, continental-range GLCMs did not. Five countries remained that were among the eventual NATO candidates—the Federal Republic of Germany, Britain, Italy, Belgium, and the Netherlands.

The HLG considered a number of specific basing issues that were important on either military or political grounds. For example, the Dutch, and to a lesser extent the other Europeans, put considerable emphasis on what later came to be known as the "shift." These countries were particularly anxious that the new deployments not increase either the total number of NATO nuclear weapons in Europe or those in any particular country. They could then argue to their publics that the new weapons merely represented a shift from one category of deployments to another. As part of this shift strategy the United States, in support of NATO's decision in December 1979, pledged to withdraw 1,000 nuclear warheads from Europe, a gesture with political significance. The removal was easy enough to accomplish since the existing NATO inventory of about 7,000 warheads in Europe was more than sufficient.

Cost and the related question of coproduction also consumed much of the HLG deliberations. In principle, the United States was willing to deploy the new systems under the "dual-key" arrangement, one in which the launchers were owned by the host country and the United States retained control over the warheads. Given NATO practice, that meant that the host country would have bought the launchers, an additional attraction from the U.S. point of view. The German government apparently decided early that its political problem would be lessened if the systems could be advertised as completely American, but other countries were interested in the dual-key arrangement. In the end, however, cost seems to have been an overriding factor for all countries, and all opted for a "single-key" plan, with the United States providing both launcher and warhead. That made financial sense at the time but complicated future politics. It made the new deployments appear to be a U.S. scheme, when that was not the case, and it provided an opening for arguments by opponents that the European countries might be dragged into nuclear war against their will. In fact, with or without the dual-key plan, no U.S. president would fire nuclear weapons from Europe without consulting his European counterpart in the host country. British Secretary of State for Defence Francis Pym made that implicit understanding explicit in discussing the new deployments, with the argument that the British government would in any case have an effective veto over firing weapons.[13]

Coproduction arrangements were obviously bound up with how the cost of the new systems was to be shared. The European allies were and remain interested in some coproduction of cruise missiles, both on economic grounds and to gain access to the technology. However, once the

13. For details on a possible medium-range ballistic missile (MRBM), see *The FY 1980 Department of Defense Program for Research, Development and Acquisition* (Department of Defense, 1979), p. VII-9, and *Fiscal Year 1980 Arms Control Impact Statements,* Joint Committee Print, 96 Cong. 1 sess. (Government Printing Office, 1979), p. 138.

Europeans decided against dual-key arrangements, their case for co-production became weak.

It was difficult to keep arms control and political considerations abreast of force planning. During 1978 there was periodic interest within NATO in analysis of arms control possibilities, but with scant results. Then, in the late spring of 1979, NATO formed a foreign office counterpart to the HLG body of defense ministers—the so-called Special Group —to look systematically at arms control and political considerations.[14]

Force planning in the HLG first lagged behind arms control, during the period when reassuring Europeans on SALT II was the dominant theme, then ran well ahead of it. By 1979 it appeared, especially in the Federal Republic of Germany, that NATO was on the verge of deploying new weapons in Europe capable of striking the Soviet Union with little evidence of having analyzed the prospects of arms control or the impact of new Western weaponry on East-West relations.

The Special Group operated in much the same way as the HLG, by attempting to link technical analysis to political reality and to build a consensus in support of the emerging NATO plan. It wrestled with the dilemma that threatens the future of the NATO TNF plan—arms control negotiations limited to continental-range systems are hardly attractive, given the rapid pace of Soviet SS-20 deployment and the fact that U.S. GLCMs, even if approved, would not begin arriving in Europe until late 1983.

Yet a serious arms control effort was regarded in Europe as a necessary condition for deployments. If NATO negotiating proposals were purely cosmetic, certain to be unappealing to the Soviet Union, they would be viewed as a mere fig leaf covering the NATO deployments, hence unlikely to serve even that role. But serious proposals were difficult to develop, and they opened the possibility of real disagreement across the Atlantic, with Americans regarded by Europeans as insensitive to European nuclear politics and Americans chiding Europeans for a naive attachment to arms control for its own sake.

Behind the immediate dilemma lay thorny practical questions and issues of doctrine. A negotiation seeking some parity in Eurostrategic systems was unrealistic in practice and disturbing in doctrine for the reasons outlined above. How should NATO respond if the Soviet Union

14. *Parliamentary Debates,* Commons, 5th series, vol. 977, session 1979–80, January 24, 1980 (Her Majesty's Stationery Office, 1980), col. 769.

sought to include in the negotiations so-called forward-based systems (FBS), that is, U.S. aircraft with nuclear capability based in Europe or in surrounding waters? That response was predictable given the long history in SALT of Soviet efforts to constrain FBS. Moreover, including some FBS seemed necessary if NATO sought limits on the Soviet Backfire bomber beyond those agreed upon as part of SALT II. Beyond that, there were arguments for broadening the negotiations to include shorter ranges of TNF. After all, negotiations over continental systems might only accomplish for shorter-range TNF what SALT had done for the SS-20: raise public concern about Soviet shorter-range systems unconstrained by arms control negotiations, the SS-21, SS-22, and SS-23 missiles in particular.

In the end, the Special Group chose a limited approach, the second part of NATO's December 1979 decision. The United States was to seek negotiations, linked to SALT, focusing on the continental-range systems of greatest concern—modern, land-based missiles. In practice, that meant the Soviet SS-20 and the planned NATO deployments. NATO was to address warheads rather than launchers, given that each SS-20 has three warheads while all new NATO systems will have a single warhead. Movement toward rough parity was the presumed objective. If agreement could be reached at a high level, that at least would provide incentive for NATO to build toward its total of 572. On the other hand, if Soviet offers were forthcoming with respect to the SS-20, the implicit logic of the proposal was that NATO would be prepared to scale down its projected deployments. That possibility was stressed both before and after December 1979 by European leaders, Helmut Schmidt in particular.

NATO never developed a clear rationale on the force planning issue regarding new deployments of either GLCMs or Pershing IIs. In part, that reflected the inherent ambiguity of NATO nuclear doctrine and nuclear deterrence in general. However, while military arguments were important, political and psychological factors were decisive and, as a result, there were no clear rationales. One rationale for new continental systems was plain enough and could be traced back to the Mulley letter: although NATO did not have much weaponry based in Europe capable of nuclear strikes on the Soviet Union, it did have some aircraft—U.S. F-111s and British Vulcan bombers—many of them aging and of dubious survivability, certain to encounter increasing difficulty penetrating Soviet air defenses, and badly needed for conventional missions in any case. Hence the most straightforward rationale for GLCMs and Pershings was a new means of accomplishing an old mission.

In retrospect, it is interesting to speculate whether NATO could have carried out its modernization plans based on that simple argument and whether the attempts to do so would have been preferable to the outcome that actually ensued. Probably the conjunction of events—SALT II, the threat of the Soviet SS-20, and the concerns reflected in the Schmidt speech—inevitably meant that the allies would move from military to more political rationales. Nuclear weapons became, as they so often have been, tokens of U.S. commitment. In the end, NATO had to reach a positive decision on GLCMs and Pershings because it had made the decision a political test of its ability to take a joint action in the face of Soviet hostility.

It is clear that once the focus of argument moved to political terrain, the rationale for new systems became clouded. The discussion became mired in the arcane language of "gaps" in the ladder of escalation. And when looking at weaponry level by level in terms of range, it was tempting to believe that NATO should somehow match the Warsaw Pact weapon for weapon. If NATO needed continental-range nuclear weapons certain to be able to strike the Soviet Union, why were the 400 Poseidon submarine-launched ballistic missile (SLBM) warheads assigned by the United States to NATO not sufficient, even granted that they were limited by SALT? More to the point, if Europe feared that the United States would not press the GLCM button, why should there be less concern about U.S. GLCMs in Germany than about U.S. Poseidons in the Atlantic? If it would not be easy for an American president to push the GLCM button, then new weapons were irrelevant. If it was, then they could be seen as dangerous and as providing the United States with ways to fight nuclear wars limited to Europe.

To be sure, there were counters to many of these qualms. The fact that the new weapons were American was viewed as coupling, not as decoupling, because no one could be sure that the Soviet Union would respect the neat categories of Western strategists and, in fact, that country might respond to a GLCM strike by hitting the United States proper. It was impossible to know how the Soviet Union would respond, and new systems surely would increase Soviet uncertainty by adding to Western NATO options. NATO would become a more difficult beast with which to deal. Yet the argument for the new deployments was neither simple nor easy to make compelling to public opinion in Western Europe. And it did not indicate why 572 was the magic number.

Processes, Politics, and Policies

Neither of the cruise missile episodes described above is particularly encouraging about the ability of the alliance to reach outcomes on sensitive nuclear issues at acceptable political cost. Both instances were "successes": Europeans ultimately accepted reassurances from the United States on the cruise missile provisions of SALT II, and NATO reached a positive decision on TNF in December 1979. Yet the successes were fragile, successes that can turn to failures. In both cases the costs were painfully plain. The process of reassuring the Europeans about the cruise missile provisions of SALT II complicated the task of reaching sensible decisions about the role of cruise missiles in NATO defenses. Coming on the heels of the neutron warhead dispute, the TNF decision elevated nuclear force planning into a "make-or-break" test of NATO cohesion, and it encouraged a miscasting of the TNF issue.

The handling of cruise missiles in SALT II was more or less nuclear business-as-usual within the alliance. U.S. consultations with Europeans, both within NATO and in bilateral negotiations between European NATO members and the United States, were meticulous in detail and supplemented by so-called reinforced meetings of the North Atlantic Council, with experts from respective capitals present. Yet the consultations had the same pattern as the previous ones: the United States stated its intentions and gave the Europeans a chance to object. It is not clear that this pattern was adequate. Many Europeans, for instance, remain disturbed by the sequence of events in 1977 that led to the firm inclusion of cruise missiles in the years ahead. When European interests, including cruise missiles, are even more directly affected by a future SALT or by TNF discussions outside SALT, former practices will not suffice, even if they have been well executed.

After the December 1979 decisions, the Special Group was reconstituted as the Special Consultative Group, with the same procedures. As preliminary U.S.-Soviet discussions began in Geneva in October 1980, the United States resisted European suggestions that the Special Consultative Group should make formal decisions on the consensus principle, as is the case with NATO arrangements for the mutual and balanced force reduction (MBFR) talks. In form, the United States will continue to decide negotiating approaches, although after consultation in detail with allies and on the presumption that clear European desires will not be overridden. So long as Europeans and Americans are in reasonable agreement on substance, this process should suffice. However, if Europeans begin to worry that the United States is not seriously pursuing the negotiations or, alternatively, believe the United States is trading European interests—in conventional cruise missiles, for instance—for negotiating objectives of special concern to the United States, they will insist on a more direct role.

The TNF decision was more of a departure in alliance practice. Washington's role was still predominant, but the process of analysis by the HLG and the Special Group was a joint one in which even the smaller NATO countries participated actively. The Dutch and Belgians, for example, helped to shape compromise decisions but then could not obtain support for those decisions from their parliaments; both countries eventually deferred a commitment to base cruise missiles on their soil. Still, the European NATO members, especially the Federal Republic of Germany, NATO's largest nonnuclear state, had to take more direct and public responsibility than in past nuclear decisions.

The negotiation that led to the TNF decision was similar to that of the neutron warhead dispute of 1977–78, but the relatively successful outcome of the former was a striking contrast. In 1977 and 1978 Washington painstakingly put together a scenario, to be ratified by NATO, whereby the United States would announce the production of components for the enhanced radiation warhead (ERW) and European NATO countries would assent to their deployment *after* the United States first offered not to deploy them in exchange for measures of Soviet restraint.[15] The process drew European leaders further into explicit support for a nuclear decision, which made them uncomfortable. The government of the Federal Republic of Germany stated that it would not be the only continental NATO member to deploy the neutron warheads, and that put enormous pressure on Belgium, the only country in which deployment made military sense and politics might permit it.

---

15. For a description of the neutron bomb and other recent U.S.-German military issues, see Alex A. Vardamis, "German-American Military Fissures," *Foreign Policy*, no. 34 (Spring 1979), pp. 87–106. For a detailed description of the neutron bomb as an issue in alliance politics, see Lothar Ruehl, "Die Nichtentscheidung über die 'Neutronenwaffe' " (The Dispute over the Neutron Bomb), *Europa Archiv*, vol. 5 (March 1979), pp. 137–50.

President Carter evidently did not realize, and was not so informed by his advisers, that clear-cut support from European heads of government for deploying neutron warheads in Europe simply was not likely to be forthcoming. Established practice in NATO and the reluctance of European leaders to take the lead on nuclear issues made European support unlikely. Once President Carter understood that, he declined to press forward with the planned scenario and announced in April 1978 that the issue would be deferred. That, in my view, was sensible, but European leaders were bound to feel that the rug had been pulled from beneath them.

The discussions on TNF modernization came soon after this experience, and alliance leaders were well aware that they could not afford to respond in the same way. While European leaders placed most of the blame on President Carter, they realized that their own reticence and conditions had contributed. The unfortunate aspect of the ERW debate was that the weapon itself hardly merited the transatlantic row it caused. Those on both sides of the Atlantic with long memories might well have suggested that the ERW was unwise in 1977 for the same reason that was cited a decade earlier: it was a marginal military gain that was bound to be purchased at high political cost. In 1977 a U.S. newspaper article described the ERW as "the ultimate capitalist weapon, destroying people but leaving buildings intact."[16]

The ERW weapon itself was not new. It had been designed in 1958, tested in 1963, considered for ABM systems in the 1960s and revived in the 1970s as an antitank weapon once the nuclear threshold had been crossed. It was hardly a great secret before the summer of 1977. The first failure was one of early warning. The neutron bomb proceeded easily through the alliance negotiations at the technical level, buried within defense ministry relations. It apparently was discussed at NPG meetings at least as early as 1974, but communiqués from those meetings mentioned it only once, in 1976, and then only indirectly.[17] Neither the NPG nor any other alliance instrument served to provide early warning of the possible political impact or pressed the issue on political leaders of allied governments. By the time the issue emerged from the NPG for

16. Walter Pincus, *Washington Post,* June 7, 1977.
17. The communiqué of the November 11, 1976, Nuclear Planning Group (NPG) meeting: "The United States is developing a new 8-inch nuclear projectile with greater accuracy and much reduced collateral damage."

decision, opportunities to shape the domestic politics surrounding it no longer existed. However compelling the NPG's technical analysis might have been, it had little effect.

There are several reasons why the NPG seems unlikely to play such a role. First, as a defense ministry operation, the group is not one that can make decisions involving sensitive political considerations. Moreover, its ministerial participants may share with their bureaucracies an interest in not sounding warning signals that would affect new weapons on which national budgetary decisions were being made. Third, the emphasis of the NPG on security, appropriate enough, has limited the range of officials in any government who know of the issues that come before it, are in a position to draw implications, or at least are able to do so early.

The performance of the NPG was much better in the case of TNF modernization. In that instance the NPG worked together with the HLG, and the task was not early warning but achieving consensus; moreover, the careful analysis of the HLG played a large part in setting the tone of the discussions. NATO politicians were less vulnerable then to the charge that the new missiles were an American whim, were unnecessary, or had resulted from casual processes.

The NPG was the result of the principal previous instance of strain in NATO nuclear arrangements—the multilateral force episode of the early 1960s.[18] Many of the initial concerns were the same; then as now they address the unknowable: would the United States respond with nuclear weapons to conventional attacks on Western Europe? The attention of the allies first was directed to hardware "solutions" that culminated in the multilateral force—a fleet of NATO surface ships, manned by sailors of different nations, carrying medium-range nuclear missiles whose firing is under U.S. control. However, the outcome was much more political than technical. From 1963 on the United States assigned submarine-launched missile warheads from its central strategic arsenal to NATO for planning purposes, and officers from NATO countries became participants in targeting at the Strategic Air Command (SAC) headquarters in Omaha, Nebraska.

The creation of the NPG in 1966 was the crucial political outcome. Initially with a rotating membership that always included the alliance's

18. The best brief account of the rise and fall of the multilateral force is Philip Geyelin, *Lyndon B. Johnson and the World* (Frederick A. Praeger, 1966), pp. 159–80.

major members (now with a permanent membership), it provided Europeans with access to U.S. nuclear planning.[19] It built confidence without changing weaponry or procedures for its use. One testimony to its success may be that in the late 1970s, unlike the previous decade, direct West German access to nuclear weapons was not an issue. The new cruise and ballistic missiles in Europe will undoubtedly be U.S. missiles. In the 1960s the NPG managed to lay nuclear matters to rest in part because the East-West climate improved after about 1963, and also because European confidence in the United States grew—hence nuclear matters were less sensitive.

Yet the political solution, the NPG, was adequate in the mid-1960s also because the hardware alternatives evidently made little sense. The MLF was obviously a military solution to a political problem. It was too "gimmicky" to persuade, and was unconvincing on military grounds to the ostensible military experts.[20] It stands in alliance politics as a lesson about the danger of pursuing aims of one sort through instruments of another.[21]

The TNF modernization decision by NATO in December 1979 skirted some of those dangers but dominated others. Again, the concerns to which the decision responded were largely political—doubts about the credibility of the U.S. nuclear guarantee to Europe. Yet the decision to deploy cruise and Pershing missiles was based on a more solid military rationale than was that of the MLF. A straightforward need to modernize NATO's limited continental arsenal was the clearest military rationale. But the arguments for more rungs on the escalation ladder and more options, hence leading to more uncertainty in Soviet minds, had a force in 1979 that they did not possess in 1965 given parity in the U.S.-Soviet nuclear balance and the pace of Soviet TNF deployments. Still, the latter arguments were arcane and easily misconstrued. Statements that emerged from Washington later, in particular Presidential Directive 59 signed in July 1980, seemed to many in Europe to suggest that the United States

19. For a general description of the NPG and its functions, see Richard E. Shearer, "Consulting in NATO on Nuclear Policy," *NATO Review*, vol. 27 (October 1979), pp. 25–28.

20. For a strong argument that NATO's planning about nuclear weapons in Europe during the 1950s and 1960s was incoherent and its policies unwise, see Nerlich, "Theatre Nuclear Forces in Europe."

21. This point is developed at length in Gregory F. Treverton, *The Dollar Drain and American Forces in Germany: Managing the Political Economics of Alliance* (Ohio University Press, 1978), pp. 166–207.

took the prospect of a limited nuclear war seriously. That possibility suggested that cruise missiles, far from adding to NATO's deterrent, would increase the danger to Western Europe. The United States must have believed that the Soviet Union would respond to the cruise missiles by an attack on their location, Western Europe, rather than on the United States; otherwise, why would the cruise missiles differ from American Poseidon submarines already assigned to NATO? These arguments gained force as the nuclear debate in Europe gained momentum. To many in Europe, especially those in the Low Countries (Belgium, Luxembourg, and the Netherlands) or on the left wing of the German Social Democratic party, the new deployments seemed unnecessary at best, merely an accumulation of weapons beyond reason, or provocative at worst, with the creation of additional targets for Soviet missiles.

Looking toward the Future

The two episodes from the recent history of cruise missiles in alliance politics avoided the serious misadventures of previous nuclear dealings across the Atlantic. Still, they do not augur well for the future. It has been difficult for the allies to reach agreement on cruise missile missions when the technology is new and ambiguous and when clear precedents and military service advocates are lacking. It has been even more difficult to come to some agreement under the pressure of ongoing arms control negotiations.

When NATO approached its decisions of December 1979, the fashionability of cruise missiles had waned. There was a reaction in Europe to the previous excessive enthusiasm about what cruise missiles might do for NATO. Yet that issue is far from settled. Enthusiasm in the Pentagon for cruise missiles gathered steam in 1980. The issue of conventionally armed cruise missiles is yet to come, and it may become entangled with possible future arms control negotiations.

In the near term, NATO's December 1979 decisions commit it to ensure the continental-range nuclear mission for cruise missiles in any subsequent arms control negotiations that may follow the preliminary U.S.-Soviet discussions of late 1980. Depending on what measures of restraint the Soviet Union is willing to offer, NATO may decide to scale down its intended deployment of continental systems. That might affect the number of cruise missiles deployed, but by the military logic of

NATO's decisions, some cruise missiles should be deployed. If there is a military rationale for deploying continental-range cruise missiles in Europe, that case exists almost independent of the Soviet SS-20. Even if the Soviet Union agreed to hold the SS-20 to, say, 150 launchers, NATO should not, on military grounds, reduce its own new deployments to zero.

On this score, however, politics diverges from technical judgment. To the extent that public opinion in Western Europe supports the NATO plan, it does so in the belief that it is necessary to counter the SS-20. That miscasts the TNF issue, and NATO is thus vulnerable to Soviet manipulations—even more so because for many European leaders, including those in the Federal Republic of Germany, the planned NATO deployments are a source of political discomfort. Those leaders will have an incentive to seize on Soviet offers as a possible solution to the problem.

Such a possibility will not be easy to avoid. Cruise missiles and Pershings will not begin to arrive in Europe until late 1983 or 1984 and will not be completed in the case of GLCMs until mid-1989. That will give the Soviet Union abundant opportunities to try to chip away at the NATO decision. The Soviet effort began even before the decision, with Soviet President Brezhnev's October 6, 1979, speech in East Berlin setting forth what served as the basic Soviet position.[22] That position was to discuss reductions in Soviet medium-range missiles if NATO did not go ahead with its intended deployments.

The perilous state of the SALT process compounds NATO's problem. Europeans assumed in December 1979 that SALT II would be ratified soon and that the TNF negotiations that NATO called for would take place as part of SALT III. SALT II ratification was then suspended after the Soviet invasion of Afghanistan, President Ronald Reagan firmly rejected the treaty, and the entire process is now in doubt.

Brezhnev's October speech was too little, too late. And there was scant evidence that the Soviet Union was prepared to make offers that would have been difficult for NATO to handle, such as an offer to freeze SS-20 deployments. Early in 1980 Moscow altered its position by saying that NATO did not need to rescind, but rather to suspend its December decisions formally before negotiations could begin.[23] During Chancellor Schmidt's visit to Moscow in July, the Soviet Union retreated from that

22. President Brezhnev's speech is excerpted in *Survival,* vol. 22 (January–February 1980), pp. 28–30.
23. See, for example, Soviet Foreign Minister Gromyko's remarks on February 18, 1980, reproduced by Tass.

position, indicating that preliminary U.S.-Soviet talks could begin but any agreements would have to await ratification of SALT II.[24] At the same time, however, Moscow returned to a demand that it had made since the beginning of SALT I—that any negotiations on theater nuclear forces would have to include the so-called American FBS, U.S. aircraft with nuclear capability based in Europe.[25]

No doubt the momentum of Soviet weapon programs made and continues to make it unlikely that Moscow could initiate proposals seriously affecting the pace of SS-20 deployments. To that extent, NATO may be saved from errors of its own by miscalculations on the part of the Soviet Union. Soviet leaders may have regarded such proposals as unnecessary in any case, while still calculating that internal strains would prevent NATO from going forward without Moscow exerting its influence. It is not yet clear that they are wrong. Afghanistan and continuing East-West tension notwithstanding, domestic politics within European countries will make it hard for NATO to stay on course. During its first months in office, the Reagan administration committed itself to pursue the TNF talks with the Soviet Union. That was reassuring to Western Europeans, but there remained doubts about how serious the administration was about those talks in particular and nuclear arms control in general. It was painfully clear that beyond the initial stages, TNF arms control made little sense without some approach to strategic arms control: why limit the Soviet SS-20 while the Soviet SS-17, SS-18, and SS-19 were unconstrained?

Moreover, even if serious negotiations over continental TNF are begun, it is far from obvious that the outcome will be desirable from NATO's point of view. Soviet SS-20 deployments will proceed apace, and NATO will be in the position of trying to trade its prospective systems—cruise and Pershing missiles—for Soviet systems that already exist. By 1983, when the first Pershings and GLCMs begin arriving in Europe,

24. The Soviet response was complicated. As outlined in *Pravda,* July 15, 1980, Moscow still preferred its original position. Its second preference was to negotiate continental TNF as part of SALT III—that is, after the ratification of SALT II. But it was willing to engage, as a fallback, in preliminary discussions.

25. Gromyko laid down a marker on this score at his press conference after the signing of SALT II, on July 25, 1979, when he said that "success [in SALT III] is possible only when the talks cover the question of the American forward-based facilities, i.e., the U.S. military bases, of which there are enough, both in Europe and outside Europe, and which are known to be trained in the military-strategic respect on the Soviet Union." The Soviet position after Schmidt's visit is described in *Pravda,* July 4, 1980.

the Soviet Union could have deployed about 300 SS-20s, two-thirds of them within range of Western Europe. There will be long debates about what is to be included in the negotiations. For instance, should all Soviet SS-20s be included, or should those deployed in the Far East out of range of Europe be exempt even though they could be moved westward in a short time? What to do about FBS and comparable Soviet systems will compound the problem. So also will questions of verification. The standards of SALT will be precedents, but those will be much harder to implement for TNF systems that are mobile, small, and frequently usable for both nuclear and conventional purposes.[26]

At best, negotiations will be measured in years, not months. Although some negotiation may make it easier for Europeans to move forward with deployments of the new U.S. missiles, the politics surrounding the issue could produce the opposite outcome—negotiation might abet the feeling that NATO should pause to see what the USSR offers or that arming while negotiating is inappropriate, despite the fact that the Soviet Union does just that.[27] Again, apparent political requirements may diverge from what makes military sense.

After the NATO decision, the focus of Soviet propaganda shifted from cruise missiles to Pershings, based on the argument that the entire deployment was nothing but more U.S. strategic forces, no matter where they were located.[28] In that light, the Pershings were more menacing because they cut the warning time of an attack on the Soviet Union from almost half an hour to several minutes. That suggests the possibility that NATO might scale down or even eliminate its planned Pershing deployments in exchange for Soviet constraints on the SS-20 while moving forward with GLCM basing, since Soviet anxieties about the surprise attack potential of slow cruise missiles do not seem as legitimate to Westerners as the concern about the fast ballistic weapons. However, there will be strong arguments for retaining some Pershings: their deployment will be com-

26. These issues are discussed at length in Gregory F. Treverton, *Nuclear Weapons in Europe,* Adelphi Paper (London: IISS, 1981). See also Lawrence Freedman's interesting proposals in "The Dilemma of Theatre Nuclear Arms Control," *Survival,* vol. 22 (January–February 1981), pp. 2–10.

27. Before December many of those critical of the NATO program argued that decisions on producing GLCMs and deploying them should be separated to give the Soviet Union an opportunity to demonstrate good faith. See, for example, Klaas G. de Vries, "Responding to the SS-20: An Alternative Approach," *Survival,* vol. 21 (November–December 1979), pp. 251–55.

28. See, for instance, the article in *Pravda* by Soviet Defense Minister Dmitri Ustinov, October 25, 1979.

pleted several years before that of the GLCMs; they serve as a hedge against advances in Soviet air defenses; and the Soviet Union is likely to retain its European ballistic missiles in any case.

Beyond the immediate question of whether NATO will follow through on its planned missile deployments, the United States and its allies in Europe will continue to face difficult cruise missile issues in arms control negotiations, especially that of conventional cruise missiles. One specific nuclear issue could arise if the French or, more likely, the British sought U.S. cooperation in building cruise missiles as part of their independent deterrents. Another problem lies in the uncertain future of conventionally armed cruise missiles. On this issue there are disturbing parallels with the issue of nuclear cruise missiles in the mid-1970s. Exactly what purpose the alliance might serve by opting for conventionally armed missiles remains unclear. (Roger Palin offers suggestions in chapter 6.) While enthusiasm for nuclear cruise missiles wanes, hope for conventional versions remains. For the moment, the absence of serious arms control negotiations in Europe creates time for clear thought. However, negotiations in the near future could again return the United States and its allies in Europe to their position during SALT II: eager to protect some cruise missile options, in this case conventional, but uncertain of which or how important each may be. There will also be the practical impossibility of distinguishing conventional from nuclear deployments.

CHAPTER FOURTEEN

The European Nuclear Powers: Britain and France

LAWRENCE D. FREEDMAN

BY THE mid-1970s the cruise missile represented all the problems that technological advance had brought to arms control. Unexceptional in payload, accuracy, range, or speed, its key features were low cost and versatility. These qualities were expected to lead to a profusion of missiles, which would appear in a bewildering variety of forms and be prepared for a great variety of missions. The standard categories (strategic or tactical, conventional or nuclear) by which nuclear weapons had been understood, and upon which arms control negotiations had been based, were inappropriate for the new missile. Moreover, it was asserted, the relative inexpensiveness of cruise missiles would encourage a new round in the arms race and drastically complicate attempts to inhibit the spread of nuclear weapons.

For all these reasons Christoph Bertram described cruise missiles as the "most obvious example" of a trend toward "multi-category, multi-mission weapons" that constituted a challenge to "notions that have been essential to arms control policies of the past twenty years. It is blurring the distinction between strategic and non-strategic weapon systems and making the verifiability of agreements uncertain."[1]

In the early 1980s it is possible to assess the extent to which the

Lawrence Freedman is head of policy studies at the Royal Institute of International Affairs, London.

1. Christoph Bertram, "The Future of Arms Control," in *Arms Control and Technological Change: Elements of a New Approach*, pt. 2, Adelphi Paper 146 (London: International Institute for Strategic Studies, 1978), pp. 4, 5.

claims made for the cruise missile by both proponents and opponents are justified. This chapter addresses one particular claim—that the important beneficiaries of the advent of cruise missiles will be the small nuclear powers, Britain and France, for which cruise missiles offer an inexpensive means of at least remaining in the nuclear arena and possibly a means of substantially enhancing existing capabilities. This claim was quickly tested; in the late 1970s both Britain and France were engaged in major studies on the future of their nuclear forces in which serious consideration was given to possible roles for cruise missiles. In both countries it was concluded that cruise missiles offered far less than had been supposed.

Cruise Missiles and Proliferation

The strategic and political significance of possible British and French acquisition of cruise missiles was, in line with the general discussion of the impact of these weapons, viewed largely within the context of arms control. This tended to limit the analysis in three ways. First, other considerations were sometimes neglected. For example, if cruise missiles did offer an inexpensive nuclear option, as was often supposed, an important implication for the balance of defense expenditures in Britain and France was that it would be possible to devote additional resources to conventional forces.

Second, the issue of British and French acquisition was often subsumed under the broader issue of whether the prospect of inexpensive delivery vehicles would encourage nuclear proliferation. It was almost taken for granted that cruise missiles would soon appear in the British and French arsenals, yet this was a presumption that deserved to be examined with care, for these were critical cases. If neither country was interested in cruise missiles, it was unlikely that others that lacked developed nuclear forces would be attracted.

Third, the arms control issue of greatest concern in the 1970s was SALT, which provided the focus for much of the discussion of cruise missiles. As a result, most attention was devoted to the direct effects of introducing the cruise missile into the U.S. force structure, with the consequences of its appearance in the British and French force structures as a subsidiary matter.

The development of these views on cruise missiles is worth noting briefly, inasmuch as such views were commonly expressed only a few years ago. Kosta Tsipis did much to draw attention to the new technology; he argued in 1975 that "the relative ease and low initial cost of its production will almost certainly induce several near-nuclear states to attempt acquisition of long-range cruise missiles." Tsipis was fatalistic about the extent to which military establishments would pressure their governments to this end and the extent to which the net result would be to diminish the security of all.[2]

Richard Burt, then at the International Institute for Strategic Studies, did much to implant the notion of cruise missiles as an inexpensive and interesting option for Europeans. Burt also observed that cruise missiles would be relatively inexpensive and made explicit the relevance of this for Britain and France as "an efficient means of enhancing existing capabilities." Britain, he asserted, using existing attack submarines "could effectively quadruple the size of her small and hence vulnerable sea-based missile force." Such improvements, he expected, would compel those currently inclined to dismiss these forces to take notice. Thus cruise missiles threatened to "change the situation" in which it was believed "that strategic nuclear weapons are the virtual monopoly of the two superpowers." When Britain and France deployed cruise missiles "in large numbers," the deployment would affect the "bilateral nature" of SALT.[3]

Later in 1976 Alexander Vershbow repeated, and to some extent exaggerated, the arguments of both Tsipis and Burt. He asserted that cruise missiles would "soon offer an effective and inexpensive delivery system to many countries." Their acquisition by "America's nuclear allies would transform their present token nuclear deterrent into a potent strategic force." This would affect the balance of political power within NATO

2. Kosta Tsipis, "The Long-Range Cruise Missile," *Bulletin of the Atomic Scientists*, April 1975, pp. 14–26; and Stockholm International Peace Research Institute, *World Armaments and Disarmament: SIPRI Yearbook 1975* (Cambridge, Mass.: MIT Press; Stockholm: Almqvist & Wicksell, 1975), pp. 332–34. There was no direct consideration of the European nuclear powers. Tsipis argued that U.S. deployment of air-launched cruise missiles (ALCMs) would validate the concept for others. He assumed this would, in turn, stimulate the United States to build up its air defenses. See also Kosta Tsipis, "Cruise Missiles," *Scientific American*, February 1977, pp. 20–29.

3. Richard Burt, "The Cruise Missile and Arms Control," *Survival*, vol. 18 (January–February 1976), p. 16. See also his "Technology and East-West Arms Control," *International Affairs*, vol. 53 (January 1977), p. 66: "At the minimum, nuclear-armed cruise missiles might provide a cost-effective approach to maintaining the viability of existing European 'minimum deterrent' forces in the 1980s and beyond."

because the U.S. nuclear role would be less dominant. SALT's bilateralism would also become "anachronistic" and the negotiations would have to be "multilateralized," apparently a retrograde step.[4]

In early 1977, as Robert L. Pfaltzgraff, Jr., and Jacquelyn K. Davis pointed out: "The sea-launched cruise missile could . . . constitute a new generation delivery system, less expensive in unit cost than alternative systems, for the nuclear forces of Britain and France in the late 1980s, either as independent national capabilities or merged into a joint European nuclear force."[5] Thus analysts from all sides of the strategic debate expressed their views, in what were taken to be the seminal articles on the subject, almost all taking for granted the attraction of cruise missiles for Britain and France.

Three basic propositions prevailed by early 1977: cruise missiles were relatively inexpensive; this was true even if they were developed and produced independently rather than purchased; and they offered a means of greatly enhancing the capabilities of small nuclear powers. None of these propositions had been seriously challenged, and they were beginning to gain wide acceptance. For example, in 1977 a British book, coauthored by a Conservative member of Parliament who now has ministerial responsibility, included a chapter on the cruise missile subtitled "The Vital Option," in which low cost and versatility were emphasized.[6] The *Economist,* with a keen eye for nuclear fashions, stated that Britain "almost certainly" would not be able to afford to replace Polaris by 1990 and reached the conclusion that cruise missiles "may be the answer."[7]

In June 1977 a significant boost was given to this enthusiasm when President Carter decided in favor of cruise missiles as a means of extending the active life of B-52s rather than producing the new B-1 bomber. This strengthened the belief that cruise missiles were associated with remarkable cost-effectiveness.

The position of cruise missiles at the center stage of SALT also ensured that they were noticed by the Europeans. The efforts of the Soviet

4. Alexander R. Vershbow, "The Cruise Missile: The End of Arms Control?" *Foreign Affairs,* vol. 55 (October 1976), p. 142.

5. Robert L. Pfaltzgraff, Jr., and Jacquelyn K. Davis, *The Cruise Missile: Bargaining Chip or Defense Bargain?* (Cambridge, Mass.: Institute for Foreign Policy Analysis, January 1977), p. 24.

6. James Bellini and Geoffrey Pattie, *A New World Role for the Medium Power: The British Opportunity* (London: Royal United Services Institute for Defence Studies, 1977), pp. 37–42.

7. *Economist,* March 26, 1977, p. 58. This idea became quite widespread among informed journalists.

Union to constrain the introduction of these weapons encouraged the view that they must be worth having (see chapter 11). One consequence was that the political pressure on the United States from its European allies neither to accept the general principle of a nontransfer clause, which would permit Soviet interference in the most intimate alliance relations, nor more specifically to foreclose their cruise missile option, created an impression of great European interest in exercising this option before any of the relevant countries had decided whether they actually wanted to do so.[8] Another consequence was that there was initial suspicion of any U.S. argument that cast doubt on the practical value of cruise missiles for Europeans, especially if it came from anyone associated with the Carter administration; such arguments were viewed as an attempt to remove some of the objections to a SALT accord.[9]

It was in this context that Britain and France began to consider seriously deployment of the cruise missile. Although policymakers in both countries have been impressed by similar limitations, as is shown below, there are important national differences in the approach of each country to all strategic questions, and they need to be considered separately.

Britain

There was considerable comment in the British media over the cruise missile, its possible use for Britain, and the extent to which it was entering SALT negotiations. It was regularly described as a major technological breakthrough, a "wonder weapon" or "military marvel."[10]

Those who were responsible for Britain's strategic force were kept well informed of the U.S. program for long-range cruise missiles through close

8. I have noted elsewhere the "Midas touch" of SALT I: "Anything in danger of being affected by the negotiations is soon represented as being particularly precious and requiring special protection." See Lawrence Freedman, "The Rationale for Medium-Sized Deterrence Forces," in *The Future of Strategic Deterrence*, pt. 1, Adelphi Paper 160 (London: IISS, 1980), p. 50.

9. This was probably less true in Britain than elsewhere. One reason may be the skepticism about cruise missiles contained in Ian Smart's influential paper, *The Future of the British Nuclear Deterrent: Technical, Economic and Strategic Issues* (London: Royal Institute of International Affairs, 1977).

10. For example, the *London Sunday Times*, September 26, 1976, stated: "wonder missile . . . amazing new cruise missile . . . a striking capacity hitherto only found in science fiction . . . the spread of this deadly weapon is now regarded by most analysts as inevitable." See also notes 6 and 7.

contact with their American counterparts. In 1974–75, as enthusiasm for the missile began to grow in defense circles of the United States, Britain made an unofficial effort through its American contacts to keep abreast of developments there.

The British defense industry also began to take notice. At what is now British Aerospace Dynamics at Stevenage a small team was put together to investigate the possibilities of cruise missiles. Their studies were extremely limited in scale but did analyze important features of a modern cruise missile, such as terrain contour matching (TERCOM) guidance and a variety of roles, including a conventional antiship role, but the studies gave little attention to a future strategic requirement. Some of the work of this group was supported by contracts from the British Ministry of Defence in 1976–78. The contracts were justified in July 1977 as clarifying "some of the options and limitations that would be involved in the possible development of a weapon system."[11]

Enthusiasm for cruise missiles within the Ministry of Defence was muted for two political reasons. First, there was suspicion within the Royal Air Force (RAF) of any move toward pilotless aircraft.[12] Second, the matter was difficult for the Labour government, in power from 1974 to 1979, because of the opposition of members of the party to any improvement in the British nuclear forces.

SALT and the Preservation of an Independent Deterrent

Official party policy was to maintain the effectiveness of a deterrent while renouncing a new generation of strategic nuclear weapons. To many on the Labour party's left wing, cruise missiles constituted not only a new generation of strategic nuclear weapons, but a particularly troublesome development that threatened to undermine all attempts at arms control. Fred Mulley, as Secretary of State for Defence, was anxious to downplay any interest in the matter within the ministry. He was displeased to dis-

11. *Parliamentary Debates,* Commons, 5th series, vol. 936, session 1976–77, July 28, 1977 (London: Her Majesty's Stationery Office, 1977), col. 396.

12. A hint of this is found in an admonition issued by the then chief of air staff, Air Chief Marshal Sir Neil Cameron, to the Royal Air Force Association in May 1977: "It is important to remember that advanced systems such as the Cruise Missile are still at the experimental stage. But we seem to be at the beginning of something new. The Royal Air Force is not necessarily in business to put a crew into every machine that flies. If unmanned vehicles can be developed to take on some of the roles of air power then we welcome it." *Observer,* May 8, 1977.

cover that studies had been commissioned on cruise missiles by British Aerospace Dynamics, and when asked about these studies in Parliament he described them as "limited" and intended "to enable us to participate in NATO discussions on the defence potential and arms control implications of these systems,"[13] and suggested that they were not actually being assessed as a possible British weapon (although they were).

He was correct, however, in stating that the studies were used in preparing the British position for consultations with the United States on SALT. The British were aware of the extent to which various limitations on cruise missiles were being discussed in SALT. Their minimum aim was to prevent the inclusion of a nontransfer clause, which would, as it was proposed by the USSR, involve a direct ban on the transfer of strategic missiles and "components, technical descriptions, and blueprints for the arms" to third parties. This could obstruct any form of nuclear cooperation, whether on ballistic or cruise missiles, that Britain might request from the United States. Moreover, Britain hoped to discourage restrictions that, while not legally binding, would nevertheless entail acceptance of an obligation in recognition of the moral force of an arms control agreement.

There was a disinclination on the part of the British government to address the problem of the future of the nuclear force; views were not firmly formed on what might be the most appropriate system to adopt should a Polaris replacement be required. Because no definite position had been taken against the nuclear force, officials took the view that it was their duty to preserve options in case the government wished to exercise them in the future. The British Aerospace studies provided some guidance on what cruise missile options might usefully be protected. One suggestion was that if cruise missiles were to be introduced, they were within indigenous capabilities, and that the best course might be to skip the current stage of U.S. development of subsonic cruise missiles and move directly to a supersonic model. Officials viewed such claims with considerable skepticism, particularly with regard to the cost and time scale of an indigenous British project. Nevertheless, Britain did ask the United States

13. The chairman of British Aerospace Dynamics, Admiral Sir Raymond Lygo, described studies on cruise missiles up to 1,500 kilometers as "internal": "We have studied the whole range of these options and the brochure we used for the study was made available to the Ministry of Defence. They did not ask for it but we let them have a copy." *Strategic Nuclear Weapons Policy,* 4th Report from the Defence Committee (HMSO, May 1981), pp. 185–86. See also *Parliamentary Debates,* Commons, 5th series, vol. 946, session 1977–78, March 21, 1978 (HMSO, 1978), col. 1314.

for assurances that supersonic cruise missiles would not be prohibited by SALT. When serious consideration was being given within the Ministry of Defence to air-launched cruise missiles (ALCMs), alarm was generated by proposals within SALT to designate all bombers carrying cruise missiles as heavy, regardless of the range and capacity of the bombers. This would mean that any British bombers carrying cruise missiles could be judged as exceeding SALT ceilings.

The variety of options the British seemed anxious to preserve surprised and sometimes irritated the Americans, but this was a consequence of the conjunction of SALT with the early stages of deliberations on the Polaris replacement issue before those deliberations had led either to authorization of a replacement or the identification of the preferred successor system.

The issue of delivery vehicles had been reviewed since the agreement on British purchase of the Polaris submarine-launched ballistic missiles (SLBMs) from the United States in December 1962 and had been confirmed in the Polaris Sales Agreement of 1963. Between 1967 and 1973 there were discussions of the problems posed by the development of a Soviet antiballistic missile (ABM) system. During this period there was little interest in a new launch platform, so the options were limited to SLBMs that could be fitted into the launch tubes of the four existing strategic ballistic missile submarines (SSBNs)—essentially a revised Polaris system or Poseidon. In 1973 Britain decided not to purchase Poseidon but to develop a new indigenous warhead for the Polaris A-3 that would be designed (using decoys and in-flight maneuvers) to penetrate the Galosh ABM system around Moscow, now limited by the 1972 U.S.-Soviet ABM treaty.[14] Cruise missiles were not relevant to this particular problem.[15] It is an indication of the speed with which cruise missiles appeared as an option that the major study in the mid-1970s on nuclear forces for medium-sized powers did not even consider cruise missiles.[16]

14. For the history of British policymaking on its strategic force, see Lawrence Freedman, *Britain and Nuclear Weapons* (London: Macmillan, 1980).

15. Cruise missiles were not mentioned in the only parliamentary analysis of the nuclear program in the 1970s before the debate at the end of the decade. *Nuclear Weapon Programme*, 12th report of the Expenditure Committee, session 1972–73 (London: HMSO, 1973).

16. Geoffrey Kemp, *Nuclear Forces for Medium Powers, Parts II and III: Strategic Requirements and Options*, Adelphi Paper 107 (London: IISS, 1974).

Later in the decade the problem of the future of the entire force began to be considered. The four SSBNs of the British Polaris fleet, each carrying sixteen Polaris A-3 SLBMs with three nonindependently targetable reentry vehicles of 200 kilotons, were in service within about two years at the end of the 1960s, unlike the comparable French SSBN fleet that was introduced over an extended period. This meant that the British boats would all begin to show the effects of wear and tear at the same time, a process originally calculated to be twenty years after launch but later estimated at about twenty-five years, that is, in the early 1990s. Furthermore, the pattern of patrols and the necessity of long periods of refitting had made it difficult to keep more than one boat on station for more than six months of each year. Consequently, the loss of one boat seriously undermined the credibility of the entire force. The sense of impending obsolescence in the 1990s was compounded by the withdrawal of the U.S. Polaris SSBNs from service by 1982 and the cessation of the production of SLBMs at Lockheed in the United States. Ways could be found to ensure that Britain would have sufficient missiles and spare parts until the 1990s but not much beyond that.

The complete British force, both boats and missiles, would thus need to be phased out in the 1990s. The fact that no element would remain serviceable meant that a clear decision was needed on whether Britain should stay in the strategic nuclear arena; if so, it would be necessary to consider all possible options for a successor system.

The analysis of both these issues began in earnest in 1978. In 1977 British government ministers were convinced of the need to identify the key issues associated with the future of the nuclear force. A small group of ministers was assembled to consider the matter—Prime Minister James Callaghan, Secretary of State for Defence Fred Mulley, Foreign Secretary David Owen, and Chancellor of the Exchequer Denis Healey. This committee authorized the establishment of two working groups on the political and technical aspects of the replacement question; the task of organizing these groups was undertaken by senior officials throughout 1978 and was headed by Sir Anthony Duff of the Foreign Office and Professor Ronald Mason, chief scientific adviser in the Ministry of Defence, respectively. The studies that resulted were discussed, somewhat inconclusively, by the committee of Labour party ministers in November 1978. Results were then presented after May 1979, with slight amendment, to a committee of the new Conservative cabinet that had a composition similar to that of ministries of the Labour group.[17] Studies continued until the issue was decided in the summer of 1980 in favor of replacement by means of Trident SLBMs.[18]

The basic analysis of the possible utility of cruise missiles for Britain was examined with greatest care by the group headed by Ronald Mason with the aid of technical studies prepared for that purpose. The following paragraphs present essentially the same arguments concerning cruise missiles that were developed in the Ministry of Defence by the summer of 1980.

Rethinking Costs and Benefits

The case for cruise missiles had to be made against a powerful argument for SLBMs. The success of the Polaris program was widely recognized: it provided a reasonably invulnerable, minimum deterrent at tolerable cost that was not too difficult to maintain, also at tolerable cost. An infrastructure existed for basing, refitting, controlling, and training to cope with SSBNs. All this created strong incentives for continuity, strengthened by the existence, presuming the special relationship with the United States could still be relied upon, of an obvious successor—Trident I—which was improved in both range and warhead versatility and was a known and proven system.

Cruise missiles presented an experimental, and therefore risky, option. The Ministry of Defence was in no position to repeat the experience of the 1950s and the 1960s when major new programs were canceled because resources could not match ambitions. If an experiment failed, in all probability there would be neither the time nor the money for another attempt. The case for cruise missiles therefore had to be extremely convincing and promise substantial savings in cost. It is important to recognize that the British debate has largely focused on cost-effectiveness rather than strategic doctrine. Because there is no interest in counterforce strategies, the concern has been to achieve a minimum deterrent at the

17. The relevant ministers were Prime Minister Margaret Thatcher, Secretary of State for Defence Francis Pym, Foreign Secretary Lord Carrington, and Chancellor of the Exchequer Sir Geoffrey Howe. Deputy Prime Minister and Home Secretary William Whitelaw was also involved. The Conservative committee was known as MISC-7.

18. The announcement was made on July 15, 1980. See the letters between the prime minister and the president of the United States and between the British secretary of state for defence and his U.S. counterpart in *The British `Strategic Nuclear Force,* Cmnd. 7979 (London: HMSO, July 1980).

lowest possible cost. The doctrinal issue has only been touched upon in considering how "minimum" a deterrent can be.

Proponents of cruise missiles contended that the unit cost of an individual cruise missile might be as little as 15 percent of that of a ballistic missile. It was argued that the possibility of a lower-cost nuclear force was neglected by the Ministry of Defence because of an instinctive desire for a "Rolls-Royce" deterrent when a "mini" deterrent would suffice. The benefits from the low unit cost of cruise missiles would be lost if large numbers had to be deployed on expensive launch platforms. The ministry strongly argued that this would be necessary if the previous requirement of an assured second strike capability to impose unacceptable damage was not to be relaxed. The proponents of cruise missiles stated that the only way Britain in its dire economic position could sustain its conventional forces was to purchase the absolute minimum nuclear force. In this way Britain was prepared to contemplate fewer weapons getting through, some vulnerability against surprise attack, and an increased dependence on the United States.[19]

Another issue that was debated, although not a major source of controversy, was TERCOM guidance. If it was to be employed, Britain would be dependent on a continual supply of up-to-date topographical information on the routes to Soviet targets from the United States, digitized for use. It was thought that Britain could construct indigenously, but at enormous expense, all components of a cruise missile, including the complex electronics of TERCOM.[20] But the basic satellite information

19. See, for example, David Fairhall, "How Latter-Day Doodlebugs Could Save Britain Millions," and "A Deterrent That Is Both Cheap and Flexible," *Guardian* (London), November 5, 1979, and March 4, 1980.

20. British Aerospace Dynamics Group (BAe D) informed a parliamentary committee that: "On the basis of existing UK technology and resources, and particularly the work BAe D has already carried out, we are confident that we can develop a cruise missile system acting as a prime contractor in a national programme." *The Future of the United Kingdom's Nuclear Weapons Policy,* 6th Report from the Expenditure Committee, Minutes of evidence taken before the Defence and External Affairs Sub-Committee, session 1978–79 (London: HMSO, 1979), p. 241. In a memorandum submitted to the same committee by the International Institute for Strategic Studies it is suggested that such a national venture could cost four times as much as purchasing from the United States (pp. 89–92). In a subsequent memorandum submitted in December 1980 British Aerospace again claimed that British industry "possesses the capability to design and build a cruise missile system within the required time scale, comparable to the current US cruise missiles." It also suggested that a "supersonic cruise high-lo missile" could be constructed, but at a higher cost than that of a subsonic missile. *Strategic Nuclear Weapons Policy,* p. 182.

and the TERCOM software were quite beyond British resources.[21] Thus there would be far greater dependence on continual cooperation from the United States than that currently necessary to provide targeting information for SLBMs.

The penetration of air defenses and the most appropriate launch platform were two additional concerns. An assessment of the air defense problem depends on a judgment both of the possible means available to the Soviet Union to counter cruise missiles and the extent to which it would be likely to deploy such means in response to the expected U.S. development of ALCMs and ground-launched cruise missiles (GLCMs). It is noteworthy that the British analysts were more impressed by the possibility of a serious air defense barrier than U.S. analysts were, but this may have been a result of the greater American confidence that this barrier could be overcome. The means to do so would not necessarily be available to Britain. The technique of saturation against defenses requires extra missiles for a set of targets, particularly given the fact that at present cruise missiles have single warheads.[22] Furthermore, the steady improvement of penetration capabilities (such as lower radar signatures) indicated that there would be less value from the purchase of the initial missiles. While ballistic missiles could last for two decades, cruise missiles might need replacing before one decade. This was stated in a government document accompanying the decision to purchase the Trident:

> It is impossible to put precise figures on what proportions of CMs [cruise missiles] Soviet air defences in the two decades from the early 1990s—roughly the timeframe we want for our new strategic system—might succeed in shooting down; but we must reckon with the possibility that it could progressively become very substantial, especially since we probably could not afford to re-equip with new and better CMs as often as the United States may well do to keep pace with defences in this new and rapidly changing field. We have to take into account also that whereas the United States ALCM force can plan to saturate the defences of key strategic targets, we could not operate on the same scale.[23]

21. It has been suggested that once the basic targets have been chosen, continued access to U.S. maps is not necessary. This is not the case. The "contours" used in terrain contour matching guidance are subject to change because of climatic and seasonal factors as well as the effects of civil and military construction and demolition projects. Furthermore, the mapping technology still has wide scope for improvement and any cruise missile force would require access to new developments.

22. Multiple independently retargetable reentry vehicles (MIRVs) on cruise missiles were forbidden in the abortive SALT II treaty.

23. *The Future United Kingdom Strategic Nuclear Deterrent Force,* Defence Open Government Document 80/23 (London: Ministry of Defence, 1980), p. 15.

This presumption of a substantial Soviet defensive capability against cruise missiles is a rare example of the British Ministry of Defence anticipating a major change in the strategic environment. In general a static picture is presented, without decisive breakthroughs in either ABM or antisubmarine warfare (ASW) technology. A major error in the balance of these predictions, particularly the reemergence of a ballistic missile defense without a substantial cruise missile defense, would confound the British calculations. From current evidence, however, it is difficult to quibble with this judgment. Another, more serious criticism is that it is assumed that the "saturation" requirement against air defenses for the British force would have to be the same as that of the U.S. force. Because Britain is interested in a limited set of targets, it is argued, it will have to pass through only a limited corridor en route and will thus have to cope with only those Soviet defenses covering that specific sector.

This criticism is often overstated. First, even if the air defense problem is limited, it still has to be overcome, and this raises the numerical requirement for cruise missiles as opposed to ballistic missiles, which are presumed to have a "free ride." Second, it should not be assumed that the force requirement is simply proportional to the target structure to be attacked. Depending on the range of the interceptor missiles, a small force operating in isolation is likely to attract the attention of defenses apparently with duties beyond the particular corridor under attack. Third, this type of air defense places a premium on a concentrated attack. A dispersed set of targets would mean penetrating the defensive barrier at a number of points with only a few missiles. A concentrated attack would reduce the flexibility in British target plans. The most important target would be Moscow, which would undoubtedly be the most heavily defended.

The uncertainties about Soviet air defense make it difficult to calculate the numbers of cruise missiles needed to ensure that a given target will be reached. Those arguing for cruise missiles contend that as long as the Soviet Union had to assume that some missiles would get through, a deterrent system was in operation. Furthermore, the cruise missile's versatility in basing would make possible a deployment on simple launch platforms. Thus an SLBM force, in which four expensive submarines were needed to ensure that one with sixteen SLBMs would be on patrol at all times, was contrasted with the possibility of a British GLCM or one based on surface craft or possibly based on existing types of aircraft and submarines.[24] Mobile ballistic missiles are possible, but the simpler the basing mode the more cost advantages cruise missiles have because of their smaller size.

One serious objection to this approach was the question of survivability. In an age of accurate missiles, fixed systems are vulnerable to a surprise attack. Keeping aircraft on airborne alert is extremely expensive in fuel, airframes, and personnel, and potentially politically awkward because of objections to continual patrols of nuclear-armed aircraft, especially with the publicity given recently to crashes of RAF aircraft.[25] The Ministry of Defence estimated that to have about 300 ALCMs carried on a dozen aircraft on constant alert it would be necessary to purchase 40 to 50 large and expensive aircraft: "We did not do a detailed costing of that because it was quite clear . . . [it was] . . . going to be huge."[26]

The protest generated by proposals to deploy 160 U.S. GLCMs in Britain as part of NATO's program to modernize its theater nuclear force (TNF) indicated this was another option that would raise political difficulties. Nevertheless, the fact that GLCMs offered the least expensive basing mode and that American GLCMs were to be deployed in Britain anyway did make a British purchase of a number of them appear an attractive option. With the air defense problem in mind, it was again suggested that 300 GLCMs might suffice. This point was countered by distinguishing between the role to be played by the U.S. GLCMs and that of a national strategic deterrent.

GLCMs would be vulnerable to a surprise attack, even if they were being moved around the country, because the area in which movement would be possible in a country of Britain's size and population density would be limited. However, the American GLCMs were to be used in a stage in the escalation ladder before all-out attacks, when both sides were presumed to be concentrating their strikes on predominantly military targets. It was assumed that in these circumstances the area bombardment involved in a surprise attack against GLCMs would be eschewed by the USSR because of the likelihood that it would lead to comparable retaliation and thus all-out war. However, if British GLCMs were the only

24. The full range of options is discussed in Peter Nailor and Jonathan Alford, *The Future of Britain's Deterrent Force*, Adelphi Paper 156 (London: IISS, 1980).
25. The accident rate for fixed-wing aircraft of the RAF has averaged more than twenty a year.
26. Evidence of Michael Quinlan, presented in *Strategic Nuclear Weapons Policy*, p. 102.

possible means of retaliation, destroying them through area bombardment would effectively disarm the country. GLCMs thus failed the test of
survivability. The option was considered, as is shown below, but only as a
British contribution to NATO's TNF and not as a successor to Polaris.

All this pointed to sea-launched options. Before examining these various possibilities, it should be noted that there were very serious technical
doubts concerning the ability of the guidance system to cope with long
journeys over the sea: "Beyond a certain distance cumulative inertial-
navigation errors may mean too high a risk that the missile will fail to
make its landfall accurately enough to initiate the overland navigation
phase successfully."[27] Because the United States was concentrating on air-
launched and ground-launched systems, there was concern in Britain that
this particular problem might not receive sufficient attention and might
introduce a more difficult issue—whether it would be necessary to undertake nationally some of the development work for the missile and support
systems. (In 1981, however, it was acknowledged privately that the progress of the U.S. SLCM program had been underestimated.)

Of the various sea-launched options, the notion of mounting cruise
missiles on small surface ships failed the survivability test. Another problem, which also characterized "minisubmersibles," lay in command and
control.[28] Not only would communication with many different vessels be
difficult, but there would be problems of finding the necessary manpower
for all these systems and maintaining the high quality control among
senior officers that is necessary for nuclear responsibilities.

All these considerations pointed toward a submarine-launched system,
although a move to submarines would negate the cost advantages of cruise
missiles. Because more cruise missiles than ballistic missiles would be
needed to attack a given target, more submarines would be needed—even
more submarines given the additional number required to ensure that a
sufficient number of boats were on station at all times.

It was this line of argument that led Ian Smart, in one of the first critical
appraisals of the cruise missile option, to conclude that it would be as expensive as, perhaps even more expensive than, the SLBM option. He calculated that to have an SLCM force equivalent in destructive power to
one out of five submarines, each carrying sixteen modern ballistic missiles

27. *The Future United Kingdom Strategic Nuclear Deterrent Force*, p. 16.
28. The argument for minisubmersibles is contained in a memorandum submitted
to the Expenditure Committee by Richard Garwin in *The Future of the United Kingdom's Nuclear Weapons Policy*, p. 246.

with three warheads of 170 kilotons, would require seventeen submarines, each carrying twenty-four single-warhead cruise missiles.[29] Ministry of Defence calculations, using a more demanding standard by assuming Trident I SLBMs, each with eight warheads of 100-kiloton yield, came to an even more startling force requirement—eleven submarines, each carrying eighty SLCMs. The smaller number of submarines was a consequence of an attempt to be realistic about cost and construction capacity—the number of boats that could be constructed in British yards over a decade —but that estimate had the effect of making the option appear even more preposterous. There would be a limited number of launch tubes, perhaps a maximum of twenty, so it would be necessary to reload and fire a number of times.[30] The length of time this would take (perhaps hours) would be sufficient to alert enemy attack submarines to the position of the boats and render them vulnerable. The probability of this happening was increased by the limited range of the SLCMs (reinforced by the navigational problems of flying for too long over sea) and thus by the limited patrol area available to the submarines. It could be argued that a less demanding standard would provide a less preposterous proposal, but even forty SLCMs per boat would raise similar problems.[31]

The Ministry of Defence stated that a force of eleven boats, each carrying eighty SLCMs, would "cost at least a third as much again to acquire and about twice as much to run" as a force of five boats each with sixteen Trident SLBMs. This suggests costs of about £7,500 million and £500 million respectively (compared to £5,600 million and £250 million for the Trident).[32]

Proponents of the SLCM argued for placing them in the torpedo tubes of existing strategic nuclear submarines (SSNs). There were a number

29. Smart assumed that no more than half the SLCMs would reach their targets. See Smart, *The Future of the British Nuclear Deterrent*.

30. *The Future United Kingdom Nuclear Strategic Deterrent Force*, p. 16. This assumed that torpedo tubes would be adopted as the launch mode: "Alternative launch modes, such as vertical launch on the SLBM pattern, would require extensive new system development and submarine design. The United States has made a preliminary study of using such modes on a limited scale in hunter-killer submarines, but there is no United States development programme. Without such a programme . . . the burden of development would fall entirely on us if we wanted such a solution."

31. Nailor and Alford consider a force of seven or eight boats, each carrying twenty-four SLCMs, in *The Future of Britain's Deterrent Force*, p. 33.

32. *The Future United Kingdom Strategic Nuclear Deterrent Force*, p. 17. Official estimates put the cost of a four-boat Trident force at £5,000 million, with £600 million for the fifth boat (authorization of which remains in doubt). No official estimates have yet been released on the operating costs of the Trident.

of problems with this approach also. First, these SSNs contained an average of only eight torpedo tubes. Second, the number of boats required would use up the existing stock and more. Third, if SSNs were converted to SLCMs and dedicated to the strategic role, something would have to be done to deal with their previous responsibilities. If, however, they were to have dual capabilities, there would be the general problem of dual-capable systems, aircraft, and submarines that would be required for both roles at the same time. When the boats were needed for anti-submarine and antiship roles they should also be on station and serve as a deterrent. There would be a reluctance to commit the SSNs to conventional engagements because of the chance that a critical part of the strategic force would be lost in the process. Last, there would be dangers of miscalculation if an attack on these SSNs, understood by the attacker to be operating in a conventional mode, was perceived as a preemptive strike against the nuclear force.

Objections were raised to many of these arguments against cruise missiles. However, it is important to remember the point made above: to those considering the replacement issue, the most obvious, straightforward, and safe option was a modern version of the previous force. The onus was on the cruise missile proponents to prove that their approach would be significantly less expensive. This they failed to do.

When the Defence Committee of the House of Commons reviewed the decision on the Trident, it concluded: "The evidence does not suggest that Cruise Missiles offer a credible alternative as a strategic deterrent to an SSBN force. Substantial savings could be made only by adopting a land-based cruise missile system or by placing such missiles in small surface ships or submersibles which could operate in coastal waters but to do so would involve operating difficulties, and relaxing the survivability criterion for the weapons so that they would be vulnerable to a surprise attack." Even the minority Labour group on the committee wrote in their dissenting report: "We accept the arguments for ballistic over cruise missiles."[33]

Additional Strategic Considerations

In the late 1970s the future of the Vulcan bombers was also under consideration. The Vulcan had been superseded by the Polaris as the mainstay of the deterrent in 1970, but Vulcans had been retained as long-range strike aircraft. By 1979 the forty-eight Vulcans were scheduled to

33. *Strategic Nuclear Weapons Policy,* pp. viii and xlii.

be phased out in the early 1980s. Replacing them was to be one of the many roles of the new Tornado-class combat aircraft, but there was dissatisfaction within official ministries at Whitehall over the limited range of the Tornado and its inability to mount attacks against targets in Soviet territory.

Some thought was given to the possibility of putting cruise missiles on Vulcans to extend their active life in the same way that the United States was planning to do with its B-52s. However, the Vulcans were not worth preserving in this manner, primarily because their large crew requirements placed too many demands on scarce RAF manpower. Tornados were not well designed for cruise missiles and could not carry many. Fitting them in this way would also mean that they would not be available for their many other roles.

During 1978 and 1979, when NATO was moving toward the adoption of GLCMs to be produced in the United States and based in Europe as part of the TNF, the issue was raised of whether Britain might purchase some GLCMs of its own to provide a Vulcan replacement benefiting again from a U.S. production line and logistics support.

Although this idea was energetically canvassed by British senior policy-makers, including the chief of defence staff, Air Marshal Sir Neil Cameron, they failed to gain acceptance of their view. In part this was due to doctrinal objections: it was argued that the Tornado was sufficient for most purposes and that there was no overwhelming requirement for a British theater capability against Soviet territory. However, the more effective objections were more practical in nature. First, as the share of the defense budget appropriated by nuclear forces was about to grow significantly because of replacement of the Polaris there was little inclination among the chiefs of staff, who were concerned about the state of their conventional forces, to endorse an even larger outlay for nuclear weapons. The cost of a small British GLCM force would have been between £500 and £1,000 million. Second, there was an important question mark regarding the ability of British nuclear weapon research establishment at Aldermaston, which has had serious manpower problems, to cope with warhead programs for both Trident and cruise missiles. It was this second problem that apparently brought the debate to a negative conclusion.

There was some support for adopting a limited GLCM force as an alternative to a full strategic deterrent. This idea appealed to those who did not want to abandon nuclear weapons but were unhappy about the likely costs of a full Polaris replacement. On doctrinal grounds some disliked the notion of an "independent" deterrent, which suggested the possibility of using force separately from the United States and created the requirement for a complete second-strike capability. As a means of remaining a nuclear power, saving money, and demonstrating greater faith in NATO and the U.S. nuclear guarantee, an unambiguously theater force could be developed.

The proponent of this view with the most seniority was the chief of defence staff, Field Marshal Lord Carver.[34] Another advocate, David Owen, foreign secretary, may have been inclined to take a similar position.[35] In general, however, there has not been much support for this compromise, and it has not been seriously discussed publicly. One objection was that a limited nuclear capability would lack credibility if it could not be covered by a full strategic deterrent. The real difficulty, however, is that the proposal takes the official confidence in NATO too much at face value and does not address the "insurance policy" aspect of an independent deterrent.

One advantage of the approach might have been in defusing some of the opposition to NATO's TNF modernization. Under this plan, as approved by the NATO Council in December 1979, 160 GLCMs are to be based in Britain. This force is to be completed before others in Europe. The British hospitality may be due to its own nuclear status, the fact that current TNF (F-111s) are based on British soil, and the absence of any early evidence of serious domestic opposition.

Domestic Political Constraints

It was not until after the December 1979 NATO decision that the basing of U.S. cruise missiles was debated in Parliament. The leadership of

34. See his contribution to a seminar at the Royal United Services Institute in April 1980 on a Polaris successor: "My solution to the problem is . . . to regard our nuclear weapons not as independent and strategic but as they have been described in every Defence White Paper over the last X number of years, as a contribution to NATO, and therefore regarded as a theatre force." He did not advocate any particular system as being suitable for this role. Lord Carver, "Polaris Successor," *RUSI: Journal of the Royal United Services Institute for Defence Studies*, vol. 125 (September 1980), p. 24. See also his "Europa and the Yankee Bull," *New Statesman* (London), August 15, 1980, p. 12.

35. See Freedman, *Britain and Nuclear Weapons*, p. 75. In a recent pamphlet Owen suggests keeping the existing Polaris squadron operational for as long as possible. David Owen, *Protect, Protest, Negotiate and Survive* (London: Campaign for Labour Victory, 1980), pp. 26–27.

Lawrence D. Freedman

the Labour opposition did not challenge the decision. In government the Labour party had been sympathetic to the argument for TNF modernization. Moreover, to question the decision would have made Britain vulnerable to accusations of disloyalty to NATO.[36] "Back bench" members of Parliament did, however, express concern over the possibility of U.S. missiles being launched from Britain (thereby inviting retaliation) without proper consultation.[37]

This concern gradually grew into complete opposition to the basing of U.S. missiles, a position that has been endorsed by the Labour party's National Executive. The criticism has been essentially that the United States is becoming a dangerous ally, ready for a confrontation with the Soviet Union but hoping to reduce the risk to its own territory by containing any resultant nuclear war in Europe. This line of reasoning was used to explain the U.S. desire to place cruise missiles in Britain.[38] It is difficult to assess the extent of public support for such a position. In October 1980 about 40 percent of the population held this view. There is more support for the NATO cruise missiles than for the Trident, though it is the former that have most stimulated the recent protest movements. There has been a growth in vocal opposition to the basing of cruise missiles in areas where they are (or were thought likely to be) located, although local polls have not found majorities against the missiles.[39] The two sites for the bases are

36. Because support for a British nuclear force is not synonymous with support for NATO, and also costs money, the Labour "front bench" has been much more skeptical about the advisability of the purchase of the Trident. For example, see the speech by the defense spokesman for Labour and one of the leaders of the party's right wing, William Rodgers, "Yes to Cruise. No to Trident," *RUSI: Journal of the Royal United Services Institute for Defence Studies,* vol. 126 (March 1981), pp. 8–13.

37. Labour foreign affairs spokesman Peter Shore, a supporter of theater nuclear modernization, stated: "There seems to be a strong case for joint control." See his comments in *Parliamentary Debates,* Commons, 5th series, vol. 977, session 1979–80, January 24, 1980 (HMSO, 1980), col. 769.

38. E. P. Thompson and Don Smith, eds., *Protest and Survive* (London: Penguin Books, 1980). The campaign has inevitably become generalized against anything to do with nuclear weapons.

39. *New Society* conducted a survey on popular attitudes to nuclear weapons and war; it showed, among other findings, that 67 percent of the sample was opposed to unilateral nuclear disarmament. The report included the comment: "Only 59 per cent of our sample claimed to have heard of cruise missiles. Further probing suggested that some of our respondents weren't as knowledgeable as they said, or thought they were. 18 per cent could not or would not specify *anything* that made cruise missiles special. 4 per cent thought that the special thing about cruise was that it was launched from submarines. Only 12 per cent of the whole sample rightly

Greenham Common (Newbury) and Molesworth (Northampton). The original American desire (based on cost efficiency) was to have only one base, but the British government insisted that the risks should be spread. Whatever the extent of the opposition, there has never been any possibility of its being defused by the development of British cruise missiles instead of or with American cruise missiles. Although such a move might in principle address the concern about the lack of sovereignty over missiles capable of being fired from national territory, it would not calm the emotional wellsprings of the opposition or deal with other aspects of the campaign such as the fear that the location of the missiles would endanger people living nearby.[40]

This does not mean that a cruise missile program is definitely ruled out over the long term. The problem of maintaining a long-range strike capability may focus attention once again on the merits of cruise missiles. In the future, GLCMs may appear an attractive alternative to another generation of sophisticated aircraft. Other ways may be found to extend the effective life of existing aircraft through standoff cruise missiles. The value of such ALCMs, and the range required, would depend on the development of Soviet air defenses capable of engaging both cruise missiles and the carrier aircraft before the missile's release.

There has been even less interest in cruise missiles with conventional warheads, apart from some support in the Royal Navy for a long-range antiship cruise missile. Such a missile seems to face navigational problems in using TERCOM over the sea that are similar to those mentioned earlier. The Sea Eagle antiship missile developed by British Aerospace Dynamics for the Royal Navy and the RAF, to be launched from the air by the Tornado, the Buccaneer, and the Sea Harrier, has been described as having "the same kind of aero-dynamic principles as a cruise missile" and adaptable to a "tactical cruise missile role." Private studies by British Aerospace have investigated the possibility of such a cruise missile for

---

identified its most distinctive feature: low flying to avoid radar." David Lipsey, "What Do We Think about the Nuclear Threat?" *New Society*, September 25, 1980, pp. 603–06. For further discussion of the development of the British debate, see Lawrence Freedman, "Britain: The First Ex-Nuclear Power?" *International Security*, vol. 6 (Fall 1981).

40. See Duncan Campbell, "World War III: An Exclusive Preview," *New Statesman*, October 3, 1980, pp. 5–6. Campbell notes that, whereas Ministry of Defence pamphlets suggest that because of the mobility of the missiles "the precise locations of the peacetime Cruise Missile bases are not . . . likely to be a priority target," recent civil defense exercises have assumed early obliteration of these bases.

use over land and with a range of up to 600 kilometers. The company's chairman, Admiral Sir Raymond Lygo, has stated his belief that "it is clear beyond any possible doubt that before halfway through this decade this country will need cruise missiles." The cruise missiles needed would be tactical and not necessarily with nuclear warheads for "use in the central front in Germany to be used against armour, for use against airfields in the area beyond the Elbe, for deep penetration where it is going to be increasingly unrealistic for aircraft to go."[41] Despite Sir Raymond's enthusiasm, there is as yet no evidence that it is matched in government. There the only serious interest is in cruise missiles with nuclear applications and, as mentioned above, for the moment none of this interest has yet turned into an operational requirement. The disposition within the Ministry of Defence, however, is to treat short- and long-range cruise missiles as raising quite distinct technical and tactical issues.

France

Despite the obvious similarities, Britain and France have quite distinct national approaches to their nuclear forces. Britain, as shown above, seeks to maintain a minimum deterrent force with the minimum of trouble and expense and has few qualms about turning to the United States for assistance in pursuit of this objective. The nuclear force is not relied upon as a symbol of national strength and independence; indeed, considerable ingenuity has been devoted to reconciling an independent deterrent with loyalty to NATO.

In France, on the other hand, the nuclear force is surrounded by political symbolism. The *force de dissuasion* is a vital part of de Gaulle's legacy that is jealously guarded by his followers who, accordingly, scrutinize all official pronouncements for deviation from orthodoxy. This renders matters that might seem to be either technical or of a rather abstract, doctrinal nature to be of far greater political sensitivity than they would be in Britain.

One example of this symbolism is the desire for independence in the production as well as the operation of the nuclear force. This self-sufficiency is taken by the French to illustrate both the nation's political autonomy, particularly from the United States, and its technological

41. *Strategic Nuclear Weapons Policy,* pp. 185–86 and 195–96.

prowess. The second of these attributes leads to a disinclination to renounce any particular weapon option until it has been made clear that France would be perfectly capable of exercising it if it chose to do so and if sufficient funds were available. This public maintenance of a wide range of choices is one difficulty for those attempting to predict the future course of French policy; another is the tendency of the French to combine an open and vigorous debate on the broad outlines of nuclear policy with great secrecy about the details of the process and the conclusions of decisionmaking.

France has developed a more diversified nuclear force than that of Britain, but at far higher cost. It is common to describe Britain as being wholly dependent on its SSBNs while France has a triad. However, the force of thirty-three French Mirage IV-class aircraft[42] is comparable, in its size, age, and inadequate capacity to penetrate Soviet air defenses, to the forty-eight British Vulcan bombers, and can be expected to survive them by only a few years.[43] The only unique French possession is a force of eighteen intermediate-range ballistic missiles (IRBMs) based in fixed silos on the plateau d'Albion in Haute-Provence.[44] Both powers are primarily reliant on SSBNs for their assured means of retaliation. France now has five of these; Britain has four. A sixth should be ready by 1985, and the new Socialist government has promised that there will be a seventh.

It is the demanding development effort in France rather than the quantity and variety of weapons that has been the main reason for the expense. From 1977 to 1981, 16 to 19 percent of the defense budget was devoted to the nuclear force, compared with less than 2 percent in Britain.[45]

42. The Mirage IVA was first deployed in 1963. It has a maximum speed of Mach 2.2 but an insufficient range to reach major Soviet targets without in-flight refueling (provided by eleven KC-135 tanker aircraft).

43. In 1976 a program was begun to extend the operational life of the force until 1985. It now seems likely that those aircraft will be phased out after 1985 (with twelve being redeployed for reconnaissance purposes and fifteen assigned to tactical roles) and not replaced by a new bomber. This replacement possibility is discussed in the next section.

44. A new missile, the S-3 with a range of 1,850 nautical miles and a 1.2 megaton warhead, is currently replacing the S-2 with a range of 1,700 nautical miles and one warhead of 150 kilotons.

45. Comparisons have to be made with care because the budget specification for strategic nuclear forces in Britain excludes both research and development and the costs of operating and maintaining the Vulcan force. On French defense budgetry see David S. Yost, "French Defense Budgeting: Executive Dominance and Resource Constraints," *Orbis,* vol. 23 (Fall 1979), pp. 579–608.

The program is guided currently by the Loi de Programmation, 1977–82, under which spending on nuclear forces is expected to decline as a proportion of the budget from 16.6 percent in 1977 to 15.7 percent in 1982.[46] However, in practice this proportion rose to 18.2 percent in 1979 and 19.1 percent in 1980. In absolute terms expenditure has been rather static: at constant 1969 prices it has moved from 4,961 million francs in 1969 to 4,887 million francs.[47] This constant level of spending involves regular investment in new equipment, although the proportion devoted to operation and maintenance of existing equipment has grown.

Initial Views

If the cruise missile had been as inexpensive as generally assumed in the mid-1970s, it would have appeared to be a natural requisition for France. In strengthening the *force de frappe,* there would be another opportunity to demonstrate that it was within France's technical capacity to do anything that the superpowers could do. There were a number of hints from the French government that it was considering the cruise missile as an attractive possibility for the future. The most widely publicized of such hints was by General Guy Méry, chief of staff of the French Armed Forces, in a lecture in March 1977 to the Institut des Hautes Etudes de Défense Nationale, in which he spoke of cruise missiles and observation satellites being given priority in studies on the future development of the nuclear force.[48]

There appears to have been some confidence that French cruise missiles could be produced during the 1980s. This confidence was supported by reports of official U.S. estimates (which now appear extremely optimistic) that France could produce a cruise missile within ten years at the manageable cost of about $650 million.[49]

46. *Rapport sur la Programmation des Dépenses Militaires et des Equipements des Forces Armées pour la Période 1977–1982* (Report on the Programming of Military Expenditures and Armed Forces Equipment for the 1977–82 Period) (Paris: Service d'Information et de Diffusion du Premier Ministre, 1976).
47. *Le Monde,* February 23, 1979, and October 5, 1979.
48. *Le Monde,* June 11, 1977. See also a speech given by President Valéry Giscard d'Estaing to French Air Force cadets in which he spoke positively of cruise missiles, reported in *NATO's Fifteen Nations,* vol. 23 (April–May 1978), p. 100.
49. *Aviation Week and Space Technology,* March 27, 1978, p. 17; *International Herald Tribune,* December 31, 1977.

There was, however, little evidence of a major research effort. The 1978 French budget contained the equivalent of $400,000 to initiate studies on cruise missiles, a figure that does not suggest a particularly intensive effort.[50] A number of studies were commissioned, including a general analysis of the feasibility of cruise missiles by the Société Nationale Industrielle Aerospatiale (SNIAS). There also have been analyses by Aerospatiale and Dassault-Breguet of the airframe, by Matra, Thomson, and Dassault of guidance systems, and by the Société Nationale d'Etude et de Construction de Moteurs d'Aviation (SNEMCA) and Turbomeca of possible power plants.[51]

There was little concern about France's ability to develop a sufficiently small and compact missile with a miniature nuclear warhead. Work on a suitable turbojet engine, designed by Turbomeca and designated Arbizon IV, had been under way for some time. The engine had been tested at the National Gas Turbine Establishment early in 1977.[52] The eventual design was for a missile similar in shape to that of the American cruise missiles—a body with a small diameter for a small radar signature, but long in length to include all the equipment. The engine would have a thrust of about 350 kilograms (772 pounds) and a flight time of about four hours. The missile would not be very heavy and so could be launched from trucks, ships, submarines, or aircraft. The ground-launched version would be 6 to 7 meters long, 0.6 to 0.7 meter in diameter, and have a span of 3 to 4 meters.[53]

The major difficulty was the guidance system. Again the electronics industry was sure that it could develop the hardware for a TERCOM system, but the effectiveness of TERCOM depends more on the software. It had always been understood that satellites would be necessary to provide the topographical information. A satellite program was already

50. *Aviation Week and Space Technology*, March 27, 1978, p. 17, which notes that these funds were blocked until after the March 1978 general election.

51. Edward W. Bassett, "France to Modernize Nuclear Forces," *Aviation Week and Space Technology*, June 16, 1980, pp. 265–69. The discussion below provides background to these studies.

52. *Flight International*, June 18–25, 1977, p. 1785.

53. *Le Matin*, July 14, 1980; *Aviation Week and Space Technology*, June 23, 1980, p. 13. The engine would be small, using special fuel and having a low specific consumption. Range would be several thousand kilometers, at low altitudes and slow speed (Mach 0.7 to 0.8). The total weight would be 1,500 to 2,000 kilograms. Germain Chambost, "French Nuclear Weapons Choices for the Next Twenty Years," *International Defense Review*, vol. 13, no. 7 (1980), p. 982.

under way for telecommunications purposes, and navigational or reconnaissance satellites seemed a natural development.[54] However, this was estimated to be a costly operation: a projection in 1979 was that it would need about 500 million francs annually at that year's prices simply to maintain two satellites (one for navigation and one for reconnaissance) in addition to the 1,500 million francs necessary for construction and launching. Beyond that, the preparation of the information from the satellites for use in a TERCOM system would be an immensely expensive and difficult undertaking, possibly beyond French means.[55] Because French strategy does not include a requirement for high accuracy, it would be possible to do without a system of the precision envisaged by the United States for its cruise missiles. Nevertheless, to fly at low altitudes and thus complicate the adversary's air defense problem, an extremely sophisticated guidance and navigation system is required.

There was some early French exploration of the possibility of reducing development costs by collaborating with West Germany. However, this effort produced no results. There was some German interest (not shared by the *Luftwaffe*) in a cruise missile to replace the F-104 Starfighter, and eventually the Tornado. But the need was for a weapon with a shorter range than that required by France, and with only a conventional warhead, so there was not really a shared interest. Moreover, the Germans, impressed by the complexities of TERCOM, saw little point in efforts to develop cruise missiles without substantial U.S. assistance. This was quite contrary to French thinking.

Second Thoughts

These investigations soon raised important doubts about whether cruise missiles would be quite as inexpensive as had been originally supposed. A subsequent question was whether there was an obvious requirement that might justify whatever expense would be involved. With its triad, France might have an interest in a sea-, ground- or air-launched cruise missile.

54. Two communications satellites are to be launched in 1983. They may have some navigational capabilities. The development of a full military program is to be studied between 1980 and 1982 for possible funding in the next six-year military plan.

55. Testimony in the United States suggests that the cost of acquisition of topographic data and the digitizing of maps for the TERCOM systems was "extraordinarily greater" than that of the cruise missile itself. Desmond Ball, "The Costs of the Cruise Missile," *Survival,* vol. 20 (November–December 1978), p. 245.

Unlike Britain, there has never been any serious question of an SLCM force replacing the current SLBM force. The French SLBM force has developed in a much more gradual manner than it has in Britain. Rather than being brought into service during a short period in a concentrated program and in conjunction with the introduction of a particular missile, there have been some quite long intervals between the introduction of individual SSBNs.[56] This allows for incremental improvements. Thus the authorization for the sixth in the French series, *L'Inflexible,* was delayed and will not be in service until 1985. It has been described as being in an "intermediate" class of its own with, for example, greater depth and less noise than its predecessors but not the quality anticipated for the new class of submarines to be introduced in the 1990s.[57]

Meanwhile, there has been continual refinement of the French SLBMs. In 1971 the first missile, M-1, had a range of 1,350 nautical miles and a yield of 500 kilotons. By 1974 the M-2 had extended the range to 1,650 nautical miles, and in 1977 the M-20 increased the yield to one megaton. For *L'Inflexible* in 1985 the M-4 will provide a range of 2,500 nautical miles and six or seven warheads of 150 kilotons (but not MIRVs). Another missile, the M-5, has already been suggested for the 1990s. This incremental pattern of development leaves little scope for a fundamental change in the character of the sea-based force required by a move to cruise from ballistic missiles.

A more likely candidate for replacement by cruise missiles has been the fixed land-based IRBM force.[58] These eighteen missiles have a sensitive position in the French force, for they justify the claim to a triad yet are widely believed to be so vulnerable to preemptive attack that they are virtually useless.

The role allotted to the IRBMs within the overall *force de frappe* has diminished since it was first conceived in the early 1960s. In 1964 the intention was to construct six fields, each with nine missiles. By the end of the decade it had been decided to go forward with only the first phase of twenty-seven missiles, and by the early 1970s this first phase had been reduced to eighteen missiles. The French government nevertheless has

---

56. The French term is SNLE (sous-marines nucléaires lanceurs d'engins). Their equivalent for SLBMs is MSBS (mer-sol balistique stratégique). The total force is known as the forces océanique stratégique (FOST).

57. *Jane's Fighting Ships, 1979–80* (New York: Franklin Watts, Inc., 1979), p. 161.

58. The French term is SSBS (sol-sol balistique stratégique).

claimed that these missiles play an important deterrent role and that the problem of their vulnerability has been exaggerated.

This optimism does not stem from a belief that the IRBMs in Haute-Provence could withstand a Soviet attack, but from the belief that the consequences of this attack would go against Soviet interests. The silos are spread over 90 square miles and designed to withstand a near miss of one megaton at 500 yards. It was calculated that hundreds of megatons would be needed to destroy all the silos, and that the resulting fallout would be carried back to the Soviet Union by the prevailing winds, thus ensuring automatic retaliation. This rationale is now being eroded by the modernization of the Soviet IRBM forces with the SS-20, which is capable of a more precise attack producing less fallout.[59]

The future of the French land-based force has been under major review since 1977, and it is in this context that cruise missiles have been most actively considered. Although the French have decided to concentrate on SSBNs as the most survivable element of the nuclear force, the option of abandoning the land-based component altogether was rejected, at least while Giscard was president. This is particularly because of the reasons outlined above and partly because of a more fundamental point of dogma —that at least some of the deterrent must be based on national territory to stress the close link between aggression against the nation and the mode of retaliation.

To preserve the land-based component of the deterrent it will be necessary to reduce its vulnerability. Various approaches to this have been considered.[60] The major studies of alternative approaches were initiated in 1978, including those on the cruise missile mentioned earlier and a study conducted by SNIAS and Aerospatiale on a new mobile ballistic missile known as the S-X. The main analysis of the alternative options has been conducted by the Ministry of Defense. By early 1980 the preliminary studies were completed, with the general staff tilting toward the S-X. It was not expected that a final decision would be reached before the end of 1980 but at the meeting of the Conseil de Défense on June 10, 1980, there was a clear preference for the S-X. The S-X proceeded to the development stage while the cruise missile, though not abandoned alto-

59. See General Pierre M. Gallois, "The Future of France's Force de Dissuasion," *Strategic Review*, vol. 5 (Summer 1979), pp. 34–41.

60. For example, a report in 1977 mentioned a concept for moving missiles through tunnels in mountains. *International Herald Tribune*, June 7, 1977. A multiple-silo option has also been assessed; see *Le Matin*, July 14, 1980.

gether, remained under study but with reduced interest; little more was done than to keep up with technological developments in this field.[61]

Development work on the S-X was expected to start in early 1981 with plans for full development and production to be put to the Conseil de Défense in 1982. The new system was expected to become operational in 1992. All the features of the system have yet to be decided (and those familiar with the history of its American cousin, the M-X, will be aware of how frequently dominant concepts can change), but a number have been reported. The proposal is to produce about 100 missiles to be carried on tractor-trailers and moved on existing roads in protected zones in suitable areas of the country. This is less complicated and expensive than building a special system of shelters and roads.[62] One of the problems is finding a suitable area of the country that does not put considerable demands on the missile's range. A range of about 2,500 nautical miles is being considered. Another problem is the need for a reliable command and control system, and for a capacity for fast realignment of the missile's guidance system before firing, to take account of the new launch position. The S-X will have to be a derivative of the existing family of IRBMs and SLBMs, probably drawing mainly on the M-4. The range requirement will result in a smaller payload than these, with either one 200-kiloton warhead or three warheads of 50 kilotons each.

One of the main arguments used by proponents of the cruise missile was that it is unwise to be too dependent on one particular type of missile. It would be valuable to have diverse means of penetrating Soviet territory in case there was a breakthrough in Soviet ABMs. While it is difficult to

61. Initially on June 26, when President Valéry Giscard d'Estaing announced the decisions of the Conseil de Défense (which included the development of the neutron bomb), he spoke only of "preparatory work on a new strategic missile," but a month later Minister of Defense Yvon Bourges made it clear that a much more firm decision in principle had been made in favor of the S-X. These deliberations have been followed particularly carefully by Jacques Isnard in *Le Monde*. See his articles on February 23, 1979; March 17, 1980; June 11, 1980; and August 1, 1980. An influential analysis is found in Gallois, "The Future of France's Force de Dissuasion," but this does not fully reflect official thinking. A detailed account of some technical considerations and decisionmaking relevant to mobile missiles is found in Bassett, "France to Modernize Nuclear Forces." See also Justin Galen, "French Defense: The View from the Ministry of Defense," *Armed Forces Journal International*, October 1979, pp. 44–47.

62. Another suggestion is to put the missile on small ocean-going vessels; see Bassett, "France to Modernize Nuclear Forces," p. 269. This does not seem likely to be taken seriously; nor does the suggestion for a large number of silos connected by tunnels. Chambost, "French Nuclear Weapons," p. 982.

imagine this taking place without a comparable breakthrough in defenses against cruise missiles, at least there would be opportunities for variations in offensive tactics that would increase the chances of some weapons reaching their targets. This presumes that the complex problems of targeting the different systems in these circumstances could be managed. (For example, would the commanders hold back one type of missile to see how the other had fared or launch both cruise and ballistic missiles simultaneously? Would they have the same or separate targets?)

Another argument was that GLCMs would be easier to conceal than the S-X and thus would reduce the vulnerability to surprise attack, particularly if there was no concern for Soviet problems of verification.

These arguments have been insufficient to counter the major argument against cruise missiles, which is, as in Britain, the prospect of extensive Soviet air defenses. As one French official noted: "A French cruise missile would seem a better idea if the United States was not developing one," the logic being that the large-scale U.S. deployment will stimulate a major Soviet defensive effort in a way that a small French deployment would not. It is generally assumed that the option of saturating air defenses is not readily available to France. Industrial and financial constraints would limit the number of missiles that could be produced, which means that only a sufficient number would be available for a reduced set of targets.[63] The option considered by French planners appears to require twice as many cruise missiles as ballistic missiles (200 versus 100), which is a much more favorable ratio than deemed necessary in Britain. The number of cruise missiles may, however, be determined by what is practicable rather than the requirement for achieving a similar destructive effect to that promised by the S-X force.[64]

The cruise missile, especially if ground based, would face similar problems of range and secure zones for movement as the S-X. (The Com-

63. French comment on this option points out that thousands of missiles would be considered necessary by the United States to saturate Soviet air defenses, and compares this with the hundreds France could produce. However, the ratio need not be so surprising—it is the same for ballistic missiles—because the United States expects to reach a wider range of targets than France does. Concentrating on a few targets means saturating fewer air defenses (assuming the few targets are not too widely dispersed).

64. Some observers in the Ministry of Defense believe that the air defense problem has been exaggerated. It has been suggested that if close defenses around key targets appeared to be impenetrable, the weapons could be detonated early, which would still cause immense damage though not quite where intended.

munist party is the strongest local party in some of the more attractive areas for deployment.) Cruise missiles would also be difficult to test because testing could not be done over the sea, and there are few areas of land where flying at low altitudes would be safe.[65] They would also cost more because of their large numbers, and the development effort would be more demanding because there is less experience to draw upon. One estimate is that it would cost about $1 billion to develop and produce 100 cruise missiles over a ten-year period.[66]

The cruise missile option requires 200 missiles, either ground or air launched (GLCM or ALCM). The ALCM option, perhaps calling for a wide-bodied jet, has been advocated more outside the French government than within it. General Gallois, for example, has offered the ambitious suggestion that an efficient use of 100 aircraft, each carrying 10 ALCMs, which could be constructed for about $1 billion, could ensure that 50 were kept airborne continually.[67] Within the government, the GLCM option has been taken most seriously.[68]

The Gaullist critique of this option questions whether sufficient cruise missiles could be launched in circumstances when traditional French doctrine indicates the nuclear retaliation must be launched—when NATO defenses have been breached and the enemy is penetrating, or about to penetrate, national territory.[69] The missiles (air or ground launched) not caught in a preemptive strike would have to be launched in a few hours and then travel 1,500 to 2,500 kilometers through hostile (and probably overcrowded) airspace controlled by an enemy enjoying the initiative.

The Gaullists had even less confidence in a sea-launched cruise missile because, they argued, a subsonic missile flying over the sea would be easy

65. One solution would be to conduct the test primarily at high altitudes, with a fighter aircraft covering the low-altitude phase of the test that could abort it quickly if something went wrong.

66. This estimate excludes launch platforms. See Michel Aurillac, *Réflexions sur la Défense* (Paris: Rassemblement pour la République, 1980). This thoroughgoing Gaullist discussion of all defense problems provides the major published French critique of the cruise missile option.

67. The suggestion was made, however, assuming a Mirage IV aircraft and no intermediate-range ballistic missile (IRBM) replacement. Gallois, "The Future of France's Force de Dissuasion," pp. 39–40. See what appears to be a report of his views in *Defense Electronics,* September 1980, pp. 55–56.

68. A suggestion was made to use Transall transports to carry GLCMs around the countryside to improve mobility.

69. See note 62. Aurillac mentions a "missile stratégique aérobie" rather than a "missile de croisière."

to detect and intercept. They found a more promising option to be an ALCM on the Mirage 4000, a twin-engine aircraft currently being promoted by Dassault as a private venture in the 1990s. The French Air Force is interested in this as an eventual replacement for Mirage IV, preferring, as do all air forces, manned aircraft to missiles. However, there are already indications that the French government considers the Mirage 4000 too expensive and has ruled it out.[70]

If it were deployed, a standoff nuclear missile would be available. The ASMP (air-sol moyenne portée) is being developed as a tactical weapon for use with the Mirage 2000 and with fifteen of the old Mirage IVs that will be assigned to a tactical role. The ASMP is said to have a range of 65 miles with a Mach 2.5 speed and a warhead of 100 kilotons. It has been suggested that two or three ASMPs could be carried on a Mirage 4000 (versus only one on the Mirage 2000). Furthermore, the ASMP contains elements of a cruise missile including a liquid fuel ramjet, which shares the propulsion function with a solid-fuel booster, and an advanced guidance system designed for low altitudes. It is argued that a future ALCM could be developed out of the ASMP by concentrating on these particular features. However, any derivative would only be short-range and thus would be dependent for any strategic use on a high-quality manned aircraft capable of penetrating air defenses by itself. Without the Mirage 4000 this option will collapse.[71]

Strategy and Weapons Choices

With the possible exception of the electronics industry, which finds in a cruise missile a more challenging set of technical problems than that posed by the S-X, there does not appear to be a strong lobby for cruise missiles in France. The French Air Force, as air forces elsewhere, dislikes the

70. There is still a considerable lobby for the Mirage 4000 as a means of ensuring diversity in the French deterrent. See Xavier Delfine, "La Vecteur Aerien dans la Discussion de Demain" (The Aerial Vector in the Discussion of Tomorrow), *Défense Nationale,* June 1979; and Alexandre Sanguinetti, "L'air et la Mer" (The Air and the Sea), *Le Monde,* October 30, 1979.

71. *Rapport d'Information Déposé en Application de l'Article 145 du Règlement par la Commission de la Défense Nationale et des Forces Armées: (1) Sur l'Etat et la Modernisation des Forces Nucléaires Française* (Information Report Submitted in Accordance with Article 145 of the Regulations of the Commission on National Defense and the Armed Forces: [1] On the State and the Modernization of the French Nuclear Forces), National Assembly, Sixth Legislature, Second Ordinary Session of 1979–80, no. 1730 (National Assembly, 1980), pp. 239–41.

notion of pilotless aircraft. Moreover, some of the advantages of the cruise missile, such as high accuracy, seem disadvantages to Gaullist purists.

The most controversial issue in French defense policy is the French role in NATO's plans and strategy. President Giscard and his supporters argued strongly for a greater readiness to participate in any NATO forward battle on German territory against a Soviet invasion on the assumption that France's security is indivisible from that of its neighbors. The Gaullists resisted this movement in policy, preferring to rely on the threat of massive and automatic nuclear retaliation to deter the Soviet Union from making any encroachments on French territory. The only point of engaging Soviet forces on German soil is for "trip-wire" purposes.

In terms of force planning rather than declaratory policy, the argument is to some extent over the balance between conventional and nuclear forces. However, even those interested in improving relations with NATO have not proposed adoption of a flexible response strategy: rather the objective would be to enable NATO to lower the nuclear threshold through early use of tactical nuclear weapons. The Gaullists are suspicious of any move to employ nuclear weapons against military targets in a battle because this would detract from their role in deterring attack on France through the threat of retaliation against cities.

The very development of short-range tactical nuclear weapons (the Pluton missile) compromised this purist position, but this was dealt with by first insisting that these weapons would be used only to signal an intent to "go nuclear" rather than an attempt to change the course of the land battle, but then accepting that the warning would only be effective if something of military value were destroyed. The Gaullists have been unwilling to go much beyond this formulation and have been wary of proposals such as those for a French "neutron bomb" on the grounds that it would be more relevant to a NATO strategy of graduated response than to a French strategy of dissuasion. The cruise missile can be seen in a similar light: most useful for attacking the Soviet lines of supply as part of a defensive effort against an invasion but not particularly suitable in providing for assured, massive, and quick retaliation against Soviet cities.[72]

Plans to deploy both the neutron bomb and cruise missiles would probably be too much for the Gaullists and the defense establishment (which is generally conservative on these matters) because together they

72. See, for example, *Le Monde,* March 17, 1980.

would indicate a clear shift toward a strategy of graduated response. Those following the more pro-NATO line of Giscard concentrated their efforts on the neutron bomb. On June 26, 1980, Giscard announced that a prototype neutron bomb had been developed and tested, and that within two to three years a decision would be made on production. Given all the problems with cruise missiles, there did not seem to be much interest in taking a strong stand on this particular weapon.[73] The policy of the government of President François Mitterand remains unclear. There have been signs of an approach to European security problems more in line with NATO orthodoxy (for example, in endorsing NATO's long-range TNF modernization program). The contrast with the views of socialists elsewhere in Europe is heightened by the determination to continue with the *force de frappe.* However, there are indications that this force may not be a central feature of French defense policy and that, while no decisions have yet been taken on the neutron bomb[74] or the S-X, the greatest emphasis will be on the sea-based force. This suggests an even dimmer future for cruise missiles than might have been expected under Giscard.

As in Britain, the conclusion for France must be that cruise missiles have not been found to offer an attractive solution to the problems of nuclear force planning and that, therefore, they are unlikely to be adopted in the foreseeable future.

Conclusion

As late as 1977 it was widely assumed that cruise missiles were a uniquely attractive option for near-nuclear and small nuclear powers because of their extraordinary cost-effectiveness. The generally negative evaluations of this option reached by cost-conscious force planners in both Britain and France may turn out to have been misguided or be overtaken by yet more spectacular developments in the relevant technology. Nevertheless, the fact that the option has been rejected for central strategic tasks by these two countries does make the predictions of massive proliferation seem premature to say the least.

73. See Union pour la Démocratie Française, "Une Doctrine de Défense pour la France," May 1980. The Gaullist reply is found in Aurillac, *Réflexions sur la Défense.*

74. As this book went to press, the French government announced that it would develop the neutron bomb. Edward Cody, *Washington Post,* September 15, 1981.

The proliferation question was a side issue for analysts mainly concerned with the impact of cruise missiles on the U.S. force structure and SALT. The propositions on the ease with which other powers might acquire cruise missiles and put them to effective use were not backed by substantial analysis. Yet, if valid, these propositions potentially had immense political significance, and even if they were not valid they had actual political significance in stimulating intense interest in the cruise missile option among Europeans who tend to take their cues from Americans on the more technical aspects of contemporary strategy.

The attraction of cruise missiles depends on the presumption of low cost. This benefit would be available only for European nuclear powers with access to much of the U.S. technology; assurances of continued U.S. assistance would enable provision of the data for the TERCOM guidance system, deployment on relatively inexpensive launch platforms, and a manageable air defense problem. Each of these points deserves examination.

While indigenous development and production of cruise missiles has always been within the capabilities of British and French industry, without the benefits of the U.S. technological base and economies of scale, the unit costs will inevitably be much higher. The French initially appeared more eager to exercise the cruise missile option but they would be confined for political reasons to an expensive self-sufficiency whereas the British were always more likely to be able to procure the relevant U.S. technology.

The most serious problem with a national program for either Britain or France is the provision of the requisite information in the necessary form for the TERCOM system. It is difficult to imagine how a missile expected to fly at low altitudes over a long distance can do so without some form of TERCOM system, yet the operation of such a system is quite beyond the means of either power without sizable and continual assistance from the United States. This is not to say that such assistance is not forthcoming, again particularly in the case of Britain, but it does confirm the extent to which any serious proliferation of modern cruise missiles, even for the European nuclear powers, depends on clear policy choices to be made in Washington.

The main determinant of the overall costs of the system is the launch platform. There was a presumption in some of the early analyses of cruise missiles that they could be launched from a wide variety of platforms—from a raft to a jumbo jet. However, those pointing to the advantages of cruise missiles for small powers did not always assume an inexpensive launch platform; in fact, the traditional, and expensive, platforms of aircraft and submarines were suggested. Yet the adoption of these systems would squander many of the cost advantages accruing to cruise rather than ballistic missiles. For countries considering cruise missiles as their primary strategic systems, the question of survivability was paramount. Thus, though it was possible to design simple and inexpensive launch platforms (like those being adopted for NATO's TNF), such platforms would not be able to survive a determined enemy attack. This did not rule out the adoption of a cruise missile force launched from a simple platform, but it did suggest that such a system would have to be subordinate to one that was less vulnerable. This in turn meant that cruise missiles were unlikely to transform the character of the nuclear arsenals of Britain and France to the point that they would be respected by third parties who had derided or dismissed them in the past. If, on the other hand, the missiles were to be deployed on survivable platforms, which essentially meant submarines, their relative cost-effectiveness would depend on the overall missile requirement and, in consequence, the submarine requirement.

A major disadvantage of cruise missiles in taking up space in a submarine was the limits to their payload. Although France was considering a ballistic missile with a limited payload (that is, without MIRVs) for its IRBM replacement, Britain's alternative for its Polaris replacement was the eight-warhead Trident. Another major disadvantage was the anticipated air defense problem. In both Britain and France policymakers have been reluctant to support cruise missiles because of their nervousness about having to cope with Soviet air defenses in a state of continual evolution; this tends to increase not only the numerical requirement for cruise missiles, but also the qualitative requirement leading to regular innovation. There has been great pessimism on the capacity of Soviet air defenses to cope with cruise missiles—more so than in the United States. Presumably this is a matter that will be partly cleared up during the 1980s. If the Soviet Union takes only modest measures to counter the U.S. GLCM and ALCM deployment, there could well be a revival of interest in national cruise missile programs in Britain and France.

The point is that, whatever the promise of low cost, neither country was either willing or able to rush into an unproven technology that would have to operate in an uncertain environment. Until the unknowns can be clarified—the problems of development and production, the efficiency of the TERCOM system and the performance in hostile conditions, and the extent of any SALT-imposed controls—it does not seem feasible to risk a limited budget for nuclear weapons on what would be an experimental option. Britain and France can change their minds once the element of risk has been reduced, but even then it is unlikely that the interest will extend beyond a subsidiary system. Both countries now have SSBN programs that are expected to provide effective deterrents well into the next century. So cruise missiles seem unlikely to be the vehicle by which the bilateralism of SALT is undermined and countries with recently acquired nuclear weapons are unlikely to find them an effective means of delivery. These two case studies should therefore be taken as a salutary lesson on the danger of becoming so impressed with the promise of new technology that unwarranted conclusions are drawn on its likely strategic and political effects.

CHAPTER FIFTEEN

West Germany and the Nonnuclear NATO Countries

CATHERINE MCARDLE KELLEHER

OF ALL THE issues pertaining to force modernization facing the NATO alliance in the early 1980s, the questions surrounding cruise missile deployment are perhaps the most difficult.[1] At a minimum, there are new doubts about the military effectiveness of these systems, labeled "wonder weapons" in the early 1970s. More significant perhaps for the long term are queries about the political costs, domestic and international, that will accompany acquisitions or basing on national territory. And there is a need for recalculation of the contribution these systems will make toward stabilizing the East-West military balance, achieving détente and arms limitation in Europe, or reinforcing transatlantic consensus.

Vital to whatever resolutions emerge will be the policies of the Federal Republic of Germany, not only because of Germany's centrality in all alliance policymaking but also because of the leading role taken by the

Catherine Kelleher is professor at the Graduate School of International Studies, University of Denver.

1. Material for this chapter is drawn from a continuing research project on European attitudes on tactical nuclear force modernization. Major background sources include a series of interviews conducted in Washington, D.C., and in Europe during 1979 and 1980; a previous research report, "Alliance Politics and Theater Nuclear Modernization," which I presented to the New York Arms Control Seminar at Columbia University in December 1979; and my article, "The Present as Prologue: Europe and Theater Nuclear Modernization," *International Security*, vol. 5 (Spring 1981), pp. 150–68.

government of Chancellor Helmut Schmidt in the NATO long-range theater nuclear force (LRTNF) decision of December 1979. German actions sparked initial alliance discussion, shaped definition of the political and military requirements, and structured the final commitment to both deployment and attempts at LRTNF arms control. Bonn thus has assumed three separate, not always congruent, roles: it speaks for unique German interests, supports joint German-American priorities, and acts as interlocutor of the other European nonnuclear states.

Some major factors are identified in this chapter that have influenced both the substance and the procedural patterns of German decision-making on cruise missile issues. A comparison is made with the factors shaping the policies of Holland, Belgium, Norway, Denmark, Italy, and the other nonnuclear countries with interests in cruise missile technology. The principal framework for the discussion is the development of policy positions in the LRTNF debate from 1977 to 1980 because that period was characterized by the clearest and most controversial choices on cruise missiles in the short term. Of at least equal interest is the potential impact on future decisionmaking in areas of increasing European interest, notably shorter-range conventional cruise missiles in either a medium-range air-to-surface missile (MRASM) or a land-attack sea-based configuration, the Tomahawk land-attack missile (TLAM).

An examination of this breadth must be hedged by caveats. One set of caveats arises directly from the continuing evolution of allied positions even on the December 1979 LRTNF decision. The countries under study have coalition governments vulnerable to shifting parliamentary majorities. A number, notably Holland, Belgium, and perhaps Denmark, face critical elections or coalition tests in which the LRTNF decision will figure prominently. Chancellor Schmidt faces continuing doubts within his own parliamentary party. Moreover, all these countries are troubled by the current uncertainties of détente and the future limitations that events in Poland or major Reagan reversals of the SALT process may impose. Many fear and vigorously oppose a major shift away from détente in national decisionmaking—and perhaps in alliance outcomes also.

This political uncertainty for present and future decisionmaking on cruise missiles has several implications. First is the probability of continuing policy change or even governmental paralysis. It appears that the December 1979 LRTNF decision to deploy ground-launched cruise missiles (GLCMs) will be implemented, with basing assured in at least West Germany and Italy. But there are still reasonable doubts about the stability of the Italian basing decision and the probability of eventual Dutch or Belgian participation.

A second set of caveats about these European positions is rooted in the nature of the decisionmaking process. The chances of policy reversal lie not, as some have argued, in the disingenuousness or irresponsibility in national decision processes. Rather they are inherent in the difficulties of overcoming both the inadequate flow of information and a longer strategic "grasp time," even among groups of experts. Unlike the situation in the United States, education about weapon systems decisions outside a limited group of technical specialists often begins only after initial high-level NATO consultations. The Federal Republic of Germany is clearly in the forefront of the European nonnuclear countries; yet even there the number of defense experts is relatively small and often dependent on American sources and materials for current information. In part this reflects a more episodic European concern with security questions; in part, many Europeans still look to the United States for leadership on programs involving new technology or nuclear systems generally. Moreover, nuclear issues elicit particularly strong emotions and create substantial domestic political risks so they are frequently postponed or ignored as long as possible. Broad governmental participation, as well as public discussion, may well occur only at the point (often set by the United States) at which binding national commitment to an alliance decision is required.

The consequence is that there may be a critical last-minute shift or at least a significant gap between final national action and the position previously taken by national experts in alliance working groups. This does not happen often; in most parliamentary systems, points of political responsibility and of authority usually coincide. Yet, on points of major domestic political sensitivity or under conditions of coalition parliamentary vulnerability, the probability of policy reversal is high. On LRTNF issues, policy reversals by several alliance partners have occurred at least twice: most spectacularly, the negotiations from 1962 to 1965 leading to the creation of a NATO multilateral force (MLF); less dramatically, the responses to the European deployment of medium-range ballistic missiles (MRBMs) from 1956 to 1958.[2] Current Dutch and Belgian delays regarding GLCM stationing on their territories allow time and opportunity for perhaps yet a third reversal.

2. For further details, see Catherine M. Kelleher, *Germany and the Politics of Nuclear Weapons* (Columbia University Press, 1975).

The interaction of these caveats points to the problem of properly assessing the impact and outcome of U.S. leadership in sensitive areas. Clearly, despite increasing German and continental self-confidence, an American proposal and timetable are still the key stimuli to decision. But U.S. influence is not and has not been necessarily sufficient since the early 1960s to produce NATO action or even consensus. The American notion of educating and persuading through specialized working groups or high-level briefings—such as in NATO's High Level Group (HLG)—is not adequate for situations of genuine domestic policy disagreement or of significant electoral risk. The issue in NATO decisionmaking is not always the management of agreement; at times it is indeed the recognition of the limits of political risk-sharing and the mitigation of the consequences of disagreement, both within individual nations and throughout the alliance.

The Federal Republic of Germany and Cruise Missiles

In sorting out the factors critical for West German policymaking on cruise missiles, it is important to distinguish between those specific to the LRTNF debate and those more broadly applicable to its future decision-making on cruise missile projects. Accordingly the following discussion of German policies and the comparative positions of the other continental nonnuclear countries considers the issues of substance and processes at stake in the LRTNF debate; the domestic political limits, present and foreseeable, within which cruise missile decisions are embedded; and the influences on future changes in policy.

The LRTNF Debate, 1978–80

Once the issues of GLCMs and LRTNF modernization surfaced in NATO, the critical alliance member became West Germany. Its political, military, and economic strength made it the key to any new NATO undertaking, and its territory was to be the principal site for any new ground-based systems. Indeed, the spark to NATO discussions and the formation of the HLG was a German initiative, Chancellor Schmidt's October 1977 address to the International Institute for Strategic Studies. Similarly, the German debate was the forerunner of many later challenges to LRTNF modernization. The issues raised by left-wing détentists in the chancellor's own Social Democratic party in the February 1979 parliamentary debates set the tone for the opposition arguments that Dutch and Belgian governments have still to overcome.[3]

As subsequent heated alliance interactions have proven, it is easy to overestimate the extent of German initiative. Schmidt's remarks were only the proximate cause and reportedly were included largely to reflect irritation at what West Germany and several other European countries perceived as an American failure to consult seriously on SALT II provisions and processes. Questions of theater nuclear balance and the role of cruise missiles had already surfaced in alliance and bilateral forums. Of particular significance were the analytic efforts begun within the framework of the Carter NATO initiatives in 1977. Throughout the discussions there had been a strong U.S. lead, a result of the briefings and preferences of earlier planners in the U.S. Department of Defense under Secretaries James R. Schlesinger and Donald H. Rumsfeld, the continuing interactions of the transatlantic community of defense intellectuals, and initial Carter administration concerns about the need to modernize tactical nuclear weapons across the board.[4] Nonetheless, the active role of the Federal Republic of Germany was matched only by Britain among the European allies.

The New Soviet Threat

The obvious basis of German calls for an LRTNF capability was the widespread perception of a new threat to Europe reflected by the increasing deployments of Soviet SS-20 missiles. Whatever the public rhetoric,

3. See the arguments raised by the Social Democratic party in its Grosse Anfrage (Bundestag, 8th electoral period, document 8/2195), the reply of the Schmidt government (document 8/2587), and the subsequent parliamentary debate (*Verhandlungen,* March 8–9, 1979). Earlier statements are summarized in Gert Krell and Peter Schlotter, *Zur Diskussion über die taktischen Nuklearwaffen in Europa* (On the Discussion about Tactical Nuclear Weapons in Europe) (Frankfurt am Main: Haag und Herchen, 1977). Subsequent critical commentary is contained in the volume prepared by the Studiengruppe Militärpolitik, *Aufrüsten, um Abzurüsten?* (Arm to Disarm?) (Hamburg: Rowohlt Verlag, 1980), especially the essays by M. Leitenberg, A. Mechterscheimer, and H. G. Brauch.

4. Compare with the analysis advanced by Fred Kaplan in his essay, "Warring over New Missiles for NATO," *New York Times Magazine,* December 9, 1979; that of Kevin N. Lewis, "Intermediate-Range Nuclear Weapons," *Scientific American,* December 1980, pp. 63–73; and that of Uwe Nerlich, "Theater Nuclear Forces in Europe: Is NATO Running Out of Options?" *Washington Quarterly* (Winter 1980), pp. 100–25.

the German push for LRTNF and for GLCMs was primarily focused on the political and psychological impact that these new deployments would have. The aim was to close a symbolic gap in the spectrum of deterrence —not to develop a countercapability to the SS-20 or meet specific war-fighting military requirements. Although there were occasional lapses, official German statements were confined to interpretations of flexible response doctrine and the role of theater nuclear forces (TNF) enunciated throughout the 1970s.[5] Escalation involved a continuum, not a step-by-step ladder; NATO doctrine was based on the range of capabilities, not on the exclusive sufficiency of any single misdefined rung in the escalation ladder.

Thus it was not surprising that Schmidt and proponents of the German official position quickly abandoned the concept of a Eurostrategic balance, which seemed to imply the acceptability of a nuclear war limited to Europe or of a Soviet "sanctuary" in such a conflict. The emphasis was placed on "coupling," on new evidence of alliance determination and the continuing U.S. nuclear guarantee, and on the avoidance of any temptation for European acceptance of finlandization. Questions of targeting or of redundancy with existing nuclear-capable forces—U.S. forward-based systems (FBS) and European systems—were of secondary significance.

GLCMs provided a number of advantages for such a force. Analysis, largely American, indicated that the GLCMs would have an initial operational capability at least as early as any alternative system. More significantly, this would be the first deployment of a major new weapons technology, promising not only visibility in deployment but also force characteristics (such as accuracy and responsiveness) superior to the existing Poseidon force assigned to the Supreme Allied Commander, Europe. Multinational ground basing would also clearly demonstrate alliance resolve, with numbers in the range of 200 to 600 estimated as sufficient to underscore this commitment.

The primacy Bonn accorded these political characteristics was even more evident in two later episodes. The first was the occasional messages (both semipublic and private) by Chancellor Schmidt about the potential attractiveness of a sea-launched cruise missile (SLCM)–LRTNF element. His remarks at times suggested that if the SLCM option could have

5. On this difference in the U.S.-German interpretation of flexible response, see Alex A. Vardamis, "German-American Military Fissures," *Foreign Policy,* no. 34 (Spring 1979), pp. 87–106.

been implemented by 1983, it would have been a way to involve more allies (for example, even indirectly through maneuvers in coastal waters, port calls, and joint exercises) and to ensure greater safety, security, and survivability. The chancellor seemed willing to trade ground visibility for these advantages and rejected the arguments of some in Washington that the SLCM, like the MLF, would prove an escape hatch of infinite delay for reluctant continental allies. But the determining characteristic was the speed and certainty of deployment—both promised by the GLCM program.

The GLCM's symbolic deterrent value was also underscored by the relatively relaxed German attitude toward force sizing. The initial definition of force requirements was left largely to American HLG support teams working within general constraints to encompass both GLCMs and Pershing IIs.[6] The actual assignment of GLCM flights to host nations reportedly was influenced by considerations of both political dispersion and risk sharing. West Germany was to host all Pershing IIs but only 40 percent of the GLCMs.[7] Moreover, when Dutch and Belgian basing became less certain in 1979–80, Bonn indicated its willingness to accept a smaller final number of GLCMs as sufficient.

These broad official views were shared by most across the the German political spectrum. The government and the coalition of the Christian Democratic Union and the Christian Socialist Union parties (CDU-CSU) disagreed only on the timing of a Western response to the new Soviet threat. Characteristically, the CDU pressed for rapid, direct action by West Germany and the United States alone if necessary. Echoes of this argument could also be heard occasionally in the remarks of West German Foreign Minister Hans-Dietrich Genscher and his colleagues in the small Free Democratic party (FDP), the junior coalition partner generally following a harder line in foreign and defense policy than the Social Democratic party (SPD). The only real dissent came from the left wing of the SPD, both its representatives in the Bundestag and the large group on the party's national executive bodies.

6. The effective limit on the Pershing II was one-to-one replacement of the existing U.S. Pershing I. See John Borawski, "Towards Theater Nuclear Arms Control?" *Washington Quarterly*, vol. 3 (Winter 1980), pp. 84–99.

7. At one point, interview reports indicate that the number of ground-launched cruise missile flights to be assigned to Britain was increased in order to avoid an overburdening (for example, over 50 percent basing) of the Federal Republic of Germany.

The Requirements of Détente and Defense

An issue on which far less domestic consensus prevailed was how the requirements of countering Soviet capability were to be meshed with those for securing ahd expanding the process of détente in Europe. These positions were not easy to sort out because the broad German and indeed continental consensus in 1977–78 (and to a lesser extent today) favored the priority of détente. Moreover, political expediency provided for an even more complex tangling of excuses and real reasons than is the norm for contemporary European politics. Yet at their core, the differences between participants in the issue were based on critically different assumptions about the nature and goals of the détente process, its significance for future European security, and its divisibility in terms of regional or sectoral relations.

The majority of the German political elite supported Schmidt's view that arms limitation, and especially stabilization of the nuclear balance at the lowest possible level, was a necessary building block for the next stage of détente. At issue was the preservation and expansion of the gains of the past decade, the change in the human and political landscape of Europe initiated by Ostpolitik and sustained by increased economic and political relations between East and West.[8] To reverse this process, to retreat to the frozen confrontations of the cold war, was not only to abandon the other half of Europe and perhaps Berlin, but to invite electoral retaliation. However necessary or promising, therefore, the deployment of any new military capability must be perceived as compatible with these broad goals and allow maximum opportunity for negotiation and eventual reduction.

A number of Schmidt's political advisers argued that this view involved a fundamentally different vision of détente as a process from that pursued by the United States. On the one hand, the original Kissinger-Nixon concept of a global détente was naive and somewhat mechanistic. The fatal flaws of that concept lay in its emphasis on a series of progressively more comprehensive and significant arms control agreements, the development (if not deployment) of weapon systems as "bargaining chips," and the linkage of political incentives in Europe to Soviet good behavior outside Europe. Equally flawed were the attempts of the Carter administration to define a more limited vision of détente. Détente could not sim-

8. See Stanley Hoffmann, "The Crisis in the West," *New York Review of Books,* July 17, 1980, pp. 41–50.

ply be an arbitrarily regulated process, characterized by stops and starts and hostage to events largely outside Europe that did not threaten basic Western interests.

From Schmidt's perspective, acquisition of even new weapon systems such as the GLCMs and efforts to achieve mutual arms limitation should and could proceed simultaneously. The ultimate goal of new systems as well as old was probably not a total ban on deployments. The long-term goal must be agreement on a mutually acceptable rough balance in Europe at the lowest possible level of military capability, European and superpower. The West must not allow limits on its freedom of action or cede the Soviet Union advantages in capability, in protection against surprise, or in verification. But the West must also not remain rigidly bound to preferred bargaining arenas, projected force levels, or desirable attributes of weapon systems.

In the short run, moreover, the process of limitation and therefore of support for détente required an ongoing exchange of views and continuing dialogue, at whatever political level was appropriate and under whatever political rubric was available at the lowest political risk. Without the NATO Special Group to prepare and consult on terms of a possible reduction, alliance plans for LRTNF deployment would lack broad public support and ultimately, therefore, international political utility.

Support for this Schmidt position was substantial. Joining with officials of the other European nonnuclear countries, Schmidt helped create the Special Group and achieved the assured Western bonding of LRTNF acquisition plans and limitation proposals. The chancellor enjoyed more mixed support but a similar measure of success in his July 1980 mission to Moscow.[9] His avowed goal was to open the way for an East-West exchange of views of European arms limitation, a process halted by the Carter post-Afghanistan sanctions and the continuing U.S. Senate opposition to ratification of the SALT II accords.

Challenges to the Schmidt definition of the LRTNF acquisition-reduction nexus, however, poured in from all sides. In the view of the more militant CDU opposition and a few FDP coalition partners, Schmidt remained naive about the Soviet interests in real détente or the process of arms limitation, in either the long or short run. Would not the result,

9. See Thomas Kielinger, "Ein Bild der Wirrnis" (A Picture of Confusion) and "Der Kern atlantischer Störungen: Amerika fragt zuerst nach der Freiheit, Europa nach dem Frieden" (The Core of Atlantic Disruptions: America Asks First for Freedom, Europe for Peace), *Die Welt* (Hamburg), June 18, 1980.

especially in the post-Afghanistan era, be Soviet use of an infinite, fruit-less dialogue to cover further increases in Soviet capability? Especially with a new promising technology like cruise missiles, might not Soviet manipulation make the potential for limitation appear at every stage to outweigh the tactical advantages of deployment? And would not the Soviet approach, particularly efforts like those exhibited in SALT, be focused to prevent any further developments (such as conventional cruise missiles) that could be portrayed as upsetting the existing balance, the chances for eventual agreement, and détente itself? The example of the mutual and balanced force reduction (MBFR) negotiations showed that continuing dialogue meant Western paralysis and little Soviet restraint. Negotiation was therefore appropriate only after deployment or when the issues were clear, limited, and sufficiently ripe for agreement on both sides.

Criticism from the CDU clearly reached its height during the initial phases of the 1979–80 election campaign, when Franz Josef Strauss, the CDU candidate for chancellor, was quick to castigate Schmidt as soft on détente. Priority targets for Strauss were Schmidt's public musing about a possible immediate Soviet SS-20 moratorium, which would necessitate a Western renunciation of some (if not all) of the planned LRTNF deployments;[10] the chancellor's Moscow visit in the face of U.S. opposi-tion; and hints of a German "sell out" on LRTNF. Schmidt was con-tinually portrayed as a man of appeasement, an uncritical captive of Ostpolitik illusions from the early 1970s, and one who was deluded about the divisibility of détente. Judged by the silence of other CDU-CSU coalition candidates later in the electoral contest, however, the Strauss campaign elicited limited public support.

A radically different critique came from the smaller but highly asser-tive left and center-left groups within the SPD associated with Herbert Wehner, Egon Bahr, and Willy Brandt.[11] In this view, détente itself was

10. For a view close to the chancellor's thinking, see Lothar Ruehl, "Moskau müsste seine Raketenrüstung stoppen" (Moscow Must Bring a Halt to Its Missile Armament), *Die Zeit,* June 13, 1980.

11. See, for example, the statements on the SPD conference, as reported in the *Washington Post,* December 10 and 11, 1979, and the description of Schmidt's later Moscow trip, *Washington Post,* July 4, 1980. In speeches in the spring of 1980 (in Essen on April 11 and Hamburg on April 12) the chancellor seemed to move closer to this view and to call for negotiations on the basis of a mutual East-West moratorium. In the face of questioning, particularly from Washington, Schmidt quickly restated his support of deployment as well as negotiation (see his Cologne speech, April 20, 1980).

ultimately the only guarantee of European security and stability. No matter how promising the technology, cruise missiles were just more weapons, more pressure for Eastern response, and therefore a further upward spiral in arms accumulation in Europe. The general view was that every avenue toward limitation must be explored before deployment to prevent destabilization; the reasons were clear: the process was largely irreversible, systems planned as bargaining chips tended to be deployed, and devising acceptable balance after deployment was an arcane, if not impossible, task for alliance decisionmakers.

If deployment itself could not be halted, the second goal became limitation of any further accumulation of nuclear capability and stockpiles. Germany and Central Europe were already a nuclear tinderbox with sufficient nuclear warheads to ensure total destruction. If new nuclear-capable systems like GLCMs were to be introduced, an equivalent number of warheads for existing systems would have to be withdrawn or destroyed. The preferred method might be unilateral reduction to achieve the most rapid stabilization of existing levels of destructive potential. Ultimately, however, the process would be one of step-by-step mutual restrictions—first of LRTNF and the destabilizing of new GLCMs, and then, presumably, of other European-based U.S. nuclear capabilities (for example, FBS).

Schmidt, therefore, walked a difficult tightrope in building a national consensus on the relation between the deployments and the future of détente. Despite the polemics of the election campaign of 1980, the lines of agreement remained clear. All but a very few on the CDU and FDP fringes agreed on the priority to be accorded to all reasonable efforts to keep Central Europe a "safe zone"—politically, militarily, and economically. The gains at stake were enormous, and while the probabilities of success were uncertain, the West and indeed Europe had a number of available means to induce Soviet cooperation. The LRTNF deployment of GLCMs was only one option—necessary and significant as a symbol of Western ability to respond to Soviet moves but clearly susceptible to limitation through agreement, even if a limited postponement of actual deployment was required. In the view of many on the left and the right more important means to restrain Soviet behavior were European economic and technological assets and the increasing dependency of both the Soviet Union and Eastern Europe. From this perspective, the LRTNF deployment of GLCMs was primarily to be valued as an instrument in the dialogue among the nations of the West to promote greater cohesion in the wake of the enhanced radiation warhead (ERW) debacle and to achieve a more equitable sharing of risks and benefits in the alliance.

The Sharing of Risk and Benefit

A similarly complex consensus undergirded the Schmidt concern that in these new political and military conditions there be a much more equitable sharing in the alliance of political risk as well as political benefit: West Germany would not stand alone in the response to the new Soviet threat or in the safeguarding of détente. At the simplest level, this German policy of nonsingularity implied two requirements. The first was that at least one other nonnuclear continental power (Holland, Belgium, or Italy being the only real candidates) must share directly in the deployment of any new countering systems. Pershing IIs could be presented as the logical successors to existing systems; GLCMs, with all the claims of a new technology, could not. There must be at least one other partner to help absorb any political fallout, to deflect either potential Soviet blackmail against West Germany or concerns among the countries of the West about the possible finlandization of Bonn.

The second requirement was that there be the widest possible alliance support for any force deployment decision. The endorsement of the nuclear powers, but also that of the Scandinavian countries with their restriction on nuclear participation or deployment on their soil during peacetime, was vital. Important, too, was the need to define deployed capabilities (and eventual arms reductions) as alliance responsibilities—a sharing of burdens that went beyond the American definition of security requirements and the risks accepted by the countries agreeing to basing on their territories.

The political consensus surrounding these requirements reflected both traditional German concerns and a new, more assertive foreign policy stance. The nonsingularity formula had been most publicly voiced in the ERW debate both to reassure domestic critics and to hedge against future external burdens. It had, in fact, been a provision of a number of earlier weapon acquisition and deployment plans.[12] In all probability,

---

12. Admittedly an awkward term, "nonsingularity" is indeed a long-standing German policy concern dating back to the restrictions on weapon deployment and production imposed under the European Defense Community in the early 1950s. See Kelleher, *Germany and the Politics of Nuclear Weapons,* pp. 9–59.

the formula will continue as a German requirement for any new system, including shorter-range cruise missiles with nuclear capability.

This approach has not always met with success, most notably in the case of the ERW and MLF.[13] In the latter instance Britain, the only assured partner of the United States, proved ultimately to have pressing interests in other areas. German willingness to proceed only with the United States left Bonn with a disproportionate economic burden and attracted criticism from both East ("the nuclear revanchists in Bonn") and West ("Bonn's nuclear back door"). The final MLF discussions in 1964–65 found an increasingly doubtful West Germany tied to an American decision over which it had only limited influence.

Bonn is now willing to apply pressure directly and confidently to be sure its political requirements are met. German concerns about non-singularity are currently far more tactical in nature and limited in intensity, whether the potential critics are internal or external. Schmidt has made little special effort to conceal his attempts to persuade fellow socialists in Holland, Belgium, and Italy through personal diplomacy, discreet pressure, and traveling teams of experts.[14] German initiatives within the HLG and Special Group were limited and generally in line with U.S. preferences but were straightforward and couched in terms of independent national analysis. Perhaps the only taboos left were the avoidance of any public action or statement on TNF that would significantly challenge or disrupt continuing relations with the East, and the necessity of references to Germany's special position—politically in terms of history and its relation with East Germany and militarily as NATO's present theater nuclear storehouse.

The new West German assertiveness was particularly clear in Schmidt's claims for more direct U.S. risk sharing, provoked by pervasive German resentment of recent American failures of alliance leadership. The issue of greatest political neuralgia was the Carter administration's introduction of another new technology perceived as critical for European security, the ERW, or neutron bomb.[15] Reportedly from Schmidt's personal

---

13. Ibid., pp. 179–202.

14. Involved in these teams were persons drawn both from the party organization and from intellectual circles close to the chancellor.

15. On the neutron bomb episode, see Alton Frye, "Nuclear Weapons in Europe: No Exit from Ambivalence," *Survival,* vol. 22 (May–June 1980), pp. 98–106; and Lothar Ruehl, "Die Nichtentscheidung über die Neutronenwaffe" (The Nondecision on the Neutron Weapon), *Europa Archiv,* vol. 34 (March 10, 1979), pp. 137–50.

perspective the U.S. president had inflicted on the nonnuclear allies two major political costs without their consent or even much notification. The first had been the leak of the pending ERW deployments, information shared in Germany only at the cabinet level (and not even there in other continental countries). The second was the abrupt, arbitrary canceling of ERW production, even though the heaviest European domestic political costs had been paid. Bonn officials were determined not to allow a second similar experience with cruise missiles or any other weapon system.

Ultimately of greater consequence had been the clear hegemonic thrust of U.S. negotiation in SALT II, similar to its behavior in SALT I. At the point when U.S. Senate ratification still seemed possible, Schmidt and other European leaders had, on request, pledged their unqualified support of the SALT treaty and their opposition to any substantive or procedural changes. Less publicly, however, Schmidt had voiced concern about the continuing tendency of the United States to give first priority to U.S.-Soviet central system limitation at the expense of negotiating limitations critical to European security and détente. Some political figures close to Schmidt had pointed—incorrectly—to American willingness to accept limitations on GLCMs and SLCMs in the SALT II protocol in a vain effort to gain restrictions on the potential intercontinental or anti-FBS roles of the Backfire bomber. Such "America-first" tendencies could only be expected to grow, they argued, given increasing U.S. stakes in limiting major new Soviet assets and the promise of the USSR to pursue limitations on FBS and, perhaps, on European nuclear forces in the next round of negotiations. West Germany was, therefore, in the forefront of the European allies demanding that there be no extension of the SALT protocol limitations on cruise missiles (for example, ranges above 600 kilometers) without extensive consultations and new Soviet concessions on equivalent Soviet-based systems.

The Carter reversal on SALT in the wake of the invasion of Afghanistan demonstrated, however, that what was needed was a stronger hedge against further sudden shifts in U.S. policies. In the view of many of Schmidt's advisers, the problem lay at the heart of the contemporary American political process. Whether LRTNF or any other defense issues were being considered, there were new and unpredictable domestic constraints on U.S. positions, as demonstrated by the inability to stem inflation and oil consumption, the strident assertiveness of a leaderless U.S. Congress, and the general mood of uncertainty and confusion in the United States over the next steps in defense, arms control, or Western economic cooperation. How willing or able would any U.S. president be to make hard choices in balancing international and domestic requirements? What kind of U.S. consensus would be necessary to both confront the Soviet Union and pursue the long-term goals of détente and arms limitation?

Almost equally feared were forceful U.S. policy initiatives that ignored the particular political and economic constraints faced by the West German government—or the other European allies. The LRTNF plan, as developed in December 1979, called for very limited cost sharing among the allies, largely on matters of infrastructure. But it was quite possible that the Americans would show the prevailing tendency, especially in Congress, to assume that the Germans were not shouldering their fair share in other ways or in offsetting systems. Indeed, in the view of many in the German political center (CDU and SPD), the real threat of American decoupling would come in the almost certain revival of "Mansfieldism" in the Congress during the next few years.[16]

At least as troublesome for this political center was a set of options more directly related to cruise missile acquisition. Among those considered conceivable were a new independent SALT proposal (as in March 1977), which proceeded without previous consultation and both gutted the 1979 GLCM decision and ignored the Special Group's "integrated package" guidelines; a U.S. decision (as in the 1962 Skybolt air-launched ballistic missile case) to drop the GLCM basing program for a more promising, "America first" solution; and new American insistence to push ahead on further nuclear force modernization, including shorter-range cruise missile systems, before the LRTNF issues had been adequately resolved or East-West negotiations attempted. The range of actions thought possible was (and is) itself a measure of the anxiety and the lack of confidence in the United States felt by the German elite.

Basic support for these positions came from all but the most militant left- and right-wing elements, albeit for quite different or even opposite reasons. The left wing of the SPD saw Schmidt's nonsingularity demand as a probable barrier to rapid GLCM deployment. The right wing of the CDU, on the other hand, saw nonsingularity as a way of obtaining due regard in the alliance for German accomplishments and the special politico-military position of West Germany. If others failed to join, the Germans could hardly be said to be at fault. Similarly, the SPD left saw

16. "Mansfieldism" has become a shorthand expression for the American force withdrawals from Europe. Senator Mike Mansfield proposed legislation in 1971 to bring home half the U.S. troops stationed there.

Schmidt's policies as providing a hedge against U.S. dominance or overly rapid German responsiveness to American demands. The more conservative CDU elements, however, saw this as a way of ensuring the continuing, essential U.S. involvement in European security arrangements and in the defense of European interests against both Soviet manipulation and domestic left-wing weakness.

Domestic Political Constraints

The new domestic political constraints on all arms acquisition that the LRTNF debate displayed were of perhaps greater long-run significance for cruise missile issues. Major shifts have occurred in the postwar German consensus on defense issues and in the ordering of national priorities between domestic and international elements in German national security strategies.

Coalition Management

One of the clearest difficulties that the Schmidt government faced was how to maintain a consensus in support of GLCMs or indeed any new defense effort. For much of the period from 1977 to 1979, Schmidt enjoyed a tenuous majority in the Bundestag of six votes and faced an advisory upper house (the Bundesrat) increasingly dominated by the CDU-CSU coalition. His control of the SPD was always a strong, articulate left wing within the Bundestag, threatened by SPD bodies, and the SPD bloc of voters. This wing had a long tradition of pacifism, separatist tendencies, and a vocal claim on the party's ideological identity in the leadership of Willy Brandt, Herbert Wehner, and Egon Bahr. Schmidt's FDP coalition partners not only were less well disciplined in their parliamentary voting but also espoused more laissez-faire domestic programs and pro-American postures than were generally acceptable to the SPD left. The FDP also appeared increasingly vulnerable electorally; there seemed to be a real danger that it would not secure minimum parliamentary representation in the October 1980 elections. Schmidt's victory in 1980 and the marked increase in FDP votes resolved many of these concerns.[17]

17. Schmidt did, however, face considerable criticism from within his own party because of his efforts before the election to ensure a good margin for the FDP above the 5 percent mandated by the basic law. For a further discussion of the ensuing coalition difficulties this brings, see Rolf Zundel, "Ein holpriger Anfang" (A Rough Beginning), *Die Zeit* (overseas edition), November 14, 1980.

A number of more fundamental factors, however, were at issue. The first was the difficulty of maintaining coalition discipline on any proposal involving additional nuclear capability, whether cruise missiles or other new systems were involved. The threat of a vote of no confidence was never as strong in Germany as it was in, say, Holland. Nor did the SPD disaffection extend—as it did in Norway and in Holland—to demands for a review of all nuclear weapons commitments and a binding commitment to phased stockpile reductions beyond those mandated by the Special Group's negotiating formula. But there were echoes of the nuclear debates of 1956 and 1958 and a notable number of attempts to mobilize public opposition to the LRTNF deployments of GLCM. There was also the sharpest questioning in over a decade about the specific political impact and military rationale for these alliance decisions. And there were moments of some uncertainty in 1979, particularly about a possible party revolt at the December 1979 party conference if the Schmidt leadership strategy did not succeed.

Thus, to the extent that cruise missiles are identified primarily as nuclear delivery vehicles, they will face continuing challenges, if not determined resistance from the left and some elements of the German political center. The sine qua non for broad parliamentary and public acceptance of the GLCM–Pershing II proposal was a simultaneous attempt to reach meaningful East-West limitation before deployment in 1983. Criteria for success were noticeably vague; the questions of Soviet manipulation and delay were barely raised. But for the large proportion of both the elite and the attentive public, this was a clear precondition.

A related question involved the GLCM range—specifically its ability to strike targets in the western Soviet Union. Most of the public and parliamentary debate touched on this only tangentially. There was little effort made by either the Schmidt government or its critics to explore what the rationale was for this range in terms of expected targets or how the effect of the GLCM would differ from that, say, of existing aircraft or Poseidons already assigned to Soviet homeland targets. Few seemed interested in or even informed about the historical precedents of the Mace missiles in the 1960s and the MRBM discussions of the Adenauer government in the 1950s. But the emphasis was on the range as an additional characteristic in the military profile of the West—whether this was viewed as a stabilizing or destabilizing element. Future cruise missile programs will confront this problem, even if the issue is how new systems of shorter range can be distinguished (or verified as being different) from long-range GLCMs.

These are only some specific concerns within a much broader set surrounding future coalition management. They are hardly the most vital;
indeed, defense decisions in general are only one of the items on the overcrowded German national agenda. Until recently, the veneer of economic
prosperity, the weakness of the CDU-CSU opposition, and the tough
image of Schmidt have all contributed to an illusion of political vigor and
governmental success.

But as both the LRTNF debate and subsequent events have shown,
Bonn, too, is suffering from what conservative critics call "the crisis of
governability."[18] Neither the SPD nor the CDU is strong enough to govern
alone; the size of the FDP is subject to the slightest of political winds.
Each new issue may therefore test the existence of the coalition—whether
it is LRTNF basing, future cruise missile acquisition, or the overall level
of defense expenditure. Despite cabinet commitment, the final parliamentary outcome on a troublesome issue may remain in doubt until the final
vote. There are also strong incentives to delay or take no action rather
than risk failure and face the problem of negotiating a new coalition.

The deepest political rifts and the more significant sources of governmental immobilism involve the nature and goals of the postindustrial welfare state. At issue are choices about requirements of external security
and appropriate trade-offs with the demands of domestic welfare,
prosperity, and distributive justice. The crisis has been precipitated
in Germany as elsewhere by what seems to be the end of a remarkable
period of postwar economic growth, by an increasing degree of Western
economic interdependence and resource vulnerability, and by unending
assertion of individual economic and social rights.[19] Thus, at a time when
the basic issues on the national political agenda are beyond Bonn's capacity to resolve, any West German government will face an increasingly
fragmented and mobilized electorate, with each of numerous groups demanding solutions carefully responsive to its interests or guaranteeing it a
veto. Moreover, for the foreseeable future, it appears that the political

18. See Samuel P. Huntington, "The United States," in Michel Crozier, Samuel P.
Huntington, and Joji Watanuki, eds., *The Crisis of Democracy* (New York University Press, 1975), pp. 59–118; and Walter Laqueur, *A Continent Astray: Europe,
1970–1978* (Oxford University Press, 1979).

19. A related analysis on the interrelationship between economic growth and
defense expenditures in the 1960s and 1970s is presented in Catherine M. Kelleher,
William Domke, and Richard Eichenberg, "Guns, Butter, and Growth: Expenditure
Patterns in Four Advanced Democracies," *Zeitschrift für Soziologie*, vol. 9 (April
1980), pp. 149–58.

spectrum in West Germany will remain to the left of the Adenauer model that prevailed for NATO's first two decades and that provided a relatively automatic majority for even acquisition of controversial weapons.

A particularly bloody Soviet invasion of Poland or an unequivocal return to a confrontation strategy vis-à-vis the Soviet Union by the Reagan administration will produce short-run reversals in these German political trends. Such events will dramatically undermine the premises of Bonn's détente policy and sharpen the review of national priorities and allegiances. But if German behavior after Czechoslovakia in 1968 is any guide, the long-term effects are less clear. These developments might well not be sufficient to shift the Federal Republic of Germany from the joint strategy of Ostpolitik-Westpolitik it has followed since the late 1960s.[20]

Constraints within the Defense Sector

More specific constraints on future cruise missiles will arise from within the German defense sector itself. Those of greatest interest are questions of cost and possible coproduction or standardization arrangements. Neither issue was directly touched upon during the LRTNF debate and both are sensitive to American decisions not yet made or even debated. Yet there is continuing interest among German defense planners in cruise missile applications beyond LRTNF, motivated by inevitable German pressure to share in the latest technological development, the growing pressure on the defense budget, and the still unresolved question of the "two-way street" in alliance and bilateral weapon development.

West Germany has expressed perhaps the greatest interest of all the European countries in coproduction, beginning almost as soon as discussion of the potential of cruise missiles in the early 1970s. More specific initiatives were developed with the specialized NATO working group of the mid-1970s and from 1977 onward, in detailed explorations with both Britain and France. The approach was consistent with past German policies reflecting a mix of cost considerations, demonstration of alliance loyalty, and the restrictions placed on independent German armament production under the 1954 Western European Union agreements.[21] Cruise

20. There are essays that differ on this point in Wolfram Hanrieder, ed., *West German Foreign Policy* (Westview Press, 1979).

21. Under the existing Western European Union restrictions, cruise missiles may not be held by German forces or produced on German soil. Progressive amendments—new and largely pro forma—have led to the lifting of many similar prohibitions during the past decade.

missiles had also been of historical interest (the V-1) and had already attracted a policy constituency among some in the Luftwaffe.[22] These principally were planners and commanders interested in conventional air-to-surface applications (for example, against airfields) to extend both the range and the life of the much-troubled European multirole combat air-craft, the Tornado. Less visible was a small number of Navy planners in-terested in the possibilities of TLAM, conventional or perhaps nuclear, for German destroyers.

German expectations about coproduction possibilities have lessened considerably, given the lack of a European consensus on cruise missile applications, let alone production. Never enthusiastic, British planners have become even less interested in the wake of the Trident decision, the lack of a significant Royal Air Force constituency, and the yawning eco-nomic deficits faced by the Thatcher government.[23] For France, cruise missiles are only one, relatively secondary, element in a complex, ambi-tious modernization program that is already meeting financial barriers.

The major cause of decline in interest has been the perception of Amer-ican opposition or at least noncooperation. There has been considerable irritation throughout Europe at the formal restriction on the transfer of terrain contour matching (TERCOM) technology—or the possibility (hinted at in 1978–79) that only Britain would receive the requisite data. More central for German planners is what they perceive as unilateral American decisions that limit European options in terms of cost alone. The selection of the MRASM missile by the American Joint Cruise Mis-sile Project Office in effect shook the NATO working group discussions on conventional cruise missiles and seemed to contradict the earlier Car-ter pressure for meaningful standardization, if not "two-way street" efforts.

Even the low unit costs promised by coproduction may not meet the new financial constraints imposed on all future German weapon acquisi-tion. The bickering between West Germany and the United States on the level of German defense effort resulted largely from Schmidt's complex tactics.[24] One aspect was a familiar German ploy of citing domestic costs

22. Some German interest was reportedly developed in preliminary discussions with other European planners and with representatives of American producer candi-dates, notably McDonnell Douglas, which had a long-standing interest in a MRASM project.

23. See chapter 14 in this volume.

24. See, for example, the series of critical reports in the *Frankfurter Allgemeine Zeitung* in mid-November 1980. There was a parallel earlier effort on American demands for greater German expenditures in September 1979 and September 1980.

and previous exemplary behavior while eventually responding grudgingly to American pressures for compliance. Another was Schmidt's effort, in the face of real coalition disagreement over domestic priorities, to demonstrate that the economic situation was paramount and that all programs would have to be financially constrained.

But current trends suggest that there will be significant deficiencies in resources for new hardware throughout the 1980s. The coproduction arrangements for the Tornado have not been cost-effective. Estimates now show at least a doubling of unit costs that will unquestionably absorb funds for additional weapons (for example, the MRASM) for the Tornado and extensive innovative programs in other areas (such as the TLAM-C). In the German 1981–82 fiscal program there are already funding shortfalls for current deliveries of frigates, tanks, and planes. Support by the military services for new programs, especially in the Luftwaffe, has lessened as systems of primary interest have come under attack.

Although far stronger than most Western European economies, the West German economy is perceived by most of its citizens to be in the gravest difficulties of the postwar era. Critics on the left argue that defense expenditure levels cannot be left unscathed, that domestic social support is of far greater importance. It was this type of criticism that led to a partially successful Bundestag revolt just before the 1980 elections on economic assistance to Turkey, presented as a substitute for a German military involvement in Persian Gulf security arrangements. The mounting costs of economic support for Eastern Europe and the increasing stalemates on economic issues within the European Community have and will continue to increase domestic perceptions of economic gloom and pressures to control defense spending.

The range of likely outcomes is still fairly open, although the probability of major investment in cruise missile technology seems low overall. One possibility would be the institution of stretched-out service-balanced weapon acquisition—similar to the program adopted under the Middle Term Financial Plan of the mid-1960s.[25] This might actually enhance the attractiveness of limited MRASM purchases (based on a favorable price) as a way of extending the effective life of the Tornado. More likely, at least in the short term, would be a moratorium on any investment in new projects or new technologies. Funding might then gradually become avail-

25. For a more complete discussion, see Gregory F. Treverton, *The Dollar Drain and American Forces in Germany: Managing the Political Economics of Alliance* (Ohio University Press, 1978).

able for evolutionary system improvements, especially those with visible advantages in terms of domestic employment or maximization of past hardware investments.

The Smaller European Nonnuclear Countries

A direct comparison of German cruise missile interests and constraints with those of the other European nonnuclear countries is, by definition, somewhat artificial. The nonnuclear status of the Federal Republic of Germany is a historical anomaly in view of the country's size, military requirements and capability, and centrality to NATO decisionmaking. Moreover, Bonn is the unchallenged European discussion partner of the United States. (The British retain some special status for sentimental reasons.) But in both substantive and procedural questions within NATO, it is West Germany that sets the European standard, presses projects to successful completion, or forces reconsideration (or even reformulation) of American demands on its alliance partners.

Yet Germany and the smaller nonnuclear countries share a number of common political concerns. Their views are shaped by continental location and by similar domestic political alignments. Moreover, except for a limited group of experts the leaders in all these countries are primarily interested in the political choices and stakes involved, rather than the full range of cruise missile applications, conventional or nuclear, or the latest technological information.

Indeed, the trends observed in Germany are more pointed in these smaller countries. In both the Low Countries (Belgium, Luxembourg, the Netherlands) and Scandinavia the political spectrum is unquestionably to the left of the German political consensus and even more susceptible to the influence of socialist strategies and concerns. Italy remains in many respects the exception, at least as responsive to considerations of alliance status and a pro-American posture as to domestic immobilism and popular drift. All these countries, furthermore, are operating close to the political and economic margin in terms of coalition stability and the present and future resources available for defense. These combine to make national choices about cruise missiles—like decisions about all defense programs—both more difficult and more significant for long-term military and political postures.

The LRTNF Decision

These patterns are demonstrated in the national debates preceding the December 1979 GLCM decision. Of all the continental states, only Italy was able to secure full parliamentary approval of GLCM basing before NATO action. Full Dutch and Belgian approval was postponed after intense debate and extensive public discussion in both countries. Norway and Denmark were never seriously considered for basing because of their traditional policy of no peacetime nuclear involvement. Although in the end both governments were successful, they had difficulty even in ensuring full support for the general LRTNF program.

The reasons for this ambivalence and delay were not rooted in fundamentally different assessments of the new Soviet challenge or the desirability of some symbolic alliance response but in the primacy assigned by the left in these countries to the maintenance of European détente. Ultimately, these differences became questions of coalition management. Traditional leftist groups almost constitute majorities in Norway and Denmark; in Belgium and Italy, they are major coalition partners; in Holland, they span government and opposition. In dramatic contrast to British Thatcherism, for example, their goals include a basic commitment to the pursuit of détente and a conviction of the primacy of the domestic social and economic agenda.

The debates about ERWs and LRTNF in all countries except Italy suggest that resistance to cruise missiles will be great simply because of their potential nuclear capability. For the foreseeable future, these governmental coalitions will be even less able than the SPD-FDP government in Bonn to accept any acquisition or basing plan not tied to full exploration of arms control options. Traditional socialist skepticism about nuclear weapons has now been reinforced by conclusions that nuclear parity will only increase Europe's vulnerability to nuclear devastation by the superpowers.[26] The challenge is not to the legitimacy of national defense programs, as it was in the 1950s, or even to the maintenance of a deterrent posture in the form of mutual assured destruction, but to the necessity of involvement in further nuclear programs given the enormous stockpiles that already exist in Europe.

26. Klaas G. de Vries, "Responding to the SS-20: An Alternative Approach," *Survival*, vol. 21 (November–December 1979), pp. 251–55. For the more pragmatic Belgian views, see the reports in *Le Monde*, especially those from mid-November through mid-December 1979.

What is striking is that in the Low Countries and Scandinavia these concerns extend beyond the left.[27] Holland is the most dramatic case. In less than two weeks, for example, more than one million Dutch citizens (out of fourteen million) signed a petition condemning ERW weapons as immoral and calling for the abandonment of any new nuclear-capable weapons acquisition and for stockpile reduction. Within the parliament, the coalition of Prime Minister Andreas von Agt faced a significant group of nuclear pacifists within government ranks, especially the Christian Democratic left. The premier skillfully overcame the advisory vote of no confidence against GLCM basing participation. But the price was re-affirmation of the primacy of military reductions by negotiation and a two-year delay in a final Dutch participation.

The issue was among the most critical in the spring 1981 elections in Holland. The progress of East-West exchanges on GLCMs and FBS reductions as well as the seriousness of alliance efforts to achieve negotiating success have been fully discussed. It seems clear that the present coalition and certainly a socialist-led successor government will delay simply because of the mechanics of coalition formation.[28] The vaguely articulated interest of some Dutch military leaders in future conventional cruise missiles will take a back seat to these overwhelming political constraints.

The extent of what might be called nuclear neuralgia is more limited in Belgium. The Flemish parties are influenced by Dutch political trends, traditions, and conceptions. For the Flemish Socialists, the LRTNF issue proved a convenient set of issues on which to separate themselves from their French-speaking colleagues. The result was a reformulation of the Belgian government (especially the departure of Foreign Minister Henri Simonet) and an initial postponement of six months for a Belgian decision on GLCM basing. Neither the new coalition nor any currently fore-

27. See Philip P. Everts, "Reviving Unilateralism: Report on a Campaign for Nuclear Disarmament in the Netherlands," paper presented to the Moscow International Political Science Association Congress, August 1979, which summarizes not only the relevant working papers of the Nederlands Institut voor de Publieke Opinie en net Marktonderzoek but also the thesis of Pieter Maessen, "Wie stopt de Neutronbom? Besluitvorming en pressie rond de invoering van de Neutronbom" (Who Stopped the Neutron Bomb? Decisionmaking and Pressure surrounding the Introduction of the Neutron Bomb), presented at Leiden, Netherlands, in 1979. A typical publication of the coalition against the enhanced radiation warhead is "The Amsterdam Appeal," issued by the International Forum, entitled "Stop the Neutron Bomb," Amsterdam, March 18–19, 1978.

28. The present coalition took approximately five months to complete its preliminary negotiations and contract.

seeable successor seems able to disentangle the question of the GLCM delay from more critical linguistically based cleavages on domestic issues. The postures of Holland and Belgium on nuclear cruise missiles approach the traditional antinuclear attitudes of Norway and Denmark; such attitudes have, if anything, intensified under the events of the LRTNF debate. The minority socialist government in Norway began in strong support of the NATO modernization program but moderated its stand in the face of both domestic criticism and the more militant Dutch and Danish criticism. There is still lingering left-wing disquiet about Norwegian approval of the December 1979 decision, as was evident in the divisive debate on a far simpler issue, the pre-positioning of military equipment for U.S. Marines in Norway.[29] Public discussion did flare up again in the context of the fall 1981 parliamentary elections.

One of the most effective challenges to the December 1979 decision was the Danish proposal to opt instead for a six-month moratorium even on an endorsement of an eventual alliance decision to deploy. In the end, Denmark did support the alliance action, but with clear reservations. Subsequent events—particularly press accounts of Presidential Directive 59 and its purported implications—suggest that even the hint of nuclear use on or from Danish soil will initiate sharp, divisive debate about all nuclear-capable weapons and new destabilizing systems. Links between Danish antinuclear groups and those in Norway and the Low Countries have grown in response to the LRTNF discussion and show every sign of continuing.

This development introduces new uncertainty into alliance consensus building, already a cumbersome process. Perceptually, at least, this will suggest indecision and weakness, even if the final decision is favorable. It implies the emergence of concerted Scandinavian-Benelux pressure for the linkage of acquisition and negotiation efforts, for progressive limitation on existing stockpiles, and for ceilings on any nuclear modernization. Present Dutch and Belgian nuclear-capable forces, which are limited in size but symbols of alliance deterrence, will come under increasing pressure for limitation or substitution of conventional weapons.[30]

29. See the scattered reports in the *New York Times* in November and December 1980.

30. A large proportion of the Dutch political elite would like to see an overall reduction in Dutch functional participation in nuclear weapon planning and use. See Everts, "Reviving Unilateralism," and the press analyses after the NATO December 1979 decision.

All this will simply intensify the difficulty of any alliance initiatives on cruise missiles, coproduction, or basic negotiation. It will also raise the specter of German isolation or the dominance of interests of the United States, West Germany, and Britain in alliance decisionmaking. Such German predominancé is unacceptable not only to the populations in the other nonnuclear states but also to most Germans, if only in the interests of continuing normalization with the East.

These trends only throw into sharper relief the unique posture of successive Italian coalitions in favor of GLCM basing. The reasons for this continuity are uncertain, given both the increasing strength of the Italian Socialist party and the widespread commitment to European détente. These become all the more interesting, however, in light of the probable Dutch or Belgian delay or default in participation in GLCM basing.

One set of conditioning factors depends on the electoral strategies of much of the Italian left, which considers demonstration of loyalty to the alliance in all its requirements and responsiveness to the lead of the United States to be vital. For the Socialists as for many of the Italian Communists (PCI) to a lesser extent, these are the marks of coalition acceptability.[31] With occasional exceptions, the Socialist leadership held to strict party discipline in support of the LRTNF decision, including GLCM basing in Italy. While opposed, the PCI was remarkably restrained and even cited the need to remove the "destabilizing" factor in the European balance, the Soviet SS-20s.[32]

The determination of the Christian Democrats and their traditional allies to avoid (or overcome) second-class NATO status for Italy is of almost equal importance. It is therefore essential that Italy seek equality in armament and participation in new military and arms control efforts by the alliance. The Christian Democrats' stance on LRTNF was a "buying-in" to the top circles of a critical alliance decision. This position reportedly enjoys widespread political support among the segments of the public attentive to foreign policy. This is true despite economic constraints, domestic crisis, and political bureaucratic paralysis in social decisionmaking—or perhaps because of them. In the past, successive Christian Democratic leaders have sought refuge in alliance politics as a way

31. This reportedly is the position of the current Craxi leadership of the Italian Socialist party. See, for example, reports in the *New York Times,* March 19–20, 1980.
32. See the PCI statements of November 6–7, 1979, especially that of Antonio Rubio.

of mobilizing external influence, especially by the United States, to force domestic agreement on new programs and hardware. It is thus a way to overcome domestic opposition and deflect domestic criticism or unresolvable disputes on social and economic programs.

To a number of Western observers there still seems to be good reason to doubt final Italian participation in GLCM basing—or indeed in anything to do with cruise missiles in the future. The informal veto power of the PCI, if it remains outside the government, will be a limiting factor of increasing importance, since continued Socialist support for the government is uncertain. If the PCI enters a governing coalition, implementation may well be impossible because of American opposition. The fate of Western arms control initiatives will also aggravate the long-pursued search for bridges among the Christian Democrats, the Socialists, and the PCI.

In sum, the probability of Italian participation in present and future alliance cruise missile projects is uncertain, despite the thrust of all present Italian declarations—both by the governing coalition and by the opposition on the left. The tolerance of the Italian political leadership for both ambivalence and certainty in the face of contravening evidence is legendary.

Conclusion

The assessment of nonnuclear European interest in cruise missile applications, present and future, must be pessimistic. The notable exception is the Federal Republic of Germany, which has both a major stake in the implementation of the December 1979 LRTNF decision to deploy GLCMs and some specific interests in future projects. But even Bonn's interests are constrained by the political and economic context in which these decisions are embedded. This pessimistic outlook, however, does not fully account for the potential impact of an energized Chancellor Schmidt. His management of the LRTNF decision was adroit and constant and involved the careful calibration of several political strategies— vis-à-vis his coalition, his own party, and general public opinion in Germany as well as within the framework of NATO and East-West diplomacy. In the 1980s he will undoubtedly face new limitations from the economy and on the SPD succession question. Yet his capacity to overcome domestic and international opposition cannot be overlooked. In tandem with an interested U.S. leadership, responsive to European requirements, Schmidt's backing for, say, a conventional TLAM would have a high probability of success.

It is striking how many of the potential constraints are old concerns. The most obvious are the external limits: the questions of U.S. political and technological dominance of alliance decisionmaking, the balance to be struck between U.S.-Soviet agreement on arms limitation and agreement among nations in the West on the negotiation agenda, and the apportionment within the alliance of political-military risk and advantage. These are points that have been debated on virtually every major alliance proposal for weapon acquisition and that have almost never been resolved to the satisfaction of all alliance partners. Their very familiarity leads many officials and observers to a confidence in continuing alliance cooperation and initiative, whatever the specific outcome of the LRTNF program or any future proposed application of cruise missile technology. Such confidence is hard to dispute. The prospects for at least partial implementation of the December 1979 decision seem strong. While European nonnuclear skepticism about the relevance of cruise missile technology has increased, it is consistent with doubts expressed in Britain and in France as well as in the United States.

Yet there are some trends in the patterns of national decisionmaking in these countries that suggest new and somewhat larger areas of disagreement and discontinuity between the nuclear and nonnuclear allies. The three that emerge most clearly are the marked negative trend in support for new defense projects among the continental electorates that were never enthusiastic, the growing immobilism that problems of coalition management and financial constraints impose on national decisionmaking, and the increasingly exposed and anomalous nonnuclear position of the Federal Republic of Germany, both among the nonnuclear states and vis-à-vis Britain and France. Viewed singly, each is a development that can be accommodated within the present alliance structure and patterns of expectations. Occurring together, they suggest that the underpinnings of alliance structure are already in a period of significant change. The ramifications go far beyond the problems of either implementing the LRTNF decision or securing maximum military and political advantage from the exploitation of cruise missile technology.

PART FOUR

Conclusions

CHAPTER SIXTEEN

Complexities, Uncertainties, and Dilemmas

RICHARD K. BETTS

CRUISE MISSILE policy is a bucket of worms. The weapons themselves have been continually changing. The difficulty of tracking and evaluating technical refinements is compounded by related issues: the choice of delivery systems, the merits of alternate weapon systems, the political constraints imposed by alliance relations, and the possibility of arms control formulas that could improve security or reduce its price. One thing is clear: neither the benefits nor the disadvantages of cruise missiles are as revolutionary or as simple as either advocates or opponents originally believed. A better view of what cruise missiles do offer depends on an appreciation of the interacting strategic, political, diplomatic, and budgetary implications of the new systems.

Technology and Cost

Cruise missiles became important because they seemed cheap. Otherwise, reliance on ballistic missiles and aircraft would have remained the bedrock of long-range firepower. Thus the larger the prospective investment in cruise missiles, the more their true costs demand examination. Reliable cost-effectiveness analysis, however, has always been difficult.[1]

1. "The problem dealt with in systems analysis is essentially an old one. Clausewitz, in one fascinating chapter of *On War* . . . attempts to analyze the appropriate mix of the three services existing in his time—infantry, cavalry, and artillery—and he understands that the only sensible way to compare them is on the basis of their

511

On this issue it is almost infinitely complex, given the profusion of missile types, potential missions, and conceivable launch platforms, and the lack of lessons from relevant battlefield experience (the V-1 is not comparable).

Performance versus Price

Many variants of the modern cruise missile have been developed in the past few years because it has been easy to capitalize on the basic common elements of design—airframe, propulsion, and guidance. This has increased the apparent military versatility of the weapon, making it useful for a broad spectrum of missions. Over time, however, commonality accompanies versatility only within limits.

One limit is the relative emphasis on the two factors. The more versatility is stressed as a requirement—expanding the number of missions and performance standards for each one—the more strain is placed on commonality. It is cheaper to produce a large number of a single version of a cruise missile than to produce smaller numbers of many versions with more sophistication. Optimizing capabilities for each of many missions makes changes in design and components more attractive. The designs of the basic models now programmed are constrained by their origins, for reasons that are anachronistic. The airframe of the Tomahawk was designed to fit the dimensions of submarine torpedo tubes, and the trapezoidal Boeing air-launched cruise missile (ALCM) was derived from the earlier subsonic cruise armed decoy (SCAD) which had in turn been shaped to fit short-range attack missile (SRAM) rotary launcher racks. Such constraints can compromise performance, and they become progressively less acceptable as the original reasons for them become outmoded and as more ambitious applications are envisioned for the missile. The Tomahawk's tubular shape is far from aerodynamically ideal. It limits the speed of response to sharp changes in altimeter readings, requiring the missile to fly higher when over jagged terrain, which increases its detectability by radar. Yet today the torpedo-tube launch mode that was

---

respective unit costs, on the one hand, and their tactical effectiveness on the other. Determining their costs he finds easy, but determining their comparative effectiveness he finds extremely difficult. . . . predicting the cost side of the equation, which was so easy in Clausewitz's time, can now be at least as difficult as predicting effectiveness." Bernard Brodie, "Technological Change, Strategic Doctrine, and Political Outcomes," in Klaus Knorr, ed., *Historical Dimensions of National Security Problems* (University Press of Kansas for the National Security Education Program, 1976), p. 303.

originally envisioned may not be among the most important for the future.[2]

According to an Air Force officer quoted by one reporter, commonality "is sometimes held out as an absolute virtue. But how much is artificial commonality, and how much is to be given up for it? The F-111 is a classic case of pursuing commonality for its own sake. We still carry 300 lb. of angle iron in the tail to accommodate carrier landings."[3] Commonality is a "technical push" criterion for cruise missile programs. If "strategic pull" criteria come to dominate—which they should if cruise missiles do become major elements of force structures—there will be greater pressure to slough off the old constraints and to reconfigure future models to accord more closely with specific operational requirements.[4] If so, cost advantages may recede along with commonality, and the combination of low cost and high military utility may diverge. One can only guess whether the divergence would be significant, but there is, at least potentially, a vicious circle that would cast doubt on the proper extent of investment in cruise missiles: cheapness drove commitment to the systems, but increased commitment may vitiate cheapness.

Even if the divergence between cost and utility is not great it can be significant as long as doubt persists about the cost-effectiveness of the missile in comparison with other systems, such as tactical aircraft, which are more expensive but also offer more flexibility per unit. In systems analysis it is difficult to incorporate the value of unit flexibility.[5] If uncertainties about respective capabilities remain high while apparent cost differentials decline, there will be stronger reasons to favor the more flexible alternative.

2. In recent years doubt developed that *any* cruise missile models would ultimately be deployed aboard submarines. The Reagan administration, however, has reportedly moved to put great emphasis on submarine-launched cruise missiles. "Navy to Arm With Cruise Missiles," *Baltimore Sun,* June 5, 1981.

3. Quoted in David R. Griffiths, "Proposal Set on Air-to-Surface Missile," *Aviation Week and Space Technology,* December 29, 1980, p. 24.

4. Differentiation of design for military reasons could also facilitate arms control by making observable distinctions a more credible basis for counting rules.

5. For a criticism of cost-effectiveness methodology's insensitivity to the value of weapon flexibility that is stimulating though marred by reliance on a straw-man characterization of the role of systems analysis in decisionmaking, see Eliot Cohen, "Systems Paralysis," *American Spectator,* vol. 13 (November 1980), pp. 23–27. Even if Cohen's caustic critique is not persuasive, there is still the problem that systems analysis techniques are most appropriate for dealing with trade-offs in force structure when doctrine is defined simply and held constant; it is much less applicable when integrated operational concepts are complex and strategy stresses multipurpose forces.

The vicious circle cannot necessarily be broken simply by reducing the emphasis on versatility. Much of the attractiveness of cruise missiles arises from their capacity to substitute for other more expensive systems in performing military missions. If simplicity and commonality are emphasized more than adaptability to multiple missions, cruise missiles become less substitutable for other weapons, except at the price of compromising effectiveness. For example, the Air Force and the Navy resisted pressure (based on cost considerations) from the Office of the Secretary of Defense to accept the Tomahawk medium-range air-to-surface missile (MRASM), preferring a supersonic ramjet missile—at least as a complement if not as an alternative—in order to widen the envelope Soviet tactical air defenses would have to cover (by striking from high as well as low altitudes).[6] This echoes the argument presented by Bennett and Foster that the ALCM is more valuable in tandem with a penetrating strategic bomber than alone, because the combination places greater demands on Soviet strategic air defense investments. Thus the appeal of cruise missiles in terms of their synergy with other systems reduces their attractiveness in terms of substitutability.

What Are the True Costs?

Cruise missiles do not seem so cheap when their unit flyaway cost grows and when the associated costs—especially for delivery systems—are considered. The significance of associated costs depends both on the scale of cruise missile deployments and on the life cycles of the delivery systems. It would be illusory to expect infinite economies of scale from the missile production learning curve, given the limited number of adaptable launch platforms.[7] Although large-scale deployment of the

6. "Pentagon Split on New Medium-Range Missile," *Flight International,* September 20, 1980, p. 1172. Air Force preference for advanced conventional standoff missile options other than the MRASM, which was directed by Under Secretary of Defense William J. Perry toward the end of the Carter administration, led to a suggestion for a compromise—procurement of 200–300 MRASMs for use against hardened command, control, and communications targets, with a "follow-on competition between General Dynamics and McDonnell Douglas to develop an anti-runway weapon." Mark Hewish, "Tactical-Missile Survey Part 1: Ground Targets," *International Defense Review,* no. 6 (1980), p. 858. Such a compromise could reduce the ability to capitalize on the MRASM production learning curve.

7. Even without associated costs, economies of scale are not in themselves reasons for increased procurement. The incremental savings at each point must exceed the diminishing returns in military utility from incremental increases in force levels. As one reporter argued after Secretary of Defense Caspar Weinberger touted the

ALCM reduces its unit costs, major increases in numbers beyond those planned would require dedicated platforms. Such new delivery systems (as opposed to B-52s, for which only modification costs are attributable) would dramatically raise the true cost of each cruise missile. Whether or not missile deployment can capitalize sufficiently on the sunk costs of adaptable platforms depends on strategic concepts and mission requirements and, most important, on changes in the role of the other legs of the triad or various components of naval and tactical air forces.

The current surge in U.S. defense investments raises questions across the board about what changes will evolve in doctrine and force structure. This compounds the difficulty in attempting to make reliable assessments of the cost-effectiveness of cruise missiles, especially conventionally armed variants. They appear potentially applicable to a wide range of military missions, but their relative utility depends on decisions about force structure at a much more general level. Enthusiasm for cruise missiles should not automatically be allowed to determine much larger decisions about force structure. As MccGwire notes in chapter 8, for example, it would be a mistake to let Tomahawk loadings take precedence over air defense systems on surface ships. At the same time, a long-term view of the potential of conventionally armed sea-launched cruise missiles (SLCMs) could warrant significant departures in ship design and naval force structure. Integrating cruise missiles into strategy, in short, requires judicious and carefully honed planning, rather than a leap to take advantage of the superficially obvious benefits of the weapons.

Ground-launched cruise missiles (GLCMs) appear to be inexpensive choices for theater nuclear force modernization only when compared to SLCMs on new, dedicated submarines rather than on partially converted old nuclear attack submarines (SSNs). Doubt about the latter option, because of the demands on existing submarines to perform other missions, helps to validate the GLCM choice. Full GLCM system costs per missile might also be reduced if fewer transporter-erector-launchers were procured and provision was made for multiple refiring, although appar-

---

"savings" that would be achieved by increasing procurement of several weapon systems beyond numbers planned by the Carter administration, "This, explained Weinberger's memo, is 'economies of scale.'. . . If a dozen doughnuts cost 60 cents but doughnuts bought singly cost 6 cents, and you have 12 doughnuts for breakfast instead of the two you originally intended to eat, you 'save,' in Pentagon mathematics. You also get fat." James Coates, "The Pentagon's Formula for 'Saving' by Spending More," *Chicago Tribune*, March 19, 1981.

ently this option is not being considered. For the conventional GLCM system discussed by Palin in chapter 6, multiple reloads might seem even more necessary for cost-effectiveness. But there is a limit to how far extra rounds might spread the costs. The number of fixed targets appropriate for cruise missiles is finite, and if the missiles are militarily effective most of those targets (with the exception of airfields) would not have to be hit again frequently. Moreover, the incremental costs for the GLCM convoys that would be required to carry and load extra rounds might not be trivial.

The smaller number of systems that make up U.S. strategic forces should make trade-offs in that area somewhat easier to grasp. But trends in cost advantage and military efficacy may be disjoined. Bennett and Foster's analysis in chapter 5 suggests that the first phase of ALCM deployment is the period in which the maximum cost advantage is obtainable from the adaptable platforms (B-52s), but this is also the period in which the contribution of the missiles to target coverage is least impressive. While the number of ALCMs deployed rises in the 1990s, the reliability of the by-then ancient B-52 carriers declines, so a larger ALCM force is not necessarily equivalent to a larger force on target. Improving the prospects requires a new carrier with greater payload and faster flyaway time. And a carrier that is new, dedicated, and more capable reduces the ALCM's cost-effectiveness vis-à-vis a manned bomber—the principal original rationale for commitment to the ALCM.

Baker's figures in chapter 4 indicate that the platform cost per ALCM space on the B-52 would almost triple in a wide-bodied cruise missile carrier aircraft and quintuple in a B-1 derivative strategic weapons launcher. (This does not mean the wide-body would be more cost-effective, because the B-1 derivative would have substantially greater prelaunch survivability.) Matched with the analysis in chapter 5, this suggests that the ALCM's major cost advantage only obtains during the 1980s "window of vulnerability,"[8] rather than indefinitely. Over the long term, however, a new ALCM carrier or bomber will have to be procured anyway if the air-breathing leg of the triad is to be preserved. So while the cost advantage of the ALCM will decline, the weapon will not become cost-ineffective unless new manned bombers turn out to be *more* pene-

8. This catchphrase refers to the period in the 1980s (before the resurgence of American capabilities when major new systems are deployed) during which U.S. forces are in their lowest position (according to standard indexes) relative to Soviet forces.

trative than cruise missiles or the air-breathing leg is abandoned. In view of the uncertainties about how effective Stealth technology will be and the enduring obstacles to devising a faultless MX basing mode, neither of those conditions seems likely to obtain.[9] Thus even when the ALCM is no longer comparatively impressive, it will still probably be a worthwhile investment.

To shrink the apparent vulnerability in the 1980s "window" period, however, there might be temptations to proliferate first-generation ALCMs to the outside limit, increasing the total investment in air-breathing strategic forces to compensate for perceived inadequacies in the other elements of the triad. But if cruise missiles are to be important over the longer term, there is a counterincentive to restrain commitment to first-generation models and to wait and capitalize on a more capable second generation that incorporates greater fuel efficiency, range, speed, penetration aids, or other advances. But as Toomay notes in chapter 1, technical improvements in altitude and radar cross section are already near the point of diminishing returns; at the point where increases in penetrativity depend on greater speed, rocket-powered systems will become more attractive.

All this suggests that the relative cost-effectiveness of cruise missiles is more certain in the near term than in the long term. To appreciate the issue fully, the strategic considerations governing the weapons' integration into force posture must be considered in more detail.

Nuclear Strategy

Bennett and Foster described many of the factors that cast doubt on the optimistic assumptions made by the most vigorous advocates of cruise missiles early in the weapons' development. In looking at feasible alternatives for achieving strategic goals, however, policymakers should not infer that air-launched cruise missiles are a poor investment. In theater nuclear

9. Ball presents rough computations suggesting that in the future, with both a survivable American MX system and a Soviet look-down–shoot-down air defense that would reduce cruise missile penetrativity, the costs per warhead on target favor the intercontinental ballistic missile (ICBM) with multiple independently targetable reentry vehicles (MIRVs) over the ALCM. He notes, though, that the value of preserving the triad would mitigate the negative inference about long-term investment in cruise missiles. Desmond Ball, "The Costs of the Cruise Missile," *Survival,* vol. 20 (November–December 1978), pp. 245–46.

force modernization the issues are primarily political, but the military roles of theater cruise missiles must be further clarified in order to judge how great an effort should be made to overcome political obstacles to their deployment.

Capability

In the long term cruise missiles buttress U.S. assured destruction capacity by reinsuring strategic forces against an unlikely but hypothetically possible combination of a Soviet antisubmarine warfare (ASW) breakthrough and an American inability to find any solution to the vulnerability of intercontinental ballistic missiles (ICBMs). In the near term, however, the assured destruction element in U.S. strategic force requirements does not make cruise missiles essential, since submarine-launched ballistic missiles (SLBMs) are not threatened, manned bomber penetrativity will only decline incrementally, and the 100–250 warheads from as few as 50–100 surviving Minuteman II and III ICBMs could make an impressive contribution to simple countervalue target coverage. Quick remedies for the eroding U.S. position in the strategic balance are not needed for assured destruction purposes, unless one assumes the most extreme capabilities that have been alleged for Soviet civil defense and industrial hardening. Remedies are needed, if at all, only for the political purposes of maintaining parity or for the strategic purposes of improving capabilities to strike military targets. The contributions of ALCMs to the former are more obvious than those to the latter.

Another constraint on the notion that a quick repair of the strategic balance could be obtained by proliferating ALCMs beyond the numbers and rate of deployment projected by the Carter administration is the possible shortage of special nuclear materials for warheads.[10] Paul Nitze

10. The shortage follows from the sharp increases scheduled in the late 1970s (Mark 12A for Minuteman modernization, the new B61 bomb, and Lance missile warheads) and resistance to starting a new plutonium reprocessing plant (resulting from Carter's nonproliferation policy). Walter Pincus, " 'Technical Problems' Cause Delays in Delivery of New Nuclear Weapons," *Washington Post,* September 28, 1980. B. T. Plymale, of Boeing, claimed that this was the only limitation on deploying extra ALCMs since there were no constraints on potential missile production within the limits of prospectively available carriers; "Strategic Alternatives: Airbreathing Systems," in William R. Van Cleave and W. Scott Thompson, eds., *Strategic Options for the Early Eighties: What Can Be Done?* (New York: National Strategy Information Center, 1979), pp. 54–56, 58, 67, 69.

argued at one point that, given this limiting factor, extra cruise missiles could be used as unarmed decoys to soak up Soviet defenses.[11] Only desperation about the window in the military balance could make such a solution economically rational; the same can be said of the option to convert Polaris SLBM tubes to SLCM launchers, which would have a high life-cycle cost because of the short time that the converted submarines would remain operational.[12]

The principal question about ALCM capability is its potential for hard-target destruction. For a long time cruise missiles were considered by both their strongest advocates and their strongest opponents to be excellent counterforce weapons. The decline in estimates of ALCM accuracy has tempered these expectations.[13] Bennett and Foster's calculations demonstrate that high-confidence effectiveness against very hard targets will require a warhead yield of 200 kilotons and a missile circular error probable (CEP) of 200 feet. Figuring an arrival probability of 80 percent, they conclude that an alert force of 1,350 ALCMs would be needed to damage 70 percent of Soviet silos (2,650 to damage 90 percent).

As long as U.S. war plans stipulate significant counterforce second strikes without launching the Minuteman force on warning, the ALCM's contribution will rest on one or more of the following possibilities: (1) an assumption that strategic warning will be provided, allowing most of the bomber force to be alerted before Soviet attack (efficient queuing and flyaway of the larger numbers of aircraft would also be necessary); (2) some scheme for preferential targeting of ALCMs against the highest priority Soviet silos; or (3) reduction of the CEP of the ALCM to improve the probability of destruction. The first is a risky strategy, and the

11. Paul H. Nitze in "Discussion: Strategic Alternatives: Airbreathing Systems," in Van Cleave and Thompson, *Strategic Options*, p. 72.

12. This choice is not persuasive even if cost considerations are ignored. The conversion option (four to seven SLCMs in each tube) was an attempt at compliance with SALT constraints. If these constraints continue to apply, why should nuclear SLCMs be more compatible than SLBMs? And if they do not apply, it makes more sense to retain the SLBMs, whose speed and assured penetration outweigh the marginal increase in the number of warheads from the SLCMs.

13. One 1978 congressional staff analysis attributed substantial effectiveness to ALCMs in a counterforce role, but against military targets other than ICBMs. In calculations made by John B. Shewmaker and Mary R. Tietz it was estimated that 650 surviving cruise missiles (on only 40 surviving bombers) could destroy 50 percent of such military targets. Congressional Budget Office, *Retaliatory Issues for the U.S. Strategic Nuclear Forces* (Government Printing Office, 1978), pp. 54, 56–57. However, it is the hardened military targets that are most important.

second places a high premium on correctly guessing Soviet operational priorities and the different dangers to U.S. targets attached to alternate combinations of surviving Soviet ICBMs.[14]

Ensuring high ALCM accuracy would be the simplest and most direct improvement, though it would not offer a full "solution." At first glance one might consider fitting the missiles with the digital scene matching area correlator (DSMAC) system designed for conventionally armed variants. Reducing the CEP to a few meters could also allow lower yield warheads, which could be tested within the threshold test ban limit of 150 kilotons and which would produce less collateral damage. Doubts about the DSMAC's cost-effectiveness for strikes with conventional munitions would clearly not apply for strategic missions. The DSMAC, however, is sensitive to time of day and seasonal changes in the target area; thus plans for conventional missions rely on prestrike reconnaissance for digital updates. Though theoretically possible, this would probably not be practical for strategic Soviet targets, of which there are thousands. Another hypothetical alternative to increase ALCM accuracy might be the use of global positioning system satellites. Even if practical, however (and it could not be before the end of this decade), this option would increase the ALCM's dependence on sophisticated support systems, an undesirable condition for the unpredictable circumstances of nuclear war. One might also consider improving the CEP by placing the missile's last terrain contour matching (TERCOM) update map close to the silo, al-

14. One rationale might be to concentrate on missiles apparently intended for military targets—SS-17s, -18s, and -19s with MIRVs. The disadvantage would be that most of them might already have been fired in the Soviet first strike, so the ALCM force would be expended solely to prevent Soviet reloading. (One theoretical alternative would be to develop real-time surveillance and communication capabilities that could function under nuclear combat conditions; together with in-flight ALCM retargeting capability, this could permit attuning cruise missile strikes to the pattern of Soviet ICBM launches in their first strikes. This would require not only challenging technical innovations, but also heroic confidence in the smooth integrated functioning of crews and equipment in unprecedented conditions of wartime stress and confusion.) Moreover, if SS-11s are replaced by larger missiles, within a few years *all* Soviet ICBMs may be "high priority." Ignoring this, one might search for a theoretical advantage; for instance, by sparing the ICBMs judged to be part of the Soviet assured destruction reserve, the U.S. second strike would be less likely to invite destruction of American cities by prompting the Russians to launch that reserve under attack. These sorts of judgments are so sensitive to technical evolution—and so dependent on guesses about Soviet operational doctrine and reactions under attack and on hyperrefined game theory about intrawar coercion and escalation control—that they would be a very risky basis for planning. *Any* scheme for a counterforce second strike, however, runs many of these risks.

though this might increase its vulnerability to jamming. Finally, it is important to remember that, although ALCM counterforce capability is most sensitive to accuracy, improved CEP alone would not compensate fully for other factors in the equation such as prelaunch survivability, reliability, and penetrativity.

It is apparent that no neat solution exists for increasing confidence in the cruise missile's ability to destroy hard military targets. Even so, despite Bennett and Foster's debunking of the high expectation about ALCM counterforce capability, they admit that it may offer better hard-target destruction potential than the other legs of the triad when prelaunch survivability is considered. At this point the question of probable cruise missile attrition from air defenses becomes central.

MacDonald, Ruina, and Balaschak in chapter 2 offer a confident view of the prospects for cruise missile penetrativity against large area targets. A devil's advocate with more pessimistic instincts might still find grounds for concern about Soviet air defenses. Official testimony leaves some doubt. According to former Under Secretary of Defense William Perry, the Soviet SA-10 could "have a formidable capability against the cruise missile," and by the late 1980s "it will be imperative for us to find the suitable countermeasures."[15] Chapter 2 notes the possibility of "corridor cutting" to suppress defenses along cruise missile flight paths, but this is a questionable comfort. In a second strike the United States might have few surviving ICBMs left, and SLBMs would be husbanded as a reserve force or would have their own targets to cover. And unless each ballistic reentry vehicle expended on an air defense installation could clear the way for a significantly larger number of cruise missiles, corridor cutting would not be cost-effective; otherwise, why use a warhead with 100 percent penetrativity merely to assist a cruise missile that is less sure to arrive? Moreover, if Soviet SA-10s are mobile, it might be impossible to plan reliable defense suppression. Nevertheless, vaunted Soviet progress in air defense would have to be tremendous—far greater than the incremental evolutionary improvements of past decades—to raise major doubts about the ALCM's efficacy against city-size targets.

A point on which the authors of chapters 2 and 5 agree is the greater difficulty the cruise missile would have in attacking hardened point targets

15. *Hearings on Military Posture and H.R. 1872 [H.R. 4040]: Department of Defense Authorization for Appropriations for Fiscal Year 1980,* Hearings before the House Armed Services Committee, 96 Cong. 1 sess. (GPO, 1979), pt. 3, bk. 1, p. 211.

protected by terminal defenses. Such defenses can be saturated, but only at the price of reducing the number of targets that can be covered, already a problem if ALCMs are allocated against ICBM silos. Thus a great deal rides on chapter 2's point, not well documented in unclassified sources, that defenses are not known to be deployed around Soviet ICBMs, as well as on the assumption that they will not be deployed in the future.

There remains the argument that U.S. cruise missiles will help restrain Soviet offensive capabilities by draining additional resources into air defense investments. While valid to some extent, the assessment of costs to the USSR is overstated if "no allowance is made for the measures that are planned or underway in any case."[16] And if the extra investments are those that dramatically alter the odds on penetration (as new defenses around silos might though limited additions to city defenses would not), the cost-benefit ratio might not favor the United States.

Despite all the limitations and uncertainties, it would still be erroneous to conclude that cruise missiles have no utility for counterforce targeting. Just because they cannot satisfactorily cover all sites in a category does not mean they should not be used to cover some, especially if there are similar or greater limitations in the capabilities of alternate systems. More complete appreciation of the potential contributions of cruise missiles depends on the overall U.S. strategy for deterrence and war.

Doctrine

Some theorists view the requirements of deterrence as different from those of fighting a war if deterrence fails. This distinction has some merit when discussing the impact of weapon programs on crisis stability, but in the largest sense it is incorrect. Deterrence depends on what the adversary believes a victim would do—that is, how surviving forces would be employed—if attacked. The credibility of deterrence thus rests on the credibility of war plans. Despite the alarm of those who believe assured destruction is a sufficient basis for deterrence, the drift of U.S. policy toward greater emphasis on counterforce options and targeting selectivity has

16. Ron Huisken, *The Cruise Missile and Arms Control,* Canberra Papers on Strategy and Defence 20 (Canberra: Australian National University, Strategic and Defence Studies Centre, 1980), p. 13. Huisken estimates that if costs are spread over ten years "a dedicated Soviet defensive response . . . could absorb $6–7 billion a year."

been rationalized as a contribution to deterrence—a rationale motivated not only by the changing strategic balance, but also by changing beliefs about Soviet conceptions of nuclear war.

Given the durability of simple U.S. assured destruction capabilities over the coming decade, the magnitude of the ALCM's role depends largely on its value for striking military targets. To some extent the ALCM's efficacy against silos or other small-area targets hinges on the lack of terminal defenses. If the Soviet Union perceives the ALCM as a worrisome threat, it may deploy such defenses, reducing the attraction of expending ALCMs against such targets. If the silos remain undefended in the face of ALCM deployments, however, this also provides grounds for doubt. It suggests either that Soviet planners do not consider the silos significantly vulnerable to cruise missiles or place little value on reloading them (in which case the deterrent logic for allocating ALCMs in that way is negated) or that they would plan to launch on warning and count on the reserve in surviving submarines.

The larger question is whether it is wise to threaten Soviet ICBMs even under the logic of the "countervailing strategy." The rationale for doing so is rather convoluted.[17] Escalation control might argue against a threat large enough to provoke launch on warning. One argument is that

even if Soviet missiles held in reserve as a form of blackmail against unattacked U.S. cities were attacked by cruise missiles, the Soviet leadership might prefer to ride out the attack. This would leave a depleted but still existent blackmail capability of launching such missiles. A premature launch would remove the blackmail capability and result in a U.S. response against Soviet cities.[18]

This, however, suggests that the U.S. counterforce threat should be *limited,* so that the Soviet "ride out" option would be reasonable. In this case the modest ALCM counterforce capabilities in Bennett and Foster's

---

17. Promoting a silo-destroying MX, General Alton Slay said of a Soviet decision-maker faced with the missile: "If he attacks at this time he will say to himself the United States will still have the capability to attack his residual ICBM forces and countervalue targets. . . . He would then have to use his residual forces or lose them. That would escalate the conflict and invite further retaliation . . . in this case he would decide that an attack probably is not worth it. . . . our strategic policy and programs ought to work on his mind and not on the silos. If we have to work on the silos, the policy has failed . . . [but] in order to work on his mind, we want to be able to work on the silos." Quoted in *Defense/Space Daily,* November 21, 1978, p. 96. As some proponents of assured destruction have argued for the "rationality of irrationality," this appears to argue for the "stability of instability."

18. Jeffrey T. Richelson, "Evaluating the Strategic Balance," *American Journal of Political Science,* vol. 24 (November 1980), p. 790 note.

assessment may be an advantage rather than an inadequacy.[19] In any case the uncertainties suggest that the public explanation of how ALCMs will be targeted should be left ambiguous.

A more prevalent pair of arguments has been that the ALCM is not good for striking ICBMs because it is too slow and that, on the other hand, the lack of first-strike capability caused by this slowness makes the weapon stabilizing. Neither argument is completely persuasive, even if Soviet views are discounted. It is doubtful that Soviet leaders who have decided to gamble on a first strike would be less prepared to launch their reserve ICBMs upon short warning of incoming retaliatory ballistic missiles than upon longer warning of approaching cruise missiles. Unless Soviet leaders can be expected to have warning information sufficient for a perfect evaluation of an ALCM attack in progress, however, the categorical arguments sometimes advanced for the "stable" character of the cruise missile are compromised. To maintain the missile's penetrativity, Soviet air defenses must be kept from tracking it consistently after launch and knowing immediately its final destination. Without confidence in such tracking and attack-assessment capability, Soviet leaders have less reason to dismiss the utility of ALCMs for a first strike. Soviet capacity to monitor the carriers and anticipate attack, without knowing the complete

19. One possible contribution of cruise missiles to a deterrence-by-denial strategy could be rhetorical. In the context of asymmetrical U.S. and Soviet capabilities (at least until the late 1980s) in the time-urgent counterforce capabilities unique to ICBMs, declaratory policy may be the only way to limit the perceived disadvantage. In theory, U.S. leaders could change course and emphasize the importance of uncertainties about ICBM accuracy caused by the "bias" problem—the potential degradation of estimated accuracy by geophysical anomalies in the wartime flight paths of ICBMs (over which they have never been tested). They could also attribute to cruise missiles optimistic CEPs that are not subject to the bias phenomenon (though statements would have to ignore comparable uncertainties because TERCOM mapping was carried out on denied territory). Soviet leaders might then have less reason to feel confident that they had a net advantage in hard-target destruction capabilities. U.S. military leaders tend to dismiss the bias problem, but some scientists consider it significant. For an example of the former position, see the interview with Air Force Deputy Chief of Staff Kelly Burke in "Air Force's Chief Armorer Plans Sortie in Multi-Year Buying," *Defense Week*, February 2, 1981, pp. 4–7. For the latter, see James Coates, "Some New Questions About the Accuracy of Missiles," *Chicago Tribune*, March 5, 1981; and Kosta Tsipis, "Precision and Accuracy," *Arms Control Today*, vol. 11 (May 1981), pp. 3–4. President Reagan's unwillingness to accept demanding schemes for MX basing and Secretary of Defense Weinberger's generally more relaxed attitude about the strategic balance than that of Reagan's preelection defense advisers suggest that a rhetorical ploy of this sort may not be politically infeasible.

flight paths of the ALCMs, might be sufficient for the stability attributed to the system. But confident categorical judgments about the Soviet assessment of the ALCM threat remain doubtful. Taken all together, these considerations suggest simply that the probable impact of ballistic and cruise missiles on deterrence or arms control may be too ambiguous to be used as criteria for procurement.

In chapter 5 it is argued that the ALCM's contribution to evolving operational doctrine is not only modest but depends on the complementarity of other forces. The justification for a mixed force of cruise missiles and penetrating bombers extends beyond the need to stress Soviet air defenses, as long as the flexibility and endurance mandated by Presidential Directive 59 are criteria for the adequacy of strategic forces. The enduring reserve force[20] would probably have to be constituted primarily of SLBMs. Before the deployment of a mobile ICBM at least, the flexibility would probably have to lie in the manned bombers. ALCMs would bolster such flexibility indirectly, allowing bombers in the penetration phase to concentrate more on in-flight damage assessment and restrike or, when and if reconstituted, to attack targets of opportunity or newly acquired targets.[21] Like much of the logic of Presidential Directive 59, this would require much improved survivability and efficiency of reconnaissance, command and communication channels, and mission planning facilities.

ALCMs offer little for the element of the directive that has attracted most attention: the targeting of hardened Soviet strategic communications and leadership bunkers, which would logically be last (in time) on the list of military targets since striking them would be counterproductive before escalation control had failed and the war had become unlimited.

20. The reserve force requirement is discussed in *Department of Defense Annual Report, Fiscal Year 1982* (Department of Defense, 1981), p. 42.

21. Until the end of the 1970s U.S. strategic nuclear debate was fixated on the role of ICBMs with MIRVs. Some skeptics also interpreted Presidential Directive 59 as a cynical brief for the MX. However, the only novel operational emphases implied in public reports of the directive—selective targeting executed over a long time span—are more conducive to single-warhead systems than to the footprint of an ICBM with ten MIRVs. What a single-reentry-vehicle cruise missile offers in avoiding warhead waste, though, it loses in slowness, since movable assets are the ones target acquisition would be most likely to seek in the later phase of war. These problems may be part of the reason behind official interest in the development of a new, small, single-warhead ICBM. See Clarence A. Robinson, Jr., "U.S. Strategic Missile Options: U.S. Weighs Small ICBM Development," *Aviation Week and Space Technology*, May 4, 1981, pp. 49–52.

The ALCM force could not easily be withheld beyond the first U.S. retaliatory counterstrike. The limitations of ALCMs under the criteria of the countervailing strategy, however, are not exceptional when one considers the overall inadequacy of the strategic forces' support systems for such criteria (especially command, control, and communications) and the lack of full commitment to the concept (greater investment in civil defense would probably be consistent with plans for selective exchanges). As some observers have noted, the capabilities to implement the directive will remain an aspiration rather than a reality for quite a while. Thus cruise missiles are not an independent solution to doctrinal dilemmas, but in the context of force modernization constraints as a whole, they represent a useful partial improvement at least into the late 1980s.

Theater Nuclear Forces

The December 1979 NATO decision on ground-launched cruise missiles derailed movement toward sea-launched cruise missiles for theater nuclear forces. But if domestic politics in Europe (together with further deterioration of U.S.-Soviet relations) unravel that deployment decision, nuclear SLCMs could become important again. Indeed, some U.S. defense planners fear that the sea-launched option leaves a way for European governments facing political resistance to wriggle out of the GLCM commitment and that further controversy over long-range theater nuclear forces (LRTNF) could produce a "rush to the sea."

It is useful to remember, though, that the SLCM was originally justified as an adjunct to U.S. central strategic forces. Some U.S. officials argued that deploying "a few SLCMs on some SSNs would force the Soviet Union into a disproportionate response," because even with only two or three per boat the Russians could not be sure that there might not actually be as many as twenty.[22] The assumption that this would place stress on Soviet defensive investments, however, is questionable. It would not increase the necessary scope of Soviet antisubmarine coverage (close in as well as the open-ocean operating area of Trident) as long as U.S. Poseidons remain deployed. On the other hand, U.S. submarines dedicated to strategic antisubmarine warfare would have to penetrate Soviet home waters to get at long-range SLBMs, in which case they would at the same time come within cruise missile striking range. This might seem to lessen the problem for dual-mission attack submarines of being in two

22. Huisken, *The Cruise Missile and Arms Control,* pp. 13–14.

places at once.[23] Coincidental striking range, though, is hardly enough; chasing Soviet submarines may not be compatible with moving to a planned launch point. (And all this ignores the arguments that strategic antisubmarine warfare destabilizes deterrence and should therefore not be promoted.)

Previous chapters have demonstrated how weak the concepts are for using SLCMs for central strategic forces. Other missions compromise the number of SSNs that could be dedicated to strikes programmed in the single integrated operational plan (SIOP), even if the cruise missiles could be loaded (for example, in ballast tanks) without penalizing weapons for sea control. Even if trade-offs in positioning and weapon loading could be solved, SLCMs on attack submarines would be inadequate for limited nuclear war (too few to saturate defenses) and redundant for assured destruction (given SLBMs). One alternative might be to make a small number of SLCMs in attack submarines a last-resort strategic reserve force. The submarines would concentrate on antisubmarine warfare in the early phase of war and divert to the strategic mission only after unlimited nuclear war had begun and most bombers and ballistic missiles had been destroyed or used up; by this time the Soviet antisubmarine capabilities that threatened penetration of coastal waters would also be degraded. The problem in this case is that the submarines could not rely on planned targeting data, since the massive nuclear exchanges that had already occurred would determine what needed to be struck. Even under the unrealistic assumption that command integrity, yet-to-be-perfected damage assessment systems, and retargeting capabilities remained intact at this late stage, submarines' unique communication problems would frustrate this option. Nevertheless, despite all these considerations, the administration is reportedly forging ahead with plans for SLCMs on submarines to augment strategic forces.[24]

Some within the Navy remain interested in nuclear SLCMs for reasons distinct from land attack or strategic missions as normally conceived. The primary vulnerability of the fleet is to a Soviet nuclear attack, and some believe that the president would more readily authorize retaliation if it appeared that the use of nuclear weapons could be confined to the sea. Thus nuclear SLCMs would theoretically deter the escalation of conventional naval engagements, not just deter Soviet nuclear attacks on Europe or the United States. If this should prompt a move to loading destroyers

23. Ibid., p. 15.
24. "Navy to Arm with Cruise Missiles."

or reconditioned battleships with hundreds of nuclear rather than conventional cruise missiles, the complications for potential arms control agreements would be tremendous, especially following GLCM deployments in Europe so closely.

Although the possibility has not been widely discussed, any priority placed on a quick revitalization of U.S. nuclear capabilities against the Soviet homeland might encourage an expansion of GLCM deployments. The limited number of B-52s militates against increased numbers of ALCMs in the near future. Large numbers of strategic SLCMs are also impractical because dedicated submarines are expensive, shipbuilding capacity is already strained by other requirements, and adapted surface platforms would not be survivable. In theory divorced from political realism, though, GLCM launchers could be proliferated, and provisions for reload could further expand the number of missiles targeted against the western USSR.

Allied sensibilities make this a fanciful notion, but the idea emphasizes the problems inherent in even the currently planned level of GLCM deployment. The range that gives the cruise missile its military edge also changes the qualitative nature of theater nuclear forces. Multiplying GLCM numbers beyond those ostensibly aimed (with the Pershing II) to match the SS-20 would validate the Soviet definition of U.S. LRTNF as strategic forces. Even without any tendentious plans for large numbers, the United States openly admitted the change in quality of the force structure. Former Assistant Secretary of Defense David McGiffert noted that the theater modernization plan would produce "a shift of emphasis within a reduced stockpile from shorter-range to longer-range nuclear systems."[25] The military advantage that Western elite groups see in retaliatory terms must logically be seen by cautious Russians as a more impressive threat. Thus the military advantage offered by new GLCMs encourages its own limitation as long as any hope remains for negotiated solutions to mutual security.

It was once thought that this tension between strictly military considerations and broader strategic calculations would adversely affect the role of cruise missiles in the modernization of European independent strategic forces. The SALT II protocol was spurred by Soviet apprehension about

25. Interview with David E. McGiffert in *U.S. News & World Report*, December 24, 1979, p. 36. The difference in range can hardly be justified as a mirror-image response to the SS-20, which, while more capable than old SS-4s and -5s, does not cover a much wider portion of Western Europe.

significantly increased Western striking power if Britain and France were to acquire cheap cruise missiles. Although many on this side of the Atlantic doubt it, one can argue that it is in the American interest that these allied forces remain viable. As U.S.-Soviet nuclear parity has eroded the credibility of American extended deterrence, it has become more advantageous to reinforce Soviet doubts that a conventional attack could succeed without precipitating nuclear retaliation. Multiplying the number of independent decision centers capable of launching nuclear weapons contributes to this reinforcement.

Hopes for stabilizing the arms race, however, create an American interest in not making these independent deterrents appear to be too highly effective. A profusion of cruise missiles that could cover more targets than SLBMs (whose numbers are limited by platform costs) might have done this. If so, and if the Soviet response was a stronger effort to match or exceed the combined total of Western forces, the result would rebound against conservative American calculations of advantage. Extremely cautious planners would then focus on the *disadvantage* of dispersing the allied deterrent across several independent forces. In a nuclear war release of *all* those forces would be less likely, so the USSR would be suspected of having "escalation dominance in detail." Fragmented command is useful for deterrence credibility, but unitary command is more credible for effectiveness in actual force employment. If any of this makes sense, then, it may be propitious that the British decided for Trident instead of cruise missiles, even if worries about the prelaunch survivability or vulnerability to Soviet air defenses of cruise missiles were unfounded.[26]

Soviet Cruise Missiles—Threat or Relief?

Another question that bears on the security implications of U.S. investment in cruise missiles is the probable Soviet response discussed by Garthoff in chapter 11. What would be the strategic consequences if the USSR decided to deploy ALCMs of its own? This issue has received scant

---

26. As long as British or French nuclear doctrine rests on finite deterrence and countervalue targeting, MacDonald, Ruina, and Balaschak's assessment of high cruise missile penetrativity against city-size target areas would deflate some of the arguments about the probable attrition of a limited cruise missile force unless the target list was large (say, forty cities). In chapter 14, however, Freedman notes that prelaunch survivability was a major concern (since the restricted deployment areas available to GLCMs could be barraged), and Ian Smart's calculations showed SLCMs to be less cost-effective than SLBMs in terms of deliverable megatonnage.

attention in strategic discourse. Modern long-range cruise missiles could make the intercontinental capability of the Backfire unambiguous. The Soviet Union has also reportedly been developing a new long-range bomber to replace its ancient Bears and Bisons.[27]

If Moscow's choice was between augmenting its forces with cruise missiles or not augmenting them at all, the United States obviously should view the prospect of Soviet cruise missiles with alarm. Conceivably this could happen if the Soviet decision was spurred by a desire to respond to the qualitative Western innovation rather than by cold strategic calculation of military requirements. In this case, if U.S. restraint could forestall a Soviet venture into a whole new dimension of weaponry, one might argue for more Western flexibility in the scale and timing of cruise missile deployments in the hope of reaching an arms control agreement that could satisfy U.S. and NATO requirements without driving the Russians into the cruise missile game. If one believes that Soviet decisions are determined primarily by careful strategic judgment, however, the desirability of cruise missiles will probably be measured against the apparent utility of alternate weapon choices and a decision will be subordinate to a more general determination of desired force levels. Soviet cruise missiles would then be less worrisome to the West.

Analysts who interpret U.S.-Soviet arms competition in terms of an "action-reaction" model might rate the chances of a Russian move toward cruise missiles as quite high. They would argue that a major self-defeating fault in some previous innovative U.S. programs (such as MIRV) was the failure to look ahead to the next stage, when Soviet imitation would neutralize the advantage or increase the threat. An action-reaction prediction, however, would not in itself be compelling. Consider the earlier difference in American and Soviet interest in old naval cruise missiles. The comparative U.S. lack of interest was due to the asymmetry of the two nations' naval missions and force structures. The reversal of interest when it came to modern long-range cruise missiles can also be understood in terms of larger trends and traditions in the organization of the countries' strategic forces. As the dominance of aircraft carriers discouraged early U.S. commitment to antiship cruise missiles, the dominance of the strategic rocket forces and ballistic systems discouraged Soviet commitment to air-breathing intercontinental delivery vehicles. The USSR did not emulate U.S. Air Force attachment to intercontinental bombers in its own strategic buildup.

27. George C. Wilson, "Soviet Bomber Development Reported," *Washington Post,* June 27, 1979.

Of course, the U.S. Navy now favors the Tomahawk antiship missile (TASM), and the Soviet Union might be driven toward ALCMs, not out of emulation but perhaps for the same reasons that concern American strategists: vulnerability of fixed ICBMs (although it would be just as likely that the USSR would respond, like the United States, by developing mobile ICBMs). There have indeed been some public indications of Soviet development of an ALCM.[28] Even inferior ALCMs on new Soviet bombers could be a credible threat against the continental United States, since U.S. air defenses are very weak.[29]

Does this mean that the United States should consider potential Soviet deployment of ALCMs a severe military danger? No. They would simply be a redundant threat in a first strike.[30] Indeed, the principal reason that Washington dismantled much of the U.S. air defense system is that the Russian ICBMs made the Soviet bomber threat only incidental. As long as the Soviet ICBM force remained substantial, ALCMs would not change that reasoning, unless it was assumed that increased air-breathing forces would offer significant options for a limited Soviet attack that would make U.S. air defense investments significantly more attractive. Washington should certainly prefer Soviet deployment of ALCMs to additional ballistic missiles. And if cruise missiles served only to buttress Soviet second-strike capabilities, so much the better for the stability of mutual deterrence. That, after all, is the popular justification for why the USSR should not see American slow-flying ALCMs as a threat to stability. It is true that Soviet cruise missile deployments might be less susceptible to U.S. intelligence monitoring. But the idea that "the threat we know" is preferable to one we do not know is questionable if the technical capabilities of the former (modern large ballistic missiles) are more dangerous.

28. When asked during Senate testimony whether the USSR had an ALCM in research and development, Chairman of the Joint Chiefs of Staff David Jones replied, "We have some very limited evidence that I would not like to discuss in open session." *Military Implications of the Treaty on the Limitation of Strategic Offensive Arms and Protocol Thereto (SALT II Treaty),* Hearings before the Senate Armed Services Committee, 96 Cong. 1 sess. (GPO, 1979), pt. 1, p. 294.

29. Huisken, *The Cruise Missile and Arms Control,* p. 51.

30. Some have suggested that blind spots in U.S. radar coverage could allow Soviet bombers to sneak through in a surprise strike. The risks to the Russians in such a plan, if it were not simply complementary to an ICBM attack, would be extreme. If it was complementary, the incremental threat to U.S. targets would be small. One scenario sometimes cited to justify concern is that the bombers could sneak through before ICBMs were launched, striking command and communications targets and bomber bases and preempting U.S. capacity to launch forces on warning.

Some observers worry about the budgetary pressure that might result if Soviet cruise missiles prompted stronger interest in continental air defense. This might be significant politically if larger Soviet air-breathing forces highlighted the disparity in air defense, but it would not change the military reasons for Western limits on such defenses as long as vulnerability to Soviet ballistic missiles is so great. The relative cost-benefit attractiveness of diverting U.S. resources back to air defense would vary directly with the extent to which Soviet ALCM deployments *replaced* more worrisome ICBMs. In that context incentives to improve defenses would be no more worrisome than welcome. Fear of the USSR's investment in cruise missiles would rest on the assumption that its alternatives were either adding ALCMs and increasing the threat or keeping the threat at the present level. It is more likely that the choice would be between adding cruise missiles or adding ICBMs; the latter would be worse for the United States.

Similarly, for theater nuclear deployments Soviet GLCMs would be less threatening to NATO than a comparable number of additional SS-20s. (By the same token, it is unclear what the military attractiveness of cruise missiles over SS-20s would be to Soviet planners. Unlike NATO Moscow does not need the increased range of cruise missiles to broaden its coverage of European targets.) When the nuclear alternatives are considered—for either replacement or additions to force levels—it is reasonable to argue that in military terms the West should encourage a Soviet move from ballistic to cruise missiles. This felicitous conclusion, however, may not carry over to the realm of conventionally armed cruise missiles. If Moscow matches Western investments in such systems (already of tenuous potential cost-effectiveness), the improvements such systems promise for NATO's position in the conventional military balance might well be neutralized. More than the technically different force elements in the strategic nuclear area, conventional cruise missiles offer as much for initiative and counterforce war-fighting as they do for retaliation and deterrence. If the Russians use conventional cruise missiles to threaten airfields in Western Europe and to interdict reinforcement choke-points more effectively (as Palin's suggestions in chapter 6 aim to do against the Warsaw Pact countries), the United States will be just as hampered in prosecuting a war as the Soviet Union will. As one anonymous defense expert said, "If it's cheap for us, it's cheap for them."[31]

31. Quoted in David Fouquet, "Cruise Missile: Launcher for Next Arms-Control Talks?" *Christian Science Monitor,* December 17, 1979.

Conventional Strategy

Early assumptions were that cruise missiles would be relatively cheap as delivery vehicles for nuclear weapons but prohibitively expensive for tactical conventional munitions. In one of the first revisionist assessments Desmond Ball reversed the conclusions, arguing, "It is interesting that the cruise missile may be least cost-effective in the very areas [nuclear] that cause most concern."[32] Chapter 5 supports the deflation of expectations about the ALCM's relative value, but doubts about the cost-effectiveness of conventional models are still greater than Ball indicates. Moreover, the lack of controversy about conventional applications was largely due to the modest amount of interest in them until very recently. The implications for arms control of a profusion of conventional cruise missiles could cause as much or more hand-wringing as the issue of ALCMs in SALT.

NATO Defense

One major contribution of nuclear GLCMs would be to augment conventional capabilities for defense in the central front by releasing quick-reaction-alert aircraft for missions with nonnuclear ordnance. The value of conventionally armed cruise missiles varies principally according to two criteria: the desirable depth of interdiction strikes, and the priority given targets that are well defended and hence forbidding to manned aircraft.

The first criterion places a progressively higher premium on the technical refinement of aerodynamic and munition capabilities beyond those of the current generation of cruise missiles, since the range-payload trade-off becomes more exacting as the depth of operation increases. To the extent that such refinements are difficult or expensive, the scope of advisable applications for conventional cruise missiles declines, especially in view of the general skepticism about deep interdiction warranted by historical experience.[33] (Moreover, assumptions are often too blithely

32. Ball, "Costs of the Cruise Missile," p. 247.
33. F. M. Sallagar, *Operation "Strangle" (Italy, Spring 1944): A Case Study of Tactical Air Interdiction*, R-851-PR (Rand Corp., 1972); Malcolm W. Cagle and Frank A. Manson, *The Sea War in Korea* (U.S. Naval Institute, 1957), pp. 222–80; Gregory A. Carter, *Some Historical Notes on Air Interdiction in Korea*, P-3452 (Rand Corp., 1966), pp. 15–19; Colonel Ray L. Bowers, USAF (ret.), "Air Operations in Southeast Asia: A Tentative Appraisal," in Colonel Alfred F. Hurley,

made about how appropriate the target arrays deep in Eastern Europe would be for conventional strikes. Some would be area targets, and some point targets—especially bridges—are too hard for their destruction to be assured with less than perfect accuracy.)

In central strategic force planning, improvement of Soviet air defenses would cast doubt on the comparative value of ALCMs and ballistic missiles. The same trade-off applies with even more force to tactical Soviet air defenses. Conventional cruise missiles become more attractive, however, if the alternative is reliance on manned aircraft rather than rocket-powered tactical missiles. For missions such as striking airfields (by dispensing submunitions along a horizontal attack profile), conventionally armed ballistic missiles may not offer the range-payload combinations and effectiveness per unit that would make them competitive with cruise missiles or fighter-bombers.

Cruise missiles are of course not immune to attrition en route, and the density of Soviet tactical air defenses presents a much greater barrier than simple extrapolation from the assessment in chapter 2 of strategic defenses in the Soviet homeland would suggest.[34] If Soviet theater air defenses improve, there will be a stronger incentive to incorporate more agility and "intelligence"—for example, electronic countermeasures—into the missile. Thus the pressure to make conventional cruise missiles more sophisticated—and therefore less certainly a cost-effective investment—comes from all directions.

Simplified comparisons such as Baker's in chapter 4 demonstrate how sensitive the value of first-generation conventional cruise missiles is to assumptions both about required numbers per target and about manned aircraft attrition rates. If estimates of aircraft losses are very optimistic, airfield attack with very few cruise missiles would have to be feasible for the latter to be sensible for that purpose. If one considers the high Israeli

---

USAF, and Major Robert C. Erhart, USAF, eds., *Air Power and Warfare: The Proceedings of the 8th Military History Symposium, United States Air Force Academy, 18–20 October 1978* (GPO, 1979), pp. 310, 318–20; Colonel Herman L. Gilster, USAF, "Air Interdiction in Protracted War: An Economic Evaluation," *Air University Review,* vol. 28 (May–June 1977), pp. 2–18; and Gilster, "On War, Time, and the Principle of Substitution," paper prepared by the Office of the Assistant Secretary of Defense (June 1977), pp. 15–16.

34. A 1977 study made at the Los Alamos Scientific Laboratory, "The Cruise Missile as a Battlefield-Support Weapons System," raised doubts about tactical cruise missiles' comparative cost-effectiveness. See the discussion of this and related studies in Robert S. Metzger, "Cruise Missiles: Different Missions, Different Arms Control Impact," *Arms Control Today,* vol. 8 (January 1978), pp. 2–3.

loss rates during part of the October 1973 war to be grounds for expecting attrition of 7 percent or more, on the other hand, cruise missiles are certainly competitive with the option of purchasing additional aircraft—especially when related costs of pilot training and the inestimable value of pilots' lives are factored into the equation.

Cruise missile investments appear sensible at the theoretical attrition "break-even" point, whatever it is, because a mixed force provides more adaptability when neither element has a decisive advantage over the other. But if budget limitations required that such investments be balanced by significant *reductions* in manned aircraft (rather than simply adding different capabilities to force levels in the current structure), estimated aircraft losses would have to be discernibly higher than the break-even point to justify shifting reliance to cruise missiles. The value of manned systems' flexibility—to roam on or behind the forward edge of the battle area, strike mobile targets of opportunity, and cope with mobile defenses[35]—is substantial. Cost-effectiveness methodology breaks down as a reliable basis for procurement decisions at this level, since the effect of intuition varies directly with the emphasis on flexibility, which by definition involves a large number of variables and subjective judgments not amenable to clear quantification. Systems analysis calculations offer sufficient grounds for reducing the number of aircraft in this case only to the extent that doctrine shifts toward more reliance on preplanned (planned before the outbreak of war) strikes and greater division of labor within force structure, and less emphasis on wartime adaptability in executing missions. Finally, aircraft are not cruise missiles' only competitors. Many other types of missiles, with rocket power, could be attractive.

Palin's and Baker's analyses (both of which leave arms control complications in abeyance) favor deployment of conventionally armed cruise missiles. But what should be their principal launch mode? The advantages offered by the MRASM are (1) higher explosive payload allowed by lower missile fuel requirements resulting from the carrier aircraft's ability to launch the missile closer to the target; (2) the avoidance of GLCM support costs, which would be greater than the incremental costs attributable to the aircraft from the missile; and (3) possibly greater compatibility with arms control verification schemes (aircraft may seem more readily countable than wandering or warehoused transporter-erector-launchers). The advantages of a hypothetical conventional GLCM are

---

35. The pilot can react when his radar lights up, while current cruise missiles must rely on preprogrammed flight profiles.

(1) increased availability of aircraft (which otherwise would use flight time carrying the MRASM and would carry less ordnance of other types that could be used during the balance of the flight) for missions that make the best use of their unique flexibility; and (2) possibly increased pre-launch survivability (which in the MRASM is identical to that of its carrier). SLCMs could be a possible complement, but perhaps only from surface platforms. The contradiction between flexibility and mission over-load (sea control and land attack competing for the platform) argues against adapting existing attack submarines. Dedicating additional attack submarines to conventional cruise missile missions would be a poor choice because of platform costs and the communication problems that would limit the responsiveness vital to tactical employment.

Flexibility is desirable because of the unpredictability of operations with a modern force structure untested in such a war as would occur between NATO and the Warsaw Pact. This argues for a mixed MRASM-GLCM-SLCM force. If a choice must be made, or the relative emphasis between the two variants be determined, decisions should hinge on two variables on which there is as yet insufficient evidence. The principal one is whether East-West arms control negotiations have any future and, if so, whether conventional GLCMs or SLCMs would be compatible with an agreement. The second is whether simple mechanisms for multiple reload of GLCMs, which would allow reliance on a small number of launchers and limit infrastructure costs, are feasible.

Palin favors the GLCM, but its potential for frustrating arms control is tremendous. The logical solution is to configure the missile with func-tionally related observable differences (FRODs) to differentiate it from the nuclear variant. FRODs, however, have been suggested in principle but not well defined in practice, and it is difficult to envision what they would be. (If future conventional cruise missiles are redesigned and tailored specifically to certain tasks, the differences might be persuasively "functional.") A more feasible alternative would be simple external ob-servable differences (EODs)—any appurtenances not visible on the nuclear GLCM, even if the difference did not physically preclude a nuclear mission. While more feasible than FRODS, EODs would be less credible for verification, but offer a better basis for bargaining than no observable differences at all. One form of EOD not integral to the missile but perhaps reasonably convincing would be the lesser security measures associated with GLCM convoys containing no nuclear material. Or, simi-lar to a suggestion made by Palin, conventional GLCMs might be deployed in a fixed or limited mobile mode at air bases—no more vulnerable to conventional preemption than aircraft—while fully mobile nuclear GLCMs remained theoretically more survivable and thus more of a deterrent against Soviet nuclear preemption.

A final alternative would be to make nuclear GLCM launchers dual-capable. This could entail a penalty in negotiating a theater nuclear balance if all the launchers were counted as nuclear, but it might actually offer a reasonable combination of effective deterrent and flexible response capability if deterrence failed. The penalty would reinforce the former: dual-capable GLCMs might symbolize the "seamless web" of flexible response strategy. And if deterrence failed, the theater nuclear balance per se would be less crucial than the mix of options available for escalation control. The conventional rounds would provide limited capability for strikes on fixed targets in Eastern Europe, and the limitation would not be crucial since NATO already relies on complementary tactical systems. In the evolving discussion about modernizing theater nuclear forces the notion of dual-capable GLCMs sounds bizarre. But is it really any more so than the current reliance on dual-capable aircraft? (Dual-capable aircraft are in fact much less desirable, since they cannot shift quickly back and forth between conventional strike and nuclear deterrent missions; and the longer they are withheld for the latter, the more likely they are to be destroyed by Soviet conventional attacks.)

The tension between the near-term economic benefits of deploying large numbers of first-generation cruise missiles and the longer term military benefits of concentrating investments in more advanced models is as great in the conventional as in the nuclear area. If the long-term consideration takes precedence and the conventional cruise missile is to be a major and enduring element of the general purpose force structure, the airframe may have to be reconfigured to rid it of the constraints in the Tomahawk's design. As Burt notes in chapter 7, this could defer investments in systems like the vertical launching system, so as to make the launch tubes compatible with next-generation missiles. (Armored box launchers could be used in the interim, though that would reduce the number of missiles.)

Force Projection

Early in the Reagan administration plans were announced to recommission two *Iowa*-class battleships, and this decision was explicitly justified by the availability of cruise missiles to give the ships long-range firepower.[36] Even if such platforms for SLCMs are unusually survivable in conventional engagements (the battleships have extremely heavy armor), planning to use them as substitute aircraft carriers for penetration of Soviet home waters (for example, to strike the Kola Peninsula or Petropavlovsk) may be foolhardy. To get close enough to fire missiles inland, the ships would put themselves within the range of Backfire bombers, and this argues for protection by carriers, thus bringing the original rationale for deploying the battleships full circle. If the crunch really came, even peacetime deterrent rhetoric about using carriers in these areas would probably evaporate; per unit they constitute too large a proportion of the service's striking power to risk in missions that could turn into a naval Charge of the Light Brigade. Planning to use the platforms to attack coastal rather than inland targets would avert interservice conflict over role assignments (the Air Force cedes only naval infrastructure targets on land) and would allow the ships to remain further back, though not enough to measurably decrease their vulnerability. Moreover, conventionally armed cruise missiles would be wasted on large target areas such as shipyards or hardened ones such as submarine pens.

Large surface platforms like battleships make more sense for contingencies in remote areas where aircraft carriers are unavailable, but the value of this option depends on the priority placed on intervention in third world regions like the Indian Ocean or Southeast Asia. The narrow confines of the Persian Gulf make it a dubious candidate. If any ship with cruise missiles is to be put at risk there, it would probably be more sensible to use one or more of lower unit value, such as a destroyer. Firing from outside the Gulf, SLCMs could cover few of the targets relevant to most Middle Eastern or Iranian contingencies.[37] MRASMs might reduce the limitations but would require a carrier rather than a battleship.

36. According to Under Secretary of the Navy Robert J. Murray, "The battleship is returning because the new technology of cruise missiles . . . opens up a new role for the battleship." "Bring Back the Battleships," *Washington Post*, April 12, 1981. See also George Wilson, "President to Seek Major Increase in U.S. Naval Power," *Washington Post*, March 4, 1981.

37. R. James Woolsey justifies the SLCM option by citing Aden—with Cuban, East German, and Soviet advisers present—as a potentially lucrative target. "The Case for Sea-Launched Cruise Missiles," *Armed Forces Journal International*, vol. 118 (December 1980), p. 22. The U.S. military, however, is by no means united behind the old battleships. " 'There is nothing more impressive than those big guns in Mombasa,' says a destroyer skipper. 'But it's a waste of manpower.' And an Air Force official put it this way: 'They're great for pounding a beach, but who wants to do that?' " Joseph Volz, "The American Navy: Is It Setting Sail for the 21st Cen-

It is far from clear that the battleship option is justified. In low-threat environments weaker task forces might suffice, yet it is doubtful that the stronger battleship could make use of its unique mix of capabilities (such as the sixteen-inch guns that require close approach to the shore) in any other than low-threat environments. And in such "easy" areas the advantage of the cruise missile's penetrativity against air defenses is also likely to be superfluous and thus less cost-effective than alternatives. Even if aircraft carriers are unavailable, quick-reaction B-52s with old-fashioned iron bombs might do the job just as well. Indeed, the Strategic Air Command has been planning this sort of option.[38] This might be an attractive and cheaper alternative to Burt's suggestion of equipping B-52Ds with conventional ALCMs, which would raise countability problems in SALT.

In chapter 8 MccGwire demonstrates the complexity of assessing cruise missiles' comparative advantage for war at sea. While they are useful for sinking ships, they do not counter the Soviet threat to the missile-launching ships themselves. Thus the critical trade-offs in weapon loadings are not simply those involving the mix of offensive systems (such as Tomahawk antiship and land-attack missiles and Harpoon), but also the balance with defense weapons. One contribution offered by SLCMs is comparable to that on land—reduction of the offensive assignments of tactical aircraft, releasing them for other purposes (in this case, fleet air defense and other maritime warfare tasks). For submarines operating against surface ships, torpedoes are more effective weapons unless the submarine is prevented from getting close to the target. Finally, MccGwire's notion of deploying shore-based TASMs around choke-points is a novel idea that warrants serious consideration even if it seems likely to provoke

---

tury?" *New York Daily News,* March 22, 1981. Reconditioned battleships may be less expensive than new destroyers, but their much larger crews would magnify the loss if they were sunk.

38. Plans reportedly call for using the B-52H because of that model's 8,000-mile range. From bases in Spain or, better, Egypt, they could fly missions to the Persian Gulf without refueling. The planes now assigned this mission have been christened "the Strategic Protection Force." Howard Silber, "B-52s Able to Speed to Mideast Hot Spots," *Omaha World Herald,* January 25, 1981; and George C. Wilson, " 'Anytime Anywhere': A New Conventional Role for B52 Bombers," *Washington Post,* March 31, 1981. The strategic mission makes the H-model a dual-capable aircraft. If these reports are accurate, however, SAC planners must consider the political fact that Spain (with close ties to Arab states) or Egypt could easily forbid the use of those bases. Moreover, the use of the B-52H for conventional strikes would probably have to be limited to contingencies that did not involve probable combat with Soviet forces; otherwise those aircraft might be withheld for the SIOP. If not, and if SAC can afford to take a number of the best B-52s out of the SIOP under present conditions, the need for a new bomber seems harder to justify.

interservice squabbling over roles and missions. All of this suggests that the trade-offs in naval applications are complex and that the administration's plans to rush into wide-scale deployments[39] could be premature if the most cost-effective mix of options is to be achieved.

Politics and Diplomacy

Procurement and changes in force structure should logically be consistent with military operational doctrine and the broad goals of strategy. These are necessary though not sufficient conditions for judging how and to what extent cruise missiles should be integrated into U.S. defense posture. The cruise missile's multipurpose nature makes the third group of variables—political factors—dominant. The analyst's temptation to address problems from the pure perspective of "Strategic Man" must be subordinated to the realities of political disagreement and competition where budgets are finite and negotiations or adversary and allied reactions affect the balance of power as much as unilateral initiatives do.

The political aspects most easily controlled by American leaders are internal. In contrast to weapon programs such as the MX, there is negligible controversy about cruise missiles—and thus no appreciable basis for constraint—in the body politic. Only the intragovernmental politics of legislative-executive relations, organizational interests, and bureaucratic bargaining apply. In chapter 12 Art and Ockenden demonstrate how sensitive the origin and evolution of cruise missile programs were to such factors. Much of the gestation of the cruise missile, however, is past. Henceforth, bureaucratic politics are likely to be a less significant determinant of policy (compared with external factors) for cruise missiles than for other weapons less formidably enmeshed in alliance politics and U.S.-Soviet relations.

The latter two factors could compromise the logic of strategic calculation. If serious nuclear arms control remains possible, some conventional applications of cruise missiles may have to be sacrificed, their relative contribution to theater nuclear forces may be scaled down, and potential interest in proliferating ALCMs beyond levels planned under SALT II would be squelched. Yet if arms control dies the United States will not be free to capitalize fully on cruise missile deployments. Although allies pushed commitment to these weapon systems in the late 1970s, they could

39. See Henry S. Bradsher, "Navy to Proceed on Long-Range Cruise Missiles," *Washington Star,* June 4, 1981.

derail the programs in the early 1980s. Any interment of SALT or theater nuclear force negotiations for which Washington appears more responsible than Moscow could demolish the fragile December 1979 plan for GLCM deployment and might fracture the Atlantic Alliance. Policy cannot be made with the coherence or decisiveness of a unitary Strategic Man in an alliance of sovereign states with varying government views, priorities, propensities to take risks, and domestic constraints.

American Defense Planning

Professional military demands for cruise missiles or resistance to them is determined in part by objective assessments of their utility, in part by the influence of doctrinal predispositions under conditions of uncertainty in those assessments, and in part by anticipatory suspicions about the effect of innovative programs on other valued elements of force structure under conditions of budgetary stringency. As long as a new weapon appears to be "free" (unthreatening to other programs and to traditional attachments to doctrine), it will be welcomed enthusiastically.[40]

In the early 1970s defense budgets were declining and cruise missiles seemed a cheap alternative for executing some missions, and service support for the weapon was limited, conditional, or nonexistent. Attack submariners liked it in principle but opposed it because of the competition for dollars and the pressure to trade off such new weapon loadings against others. Chief of Naval Operations Elmo R. Zumwalt, Jr. (a surface sailor), liked it in principle but opposed it as a justification for new submarines. Similarly, through the late 1970s the ALCM was promoted as a substitute for penetrating bombers, so Air Force officers opposed it. Throughout the decade the Pentagon's push for cruise missiles came from the Office of the Secretary of Defense rather than from the military.[41]

Today the defense budget is growing, the issue of substantial commitment to cruise missiles is closer to being settled, and some new manned bomber seems safely on the horizon. While cruise missiles may be bought

40. "The conservatism of the military . . . seems always to have been confined to their adaptation to new weaponry rather than to their acceptance of it. The commander . . . knows a superior weapon . . . when he sees it, and he has rarely been lacking eagerness to have it." Brodie, "Technological Change," p. 299.

41. The original rationales sound archaic today: "Pentagon spokesmen generally plugged away at the three broad themes; negotiating leverage, the potential vulnerability of ballistic re-entry vehicles to future ballistic missile defence systems and even surface-to-air missiles, and the strategic potential of the Soviet arsenal of cruise missiles." Ron Huisken, "The Origins of the Strategic Cruise Missile: Perceptions and the Strategic Balance," *Australian Outlook,* April 1980, p. 32.

at the price of *additions* to other elements of force structure, offsetting reductions are unlikely. Service resistance, therefore, probably figured more in the genesis of cruise missile programs than it will in their fruition. Helped along by "commercial push" (industrious salesmanship by cruise missile manufacturers who have been touting the system as a panacea, wonderful for attacking everything from tanks to submarines) and by "conventional push" (multiplying plans for tactical applications reinforce the general level of interest in the basic system), momentum now characterizes the weapon's progress more than sluggishness. Momentum raises the possibility of unforeseen diplomatic ramifications and dynamic effects on Soviet defense policy reactions.

In this context the Office of the Secretary of Defense may act more as a restraint (or arbiter) than as the prod it was in the past decade. Otherwise, if the administration relies heavily on recommendations from military staffs instead of judgments by units such as the Office of Program Analysis and Evaluation in the Defense Department, investment in different cruise missile variants may follow a general pattern of aggregation —procuring every variety favored by the three services, with numbers arbitrarily limited according to the incremental funds available—rather than discrimination according to cost-effectiveness analyses that cut across service lines. Historically, weapon innovations were often incorporated in force structures without appropriate doctrinal adjustments because of the inadequacy of organizational arrangements for evaluation.[42] The American military does not have a genuine General Staff, of the sort for which the German tradition is renowned, to deal trenchantly with

---

42. I. B. Holley, Jr., *Ideas and Weapons: Exploitation of the Aerial Weapon by the United States during World War I* (Yale University Press, 1953), pp. 16–17, 19–22, 176. Development of early cruise missiles in the 1950s was hampered by a management system that dealt with them as a simple extension of aircraft research and development; this did not optimize the use of subsystem technologies. In contrast, ballistic missiles, which were seen as "different," were handled in a more flexible project-centered organization, which allowed "high-level intervention to lift their development out of standard organization." Robert F. Coulam, *Illusions of Choice: The F-111 and the Problem of Weapons Acquisition Reform* (Princeton University Press, 1977), pp. 354–59. In the early period, "development of the cruise missile as a weapons system did not keep pace with the evolution of its component parts." The present ALCM and SLCM programs, however, "began in 'crisis' periods during which normal weapon development routines were disrupted. This permitted extra-service organizations with interests in promoting cruise missiles and their associated technology to exercise important influence. A new 'action-channel' was momentarily created and exploited to achieve a reorientation of ongoing service-sponsored programs." Henry D. Levine, "All Things to All Men: The Politics of Cruise Missile Development," *Public Policy,* vol. 25 (Winter 1977), pp. 125, 122.

mission and force structure trade-offs across service lines.[43] Without fully integrated programming decisions, ambiguities in assessment of cruise missile utility will compete with uncertainties in the achievable levels of procurement for other systems.

This may not matter if political complications or strategic utility are primarily sensitive to the overall levels of conventional cruise missile deployment rather than to the specific variations within that level. And in any case the significance for future policy outcomes of the bureaucratic decisionmaking process is likely to be marginal. The important political constraints are not intradepartmental staffing procedures, but the external pressures that will figure in interagency discussion and presidential decisions.

Cross-Pressures in Arms Control

Even before the 1980 election the future of the strategic arms limitation talks was in doubt. The rhetoric of the Reagan campaign provided even stronger grounds for doubting that the negotiations themselves, let alone the prospects for a viable treaty, would survive. But now that the president's task has shifted from criticizing past arms control agreements to finding ways to cope with the prospective as well as the present Soviet nuclear threat, SALT should remain an attractive option in principle. Pressure from U.S. allies and the desire to prevent LRTNF modernization plans from falling apart also encourage serious pursuit of arms control. The formidable challenge for future negotiation is to devise formulas that make more ambitious criteria for adequate American nuclear forces compatible with the Soviet Union's minimum criteria for an acceptable balance. Otherwise, the Soviet leaders' greater domestic political freedom of maneuver may compensate for their inferior productive potential and allow them to make additional military investments that will neutralize American improvements, which will still be somewhat constrained by competing domestic demands.

Cruise missiles are a secondary element in this problem where intercontinental forces are concerned (for theater nuclear forces, cruise mis-

---

43. Tours on the Joint Staff lack the duration and prestige to enable that unit to transcend service loyalties. Of course, even if the United States did have a Prussian-style general staff, the fact that the U.S. military comprises three services relatively balanced in size and importance (as opposed to the army-dominated military establishments of continental Europe) would still limit the capacity for integrative analysis.

siles are more important). Soviet ICBM development is the principal concern of Washington, and the future MX is therefore the responsive system on which most attention is focused; since the availability of carriers for ALCMs is limited, restrictions akin to those in the SALT II treaty would not be especially problematic for the new administration until much later in this decade. The GLCM is another matter, since it brings strong Soviet and Western European sensitivities into the picture, but this involves the linkage between SALT and theater nuclear arms control.

It is ironic that until the last few years the arms control advocates most firmly committed to institutionalizing a situation of mutual assured destruction saw ALCMs as a major threat to stability. The ALCM appeared to derail the Vladivostok agreement, augur a proliferation of U.S. weapons that would drive up force levels on both sides, destabilize the balance by dramatically increasing U.S. counterforce capability, and frustrate verification. But SALT II managed to produce a formula for verification, and degradation of early popular estimates of the ALCM's hard-target destruction potential combined with the missile's association (in the Carter administration) with the cancellation of the B-1 bomber to make it appear more compatible with the mutual assured destruction theory's norms of arms restraint, while the evolving doctrinal trends highlighted by Presidential Directive 59 made the MX a much more salient issue.

Cruise missiles became less problematic in the restricted frame of reference of SALT I and II negotiations (intercontinental bombers and missiles and SLBMs), but the frame of reference itself has become more problematic, in part because of the cruise missile's prospective role in theater nuclear forces. This highlights the question implicit in Quester's discussion in chapter 9. Might the difficulties for negotiated limitations posed by cruise missiles be outweighed by the contribution to deterrence the weapons may offer through unilateral adjustments in force posture? Is formally regulated arms race stability necessarily preferable to a sort of unregulated "free market" stability, which might require giving up the aim of leveling off arms competition and reducing innovation and procurement on both sides? Negotiated arms control does not ipso facto create greater deterrence stability than competitive innovation and deployment does.[44] Quester notes what has become an increasing suspicion

44. Samuel P. Huntington, "Arms Races: Prerequisites and Results," in Carl J. Friedrich and Seymour E. Harris, eds., *Public Policy: A Yearbook of the Graduate School of Public Administration, Harvard University* (GSPA, 1958), pp. 41–86.

among some observers: by focusing on monitoring and verifiability, SALT may have perversely made the achievement of acceptable stability more difficult by aggravating anxieties about specific inequities and encouraging impossible demands to cover every nuance of disadvantage in the aggregate balance of forces.

In chapter 10, however, Kincade reminds us of the long-term potential for self-defeating boomerang effects from the urge to capitalize on technological advantages in the short term. And even if the problem could be kept within the old SALT frame of reference, the cruise missile presents challenges for future negotiation: the potential for proliferating ALCMs grows over time, and the system will be linked with the ICBM problem (implicit in the sublimit counting rules for MIRVs of the SALT II treaty) even if Washington manages to solve the MX basing problem and begins to deploy the missile, and even more so if it does not. For the long term, both the significance of the ALCM for maintenance of the American deterrent and its relative importance in arms control negotiations will vary with the role of the MX. If the MX program is carried out, the United States will have less incentive to push larger numbers of ALCMs into the strategic force, and they will therefore constitute relatively less of the Soviet concern about U.S. capabilities. If U.S. ICBM modernization remains frustrated, on the other hand, there will be temptations to temporize by augmenting the other legs of the triad. Since the possibility for extra submarine construction is less elastic than that for cruise missile carrier aircraft, and since the rigors of submarine duty make it unlikely that the United States could field crews in sufficient numbers even with a larger number of submarines, boosting the number of ALCMs would be a more likely option.

Kincade's suggestion of a SALT formula tying the average number of ALCMs on U.S. aircraft to the number of MIRVs on Soviet ICBMs makes some sense in either case, but especially if the ICBM element in the U.S. force is degraded. In that event, though, it would be all the more vital to hold out for a differential in the comparison—allowing a higher average of ALCMs per delivery vehicle than Soviet MIRVs—because air-breathing missiles are less penetrative than ballistic reentry vehicles. As long as the antiballistic missile (ABM) treaty remains in force, Moscow could hardly deny the logic of a differential without denying the utility of the Soviet air defense system (and denial would give Washington grounds for a demand to limit such air defense deployments).

This rationale also helps to meet U.S. concern about the greater threat posed by "time-urgent" counterforce capabilities of Soviet ICBMs without resting on the distinction—which Soviet spokesmen do not accept—that "slow" bombers and cruise missiles are only retaliatory weapons without first-strike utility. Moreover, if a survivable MX deployment does go forward and Soviet negotiators are more worried (as they logically should be) about that system than about ALCMs, a differential average for trade-offs between ALCM carriers and ICBMs with MIRVs should be a reasonable compromise, mitigating Soviet anxiety about vulnerability (given the alternative U.S. choice of emphasizing the MX in the force mix) and U.S. qualms about bomber prelaunch survivability and ALCM penetrativity. Such a formula of course does not solve many potential negotiating problems, and neither side is likely to welcome it enthusiastically, but both could see it as a second-best solution—and more feasible than alternatives.

Theater Arms Control

Outside the realm of central strategic forces as traditionally defined by Americans, the interlocking military, political, and diplomatic challenges posed by cruise missiles appear less tractable. Many U.S. arms controllers prefer to keep theater cruise missiles nuclear, because significant deployments of conventional models would threaten negotiated agreement by muddying the verification problem. As Kelleher points out in chapter 15, however, it is the nuclear cruise missiles that provoke the most opposition from the Western European Left. The whole problem of grappling with long-range theater weapons in arms control is, compared to the more than ten-year history of SALT, relatively new, and it raises the ambiguities and dilemmas in alliance relations more insistently than the earlier negotiations. In the 1950s the Soviet deployments of medium and intermediate range missiles

were more than offset by a substantial U.S. intercontinental superiority. So much so, that they were largely forgotten. After the beginning of MBFR [mutual and balanced force reductions], there even emerged, for a period, an image of massive Western superiority in theater nuclear forces stimulated by the artificial delimitation of the area to which MBFR is to apply, the so-called NATO Guidelines Area . . . [which] excludes the Soviet Union but includes the Federal Republic of Germany, and since the Soviets have been hesitant to deploy nuclear weapons beyond their borders.[45]

45. Stanley Sienkiewicz, "Foreign Policy and Theater Nuclear Force Planning," *Journal of Strategic Studies,* vol. 2 (May 1979), p. 28.

Indeed, the recent push to engage in theater nuclear arms control reverses the earlier alliance position, when Europeans preferred to keep U.S. theater nuclear forces out of SALT to avert a decoupling of U.S. strategic forces.[46] The reversal was not accompanied by resolution of the old worry, so European ambivalence toward theater nuclear forces was heightened. Many European leaders want nuclear GLCMs (and Pershing IIs) to be strategically coupling, but they do not want them to unnerve the Soviet Union by being strategically threatening. In a sense, therefore, they want GLCMs to be strategic but not too strategic. This contradiction does not augur well for the possibility of comprehensive arms control that is already slim because of the fate of the SALT II treaty and the vagaries of American domestic politics.

While Carter's opponents damned the SALT II treaty as a codification of U.S. weakness, many European leaders tended to see the potential rejection of the treaty as evidence of weakness in America's capacity for leadership.[47] The divergence of European and American views is often explained by Europeans' greater concern with the political and diplomatic elements in the problem of nuclear policy and Americans' greater concern with the technical and military elements. This simple distinction masks a deeper difference in dominant views of deterrence. It implies to some Americans that the problem is basically one of weak will, that European governments are more inclined to appease their own pacifist and leftist opposition movements and the USSR as well, and that stronger assertion of leadership from Washington can overcome the problem.

Even without European leaders' desire to avoid provocation, however, there is the old problem of difference in *objective* interests between Washington and NATO capitals: the American interest in a nuclear strategy that promises to keep combat confined to the European continent as long as possible, and the allies' interest in ensuring that escalation occur as soon as possible. The Europeans' emphasis on the political component of strategy over the operational one goes logically with the emphasis on rhetoric about extended deterrence and the import of declaratory policy as a pillar of such deterrence. This long-standing latent tension in the alliance explains some of the confusion over whether the greater "visi-

46. Lawrence Freedman, "The Dilemma of Theatre Nuclear Arms Control," *Survival,* vol. 23 (January–February 1981), p. 3.
47. *SALT and the NATO Allies,* Committee Print, Staff Report to the Subcommittee on European Affairs of the Senate Foreign Relations Committee, 96 Cong. 1 sess. (GPO, 1979), pp. 8–10.

bility" of GLCMs (as opposed to SLCMs or old SLBMs assigned to Supreme Allied Commander, Europe—SACEUR) was of real concern to European leaders or simply anticipated by U.S. planners. In terms of the domestic political constraints faced by European governments in the wake of the 1979 LRTNF decision, in fact, visibility emerges as more of a liability than an advantage.

Domestic politics have militated against serious theater nuclear arms control negotiations on both sides of the Atlantic. The potential for wringing a reasonable agreement out of Moscow depends to some extent on the durability of NATO deployment plans for the GLCM and the Pershing II, yet the advent of negotiations could give the NATO swing countries (the Netherlands and Belgium) an excuse to bail out of participation in the deployment. In the United States, Carter wanted to postpone theater negotiations until after the 1980 election; not only was he pressed by Reagan's campaign criticism of the softness of U.S. defense policy, but there was also the worry that early negotiations would tip the Belgian decision against deployment.[48] And Reagan's record now makes it even more difficult for Washington to consider serious negotiations if "serious" means willingness to make meaningful compromises.

The complications within the alliance simply increase the difficulties in negotiating with the Russians. Earlier fears among arms controllers that cruise missile technology would lead to horizontal proliferation of modern nuclear delivery systems appear now to be unfounded. Freedman demonstrates why the Western European nuclear powers' interest in cruise missiles cooled, alleviating earlier Soviet concern about U.S. technology transfers that might circumvent SALT. Fear that third world countries will seek sophisticated cruise missiles, on the other hand, does not appear economically or militarily logical.[49]

48. John M. Goshko, "Brezhnev Hits NATO Delay on Missile Talks," *Washington Post*, August 27, 1980.

49. For third world countries with limited resources, smaller and less diversified force structures, and contiguous enemies, multipurpose tactical aircraft with greater payload, flexibility, and reusability are a far more rational investment. Even if the propulsion and guidance technologies of the cruise missile itself do not constitute a barrier, TERCOM mapping requirements and computer support for mission planning systems are daunting. Nevertheless, there have been rumors reportedly emanating from "U.S. intelligence agencies" that Israel, South Africa, and Taiwan have been collaboratively seeking to develop cruise missiles. Jack Anderson, "3 Nations to Begin Cruise Missile Project," *Washington Post*, December 8, 1980. These "pariah states" have unique strategic concerns, however, and in economic and scientific development are beyond third world status. Moreover, these rumors do not

The prime issue for the Soviet Union now is not horizontal proliferation among many of its enemies, but vertical proliferation of American cruise missiles in Europe or at sea. Future progress in negotiation therefore requires either opening up the fractious issue of U.S. forward-based systems (FBS), which stalemated SALT until it was put aside, or finding a new formula that would mollify Moscow's anxiety about "equal security" without harming the West's position in the aggregate nuclear balance. The latter possibility is more attractive, not only because legitimating the Soviet definition of LRTNF/FBS weakens the integrity of the Western alliance, but because the potential for overloading the SALT mechanism (or a theater arms control forum) beyond its ability to cope varies directly with the diversity and complexity of military force structures subject to negotiation.

Theater nuclear arms control, however, by definition precludes brushing aside Soviet objections to forward-based systems with the same rationales used earlier in SALT. One does not have to sympathize with Soviet concern about security or strategy to recognize why the fixation on LRTNF in Western Europe is more than a disingenuous ploy to gain military advantage or split NATO. Washington has never conceded analogous "rights" for forward-based systems to Moscow (although exclusion from SALT of Soviet naval cruise missiles technically capable of striking U.S. coastal targets might be seen in this light).[50] Indeed, the United States went to the brink of war in 1962 to remove Soviet missiles forward-deployed in Cuba.

If NATO were to accept inclusion of U.S. forward-based aircraft in theater negotiations, it would be reasonable to insist on the incorporation of nuclear-capable aircraft based in the western USSR as well. Broadening the scope this far would make it hard to avoid bringing in British and French strategic forces. Probably the only hope for a feasible agreement when such complex systems must be covered would be a combination of a simple counting standard (such as numbers of launchers, the basis for early SALT negotiations) and a generous freedom-to-mix provision. Lawrence Freedman has proposed an ingenious scheme of this sort that

---

make clear that they are seeking modern TERCOM-guided cruise missiles, rather than the older, less sophisticated kinds that have long been practical for many countries. India, for example, tested a cruise missile some years ago (and has apparently gone no further in developing it for military applications).

50. Huisken debunks the significance of that threat in "Origins of the Strategic Cruise Missile," p. 33.

has the added virtue of transcending the U.S.-allied tension over de-coupling, differences in U.S. and Soviet definitions of "strategic" weap-ons, and the issue of whether parity in theater nuclear forces is desirable. He suggests doing this by lumping intercontinental and theater nuclear forces together, which may appeal less to Washington than to its allies or adversary, but may be worth considering nonetheless:

If an all-inclusive ceiling can be achieved within SALT III with a freedom-to-mix arrangement, then the allies can sort out the proper balance between cen-tral and theatre systems among themselves. . . . The proposal is to add 400, either to the eventual ceiling for central systems under SALT II, 2,250, or to a lower figure if further cuts in central system levels are agreed. . . . The United States, for example, might still be interested in going beyond 400 in theatre systems to take up some of the gap between the SALT II ceiling and the cur-rently planned force levels.[51]

As with other arms control ideas, such formulas seem elegantly suited to cutting the Gordian knot of negotiation because of their simplicity, but they might not survive the internal and diplomatic wrangles provoked by anxiety about specific inequities in other aspects of the weapons systems. And in any case the notion suggested is one in which cruise missiles per se do not present notable opportunities or difficulties; the advantages and pitfalls of that new technology would be submerged in the more general categorization of the systems. Cruise missiles, however, could still spoil such a formula if the United States deployed large numbers of conven-tionally armed models. If the Soviet Union deployed its own conventional cruise missiles, the situation would be even worse. While agreement on excluding such missiles from negotiation might appear feasible on grounds that they mutually cancel each other out, making the verification prob-lems they pose more acceptable, the West would have more reason than the East to fear cheating—clandestine substitution of nuclear warheads—because of the asymmetry in available information and the probability of exposure in open Western societies. Moreover, even if Soviet counter-deployment of cruise missiles washed out the verification problem, it

51. "Because this proposal is based on launchers rather than warheads it does not take account of the SS-20's three warheads. This could be remedied by includ-ing the SS-20 under one of the existing sub-ceilings for MIRVed missiles, the most likely would be the 1,320 ceiling which currently gives the United States a 120 credit for bombers carrying ALCMs. An equivalent 120 credit for MIRVed medium-range missiles could well seem appropriate.

"Within these sorts of totals the 66 US FB-111s could not be excluded. The more politically awkward problems of the Soviet forces facing China and the British and French forces will remain. They may become linked, so that they are either brought in together or kept out together." Freedman, "Dilemma of Theatre Nuclear Arms Control," p. 8.

would also neutralize the enhanced conventional Western military capability that warrants significant expenditures on such weapons.

If NATO deploys conventional cruise missiles and the USSR does not, how can theater nuclear arms control be salvaged? One heretical possibility would be to have such conventional missiles deployed by *German* military forces alone, with SACEUR dividing the tactical labor of the alliance by allocating to the *Bundeswehr* or *Luftwaffe* the targets appropriate for those weapons. At first glance this seems to offer the worst of both worlds, given nervous Russian jokes about how the nuclear "GLCM" stands for "German-launched cruise missile." But the fact remains that West Germany, as opposed to the United States, Britain, and France, does not have nuclear ordnance. It should be credible to Moscow that West Germany's allies have reason not to want to change that situation and that, if Bonn were to decide to develop and deploy its own nuclear weapons, the availability of cruise missile delivery systems would be a negligible factor.

If the Russians, the allies, or the American military object (the Air Force's lack of enthusiasm for cruise missiles might change if a sister service had the weapons while it did not), there are alternatives, though they might be too ambitious to negotiate. Washington might simply plan and declare that certain models of NATO dual-capable aircraft were no longer assigned nuclear missions, stating that it would be logical to deploy nuclear GLCMs to release dual-capable aircraft for strikes with conventional munitions.[52] Soviet concern about verifying the nonnuclear status of conventional cruise missiles could be parried by citing observable differences in security precautions for the nuclear GLCMs. This would support the demand to simplify the negotiations by restricting them to missiles, deflecting Soviet insistence on dealing with more broadly defined forward-based systems, thus increasing the practical chances that the negotiating mechanism could cope with the issues.

Toward Some Fuzzy Bottom Lines

As a multipurpose family of weapons, cruise missiles do not lend themselves to evaluation by clear standards or binary choices. Any variant

52. Such a sweeping change could be objectionable to nonnuclear allies who now have a stake in two-key dual-capable aircraft; the arrangement gives them participation in the nuclear deterrent—a finger on the safety catch as well as on the trigger—without responsibility. The current plan is for nuclear GLCMs to be completely under U.S. control.

can be compared with other weapons within one of the relevant dimensions of analysis—technical, economic, strategic, tactical, political, diplomatic—but the many cruise missile variants and the interdependence of the different variables in the analysis preclude confidence in a comprehensive assessment. Preceding sections of this chapter attempted to integrate assessment by extrapolating the relationships between the detailed discussions in previous chapters. This final section summarizes the conflicting trends and implications, the principal strategic choices, and the principal variables to which decisions on cruise missiles should be sensitive.

Doctrinal Adaptations

The most direct way in which to summarize the promise of the cruise missile is to distill its military advantages. These advantages may be lessened, neutralized, or turned into liabilities when other considerations are applied, but the missile is above all a weapon.

For strategic nuclear forces cruise missiles offer less than early enthusiasts hoped or opponents concerned about arms control feared. But they offer more than can be inferred from narrowly focusing on the weapon in isolation from other elements of force structure or from those that could be feasible alternatives for maintaining strategic capabilities. ALCMs support the minimum requirement for strategic forces—assured destruction retaliatory capability—by buttressing one weakening leg of the triad (aging bombers whose penetrativity will decline) while deficiencies in a leg that is generally believed to be even weaker (fixed ICBMs) are remedied. Though ALCMs in the numbers planned may, by themselves, offer inadequate countervalue target coverage in the worst case (a Soviet surprise attack against bombers on day-to-day alert), they would add to it significantly in conjunction with SLBMs. Strictly in terms of assured destruction criteria, after all, the only rationale for a triad is to compensate for what many believe is happening now because of Minuteman vulnerability—emergence of a decisive preemptive threat against one leg. At the same time, if the counting rules arrived at in SALT II are a guide, ALCMs do not threaten arms control solutions for stabilizing deterrence and force levels. This, however, reflects the limits of the ALCM's contribution to military effectiveness.

The doctrinal emphasis in Presidential Directive 59, in contrast to simple mutual assured destruction criteria, poses more ambitious demands than can be met by current capabilities, and to these the ALCM's contribution is limited. It is less troubling in bureaucratic-political terms than it was through most of the 1970s because the Carter administration's move to countervailing strategy, now reinforced by the Reagan administration's commitments to a generally strengthened force posture, eroded resistance to the procurement of a new penetrating bomber. In strategic terms, the ALCM is almost neutral. Its flexibility is not the sort of flexibility stipulated by the directive because the missile depends on a delivery platform and mission planning support structure of dubious endurance. The other notable aspect of Presidential Directive 59 is the expansion of the target base (a menu of 40,000 installations in SIOP 5D, according to one report).[53] Since ALCMs replace other weapons, they offer little additional coverage, and the newly emphasized categories—command structure targets—would probably be spared beyond the firing time for ALCMs. However, in light of the overall inadequacy of current U.S. capabilities to implement the directive's requirements for enduring flexibility, the ALCM's limitations for that purpose do not discredit the weapon. And if its accuracy can be held to the higher limits of the range of uncertainty in public estimates, the ALCM offers an incremental improvement in the second-strike counterforce requirements of the countervailing strategy during the period between the erosion of B-52 penetrativity and the deployment of more survivable ICBMs.

Finally, the implications of ALCMs for deterrence stability are positive. They coincide with emphasis on counterforce-matching for deterrence by denial yet present less danger of counterproductive effects (by raising the "use 'em or lose 'em" reciprocal fear of surprise attack) than an improved ICBM because of both their slowness and their limited potential for counterforce target coverage. And by the time more impressive counterforce ballistic missiles (MX and D-5) enter the strategic force, ALCMs should not figure much in the debate over stability since their contribution to the threat against Soviet forces would be secondary, if not incidental. (If the superpowers moved to deploy antiballistic missile systems, though, air-breathing forces could become more important since they would no longer appear less capable of penetration.)

For LRTNF, the GLCM represents a clear qualitative improvement in capability by virtue of its range, which allows wider coverage of targets (more than for the Pershing II), including ones within the Soviet home-

53. Desmond Ball, "Counterforce Targeting: How New? How Viable?" *Arms Control Today,* vol. 11 (February 1981), p. 2.

land. Thus constituting a greater threat to the USSR (and as long as the Russians consider it as invulnerable to preemption as NATO planners do), the GLCM appears to offer enhanced deterrence when considered in isolation from the responses it may provoke. But it would be unrealistic to assume that GLCMs will be invulnerable. In a surprise attack they could be caught on their bases, and they might not even be dispersed upon strategic warning because of the apparent escalatory effect such a move would have in a crisis.[54] Moreover, the political and diplomatic salience of the LRTNF modernization issue complicates the military rationales for the system. Much more than the ALCM, the GLCM aggravates the tension between unilaterally improved security and negotiated stabilization through arms control.

The change in capability that GLCMs present may be seen as a logical adaptation of NATO's deterrence to the combined effect of parity at the higher level of central strategic forces and continuing Western disadvantage at the lower level of conventional forces for war in Europe. The value of the adaptation depends to some extent on its ambiguity, since Americans may see it as a decoupling protection against escalation to intercontinental exchanges while Europeans prefer to see it as a recoupling link (in a sense validating the logic in the Soviet charge that the LRTNF modernization plan circumvents the balance established under SALT II). The adaptation, however, is more inadvertent than premeditated, since it was the availability of the weapon that prompted the decision to deploy it, not a preexisting doctrinal requirement that prompted its development.[55]

These uncertainties raise the odds that arms control pressure to limit the GLCM's role could be persuasive. The combination of greater commitment in Western Europe than in Washington to salvaging détente with adamant Soviet objections to the novel threat posed by the GLCM suggests that the full military potential of the system will not be realized. Thus it appears, not surprisingly, that the cruise missile with limited utility for increasing U.S. striking power (the ALCM) is politically unproblematic, while the one with greater military significance (the GLCM) will face more unyielding constraints. Even in the unlikely event that

---

54. Richard K. Betts, *Surprise and Defense* (Brookings Institution, forthcoming), chap. 8.

55. This proposition is reinforced by the original U.S. willingness to accept the SALT II protocol. Washington made clear to Moscow that the protocol was no more than a hollow shell, with no possibility of extension, only after the U.S. SALT debate and allied pressure intensified.

vigorous U.S. leadership and adept alliance diplomacy overcame the political hesitancy of NATO governments, the consequences of Soviet reactions for the balance of capabilities might constitute valid *military* grounds for accepting limitations on the nuclear GLCM. If it became certain that East-West arms control was dead rather than in doubt, however, the overall problems would be worse but the strategic calculations would be less complicated. Without arms control, it would also be harder to contain arguments for proliferating nuclear SLCMs on sea-based platforms.[56]

The contribution of conventionally armed cruise missiles to Western defense is less certain than that of the nuclear variants. Palin's speculations offer grounds for great expectations, but must be tempered by several questions about ultimate cost-effectiveness. First, can new conventional munitions and technical improvements in capability be developed within narrow limits of acceptable unit price? Second, can deployment modes be made compatible with arms control, so as to reduce the odds of Soviet counterdeployments that would neutralize the U.S. investment? And third, can integrated operational plans be adjusted for optimal employment of complementary weapon systems? The first depends on ingenuity in research and development and efficiency in production; the second on percipient judgment of the elasticities in Soviet security concerns, military investment, and negotiating positions, and the third on confidence in the reliability of sensitive components of the cruise missile under conditions of wartime friction when more flexible systems would allow greater margin for error.[57] Commitments to conventional cruise missiles should depend on answering these questions in sequence.

Placing large numbers of conventional SLCMs on ships would highlight two fundamental issues of strategy and doctrine that should be

56. Reasons against doing so would still exist: the weapon-loading trade-offs that would compromise conventional missions of the fleet, and the danger of turning vulnerable surface ships into nuclear lightning rods. In this case MccGwire's suggestion that nuclear TLAMs would best be deployed on aircraft carriers—because those platforms already carry nuclear weapons and the change would not be as symbolically provocative as turning other surface ships into nuclear delivery systems—seems even more interesting.

57. Neither TERCOM nor DSMAC is perfect. According to recent reports by the General Accounting Office, TERCOM is more susceptible to error than U.S. tests—conducted over familiar terrain—have indicated. Questions have been raised about problems posed by Soviet terrain and seasonal changes and by deficiencies in satellite mapping. For example, the satellite pictures reportedly record the tops of trees sometimes, rather than the ground below. Therefore, when the leaves fall, the altitude reading changes. James Coates, "Flaws Found in Guidance System of Cruise Missiles," *Chicago Tribune*, September 6, 1981. Toomay's conclusions in chapter 1,

settled before deploying cruise missiles rather than letting strategy emerge by default from deployment decisions. One is the land-attack mission of the Navy. Should naval surface force structure be largely determined by the requirement to mount attacks with conventional ordnance against targets on the periphery of the USSR? If not, the rationale for major investments in cruise missile launch platforms such as battleships, even for missions in the third world, is weak, since the unavailability of aircraft carriers in remote areas assumes that they remain stationed in positions for war with the Soviet Union. Moreover, even under the third world intervention rationale, the logic implicit in big investments in capital ships with cruise missiles is questionable. Large expenditures of that sort, if unmatched by commensurate expansion of ground forces earmarked for such contingencies (if carriers need to be withheld to cover NATO or Korea, significant numbers of ground forces might need to be too), emphasize offshore assets as sufficient for operational success. Such faith in independent naval firepower may be similar to the overconfidence in the efficacy of air power of Air Force spokesmen in the past. And if the ship is meant to provide close support for ground troops, guns rather than cruise missiles (more appropriate for deep interdiction) are most relevant.

Second, should the United States continue to build the Navy around a few large ships with high unit capability (many eggs in few baskets) or a larger number of smaller vessels? A shift in the latter direction would argue for keeping the battleships in mothballs and parceling out SLCMs to destroyers or other small platforms that can be deployed in large numbers.[58] Considering all these uncertainties, if concern about military oper-

---

however, remain basically valid, since some amount of attrition from technical unreliability was always to be expected. For a nuclear attack, the failure of, say, 15 percent of the missiles en route would not be catastrophic. Allowance for the failure of conventional cruise missiles cannot be generous, however, because their cost-effectiveness is more marginal.

DSMAC guidance and transwar mission planning capabilities are even more sensitive to uncertainties in weather and wartime communications than TERCOM is. The rationale for freeing tactical aircraft to exploit fully the comparative advantage of the on-board human intelligence also depends on narrowing their missions. That in turn requires reducing the doubt about cruise missiles' capacity to execute the other missions. Readjustment of strike plans after war begins would be possible if the cruise missiles flopped, but would exact a price in timeliness and efficiency of overall operations.

58. Under Secretary Murray did argue ("Bring Back the Battleships"), however, that refitted battleships would cost no more and would be available sooner than new destroyers.

ations takes precedence over the political utility of impressive dreadnoughts for peacetime "presence" missions, battleships carrying cruise missiles seem a questionable buy.[59]

All of these doctrinal questions fade in significance (as constraints on force structure decisions) to the extent that defense budget limitations are eased. When expenditures involve only additional capabilities rather than trade-offs within existing aggregates, it is easier (though no more rational) to avoid strategic choices and indulge the simpler impulse that more (of anything) is better. Long-term sustained real growth in defense expenditures, however, cannot be assumed, even if the presidency and Congress remain in conservative hands for years. Reagan's economic program could fail or liberals in Congress could restrain the pace of reduction in domestic expenditures; in either case the consensus behind major expansion of military forces could diminish. Indeed, some observers attribute the large increases in the 1982 defense budget to the administration's fear that the defense fervor could abate, making it vital to boost total obligational authority for investment as much as possible immediately. The flap in September 1981 over cutting back defense increases illustrates the problem.

If cruise missiles were independent weapons, their unit cost could make it reasonable to pay less attention to doctrinal questions, assuming that future decisions to deemphasize their proportional role in military plans would come at a low premium. Because many variants of the missile depend on expensive launch platforms, however, their role has larger and more expensive implications for force structure. This is of more concern for conventional cruise missiles and naval applications than for nuclear variants, where the trade-offs and alternative choices seem less complex. There is some advantage in avoiding rigid subordination of force structure to concepts of warfare that could prove erroneous, and letting technological serendipity and the principle of diversity in weapon systems shape doctrine. But that advantage has limits. Where the potential utility of cruise missiles is least certain, the technical tail must not be allowed to wag the doctrinal dog completely.

Future Choices in Focus

Cruise missile types can be assessed according to numerous balances of cost and benefit: military utility against financial cost; cost advantage

59. If the "presence" function justifies the battleship, it does so because of the ship's size, not its component cruise missiles.

from commonality versus military advantage from diversification; short-term versus long-term payoff from investment; military benefit versus arms control cost; missile capability versus platform limitations; and so on. Judgments about the missiles' potential are sensitive to, among other things, the possibilities of combining technical improvement (to cope with evolving Soviet countermeasures) and cost-containment; the availability of cheap, adaptable launch platforms; the relative importance of preserving the air-breathing leg of the strategic triad; the priority in doctrine of deep interdiction or attacks on well-defended targets; the development of credible conventions for counting missiles in arms control agreements; the balance between allies' enhanced confidence in military deterrence and their desire to salvage political détente; and the prospective rates of progress in improvement of air defenses as opposed to improvement in missile penetrativity. Until the unreachable point when uncertainties about technical data and procurement costs evaporate, military strategy becomes less artful and more scientific, and policy decisions by adversaries and allies become more predictable than our own, there is no grand model that can factor in all these choices and produce an answer to how many cruise missiles the United States should buy for military purposes or how many it should give up for political purposes.

This is analytically dispiriting, but perversely revealing. When the cruise missile began to emerge in the 1970s many observers thought its implications were clear and predictable. Civilian enthusiasts believed it would be militarily good for everything, military skeptics feared it might gut commitments to preferred systems, and worried arms control advocates believed it would wreck strategic stability. The durability of the first of these assumptions and the erosion of the second and third have led to a momentum that has outstripped the analytical basis for it. Cruise missile programs are rushing forward faster than doctrinal concepts can rationalize them. The political eclipse of domestic antidefense sentiment has discredited anxiety about arms control negotiability to an extent unwarranted by the boomerang effects that indiscriminate deployments could have on the West's position in the military balance. Full recognition of the daunting complexity of technical, strategic, and political cost-effectiveness calculations should prompt foreign policy decisionmakers to pause and put cruise missile programs under the jeweler's glass. Wallowing in complexity is of course an analytical cop-out. A few particular conclusions about the variables governing choice warrant emphasis.

For strategic nuclear cruise missiles the critical uncertainty is time—

how long the weapons will provide the benefits they promise. For the ALCM the issue is less its role through the mid-1980s than its role in a refurbished triad—or a dyad by default if ICBMs cannot be deployed satisfactorily—further in the future. The three central variables are the future of land-based ICBMs, the technological race between penetrativity and air defense, and the arms control race between the technological evolution of strategic weaponry[60] and the ability of negotiating mechanisms to keep up.

The critical uncertainty for the nuclear GLCM is its compatibility with NATO solidarity—whether its clear enhancement of LRTNF capability can be accommodated to Soviet objections (at what price in other aspects of the balance?), and if not, whether Western European backsliding on deployment can be averted.[61] But if allied pressure makes some major compromise unavoidable, cruise missiles might actually have more rather than less significance as a component in theater nuclear force modernization if the Pershing II component is bargained away. And if land-based long-range theater nuclear forces are truncated by trading away Pershings for political reasons, a U.S. administration bent on improving capabilities would have more incentive to deploy some form of nuclear SLCM. In that event the crucial problems would move from the political to the strategic realm. What sorts of naval platforms should be used for nuclear land attack—invulnerable but comparatively expensive dedicated SSNs, which also lack tactical responsiveness, or more readily adaptable but exposed surface ships? And what if the USSR deploys modern SLCM systems that could strike North America as well as Europe?

Conventionally armed cruise missiles are the most challenging to thoughtful planning. How can judgment of their comparative utility be refined to ensure confidence in their cost-effectiveness compared with alternate weapon investments? How should major commitments to the conventional TLAM and the TASM affect more general and significant

60. If ABM or exotic beam weapons become more practical, cruise missiles may seem either trivial or necessary to maintain offensive penetration.

61. At this writing European commitments remain as conditional as ever. On March 17, 1981, West German Foreign Minister Hans-Dietrich Genscher "reaffirmed support for the NATO 'dual-decision' of 1979, stressing that Bonn attaches as much importance to the offer to negotiate arms limitations with the Soviet Union as to the decision to modernize the NATO arsenal. 'Military balance at the lowest possible level' must be the goal of the negotiations, said Genscher." "Foreign Minister Genscher Outlines Security Policy," *German Press Review*, 81-12 (March 25, 1981), p. 4. Soviet invasion of Poland could "solve" Washington's problem of keeping the NATO allies resolute, but the solution would hardly be worth the price.

choices about configuration of the naval force structure? How can their benefits for conventional deterrence and defense be realized without rebounding against U.S. interests in the nuclear sphere (by demolishing arms control limitations that might restrain further expansion of the already worrisome Soviet threat to the West)?

If the hard foreign policy choices about cruise missiles had to be distilled into one principal problem, it would be the tension between conventional defense and negotiated nuclear stability. Does the "conventional push" trend in cruise missile programs offer benefits sufficiently large and certain to override the costs for nuclear arms control verification? Either of three eventualities could make this problem moot: (1) if enthusiasm for conventional cruise missiles was deflected and relatively few were deployed, the consequences for the verification problem could be finessed;[62] (2) if either functionally related or external observable differences satisfactory to Moscow could be appended to conventional cruise missiles, the verification problem would be resolved; or (3) if arms control died, verification of U.S. capabilities would cease to worry Washington, although verification of Soviet forces and preservation of the allies' contribution to the NATO deterrent would become more of a problem.

The last possibility is the biggest issue. It would be ironic if conventional cruise missiles emerged as a much more significant determinant of U.S. security or danger than nuclear-armed models, and if they wrecked arms control. Modern cruise missile programs, after all, were born primarily because of civilian fixation on the nuclear roles envisioned for them and on their enhancement of U.S. arms control initiatives.[63] The alleged distinction in the nuclear sphere between strategies of deterrence and defense, often asserted by academic theorists who favor the logic of mutual assured destruction, has lost popularity in recent years as deterrence-by-denial theories underlying the countervailing strategy have come to the fore. Thus it would also be ironic if the alleged distinction became

62. This would be all the more possible if U.S.-Soviet arms control continued to be based on launchers rather than weapons as the currency of negotiation, and if conventional cruise missile deployments were based on a few launch platforms with multiple reloads.

63. Technological determinism, pressure from the armed services, and action-reaction arms competition motives were either negligible or negative influences; SALT bargaining leverage was the prime rationale. Huisken, "Origins of the Strategic Cruise Missile," pp. 33–35.

relevant to the role of conventional cruise missiles, with the side effects of those weapons eroding confidence in the stability of the nuclear balance. So perhaps the principal issues that need to be resolved definitely before final decisions on what to do with the various cruise missiles emerging from development are the new, specific question of how financially inexpensive conventional cruise missiles will really be, and the old, general question of how strategically expensive the death of negotiated arms control could be.

PART FIVE

Appendixes

Detailed Characteristics
of the Soviet Air Defense System

GORDON MACDONALD, JACK RUINA, *and* MARK BALASCHAK

IN THIS appendix the technical characteristics of selected components of the Soviet air defense system are reviewed.

Early Warning Radar

The best-known Soviet early warning radars are code-named Tall King, Spoon Rest, and NYSA-C.[1] The Tall King was introduced in 1959. It has a large antenna (50 by 80–100 feet), operates at metric wavelengths (the frequency is about 170 megahertz), and was designed to detect high-altitude aircraft, a threat against which the deployed Soviet air defenses are optimal. Its effective altitude is over 140,000 feet and its range over 350 miles. The Tall King is expected to perform poorly against cruise missiles, whose head-on radar cross section (RCS) may be one-thousandth that of an aircraft like the B-52, the aircraft this radar is intended to detect.[2] The smaller, more mobile Spoon Rest system also entered service in 1959 and was exported to Egypt and Vietnam. It operates at about 150 megahertz and has a range of about 160 miles. It is sometimes used as the target-acquisition radar for the SA-2 surface-to-air mis-

1. Except where otherwise noted, data on Soviet radars in this appendix are taken from Harry F. Eustace, ed., *The International Countermeasures Handbook, 1978–1979,* 4th ed. (Palo Alto, Calif.: EW Communications, 1978), pp. 204, 228–33; and *Jane's Weapon Systems, 1979–80,* R. T. Pretty, ed. (Franklin Watts, 1979), pp. 506–13.

2. *Hearings on Military Posture and H.R. 1872 [H.R. 4040] Department of Defense Authorization for Fiscal Year 1980,* Hearings before the House Armed Services Committee, 96 Cong. 1 sess. (Government Printing Office, 1979), pt. 3, bk. 1, p. 206.

sile system. Little has been reported of the NYSA-C early warning radar, which is deployed in Poland, East Germany, and other Warsaw Pact states. It has two rather large antennas and is thought to operate at ultra-high frequencies, which would put its operating wavelength in the 1-meter-to-10-centimeter region. Although its operating characteristics are less certain than those of Tall King and Spoon Rest, it probably has little or no capability against cruise missiles.

A very special type of early warning radar whose range is much greater than most and that is not limited by line-of-sight considerations is the so-called over-the-horizon backscatter radar. These operate at 10- to 100-meter wavelengths (longer than typical radars), which can bounce off the ionosphere like shortwave radio broadcasts. By using ionospheric reflection for the transmitted signal on the way to and from a target, backscatter radars have ranges well beyond line of sight; the transmitted and reflected signals bounce off the ionosphere and the ground in a series of hops. But such radars typically have low resolution and are sensitive to ionospheric disruptions such as those that occur during auroral displays and unusual solar activity. Their performance is therefore particularly erratic in Arctic regions, where they are needed most for air defense early warning. Nuclear explosions could cause further severe disruption. Over-the-horizon radars are large and expensive, and therefore few in number, making them attractive targets in wartime. However, their range of 1,000 miles or more greatly increases warning times when they do function properly.

The Soviet Union operates two such radars facing the United States that are presumably to provide warning of a U.S. ICBM launch.[3] Strange signals that interfered with shortwave broadcasts in 1976 and 1977 were taken as indication of continuing Soviet work in this field.[4] Although detailed knowledge of the transmissions from such radars would be necessary before detailed capability against the ALCM threat could be evaluated, even if these radars had limited capability against carriers, it is highly unlikely that the radars could detect, much less track, objects with an RCS as low as that of the cruise missile.

Interceptor Aircraft

As in other Soviet air defense equipment, interceptor aircraft were designed with the primary mission of engaging high-altitude aircraft.

The Su-9 and its later derivative, the Su-11, constitute roughly one-

3. *Department of Defense Annual Report, Fiscal Year 1980* (GPO, 1979), p. 73.
4. *Jane's Weapon Systems*, p. 506.

sixth of the total air defense forces.[5] These aircraft were introduced in 1959 and 1967, respectively, and have performed well in the high-altitude high-speed intercept role. Long-range (1,600-mile radius) interception is the job of the Tu-28P, which was introduced in 1961. These aircraft are based in the north and constitute about 5 percent of the Soviet strategic defense aircraft inventory. Some medium-range all-weather interception is done by the 320 Yak-28P interceptors, aircraft of the same vintage as the TU-28P. The Su-15 Flagon (NATO code name) is the most widely used interceptor, making up about a third of the force. First observed in 1967, it has since been produced in four successive models. A good, fast, medium-range and -altitude interceptor, its engines, electronics, and low-altitude-flight characteristics have been improved. Possibly its radar has also been improved.[6]

The MiG-25 Foxbat is a high-altitude, Mach 2.5-plus interceptor; about 330 are in service. This aircraft, though it currently has no lookdown capability,[7] is evidently serving as a testbed for new Soviet airborne intercept (AI) radars, and a version of the MiG-25 with a look-down–shoot-down capability against fighter-sized targets may enter service within the next year.[8] The MiG-23 and the MiG-25 are the only aircraft now in production for the strategic air defense forces.[9]

The MiG-23 Flogger is a variable-geometry ("swing-wing") multirole aircraft that serves as interceptor with the PVO Strany, and as a fighter-bomber and, in much modified form, as a ground-attack aircraft with the Soviet tactical air forces. With more than 600 in service with the PVO (and this number is increasing at the rate of 200 a year),[10] the MiG-23 is expected to become the most important interceptor in the Soviet inventory over the next few years.[11] It is the only aircraft that has demonstrated

5. Numbers of particular aircraft types in service are from International Institute for Strategic Studies, *The Military Balance, 1980–1981* (London: IISS, 1980), p. 10, unless otherwise cited.

6. David R. Jones, "National Air Defense Force," in David R. Jones, ed., *Soviet Armed Forces Review Annual*, vol. 2 (Gulf Breeze, Fla.: Academic International Press, 1978), p. 85.

7. *Allocation of Resources in the Soviet Union and China—1978*, Hearings before the Subcommittee on Priorities and Economy in Government of the Joint Economic Committee, 95 Cong. 2 sess. (GPO, 1978), pt. 4, p. 20.

8. J. W. R. Taylor, "Gallery of Soviet Aerospace Weapons," *Air Force*, March 1980, p. 126; and *Department of Defense Annual Report, Fiscal Year 1981* (GPO, 1980), p. 76.

9. *Department of Defense Annual Report, Fiscal Year 1979* (GPO, 1978), p. 51.

10. IISS, *The Military Balance, 1978–1979, 1979–1980*, and *1980–1981*, pp. 9, 9, and 10, respectively.

11. *United States Military Posture for FY 81* (GPO, 1980), p. 78.

the ability to engage targets flying lower than itself, and the Floggers now entering the force have upgraded radar and other improvements, giving them better low-altitude capabilities than earlier versions.[12] Still further improvements are rumored.

The Soviet air defense is expected to introduce in the 1980s a new long-range interceptor with an advanced radar[13] that permits the interceptor to track the target while in flight, look down on a low-flying vehicle, and direct its missiles against the vehicle. The new interceptor would presumably operate in conjunction with the new airborne warning and control system. An important question is whether the new fighter will be able to refuel in flight to substantially increase its range and loiter capability. No present Soviet interceptor has this capability.

The primary armaments for these aircraft are air-to-air missiles (AAMs). Some interceptors carry one pair of AAMs, others carry two. One missile in each pair uses passive infrared homing, the other uses semiactive radar homing. This means the missile looks for signals from the interceptor's AI radar that reflect off the target as it is tracked by the AI radar. The Soviet AAMs carry the designations AA-2, -3, -5, -6, -7, and -8. Of these, only the relatively old infrared homing AA-2 Atoll has been encountered in combat and its performance, even in advanced versions, has been disappointing.[14] The AA-7 and AA-8 have limited ability to engage lower flying targets and, unlike the other AAMs, were intended from the start for tactical air-to-air combat rather than strategic air defense.[15] A system currently being tested in a modified MiG-25 reputedly uses the AA-X-9 missile, which has its own small radar transmitter for use in the final stage of flight; the AI radar on the interceptor reportedly can guide missiles to four targets while tracking twenty.[16]

Surface-to-Air Missile Systems

As in the case of other components of the air defense system, the Soviet Union has deployed and maintained a large number of SAMs in a variety

12. *United States Military Posture for FY 79* (GPO, 1978), p. 38; and *United States Military Posture for FY 81*, p. 70.

13. "Soviets' Nuclear Arsenal Continues to Proliferate," *Aviation Week and Space Technology*, June 16, 1980, p. 70.

14. "World Missile Survey," *Flight International*, June 10, 1978, p. 1801.

15. *Department of Defense Authorization for Appropriations for Fiscal Year 1979*, Hearings before the Senate Armed Services Committee, 95 Cong. 2 sess. (GPO, 1979), pt. 6, p. 4413.

16. Taylor, "Gallery of Soviet Aerospace Weapons," p. 122.

of models. The SA-1 Guild, the oldest Soviet system, was introduced about 1954, and within a few years 3,200 were deployed in two concentric rings around Moscow.[17] The SA-1 may carry a nuclear warhead, reflecting the Soviet doctrine that nuclear weapons are to be used throughout the military forces. Although obsolete, it is probably being retained as a last line of defense for Moscow. The radars associated with the SA-1 system—the Gage target-acquisition and the Yo-Yo fire-control radars—work at frequencies of 3 gigahertz (a wavelength of about 10 centimeters), and the system's six antennas are reputed to be able to track twenty-four to thirty-two targets simultaneously.

The SA-2 Guideline is the best-known Soviet SAM system. It was used to shoot down Francis Gary Power's U-2 and was exported to and used in Egypt and Vietnam. Since its introduction in 1955–56, it has undergone numerous modifications, reputedly to improve its performance at altitudes of and above 1,200 feet. One version is thought to carry a nuclear warhead. It has a range of twenty-five miles and a maximum altitude of 90,000 feet, and roughly 3,000 are in service.[18] The SA-2 is now slowly being phased out. There are six models (A through F) of the Fan Song radar, which is used with the SA-2. All have two orthogonal beams that are mechanically swept across the sky, which gives the radar a track-while-scan capability; it can follow up to six targets and three interceptor missiles simultaneously. Operating frequencies have changed through the series; jammers designed to be effective against Fan Song B (3 gigahertz) would be ineffective against Fan Song E (5 gigahertz). Power, resolution, and range were increased—the range rising from 120 to 150 kilometers. Other changes have been incorporated through the series to increase the radar's capabilities against electronic countermeasures. The latest version, Fan Song F, reputedly incorporates an optical guidance system so the missile can be used despite heavy jamming.

The SA-3 Goa is a low-altitude SAM, with a range of twenty-two miles and effective altitude of between 300 and 50,000 feet. It was first deployed in 1961. Some sources credit it with a nuclear capability. It too has reportedly been modernized through its career, though details are not available. Over 4,000 are in service, and the number is increasing even

17. Missile deployment figures are from John M. Collins, *American and Soviet Military Trends Since the Cuban Missile Crisis* (Georgetown University, Center for Strategic and International Studies, 1978), p. 144, unless otherwise cited.

18. Missile performance data and technical specifications throughout are from "World Missile Directory," *Flight International,* August 2, 1980, pp. 456, 461, 472–73, unless otherwise cited.

though the system is nineteen years old. The Low Blow fire-control radar used with the SA-3, like the Fan Song series, uses mechanically scanned beams and can handle multiple targets. As the name implies, this radar reputedly performs well against high-altitude targets in the presence of clutter, as do the other two radars, Squat Eye and Squint Eye, that serve the SA-3 for target acquisition.

The SA-5 Gammon is the Soviet Union's ultrahigh-altitude SAM. It has a range of 155 miles and is effective up to about 100,000 feet, and it may have some slight antiballistic missile capability. Its introduction in 1963 into the Soviet air defense system was particularly puzzling to U.S. analysts since at that time the United States posed no high-altitude bomber threat and was not developing any after the earlier cancellation of the B-70 high-altitude supersonic bomber. The SA-5 is a very large missile—its precise homing method and whether it carries a nuclear warhead are in dispute. About 2,000 SA-5 missiles are in service and more are expected to be phased in. The SA-5 missile uses the Square Pair radar for target-missile tracking. One source reports that this radar may be frequency agile, making it more difficult to jam.[19] The Back Net radar and its associated Side Net height-finding radar, which are usually used for ground-controlled intercept guidance, perform the target-acquisition functions for this system.

The latest Soviet SAM system is the SA-10, which has been under development for about a decade and may be deployed soon.[20] The missile is reportedly canister mounted,[21] very fast (Mach 5–6), highly maneuverable (20g acceleration),[22] and designed to engage targets between 1,000 and 16,000 feet at ranges of up to thirty miles. A canister-mounted missile indicates that the SA-10 is being designed to have some mobility. A shipborne variant has been mentioned.[23] Three radars, with continuous-wave and pulse-Doppler technology, have been associated with the SA-10 and are clearly designed to handle clutter.

Besides the air defense forces inside the Soviet Union, the Warsaw Pact countries have about 1,400 interceptor aircraft of intermediate age,

19. Eustace, ed., *International Countermeasures Handbook*, p. 204.

20. *Department of Defense Appropriations, Fiscal Year 1979,* Hearings before the Senate Appropriations Committee, 95 Cong. 2 sess. (GPO, 1978), pt. 5, p. 203; and *Department of Defense Annual Report, Fiscal Year 1981,* p. 82.

21. *Hearings on Military Posture and H.R. 1872,* pt. 3, bk. 1, p. 148.

22. Collins, *American and Soviet Military Trends,* p. 152, n. 51.

23. *Hearings on Military Posture and H.R. 1872,* pt. 3, bk. 1, p. 122.

plus 700 to 1,400 SA-2 and SA-3 launchers. These are included in the USSR's air defense network.[24]

Tactical air defense systems used by field forces (mobile missile and gun systems, many of which are designed to counter low-altitude tactical aircraft) might also be available to the strategic forces in an emergency. The tactical systems have been developed to target low-flying aircraft and helicopters in battlefield situations, and the technologies represented by these tactical weapons may be more germane to the problem of cruise missile defense than those embodied in the present strategic weapon systems.

One example would be light, passive infrared homing SAMs such as the SA-7 Grail and SA-9 Gaskin. The SA-7 missile weighs about eighteen pounds. The latest version has altitude limits of 1,300 feet and a range of over two miles. The initial version, which had a top speed of Mach 1.5, could deal with targets moving more slowly than about 550 miles an hour. Its range and speed appear marginal against a cruise missile. During the 1973 Middle East war it rarely inflicted killing damage on fixed-wing aircraft; it normally damaged the jet tailpipe and tail of attack aircraft. The smaller cruise missile, however would probably be less damage tolerant, but conversely, the cruise missile's design and its small engine endow it with a smaller infrared signature than the tactical aircraft and helicopters that are the usual targets of missiles like the SA-7 and SA-9. This low signature would restrict the use of such SAMs to "tail-chasing" attack, where the SAM locks onto the cruise missile after it has passed over and presents the SAM's seeker with a direct view of the hot engine interior. This low signature could be further reduced by passive measures, such as an exhaust shroud, or by the use of active infrared jammers, which are normally fitted to helicopters and tactical aircraft. The further reduction would undoubtedly require a great increase in the sensitivity and sophistication of the SAM's infrared seeker head to achieve a reasonable kill probability against a cruise missile.

The SA-9 Gaskin weighs more than the SA-7—about eighty pounds, of which about ten pounds are warhead. It has an effective altitude of up to 15,000 feet, a range of about two miles, and speed probably near Mach 2.0.[25] This system is usually mounted in fours on the back of a light armored scout car. Although the operator normally picks up targets with

24. IISS, *The Military Balance, 1980–1981,* pp. 15–17.
25. "SA-9 Gaskin: Point-Defense for the Soviet Army," *Flight International,* August 4, 1979, p. 315.

the naked eye, there have been reports that the SA-9 is being fitted with a radar that would provide it with all-weather capability.[26] The range and speed of the SA-9 would give it some capability against a cruise missile.

The Soviet Union has antiaircraft guns ranging in caliber from 14.5 to 310 millimeters, the heavier equipment usually being of World War II or immediate postwar vintage. Two of these systems are mobile, mounted on tracked chassis. One is the ZSU 57-2, which consists of two optically aimed 57-millimeter guns. There is no provision for radar direction, which limits the system's usefulness in bad weather.

The other mobile system is the ZSU-23-4. It consists of four 23-millimeter guns linked to a Gun Dish radar (reportedly ineffective against targets flying below 200 feet),[27] which performs both target-acquisition and fire-control roles. Optical aiming equipment is also carried. This system proved very effective during the 1973 war alongside other Soviet-supplied light antiaircraft artillery and SAMs. Evasive maneuvers that were effective against tactical SAMs often brought the aircraft down within range of light artillery, where it took its toll.

These gun systems, along with the SA-4, SA-6, SA-7, SA-8, and SA-9 tactical air defense missiles, are operated by the air defense forces of the ground troops, and are under the operational command of the ground forces. The systems, particularly the SA-9, could provide some point defense capability against cruise missiles, but their use by the strategic defense forces might entail some difficulties regarding the transferability of command. Further, their removal from the ground forces would severely hinder those forces in the event that some conventional offensive action were contemplated. However, the Egyptian use of the SA-2, SA-3, SA-6, SA-7, and antiaircraft artillery in a coordinated air defense provides a precedent for mixing tactical and strategic systems.

26. Eustace, *International Countermeasures Handbook*, p. 229.
27. *International Defense Review*, no. 9 (1978), p. 1375.

Additional Data on Costs

JOHN C. BAKER

The Air-Launched Cruise Missile Program

The ALCM program is the most advanced of the six. Estimated at nearly $6 billion in 1980 dollars for procurement of 3,418 missiles (table B-1), the air-launched cruise missile is scheduled to become operational in December 1982. The currently projected purchase is based on the eventual deployment of 20 ALCMs on each of the 151 B-52G bombers, with additional missiles for spares and testing.[1] Until 1977 the Air Force had planned to procure only about 2,300 ALCMs because the B-1 penetrating bomber canceled by President Carter was to be the central element in the strategic bomber force.[2]

From February 1978 through March 1980 two firms, the Boeing Aerospace Company and the General Dynamics Convair Division, were in competition to become the prime contractor for the ALCM. Following a prototype fly-off, Boeing was selected in March 1980.[3] Important considerations in awarding the contract to Boeing included the better performance of its prototype in the flight tests and its proposed manufacturing methods, which promised greater economies in production.[4] The

1. *Hearings on Military Posture and H.R. 6495 [H.R. 6974]: Department of Defense Authorization for Appropriations for Fiscal Year 1981,* Hearings before the House Armed Services Committee, 96 Cong. 2 sess. (Government Printing Office, 1980), pt. 4, bk. 2, pp. 1814–26.

2. *Department of Defense Appropriations for 1978,* Hearings before a subcommittee of the House Appropriations Committee, 95 Cong. 1 sess. (GPO, 1977), pt. 2, pp. 287, 318–19.

3. David R. Griffiths, "Software Key to ALCM Choice," *Aviation Week and Space Technology,* March 31, 1980, pp. 18–22.

4. "Shift in Fabrication Techniques Was Factor in ALCM Win, Boeing Says," *Aerospace Daily,* March 27, 1980, p. 147.

difference in the cost estimates of the two contractors, however, was not a significant factor in determining the verdict.

Current procurement plans would build to a maximum of 480 missiles in the 1981 budget, and then decrease to 440 a year through the end of the program. At this rate, the final delivery will not be made until about 1989. The relatively large number of ALCMs to be procured is expected to yield more economies of scale, and hence lower unit costs, than can be achieved for sea-launched and ground-launched cruise missiles (SLCMs and GLCMs), which are to be bought in smaller numbers. The average unit flyaway cost of the ALCM is estimated at nearly $800,000 per missile in fiscal 1981 dollars. This figure does not include the development and production cost of its W-80 nuclear warhead. Such cost estimates are seldom publicly available for a nuclear weapon system, but they are probably substantial.

The Defense Department has designated the 151 operational B-52Gs (about 40 percent of the FB-111 and B-52 strategic bomber force) as ALCM carriers. A variety of modifications are required to convert such aircraft into carriers. Totaling some $2 billion in 1980 dollars, the primary modifications and their approximate costs are: (1) integration of an internal missile launcher and external pylons for carrying the ALCMs, $1 billion; (2) externally observable modifications to comply with SALT II verification guidelines, $100 million; and (3) improvements to the aircraft's avionics system generally related to the cruise missile system, $900 million.[5] These expenses average $12 million per aircraft.

A decision must be made on what should be the next type of ALCM launcher acquired, and when. The basic choice is whether a new cruise missile aircraft should be deployed during the mid-to-late 1980s or deferred until the next decade. During the Carter administration defense officials wanted to delay the acquisition of a new, more expensive carrier until the 1990s because of the projected high level of modernization expenditures for other elements of the strategic forces in the mid-1980s,[6] and in the meantime, to convert to ALCM carriers the 90 active duty B-52H bombers whose capability to penetrate Soviet defenses will decrease in the late 1980s. Such a course would add more than 1,800

5. *Hearings on Military Posture and H.R. 6495*, pt. 1, p. 897.
6. Speech by Under Secretary of Defense for Research and Engineering William J. Perry at the American Defense Preparedness Association, Arlington, Va., December 10, 1980, pp. 5–6.

ALCMs to present production levels, costing over $2 billion in 1980 dollars, with another $800 million in associated aircraft modifications.[7]

The alternative would be to initiate an expensive acquisition program aimed at deploying a dedicated cruise missile carrier aircraft starting about 1987. At issue is what type of aircraft this should be. For about 100 aircraft, the cost of such a program has been estimated at between $175 million and $200 million per aircraft in 1980 dollars, depending on the type selected.[8] To date, however, defense officials have not stated that a new carrier aircraft is necessary to augment the B-52s. Instead, they view it as a possible hedge against unexpected technical shortcomings in the B-52 or as a possible supplement to the B-52s if national policy dictates the need for substantial increases in U.S. strategic force capability.[9] However, depending on the Reagan administration's choice of a new multirole penetrating bomber for the 1980s, interest in deploying a dedicated ALCM carrier could probably diminish further.

The Sea-Launched Cruise Missile Program

The SLCM has been the most changeable and diverse of the cruise missile programs and priorities since its initiation in 1972. This program seeks to develop three distinct variants of the Tomahawk SLCM, for which the General Dynamics Convair Division is the prime contractor. The SLCM program also provides a technical basis for outgrowths such as the GLCM and MRASM systems.[10]

7. Author's estimate of ALCM cost based on table 4-1, and B-52H modification cost from congressional testimony. *Hearings on Military Posture and H.R. 6495,* pt. 1, p. 897.

8. Author's calculations based on *Department of Defense Authorization for Appropriations for Fiscal Year 1981,* Hearings before the Senate Armed Services Committee, 96 Cong. 2 sess. (GPO, 1980), pt. 2, pp. 1028–29; and *Department of Defense Appropriations for Fiscal Year 1981,* Hearings before the Senate Appropriations Committee, 96 Cong. 2 sess. (GPO, 1980), pt. 1, p. 597.

9. *Department of Defense Appropriations for 1981,* Hearings before a subcommittee of the House Appropriations Committee, 96 Cong. 2 sess. (GPO, 1980), pt. 3, pp. 1038–39.

10. "Perry Memo on Medium Range Air-to-Surface Missile," *Aerospace Daily,* April 4, 1980, p. 197; and *Department of Defense Appropriations for 1980,* Hearings before a subcommittee of the House Appropriations Committee, 96 Cong. 1 sess. (GPO, 1979), pt. 3, p. 711.

All three variants of the SLCM are designed to be fired from a submarine torpedo tube and certain types of surface ship missile launchers. Recent U.S. Navy plans have been to deploy the Tomahawk on most nuclear-powered attack submarines, reactivated battleships, modern cruisers, and DD-963-class destroyers.[11] While the number procured reportedly will increase substantially, the SLCM program totaling nearly $3 billion (projected in the 1981 five-year defense plan) was limited to the purchase of 439 missiles.[12] This figure may include procurement of the antiship and the conventionally armed land-attack variants.

The nuclear-armed Tomahawk land-attack missile (TLAM-N) was the highest priority when the SLCM program began.[13] Navy officials declared that separate development of a tactical antiship variant of the Tomahawk would be too expensive to justify funding on its own merits.[14] This highlights the fact that the commonality of the cruise missile variants enables defense planners to consider different types of weapon systems that would be too expensive if developed separately. Indeed, the commonality of the antiship and land-attack versions has been increased by the Navy's decision to substitute the more efficient (but more expensive) turbofan engine for the antiship missile's previously planned turbojet engine,[15] thereby increasing both the range and the cost of the Tomahawk antiship missile (TASM). In contrast to its original priority, the future of the TLAM-N is uncertain and its operational deployment date relatively tentative. The Navy appears to be giving the highest priority to the deployment in 1982 of a conventionally armed land-attack cruise missile (TLAM-C), a much more recently conceived system.[16]

Overall SLCM procurement figures have been in a state of flux. At one

11. *Hearings on Military Posture and H.R. 6495,* pt. 4, bk. 2, pp. 1497–98.

12. Ibid., pp. 1496–99.

13. *Department of Defense Appropriations for Fiscal Year 1973,* Hearings before a subcommittee of the Senate Appropriations Committee, 92 Cong. 2 sess. (GPO, 1972), pt. 5, pp. 283–86.

14. *Fiscal Year 1975 Authorization for Military Procurement, Research and Development, and Active Duty, Selected Reserve and Civilian Personnel Strengths,* Hearings before the Senate Armed Services Committee, 93 Cong. 2 sess. (GPO, 1974), pt. 7, pp. 3676–77.

15. *Hearings on Military Posture and H.R. 5068 [H.R. 5970]: Department of Defense Authorization for Appropriations for Fiscal Year 1978,* Hearings before the House Armed Services Committee, 95 Cong. 1 sess. (GPO, 1977), pt. 3, bk. 2, p. 1110.

16. Department of Defense, "Selected Acquisition Reports as of December 31, 1980" (1981), p. 4; and Department of Defense, "Highlights of Budget Revisions for Fiscal Years 1981 and 1982" (March 1981), p. 62.

time the Navy planned a baseline acquisition of nearly 1,200 SLCMs, equally divided between the TASM and the TLAM-N.[17] As of 1981 the purchase of 439 SLCMs was based on the number contained in President Carter's 1981 five-year defense plan.[18] Each annual update in the five-year defense plan will expand the overall SLCM procurement objective. This situation makes cost comparisons between the SLCM and other systems difficult to estimate and makes the SLCM's relative cost appear greater now than it is likely to be in the long run. As table 4-1 illustrates, the projected average unit cost of $1.4 million (constant dollars) is nearly 75 percent higher than that of its air-launched counterpart despite their similarities. For the most part, the disparity results from their different positions on the learning curve of production economies as a result of the much greater projected production of ALCMs (see figure 4-1).

As in the case of the ALCM, the availability of launch platforms will also be an important influence in determining the size of SLCM production during the 1980s. Initially SLCM deployment is to be limited to submarine torpedo-tube launchers and four-cell armored box launchers for surface ships. The Navy currently plans to install two armored box launchers on each of its DD-963 *Spruance*-class destroyers and on most of its cruisers for about $10 million per ship. By comparison, submarines offer one of the least expensive means for deploying Tomahawk SLCMs since direct costs are primarily limited to changes in the submarine's fire-control system (see table B-7). Current Navy procurement planning calls for eight Tomahawks per modern attack submarine.[19]

An alternate submarine launcher considered recently is the Polaris ballistic missile submarine. Because of their age, limited capacity for modernization, and the tacit extension of SALT I restrictions, the ten oldest SSBNs are scheduled to be phased out as ballistic missile launchers in fiscal 1981.[20] These could be converted into cruise missile platforms armed with four to seven SLCMs in each tube.[21] While the number of cruise missiles each platform could deliver would be substantial, conversion of these submarines with their short remaining service life would be

17. John Rhea, "Tomahawk and ALCM: Cruise Missile Decision Pending," *Sea Power*, December 1976, p. 26.
18. *Hearings on Military Posture and H.R. 6495*, pt. 4, bk. 2, pp. 1496–99.
19. Ibid., pt. 2, p. 188. See also *Department of Defense Authorization Act, 1981*, H. Rept. 916, 96 Cong. 2 sess. (GPO, 1980), p. 50.
20. *Department of Defense Annual Report, Fiscal Year 1981*, p. 131.
21. "Submarine Cruise Missile Plan Mulled," *Aviation Week and Space Technology*, June 16, 1980, p. 119.

an expensive means of deployment,[22] and this option seems to have been dropped for the time being.

Over the longer term, the development of new types of missile launchers offers the potential for significantly expanding the number of SLCMs deployed at sea. Various launcher systems are now planned for both submarines and surface ships that could supplement or supplant existing launchers. One emplaces vertical launch tubes in the forward hull section of nuclear-powered attack submarines. Twelve vertical missile launchers will be added to the SSN-688 submarine without degrading its performance or reducing its supply of torpedoes.[23] An even more significant development for the long term is the installation of vertical launching systems (VLS) on surface ships. A major surface ship could mount up to two large, blocklike VLS magazines, each composed of sixty-one individual missile canisters. These modular launching systems significantly increase the number of missiles available per ship and reduce missile reaction time and maintenance requirements.[24] While the cost of procuring and installing is high at possibly $50 million per magazine, the large number of missiles deployed makes it competitive with other launchers (see table B-7). The vertical launching system was originally designed to accommodate other naval missiles for air defense and antisubmarine warfare, although it is now being adapted to launch Tomahawk as well. The Navy now seeks to install VLS magazines on CG-47 cruisers, DD-963 destroyers, and the future DDGX destroyer.[25] Since the principal missions of these ships are fleet air defense and antisubmarine warfare, it can be assumed that their VLS magazines will carry at most only a small proportion of cruise missiles. The Navy is also considering deploying large numbers of SLCMs, possibly in VLS magazines, on the two battleships it plans to return to active service.[26]

Based on the number of cruise missile launchers the Navy plans to

22. Defense Department officials have testified that it would cost about $2 billion to convert the eight remaining Polaris SSBNs and extend their service lives by about six years. *Department of Defense Authorization for Appropriations for Fiscal Year 1981*, Hearings, pt. 2, p. 635.

23. "Statement of Vice Admiral John G. Williams, Jr., USN, Deputy Chief of Naval Operations for Submarine Warfare, before the Subcommittee on Seapower of the House Armed Services Committee on the FY 82 Budget Request for Strategic and Tactical Submarine Forces" (Department of Defense, March 5, 1981).

24. *Hearings on Military Posture and H.R. 6495*, pt. 4, bk. 2, pp. 1439–41.

25. Ibid.

26. "Cruise Missiles Planned for Battleships," *Aviation Week and Space Technology*, March 30, 1981, pp. 24–25.

modify or install during the 1980s, it can be estimated that at least 1,700 Tomahawk SLCMs will be deployed in the near future.[27] This higher production level (than the Navy's earlier projected level of 1,200[28]) can be expected to reduce the missile's average unit flyaway cost to nearly $1 million per missile in 1981 dollars, or to about 70 percent of its currently estimated unit cost. The political and military inhibitions against large deployments of the TLAM-N make it seem likely that the Tomahawk missile force will be predominantly—if not entirely—conventional.

The Ground-Launched Cruise Missile

The GLCM is a long-range nuclear-armed weapon scheduled for deployment in Western Europe as part of the program approved in December 1979 by the NATO ministers. The missiles will be mounted on large truck launching platforms, known as transporter-erector-launchers (TELs), and will be stationed on NATO air bases in peacetime under the command of the U.S. Air Force. Two of the five NATO countries scheduled to receive GLCMs have yet to fully approve deployment on their own air bases.[29] Consequently, despite the Defense Department's operational schedule for the first deployment of GLCMs by December 1983,[30] uncertainties about the program's future still exist.

27. The author's estimate of 1,700 Tomahawk missiles procured over the decade is derived from the following assumptions: (a) 8 SLCMs per modern attack submarine without vertical launchers (assumed to be 60 submarines); (b) 12 SLCMs per modern attack submarine with vertical launchers (assumed to be 30 submarines); (c) 61 SLCMs, or 2 complete VLS magazines, per reactivated battleship (2 ships); (d) 8 SLCMs per modern cruiser (18 ships); and (e) an average of 30 SLCMs, or one-half of one VLS magazine, on each CG-47 *Ticonderoga*-class cruiser and each new DDGX-class destroyer (an assumed total of 23 ships during the 1980s), in addition to 15 SLCMs, or one-quarter of the one VLS magazine scheduled to be eventually retrofitted on the DD-963-class destroyers (a total of 31 ships). This resulted in a total requirement of over 2,200 cruise missiles. The final SLCM production figure of 1,700 was derived by excluding about one-third of the launch platforms to account for ships and submarines in overhaul, and by adding 10 percent to the remaining number of missile spaces for spare missiles and flight tests. Although their prospects are uncertain, new types of cruise missile launch platforms such as converted freighters are included in these calculations.

28. *Department of Defense Appropriations for 1980,* Hearings, pt. 2, p. 320.

29. Plans call for 48 GLCMs to be deployed in Belgium and 48 in the Netherlands and both countries have expressed continuing reservations on this issue. See *Baltimore Sun,* June 4, 1980.

30. *Hearings on Military Posture and H.R. 6495,* pt. 4, bk. 2, p. 2319.

The GLCM originated as a separately funded program in 1977, when the Joint Cruise Missile Project Office (JCMPO) was directed to proceed with development of a ground-launched cruise missile based on the General Dynamics SLCM.[31] Initial funding began in fiscal 1978. Usually excluded from the program figures is additional funding for GLCM-associated military construction, which is estimated at about $265 million, to be paid through the NATO infrastructure.[32] A maximum production rate of ten missiles a month is scheduled to be achieved by fiscal 1983.

The GLCM program provides a good example of outgrowth. It was able to draw on the technical experience and sunk costs of the earlier programs, reducing its own development costs to about $200 million (less than 25 percent of that expended by either the ALCM or the SLCM program). This advantage, however, is not as great as it seems because the GLCM requires a dedicated launch system and a large portion of the procurement funds will be spent on supporting equipment instead of on the missile itself. As a result, the GLCM's average unit flyaway cost is estimated at nearly $2 million in fiscal 1981 dollars, substantially more than for either the ALCM or the SLCM. More than half of this unit cost can be attributed to support equipment, which is so high because of the more demanding levels of support and security forces required by a ground-mobile nuclear weapon system and the lack of an existing launcher system to which the GLCM could be adapted. A GLCM unit will contain not only four TELs (each carrying four GLCMs), but also a launch control van and several other vehicles for security and support.[33]

The Medium-Range Air-to-Surface Missile

The MRASM is the most recent of development programs. About the same time that Boeing was awarded the ALCM production contract, the JCMPO was directed to develop a variant of the Tomahawk for the MRASM role.[34] Like the GLCM, this missile draws upon the available

31. "Clements Memo on Cruise Missiles," *Aerospace Daily*, January 24, 1977, pp. 115–16.

32. *Military Construction Appropriations for 1981*, Hearings before a subcommittee of the House Appropriations Committee, 96 Cong. 2 sess. (GPO, 1980), pt. 3, pp. 194, 196.

33. *Department of Defense Authorization for Appropriations for Fiscal Year 1979*, Hearings before the Senate Armed Services Committee, 95 Cong. 2 sess. (GPO, 1978), pt. 5, p. 3885.

34. "Perry Memo on Medium Range, Air-to-Surface Missile," p. 197.

technology offered by the General Dynamics SLCM program, thereby constraining its estimated development costs to about $200 million.[35] The MRASM is being developed as the primary U.S. candidate to fulfill the need for an accurate, nonnuclear standoff cruise missile (although a variant may be developed for Navy aircraft).[36] The MRASM could be carried by a variety of Air Force and Navy aircraft. The primary launcher for the Air Force will be the B-52D bomber, which is expected to carry twelve MRASMs; the Air Force's F-16 tactical aircraft is likely to be armed with fewer than half that number.[37]

The initial MRASM variant, in an attempt at early deployment in fiscal 1983, will draw heavily on the existing Tomahawk SLCM technology.[38] This is certain to make it expensive for a tactical missile, thereby limiting its production. A later, less expensive variant of the MRASM land-attack weapon is a more likely candidate for large-scale production, which could bring its unit cost closer to $500,000.[39] Scheduled to become operational in fiscal 1984, it will use lower cost guidance and propulsion subsystems.

Lower cost is one of the most salient issues in determining the desired level of investment in conventional cruise missiles. To some degree, this arises from the nature of conventional warfare itself, which places a higher premium on numbers of weapons because nonnuclear targets are usually more numerous or require multiple strikes to be neutralized since the damage inflicted by conventional warheads is less.

Since it grows out of other cruise missile programs, the MRASM's development and procurement costs are reduced. Substitution or deletion of certain expensive components found in the longer range nuclear-armed cruise missiles also helps. The shorter range required for the MRASM allows the use of a less efficient, lower cost turbojet engine, and the more expensive inertial guidance system critical to a longer range flight can be

35. David R. Griffiths, "Proposal Set on Air-to-Surface Missile," *Aviation Week and Space Technology*, December 29, 1980, pp. 23, 25.

36. *Department of Defense Appropriations for 1981*, Hearings, pt. 3, pp. 1001, 1029–30; Mark Hewish, "Tactical-Missile Survey, Part 1: Ground Targets," *International Defense Review*, no. 6 (1980), pp. 861–62; and "Navy Withdraws from Joint Missile Effort," *Aviation Week and Space Technology*, February 9, 1981, pp. 32–33.

37. Griffiths, "Proposal Set on Air-to-Surface Missile," p. 23; and "Carrier Launch Tests Planned for Medium Range Air-to-Surface Missile," *Aerospace Daily*, September 19, 1980, p. 105.

38. "Perry Memo on Medium Range Air-to-Surface Missile," p. 197.

39. *Department of Defense Appropriations for 1981*, Hearings, pt. 3, pp. 1001, 1030.

replaced with less costly variants.[40] The MRASM can also avoid the high costs associated with nuclear weapons (warhead development and production, hardening of components against nuclear effects, and higher support and security costs). All these factors combined may mean that the MRASM's average unit flyaway cost could be less than $500,000 per missile in 1981 constant dollars—between one-half and two-thirds the unit cost of its SLCM and ALCM counterparts.[41]

Cruise Missile Support Systems

At least three important support systems are applicable to cruise missiles. One is the digital mapping essential to the missile guidance system. This is the responsibility of the Defense Mapping Agency, which generates both the terrain contour matching (TERCOM) data for guidance updates and the vertical obstruction data necessary for the cruise missile's low-altitude flight.[42] About $30 million a year for the near future is required for this process.[43]

A second element is the theater mission planning system, which constructs preplanned flight profiles.[44] When fully operational, this system will include about half a dozen computer analysis centers located in major American military commands around the world.[45]

Although specific costs related to the theater mission planning facilities are not available, they are likely to be modest compared to the life-cycle costs of the weapons themselves. On the other hand, if such facilities are established at lower command levels to enhance their responsiveness for retargeting against mobile and nonnuclear targets, their costs could be more significant.

40. Ibid., pp. 24–25. As an air-launched missile, the MRASM also avoids the costs related to the booster motor and special launch container necessary for the sea- and ground-launched cruise missiles.
41. *Department of Defense Appropriations for 1982*, Hearings before a subcommittee of the House Appropriations Committee, 97 Cong. 1 sess. (GPO, 1981), pt. 1, p. 1024.
42. See "DMA—The Cruise Missile's Silent Partner," *Air Force*, April 1980, pp. 60–62.
43. *Department of Defense Appropriations for 1981*, Hearings, pt. 3, pp. 695–96, 701.
44. *Department of Defense Appropriations for 1980*, Hearings, pt. 3, pp. 539, 558–59.
45. *Aviation Week and Space Technology*, March 30, 1981, p. 25.

The third support system is more specifically limited to the antishipping variants of the cruise missile: over-the-horizon targeting, a system that correlates information from satellites, undersea acoustic sensors, and patrol aircraft for targeting enemy warships at long ranges.[46] About $50 million has been spent so far on acquisition of this system and more than twice that amount is projected through 1985.[47] Installation of the special terminals required to integrate a naval ship into this general system is estimated to cost less than $1 million per ship or submarine.[48] This project may be supplanted by a more comprehensive naval ocean surveillance system that could not be attributed solely to supporting cruise missile targeting.

Tables

Eight tables provide additional data on cruise missiles and weapon delivery systems. Sources on which they are based follow them. Abbreviations used in the tables are spelled out in the list preceding page 1.

46. *Hearings on Military Posture and H.R. 6495*, pt. 1, bk. 4, pp. 228–29.

47. *Department of Defense Authorization for Appropriations for Fiscal Year 1979*, Hearings, pt. 8, pp. 6175, 6232; and *Fiscal Year 1981 Arms Control Impact Statements*, Joint Committee Print, House Foreign Affairs and Senate Foreign Relations Committees, 96 Cong. 2 sess. (GPO, 1980), p. 369.

48. *Hearings on Military Posture and H.R. 10929: Department of Defense Authorization for Appropriations for Fiscal Year 1979*, Hearings before the House Armed Services Committee, 95 Cong. 2 sess. (GPO, 1978), pt. 3, bk. 2, pp. 1266–69.

Table B-1. U.S. Cruise Missiles Planned, 1981

Type	Description	Initial operational capability	Warhead	Operational range (kilometers)	System	Launch platform	Projected production level
Air-launched cruise missile (ALCM)	Long-range nuclear-armed land-attack missile	December 1982	Nuclear	2,500	Inertial guidance aided by TERCOM	Strategic B-52G[a] bombers	3,418
Sea-launched cruise missile (TASM)	Medium-range conventionally armed antiship missile	June 1982 (submarines); June 1983 (surface ships)	1,000 pounds conventional	450	Active radar seeker	Submarines and surface ships	n.a.
Sea-launched cruise missile (TLAM-C)	Long-range conventionally armed land-attack missile	January 1982 (submarines); June 1983 (surface ships)	1,000 pounds conventional	800	Inertial guidance aided by DSMAC	Submarines and surface ships	n.a.[b]
Sea-launched cruise missile (TLAM-N)	Long-range nuclear-armed land-attack missile	Undetermined[c]	Nuclear	2,500	Inertial guidance/ TERCOM	Submarines and surface ships	n.a.

Ground-launched cruise missile (GLCM)	Long-range nuclear-armed land-attack missile	December 1983	Nuclear	2,500	Inertial guidance/ TERCOM	Ground-mobile transporter-erector-launcher	560
Medium-range air-to-surface missile (MRASM)[d]	Medium-range conventionally armed missile variants						Several thousand
AGM-109C (land attack)		Fiscal year 1983	650 pounds conventional	480	Inertial guidance/ TERCOM/DSMAC		
AGM-109H (Air Force, land attack)		Fiscal years 1984–85	1,200 pounds antiairfield submunitions	400	Lower cost guidance system/ TERCOM/DSMAC	B-52D bomber; F-16 fighter	

n.a. Not available.

a. Plans call for the conversion of the B-52G bombers to serve as cruise missile carriers. Other possible launch platforms for the ALCM during the 1980s include the B-52H and a dedicated cruise missile carrier aircraft based on a variant of the earlier B-1 bomber.

b. The current Tomahawk SLCM program is projected on the basis of missile production figures and costs through the latest five-year defense plan. As the five-year defense plan is updated each year, the cost and force level projections will change. In the defense request for fiscal 1981 the Tomahawk program cost was based on projected funding for 574 SLCMs during fiscal years 1982–86. The Reagan amendment of March 1981 added 40 SLCMs to the 1982 request.

c. As of this writing, neither a specific initial operational capability nor firm production figures have been reported for the nuclear-armed Tomahawk SLCM. The first TLAM-N cruise missile could become available in 1984 if it is decided to start production.

d. The initial MRASM variant (AGM-109C) will rely on the existing cruise missile guidance system although it will have a lower cost turbojet engine instead of the turbofan engine of the other cruise missiles. Later land-attack MRASMs will seek to use a less expensive inertial guidance system such as the ring laser gyro system while retaining the TERCOM and DSMAC terminal guidance components. Eventually an MRASM might also be developed for the Navy to use in attacking targets at sea as well as on land. It could incorporate an imaging infrared seeker guidance set and data link for the capability to attack targets at sea.

Table B-2. *Cruise Missile Life-Cycle Costs*

Costs in millions of 1981 constant dollars

Description	Air-launched cruise missile	Ground-launched cruise missile	Sea-launched cruise missile
Force levels			
Total planned missile procurement	3,418	560	439[a]
Total planned operational missiles[b]	3,020	464	384[c]
Total force costs			
Acquisition[d]	4,510	1,745	2,126
Annual operating and support[e]	365	150	40
Fifteen-year life cycle[f]	9,950	3,950	2,700
Cost per operational weapon			
Acquisition	1.5	3.8	5.5
Annual operating and support	0.12	0.32	0.1
Fifteen-year life cycle[g]	3.3	8.6	7.0

a. Force level projections for the SLCM program are based on the Department of Defense five-year defense plan, which is updated each new fiscal year. The SLCM procurement objective for the five-year defense plan submitted in the 1982 budget request was 574.

b. The actual number of weapons planned for deployment. These figures exclude the additional missiles that are purchased as spares and for testing, which are included in the line above.

c. Author's estimate based on the assumption that the 33 attack submarines and 15 DD-963 destroyers programmed to receive SLCMs in the 1981 five-year defense plan will account for an average of eight operational missiles each.

d. Includes research and development, procurement, initial spares, and military construction costs for the cruise missile programs. Acquisition costs related to the cruise missile's launch platform are included in the GLCM and SLCM programs, but not in the ALCM program. Costs directly relevant to converting the B-52G bombers into ALCM launch platforms are estimated by the author to be about $700 million, although additional funds are required for the general modernization of the B-52 force. The GLCM program has an additional $150 million (in constant dollars) to account for separate funding for GLCM support facilities through the NATO infrastructure.

e. These figures include annual operating and support costs for the cruise missiles only, except in the case of the GLCM, where they are for both the missile and its associated launch. Given its basic similarity to the Tomahawk SLCM, the annual operating costs for the missile only should be comparable to those shown for the SLCM.

f. Life-cycle costs as used here mean the sum of the cruise missile program's projected acquisition cost and fifteen years of its operating and support costs at a fully deployed level.

g. The life-cycle costs are prorated to the number of deployed or operational cruise missiles. The figures in this line cannot be strictly compared because of the different cost elements included in each program as described in notes d and e. More readily comparable life-cycle cost figures for these systems are shown in tables B-5 and B-6.

Table B-3. *Nuclear Weapon System Characteristics*

Launch platform	Weapons per launch platform	Weapon	War-heads per weapon	Warhead yield[a] (kilo-tons)	Weapon accuracy[b] (nautical miles)
Airborne					
B-52G/cruise missile carrier[c]	20	ALCM	1	200	0.015
Wide-bodied cruise missile carrier aircraft	60[d]	ALCM	1	200	0.015
B-1 bomber/strategic ALCM launcher	30	ALCM	1	200	0.015
B-1 penetrating bomber	16[e]	Nuclear gravity bomb/SRAM	1	1,100/ 200	0.15/ n.a.
F-111 fighter-bomber	2	Nuclear gravity bomb		n.a.	n.a.
A-6E fighter-bomber	2	Nuclear gravity bomb	1	n.a.	n.a.
F-16 fighter	1	Nuclear gravity bomb	1	n.a.	n.a.
Ground-based					
MX/multiple basing system	1	ICBM	10	335	0.05
Cruise missile/transporter-erector-launcher	4	GLCM	1	n.a.	0.015
Pershing ballistic missile launcher	2–3[f]	Pershing II	1	n.a.	n.a.
Sea-based					
Nuclear attack submarine	Variable	TLAM-N	1	200	0.015
Torpedo-tube launched[g]	6–8				
Hull launchers	8–12				
Surface ship	Variable	TLAM-N	1	200	0.015
Armored box launchers[h]	8				
Vertical launching system[i]	61–122				
Converted Polaris cruise missile launcher submarine[j]	64–112	TLAM-N	1	200	0.015
Poseidon ballistic missile submarine	16	Trident I SLBM	8	100	0.20
Trident ballistic missile submarine	24	Trident I SLBM	8	100	0.20

n.a. Not available.

a. For the most part, yields of nuclear warheads for theater nuclear weapons are less publicly available. Also, selectable yield warheads are frequently attributed to such weapons. Calculations in table 4-4 are not dependent on this information.

b. Similar to warhead yields, such information is not readily available for theater nuclear systems. Calculations in table 4-4 did not require this information.

c. In chapter 4, all cost calculations on the B-52G/cruise missile carrier assume a full load of 20 ALCMs even though these bombers are planned to carry internal weapons such as gravity bombs until the mid-1980s, when an internal cruise missile carriage will be installed.

Notes continued on next page

Notes to table B-3, continued

d. While a Boeing 747 type of civilian transport is credited with the capacity to carry up to 72 of the present ALCMs, a more conservative estimate of 60 ALCMs per aircraft is used here.

e. According to Defense Department reports, the normal weapon load of a B-1 penetrating bomber was calculated at 16 weapons (8 SRAMs and 8 gravity bombs) despite its total capacity to carry 24 weapons internally.

f. The range of numbers includes the author's assumption (based on historical precedent) that the Pershing II launchers could be eventually deployed with one or two reload missiles per launcher.

g. Congressional testimony has suggested that an average of either 6 or 8 SLCMs will be carried aboard nuclear attack submarines for launch from torpedo tubes, although a loading of 8 SLCMs per submarine appears to be the most commonly used figure.

h. Surface ships are planned to receive 2 armored box launchers, each capable of launching 4 SLCMs.

i. The vertical launching system magazines scheduled for installation on certain cruisers and destroyers are reported to be composed of 61 separate weapon launchers. Some ships may receive 2 VLS magazines for a total of 122 launchers. On existing warships, most of these launchers are likely to be filled with air defense and antisubmarine warfare weapons.

j. These submarines reportedly could carry 4 to 7 SLCMs in each of their 16 launch tubes, or a total of 64–112 SLCMs per submarine.

Table B-4. *Nonnuclear Weapon System Characteristics*

Launch platform	Weapon	Weapons per launch platform	Payload per weapon[a] (pounds)
Airborne			
B-52D bomber	MRASM	12	1,200
F-16 fighter[b]	MRASM	2–4	1,200
A-6E fighter-bomber[c]	MRASM	2–4	650
A-6E fighter-bomber	Walleye II gravity bombs	2	2,000
F-111E fighter-bomber[d]	Antiairfield sub-munitions	4[e]	n.a.
Ground-based[f]			
Ground-launched conventional cruise missile launcher	Nonnuclear GLCM (hypothetical)	4	1,000
Sea-based			
Attack submarine	TASM/TLAM-C	. . .	1,000/1,000
Torpedo-tube launched[g]		6–8	
Hull launchers		12	
Converted Polaris SSBN[h]	TASM/TLAM-C	64–112	1,000/1,000
Surface ship	TASM/TLAM-C	. . .	1,000/1,000
Armored box launchers[i]		8	
Vertical launching system[j]		61–122	

n.a. Not available.

a. Because of variations in warhead design and material composition, target destruction is not simply a function of the weapon's payload, although it can provide a rough measure of weapon capability.

b. The range in the number of MRASMs carried by an F-16 fighter reflects the fact that, because of the substantial penalties incurred in the aircraft's range and maneuverability, it is unlikely to carry as many such weapons as it can hold.

c. Designed for carrier-based aircraft, the Navy versions of the MRASM are planned to be smaller in size and payload than the Air Force's MRASM.

d. Calculations of the F-111E fighter-bomber's capacity to carry advanced antiaircraft submunitions are not publicly available at this time, although reports indicate that it can carry four dispensers for submunitions and mines of the JP-233 airfield attack weapons.

e. Submunition dispensers.

f. This is a hypothetical system for comparison purposes. While based on the currently planned nuclear-armed GLCM system, a nonnuclear variant would probably require fewer of the expensive items associated with deploying and securing nuclear weapon forces.

g. Although U.S. submarines have the capacity to carry a larger number of SLCMs for launch through their torpedo tubes, the Navy apparently plans to purchase SLCMs at the rate of 8 operational missiles per submarine.

h. It has been reported that 4 to 7 SLCMs could be carried in each of the 16 launchers aboard the older Polaris ballistic missile submarines if these submarines were converted to cruise missile launchers.

i. Current plans are for 2 armored box launchers (each capable of launching 4 SLCMs) on selected cruisers and destroyers.

j. Each vertical launching system magazine will be composed of 61 missile launchers, and will probably carry a mix of various air defense, antisurface, and antisubmarine warfare weapons. Plans call for some ships, such as the CG-47-class cruisers, to receive 2 VLS magazines each. Given the mission priorities of the warships designated to receive VLS magazines, it seems likely that only a small proportion of their VLS launchers will carry Tomahawk SLCMs.

Table B-5. *Nuclear Weapon System Life-Cycle Costs*

Costs in millions of 1981 constant dollars

Weapon system	Weapon	Total force acquisition costs	Total force annual operating and support costs	Total number of launchers/ operational warheads[a]	Cost per warhead		
					Acquisition	Fifteen-year operating and support	Fifteen-year life cycle[a]
Air-launched							
B-52G/cruise missile carrier	ALCM	7,700.0	1,100.0	151/3,020	2.5	5.5	8.0
Wide-bodied aircraft/ cruise missile carrier	ALCM	21,900.0	1,200.0	100/6,000	3.6	3.0	6.6
B-1 strategic ALCM launcher	ALCM	16,700.0	750.0	90/2,700	6.2	4.2	10.4
B-1 penetrating bomber[b]	Nuclear gravity bomb/SRAM	13,200.0	540.0	90/1,440	9.2	5.6	14.8
F-111 fighter-bomber	Nuclear gravity bomb	11,100.0	535.0	n.a.[c]/2 per aircraft	13.1	13.9	27.0
F-16 fighter	Nuclear gravity bomb	13,940.0	1,300.0	n.a.[d]/1 per aircraft	10.0	15.0	25.0
Ground-launched							
MX/multiple basing system[e]	ICBM	34,100.0	460.0	200/2,000	17.0	3.4	20.4
Cruise missile/trans-porter-erector-launcher	GLCM	1,745.0	150.0	116/464	3.8	4.8	8.6
Pershing ballistic missile launcher	Pershing II	1,440.0	175.0	108/216–324	4.4–6.7	8.1–12.2	12.5–18.9

Sea-launched

Nuclear attack submarine						
Torpedo-tube launched	TLAM-N	n.a.	...	90	4.9[g]	2.2
Hull launcher		...	...	n.a.	6.9–7.9[g]	3.0
Surface ship	TLAM-N	n.a.[f]	...	...	...	...
Armored box launchers		...	...	n.a.	7.3	3.8
Vertical launching system		...	...	n.a.	5.6	3.0
Converted Polaris cruise missile launcher submarine	TLAM-N	2,200	400.0	128/512–896[h]	2.4–4.3	6.7–11.7
Poseidon ballistic missile submarine	Trident I SLBM	3,500	580.0	192/1,536	2.3	5.7
Trident ballistic missile submarine	Trident I SLBM	27,200.0	680.0	336/2,688	10.0	3.8

7.2
9.9–10.9
11.1
8.6
9.1–16.0
8.0
13.8

n.a. Not available.

a. Costs are prorated on the basis of the total number of operational launchers and weapons, where this is applicable. An additional 10 to 15 percent of the weapon force is usually procured to serve as spares and for testing purposes. These are included in the total force acquisition.

b. These figures are based on recent proposals to restart the B-1 bomber program with the aim of deploying 100 penetrating bombers. Program costs before fiscal 1981 are not counted.

c. While the F-111 fighter-bomber is capable of delivering nuclear weapons, only a small portion of the about 435 total operational aircraft are likely to be dedicated to serving as theater nuclear strike systems at any one time. It is thus less appropriate to prorate the total programs costs to each nuclear-armed F-111. Instead, the aircraft's average unit flyaway cost is used as a measure of its financial cost.

d. Since only a few of F-16 fighters may ever be equipped and deployed as nuclear delivery systems, it is not appropriate to attribute the program costs to this role. Instead, the acquisition costs listed are limited to the current estimate of the F-16's average unit flyaway cost.

e. The costs assumed for the mobile MX ICBM/multiple basing systems are based on official estimates of the costs required for either a vertical silo basing system or a less mobile version of the horizontal basing mode. According to Defense Department testimony, these systems would reduce the total program costs of the recently planned horizontal basing system by nearly $2.5 billion for acquisition and about $30 million for annual operations and support.

f. Since the SLCM will be only one of several weapons deployed on various naval warships, it would be inappropriate to attribute more than the specific launcher acquisition and modification costs to the cruise missile.

g. If the SLCMs are produced in greater numbers than projected in the fiscal 1981–85 five-year defense plan, the program unit cost should be significantly reduced. For instance, assuming an eventual production objective of 1,500 SLCMs might reduce the cruise missile's program unit cost to about $2.2 million in 1981 constant dollars.

h. The total force acquisition cost to convert the 8 remaining Polaris ballistic missile submarines into cruise missile launch platforms is estimated at $2.2 billion. This figure does not include the sunk costs of the Polaris program to date. Each launch tube on the Polaris submarines reportedly would be capable of carrying 4 to 7 SLCMs.

Table B-6. *Nonnuclear Weapon System Life-Cycle Costs*

Costs in millions of 1981 constant dollars

Launch platform	Weapon	Cost per weapon[a]	Launch platform acquisition cost[b]	Launch platform modification cost[b]	Annual operating and support cost of launcher with full weapon load[c]	Fifteen-year operational and support cost per weapon
Airborne						
B-52D bomber	MRASM	0.65	n.a.	1.0	3.3	4.1
F-16 fighter	MRASM	0.65	7.7	0.2	1.1	4.1–8.2
A-6E fighter-bomber	MRASM	0.65	10.0	0.1	2.0	7.5–15.0
A-6E fighter-bomber	Walleye II gravity bomb	0.15	10.0	0.0	2.0	15.0
F-111E fighter-bomber	Antiairfield munitions[d]	n.a.[d]	26.0	n.a.	2.0	n.a.
Ground-based						
Ground-launched conventional cruise missile launcher (hypothetical)[e]	Nonnuclear GLCM (hypothetical)	0.72	8.5	0.0	0.9	3.4

Sea-based

Attack submarine					
Torpedo-tube launched	Harpoon	0.7	0.0	n.a.	n.a.	n.a.
Torpedo-tube/hull launchers	TASM/TLAM-C	1.4	0.0	1.0/25.0	1.2/1.6–2.4[f]	2.2/3.0[f]
Converted Polaris ballistic missile	TASM/TLAM-C	1.4	0.0	208.0	50.0	6.7/11.7
Surface ship					
Armored box launcher	Harpoon	0.6	0.0	n.a.	n.a.	n.a.
Vertical launching system	TASM/TLAM-C	1.4	0.0	10.0/50.0	2.0/3.0–12.2[g]	3.8/3.0[g]

n.a. Not available.

a. Costs are expressed in terms of the average unit flyaway cost instead of the broader program unit cost calculation used for most of the weapons in table B-5. This measure of cost is more appropriate to nonnuclear weapon systems since their relatively larger production numbers make marginal costs a more important consideration in choices between various weapon programs.

b. The launch platform acquisition cost is included for the various tactical aircraft for illustrative purposes, since these weapon systems can perform in a wide variety of roles besides delivering the specified munitions and cruise missiles. For the sea-based cruise missile, the launch platform modification cost includes both the acquisition cost and the modification cost of the cruise missile's specific launch system.

c. Figures include the annual operating and support costs for both the launcher and its assumed weapon load.

d. The final choice for such an antiairfield weapon for the United States is not yet firm. An example of the type of munitions considered for delivery by the F-111 is the JP-233 airfield attack system developed in the United Kingdom. Each F-111E could carry 4 JP-233 dispensers; 2 containing antirunway cratering bomblets, and 2 loaded with area mines to delay repair operations. A rough estimate of the cost of such weapon dispenser sets would be about $700 million in 1981 constant dollars.

e. All costs are author's estimates based on the assumption that a conventionally armed ground-launched cruise missile would cost the same as the MRASM with the addition of a booster motor and missile canister.

f. The range of figures results from the possibility that 8 to 12 hull launchers could be deployed on a nuclear-powered attack submarine.

g. The annual operating and support costs attributable to cruise missiles deployed in a vertical launching system will depend on what portion of the 61 launcher cells contains SLCMs. These figures illustrate the range of costs of a VLS magazine 25 to 100 percent filled with Tomahawk sea-launched cruise missiles.

Table B-7. *Cruise Missile Launch Platform Costs*

Costs in millions of constant 1981 dollars

Missile and platform	Number of missile loadings[a]	Launch platform modification or acquisition cost[b]	Platform cost per cruise missile space[c]
Air-launched cruise missile			
B-52 bomber[d]	20	18.4	0.92
B-1 strategic ALCM launcher[e]	30	144.0	4.8
Wide-bodied ALCM launcher[f]	60	154.0	2.6
Sea-launched cruise missile[g]			
Submarine (torpedo-tube launched)	6–8	1.0	0.13–0.17
Submarine (hull launcher)	8–12	25.0	2.1–3.1
Surface ship (armored box launcher)	8	10.0	1.25
Surface ship (vertical launching system)[h]	15–61	50.0	0.82
Polaris SSBN conversion[i]	64–112	208.0	1.8–2.6
Ground-launched cruise missile[j]			
Transporter-erector-launcher system	4	6.8	1.7
Medium-range air-to-surface missile			
B-52D bomber	12	1.0	0.08
A-6 fighter-bomber	2–4	0.1	0.02–0.05

a. Likely number of the current generation of cruise missiles to be carried by various launch platforms. Second-generation cruise missiles, such as an improved ALCM, are expected to be larger; therefore fewer could be carried on each aircraft.

b. This includes only the modification costs to convert the platform into a cruise missile carrier with the exceptions of the B-1 SAL bomber, the wide-bodied aircraft, and the GLCM launcher. These three are considered here as dedicated cruise missile launch platforms, which exist solely for this role, and consequently all acquisition costs related to these systems are included.

c. Figures are based on only the acquisition or modification costs related to the launch platform; neither the costs of the missiles nor the operating costs of the system are included.

d. Costs exclude the sunk costs of the earlier B-52 bomber acquisition program. The cost for modifications to the B-52 includes expenses for cruise missile launch systems and SALT verification-related design changes as well as various improvements in the B-52's offensive and defensive systems to maintain its military effectiveness. Cruise-missile-related modifications account for no more than one-half of the cost through the 1980s.

e. Based on public estimates of a possible fixed-wing variant of the terminated B-1 bomber program. Costs before program initiation in fiscal 1981 are excluded.

f. Based on Defense Department cost estimates for buying and converting a Boeing 747 type of wide-bodied commercial aircraft for use as a cruise missile launcher. The maximum ALCM capacity for such an aircraft would be 72 missiles, although a more conservative figure is used in this table.

g. Outlines modification costs for five different types of SLCM launcher systems. The first relates primarily to changes in the submarine's fire-control system. The second involves a possible plan to place up to 12 SLCM launchers in the submarine's pressure hull. The third and fourth are two different-sized launchers for surface ships. Finally, the last is based on reports that 8 aging Polaris ballistic missile submarines could be converted to launch SLCMs.

h. Each vertical launching system magazine will contain 61 missile launcher cells. The range for the force loading assumes in the high case that the equivalent of one complete VLS magazine is dedicated to SLCMs on a ship carrying two VLS systems. The lower number assumes that only about one-fourth of one VLS magazine is filled with SLCMs, and therefore the cost attributable to the SLCM is proportionate.

i. The 8 remaining Polaris SSBNs have been considered for this conversion. Reportedly, each of the Polaris SSBN's 16 launch tubes might carry 4 to 7 SLCMs.

j. A single transporter-erector-launcher (TEL) system has been chosen as a typical GLCM launch platform even though GLCM units will include 2 launch control centers as well as 4 TEL systems. Costs have been prorated to the single TEL.

Table B-8. *Characteristics and Costs of Tactical Aircraft and Conventional Cruise Missiles*

Costs in millions of 1981 constant dollars

Item	F-111 fighter-bomber	MRASM		GLCCM[a]	
		Lower cost	Higher cost	Lower cost	Higher cost
Costs					
Average unit flyaway cost	26.0	0.65	0.65	0.72	0.72
Annual operating and support cost	1.85	0.05	0.075	0.75	0.1
Fifteen-year life-cycle cost per operational weapon	54.0	1.4	1.8	1.8	2.2
Force levels					
Total force	53 F-111s	2,045 missiles; 22 F-16s	2,045 missiles; 50 F-16s	2,045 missiles; 35 TELs	2,045 missiles; 35 TELs
Total operational units	48 F-111s	1,800 missiles; 20 F-16s	1,800 missiles; 45 F-16s	1,800 missiles; 30 TELs	1,800 missiles; 30 TELs
Operational capability					
Average sortie rate per day	1.25	3	2	6 missile launches	6 missile launches
Average weapon load	n.a.	3 missiles per F-16	2 missiles per F-16	...	...

n.a. Not available.
a. Ground-launched conventional cruise missile.

Sources

Below are the sources used to construct some of the text tables and the appendix tables, arranged chronologically according to category. In most cases it was necessary to convert the figures into fiscal 1981 constant dollars. The sources and their designations are given first; the weapons and delivery systems, with their sources by designation, follow.

List of Sources and Their Designations

A. CONGRESSIONAL HEARINGS

  1. *Fiscal Year 1974 Authorization for Military Procurement, Research and Development, Construction Authorization for the Safeguard ABM, and Active Duty and Selected Reserve Strengths,* Hearings before the Senate Armed Services Committee, 93 Cong. 1 sess. (Government Printing Office, 1973).

  2. *Department of Defense Appropriations for Fiscal Year 1976,* Hearings before a subcommittee of the Senate Appropriations Committee, 94 Cong. 1 sess. (GPO, 1975).

  3. *Fiscal Year 1976 and July–September 1976 Transition Period Authorization for Military Procurement, Research and Development, and Active Duty, Selected Reserve, and Civilian Personnel Strengths,* Hearings before the Senate Armed Services Committee, 94 Cong. 1 sess. (GPO, 1975).

  4. *Fiscal Year 1977 Authorization for Military Procurement, Research and Development, and Active Duty, Selected Reserve and Civilian Personnel Strengths,* Hearings before the Senate Armed Services Committee, 94 Cong. 2 sess. (GPO, 1976).

  5. *Hearings on Military Posture and H.R. 11500 [H.R. 12438]: Department of Defense Authorization for Appropriations for Fiscal Year 1977,* Hearings before the House Armed Services Committee, 94 Cong. 2 sess. (GPO, 1976).

  6. *Fiscal Year 1978 Supplemental Military Authorization,* Hearings before the Subcommittee on Research and Development of the Senate Armed Services Committee, 95 Cong. 1 sess. (GPO, 1977).

  7. *Hearings on Military Posture and H.R. 10929: Department of Defense Authorization for Appropriations for Fiscal Year 1979,*

Hearings before the House Armed Services Committee, 95 Cong. 2 sess. (GPO, 1978).

8. *Department of Defense Appropriations for 1980,* Hearings before a subcommittee of the House Appropriations Committee, 96 Cong. 1 sess. (GPO, 1979).

9. *Department of Defense Appropriations for Fiscal Year 1980,* Hearings before a subcommittee of the Senate Appropriations Committee, 96 Cong. 1 sess. (GPO, 1979).

10. *Department of Defense Appropriations for Fiscal Year 1981,* Hearings before a subcommittee of the Senate Appropriations Committee, 96 Cong. 2 sess. (GPO, 1980).

11. *Hearings on Military Posture and H.R. 6495 [H.R. 6974]: Department of Defense Authorization for Appropriations for Fiscal Year 1981,* Hearings before the House Armed Services Committee, 96 Cong. 2 sess. (GPO, 1980).

12. *Department of Defense Authorization for Appropriations for Fiscal Year 1981,* Hearings before the Senate Armed Services Committee, 96 Cong. 2 sess. (GPO, 1980).

13. *Department of Defense Appropriations for 1981,* Hearings before a subcommittee of the House Appropriations Committee, 96 Cong. 2 sess. (GPO, 1980).

14. *Military Construction Appropriations for 1981,* Hearings before a subcommittee of the House Appropriations Committee, 96 Cong. 2 sess. (GPO, 1980).

15. *MX Missile Basing Mode,* Hearings before a subcommittee of the Senate Appropriations Committee, 96 Cong. 2 sess. (GPO, 1980).

B. DEPARTMENT OF DEFENSE REPORTS

1. Office of Director, Defense Research and Engineering, *Joint Bomber Strategic Study: Supporting Analyses* (Department of Defense, 1974).

2. *FY 76 Defense Budget Financial Summary,* prepared for the Center for Defense Information by the Department of Defense, 1975.

3. Department of Defense, "Selected Acquisition Reports as of September 30, 1980" (1981).

4. *Department of Defense Annual Report, Fiscal Year 1981* (GPO, 1980).

C. JOINT CRUISE MISSILE PROJECT

1. "The Joint Cruise Missile Project" (Washington, D.C.: Joint Cruise Missile Project Office, no date).

2. "U.S. Air Force Ground Launched Cruise Missile" (JCMPO, no date).

D. JOURNALS AND ARTICLES

1. Edgar Ulsamer, "In Focus..." *Air Force,* May 1979.
2. F. Clifton Berry, Jr., "Pershing II: First Step in NATO Theatre Nuclear Force Modernization?" *International Defense Review,* vol. 12, no. 8 (1979).
3. *Aviation Week and Space Technology,* June 16, 1980.
4. "Military Highlights from Farnborough International '80," *International Defense Review,* vol. 13, no. 8 (1980).
5. *Aerospace Daily,* September 19, 1980.
6. David R. Griffiths, "Proposal Set on Air-to-Surface Missile," *Aviation Week and Space Technology,* December 29, 1980.
7. Robert D. McKelvey and Edward A. Jordan, "Manned Tactical Aircraft and Conventional Cruise Missile Mission Compatibility and Effectiveness" (San Diego: General Dynamics Convair Division, no date).

E. OTHER SOURCES

1. Congressional Budget Office, *Retaliatory Issues for the U.S. Strategic Nuclear Forces* (GPO, 1978).
2. Colin S. Gray, *The Future of Land-Based Missile Forces,* Adelphi Paper 140 (London: International Institute for Strategic Studies, 1978).
3. Stockholm International Peace Research Institute, *Tactical Nuclear Weapons: European Perspectives* (London: Taylor and Francis, 1978).
4. *Fiscal Year 1981 Arms Control Impact Statements,* Joint Committee Print, House Committee on Foreign Affairs and Senate Committee on Foreign Relations, 96 Cong. 2 sess. (GPO, 1980).

Cruise Missiles

AIR-LAUNCHED

Force levels: A 11, pt. 4, bk. 2, p. 1814; and A 8, pt. 3, p. 717.

Force costs: B 3; and A 11, pt. 4, bk. 2, p. 1823. Annual operating and support costs derived from A 6, p. 131.

Force characteristics: B 4, p. 133; A 10, pt. 5, p. 1632; and author's estimates derived from E 2, p. 32.

GROUND-LAUNCHED

Force levels: A 12, pt. 2, p. 508, and pt. 4, p. 2447.

Force costs: B 3; A 12, pt. 4, p. 2447; and the reference for the additional $265 million for GLCM construction funded through the NATO infrastructure, A 14, pt. 3, pp. 194–96. Annual operating and support cost derived from A 14, pt. 4, p. 685.

Force characteristics: A 12, pt. 2, p. 508, and pt. 4, pp. 2477, 2480; and C 2, pp. 2–4.

SEA-LAUNCHED

Force levels: A 11, pt. 4, bk. 2, p. 1498. For my estimate of operational weapons based on 8 SLCMs per programmed launch platform, see A 11, pt. 2, p. 188, and pt. 4, bk. 2, p. 1497.

Force costs: B 3; and A 11, pt. 4, bk. 2, p. 1498. My estimates of annual operating and support costs based on interviews of July 25 and December 5, 1980.

Force characteristics: operational dates, A 11, pt. 4, bk. 2, p. 1497, and a possible deployment date of 1983–84 for the TLAM-N, D 3, p. 277; C 1, pp. 2–3; and A 8, pt. 3, p. 514.

MEDIUM-RANGE AIR-TO-SURFACE

Force costs: D 6, p. 23; and A 13, pt. 3, pp. 1001, 1030. My estimate of operating and support costs based on D 7, p. 17.

Force characteristics: D 5, p. 105; and D 6, pp. 23–25.

Air-Launched Delivery Systems

B-52G/ALCM

Force costs: Unit costs for the ALCM and associated B-52 modification from A 9, pt. 1, p. 620; and A 11, pt. 1, p. 897. Operating and support costs derived from A 6, p. 131.

Force characteristics: A 12, pt. 2, p. 520; and A 8, pt. 3, p. 717.

B-52H/ALCM

Force costs: A 11, pt. 1, p. 897.

Force characteristics: A 12, pt. 2, p. 520.

B-52D/MRASM

Force costs: Cost of B-52D modification to accept MRASMs based on an interview, December 10, 1980; annual operating and support costs derived from B 2.

Force characteristics: D 5, p. 105.

WIDE-BODIED (BOEING 747 TYPE) CRUISE MISSILE CARRIER
AIRCRAFT/ALCM

Force costs: A 12, pt. 2, pp. 1028–29. Operating and support costs estimated from A 6, p. 131.

Force characteristics: A 12, pt. 2, p. 1028; from a total buy of 111 aircraft given, I estimate that 100 would be operationally deployed. Despite the aircrafts' capacity to carry 72 ALCMs each, I use the more conservative estimate that only 60 ALCMs will be carried; A 8, pt. 3, p. 729.

B-1 STRATEGIC ALCM LAUNCHER (SAL) TYPE CRUISE MISSILE CARRIER
AIRCRAFT/ALCM

Force costs: A 10, pt. 1, p. 597. My estimate of operating and support costs derived from A 6, p. 131.

Force characteristics: A 10, pt. 1, p. 597. I estimate that, of the 100 aircraft procured, only 90 would be operationally deployed.

B-1 PENETRATING BOMBER/NUCLEAR GRAVITY BOMBS AND SRAMS

Force costs: A 11, pt. 1, p. 50. Operating costs derived from A 6, p. 131. Original B-1 program costs derived from B 1, vol. 2, p. 29.

Force characteristics: A 11, pt. 1, pp. 36, 51. For average weapon loading and assumption of 1.1-megaton yield for gravity bomb, A 6, pp. 175–76. Bomber accuracy derived from E 1, pp. 6–9.

FB-111B/C PENETRATING BOMBER/NUCLEAR GRAVITY BOMBS
AND SRAMS

Force costs: A 11, pt. 1, pp. 36, 50; and A 13, pt. 4, p. 138.

Force characteristics: A 11, pt. 1, p. 51; and A 13, pt. 4, p. 35.

F-111 FIGHTER-BOMBER/NUCLEAR GRAVITY BOMBS OR NONNUCLEAR
ANTIAIRFIELD MUNITIONS

Force costs: Average unit flyaway cost derived from chart in A 4, pt. 6, p. 3728; and A 2, pt. 4, p. 199. Operating and support costs derived from B 2.

Force characteristics: B 4, p. 93. An illustrative type of antiairfield munition is described in D 4, p. 1286.

F-16 FIGHTER/NUCLEAR GRAVITY BOMB OR MRASMS

Force costs: Average unit flyaway cost from A 11, pt. 2, p. 435. Operating and support costs from A 10, pt. 5, p. 1623.

Force characteristics: A 11, pt. 4, bk. 2, p. 2318, for nuclear loading; D 5, p. 105, for MRASM capacity.

A-6E FIGHTER-BOMBER/NONNUCLEAR WALLEYE II BOMBS OR MRASMS

Force costs: Author's estimate based on A 11, pt. 2, p. 127. Operating and support costs from B 2.

Force characteristics: D 5, p. 105; nuclear weapon load assumed to be equal to that of F-111 fighter-bomber.

Ground-Launched Delivery Systems

MX ICBM IN A MULTIPLE BASING SYSTEM

Force costs: Based on a vertical silo or lower cost horizontal multiple protective system, A 11, pt. 4, bk. 2, pp. 1854–55; and A 12, pt. 2, p. 593. Missile cost breakdown based on A 15, p. 111.

Force characteristics: A 15, pp. 59–65; and D 1, p. 25. Accuracy derived from E 2, p. 32.

PERSHING II BALLISTIC MISSILE SYSTEM

Force costs: B 3. Operating and support costs derived from my estimate of the efficiency of the Pershing II basing system over its predecessor, the Pershing I; see A 1, pt. 8, p. 5356; and D 2, p. 1304.

Force characteristics: A 12, pt. 2, p. 512. For my estimate of 1–2 reload missiles per Pershing launcher based on historical experience with Pershing I launchers, see E 3, p. 112.

Sea-Launched Delivery Systems

TRIDENT SSBN/TRIDENT I (C-4) SLBM

Force costs: B 3; and A 11, pt. 3, p. 195. Annual operating and support costs derived from A 5, pt. 4, pp. 114.

Force characteristics: A 11, pt. 3, p. 195; D 3, p. 91; and E 2, p. 32.

POSEIDON SSBN/TRIDENT I (C-4) SLBM

Force costs: Author's estimates based on A 11, pt. 3, p. 202; and A 8, pt. 3, p. 485. Annual operating and support costs derived from A 5, pt. 4, p. 114.

Force characteristics: A 11, pt. 3, p. 195; D 3, p. 91; and E 2, p. 32.

POLARIS SSGN/TOMAHAWK SLCM

Force costs: A 12, pt. 5, p. 2921. Operating and support costs assumed to be the same as those of the Poseidon SSBN.

Force characteristics: A 12, pt. 5, p. 2921; and D 3, p. 119.

NUCLEAR ATTACK SUBMARINES/TOMAHAWK SLCM

Force costs: Author's estimates based on A 7, pt. 3, bk. 2, p. 1269; and interviews of April 15 and December 5, 1980.

Force characteristics: A 11, pt. 2, p. 188, and pt. 4, bk. 2, p. 1497; and A 7, pt. 3, bk. 2, p. 1263.

SURFACE SHIPS/TOMAHAWK SLCM

Force costs: Author's estimates based on interviews of April 15, July 25, and December 5, 1980.

Force characteristics: Armored box launchers, A 11, pt. 4, bk. 2, p. 1488, and pt. 2, p. 188; and A 7, pt. 3, bk. 2, p. 1263. Vertical launching systems, A 11, pt. 4, bk. 2, pp. 1439–45; and A 10, pt. 4, pp. 86–88.

HARPOON ANTISHIP MISSILE

Force costs: Author's estimates derived from B 3; and E 4, p. 369.

Force characteristics: A 3, pt. 9, p. 4913.

APPENDIX C

Glossary

Area defenses. Defenses against bombers or missiles, organized around large areas such as cities. Effectiveness lower than for terminal defense of point targets.

Arms race stability. Reduction of the expense or pace of competition in arms deployments, through tacit or formal agreement on a mutually acceptable distribution or configuration of forces.

Assured destruction. One criterion for adequacy of nuclear retaliation, specifying some percentage of civilian targets whose destruction would cripple the enemy's society. *Mutual assured destruction* refers to the theory that stability is maximized when both superpowers' homelands are highly vulnerable to retaliation by the other's surviving nuclear forces.

Collateral damage. Destruction of civilian life and property in the vicinity of a military target. Under some theories, counterforce attacks should minimize collateral damage to avoid provoking disproportionate retaliation.

Counterforce. Attack directed against military targets, especially enemy strategic nuclear forces.

Countervailing strategy. Rationale for wartime employment of nuclear forces to prevent the enemy from achieving military objectives. Involves calibrating options to match or counter various enemy attack plans, keeping response proportional to provocation.

Countervalue. Attack directed against nonmilitary targets, especially industrial or population centers.

Crisis stability. A theory that certain technical configurations of U.S. and Soviet nuclear forces—particularly, invulnerability of the weapons of both superpowers to preemptive attack—prevent either from considering that it could benefit from a first strike in a crisis.

603

Essential equivalence. A criterion for adequacy of U.S. strategic forces based on the principle that any Soviet advantage in certain elements must be offset by different advantages in U.S. capabilities; measured primarily by static indexes of weapon system quantities and qualities.

Flexible response. NATO's strategy for deterrence and defense by sequential escalation. Soviet attack is to be resisted at first with conventional forces alone; if conventional defenses fail, theater nuclear forces will be used; if theater nuclear forces fail to check the Soviet attack, U.S. central strategic forces are supposed to be used.

Force projection. Combat intervention over long distances from home bases, moving forces by sea or air; principal means are naval forces, air transport, light ground forces, and logistical support systems.

Fractionation. Division of the payload of a ballistic missile into numerous separate warheads. Limits on fractionation for a heavy missile reduce its counterforce capability.

Hardened point targets. Military targets (such as ICBM silos) or command centers buried or protected by reinforced concrete, making them resistant to nuclear blast. Destruction requires very high accuracy or extremely high yield in the weapon aimed at the target.

Interdiction. Attacks on enemy forces or logistical assets along lines of communication behind the battle area.

Prelaunch survivability. Invulnerability of a weapon to destruction before it is launched; achieved by hardening, concealment, or rapid reaction to warning of attack.

Presidential Directive 59. Issued by President Carter in 1980, it stipulates the criteria for U.S. nuclear strategy. The directive emphasizes flexible and selective targeting throughout a protracted war, greater capability to strike military targets and command centers, and improvements in reconnaissance and communications to allow strategic target acquisition during the course of nuclear war.

Single integrated operations plan. The U.S. plan for strategic nuclear war allocating weapon systems to specific targets, with options for selective attacks as well as an unlimited one.

"Soft" area targets. Unprotected collections of valuable assets—for example, cities—more vulnerable to destruction than hardened point targets.

Standoff systems. Weapons—for example, cruise missiles—that can be launched from their carriers from outside the effective range of enemy defensive systems, thus permitting attack while protecting the carrier.

Terminal defenses. Defenses against bombers or missiles around point targets, such as military command posts. More effective than area defenses.

Triad. Organization of strategic nuclear forces in three basic components: ICBMs, SLBMs, and bombers.

Index

607

608